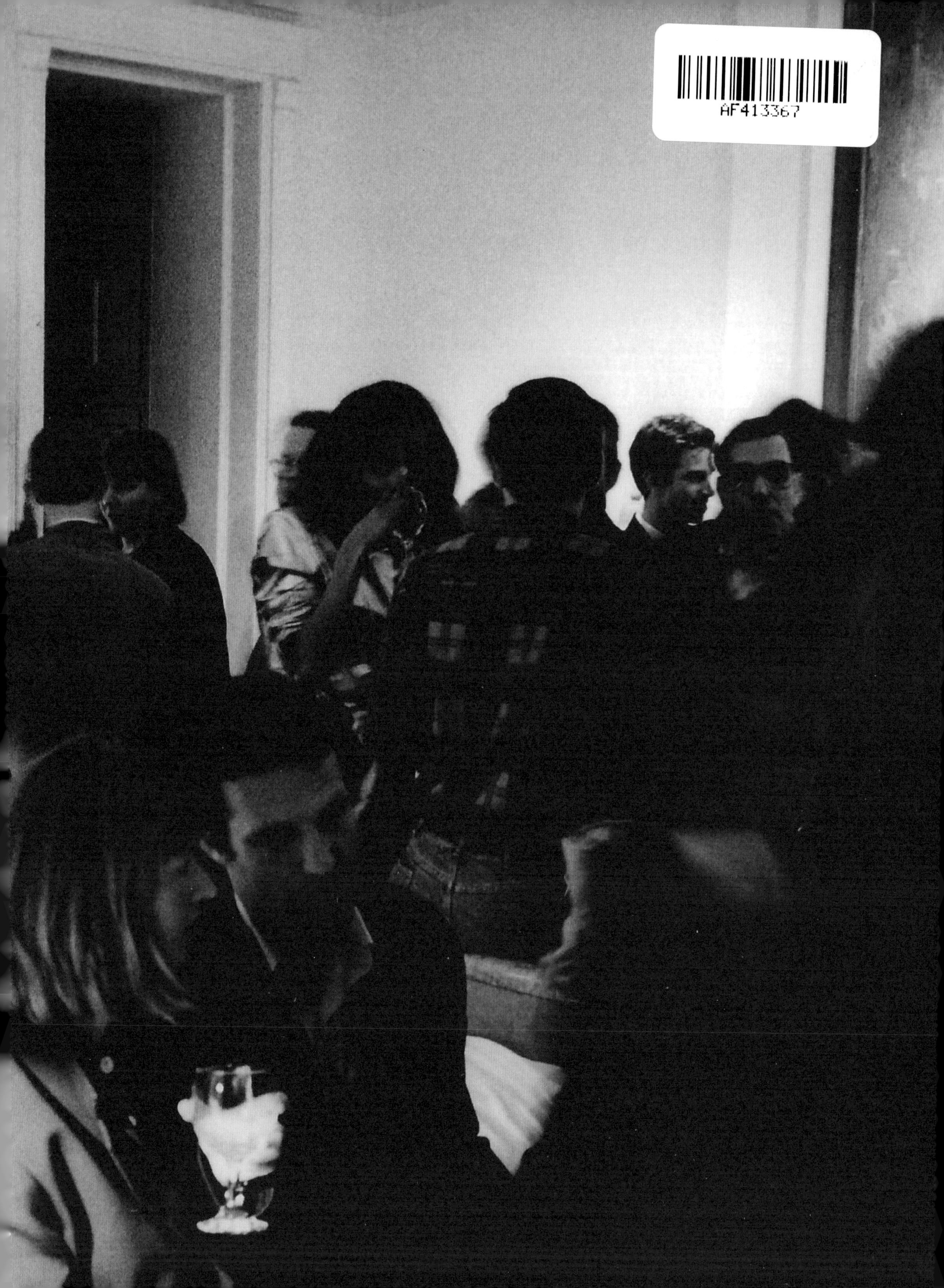

RUBELL MUSEUM

Highlights & Artists' Writings

Published in 2023 by the
Rubell Museum / Contemporary Arts Foundation, Miami, FL
© 2023 Rubell Museum

Publication
Editor: Juan Valadez
Designer and Photographer: Chi Lam
Assistant Editor: Alexandra Perez
Line Editor: Elizabeth Martinez

ISBN: 979-8-218-20298-9
Library of Congress Control Number: 2023908570

Cover: Jean-Michel Basquiat, *Bird On Money* (detail),
1981, acrylic and oil on canvas, 66 x 90 in. (167.6 x 228.6
cm), acquired in 1981, © Estate of Jean-Michel Basquiat.
Licensed by Artestar, New York.

Inside cover: Party at the New York home of Mera and
Donald Rubell following the opening of the 1991 Whitney
Biennial; artwork by John Ahearn, Keith Haring, and
Jean-Michel Basquiat; photograph by Ivan Dalla Tana.

Back inside cover: Inaugural opening, Rubell Museum,
Miami, 2019

Rubell Museum Miami
1100 NW 23 ST
Miami, FL 33127
Juan Valadez, Director
Chi Lam, Designer and Photographer
William Vargas, Collection Manager
Alexandra Perez, Exhibition Manager & Registrar
Leyden Ayure, Installation Technician
Liliana Zarif, Director of Finance
Lucy Cai, Bookstore & Visitor Services Manager
Ashley Thomas, Events Manager
Cristina Muller, Visitor Services
Lisbet Rodriguez, Office Manager
Sonia Alvarado, Facility Technician
Juan Perez, Engineer
Juan Soto, Security
Marisela Rodriguez, Security
Andrea Pendergrass, Security

Rubell Museum DC
65 i Street SW
Washington, DC, 20024
Caitlin Berry, Director
Claudia Solano, Director of Finance
Trinity Lewis, Visitor Services & Events Coordinator
MaryGrace Arlotto, Visitor Services & Operations Coordinator
Ashlie Hollis, Visitor Services & Tour Coordinator
Andres Castro, Engineer
Carlos Castro, Visitor Services & Security
Wayne Vann, Security
Ian Solano, Visitor Services Intern

CONTENTS

ARTIST INDEX

Sixty years ago, Mera and Don Rubell married and shortly thereafter, by chance, began visiting artists in their studios. Thirty years ago, with their family, they created the Contemporary Arts Foundation and made the artwork acquired from decades of studio and gallery visits available to the public. As these complicated and oftentimes highly fraught endeavors— marriage, working with family, public-facing institutions—are still ongoing and evolving in very meaningful ways, we felt it necessary to celebrate by taking the long view and presenting a limited but significant overview of our efforts.

The Foundation, with museums in Miami and Washington DC, is now responsible for over 8,200 works by more than 1,050 artists and represents more resonant perspectives and possibilities than any other post-1980 collection assembled by one family. Hence, the prospect of this volume limning the collection via a selection of works from 126 artists is tenuous at best. That said, we believe that a measure of the intent, activity, and scope of the Rubells' collection and Foundation is evidenced herein. It is also our hope that the artists' spirit, highly independent and, at times, transgressive, is present.

Mera and Don Rubell work in close collaboration, both as collectors and hoteliers, with their son, Jason, and draw insight and inspiration from their daughter, Jennifer, an artist. An additional wellspring for them has been time spent in conversation with their grandchildren. On countless occasions over the past decades, Don, Mera, and Jason have arrived, after much consideration, at that elusive port of call known as *consensus*. This consensus, reached without advisers or committees, is first and foremost what compels them, resources permitting, to acquire a specific installation, sculpture, painting, video, or photograph. Without this consensus there is no movement. Prior to this point, they educate themselves: visiting studios, galleries, museums, attending innumerable lectures, and poring over catalogs and journals. Of these, the studio visits are far-and-away the most critical and result in many long-standing friendships as well as introductions to other artists.

Since the Foundation's inception, a guiding tenet for us is to solely exhibit art that the Rubells have acquired. Everything on our walls, floors, suspended from our ceilings, traveling overseas, or crated within our storage was purchased from artists via their galleries and comprises our permanent collection. That is to say, there is a permanence within our commitment to these artists and objects. Fortunately, for the clarity of our exhibitions and viewers, when a commitment is made to acquire an artist's work it is rarely a single object but rather many. We are therefore able to present the artist in the context of their own work, their own vision. Indeed, of the artists featured in this catalog there are only three who are represented in the collection by a single object, while the majority are represented by many, including, for example, Keith Haring, Josh Kline, Hank Willis Thomas, and Kaari Upson who are represented by 72, 28, 87, and 32 works, respectively. This scale of commitment and support is profound for any collection—private or public—and this commitment is, whenever possible, ongoing throughout the artist's career.

In 1993, the Rubells' growing commitment to presenting artists, many of whom were unheralded and not widely exhibited, especially in the Southeast, led them to repurpose as exhibition space a then-derelict building in Miami that had previously held weapons and narcotics confiscated by the Drug Enforcement Agency. In creating a public site for a private contemporary art collection, the Rubells' main points of reference were the collectors Anton and Annick Herbert in Ghent, Belgium, and the artist and collector Urs Rausmüller's Hallen für Neue Kunst in Schaffhausen, Switzerland. In the early 1980s, both the Herberts and Rausmüller converted disused factories into exhibition spaces to present their collections and, in the Herberts' case, live with their art.

From 1994 to 2019, via rotating exhibitions and programs, this building in Miami was our laboratory for understanding how best to develop as an institution, champion artists, and manage the rapidly expanding collection. We started and advanced projects that are now a keystone of our efforts. These include a museum studies internship, our artist-in-residence program and its attendant exhibition, which is a generative extension of the Rubells' aforementioned studio visits, and traveling large-scale exhibitions drawn from the collection. This latter highly intensive endeavor allows us to collaborate countrywide with institutions and their communities by sharing such essential works as those which comprise our *30 Americans* exhibition, which has been presented at 22 museums.

In 2015, while scouting for additional art storage, the Rubells found a series of interconnected warehouses in Miami's Allapattah neighborhood that we determined should become our new museum. The gifted architect Annabelle Selldorf transformed these buildings into a 100,000-square-foot campus that now allows for single-artist presentations of recent acquisitions and commissions alongside thematic bodies of work from the 1980s and 1990s. In December of 2019, as we opened this new museum in Miami, we started down an equally ambitious and challenging road to open a museum in our nation's capital, the seeds of which were planted 14 years prior when the Rubells acquired a former schoolhouse in Washington, D.C.'s, Southwest neighborhood. Prior to its closing in 1978, this century-old red brick building was the Randall Junior High School, a segregated school for boys that counts Marvin Gaye among its alumni. Working with architect Hany Hassan of Beyer Blinder Belle on an extensive renovation with exhibition spaces that hewed closely to the school's original layout, we opened the Rubell Museum DC in October 2022, presenting works as poetic as they are political. Marvin Gaye's forever relevant "What's Going On" played in a gallery filled with Keith Haring paintings inspired by this very song.

Rescuing buildings from the wrecking ball, sharing an art collection, invigorating a city's arts community, welcoming thousands of students—all are highly commendable. But how might one know if the art they are stewards of is relevant outside of their walls? Perhaps the critical art of our time is elsewhere? An artwork's monetary value is certainly no indication. Younger artists referencing a previous generation's work—work that is part of the collection—is perhaps the most assured confirmation. An additional affirmation may be the unsolicited artwork loan requests we receive from many astute curators in the field. To that end, and to honor institutions large and small, we have included an abbreviated list of our artworks that have been requested and presented in public institutions.

As the works featured herein are inextricably tied to the Rubells, we look forward in the coming years to sharing, in their own words, their personal histories as they parallel and intersect with the art of our time. Our decision with this catalog to initially focus on the artist's voice reflects one of the central tenets running throughout the years I have had the good fortune to collaborate with the Rubells: artists first. Like the works themselves these artists' writings consider knots not easily untied; issues of race, gender and class are discussed throughout. Nearly all the artists we approached for this project carved time out of their schedules for us. For this, for the art itself, for our colleagues, and for our public, we are extraordinarily grateful.

Donald, eldest child of Ann, a schoolteacher, and Philip Rubell, a postman and tennis coach, is born in Brooklyn, New York. Don's brother, Steve, is born in 1943.

Don enrolls in Cornell University on a tennis scholarship, graduates in 1961 with a degree in theoretical mathematics, and begins a career in actuary science. Within a few years, Don rejects corporate life for a career in medicine.

Ranked number one on the tennis team at Cornell and named captain in his junior and senior year, Don continues to play tennis and compete to this day. In 1985, he wins the USTA Men's 45+ National Championship. In 2008 he is inducted into the Eastern Tennis Hall of Fame, and in 2022 he receives the Intercollegiate Tennis Association's David A. Benjamin Lifetime Achievement Award.

Mera and Don marry August 30th, 1964. One week later, Don enters medical school at New York University, and Mera begins teaching at Head Start in Harlem. Her $100-a-week salary is their sole means of support for the next four years.

On daily walks through their Chelsea neighborhood, Mera and Don discover art by talking to the artists working out of storefront studios. They eventually purchase their first piece of art on a $5-per-week payment plan. Thereafter, they commit to putting aside $25 every week for subsequent purchases, and a passion is born.

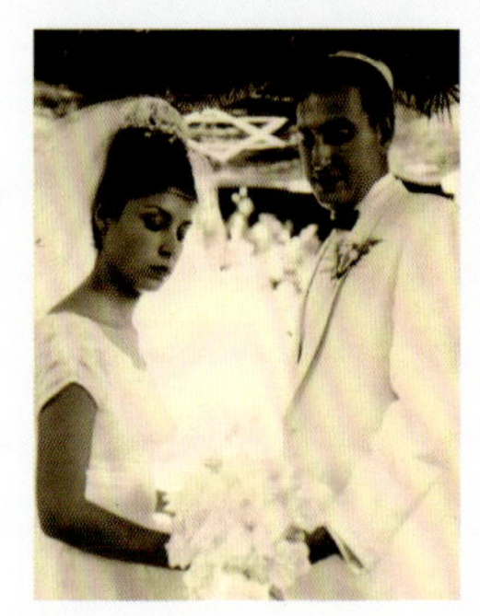

Don graduates medical school and begins his medical internship at Cedars-Sinai Hospital in Los Angeles. Their son Jason is born in L.A. in 1969.

Mera, Don, and Jason return to New York City, and Don begins his residency in obstetrics and gynecology at Bellevue/NYU Medical Center. Their daughter, Jennifer, is born in New York City.

Mera establishes Quest, a reading discussion group for women—one of her early entrepreneurial endeavors.

The family relocates to San Antonio, Texas, for Don's Air Force service. Don works at the University of Texas Medical School while serving at Lackland Air Force Base. Mera opens two tennis-themed clothing stores for women in San Antonio.

1940   1943   1956   1960   1962   1964   1968   1970   1973   1975

Mera, eldest child of Freida, a seamstress, and Albert Sosnowicz, a hairdresser and artist, is born in Tashkent, Russia (now Uzbekistan). Holocaust survivors, Mera's earliest memory is of living in a Displaced Person camp in Germany after the war. Mera's sister, Sabrina, is born in Germany in 1948. The family emigrates to the United States in 1954 and settles in Brooklyn.

After six months of sitting across from each other in the Brooklyn College Library without speaking, Don invites Mera out for a vanilla egg-cream. Upon leaving the library he proposes marriage, and Mera accepts.

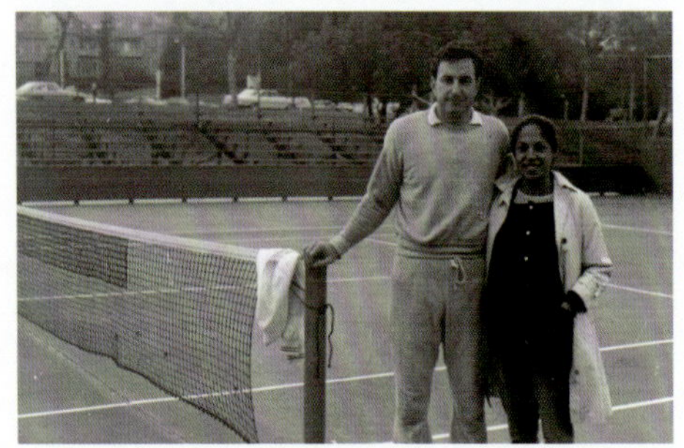

His service concluded, Don is discharged from the U.S. Air Force with the rank of Lieutenant Colonel and the family returns to Manhattan. Don joins an OB-GYN practice and within six months he continues as a solo practitioner.

Mera, having sold her two tennis apparel stores before leaving Texas, opens a new tennis-themed clothing store, Tennis Woman, on the Upper East Side. In a few years she becomes the U.S. marketing director for Fila and then the exclusive distributor of Ellesse apparel for the U.S. market. She authors *Open to Buy*, a trade book about merchandising.

Don and Mera's art collecting begins in earnest and soon becomes their overwhelming obsession. Kids in tow, they visit galleries, artist studios, and museums.

Mera enrolls in Brooklyn College and graduates in 1965 with a degree in psychology. She later earns a master's degree in education from Long Island University and begins a career as a teacher.

In 2015, on the 50th anniversary of her graduation, Mera is asked to represent the Brooklyn College Anniversary Class of 1965 at the college's baccalaureate commencement ceremony. In her address, Mera discusses the power of a college education and how art has inspired and given purpose to her life.

The family moves to a townhouse on Manhattan's Upper East Side, financing the purchase by renting the upper two floors to seven psychiatrists in private practices.

Mera opens a commercial real estate company in New York City.

Don's brother, Steve, opens Studio 54 in New York. In 1985, he opens the Palladium and commissions artwork from artists, including Jean-Michel Basquiat, Francesco Clemente, and Keith Haring.

In 1979, the townhouse becomes the setting for an impromptu Whitney Biennial afterparty, marking the first time the Rubells open their collection to the public. The Whitney Biennial afterparties continue for many years as an artworld institution and fuel the Rubells' commitment to collecting contemporary art.

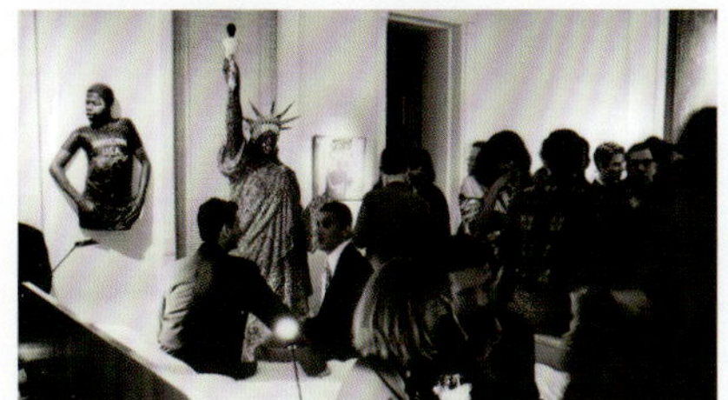

Mera closes her real estate practice and moves to Miami, with Don commuting every weekend from New York City. Don will close his medical practice in 1998 to move to Miami full-time.

Jason curates, publishes, and installs a selection of his art collection for his senior thesis at Duke University Museum of Art. The exhibition and catalog, *Contemporary Art from the Collection of Jason Rubell*, will travel to 14 university galleries within four years.

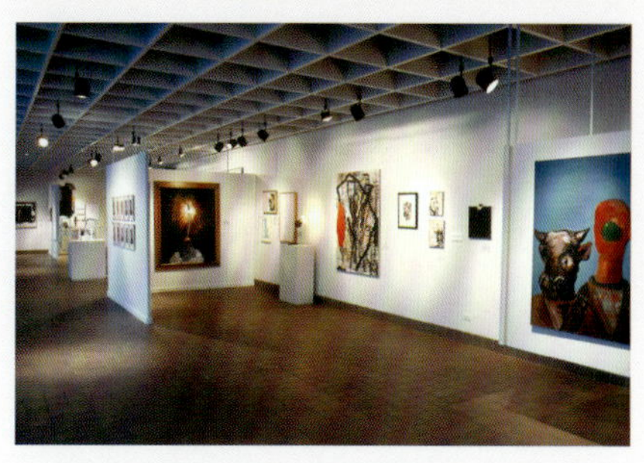

The Rubells' artwork loan program begins with the loans of Francesco Clemente's *Two Painters* (1980) to the Hallwalls Contemporary Arts Center, Buffalo, New York; and David Salle's *Rainy Night in the Rubber City* (1980) to the Allen Memorial Art Museum in Oberlin, Ohio. By 2023, more than 500 artwork loans will be made to museums in over 30 countries.

Jason, an All-American tennis player while at Duke University, graduates with a degree in art history and moves to South Florida. He opens an art gallery on 238 Worth Avenue in Palm Beach and one year later an additional gallery on 700 Lincoln Road in Miami Beach, representing artists such as Karen Davie, Peter Halley, Suzanne McClelland, David Salle, Julian Schnabel, and Gary Simmons.

In 1994, Jason closes his galleries to work with his family on their real estate business and to focus on the family's mission of sharing their art collection with the public.

1977 **1979** **1980** **1981** **1982** **1990** **1991**

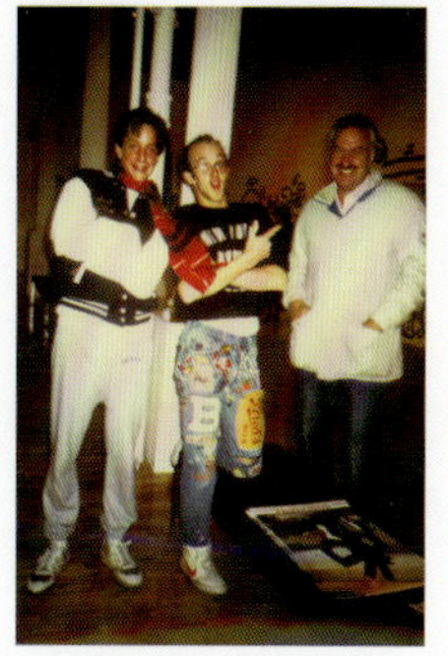

The Rubells make their first visit to Art Basel and soon regular attendance at the European art fairs, biennials, and museums follow. Mera and Don commit to collecting individual artists in depth.

The New York art scene moves from Uptown to Downtown, with a surge of galleries opening in SoHo and the East Village. The Rubells gravitate to the work of emerging artists.

The Rubells meet Keith Haring at a gallery space above the Mudd Club in Lower Manhattan and begin collecting his work and that of his contemporaries, including Jean-Michel Basquiat, who was introduced to the Rubells by Haring. They develop a close friendship with Haring that lasts until his death in 1990.

Jason receives his first artwork, a gift from Keith Haring, motivating him to pursue his own art collection. In 1983, at age 14, Jason makes his first art purchase from Pat Hearn—George Condo's *The Immigrants* (1983)—by paying weekly installments with earnings from his tennis racket stringing business. Subsequent purchases are made in the same manner and, within a few years, Jason's personal art collection grows to include more than 100 pieces of art.

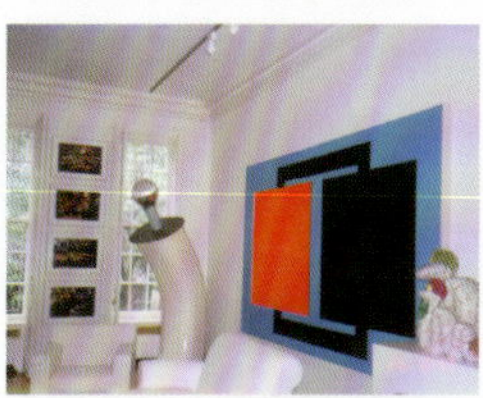
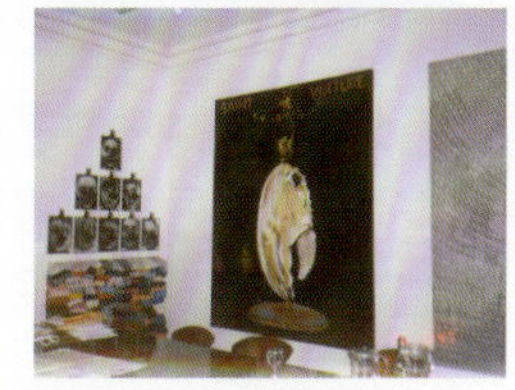

As the Rubells' collection grows so does their reputation for finding provocative work that challenges traditional conventions.

The Rubells begin welcoming and touring curators, directors, and museum groups from across the country through their townhouse. These visits inspire the Rubells as they begin their public-facing journey.

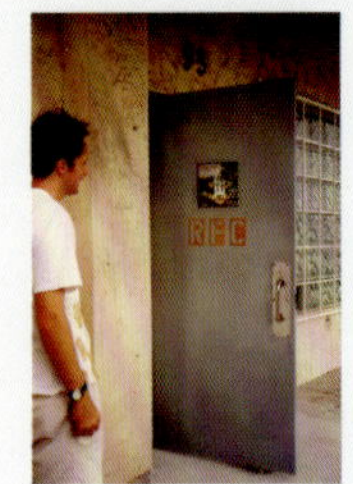

Having outgrown their art storage space in New York, the Rubells purchase a property at 95 NW 29th Street in Miami's Wynwood neighborhood to house their art collection.

This 30,000 square-foot building, a former DEA warehouse, becomes the home of the Rubell Family Collection (RFC) with the assistance of the artist Mark Handforth.

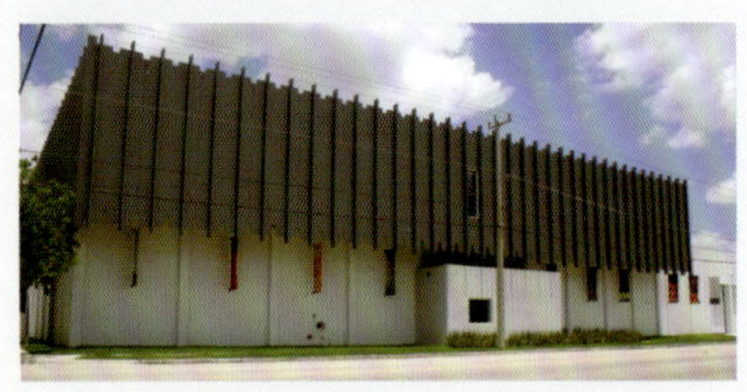

Jennifer graduates from Harvard University with a degree in art history.

She moves back to New York City in 2003. Her children Stevie and Max are born in New York in 2005 and 2012, respectively.

The Rubells initiate a delegation to Art Basel in Switzerland that includes Miami Beach commissioners and then-mayor of Miami Beach, Niesen Kasdin, to begin discussions to bring the celebrated art fair to Miami.

Jason marries Michelle Simkins. Their children Samuel, Ella, and Olivia are born in 2001, 2002, and 2005, respectively.

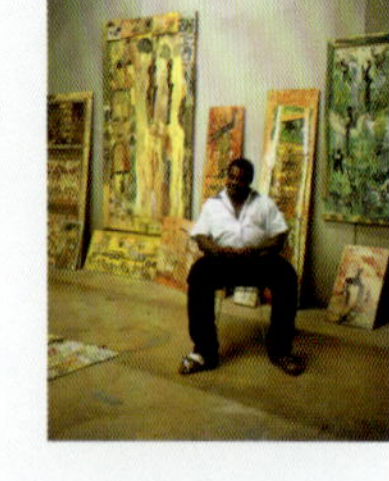

The Rubells are introduced to the work of Purvis Young and purchase the entire contents of his studio in Miami, some 3000 works that include paintings, sketchbooks, and drawings. They commit to donating hundreds of these works to museums and universities, including 116 that are on permanent exhibition in the Martin Luther King Jr. International Chapel at Atlanta's Morehouse College.

Juan Valadez, a graduate of Cooper Union in New York, is hired to assist in cataloguing Young's works. In 2009, Valadez is appointed director of the Rubell Family Collection and continues his directorship—to date, a tenure of 24 years with 14 years as director.

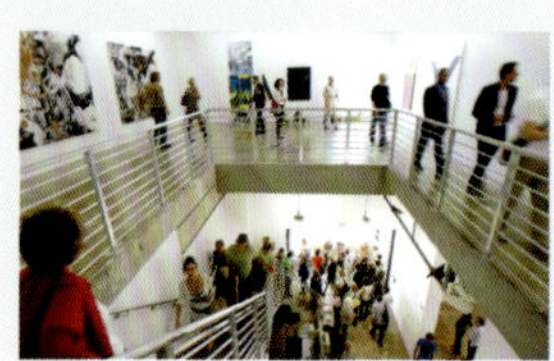

The first Art Basel Miami Beach opens in December 2002. The RFC presents a selection of artwork from the Collection and future exhibitions open concurrently with the fair each year.

Pillow Talks, a visiting-artist program dedicated to the public discussion of contemporary art, debuts at RFC. Participating artists include Jeff Koons, Maurizio Cattelan, and Rineke Dijkstra.

1992   **1993**   **1994**   **1998**   **1999**   **2000**   **2002**

After renovation, the Rubell Family Collection opens to the public, becoming one of the first private museums in America devoted to post-1980s art. The early exhibition schedule features selections from the Collection.

The RFC will undergo another extensive renovation in 2004 and begin a more ambitious public program offering thematic exhibitions and accompanying catalogs.

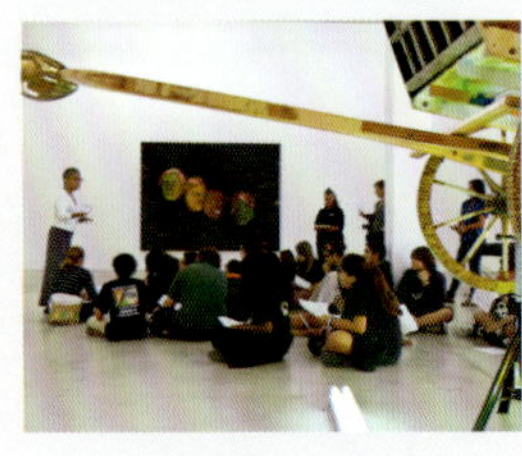

EXHIBITIONS 2004-2023:

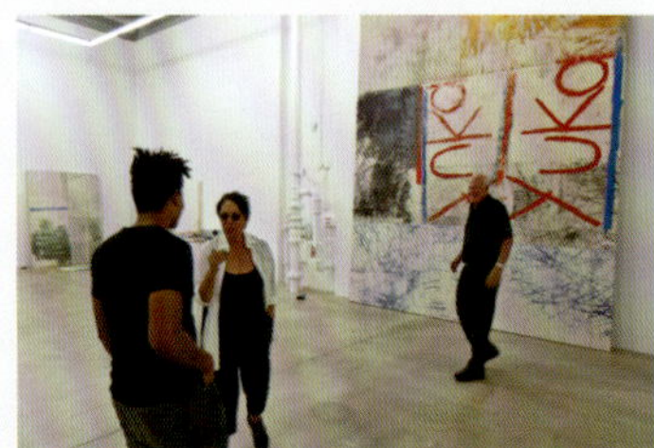

Richard Prince, 2004 (catalog)
Eberhard Havekost, 2004 (cat.)
Life After Death: New Leipzig Paintings, 2004 (cat.)
Memorials of Identity, 2004 (cat.)
Against All Odds: Keith Haring, 2005
At This Time: 10 Miami Artists, 2005
Poles Apart, 2005
Seriality, 2005
Andro Wekua, 2005
Red Eye: L.A. Artists from the Rubell Family Collection, 2006 (cat.)
Euro-Centric, 2007
Hernan Bas, 2007 (cat.)
John Stezaker, 2007 (cat.)
30 Americans, 2008 (cat.)
Beg, Borrow and Steal, 2009 (cat.)

How Soon Now, 2010 (cat.)
Time Capsule, Age 13 to 21: The Contemporary Art Collection of Jason Rubell, 2010 (cat.)
American Exuberance, 2011 (cat.)
Alone Together, 2012
Oscar Murillio: work, 2012 (cat.)
28 Chinese, 2013 (cat.)
Aaron Curry, 2014
Neil Beloufa, 2014
Will Boone, 2014
Lucy Dodd, 2014 (cat.)
Mark Flood, 2014
David Ostrowski, 2014
Kaari Upson, 2014
To Have and to Hold, 2014
No Man's Land, 2015 (cat.)
High Anxiety, 2016
New Shamans, 2016 (cat.)
Still Human, 2017
Allison Zuckerman, 2017 (cat.)
Christina Quarles, 2017
Purvis Young, 2018 (cat.)
Jonathan Lyndon Chase, 2018
Amoako Boafo, 2019

Yayoi Kusama: Infinity Rooms and Narcissus Garden, 2019
Natalie Ball, 2020
Genesis Tramaine: Sanctuary, 2020
Casja von Zeipel, 2021
Reginald O'Neal: As I Am, 2021
Kennedy Yanko, 2021
Otis Kwame Kye Quaicoe, 2021
Tesfaye Urgessa, 2022
Clayton Schiff, 2022
Jo Messer, 2022
Jared McGriff, 2022
Doron Langberg, 2022
Patricia Ayres, 2022
What's Going On, 2022
Sylvia Snowden, 2022
Alexandre Diop, 2022 (cat.)

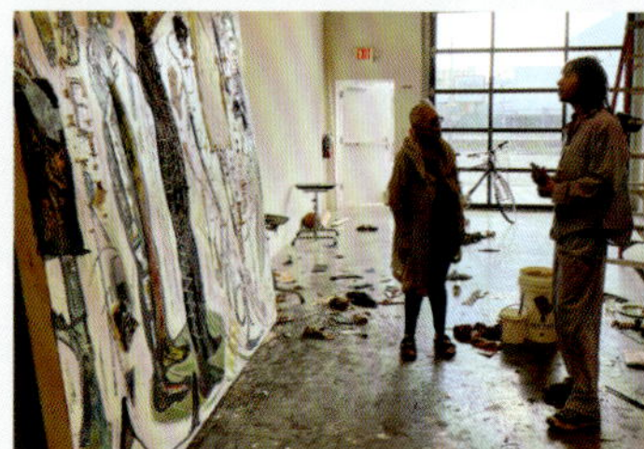

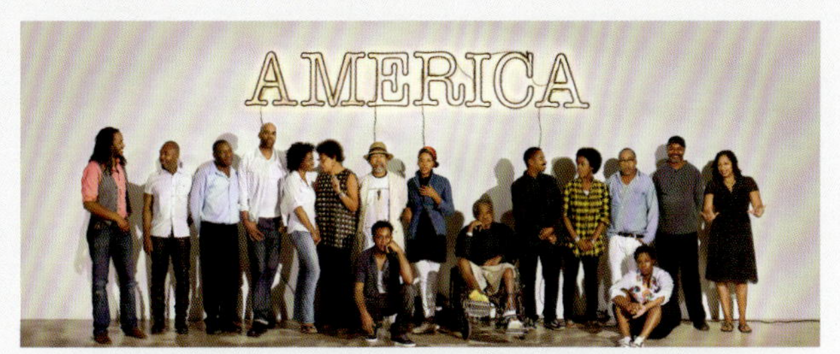

The exhibition *30 Americans*, a selection of more than 200 works by 31 artists collected over a 25-year period, is presented at the RFC and subsequently travels to 22 museums across the country. To date, *30 Americans* is one of, if not the, most traveled contemporary art exhibitions in the country, drawing an audience of over a million visitors.

In 2011, President Barack Obama and his family visit the exhibition while it is on view at the Corcoran Gallery of Art in Washington DC.

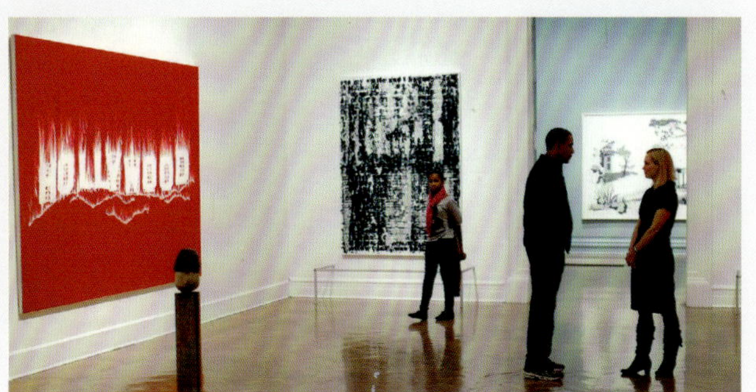

The Rubells purchase a series of adjacent food-processing warehouses at 1100 NW 23rd Street in Miami's Allapattah neighborhood, which becomes the site of the new Rubell Museum. Designed by architect Annabelle Selldorf, the new museum will feature a cohesive 100,000-square-foot-campus with 36 galleries, an extensive and publicly accessible research library, a garden courtyard, and a restaurant.

Don and Mera receive the Smithsonian's Archives of American Art Medal, which honors distinguished service in advancing the field of American art.

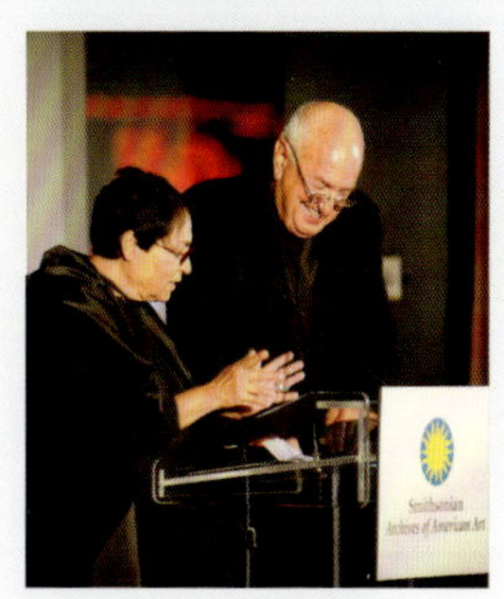

The Rubell Family Collection in Wynwood closes in June after presenting its largest single-artist-exhibition to date, *Purvis Young*.

The new Rubell Museum opens in December with an inaugural exhibition that features more than 300 works by 100 artists, highlighting key moments in contemporary art over the past 50 years.

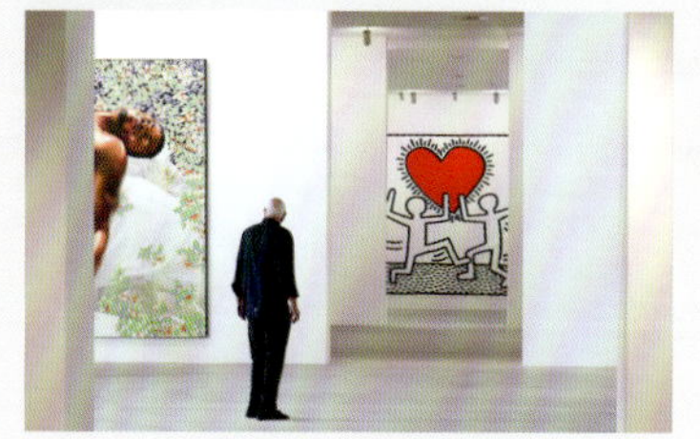

2003 · · · **2005** · · · **2008** · · · **2010** · · · **2011** · · · **2012** · · · **2014** · · · **2015** · · · **2019** · · · **2022**

The RFC establishes its museum studies internship program. Supported in part by a grant from the Knight Foundation, the program offers experiential learning for undergraduate and graduate students.

The RFC begins loaning comprehensive exhibitions to other museums, starting with *Life After Death: New Leipzig Paintings from the Rubell Family Collection* to the Massachusetts Museum of Contemporary Art. To date, 15 exhibitions have been loaned to 48 museums worldwide.

With support from the Knight Foundation, the RFC establishes its artist residency program; Sterling Ruby is the first recipient. Subsequent resident artists are Oscar Murillo (2012), Lucy Dodd (2014), Sônia Gomes (2015), Cy Gavin (2016), Allison Zuckerman (2017), Jonathan Lyndon Chase (2018), Amoako Boafo (2019), Genesis Tramaine (2020), Kennedy Yanko (2021), Otis Kwame Kye Quaicoe (2021), Alexandre Diop (2022), and Basil Kincaid (2023).

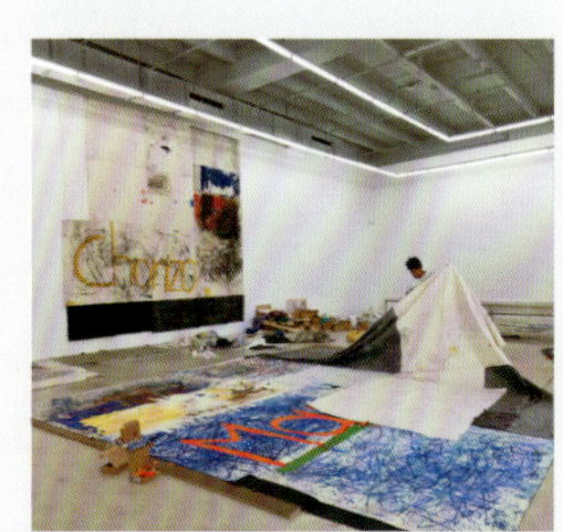

Mera and Don are honored for their philanthropy and commitment to African American artists at the Museum of Modern Art's Jazz Interlude, an annual event organized by The Friends of Education.

As a guest curator for the Washington Project for the Arts Mera visits 36 studios in 36 hours across DC and Baltimore.

The RFC begins hosting the annual Scholastic Art Awards, presenting hundreds of artworks from students across Miami.

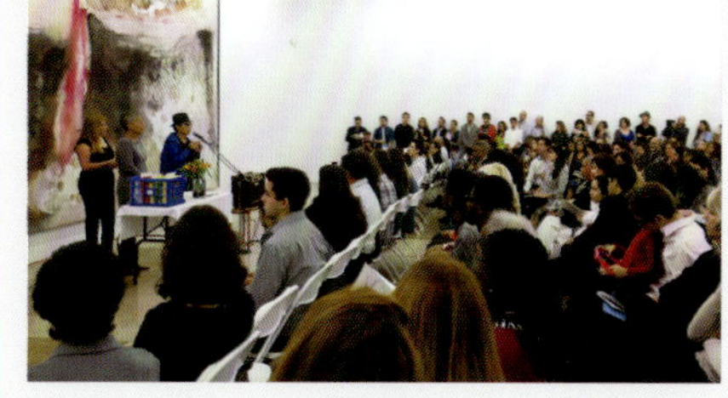

After a 14-year process, the 35,000-square-foot Rubell Museum DC opens at 65 i Street SW in Washington, DC, on the site of the former Randall Junior High School (1927-1978). The inaugural exhibition, *What's Going On*, inspired by alumnus Marvin Gaye, features nearly 200 works by a multi-generational group of 51 artists.

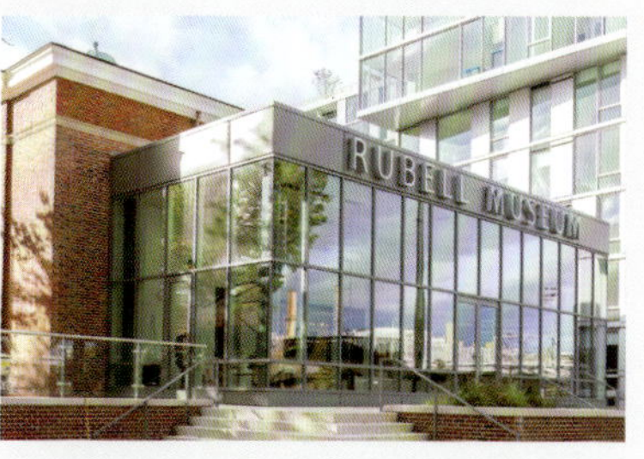

Rubell Museum exhibitions have traveled to the following institutions

30 Americans
2022 New Britain Museum of American Art, New Britain, CT
2021-22 Columbia Museum of Art, Columbia, SC
2021 Arlington Art Museum, Arlington, TX
2020-21 Albuquerque Museum, Albuquerque, NM
2020 Honolulu Museum of Art, Honolulu, HI
2019-20 Barnes Foundation, Philadelphia, PA
2019 Nelson-Atkins Museum of Art, Kansas City, MO
2019 Joslyn Art Museum, Omaha, NE
2018 Juliet Art Museum, Charleston, WV
2018 McNay Art Museum, San Antonio, TX
2017 Tacoma Art Museum, Tacoma, WA
2016 Cincinnati Art Museum, Cincinnati, OH
2015-16 Detroit Institute of the Arts, Detroit, MI
2015 Arkansas Arts Center, Little Rock, AK
2014 Contemporary Art Center, New Orleans, LA
2013-14 Frist Center for the Visual Arts, Nashville, TN
2013 Milwaukee Art Museum, Milwaukee, WI
2012 Chrysler Museum of Art, Norfolk, VA
2011-12 Corcoran Gallery of Art, Washington, DC
2011 North Carolina Museum of Art, Raleigh, NC

Beg, Borrow and Steal
2014-15 Taubman Museum of Art, Roanoke, VA
2013 Palm Springs Art Museum, Palm Springs, CA

Being Human: Contemporary Art from the Rubell Museum
2022 Flint Institute of Arts, Flint, MI

28 Chinese
2016 San Antonio Museum of Art, San Antonio, TX
2016 Asian Art Museum of San Francisco, San Francisco, CA

Eberhard Havekost: 1996-2006 Paintings from the Rubell Family Collection
2007 The Tampa Museum of Art, Tampa, FL
2007 The Art Galleries of Florida Gulf Coast University, Fort Myers, FL
2006 Katzen Arts Center, American University Museum, Washington, DC

Hernan Bas
2009 Brooklyn Museum, Brooklyn, NY

Keith Haring: Against All Odds
2023 Akron Art Museum, Akron, OH
2019 Arlington Museum of Art, Arlington, TX
2008-09 Palm Springs Art Museum, Palm Springs, CA

Life After Death: New Leipzig Paintings from the Rubell Family Collection
2008 Richard E. Peeler Art Center, DePauw University, Greencastle, IN
2007-08 Kemper Museum of Contemporary Art, Kansas City, MO
2007 Salt Lake Art Center, Salt Lake City, UT
2007 Frye Art Museum, Seattle, WA
2006 Katzen Arts Center, American University Museum, Washington, DC
2006 SITE Santa Fe, Santa Fe, NM
2005-06 Massachusetts Museum of Contemporary Art, North Adams, MA

Made in Germany: Contemporary Art from the Rubell Family Collection
2019 Vero Beach Museum of Art, Vero Beach, FL
2016 McNay Art Museum, San Antonio, TX

Memorials of Identity: New Media from the Rubell Family Collection
2007 The Tampa Museum of Art, Tampa, FL
2007 Haifa Museum of Art, Haifa, Israel

NO MAN'S LAND: Women Artists from the Rubell Family Collection
2022-23 Arkansas Arts Center, Little Rock, AR
2017 National Museum of Women in the Arts, Washington, DC

Paintings from the Rubell Family Collection
2012 Fundación Banco Santander, Madrid, Spain

Rebel/Re-Belle: Selections from the Asheville Art Museum and the Rubell Museum
2022 Asheville Art Museum, Asheville, NC

Time Capsule, Age 13 to 21: The Contemporary Art Collection of Jason Rubell
2012 Nasher Museum of Art, Duke University, Durham, NC

Rubell Museum artworks have been loaned to the following institutions

Akron Art Museum, Akron, OH
1991 'Power: Its Myths and Mores in American Culture, 1961-1991,' *Jeff Koons, New Hoover Convertible*, 1980
1984 'Robert Longo: Drawings and Reliefs,' Robert Longo, *Men Trapped in Ice*, 1979

Albright-Knox Art Gallery, Buffalo, NY
1981-82 'Figures: Forms and Expressions,' Francesco Clemente, *Two Painters*, 1980

Aldrich Museum of Art, Ridgefield, CT
1990-91 'German Photography Today,' Bernd + Hilla Becher, *Untitled (Water Towers 0)*, 1988
1987 'Post Abstract Abstraction,' Philip Taaffe, *Pharos*, 1985

Allen Memorial Art Museum, Oberlin, OH
1981 'The Young Americans,' David Salle, *Rainy Night in the Rubber City*, 1980

Art Institute of Chicago, Chicago, IL
2002-03 'Juan Muñoz,' Juan Muñoz, *Enano con Tres Columnas*, 1988

The Art Museum of South Texas, Corpus Christi, TX
1995 'Critiques of Pure Abstraction,' by Independent Curators Incorporated, Sherrie Levine, *Untitled (Golden Knots: 5)*, 1987

Asia Society and Museum, New York, NY
2010-11 'Yoshitomo Nara,' Yoshitomo Nara, *Hyper Enough (to the City)*, 1996; *Too Young to Die*, 2001

Aspen Art Museum, Aspen, CO
2017-18 'Nate Lowman: Before and After,' Nate Lowman, *Bikinicide*, 2012; *Untitled (Survivor Series)*, 2011
2017 'Adam McEwen,' Adam McEwen, *Untitled (Yoga Mat)*, 2008
1999 'Twenty Years Twenty Artists,' Francesco Clemente, *Untitled*, 1980

The Atlanta College of Art Gallery, Atlanta, GA
2000 'Post-Hypnotic,' Philip Taaffe, *Brest*, 1985

Baltimore Museum of Art, Baltimore, MD
2021 'Tschabalala Self: By My Self', Tschabalala Self, *Two Women*, 2019
2018-19 'John Waters: Indecent Exposure,' John Waters, *Beverly Hills John*, 2012; *Brainiac*, 2014; *Library Science #5*, 2014; *Library Science #6*, 2014; *Library Science #8*, 2014; *Shoulda!*, 2014

Bass Museum of Art, Miami Beach, FL
2014 'Gold', Chris Burden, *Gold Bullets*, 2003
2010 'Human Rites,' Christian Boltanski, *Untitled (Reserve)*, 1989

Berkeley Art Museum & Pacific Film Archive, University of California, Berkeley, CA
2018 'Christina Quarles / MATRIX 271,' Christina Quarles, *...Tha Color of Tha Sky (Magic Hour)*, 2017
2004 'MATRIX 213: Some Forgotten Place,' William Sasnal, *Duel*, 2001
2000 'Peter Doig/Matrix 183,' Peter Doig, *Study for Echo Lake (Screaming Cop)*, 1999
1991 'Rosemarie Trockel,' Rosemarie Trockel, *Grosse Als Form [Size as Form]*, 1984

Brooklyn Museum, New York, NY
2015 'Kehinde Wiley: A New Republic,' Kehinde Wiley, *Sleep*, 2008
2008-09 'Gilbert & George: Pictures 1971-2006,' Gilbert & George, *Apostasia*, 2004; Gilbert & George, *Finding God*, 1982
2008 'Murakami ©,' Takashi Murakami, *PO+KU Surrealism Mr. DOB-Blue*, 1998

Cantor Arts Center, Stanford University, Stanford, CA
2012-13 'Jameel Prize,' Hayv Kahraman, *Migrant I*, 2009

Carnegie Museum of Art, Pittsburgh, PA
1999-2000 '1999-2000 Carnegie International,' Gregor Schneider Ur 21, *Loch (Hole)*, Rheydt, 1997; Luc Tuymans, *Christ*, 1988

Center for Curatorial Studies, Bard College, Annandale-on-Hudson, NY
2009 'Rachel Harrison: Consider the Lobster,' Rachel Harrison, *Untitled (Hat/Broom)*, 2005
1999 'Takashi Murakami: The Meaning of the Nonsense of the Meaning,' Takashi Murakami, *Four Monks Sleep*, 1998

Center for Fine Arts, Miami, FL
1993 'Philip Taaffe,' Philip Taaffe, *Brest*, 1985
1986 'New Art of Italy,' Francesco Clemente, *Self-Portrait (Inside/Outside)*, 1979

CEPA Gallery, Contemporary Photography & Visual Arts Center, Buffalo, NY
1981-82 'Figures: Forms and Expressions,' Francesco Clemente, *Two Painters*, 1980

The Chicago Cultural Center, Chicago, IL
2022 'Art and Race Matters: The Career of Robert Colescott,' Robert Colescott, *Arab: The Emir of Iswid (How Wide the Gulf?)*, 1992; *Delacrow's Masterwork: A Mockumentary Film*, 1976
2018 'Nina Chanel Abney,' Nina Chanel Abney, *The Party's Over*, 2007; *The Boardroom*, 2008
2000 'Post-Hypnotic,' Philip Taaffe, *Brest*, 1985

Cleveland Museum of Art, OH
2018 'Kerry James Marshall: Works on Paper,' Kerry James Marshall, *Study (for party woodcut)*, 1998

Contemporary Art Center of Virginia, Virginia Beach, VA
2007 'Counterparts: Contemporary Painters and Their Influences,' Kerry James Marshall, *Vignette #10*, 2007

The Contemporary Arts Center, Cincinnati, OH
2019-20 'Art and Race Matters: The Career of Robert Colescott,' Robert Colescott, *Arab: The Emir of Iswid (How Wide the Gulf?)*, 1992; *Delacrow's Masterwork: A Mockumentary Film*, 1976
1999 'Post-Hypnotic,' Philip Taaffe, *Brest*, 1985
1986 'New Art From Italy,' Francesco Clemente, *Two Painters*, 1980
1992 'South Bronx Hall of Fame: Sculpture by John Ahearn and Rigoberto Torres,' John Ahearn, *Bobbie (Sneaker Town USA)*, 1981; *Migna*, 1981

Contemporary Arts Museum Houston, Houston, TX
2003 'Juan Muñoz,' Juan Muñoz, *Enano con Tres Columnas*, 1988
1991 'OBJECTives: The New Sculpture,' Tony Cragg, *Mother's Milk*, 1988; Jeff Koons, *Two Kids*, 1986
1991 'South Bronx Hall of Fame: Sculpture by John Ahearn and Rigoberto Torres,' John Ahearn, *Bobbie (Sneaker Town USA)*, 1981; *Migna*, 1981
1986 'Robert Longo: Sequences/Men in the Cities,' Robert Longo, *Men Trapped in Ice*, 1979

Contemporary Jewish Museum, San Francisco, CA
2001-02 'Christian Boltanski: Faces of Memory,' Christian Boltanski, *Autel de Lycee Chases [Altar to Chases High School]*, 1986-1987

The Contemporary Museum, Honolulu, HI
1992 'South Bronx Hall of Fame: Sculpture by John Ahearn and Rigoberto Torres,' John Ahearn, *Bobbie (Sneaker Town USA)*, 1981; *Migna*, 1981

Corcoran Gallery of Art, Washington, DC
1991 'OBJECTives: The New Sculpture,' Tony Cragg, *Mother's Milk*, 1988; Jeff Koons, *Two Kids*, 1986

Crocker Art Museum, Sacramento, CA
1995 'Critiques of Pure Abstraction,' Sherrie Levine, *Untitled (Golden Knots: 5)*, 1987

Dallas Museum of Art, Dallas, TX
2010 'Luc Tuymans,' Luc Tuymans, *Diorama*, 2001
1979 'Carl Andre Sculpture 1959-1977,' Carl Andre, *Llano Estacado*, Dallas, Texas, 1979

de Young Museum, San Francisco, CA
2008 'Gilbert & George: Pictures 1971-2006,' Gilbert & George, *Apostasia*, 2004; *Finding God*, 1982

Fort Wayne Museum of Art, Fort Wayne, IN
1986-87 'Robert Longo: Sequences/Men in the Cities,' Robert Longo, *Men Trapped in Ice*, 1979

Frist Arts Museum, Nashville, TN
2023 'Multiplicity: Blackness in Contemporary American Collage,' Jamea Richmond-Edwards, *Archetype of a 5 Star*, 2018
2016 'Phantom Bodies,' Christian Boltanski, *Untitled (Réserve)*, 1989

FRONT International, Cleveland, OH
2018 'Josh Kline,' Josh Kline, *Indifference*, 2017; *Politics is like the weather*, 2017; *Indifference*, 2017

Frye Art Museum, Seattle, WA
2023 'Flying Woman: The Paintings of Katherine Bradford,' Katherine Bradford, *Stripe People with Arms*, 2018
2022 'Christina Quarles,' Christina Quarles, *...Tha Color of Tha Sky (Magic Hour)*, 2017
2016 'Noah Davis,' Noah Davis, *Painting for My Dad*, 2011

Hammer Museum, Los Angeles, CA
2020 'Tishan Hsu: Liquid Circuit,' Tishan Hsu, *Closed Circuit II*, 1986
2015 'Perfect Likeness,' Elad Lassry, *Selkirk Rex, LaPerm*, 2011
1995 'Critiques of Pure Abstraction,' Sherrie Levine, *Untitled (Golden Knots: 5)*, 1987

The Harvard University Art Museums, Cambridge, MA
2000 'Landmark Pictures: Ed Ruscha/Andreas Gursky,' Andreas Gursky, *Ratingen Schwimmbad, (Swimming Pool)*, 1987

Herbert F. Johnson Museum of Art, Cornell University, Ithaca, NY
1999 'We were happy to be able to own something that wasn't easy, that was astonishing.' Selections from the Rubell Family Collection

High Museum of Art, Atlanta, GA
2013 'Rashid Johnson: Message to Our Folks,' Rashid Johnson, *The Shuttle*, 2011
1988 'Art at the Edge: Sherrie Levine,' Sherrie Levine, *Untitled (Golden Knots: 5)*, 1987

Hirshhorn Museum and Sculpture Garden, Washington, DC
2018 'Brand New: Art and Commodity in the 1980s,' Jeff Koons, *Art Ad Portfolio*, 1988-1989; *New Hoover Deluxe Rug Shampooer*, 1979; R. M. Fischer, *Elbow Macaroni*, 1979
2001-02 'Juan Muñoz,' Juan Muñoz, *Enano con Tres Columnas*, 1988
2000 'Robert Gober: Sculpture + Drawing,' Robert Gober, *Untitled (Large Sink)*, 1984; *Untitled (Pencil on Paper)*, 1984
1988 'Directions: Sherrie Levine,' Sherrie Levine, *Untitled (Golden Knots: 5)*, 1987

Indianapolis Museum of Art, Indianapolis, IN
1991 'Power: Its Myths and Mores in American Culture, 1961-1991,' Jeff Koons, *New Hoover Convertible*, 1980

Institute of Contemporary Art, Boston, MA
1991 'Rosemarie Trockel,' Rosemarie Trockel, *Grosse Als Form [Size as Form]*, 1984
1988 'The BiNational: American Art of the Late '80s,' Robert Gober, *Slanted Playpen*, 1987; Jeff Koons, *Two Kids*, 1986

Institute of Contemporary Art, Los Angeles, CA
2020 'No Wrong Holes: Thirty Years of Nayland Blake,' Nayland Blake, *Untitled*, 1990
2018-19 'Nina Chanel Abney: Royal Flush,' Nina Chanel Abney, *The Boardroom*, 2008; *The Party's Over*, 2007

Institute of Contemporary Art, Miami, FL
2019 'Purvis Young: Drawings,' Purvis Young, four *Untitled*, 1980-1990
2018 'Diamond Stingily: Life In My Pocket,' Diamond Stingily, *Entryways*, 2017
2016 'John Miller,' John Miller, *Everything is Said #8*, 2019; *Everything is Said #14*, 2010

Institute of Contemporary Art at the University of Pennsylvania, Philadelphia, PA
2017 'Myths of the Marble,' Shahryar Nashat, *Hard Up for Support*, 2016
2014 'Ruffneck Constructivists,' Lior Shvil, *Operation OZ Belev-Yam*, 2011
1994 'Face Off: The Portrait in Recent Art,' Christian Boltanski, *Autel de Lycée Chases [Altar to Chases High School]*, 1986-1987

1991 'Rousing the Rubble,' David Hammons, *Esquire (or John Henry)*, 1990

1998 'Three Stanzas: Miroslaw Balka, Robert Gober, and Seamus Heaney,' Robert Gober, *Slanted Playpen*, 1987

1985 'East Village Artists,' David Wojnarowicz, *I Use Maps Because I Don't Know How to Paint*, 1984

International Center of Photography, New York, NY
2003 'The First ICP Triennial of Photography and Video: Strangers,' Fiona Tan, *Facing Forward*, 1999

Jeffrey Deitch, New York, NY
2020 'Peter Nagy: Entertainment Erases History,' Peter Nagy, *Parasitical Clown Dough*, 1987

John and Mable Ringling Museum of Art, Sarasota, FL
1989 'Abstraction in Question,' Philip Taaffe, *Pharos*, 1985
1987-88 'Projects 1: Mike + Doug Starn – The Christ Series,' Mike + Doug Starn, *Rose with Christ*, 1982-1986,

The John F. Kennedy Center for the Performing Arts, Washington, DC
2011 'Hall of Nations,' Jitish Kallat, *Public Notice 2*, 2007

Joslyn Art Museum, Omaha, NE
1986 'New Art of Italy,' Francesco Clemente, *Self-Portrait (Inside/Outside)*, 1979

kurimanzutto, Mexico City, MX
2020 'siembra,' Felix Gonzalez-Torres, *Untitled (Join)*, 1990

Los Angeles County Museum of Art, Los Angeles, CA
2023-2024 'Woven Histories: Textiles and Modern Abstraction,' Rosemarie Trockel, *Untitled*, 1986, *Untitled*, 1986
2021 'Yoshitomo Nara,' Yoshitomo Nara, *Sleepless Night (Sitting)*, 1997
2019-20 'The Allure of Matter: Material Art from China,' He Xiangyu, *A Barrel of Dregs of Coca-Cola*, 2009; *Cola Project - 9 Sketches*, 2010
2011 'Glenn Ligon: AMERICA,' Glenn Ligon, *Untitled (America)*, 2008
1994 'Mike Kelley: Catholic Tastes,' Mike Kelley, *Screamin' Smoke*, 1985

Lowe Art Museum, Coral Gables, FL
2020-21 'NEXUS: Contemporary Art from Leading Miami Collections,' Allison Zuckerman, *The Queen*, 2017
1995 'Critiques of Pure Abstraction,' Sherrie Levine, *Untitled (Golden Knots: 5)*, 1987

MASS MoCA, North Adams, MA
2018-19 'THE LURE OF THE DARK,' Noah Davis, *Painting for My Dad*, 2011

Massachusetts College of Art, Boston, MA
2001 'Post-Hypnotic,' Philip Taaffe, *Brest*, 1985

Massachusetts Institute of Technology, Boston, MA
2012-2013 'In the Holocene,' Thea Djordjadze, *Pythagoras*, 2007

Mattress Factory, Pittsburgh, PA
1989 'Cady Noland,' Cady Noland, *This Piece Has No Title Yet*, 1989

The McKinney Avenue Contemporary, Dallas, TX
2000 'Post-Hypnotic,' Philip Taaffe, *Brest*, 1985

McNay Art Museum, San Antonio, TX
2020 'Fashion Nirvana: Runway to Everyday,' Rineke Dijkstra, *The Buzzclub, Liverpool, U.K./Mysterworld, Zaandam, NL*, 1996-1997
2018 'Transamerica/n: Gender, Identity, Appearance Today,' Frank Benson, *Juliana Prototype*, 2014-2015

The Menil Collection, Houston, TX
2013-14 'Luc Tuymans: Portraits,' Luc Tuymans, *Christ*, 1988
2009 'Marlene Dumas: Measuring Your Own Grave,' Marlene Dumas, *Imaginary 2*, 2002

The Metropolitan Museum of Art, New York, NY
2023 'Cecily Brown: Death and the Maid,' Cecily Brown, *The Only Game in Town*, 1998
2012 'Regarding Warhol: Sixty Artists, Fifty Years,' Sarah Lucas, *Hunk of the Year*, 1990-1992

Miami Art Museum, Miami, FL
2012 'Rashid Johnson: Message to Our Folks,' Rashid Johnson, *The Shuttle*, 2011

2008-09 'Objects of Value,' Chris Burden, *Gold Bullets (Roundies)*, 2003

Mildred Lane Kemper Art Museum, Washington University, St. Louis, MO
2013 'Rashid Johnson: Message to Our Folks,' Rashid Johnson, *The Shuttle*, 2011
2012 'John Stezaker,' John Stezaker, *Blind*, 1970; *The Trial*, 1978; *Tabula Rasa II*, 1983

Milwaukee Art Museum, Milwaukee, WI
2008 'Gilbert & George: Pictures 1971-2006,' Gilbert & George, *Apostasia*, 2004; *Finding God*, 1982

Modern Art Museum of Fort Worth, Fort Worth, TX
2018 'TAKASHI MURAKAMI: THE OCTOPUS EATS ITS OWN LEG,' Takashi Murakami, *PO+KU Surrealism (Blue)*, 1999
2014-15 'Urban Theater: New York in the 1980s,' Philip Taaffe, *Brest*, 1985; Keith Haring, *Untitled*, 1981; *Untitled*, 1981
2012 'Glenn Ligon: AMERICA,' Glenn Ligon, *Untitled (America)*, 2008
2007 'Pretty Baby,' Yoshitomo Nara, *Dogs from Your Childhood*, 1999

MoMA PS1, New York, NY
2013-14 'Mike Kelley,' Mike Kelley, *Extracurricular Activity Projective Reconstruction #9 (Fresno)*, 2005
2013 'EXPO 1: New York Dark Optimism,' John Miller, *A Refusal to Accept Limits*, 2007
2001 'Uniform: Order and Disorder,' Maurizio Cattelan, *La rivoluzione siamo noi*, 2000
1991 'Rousing the Rubble,' David Hammons, *Esquire*, 1990

Museum of Art and Design, Miami, FL
2020-21 'The Body Electric,' Anicka Yi, *A Box in Which Four Seasons Will Fit Again*, 2015

Museum of Contemporary Art, Chicago, IL
2022 'Christina Quarles,' Christina Quarles, *...Tha Color of Tha Sky (Magic Hour)*, 2017
2017 'Takashi Murakami, *PO+KU Surrealism (Blue)*, 1999
2013 'Homebodies,' Robert Gober, *Slanted Playpen*, 1987
2012 'Rashid Johnson: Message to Our Folks,' Rashid Johnson, *The Shuttle*, 2011
2011 'This Will Have Been: Art, Love & Politics in the 1980s,' Richard Prince, *Untitled (man's hand with cigarette)*, 1980
2010-11 'Luc Tuymans,' Luc Tuymans, *Diorama*, 2001
2008 'Jeff Koons,' Jeff Koons, *Two Kids*, 1986
1999 'Charles Ray,' Charles Ray, *Oh! Charley, Charley, Charley...*, 1992
1991 'Rosemarie Trockel,' Rosemarie Trockel, *Grosse Als Form [Size as Form]*, 1984
1988 'Jeff Koons: Works 1979–1988,' Jeff Koons, *New Hoover Convertible*, 1980

Museum of Contemporary Art, Los Angeles, CA
2014 'Mike Kelley,' Mike Kelley, *Extracurricular Activity Projective Reconstruction # 9 (Fresno)*, 2005
2008 'Marlene Dumas: Measuring Your Own Grave,' Marlene Dumas, *Imaginary 2*, 2002
2007-08 'Murakami ©,' Takashi Murakami, *PO+KU Surrealism Mr. DOB-Blue*, 1998
2002-03 'Juan Muñoz,' Juan Muñoz, *Enano con Tres Columnas*, 1988
1998-99 'Charles Ray,' Charles Ray, *Oh! Charley, Charley, Charley...*, 1992

Museum of Contemporary Art, North Miami, FL
2023 'Jamea Richmond-Edwards: Ancient Future,' Jamea Richmond-Edwards, *Shirt with Lace Heart*, 2018
2009-10 'The Reach of Realism,' Thomas Demand, *Bathroom (Badezimmer - Beau Rivage)*, 1997; *Wand/Mural*, 1999
2001 'Mythic Proportions: Paintings in the 1980s,' Ross Bleckner, *Architecture of the Sky*, 1990; Keith Haring, *Untitled (Martian Attack)*, 1981; *Untitled (Mickey Mouse on TV)*, 1981; *Untitled (Mickey Mouse over stripes)*, 1981; *Untitled (Sombrero [AKA: UFO] and Mickey Mouse)*, 1981
1999 'Great Illusions,' Thomas Demand, *Bathroom (Badezimmer - Beau Rivage)*, 1997
1998 'Keith Haring Retrospective,' Keith Haring, *Untitled (Martian Attack)*, 1981; *Untitled (Mickey Mouse on TV)*, 1981

Museum of Contemporary Art San Diego, La Jolla, CA
1995 'Sleeper: Katharina Fritsch, Robert Gober, Guillermo Kuitca, Doris Salcedo,' Robert Gober, *Slanted Playpen*, 1987

Museum of Fine Arts, Boston, MA
1994 'Self Made/Self Conscious,' Janine Antoni, *Eureka*, 1993

Museum of Modern Art, New York, NY
2014 'Robert Gober: The Heart is Not a Metaphor,' Robert Gober, *Slanted Playpen*, 1987
2012-13 'Cindy Sherman,' Cindy Sherman, *Untitled (#397)*, 2000
2008 'Marlene Dumas: Measuring Your Own Grave,' Marlene Dumas, *Imaginary 2*, 2002

Nasher Museum of Art, Durham, NC
2017 'Nina Chanel Abney: Royal Flush,' Nina Chanel Abney, *Class of 2007*, 2017

Nasher Sculpture Center, Dallas, TX
2011 'Statuesque,' Paweł Althamer, *Sylwia*, 2010

National Gallery of Art, Washington, DC
2023-24 'Woven Histories: Textiles and Modern Abstraction,' Rosemarie Trockel, *Untitled*, 1986, *Untitled*, 1986
2023 'The Land Carries Our Ancestors: Contemporary Art by Native Americans,' Natalie Ball, *Bang Bang*, 2019

National Museum of Woman in the Arts, Washington, D.C.
2017 'Revival,' Beverly Semmes, *Blue Gowns*, 1993; Sônia Gomes, *Made In America*, 2015; *Sem Titulo da série Torcao*, 2015; *Sem Titulo da série Torcao*, 2015

National Portrait Gallery, Washington, DC
2008 'Recognize! Hip Hop and Contemporary Portraiture,' Kehinde Wiley, *Equestrian Portrait of the Count-Duke Olivares*, 2005

Nerman Museum of Contemporary Art, Overland Park, KS
2004 'Dana Schutz,' Dana Schutz, *Lovers*, 2003

Neuberger Museum of Art, NYNeuberger Museum of Art, NY
2019 'Nina Chanel Abney: Royal Flush,' Nina Chanel Abney, *The Boardroom*, 2008; *The Party's Over*, 2007
2015 'GOLD,' John Miller, *The Newcomers*, 2008; *The Young and the Restless*, 2008; Chris Burden, *Gold Bullets*, 2003

New Museum, New York, NY
2023 'Wangechi Mutu: Intertwined,' Wangechi Mutu, *Non je ne regrette rien*, 2007 and *The Evolution of Mud Mama from Beginning to Start*, 2008
2022 'Art and Race Matters: The Career of Robert Colescott,' Robert Colescott, *Arab: The Emir of Iswid (How Wide the Gulf?)*, 1992; *Delacrow's Masterwork: A Mockumentary Film*, 1976
2013 'NYC 1993: Experimental Jet Set, Trash and No Star,' Paul McCarthy, *Cultural Gothic*, 1992-1993
2007-08 'Unmonumental: Falling to Pieces in the 21st Century,' Matthew Monahan, *Liberator's Retreat*, 2006
2004-05 'East Village USA,' McDermott & McGough, *Scapegoat*, 1986
1988-89 'Christian Boltanski,' Christian Boltanski, *Lycée Chases (8) [Chases High School (8)]*, 1986-1987

Newport Harbor Art Museum, Newport Beach, CA
1990 'OBJECTives: The New Sculpture,' Tony Cragg, *Mother's Milk*, 1988; Jeff Koons, *Two Kids*, 1986

New York Historical Society, New York, NY
2006-07 'Legacies: Contemporary Artists Reflect on Slavery, Leonardo Drew,' Leonardo Drew, *Untitled #25*, 1992

Norton Museum of Art, West Palm Beach, FL
1998 'Favorites,' Joseph Beuys, *Felt Suit*, 1970

NSU Art Museum, Ft. Lauderdale, FL
2022 'Confrontation: Keith Haring & Pierre Alechinsky,' Keith Haring, *Untitled*, 1988
2021-22 'Jared McGriff: Where We Are You,' Jared McGriff, *Trio as One*, 2020; *They Become the Depths Between Them*, 2021
2019-20 'Happy!,' Alake Shilling, *Cheetah*, 2018; *Did Somebody Say Wonky*, 2018; *Ladybug*, 2018; *Nicky Mouse Vase*, 2018; *Tiger*, 2018
2017 'SOME AESTHETIC DECISIONS: A CENTENNIAL CELEBRATION OF MARCEL DUCHAMP'S FOUNTAIN,' Mike Kelley, *Rewrite*, 1995; *Pink Shadow*, 1989; Elad Lassry, *Czech Girl*, 2009; *Man*, 2007; *Lipstick*, 2009; *Selkirk Rex, LaPerm*, 2011

Orange County Museum of Art, Newport Beach, CA
2013 'Richard Jackson: Ain't Painting a Pain,' Richard Jackson, *The Blue Room*, 2010/2011

Orlando Museum of Art, Orlando, FL
2022 '2022 Florida Prize in Contemporary Art,' Jared McGriff, *Pink Dream Recliner*, 2019; *They become the Depths Between Them*, 2021; *Trio as One*, 2021

Philharmonic Center for the Arts, Naples, FL
2001 'Post-Hypnotic,' Philip Taaffe, *Brest*, 1985

The Phillip & Patricia Frost Art Museum, Florida International University, Miami, FL
2011-2012 'Tour de France/Florida: Contemporary Artists from France in Florida's Private Collections,' Christian Boltanski, *Lycée Chases (8) [Chases High School (8)]*, 1986-1987; *Untitled (Reserve)*, 1989

Portland Museum of Art, Portland, ME
2022 'Flying Woman: The Paintings of Katherine Bradford,' Katherine Bradford, *Stripe People with Arms*, 2018
2020 'Art and Race Matters: The Career of Robert Colescott,' Robert Colescott, *Arab: The Emir of Iswid (How Wide the Gulf?)*, 1992; *Delacrow's Masterwork: A Mockumentary Film*, 1976
2016 'Josh Kline: Freedom,' Josh Kline, *Freedom*, 2015

Queens Museum, Queens, NY
1990 'Keith Haring: Future Primeval,' Keith Haring, *Elvis Presley Posters (4)*, 1981; *Marilyn Monroe (3)*, 1981
1990 'Queens 1990, Circle: John Armleder, Neil Campbell, Adam Fuss, Olivier Mosset, James Nares, Peter Schuyff,' Olivier Mosset, *Untitled*, 1986

Ringling Museum of Art, Sarasota, FL
2016 'Phantom Bodies,' Christian Boltanski, *Untitled (Reserve)*, 1989

The Renaissance Society at The University of Chicago, Chicago, IL
2006 'And Every Woman Will Be A Walking Synthesis Of The Universe,' Mai-Thu Perret, *Apocalypse Ballet (Pink Ring)*, 2006; *Apocalypse Ballet (Neon Dress)*, 2006; *Apocalypse Ballet (2 White Rings)*, 2006; *Apocalypse Ballet (3 White Rings)*, 2006

Rose Art Museum, Brandeis University, Waltham, MA
2006 'Dana Schutz,' Dana Schutz, *Lovers*, 2003; *Frank on a Rock*, 2002

Rowan University Art Gallery, Glassboro, NJ
2019 '7 Mile Girls,' Jamea Richmond-Edwards, *Ancestral Matrix and Black Alligator Boots*, 2018; *Archetype of a 5 Star*, 2018; *Girl Standing with Green Alligator Bag Next to Mannequin*, 2018; *Shirt with Lace Heart*, 2018

San Antonio Museum of Art, San Antonio TX
2013 'Jameel Prize,' Hayv Kahraman, *Migrant I*, 2009

San Diego Museum of Art, San Diego, CA
1991 'Rousing the Rubble,' David Hammons, *Esquire (or John Henry)*, 1990

San Francisco Museum of Modern Art, San Francisco, CA
2010 'Luc Tuymans,' Luc Tuymans, *Diorama*, 2001
2000 'Robert Gober: Sculpture + Drawing,' Robert Gober, *Untitled (Large Sink)*, 1984; *Untitled (Pencil on Paper)*, 1984
1997-98 'Keith Haring Retrospective,' Keith Haring, *Untitled (Martian Attack)*, 1981; *Untitled (Mickey Mouse on TV)*, 1981
1992 'Jeff Koons Retrospective,' Jeff Koons, *New Hoover Deluxe Rug Shampooer I*, 1979; *New Hoover Convertible*, 1980; *Two Kids*, 1986; *Inflatable Flower (Tall Yellow)*, 1979
1988 'Projects 1: Mike + Doug Starn – The Christ Series,' Mike + Doug Starn, *Rose with Christ*, 1982/1986

Sarah Campbell Blaffer Art Museum, University of Houston, Houston, TX
2009 'Existed:Leonardo Drew,' Leonardo Drew, *Untitled #25*, 1992
1995 'Critiques of Pure Abstraction,' Sherrie Levine, *Untitled (Golden Knots: 5)*, 1987

Sarasota Museum of Art, Sarasota, FL
2021 'Art and Race Matters: The Career of Robert Colescott,' Robert Colescott, *Arab: The Emir of Iswid (How Wide the Gulf?)*, 1992; *Delacrow's Masterwork: A Mockumentary Film*, 1976

SCAD Museum of Art, Savannah, GA
  2020 'Kenturah Davis: Everything that Cannot Be Known,' Kenturah Davis, *Everything that Cannot Be Known*, 2019

SculptureCenter, New York, NY
  2020-2021 'Tishan Hsu: Liquid Circuit,' Tishan Hsu, *Closed Circuit II*, 1986

Sheldon Museum of Art, University of Nebraska, Lincoln, NE
  1995 'Critiques of Pure Abstraction,' Sherrie Levine, *Untitled (Golden Knots: 5)*, 1987

SITE Santa Fe, Sante Fe, NM
  2005 'Dana Schutz,' Dana Schutz, *Lovers*, 2003; Dana Schutz, *Frank on a Rock*, 2002
  2003 'Janine Antoni: taught tether teeter,' Janine Antoni, *Eureka*, 1993

Smithsonian National Portrait Gallery, Washington, DC
  2022-24 'Kinship,' Njideka Akunyili Crosby, *Nkem*, 2021

Solomon R. Guggenheim Museum, New York, NY
  2011-12 'Maurizio Cattelan,' Maurizio Cattelan, *Not Afraid of Love*, 2000; *Mother*, 1999; *Lavorare e un Brutto Mestiere*, 1993; *Sans Titre (Philippe)*, 1999
  2010 'Haunted: Contemporary Photography/ Video/ Performance,' Christian Boltanski, *Autel de Lycée Chases [Altar to Chases High School]*, 1986-1987; *Lycée Chases (8) [Chases High School (8)]*, 1986-1987
  2008-09 'Catherine Opie: American Photographer,' Catherine Opie, *Jo*, 1993; *John and Scott*, 1993; *Justin Bond*, 1993; *Mitch*, 1994
  2007 'Richard Prince: Spiritual America,' Richard Prince, *Untitled (man's hand with cigarette)*, 1980
  1995 'Ross Bleckner Retrospective,' Ross Bleckner, *Architecture of the Sky*, 1990

Storm King Art Center, Mountainville, NY
  2013 'Thomas Houseago: As I Went Out One Morning,' Thomas Houseago, *Untitled (Striding Figure 1)*, 2007

Studio Museum in Harlem, New York, NY
  2007 'Henry Taylor,' Henry Taylor, *Watts County*, 2004

Swiss Institute/Contemporary Art, New York, NY
  2006 'Space Boomerang,' Mark Handforth, *Honda*, 2002

Tarble Art Center at Eastern Illinois University, Charleston, IL
  2016 'Hank Willis Thomas,' Hank Willis Thomas, *Priceless*, 2004

Thread Waxing Space, New York, NY
  1992 'Three Sculptors: Leonardo Drew, Lisa Hoke, Brad Kahlhamer, Leonardo Drew,' Leonardo Drew, *Untitled #25*, 1992

Tucson Museum of Art, Tucson, AZ
  2021-22 'Patrick Martinez: Look What You Created,' Patrick Martinez, *No Justice, No Love*, 2020; *Tongva Landscape*, 2019
  2018 'Dress Matters: Clothing as Metaphor,' Catherine Opie, *Justin Bond*, 1993; Christian Boltanski, *Untitled (Réserve)*, 1989; Nick Cave, *Soundsuit*, 2006

The Tweed Museum of Art, University of Minnesota, Duluth, MN
  2001 'Post-Hypnotic,' Philip Taaffe, *Brest*, 1985

The University Art Museum at California State University, Long Beach, CA
  1986 'Robert Longo: Sequences/Men in the Cities,' Robert Longo, *Men Trapped in Ice*, 1979

The Underground Museum, Los Angeles, CA
  2022 'Noah Davis,' Noah Davis, *Painting for My Dad*, 2011

University Galleries, Illinois State University, Normal, IL
  1999 'Post-Hypnotic,' Philip Taaffe, *Brest*, 1985
  1991 'Keith Haring: Future Primeval,' Keith Haring, *Elvis Presley Posters (4)*, 1981; *Marilyn Monroe (3)*, 1981

University of Michigan Museum of Art, Ann Arbor, MI
  2014-15 'Reductive Minimalism: Women Artists in Dialogue, 1960-2014,' R.H. Quaytman, *Evas Arche April 3*, 2011
  2010-11 'Mai-Thu Perret: An Ideal for Living,' Mai-Thu Perret, *Apocalypse Ballet (Pink Ring)*, 2006; *Apocalypse Ballet (Neon Dress)*, 2006; *Apocalypse Ballet (2 White Rings)*, 2006; *Apocalypse Ballet (3 White Rings)*, 2006

USF Contemporary Art Museum, Tampa, FL
  2006 'Dragon Veins,' Takashi Murakami, *Four Monks Sleep*, 1998; *Oh My The Mr. DOB*, 1998
  1999 'We were happy to be able to own something that wasn't easy, that was astonishing.' Selections from the Rubell Family Collection

Virginia Museum of Fine Arts, Richmond, VA
  1991 'Power: Its Myths and Mores in American Culture, 1961-1991,' Jeff Koons, *New Hoover Convertible*, 1980
  1984 'East Village Artists,' David Wojnarowicz, *I Use Maps Because I Don't Know How to Paint*, 1984

Walker Art Center, Minneapolis, MN
  1999 'Robert Gober: Sculpture + Drawing,' Robert Gober, *Untitled (Large Sink)*, 1984; *Untitled (Pencil on Paper)*, 1984
  1993 'Jeff Koons Retrospective,' Jeff Koons, *New Hoover Convertible*, 1980; *Inflatable Flower (Tall Yellow)*, 1979

Weatherspoon Art Museum at the University of North Carolina, Greensboro, NC
  1998 'Wild/Life or the Impossibility of Mistaking Nature for Culture,' Jake and Dinos Chapman, *Go Go Fuck Face*, 1997

Weisman Art Museum, University of Minnesota, Minneapolis, MN
  1995 'Critiques of Pure Abstraction,' Sherrie Levine, *Untitled (Golden Knots: 5)*, 1987

Wexner Center for the Arts, Ohio State University, Columbus, OH
  2019 'John Waters: Indecent Exposure,' John Waters, *Beverly Hills John*, 2012; *Brainiac*, 2014; *Library Science #5*, 2014; *Library Science #6*, 2014; *Library Science #8*, 2014; *Shoulda!*, 2014
  2018 'Mickalene Thomas: I Can't See You Without Me,' Mickalene Thomas, *Portraits of Quanikah*, 2006
  2009-10 'Luc Tuymans,' Luc Tuymans, *Diorama*, 2001

Whitney Museum of American Art, New York, NY
  2023 'Josh Kline: Project for a New American Century,' Josh Kline, *Actress/Shoplifter/Psychology Major*, 2011, *Dress Jeans*, 2011, *Creative Hands*, 2011, *Forever 21*, 2013, *Sleep Drip*, 2013, *Packing for Peanuts (FedEx Worker's Hand with Scanner)*, 2014, *No Sick Days (FedEx Worker's Head with FedEx Cap)*, 2014, *Contagious Unemployment (All the Best)*, 2016, *Normalization*, 2017, *Politics is like the weather*, 2017
  2018 'David Wojnarowicz: History Keeps Me Awake at Night,' David Wojnarowicz, *I Use Maps Because I Don't Know How to Paint*, 1984
  2014 'Jeff Koons: A Retrospective,' Jeff Koons, *New Hoover Convertible*, 1980; *Two Kids*, 1986; *Inflatable Flower (Tall Yellow)*, 1979; *Art Ad Portfolio*, 1988
  2011 'Glenn Ligon: AMERICA,' Glenn Ligon, *Untitled (America)*, 2008
  2008 Whitney Biennial, Rodney McMillian, *Untitled*, 2005; *Untitled*, 2007
  2006 'Whitney Biennial Day for Night,' Matthew Day Jackson, *Chariot (The Day After The End of Days)*, 2005-2006
  1999-2000 'The American Century,' Janine Antoni, *Eureka*, 1993
  1998 'Charles Ray,' Charles Ray, *Oh! Charley, Charley, Charley...*, 1992
  1997 'Keith Haring Retrospective', Keith Haring, *Untitled (Martian Attack)*, 1981; *Untitled (Mickey Mouse on TV)*, 1981
  1993 'Mike Kelley: Catholic Tastes,' Mike Kelley, *Screamin' Smoke*, 1985
  1991 'Whitney Biennial,' Cady Noland, *This Piece Has No Title Yet*, 1989
  1987 'Whitney Biennial,' Mike + Doug Starn, *Yellow Rose*, 1982/1986

AUSTRALIA

Biennale of Sydney, Sydney
  1990 'Readymade Boomerang: Certain Relations in 20th Century Art,' Jeff Koons, *New Hoover Deluxe Rug Shampooer I*, 1979

Tasmanian Museum and Art Gallery, Hobart
  2016 'Tempest,' Hernan Bas, *Fragile Moments*, 2003

AUSTRIA

The Albertina Museum, Vienna
  2023 'Yoshitomo Nara. All My Little Words,' Yoshitomo Nara, *Hyper Enough (to the City)*, 1996
  2018 'Keith Haring. The Alphabet,' Keith Haring (collaboration with LA II), *Statue of Liberty*, 1982

Kunsthalle Wein, Vienna
   2016 'The Promise of Total Automation,' Magali Reus, *Leaves (Amber Line, May)*, 2015
   1993 'The Art of Language,' Sue Williams, *We've Got a Lot of Work to Do*, 1992

BELGIUM

Middelheim Museum, Antwerp
   2009 'Chris Burden,' Chris Burden, *21 Foot Truss Bridge*, 2003

WIELS Contemporary Art Centre, Brussels
   2016 'Simon Denny,' Simon Denny, *Formalised Org Chart/ Architectural Model: GCHQ 3 Agile/Holacracy Workspace*, 2015
   2010 'Wangechi Mutu: My Dirty Little Heaven,' Wangechi Mutu, *The evolution of mud mama from beginning to start*, 2008
   2008 'Kelley Walker,' Kelley Walker, *Untitled*, 2007

CANADA

Art Gallery of Ontario, Toronto
   1997-98 'Keith Haring Retrospective,' Keith Haring, *Untitled (Martian Attack)*, 1981;

Illingworth Kerr Gallery, Alberta College of Art, Calgary
   1995, 'Critiques of Pure Abstraction,' Sherrie Levine, *Untitled (Golden Knots: 5)*, 1987

Montreal Museum of Fine Arts, Montreal
   1998-99 'Keith Haring Retrospective,' Keith Haring, *Untitled (Martian Attack)*, 1981; *Untitled (Mickey Mouse on TV)*, 1981

The Power Plant, Toronto
   1992 'Rosemarie Trockel,' Rosemarie Trockel, *Grosse Als Form [Size as Form]*, 1984
   1991 'OBJECTives: The New Sculpture,' Tony Cragg, *Mother's Milk*, 1988; Jeff Koons, *Two Kids*, 1986

Vancouver Art Gallery, Vancouver
   2018 'Takashi Murakami, *PO+KU Surrealism (Blue)*, 1999

Winnipeg Art Gallery, Winnipeg
   1988 'The Impossible Self,' Francesco Clemente, *Self-Portrait (Inside/ Outside)*, 1979

CZECH REPUBLIC

Galerie Rudolfinum, Prague
   2007-08 'Uncertain States of America: American Art in the 3rd Millennium,' Christian Holstad, *Corrections (make-up table)*, 2004

Prague Biennale, Prague
   2003 'Lazarus Effect,' Dana Schutz, *Lovers*, 2003

DENMARK

Herning Museum of Contemporary Art, Herning
   2007-08 'Uncertain States of America: American Art in the 3rd Millennium,' Christian Holstad, *Corrections (make-up table)*, 2004

FRANCE

Abbaye Saint-André Centre d'Art Contemporain, Paris
   1991 'Aspect of Art in the Twentieth Century: the Work Re-Produced,' Sherrie Levine, *Untitled (After Alexander Rodchenko:9)*, 1987; Philip Taaffe, *Pharos*, 1985

Bourse de Commerce, Paris, France
   2023-24 'Mike Kelley: Ghost and Spirit,' Mike Kelley, *Extracurricular Activity Projective Reconstruction #9 (Fresno)*, 2004-2005
   2022 'Charles Ray,' Charles Raye, *Oh! Charley, Charley, Charley…*, 1992

Centre Pompidou, Paris
   2014-15 'Jeff Koons: A Retrospective,' Jeff Koons, *New Hoover Convertible*, 1980; *Two Kids*, 1986
   1989 'Les Magiciens de La Terre,' Juan Muñoz, *Enano con Tres Columnas*, 1988

Hôtel des Arts, Fondation Nationale des Arts, Paris
   1992 'Sherrie Levine,' 1992, Sherrie Levine, *Untitled (Golden Knots: 5)*, 1987

Institut du Monde Arabe, Paris
   2011-12 'Jameel Prize,' Hayv Kahraman, *Migrant I*, 2009

Le Consortium, Dijon
   2014 'L'Almanach 14,' John McAllister, *Tropical Polka*, 2010; *Blushy Pushly*, 2011; *Left Turn at Albuquerque*, 2011; *Splendors Barely Flung*, 2011; *Darksome Almost Dawn*, 2011

Le Magasin - Centre National d'Art Contemporain, Grenoble
   2007 'Kelley Walker,' Kelley Walker, *Untitled*, 2007
   1988 'Richard Prince,' Richard Prince, *Untitled (Cowboys)* six works, 1987

Musée d'Art Contemporain, Marseilles
   1997 'CARL ANDRE Sculptor 1997,' Carl Andre, *Blue Eva Adams, New York*, 1983

Musée d'Art Contemporain de Bordeaux, Bordeaux
   1988-89 'Haim Steinbach,' Haim Steinbach, *ultra lite #2*, 1987

Musée d'Art Moderne de la Ville de Paris, Paris
   2019 'Thomas Houseago: Almost Human,' Thomas Houseago, *Sitting Nude*, 2006; *Standing Boy*, 2006
   2013 'Keith Haring,' Keith Haring, *Untitled (Dogs Surrounding Man) (2)*, 1981; *Untitled (Statue of Liberty)*, 1982; *Against All Odds (20)*, 1989
   2010-11 'Basquiat,' Jean-Michel Basquiat, *One Million Yen*, 1982
   2008 'Peter Doig,' Peter Doig, *Canoe Lake*, 1999
   1991 'Lieux Communs, Figures Singulieres,' Mike Kelley, *Screamin' Smoke*, 1985; *Untitled, (afghans, stuffed animals)*, 1990

Palais de Tokyo, Paris
   2022 'Reclaim the Earth,' Solange Pessoa, *Catedral*, 1990-2015
   2012-13 'Imagination Adrift,' John Miller, *Mannequin Lover*, 2002
   2007 '5 Milliard d'années,' Mark Handforth, *Honda*, 2002

GERMANY

Akademie der Kunste, Berlin, Germany
   2016-17 'Jordan Wolfson: manic / love truth / love', Jordan Wolfson, *Untitled*, 2017
   2016-17 'Uncertain States – Artistic Strategies in States of Emergency', Sigalit Landau, *Barbed Hula*, 2000

Deichtorhallen Hamburg, Hamburg
   2006 'Mama Johnny', Jonathan Meese, *Totale Revolution Am Highway (Kleinhaiway)*, 2006

Deutsche Guggenheim Museum, Berlin
   2010 'Wangechi Mutu: My Dirty Little Heaven,' Wangechi Mutu, *The evolution of mud mama from beginning to start*, 2008

Documenta, Kassel
   1992 documenta IX, Charles Ray, *Oh! Charley, Charley, Charley…*, 1992
   1982 documenta VII, Jean-Michel Basquiat, *Bird on Money*, 1981

Fridericianum, Kassel
   2014 'Helen Marten Parrot Problems,' Helen Marten, *Under blossom: B. uses frenzy*, 2014

Hamburger Kunsthalle, Hamburg
   2001-02 'Monet's Legacy: Series - Order and Obsession,' Carl Andre, *Llano Estacado, Dallas, Texas*, 1979

Haus der Kunst, Munich
   2012 'Wilhelm Sasnal,' Wilhelm Sasnal, *Duel*, 2001
   2007 'Gilbert & George Retrospective,' Gilbert & George, *Apostasia*, 2004; *Finding God*, 1982
   1995 'Mike Kelley: Catholic Tastes,' Mike Kelley, *Screamin' Smoke*, 1985

Kölnischer Kunstverein, Cologne
 2011 'Kerstin Brätsch & DAS INSTITUT, ("Nichts, Nichts!")' Kerstin Bratsch, *When You See Me Again It Won't Be Me*, 2010

Kunstsammlung Nordrhein-Westfalen, Düsseldorf
 2024 'Mike Kelley: Ghost and Spirit,' Mike Kelley, *Extracurricular Activity Projective Reconstruction #9 (Fresno)*, 2004-2005

Kunsthalle der Hypo-Kulturstiftung, Munich
 2015 'Keith Haring: The Political Line,' Keith Haring, *Against All Odds (20)*, 1989

Kunsthalle Mannheim, Mannheim
 2005 'Cecily Brown: Paintings,' Cecily Brown, *Black Painting 4*, 2003

Kunsthalle Weishaupt, Ulm
 2009 'Keith Haring,' Keith Haring, *Untitled*, 1982

Kunstverein für die Rheinlande und Westfalen, Düsseldorf
 1988 'The BiNational American Art of the Late '80s,' Robert Gober, *Slanted Playpen*, 1987; Jeff Koons, *Two Kids*, 1986

Kunstverein Hannover, Hannover
 2003 'Luc Tuymans: The Arena,' Luc Tuymans, *Christ*, 1998, *Oberammergau*, 1999

Martin-Gropiu-Bau, Berlin, Düsseldorf
 1991 'Metropolis,' Ross Bleckner, *Architecture of the Sky*, 1991

Museum der bildenden Künste, Leipzig
 2010 'Neo Rauch — Begleiter,' Neo Rauch, *Das Neue*, 2003; *Diktat*, 2004; *Demos*, 2004; *Vorfuehrung*, 2006

Museum für Moderne Kunst, Frankfurt
 2008 'Murakami ©,' Takashi Murakami, *PO+KU Surrealism Mr. DOB-Blue*, 1998

Museum Haus Lange, Krefeld
 1996 'Carl Andre Retrospective,' Carl Andre, *Blue Eva Adams, New York*, 1983

Museum Ludwig, Cologne
 2005-06 'Rosemarie Trockel Retrospektive,' Rosemarie Trockel, *Untitled (black and white wool)*, 1986; *Untitled (black and white wool)*, 1986

Pinakothek der Moderne, Munich
 2010 'Neo Rauch — Begleiter,' Neo Rauch, *Das Neue*, 2003; *Diktat*, 2004; *Demos*, 2004; *Vorfuehrung*, 2006
 2003 'Luc Tuymans: The Arena,' Luc Tuymans, *Christ*, 1998; *Oberammergau*, 1999

Schirn Kunsthalle Frankfurt, Frankfurt
 2012 'Jeff Koons: The Painter & The Sculptor,' Jeff Koons, *Two Kids*, 1986
 2008-09 Peter Doig, Peter Doig, *Canoe Lake*, 1999

Städtische Kunsthalle, Düsseldorf
 1988 'The BiNational American Art of the Late '80s,' Robert Gober, *Slanted Playpen*, 1987; Jeff Koons, *Two Kids*, 1986

Westfälischer Kunstverein, Münster, Germany
 2015 'Editions 2015,' Magali Reus, *Leaves (Peat, March)*, 2015; *Leaves (Amber Line, May)*, 2015

Westfälisches Landesmuseum, Münster
 1992 'Sherrie Levine,' Sherrie Levine, *Untitled (Golden Knots: 5)*, 1987

Zentrum für Kunst und Medientechnologie, Karlsruhe
 2001-02 'Keith Haring — Heaven and Hell,' Keith Haring, *Against All Odds (20)*, 1989

HONG KONG, CHINA

HACK SPACE, K11 Art Foundation, Hong Kong
 2016 'Simon Denny,' Simon Denny, *Formalised Org Chart/ Architectural Model: GCHQ 3 Agile/Holacracy Workspace*, 2015

ISRAEL

Haifa Museum of Art, Haifa
 2007-08 'BoysCraft,' El Anatsui, *Another Man's Cloth*, 2006

The Israel Museum, Jerusalem
 1993 'Post Human,' Charles Ray, *Male Mannequin*, 1990
 1991 'Life-Size,' Jeff Koons, *New Hoover Deluxe Rug Shampooer I*, 1979; Cindy Sherman, *Untitled Film Still (#21)*, 1978

ITALY

Castello di Rivoli-Museo d'Arte Contemporanea, Turin
 2008 'The Painting of Modern Life,' William Sasnal, *Untitled (Hunters)*, 2001
 2007-08 'Gilbert & George Retrospective,' Gilbert & George, *Apostasia*, 2004; *Finding God*, 1982

Chiesa di San Lorenzo, Aosta
 1992 'Theoretically Yours,' Allan McCollum, *Twenty Plaster Surrogates*, 1992

Fondazione Sandretto Re Rebaudengo, Turin
 2016 'Magali Reus,' Magali Reus, *Leaves (Peat, March)*, 2015

The HangarBicocca Foundation, Milan
 2007 'Urban Manners,' Jitish Kallat, *Public Notice 2*, 2007

Museo d'Arte Moderna e Contemporanea, Trento
 1991-92 'American Artists of the '80s,' Mike + Doug Starn, *Rose with Christ*, 1982-1986; Philip Taaffe, *Pharos*, 1985

Museo Nazionale delle Arti del XXI Secolo, Rome
 2006 'Rosemarie Trockel: Post-Menopause,' Rosemarie Trockel, *Untitled (black and white wool)*, 1986; *Untitled (black and white wool)*, 1986

Venice Biennale, Venice
 2011 'ILLUMInations,' Rashid Johnson, *The Shuttle*, 2011
 2001 German Pavilion, Gregor Schneider, *Ur 21, (Loch/Hole)*, Rheydt, 1997; *Ur 7 — 10, (Kuche/kitchen)*, Rheydt, 1987
 2001 Belgium Pavilion, Luc Tuymans, *Diorama*, 2001
 1999 'dAPERTutto,' Jason Rhoades with Paul McCarthy, *Proposition*, 1999
 1988 'The Place of the Artist,' Tony Cragg, *Mother's Milk*, 1988
 1993 'Aperto 93: Emergency/Emergenza,' Maurizio Cattelan, *Lavorare é un Brutto Mestiere [Working is a Bad Job]*, 1993

JAPAN

Fukuoka Art Museum, Fukuoka
 1991 'Beyond the Frame: American Art 1960-1990,' Haim Steinbach, *ultra lite #2*, 1987

The Museum of Modern Art, Saitama
 1992 'The Tenth Anniversary Exhibition: Adam and Eve,' Cindy Sherman, *Untitled (#207)*, 1989

The National Museum of Art, Osaka
 1991 'Beyond the Frame: American Art 1960-1990,' Haim Steinbach, *ultra lite #2*, 1987

Setagaya Art Museum, Tokyo
 1991 'Beyond the Frame: American Art 1960-1990,' Haim Steinbach, *ultra lite #2*, 1987

Toyota Municipal Museum of Art, Toyota
 2017 'Yoshitomo Nara: For Better or Worse,' Yoshitomo Nara, *Sleepless Night (sitting)*, 1997

LUXEMBOURG

Mudam Luxembourg Musée d'Art Moderne Grand-Duc Jean
 2011 'John Stezaker,' John Stezaker, *Blind*, 1970; *The Trial*, 1978; *Tabula Rasa II*, 1983

Kurimanzutto, Mexico City
 2020, 'SEX,' Felix Gonzalez-Torres, *"Untitled" (Join)*, 1990

Museo Tamayo Arte Contemporáneo, Mexico City
 2015 'The Third Person,' John Stezaker, *Film Portrait (Landscape) IX, Film Portrait (Landscape) VII*, 2005

MONACO

Grimaldi Forum Monaco, Monte Carlo
 2006 'New York, New York: Fifty Years of Art, Architecture, Cinema, Performance, Photography and Video,' Kara Walker, *Camptown Ladies*, 1998

NETHERLANDS

de Appel Arts Centre, Amsterdam
 2007-08 'Richard Hawkins: Of Two Minds, Simultaneously,' Richard Hawkins, *Urbis Paganus III, 3*, 2006;

Kunsthal KAdE, Amersfoort
 2021-22 'Natasja Kensmil & Sadik Kwaish Alfraji, Natasja Kensmil, *Desperate Land,* 2014; *Orca*, 2001; *Garden of Eden*, 2005

Kunsthal Rotterdam, Rotterdam
 2015-16 'Keith Haring — The Political Line,' Keith Haring, *Against All Odds (20)*, 1989

Museum Boijmans Van Beuningen, Rotterdam
 2002 'Keith Haring — Heaven and Hell,' Keith Haring, *Against All Odds (20)*,1989
 1990 'Robert Gober,' Robert Gober, *Slanted Playpen*, 1987; *Untitled (Large Sink)*, 1984
 1983 'David Salle,' David Salle, *Rainy Night in the Rubber City*, 1980

Museum de Fundatie, Zwolle, the Netherlands
 2017 'Behold the Man, Ryan Trecartin, *Negative Beach + Lizzie Fitch*, 2010

Stedelijk Museum Amsterdam
 2012-13 Mike Kelley, Mike Kelley, *Extracurricular Activity Projective Reconstruction #9 (Fresno)*, 2005

Witte de With Center for Contemporary Art, Rotterdam
 1991-92 'South Bronx Hall of Fame: Sculpture by John Ahearn and Rigoberto Torres,' John Ahearn, *Bobbie (Sneaker Town USA),* 1981; *Migna*, 1981

NEW ZEALAND

City Gallery Wellington, Wellington
 1999 'Keith Haring Retrospective', Keith Haring, *Untitled (Martian Attack)*, 1981

NORWAY

Astrup Fearnley Museet, Oslo
 2014 'Elmgreen & Dragset — Biography,' Elmgreen & Dragset, *Crash… Boom…Bang!*, 2008
 2005 'Uncertain States of America: American Art in the 3rd Millennium,' Christian Holstad, *Corrections (make-up table)*, 2004

POLAND

Centre for Contemporary Art Ujazdowski Castle, Warsaw
 2007 'Uncertain States of America: American Art in the 3rd Millennium,' Christian Holstad, *Corrections (make-up table)*, 2004

PORTUGAL

Fundação de Serralves-Museu de Arte Contemporanea, Porto
 2008-09 'Juan Muñoz,' Juan Muñoz, *Enano con Tres Columnas*, 1988

QATAR

Qatar Museums Authority (QMA), Doha
 2016 'Luc Tuymans: Retrospective,' Luc Tuymans, *Oberammergau*, 1999

REPUBLIC OF IRELAND

Irish Museum of Modern Art, Dublin
 1995 'Janine Antoni: Slip of the Tongue,' Janine Antoni, *Eureka*, 1993

RUSSIA

Moscow Museum of Modern Art, Moscow
 2012 'Things, Words, and Consequences,' Simon Denny, *Analogue/Digital Transmission Switchover: Germany*, 2012

SINGAPORE

Bodhi Art
 2008 'Public Notice 2,' Jitish Kallat, *Public Notice 2*, 2007

SPAIN

Barcelona Museum of Contemporary Art, Barcelona
 2021 'Felix Gonzalez-Torres: The Politics of Relation,' Felix Gonzalez-Torres, *Untitled (Join)*, 1990

Casa Árabe, Madrid
 2012 'Jameel Prize,' Hayv Kahraman, *Migrant I*, 2009

Fundació "la Caixa," Barcelona
 1996 'Activitats Esculturals,' Janine Antoni, *Eureka*, 1993

Guggenheim Museum, Bilbao
 2024 'Yoshitomo Nara,' *Sleepless Night (Sitting)*, 1997; *Little Ramona*, 2001; *Slight Fever*, 2001; *Too Young to Die*, 2001
 2015 'Jeff Koons,' Jeff Koons, *New Hoover Convertible*, 1980; *Two Kids*, 1986
 2009 'Murakami ©,' Takashi Murakami, *PO+KU Surrealism Mr. DOB-Blue*, 1998
 2008 'Juan Muñoz,' Juan Muñoz, *Enano con Tres Columnas*, 1988
 1999 'Francesco Clemente: A Retrospective,' Francesco Clemente, *Self Portrait (Inside/Outside)*, 1979

Institut Valencià d'Art Modern, Valencia
 1992 'Juan Muñoz: Conversaciones,' Juan Muñoz, *Enano con Tres Columnas*, 1988

Museo Nacional Centro de Arte Reina Sofia, Madrid
 2019 'David Wojnarowicz: History Keeps Me Awake at Night,' David Wojnarowicz, *I Use Maps Because I Don't Know How to Paint*, 1984
 2008-09 'Juan Muñoz: Retrospectiva,' Juan Muñoz, *Enano con Tres Columnas*, 1988
 1992 'Rosemarie Trockel,' Rosemarie Trockel, *Grosse Als Form [Size as Form]*, 1984

SWEDEN

Moderna Museet, Stockholm
 2025 'Mike Kelley: Ghost and Spirit,' Mike Kelley, *Extracurricular Activity Projective Reconstruction #9 (Fresno)*, 2004-2005
 1994 'Mike Kelley: Catholic Tastes,' Mike Kelley, *Screamin' Smoke*, 1985

Rooseum Center for Contemporary Art, Malmö
 1999-2000 'Robert Gober: Sculpture + Drawing,' Robert Gober, *Untitled (Large Sink)*, 1984; *Untitled (Pencil on Paper)*, 1984

1992 'Sherrie Levine,' Sherrie Levine, *Untitled (Golden Knots: 5)*, 1987
1989 'What is Contemporary Art?,' Sherrie Levine, *Untitled (After Alexander Rodchenko:9)*, 1987; *Untitled (Golden Knots: 5)*, 1987

SWITZERLAND

Beyler Foundation Museum, Basel
2012 'Jeff Koons,' Jeff Koons, *New Hoover Convertible*, 1980; *Serpents*, 1988
2010 'Basquiat,' Jean-Michel Basquiat, *One Million Yen*, 1982

Centre d'Art Contemporain Genève, Geneva
2001 'Lisa Yuskavage,' Lisa Yuskavage, *Northview*, 2000

Kunsthalle Bern, Bern
1975 'Carl Andre,' Carl Andre, *Forty-third Copper Cardinal*, 1975

Kunsthalle Zürich, Zürich
2009 'John Miller,' John Miller, *A Refusal to Accept Limits*, 2007
2006 'Wade Guyton, Seth Price, Joshua Smith, Kelley Walker,' Kelley Walker, *Untitled*, 2006
1991-92 'Sherrie Levine,' Sherrie Levine, *Untitled (Golden Knots: 5)*, 1987

Kunstverein St. Gallen Kunstmuseum, St. Gallen
2003 'Luc Tuymans: The Arena,' Luc Tuymans, *Christ*, 1998, *Oberammergau*, 1999

Musée cantonal des Beaux-Arts, Lausanne
2009-10 'Renée Green Retrospective Works 1989-2009,' Renée Green, *Between and Including, Set I (Trinth T. Min-Ha to Xie Jin)*, 1998

Musée d'art d'histoire, Geneva, Switzerland
2009-10 'Dana Schutz,' Dana Schutz, *Frank on a Rock*, 2002

Musée Rath, Geneva
1990 'John M Armleder: furniture sculpture,' John Armleder, *Furniture Sculpture*, 1986

Schaulager, Basel
2014 'Paul Chan-Selected Works,' Paul Chan, *The Body of Oh Girl (truetype font)*, 2008; *The Body of Oh Juliette (truetype font)*, 2008
2007 'Robert Gober. Work 1976-2006,' Robert Gobert, *Slanted Playpen*, 1987; *Untitled (Large Sink)*, 1984

UNITED KINGDOM

Centre for Contemporary Arts, Glasgow, Scotland
1995 'Janine Antoni: Slip of the Tongue,' Janine Antoni, *Eureka*, 1993

Hayward Gallery, London, England
2014 'The Human Factor,' John Miller, *Mannequin Lover*, 2002
2007 'The Painting of Modern Life,' Wilhelm Sasnal, *Untitled (Hunters)*, 2001

The Hepworth Wakefield, Wakefield, England
2015 'Magali Reus: Particle of Inch,' Magali Reus, *Leaves (Peat, March)*, 2015; *Leaves (Amber Line, May)*, 2015

Luxembourg + Co., London
2005 'At the Edge of Pictures: John Stezaker, works 1975-1990,' John Stezaker, *The Trial,* 1980; *Blind*, 1979; *Tabula Rasa II*, 1983

Modern Art Oxford, Oxford, England
2015 'Josh Kline: Freedom,' Josh Kline, *Freedom*, 2015
2005 'Cecily Brown: Seeing is Believing,' Cecily Brown, *Black Painting 4*, 2003

Saatchi Gallery, London, England
2010 'The Empire Strikes Back: Indian Art Today,' Jitish Kallat, *Public Notice 2*, 2007

Serpentine Galleries, London, England
2006 'Uncertain States of America: American Art in the 3rd Millennium,' Christian Holstad, *Corrections (make-up table)*, 2004

Tate Britain, London, England
2008 'Peter Doig,' Peter Doig, *Canoe Lake*, 1999

Tate Liverpool, Liverpool, England
2010 'Afro Modern: Journeys through the Black Atlantic,' Glenn Ligon, *Gold Nobody Knew Me #1*, 2007; *Gold When Black Wasn't Beautiful #1*, 2007

Tate Modern, London, England
2024-25 'Mike Kelley: Ghost and Spirit,' Mike Kelley, *Extracurricular Activity Projective Reconstruction #9 (Fresno)*, 2004-2005
2008 'Juan Muñoz,' Juan Muñoz, *Enano con Tres Columnas*, 1988
2007 'Gilbert & George Retrospective,' Gilbert & George, *Apostasia*, 2004; *Finding God*, 1982

Victoria and Albert Museum, London, England
2011 'Jameel Prize,' Hayv Kahraman, *Migrant I*, 2009

Whitechapel Gallery, London, England
2011 'John Stezaker,' John Stezaker, *Blind*, 1970; *The Trial*, 1978; *Tabula Rasa II*, 1983
2011 'Wilhelm Sasnal,' Wilhelm Sasnal, *Duel*, 2001
2010 'Rachel Harrison: Consider the Lobster,' Rachel Harrison, *Untitled (Hat/Broom)*, 2005

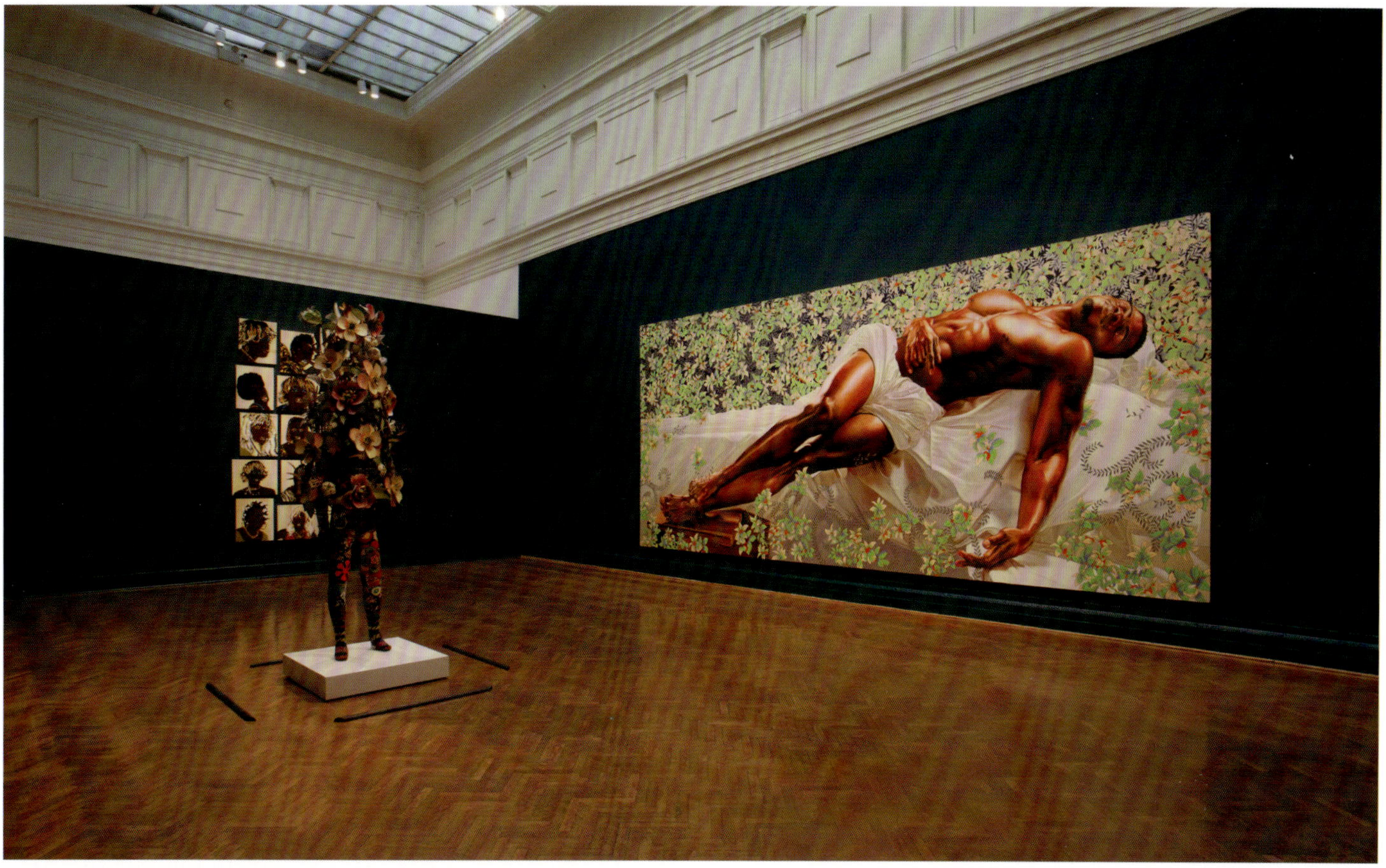

30 Americans at Corcoran Gallery of Art, Washington, DC, 2011-12

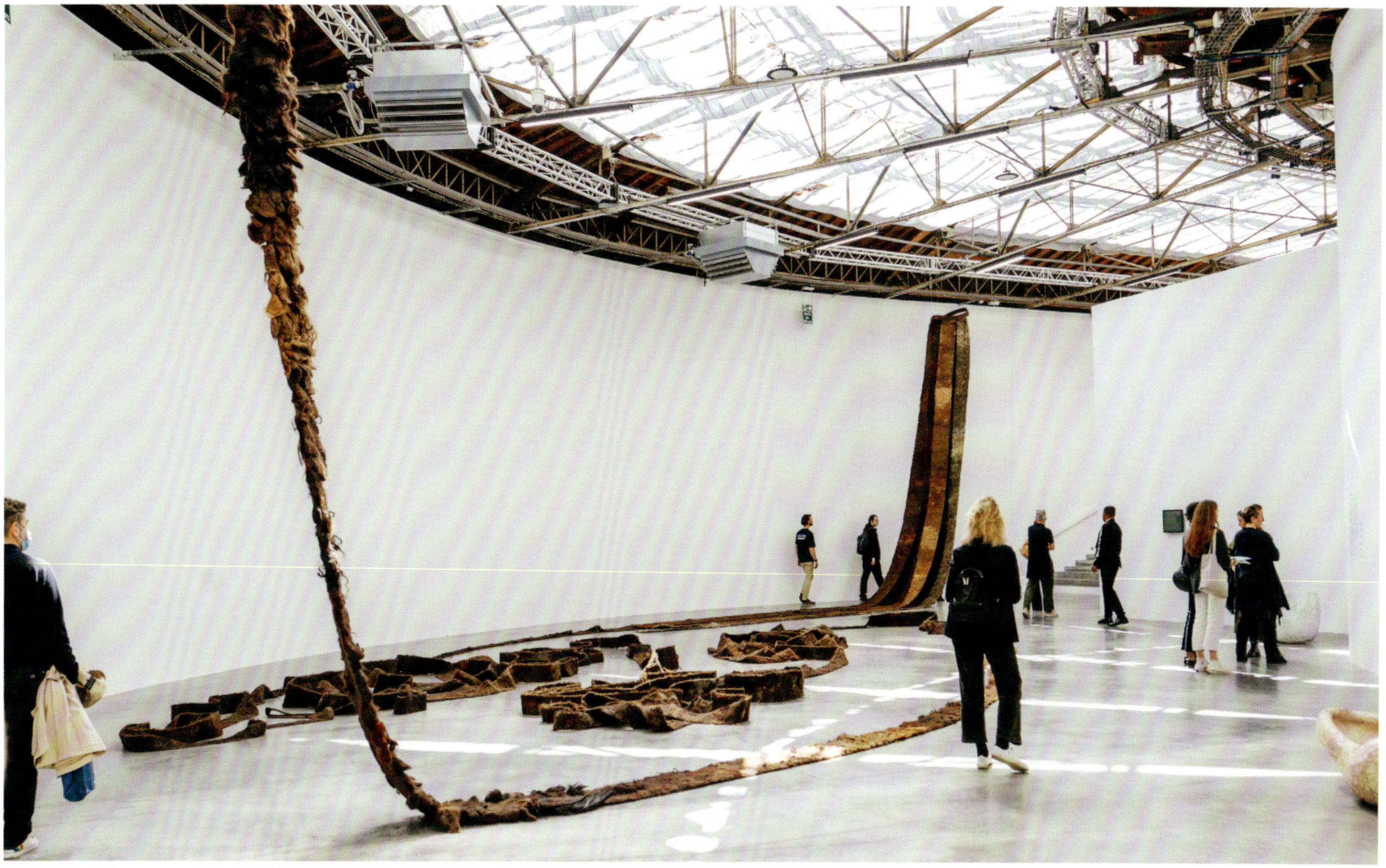

Solange Pessoa, *Catedral*, 1990-2015 at Palais de Tokyo, Paris, 2022

Artwork & Writings

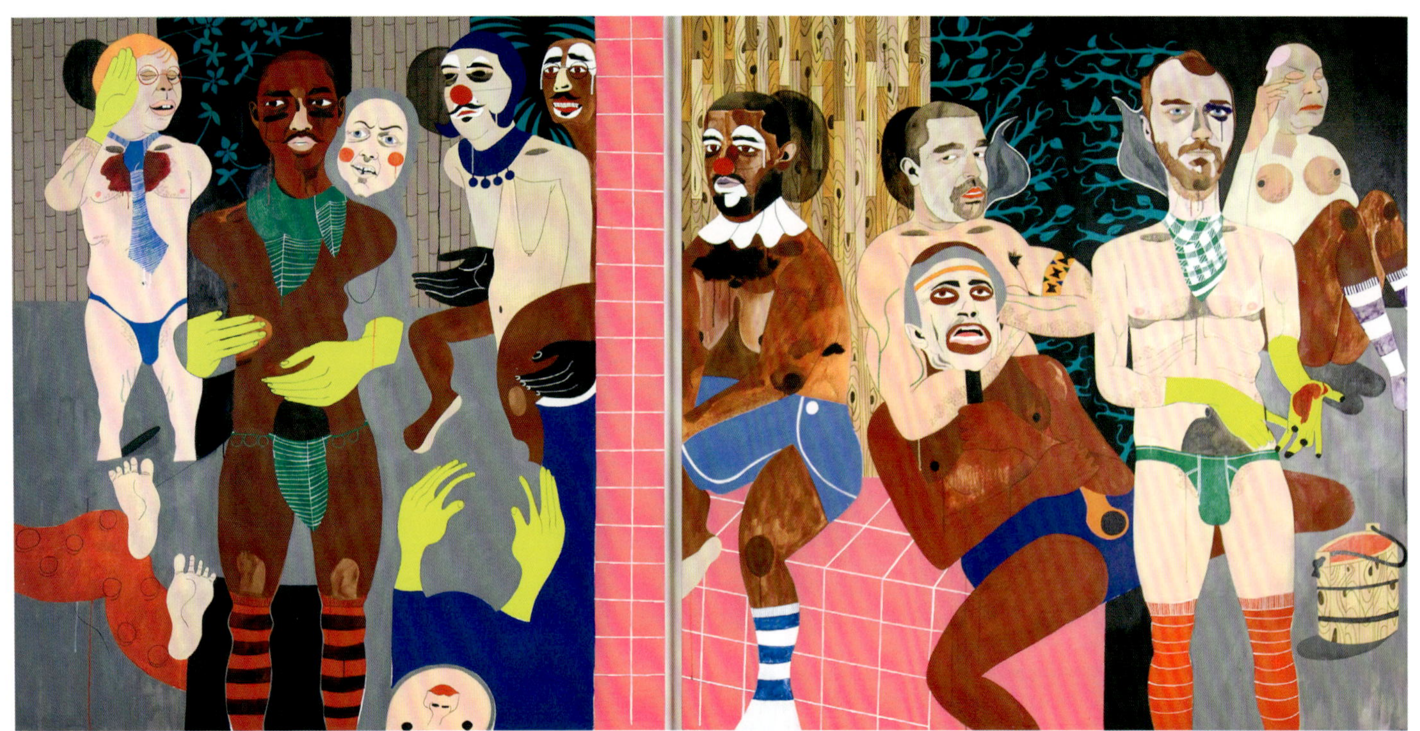

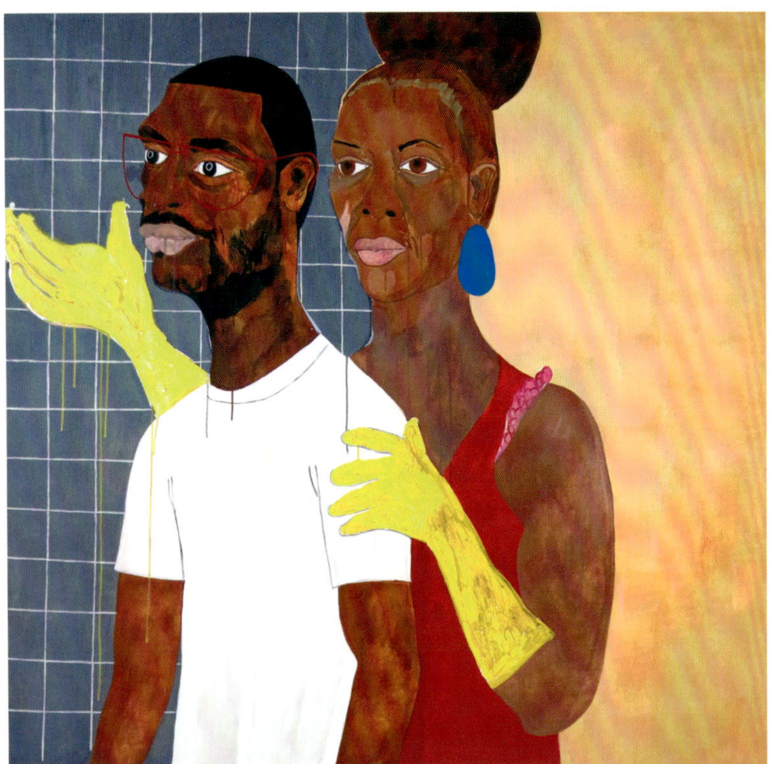

The Boardroom, 2008, acrylic on canvas, diptych, overall 77 x 156 in. (195.6 x 396.2 cm),acquired in 2008
Khaaliqua & Jeff, 2007, acrylic on canvas, 61 x 63 3/4 in. (155 x 162 cm), acquired in 2007
Opposite page: *Class of 2007*, 2007, acrylic on canvas, diptych, overall 114 x 183 in. (289.6 x 464.8 cm), acquired in 2008

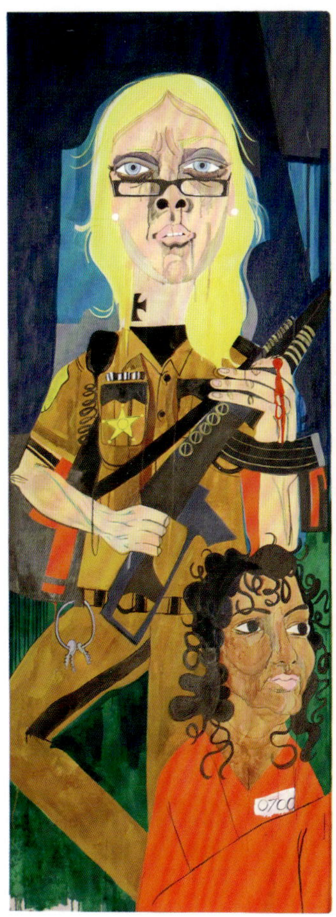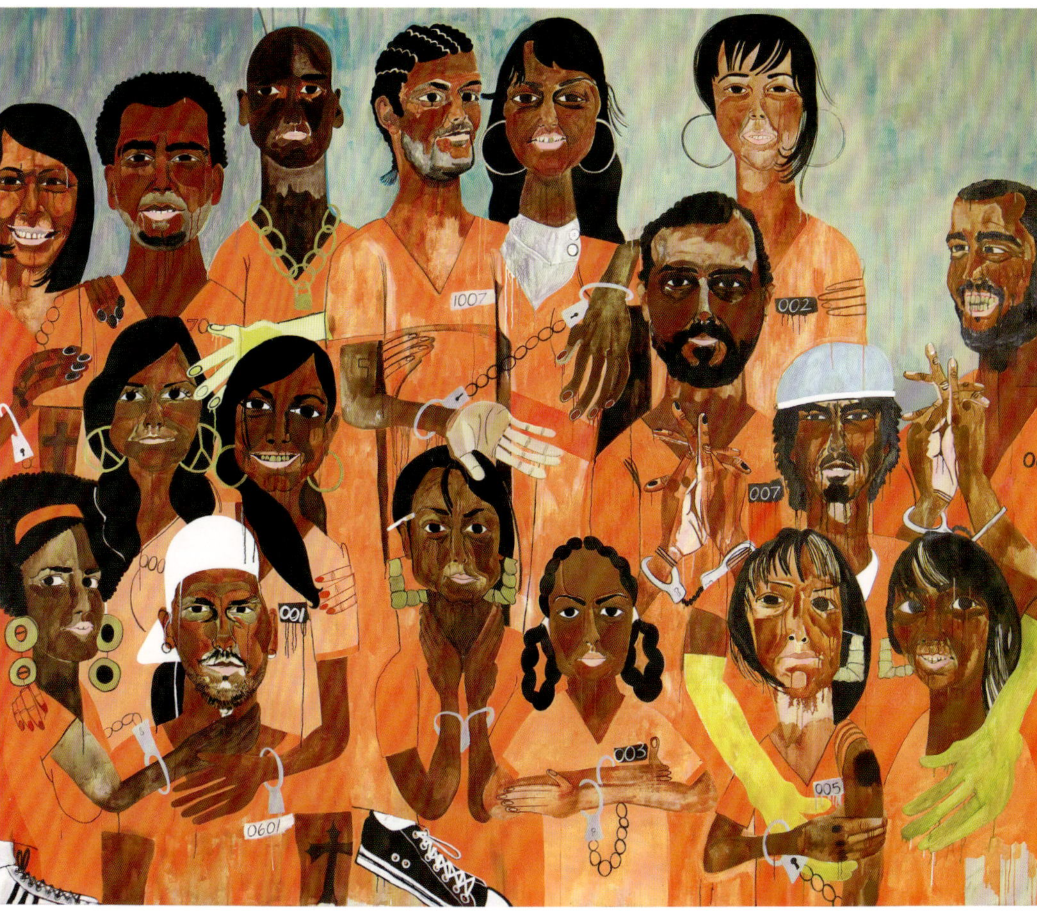

Class of 2007 was the last painting I completed as a graduate student. Therefore, I wanted the painting to be a culmination of my entire experience at Parsons. I am interested in fusing multiple issues, so I set out to address the disproportionate number of white students in MFA programs and the disproportionate number of African American males in prison. I also wanted to address the idea of creating a work that is "universal." Over the course of my time at Parsons, several of my classmates noted that they felt as though they could not completely relate to my work. They commented on how they were unable to see their role in a painting about race. So I questioned what would make a work about race issues universal until I finally came up with an answer. I figured that I would paint my classmates as African Americans. Filtering them through my vision, I would be able to create a painting more understandable to them.

My entire time at Parsons, I found myself battling against the notion of "Black Art" and the expectations for a "Black Artist." I was the only African American student in my class, and some of my classmates assumed that simply creating a class portrait would amplify that fact. They assumed the main objective of the portrait would be to show that I was the only Black student in the class. But I'm not one to do the expected, so I led my classmates to believe that I would be creating a simple class portrait. Knowing that I would secretly switch everyone's race including my own, I insisted that the painting not be revealed until the installation of the show. I admittedly wanted a mixed response: some angry, some excited. I therefore did the best I could to take everyone's personality into account to determine what skin tone, hairstyle, and accessories each student might be dissatisfied or pleased with.

During the big reveal, I got the unexpected: silence, then confusion, then laughter. Most seemed genuinely pleased, while some were visibly uncomfortable.

I had been searching my entire time in graduate school for what I consider the perfect balance: work that is conceptual, humorous, and visually pleasing, while at the same time commenting on extremely uncomfortable race issues that can be experienced by anyone. With the creation of *Class of 2007*, I had finally begun to feel like I was within arm's reach.

—Nina Chanel Abney

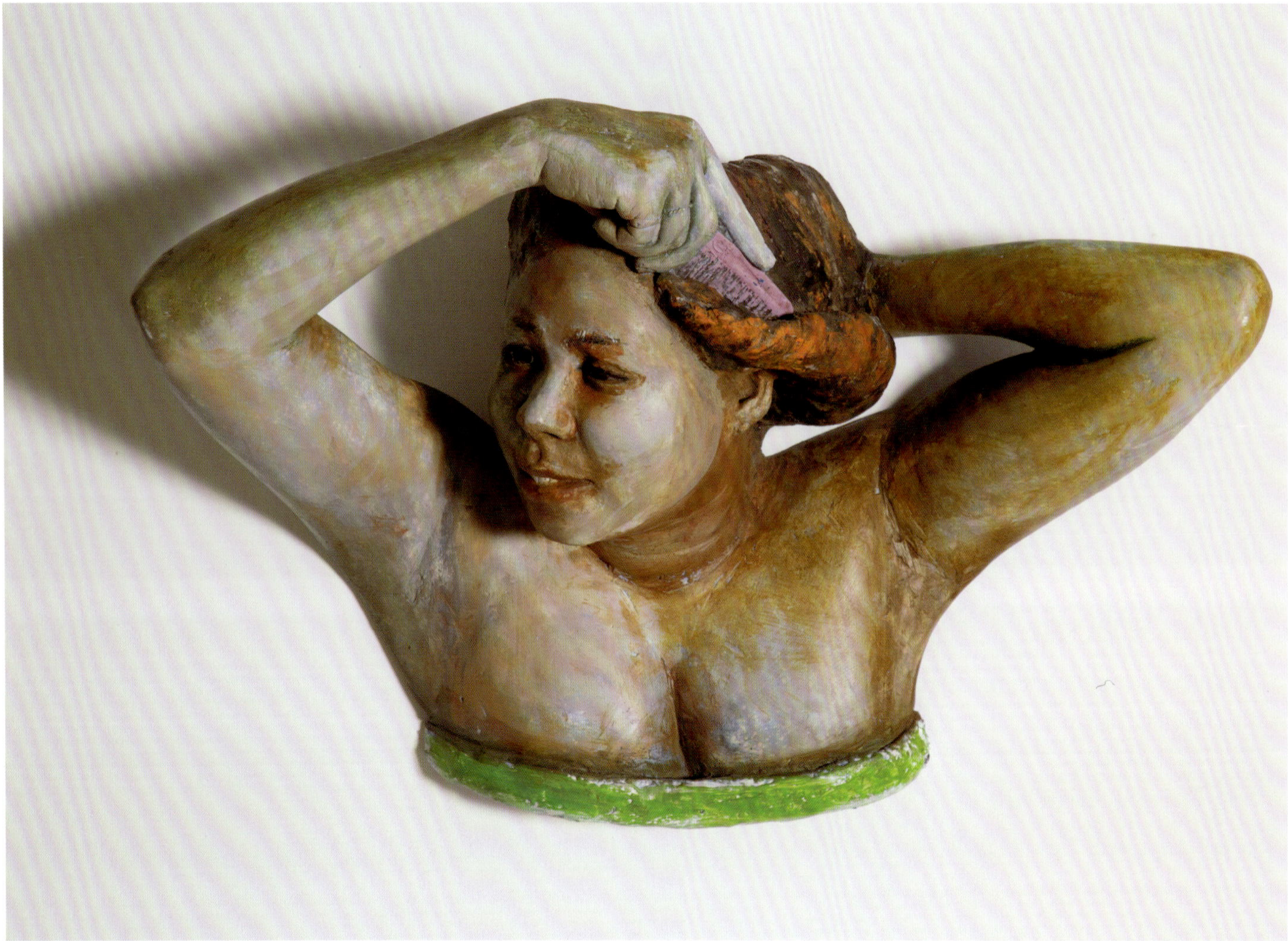

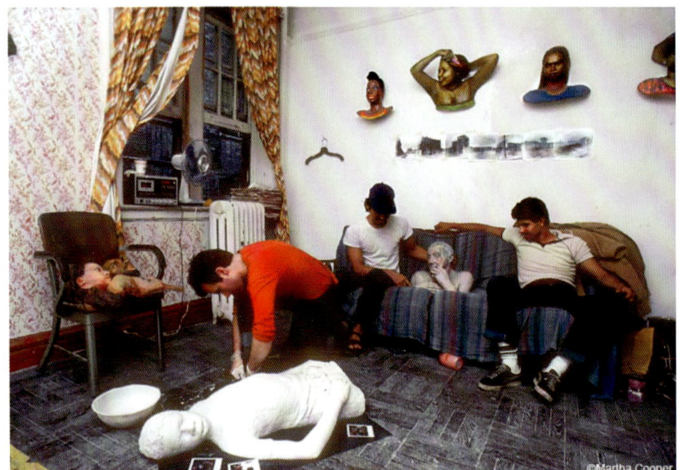

1981, Walton Avenue studio with John Ahearn working on *Bobbie (Sneaker Town USA)*; Rigoberto Torres and David Ortiz, seated.

During the *Times Square Show* in June 1980, Rigoberto Torres and I agreed to open a life-casting workshop on his Walton Avenue block in the Bronx. I rented a ground floor apartment on Walton near 170th Street and decorated the place with lots of sculptures. Whenever we would cast anyone, friends and relatives would be there to watch us or come later to see how the portrait turned out. *Sneaker Town* was the first figurative sculpture that focused more on body language. Later, in 1981, we would make full-figure reliefs in fiberglass and create neighborhood murals, such as the *Double Dutch* girls.

—John Ahearn

Migna, 1981, oil on plaster, 17 x 26 x 11 in. (43 x 66 x 28 cm), acquired in 1982
Opposite page: *Bobbie (Sneaker Town USA)*, 1981, oil on plaster, 39 x 27 1/2 x 7 1/2 in. (99 x 69.8 x 19 cm), acquired in 1981

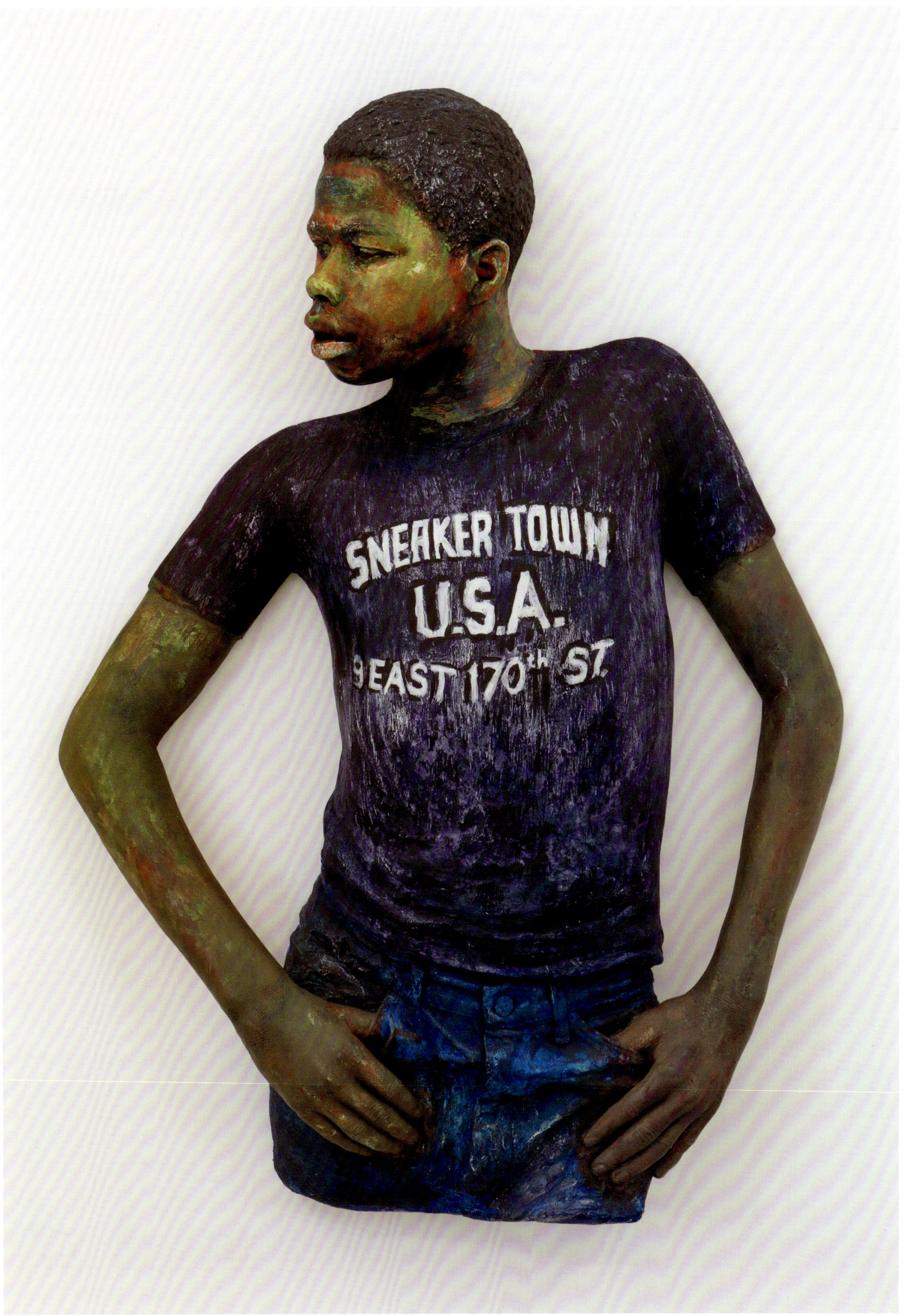

SNEAKER TOWN
U.S.A.
9 EAST 170th ST.

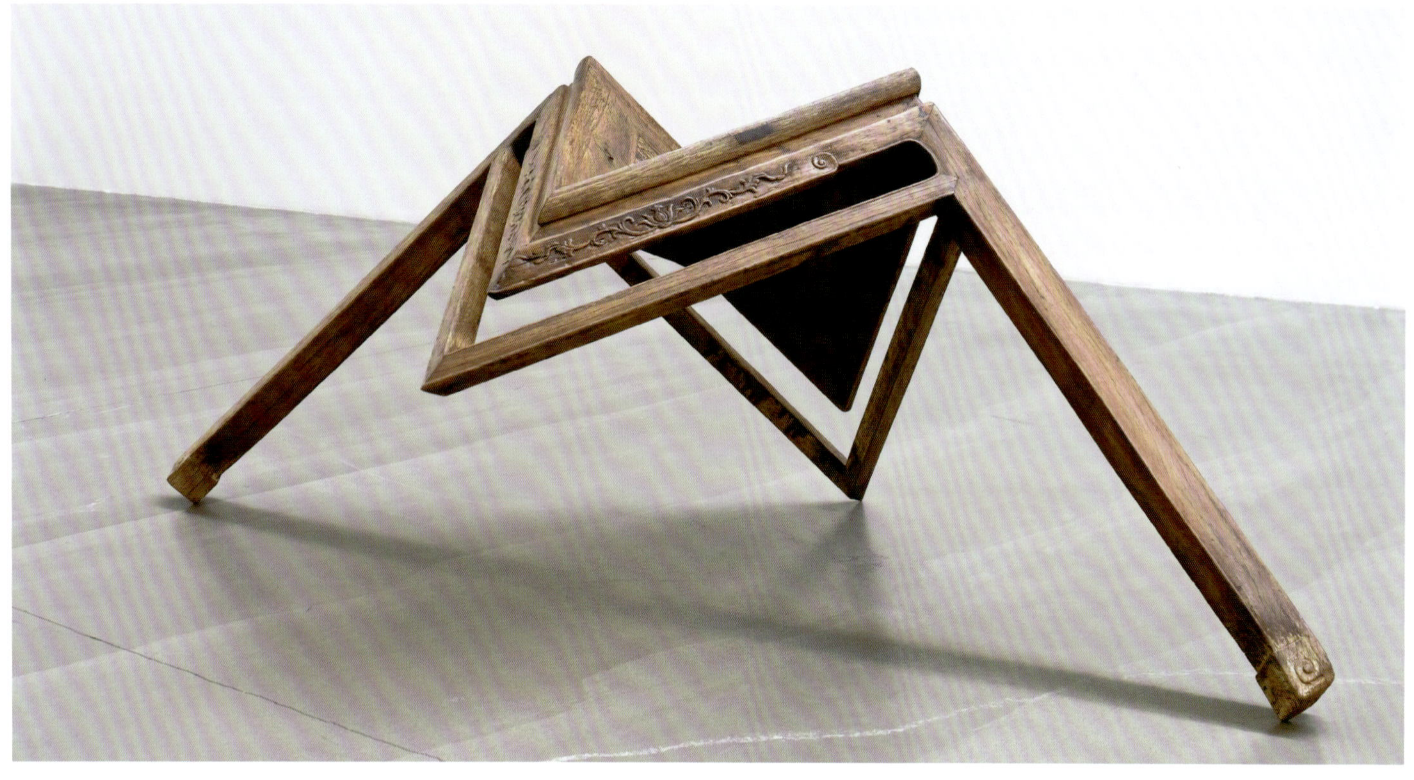

Antique tables from China are made with clear, logical principles of proportion and structure, taking careful consideration of the type of wood that is used. With traditional joinery techniques, no nails were used in building the furniture. Not only does it reflect the craftsmen's profound understanding of aesthetics and materials, these objects are also status symbols in Chinese culture. In constructing *Table with Two Legs,* I intervened and reconstructed the original structure, purposely without leaving any traces. By destroying the original form and function, the work challenges our perception and becomes some sort of mysterious object.

The idea for *Ton of Tea* originates from a visit to Kunming, Yunnan, where Pu'er tea is a famous product. The tea leaves are often compressed into blocks called *bingcha* ("tea cakes") for easy transportation along ancient routes on horseback and would travel to faraway places such as Tibet. As a play on the age-old tradition, a whole ton of tea was pressed into a cube to look like a minimalist sculpture. The work provides a different vantage point to what is ingrained in Chinese history and customs.

—Ai Weiwei

Table with Two Legs, 2008, Qing dynasty wooden table, 23 3/4 x 65 x 37 in. (60.5 x 165 x 94 cm), acquired in 2008
Opposite page: *Ton of Tea*, 2005, Pu'er tea and wood, 39 3/8 x 39 3/8 x 39 3/8 in. (100 x 100 x 100 cm), acquired in 2008

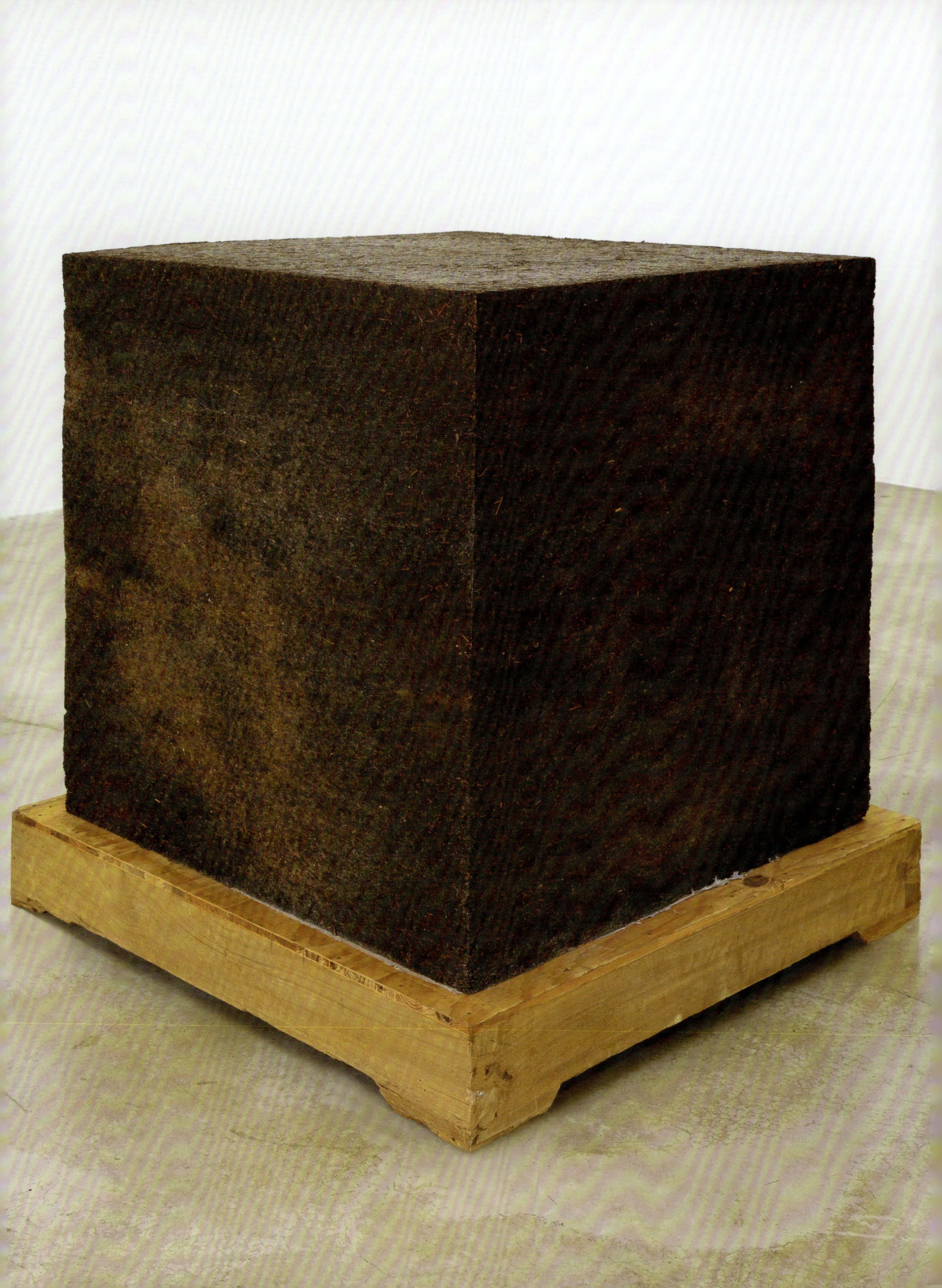

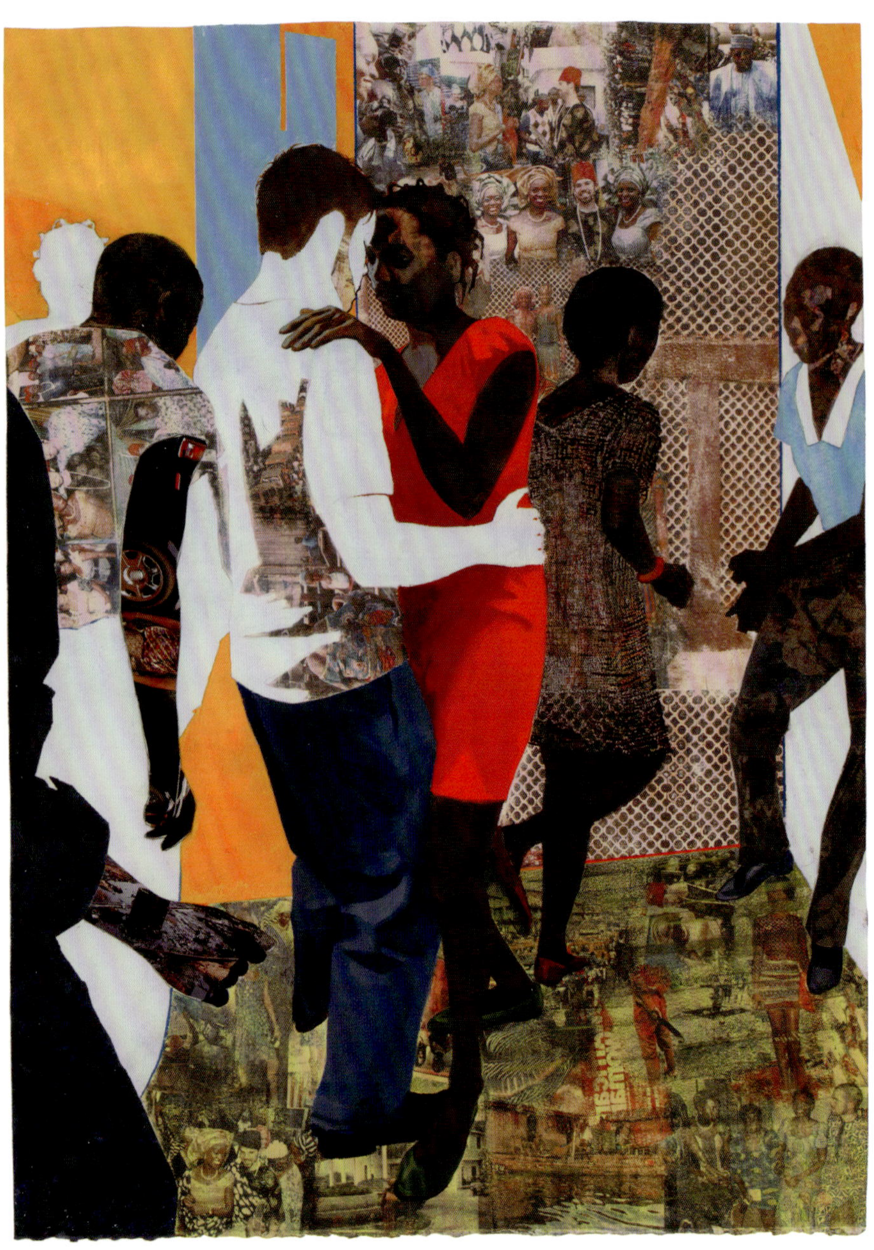

Cheryl Brutvan: Tell me about your life in Nigeria.

Njideka Akunyili Crosby: I left Nigeria after high school. I grew up in a post-colonial country— it's this weird but exciting mash-up of different things. Even within the country, there are 200-plus tribes, and the cultures of all those tribes are beginning to mesh together. That's the reason I love using images of traditional weddings, which is one place where our tradition thrives. For example, at my brother's traditional wedding, they did something called *aso-ebi* ("cloth of the family"). Everyone gets the same fabric and sews their own pattern. It's a Yoruba custom, but it was an Igbo wedding; the headscarves were tied in a style from the Eastern part of the country, and the outfit designs

were very Western— so it's just like this weird confluence. Even what people now call tradition is cobbled together from many things.

CB: What kind of references to America did you grow up with?

NAC: I grew up on Madonna, Michael Jackson, MC Hammer, The Cosby Show, Sesame Street. As Nigeria got rich and oil money started coming in, the country was able to purchase programs from the U.S., so that became part of the fabric of Nigerian life. Growing up, I could sense all that.

One big theme that I explore a lot in my work is marrying

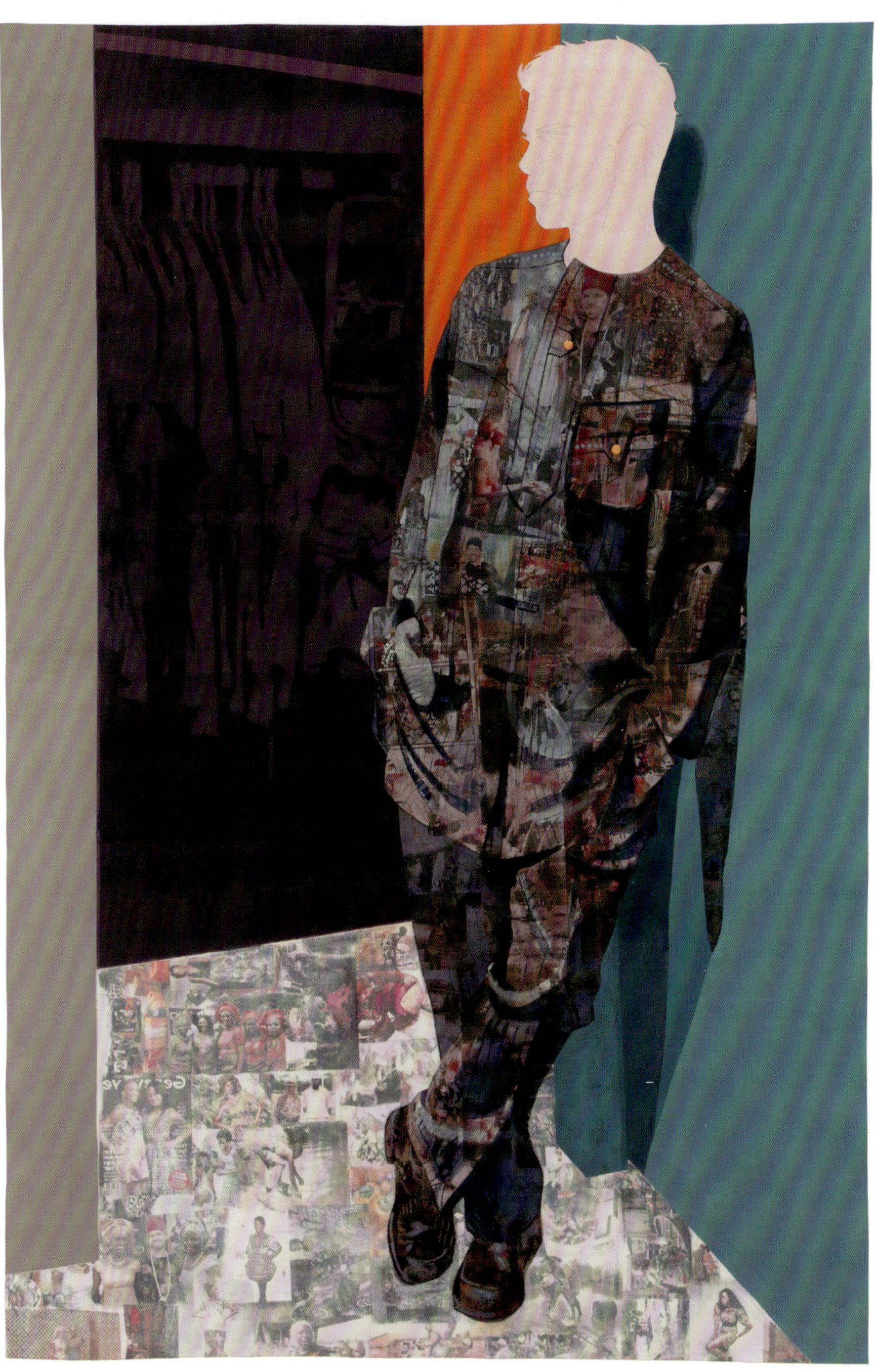

my husband, because he becomes that which roots me in America. Of course home is Nigeria and trying to think of these two notions of home and staying connected to both at once, and having to renegotiate, again, a new space for myself— a lot of those themes come out during the work.

CB: We talked earlier about the images of Nigeria, the images that resonated with you, but also this complete political connection through your mother and father and that generation. Does that enter your art?

NAC: I'm Nigerian; I grew up under too many dictatorships, but I think that *coup* is a word I have in my head about my art. It's subtle and slips in there before you even know it, so it turns out the image is changing your perception of a place before you even know what is happening. But politics can refer to things beyond the government. I'm thinking of images I didn't see, but I wanted to see more. I'm thinking of a woman of color and a white man in a very loving, intimate relationship, being depicted in a very ordinary way. This is a power structure that is different from what I've seen before.

Opposite page: *Efulefu: The Lost One*, 2011, acrylic, charcoal, collage, color pencil on Xerox transfer, 31 x 23 in. (78.7 x 58.4 cm), acquired in 2012
Nkem, 2012, acrylic and Xerox transfer on paper, 76 x 51 in. (193 x 129.5 cm), acquired in 2012

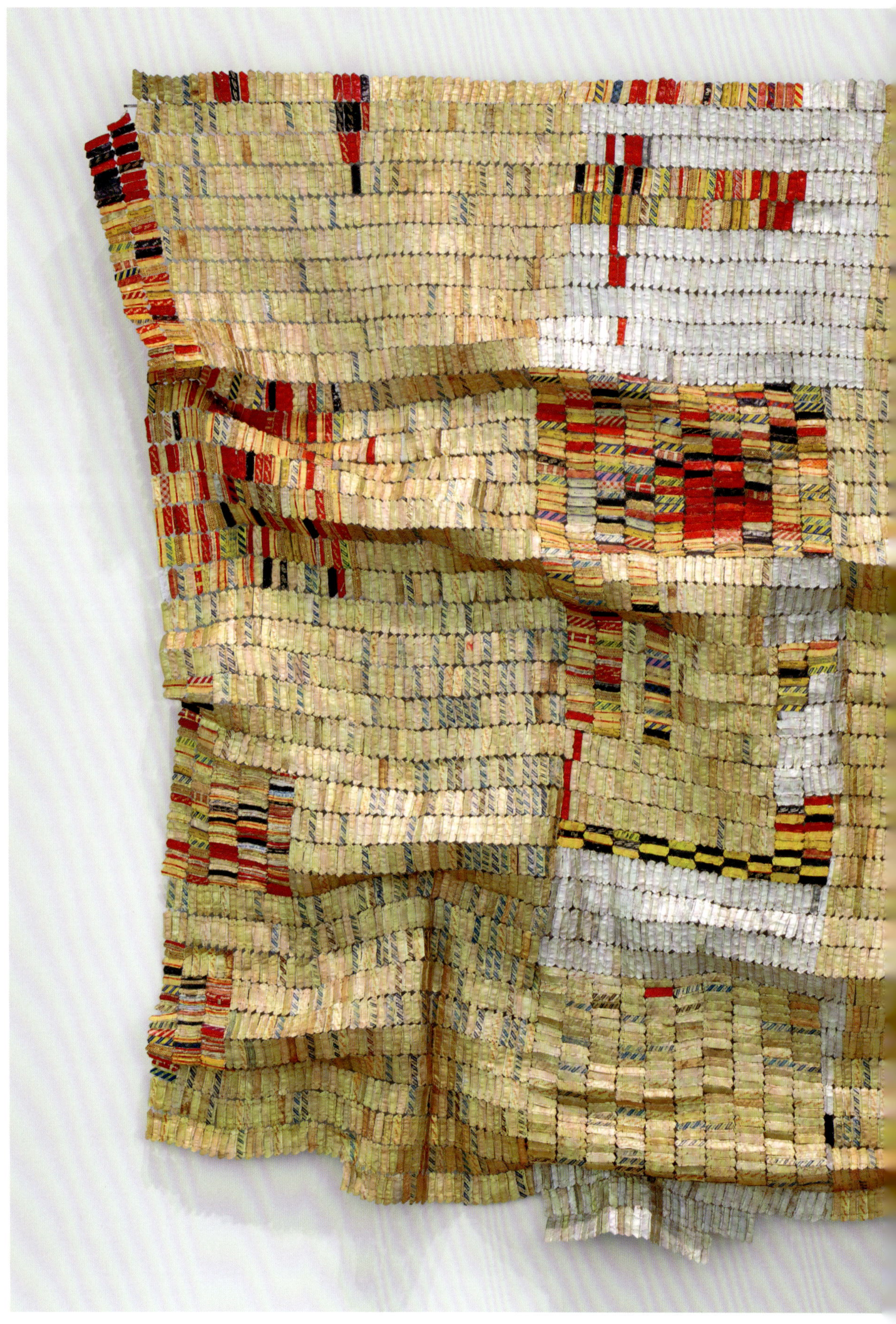

Another Man's Cloth, 2006, found aluminum and copper wire, 156 x 195 in. (396.3 x 495.3 cm), acquired in 2007

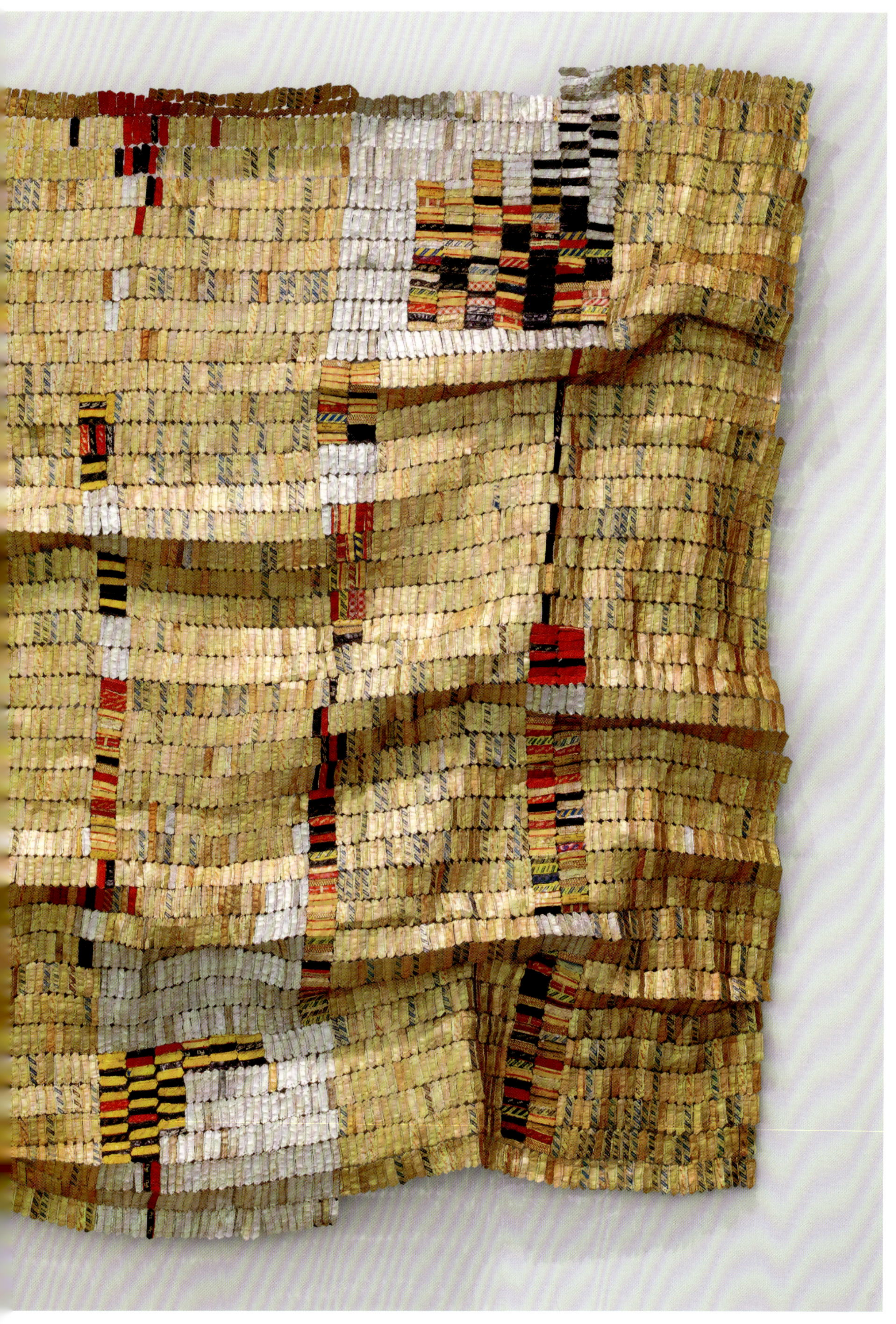

To make *Eureka*, I submerged myself in a tub filled to the brim with lard. Once submerged, I re-flattened the lard at the top of the tub, removing what my body had displaced. The removed lard was mixed with lye and water to make a cube of soap. I then washed with the cube, slowly rounding its edges by repeated bathings.

This sculpture is inspired by a story of Archimedes. One day, the king asked Archimedes how much gold was in his crown. Archimedes was killing himself trying to figure out how to answer this question when, one night while bathing, he realizes that his body is displacing the water in his tub. He could answer the king's question by doing the same experiment with the crown. The submerged crown would displace the amount of water equal to its volume. Archimedes jumps out, screams "Eureka!" and runs through the streets naked.

In Archimedes' experiment, his body, like my body, becomes both the tool for making and thus the means for understanding. In making artwork, I know that my viewer also has a body. This is why I'm known for doing extreme acts. The viewer can imagine being submerged in a tub of lard, or, as I did to make my work *Gnaw* (1992), chewing on 600 pounds of chocolate. I realize that my audience will not have a neutral reaction to this kind of behavior, and I'm interested in whether I can elicit their empathy.

This is not the approach that we typically take to conceptual art. We usually take a more subjective approach, moving through a process of decoding to find the meaning. I would rather the viewer imagine what it took for me to make the object and let the meaning arise from the empathetic position of sharing with one another our relationships to our bodies.

If I use my body volume in fat, and fat is both a material of the body and the soap, then I have metaphorically entered the cube and I'm washing myself with myself. What does it mean to wash the body with another body?

—Janine Antoni

Eureka, 1993, bathtub, lard, soap, and Corian; soap 22 x 26 x 26 in. (55.8 x 66 x 66 cm); tub 30 x 70 x 25 in. (76 x 177 x 63.5 cm), acquired in 1993

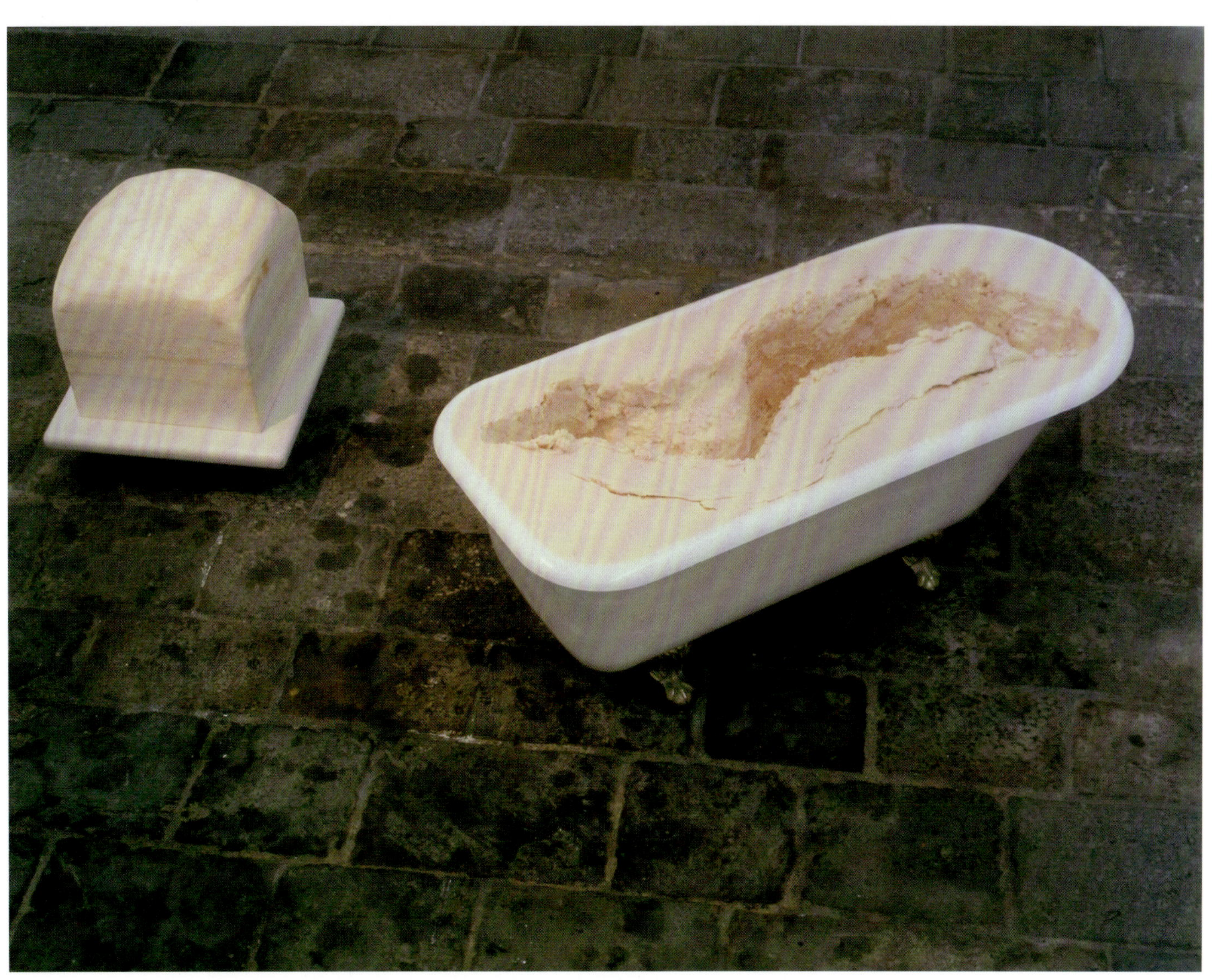

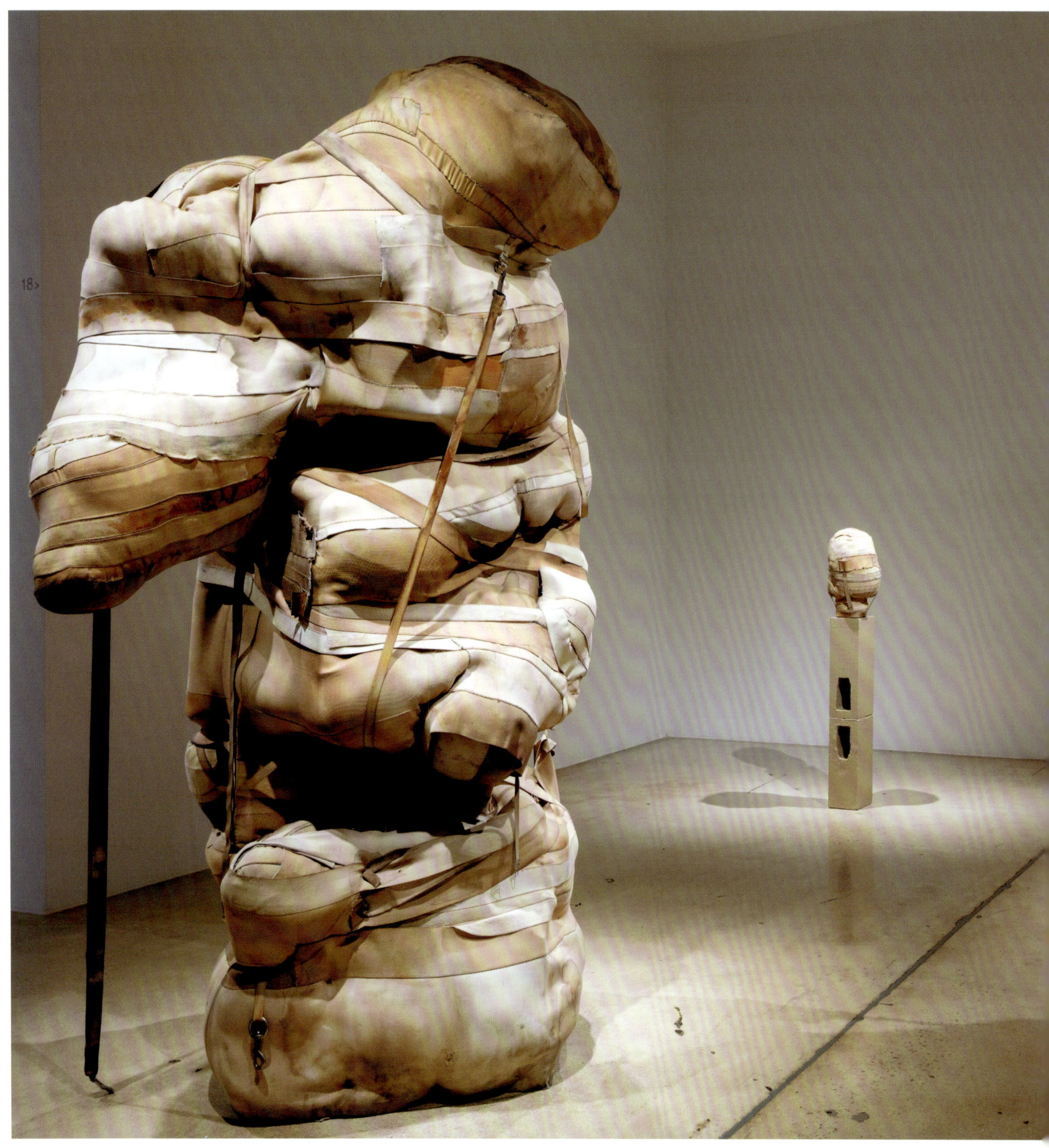

These sculptures relate to stories of isolation, separation, and confinement. I have stained, stitched, and bound elastic — a material typically used on the inside of clothing. It reminds me of skin but also of a strait jacket. I use straps to convey restraint and obscurity. The tension implies sexual dominance and control. This work is an examination of the transgressions of my family. Sister Vessels and Father Curtin, my grandparents, had a love affair while still ordained and later fled the church. I attempt to capture what the guilt of this perceived sin and disobedience might look like. In my mind, these transgressions are bound to the experience of another family member, formally incarcerated in a state prison.

—Patricia Ayres

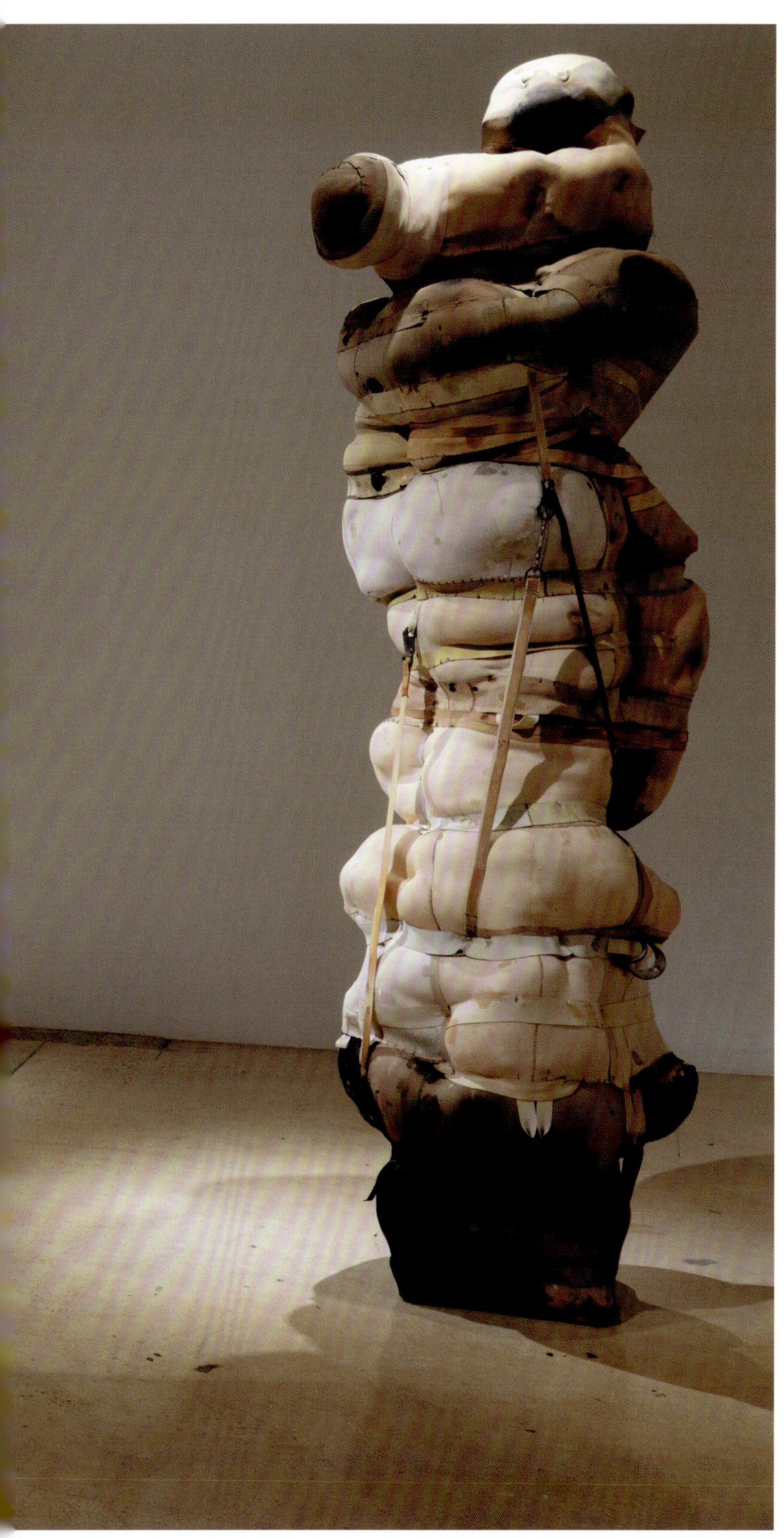

Left to right:
16-18-9-19-3-1, 2018, elastic, metal hooks, women's undergarment hardware, dye, coffee, paint, anointing oil, iodine, liquid latex, wood, padding, 90 x 57 x 46 in. (228.6 x 144.8 x 116.8 cm), acquired in 2022
4-1-14-9-5-12, 2022, elastic, paint, ink, dye, anointing oil, iodine, gunk, metal hardware, thread, wood, padding, foam, cement and plaster, 48 x 11 x 11 in. (121.9 x 27.9 x 27.9 cm), acquired in 2022
1-7-1-20-8-9-21-19, 2022, United States military elastic, elastic, paint, ink, dye, anointing oil, iodine, gunk, metal hardware, wood, padding, 102 x 42 x 36 in. (259 x 106.7 x 91.4 cm), acquired in 2022

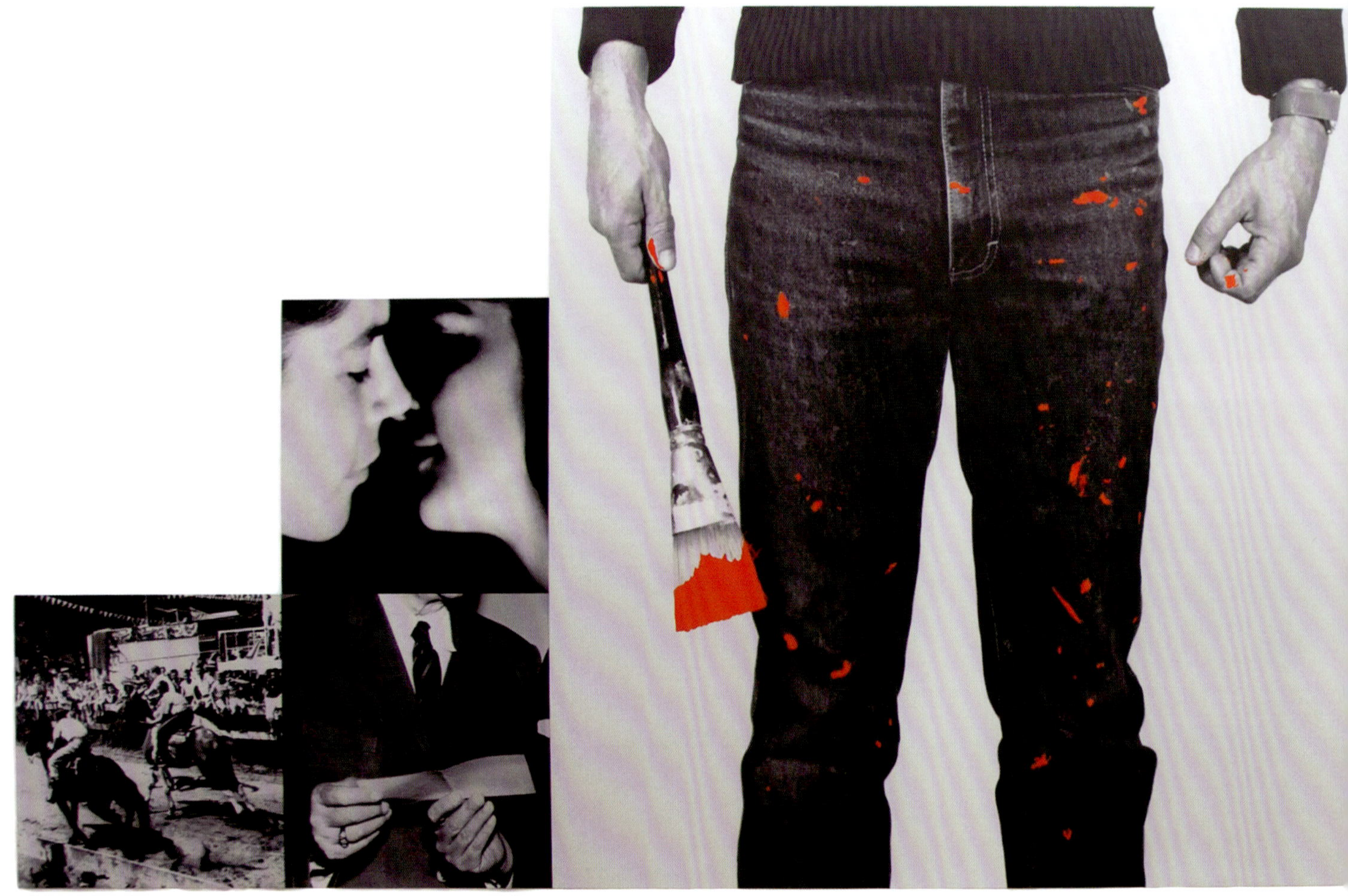

I did this piece explicitly for the Rubells, and it is a remake of an installation I made for the Biennale de Paris in 1985, which is how it originated. When I was thinking about what I would do, I heard there was a steak—a beefsteak in France—called a *palette* steak. Like a painter's palette. I found the cut, which is the steak in the piece, and then I decided to take it literally and put paint on it like a palette. The image to the right of the guy holding the paintbrush expands on the idea that the piece is somehow about painting. I made him the person that makes the painting, a *painter*, thus furthering the idea. During the Renaissance, artists made multi-panel religious paintings, and the adjoining panels of the main painting were called *predellas*. They were used to enhance the narrative of the main image, which was usually some religious subject matter. I decided to do the same thing—have predella panels that could illustrate what was on the mind of the artist—So I have several images. There's one of a couple kissing, because love and relationships are always an issue, or at least they

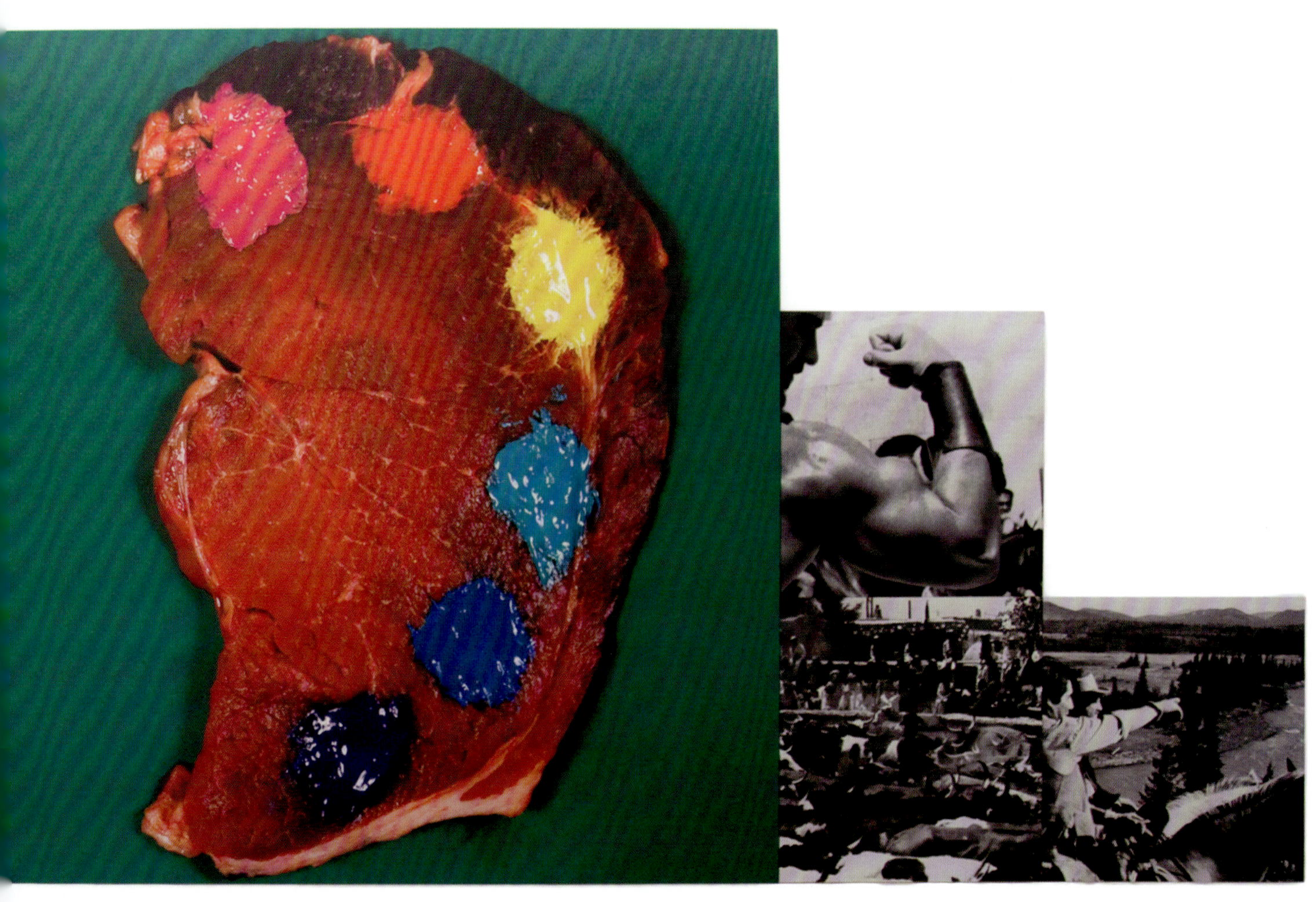

were back then. In the one below it, someone is being handed a check because money is always present in art. To the right, there's a herd of cattle, and you might think of meat coming from the cattle, but I was thinking artists are often treated like cattle, more meat for the system. The one above it, the guy flexing, is a pretty obvious symbol about power. And to the extreme left, the horse race—that's about art being a contest. Who's going to win? With collectors as well, there's a kind of contest going on. And then to the extreme right, again that is about performance, and how we as artists perform for people.

—John Baldessari

Stake: Art is Food for Thought and Food Costs Money, 1985, black-and-white photograph, color photograph, and acrylic paint, 144 x 480 in. (365.8 x 1219.2 cm), acquired in 2006

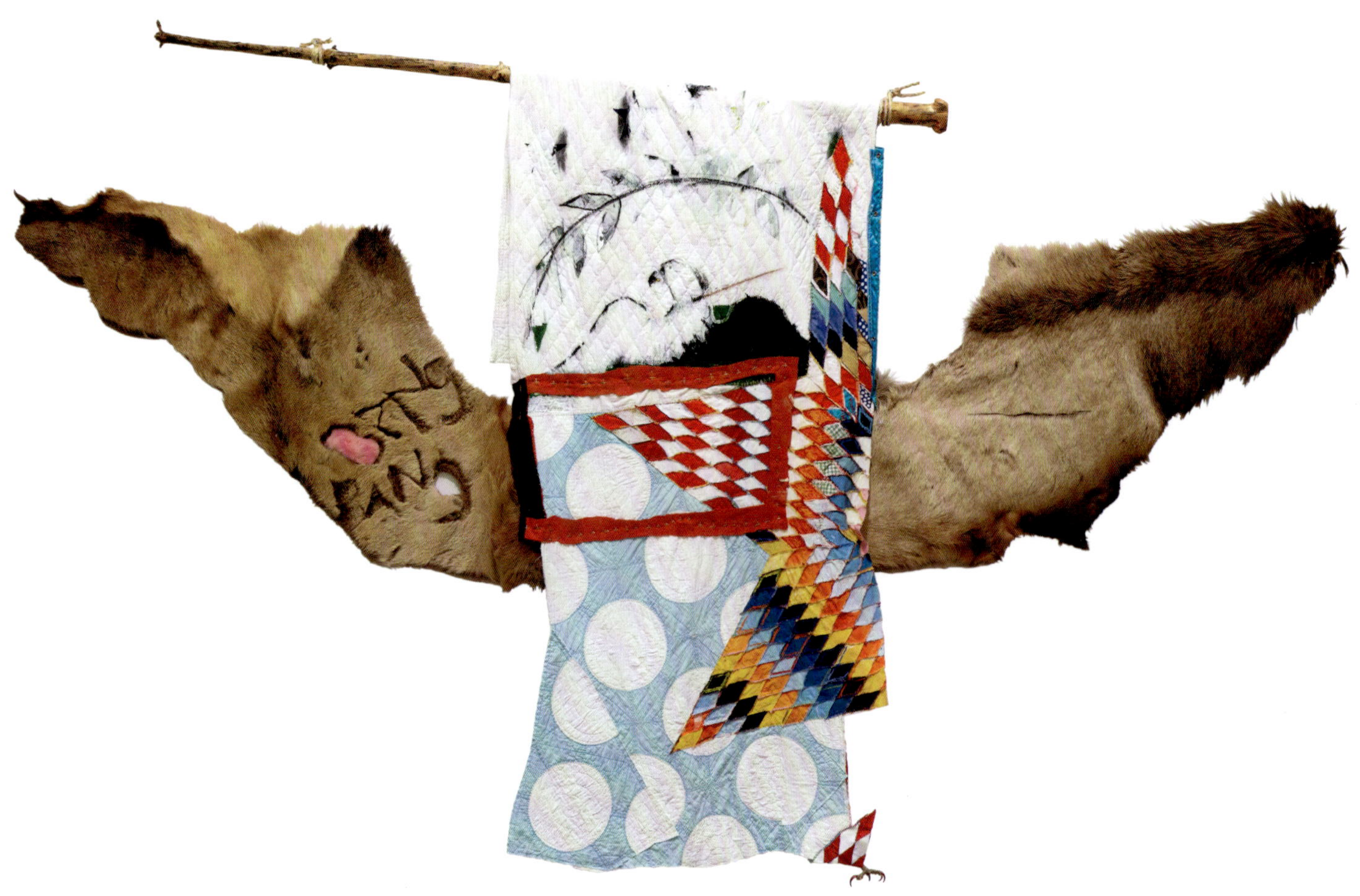

Bang Bang came from my solo exhibition in New York at Half Gallery titled *Bad Lucky Indian*. It was right after my MFA at Yale, and I was thinking through gesture, materiality, complex narratives, form, assemblage, but mostly humor.

In the studio I was looking at the Great Seal of the United States and I started to think about what that seal and its eagle means for me, what it means for our history, and what it means to be a dual citizen: to be a citizen of the Klamath Tribes, of a sovereign nation, but also a citizen of the United States. My thoughts just came back to extreme violence; it just came back to *Bang Bang*. It came back to thinking through the violence of us having to fight for our ability to access our first foods, which is represented by the elk hide. This is connected to our ability to exist.

There's a history with the settlers who have enacted extreme violence, then and now. I thought through materiality by appropriating settler quilts from my area. I deconstructed them in my studio to make new meaning and to give you my version of this American seal, but interpreted through a woman who's a mama, a matriarch, and who is connected to her territory and to these violent histories.

I was really pumping through it and going really hard and not worrying about anything in the process, which is really what I want to get back to. This work is really special to me because I wasn't worried about anything. I just was trying to say it and say it fast and say it hard: I wanted my own seal! The eagle and its symbolism have been appropriated historically. It has a significance in my culture too, and I wanted to bring that forward and honor it in a different way.

But there's also humor in the piece. There's a hawk's foot sticking out at the bottom with painted, glittered red nails. I've taken something really serious, but then I've also been able to be in a state of joy with the materials. I've had to really home in on that in the studio and cultivate that and maintain that. It's a skill set.

Since this is the first work I did when I came home to the studio after my MFA, I think that joy is a big part of this work too, even though what I'm talking about is really heavy. The materials in it are really dope. I talk about the settler quilts, but also there's leather cowboy boots in the diamonds of the star quilt. There are trade blankets in there, too. My auntie's

Bang Bang, 2019, elk hide, rabbit fur, oil stick, acrylic, charcoal, cotton, and pine, 84 x 124 in. (213.4 x 315 cm), acquired in 2019

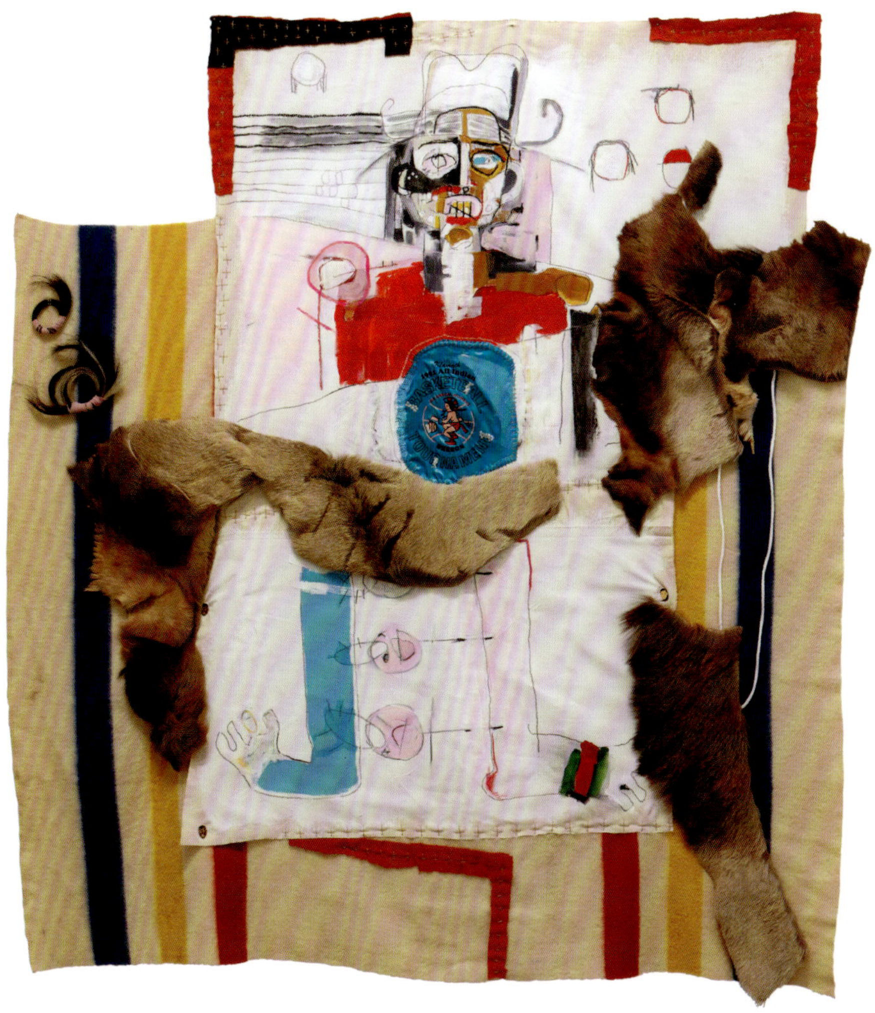

quilt is in there. We have the oldest All Indian basketball tournament in the United States here in Chiloquin, and it's on our Rez; my tribe started it. So, part of that jacket is in there, and part of it is in the other piece as well. There's some mark-making gestures to move your eye around the piece, and where *Bang Bang* is written on the piece, where the hole is on the second letter g, is where the animal was shot.

What's More American than a Cowboy? Assuming that the American cowboy is the hero, what's more American than that? In my practice I was taking that idea and spinning it. We may think of America as old, but America really isn't old in comparison to my culture and my history. Our connection to the land, our connection to our foods —our first foods— is ancient. We've known that we've been here from the beginning of time, and science is just catching up to how old our culture really is. What's more American, what's older, what's more superhero-ish than a cowboy? I was thinking about the character Billy Jack and his famous black hat. He's an Indian superhero that came into Hollywood Film in the '70s. I started with Billy Jack, referencing him in this piece figuratively, and then I went back to thinking about

our ancestors. We have this way of taking care of ourselves sustainably through our first foods without having to rely on agriculture or farming. We could feed ourselves.

In the middle of the piece, I refer back to our All Indian basketball players. Res ball is some of the toughest, most exciting basketball you'll ever see. It's a battle; they're warriors out there on the floor. I added one of the tournament jackets and also a trade blanket to reference the history of the Hudson's Bay blanket, but this one is from JC Penney— it's "fast material."

There's some humor again through the addition of the pins and the Gucci sandal. The little scalped caricatures on the piece first popped up when I was in school in New Zealand. I was just reminding myself that we're way older than these narratives, way older than these heroes that we see, and I made a set of figurative dolls that represent the projected idea of an Indian.

—Natalie Ball

What's More American Than a Cowboy, 2019, elk hide, oil stick, acrylic, pastel, charcoal, graphite, resin, horsehair, and wool, 92 x 84 in. (233.7 x 213.4 cm), acquired in 2019

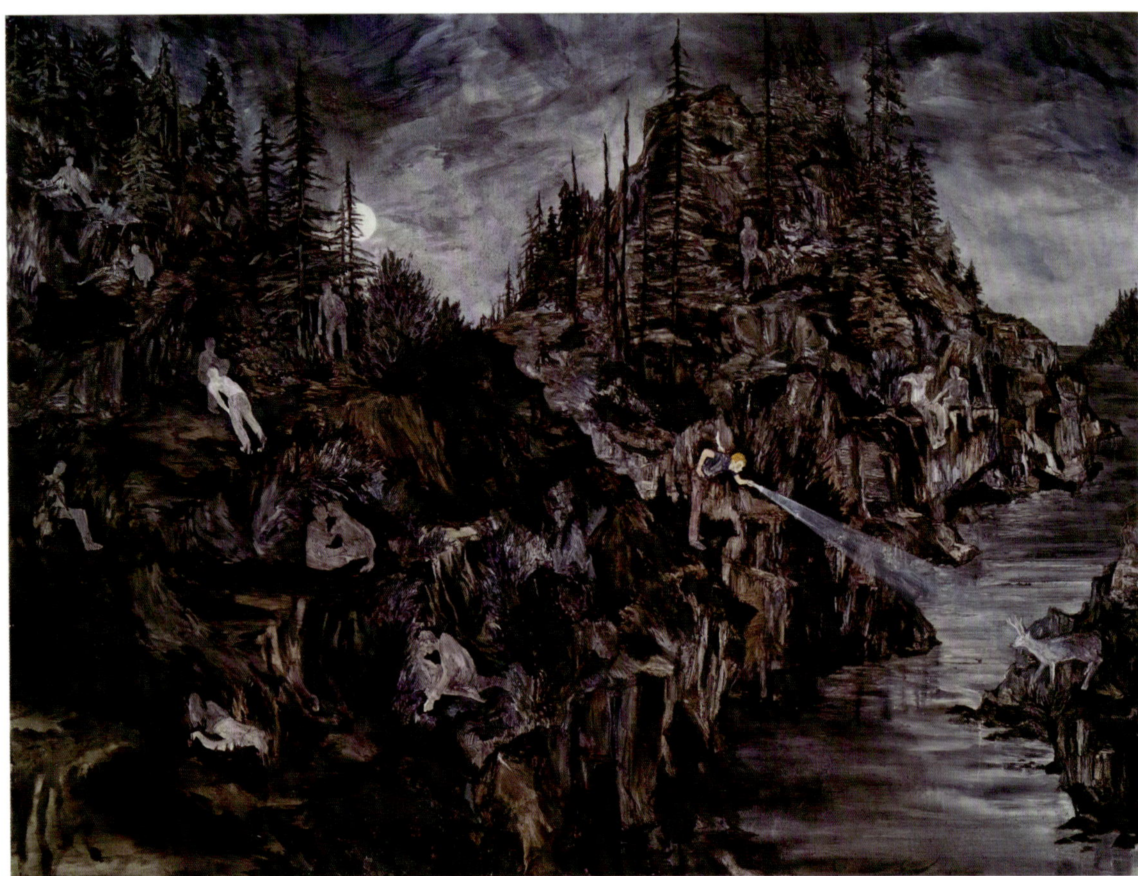

On the Jagged Shores was painted at the time I was working on a series set to be shown at my first solo museum project at MOCA Miami. The exhibition, titled *It's Super Natural*, was centered around a dimly lit installation of what appeared to be a rundown young boys' clubhouse, made of spare wood planks, etc. What wasn't immediately seen was the interior world within—what I've come to refer to as my Trojan Horse for sissies. A slit in the door revealed an opposite universe, one with pristine white walls and carpet, designer furniture, and issues of *Men's Vogue* scattered (neatly) around. The gallery walls surrounding the clubhouse were lined with small (bookish in size) black-and-white works on paper, the subject of which revolved around the ambiguous relationship of the main characters in *The Hardy Boys*, a children's book series about two handsome, young sleuths solving mysteries together. This wasn't my first foray into "willful misinterpretation," having taken on the homoeroticism of Boy Scout manuals a year earlier. But this was different, it tied into a sense of mystery, the strange, and even the otherworldly. The supernatural world played a recurring part in the storylines of the Hardy Boys mysteries and those tales combined with a liberal (arguably) re-interpretation of the boys' relationship became for me a manner of discussing homosexuality, youth, and vulnerability. Being gay was, to me, "Super Natural." This was both a play on words and a way of relating the gay character to something out of the realm of the norm. Oscar Wilde was often described as being an alien in his time, and for me this became a badge of honor. *On the Jagged Shores*

was at the time the largest work I had made and one of the first works on canvas in my professional career. I wanted it to be an epic but shy painting. As a result, I left behind the couples (Hardy Boys) I had made in the works on paper and opted for a sole protagonist. I wanted to be Caspar David Friedrich; I wanted a "Monk by the Sea" and to involve myself in the history of precipices in historical paintings. I was thinking of Romanticism, about Robert Smith of The Cure "spinning on that dizzy edge" alone on a cliff edge in the music video for their Goth crossover hit, "Just Like Heaven."

To describe the work specifically, the main character (the only one "lit" with color) has stumbled upon an innocent deer, catching its gaze in the beam of his flashlight. Meanwhile, the surrounding landscape is alive with silhouetted figures of pairs of men in compromising positions. I loved the idea of this innocent moment being surrounded by a hidden opposite. Gay culture has a long-standing history of public sex, a history that honestly frightened me a bit. I was recalling the memory of hiking through the woods (I was maybe 11) with my brother and sister at a certain Coconut Grove park and realizing we weren't alone, and stumbling on abandoned "sex pits" with the leftovers of anonymous sex and porn scattered in the mud and mangroves. We had been looking for alligators and perhaps the figure in *On the Jagged Shores* had found what he was seeking out in that deer? The answer to that question is something I would like to remain a mystery.
—Hernan Bas

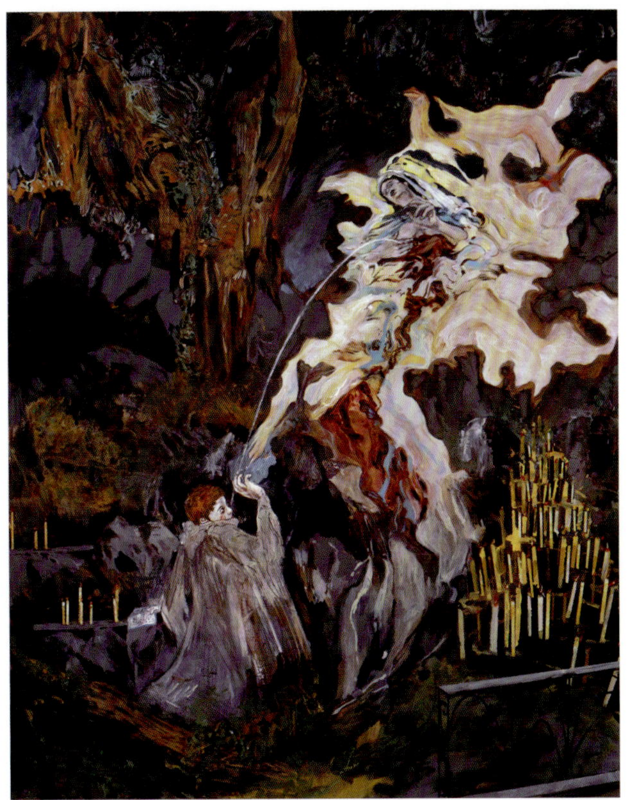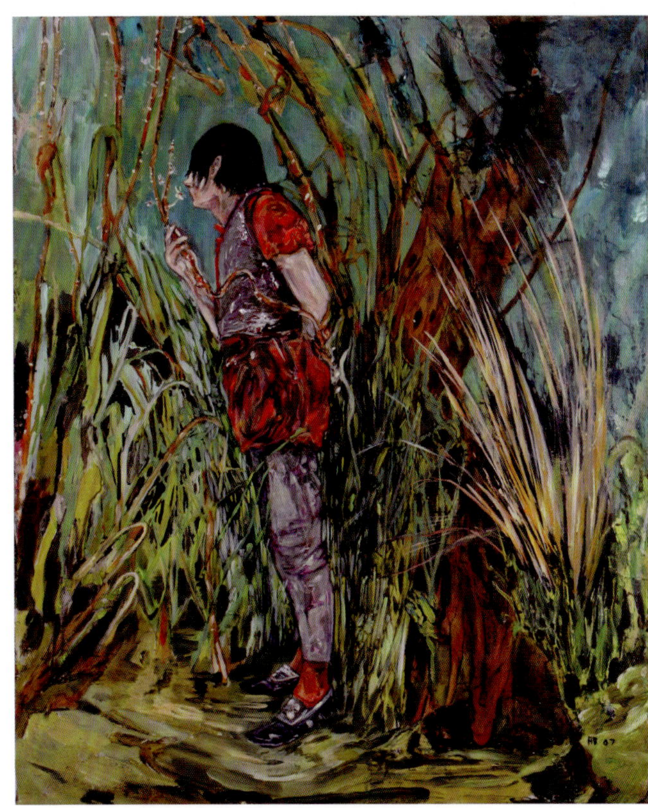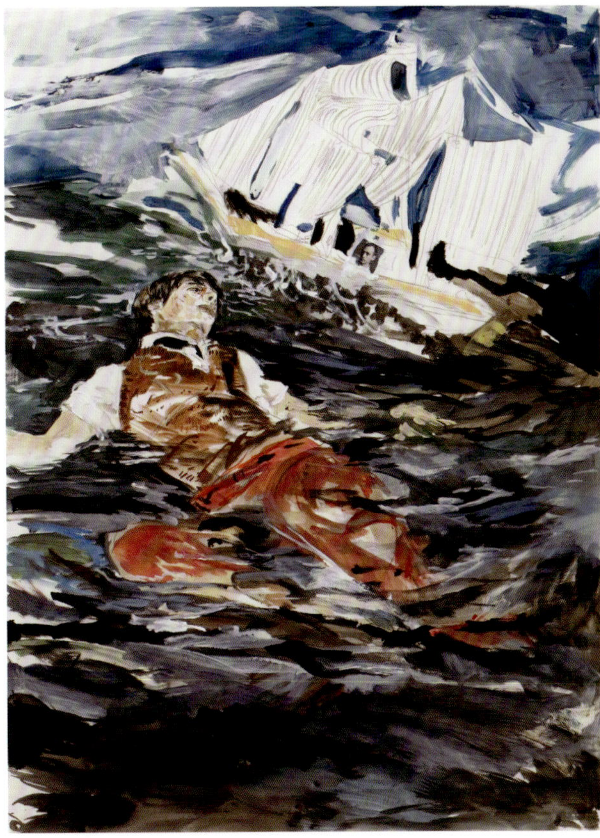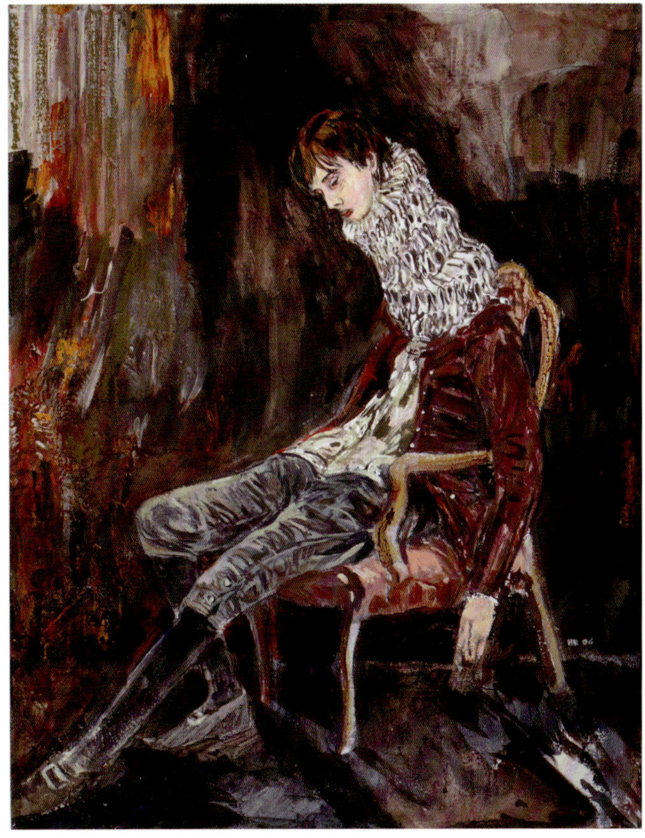

Opposite page: *On the Jagged Shores*, 2002, acrylic and water-based oil on linen, 52 x 70 in. (132 X 177.8 cm), acquired in 2002
Above, clockwise from top left: *The Immaculate Lactation of Saint Bernard*, 2007, acrylic and gouache on linen, 50 x 40 in. (127 x 101.6 cm), acquired in 2007; *Mephistopheles at 17 (In His Weed Garden)*, 2007, acrylic and gouache on linen, 24 x 20 in. (61 x 50.8 cm), acquired in 2007; *The Burden (I Shall Leave No Memoirs)*, 2006, acrylic and gouache on linen, 20 x 16 in. (50.8 x 40.6 cm), acquired in 2006; *Floating in the Dead Sea with Ghost Ship Pirated by Hedi Slimane*, 2003, acrylic, watercolor, pencil, and collage on paper, 30 x 22 1/2 in. (76.2 x 56 cm), acquired in 2004

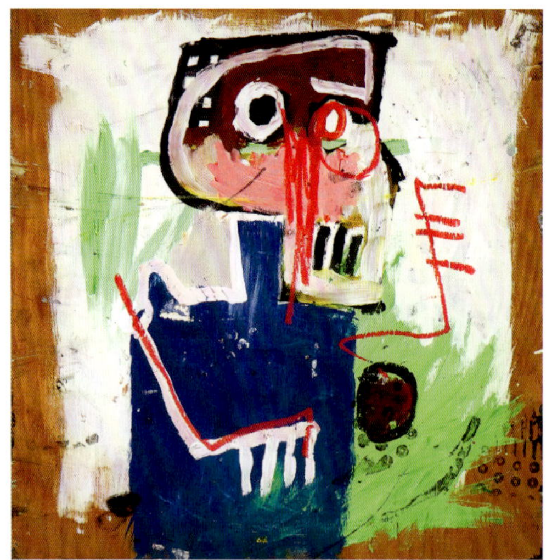

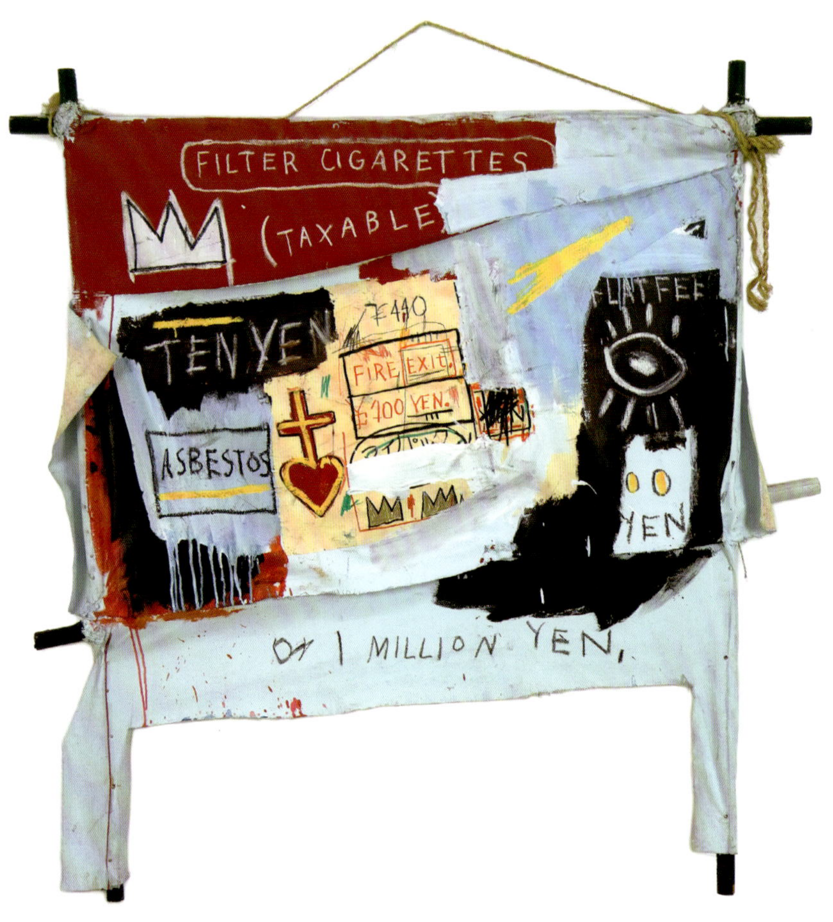

Untitled (Self-portrait), 1982-1983, oil on wood, 20 x 20 in. (50.8 x 50.8 cm), acquired in 1983
One Million Yen, 1982, oil on canvas with wood and jute, 60 x 58 x 3 3/4 in. (152.4 x 147.3 x 9.5 cm), acquired in 1982
© Estate of Jean-Michel Basquiat. Licensed by Artestar, New York.

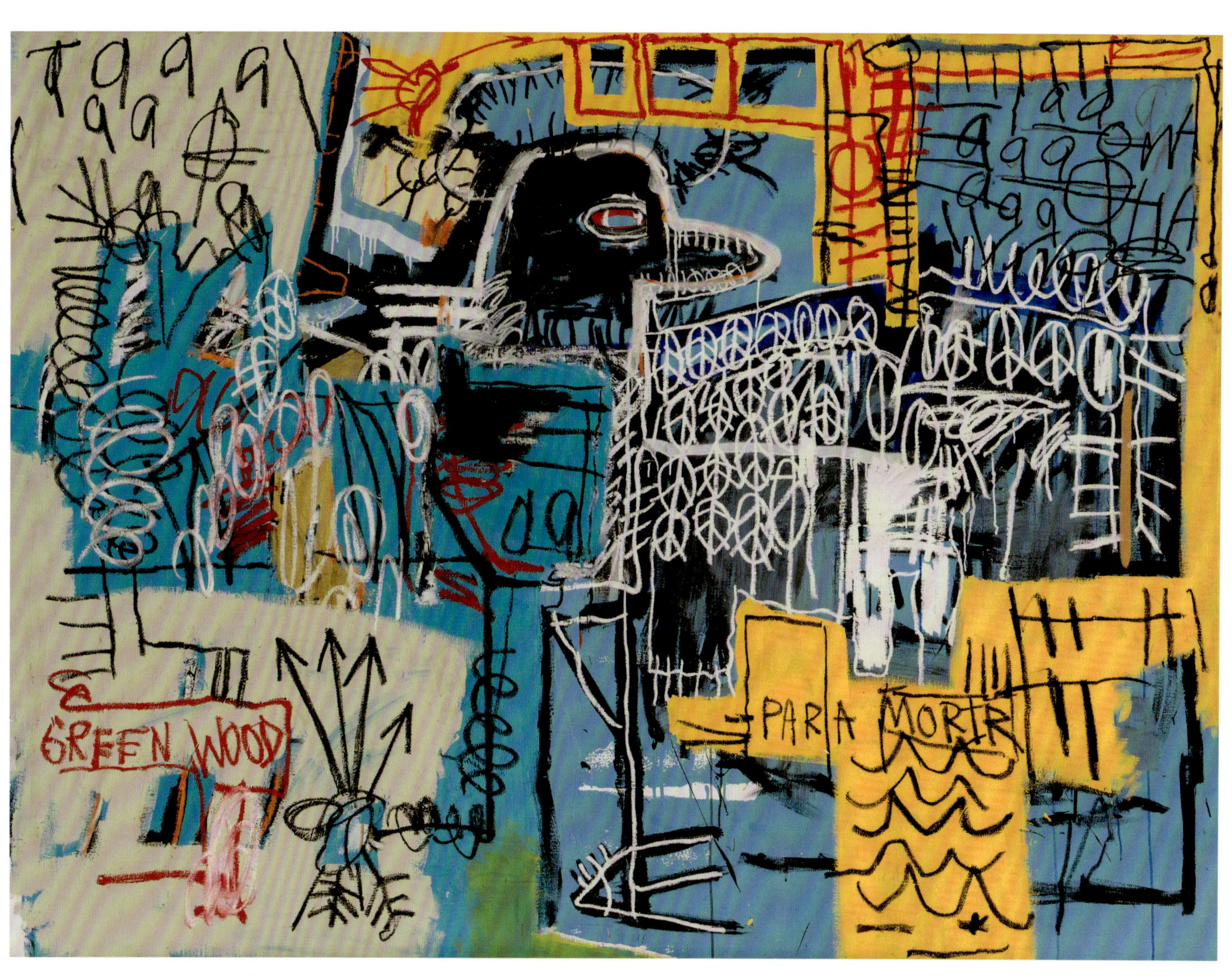

Bird On Money, 1981, acrylic and oil on canvas, 66 x 90 in. (167.6 x 228.6 cm), acquired in 1981
© Estate of Jean-Michel Basquiat. Licensed by Artestar, New York.

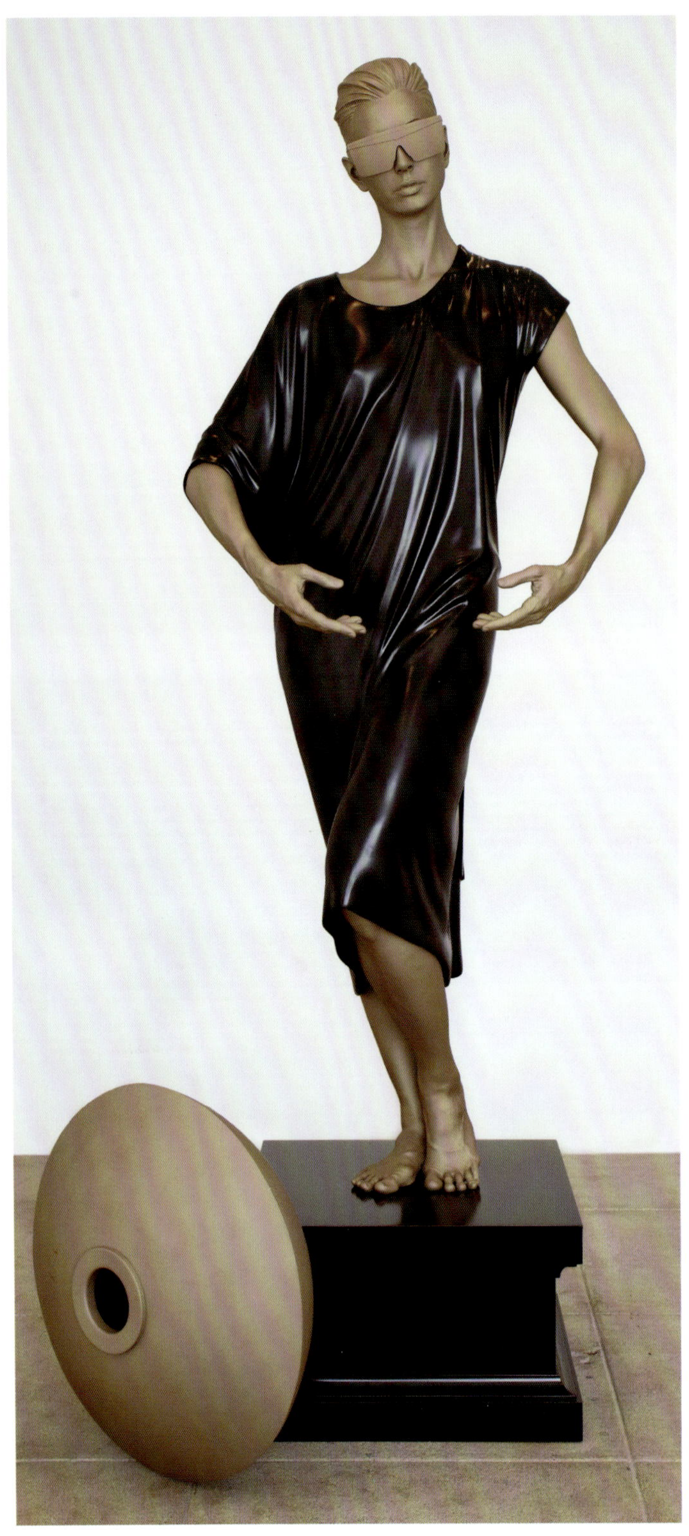

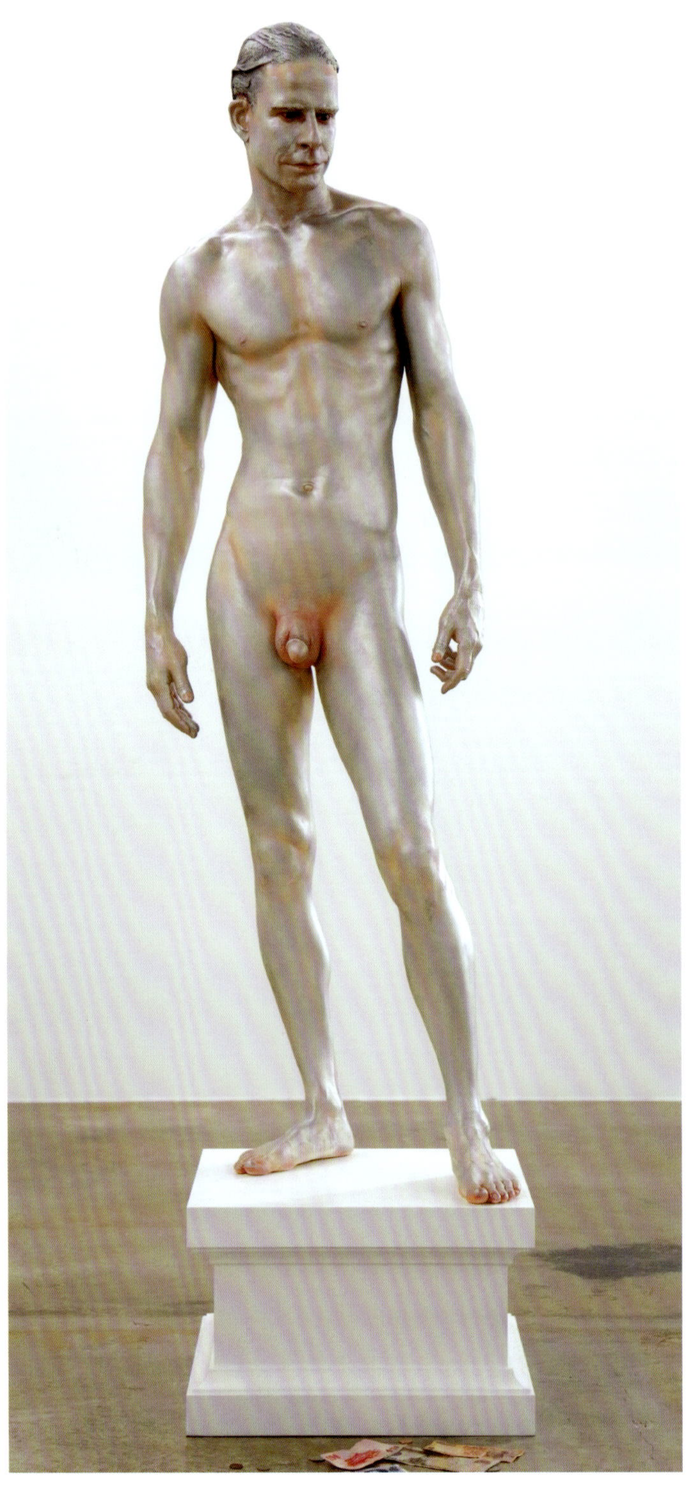

Human Statue (Jessie), 2011, is a life-size bronze figure depicting a woman in a designer dress and sunglasses holding a pose, which mirrors the circular form of the vase at her feet. I originally conceived of this work as the female counterpart to an earlier sculpture of a nude male, *Human Statue*, 2005, but departed from that work's trompe l'oeil illusionism by giving primary emphasis to the overall form of the sculpture and the natural color of its material. Both works recall figurative sculptures of the past, but the model's contemporary dress and angular pose clearly place *Human Statue (Jessie)* in the present. This interplay of modernity and classicism is reflected in the work's realization: it was first designed digitally using 3D scans of Jessie Gold, the New York–based, Miami–raised, model, artist, dancer, and musician. The scans were then used to construct a virtual model, which required months of work digitally re-sculpting the figure to achieve the lifelike

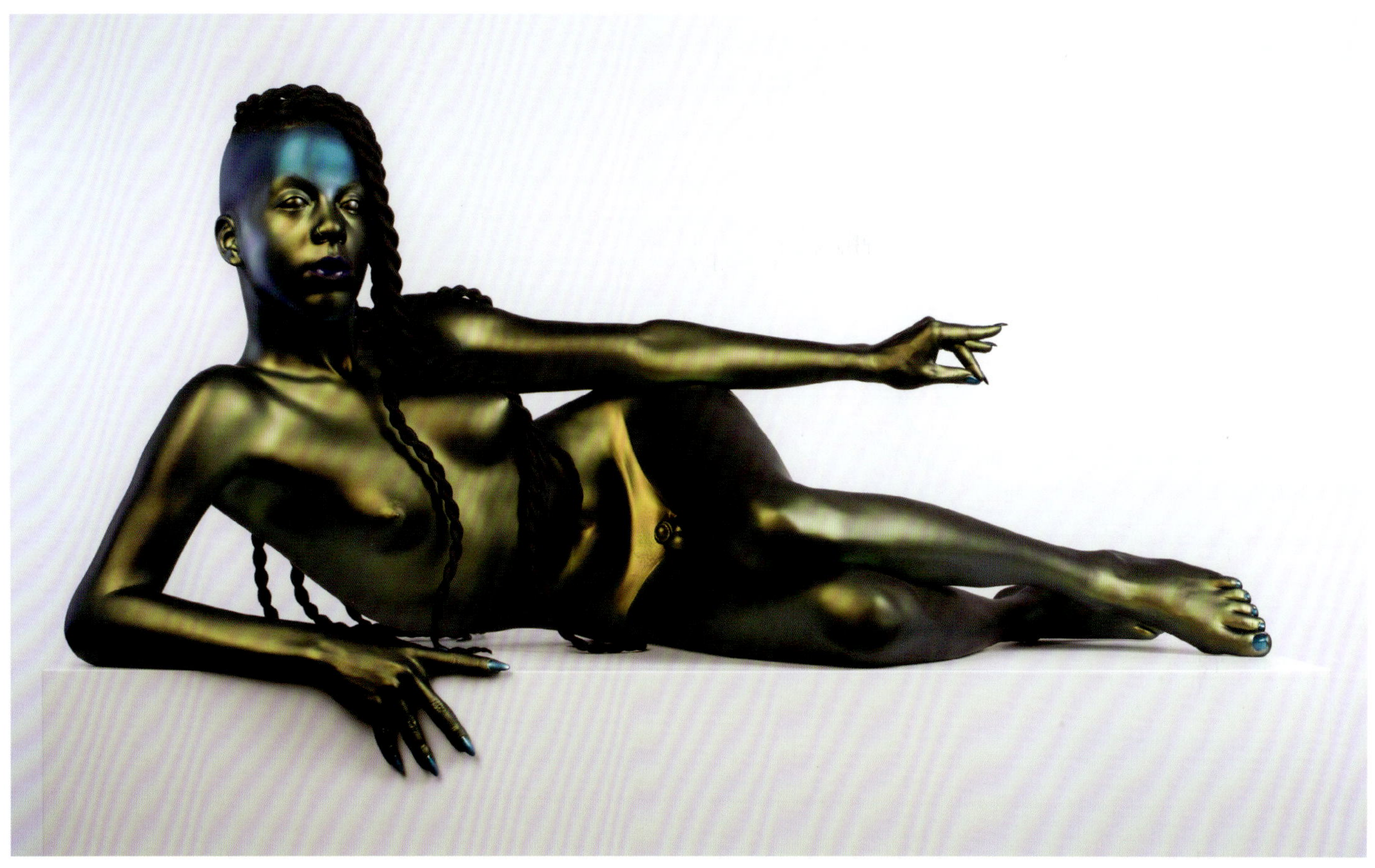

detail visible in the final piece. Once complete, the hands, head, and legs of the figure were output from the computer as rapid prototypes, and the dress was milled out of high-density foam. These models were then molded for bronze casting. The sunglasses, based on a vintage Versace design, have been milled out of solid bronze, and the vase at the base of the sculpture has been cast directly from an existing ceramic vessel. After the entire sculpture was assembled, the dress and the plinth were painted black, while the rest of the sculpture retains the natural color of the alloy of which the whole is cast, approximating the model's flesh.

Not just a means to an end, the technology used to construct the sculpture was integral to the conception of the work. The cold, mechanical data capture and the precise, physical fabrication employed to create the piece informed the model's rigid, robotic pose. The resulting work combines my interest in mechanical reproduction, sculptural objecthood, and assemblage, which is reflected in the interplay of abstracted forms comprising the sculpture. Aesthetically, *Human Statue (Jessie)* blends the neo-noir classicism of Patrick Nagel's illustrations and Ridley Scott's *Blade Runner* (both indelible

influences from my youth) with the technical advancements of James Cameron's *Avatar* to form a depiction of a young woman that is uncanny in its detail and anonymous in its formalism. For all their flaws, Nagel's ubiquitous prints of the 1980s popularized an unconventional ideal of feminine beauty. Working from photographic source material, Nagel reduced the angular figures of his austere compositions to their essential contours, gracefully merging them with the simple geometry of their clothing and accessories, and in the process, defining the style of a generation. Similarly, Rachel, the female protagonist of Ridley Scott's *Blade Runner*, is an iconic beauty of artificial origin, conceived at a time when people were just beginning to develop intimate relationships with new technology. Thankfully, the post-apocalyptic future world Scott envisioned has not arrived, but the film did accurately predict a time when we would become inseparable from our once-unimaginable technological creations. Despite these advancements, the one thing still eluding mankind is an escape from death. This desire to preserve and extend life, so central to the replicant characters of the film, is also reflected in my work, where the ephemeral is made concrete and life is cast in a material that will outlive us all. —Frank Benson

2019 Artist in Residence

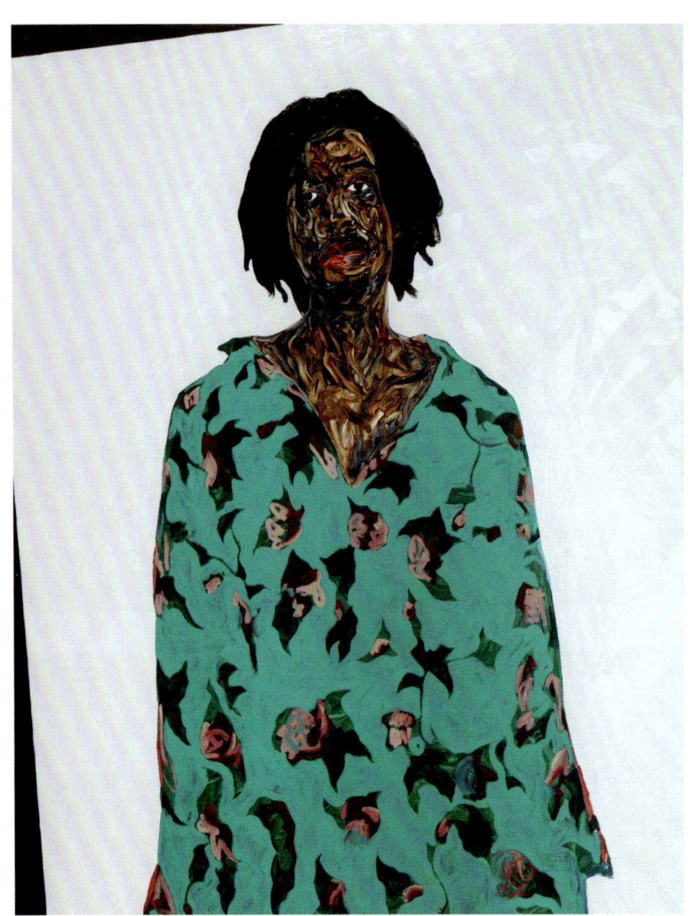

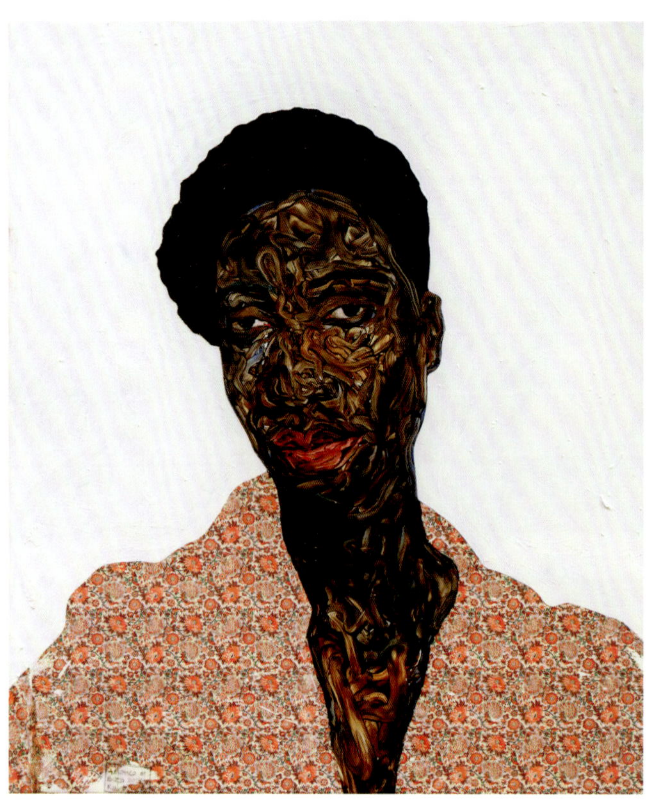

Hudson, the subject of the painting *Hudson in a Baby Blue Suit* [opposite], is a character with a lot of confidence. I wanted to be able to put something of that sort out there—a Black figure commanding a space, having such confidence and complementing it with colors that are also bold, which is where I imagine his energy comes from. I'm always thinking about color palette, which sets the mood. Part of my character is that I like looking at people when I am talking to them, so I don't waste my time with bullshitting. So I want my characters to pierce into your eyes when you are looking at them. Of course, I do have moments when I make paintings where the characters look away, but I think the majority of my paintings are paintings that look back at you.

The subject in the painting *Missy May* is a Ghanaian friend of Otis's [Kwame Kye Quaicoe]. I liked the confidence that I saw on her Instagram page. That's the energy she puts out and I just wanted to connect myself to it. For me, it's not really about painting the resemblance but more the character that I see and how I am able to put it out there. I want to find ways

where I can make images that suggest confidence. I want to suggest beauty in all its complex ways. I also want to show that we don't always have to laugh or smile.

I'm always thinking about making paintings that suggest something. I think of format, space, and size. With *Jeremy*, I was interested in pattern making and how it could be a form of abstraction. I was also interested in how the painting would look if you just moved a little bit away from making a flat surface by adding some off-palette color in the background that suggests that the painting is a bit tilted. I was just trying to push myself a little bit from what I know because of late I've been thinking a lot about painting.

I know, for me, drawing is the beginning of painting, but is drawing really necessary to make a painting? I know I'm good at painting, so I've been asking myself, should I not go straight to painting? Why do I have to sketch? But over the years I realized that, for me, drawing is a much more intimate process than I had thought. When I'm drawing, I'm much

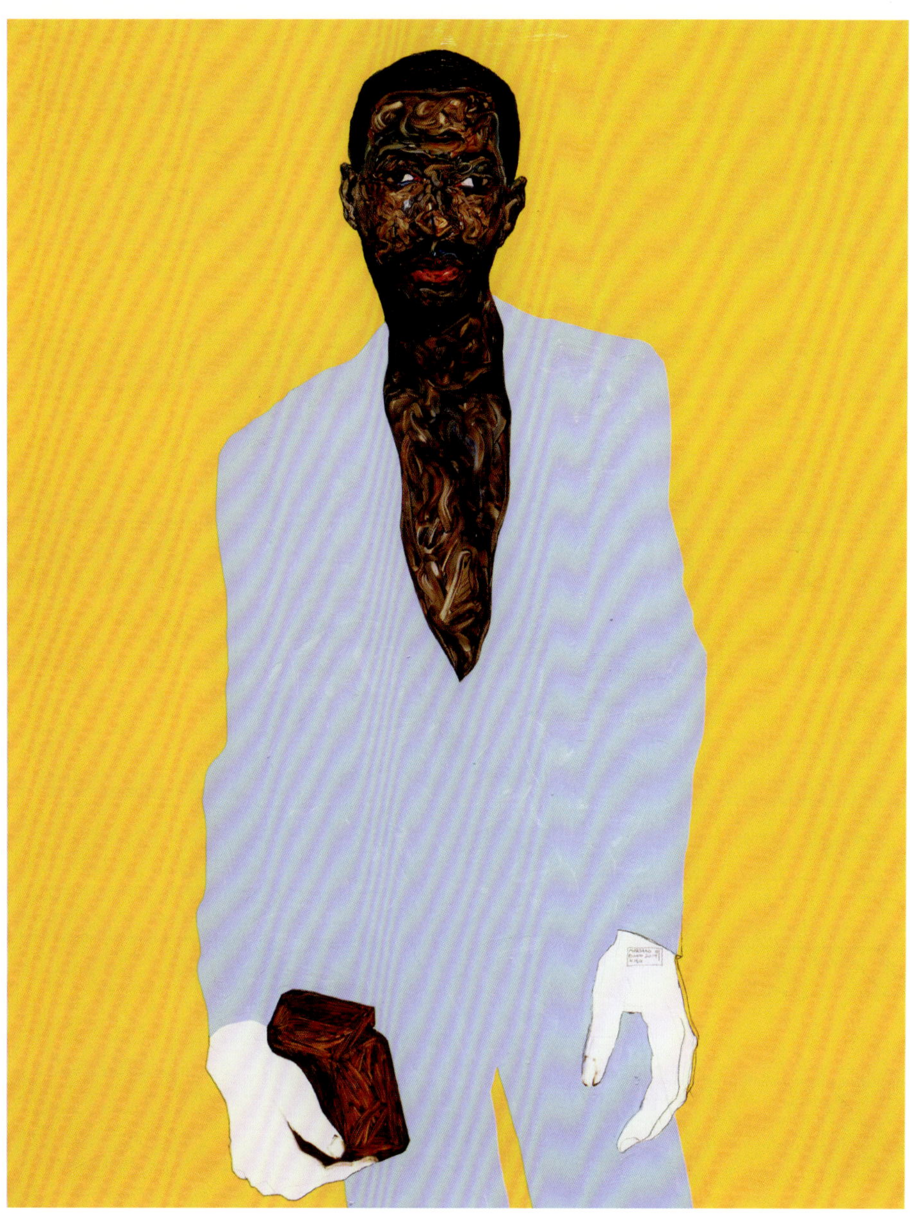

closer to the person because I think of all the strokes and all the corrections that I have to make, and those are the times that I bond with the subject. Adding the colors is just a feeling. In this painting, you will see that there's a lot of drawing, not just painting. One thing that makes it quite special is that if I should try to repeat this particular image again, it will not be the same because that's the thing with drawing freely. I like to free-sketch where I don't have control. When you have no control, it always shows a form of maturity.

My process suggests almost everything from drawing to sculpting to molding; it has all the elements in it. Sculpting is the same process of adding and taking out, and that's exactly what I do with my finger when I am painting. I always want to find ways to make the work interesting with patterns. Of course, I did try a few ways to draw or paint the patterns on these pieces myself, and then I decided I wanted to try this transfer technique where there are rules to follow. But the way I work best is to understand the basics and then to find my own way, which, in *Missy May*, was to apply a liquid, add the material, wait for a certain amount of time, and then rub it all off. The pattern stays and whatever comes up, comes up. It's a raw process because it cannot be repeated. Sometimes you have a moment where everything stays and then you have other surfaces where nothing stays. But everything comes out the way it's supposed to, and I like the fact that I don't have control over the process. Anything that will guarantee or allow me freedom is what I am leaning towards.

—Amoako Boafo

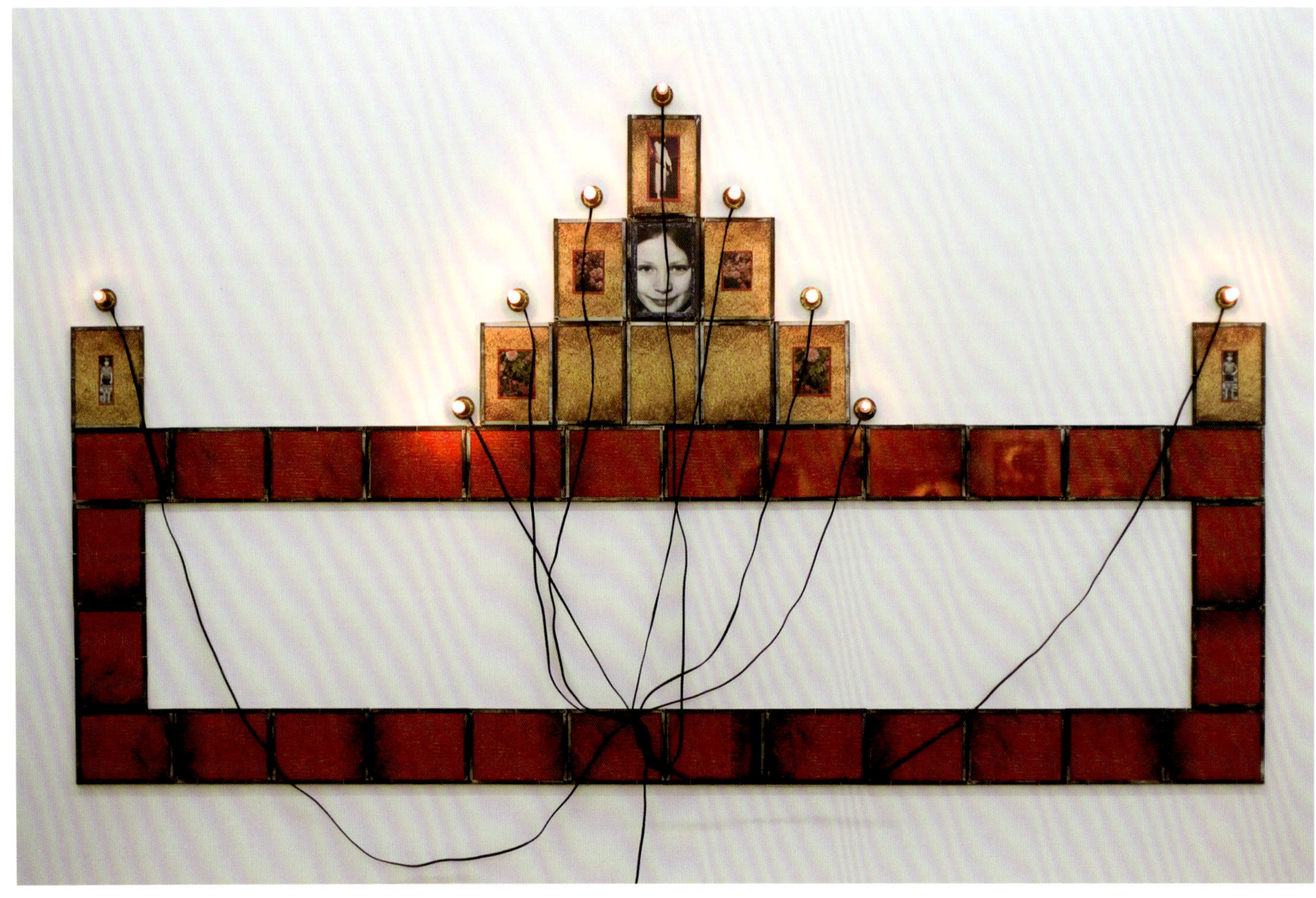

This series of works titled *Réserve* conveys the idea of archive and conservation. The photographs are close-up portraits of Jewish children taken before the Second World War on the day of the Purim holy day, and this might have been the last holy day in these children's lives. The work in the Rubell Collection, *Untitled (Réserve)* (1989), includes piles of folded clothes and prefigures the monumental installations I made at the Park Avenue Armory in New York and at the Grand Palais in Paris, both in 2010.

—Christian Boltanski

Monument, 1985, photographs, light bulbs, and fixtures, 55 x 96 7/8 x 2 3/4 in. (139.7 x 246 x 7 cm), acquired in 1988
Opposite page: *Autel de Lycée Chases [Altar to Chase High School]*, 1987, six photographs with six electric lamps and twenty-two tin boxes, 81 x 83 1/2 x 8 3/4 in. (205.7 x 212 x 22.2 cm), acquired in 1988

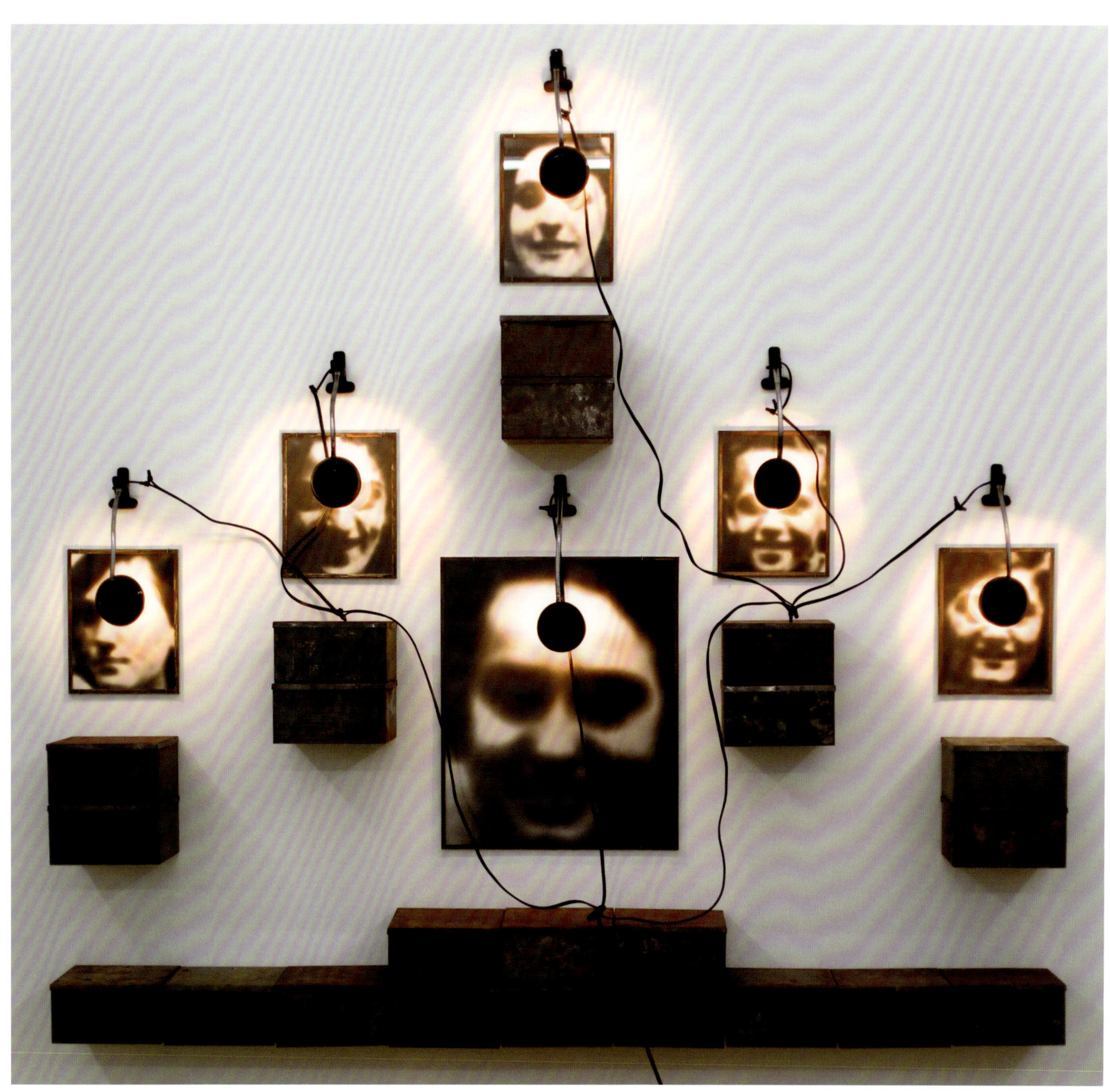

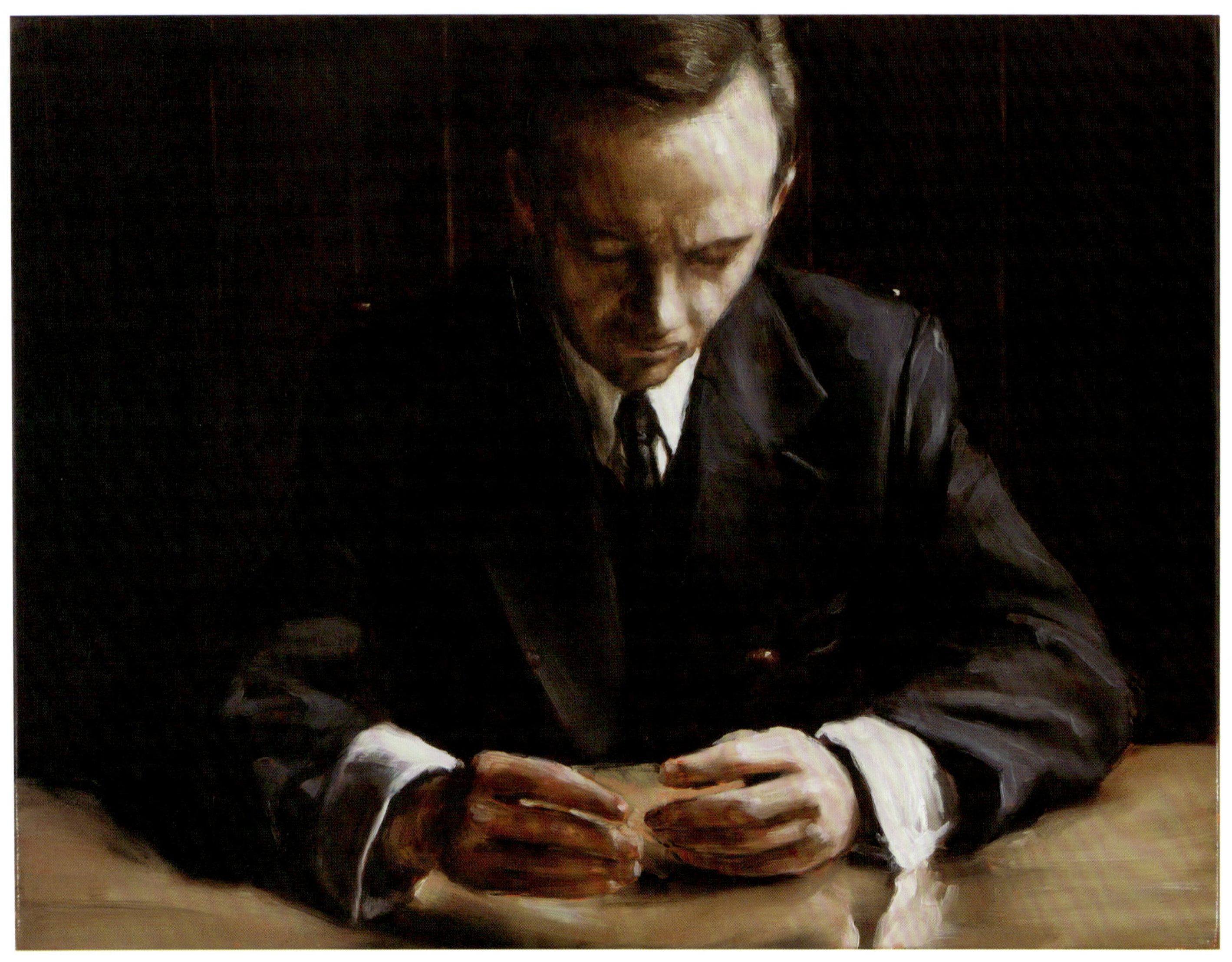

The Slide, 2004, oil on canvas, 23 1/2 x 31 1/2 x 1 in. (60 x 80 x 3 cm), acquired in 2004
Opposite page: *The Constellation*, 2000, oil on canvas, 39 x 47 in. (100 x 120 cm), acquired in 2002

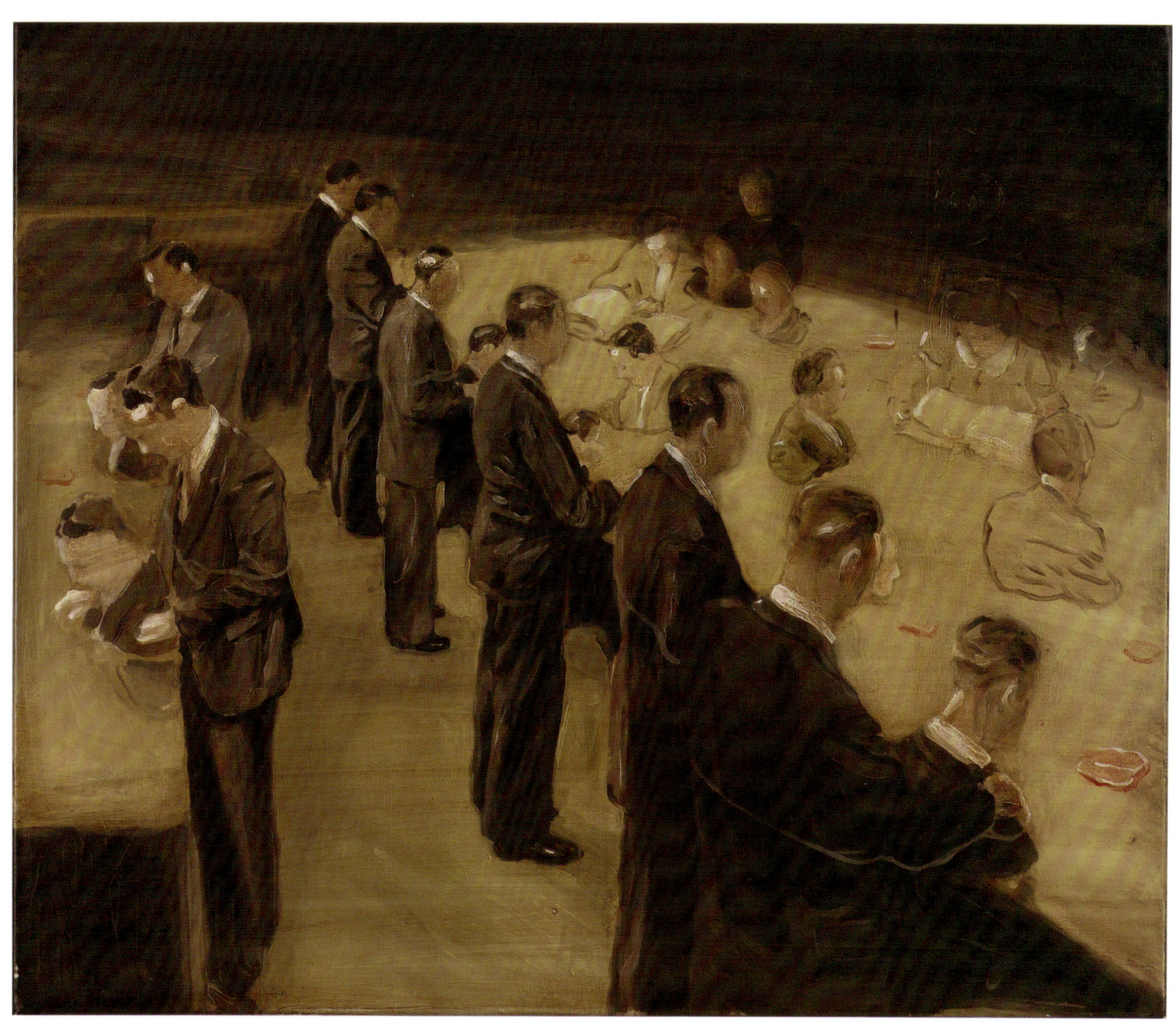

This painting is about sculpture and performance, many of
the early paintings are.

The later paintings are about painting mostly, and the painting
in the painting and in the painting.

—Michaël Borremans

This painting is about the feelings I was having regarding my work within the larger context of painting and history. It felt like everything I was doing was kind of impure, and I had this desire to engage with painting; not collage, not found material, but with the history of paint.

Since the early days of my art school education, I have wondered why the very first gesture—the material *paint*—is never questioned nor critiqued. That interested me: why paint itself is so highly fetishized and discussions focus solely on the imagery within a painting. The fact that paint itself is never questioned is just another way of reinforcing hierarchic relationships. The way those relationships are constructed is connected to power. So I wanted to explore this problem. The materials I have always used were so impure, and using them felt at first like I was a whore in the holy church of modernism.

This is an important work. It is one of the first paintings that came together compositionally and topographically. This was the first work in which I used silver paper, and probably the first where I used bathroom caulking instead of string. It has a really interesting graphic quality. I divided the canvas in a very horizontal way; the background is divided in two, and then the image is in the foreground, front and center. The canvas is unstretched, which allowed me to move away from a traditional way of framing an image and to see different, interesting things for a minute. I used a lot of map imagery in this painting. I would take a lot of maps and cut them up until they started to look like abstract paintings, and then I would draw them back into the work.

—Mark Bradford

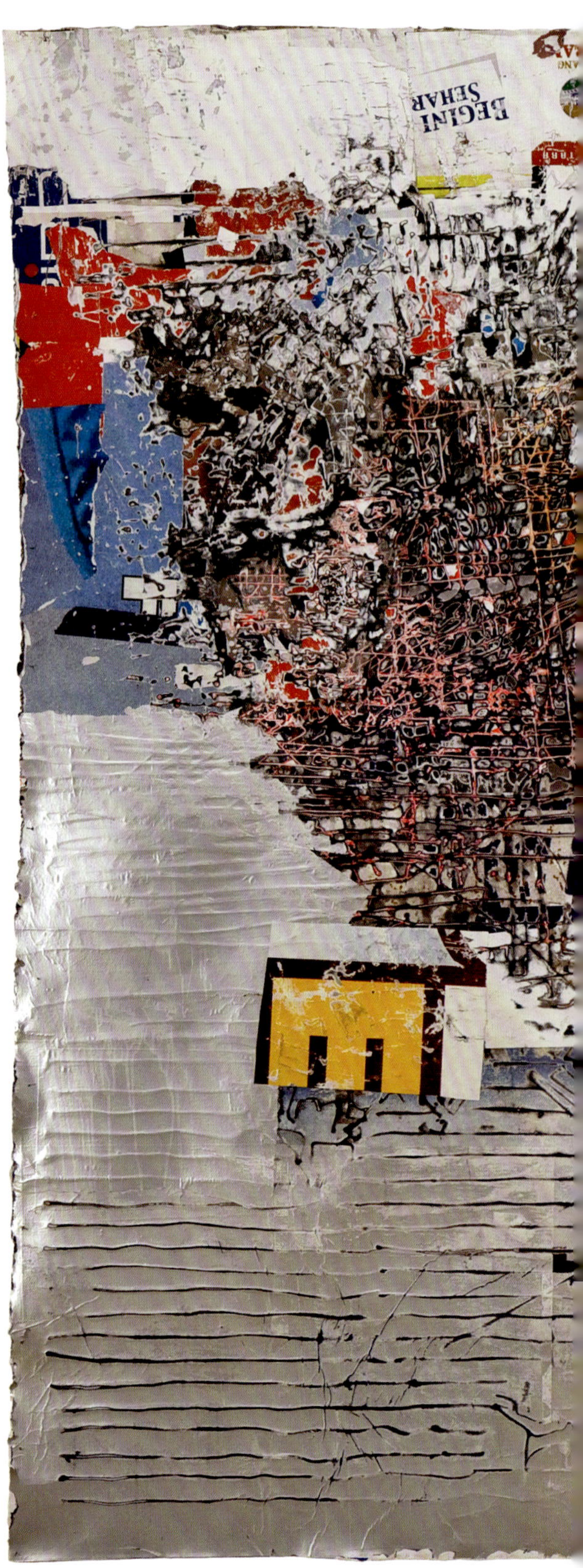

Whore in the Church House, 2006, mixed media collage on canvas, 103 x 142 in. (261.6 x 360.7 cm), acquired in 2006

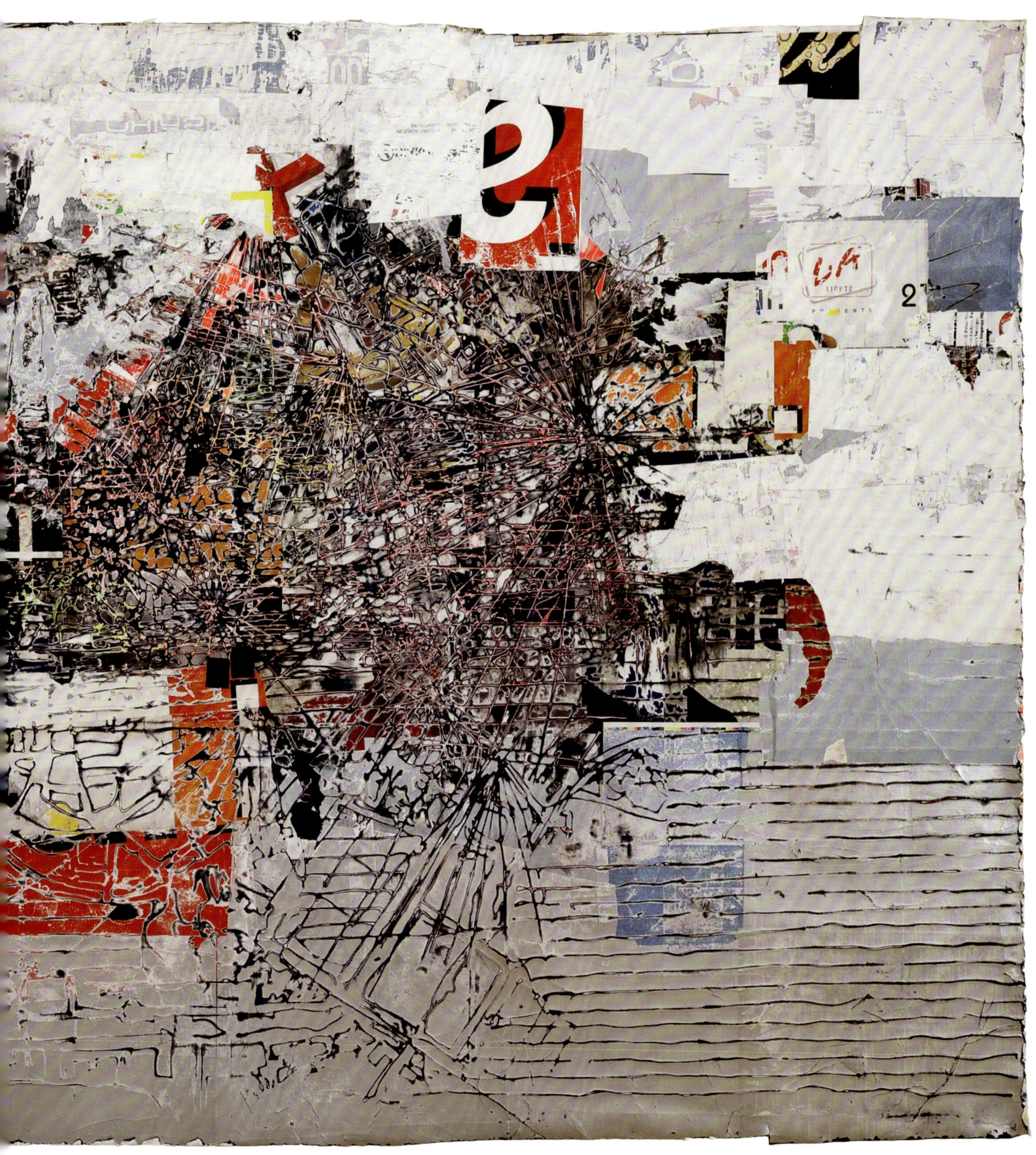

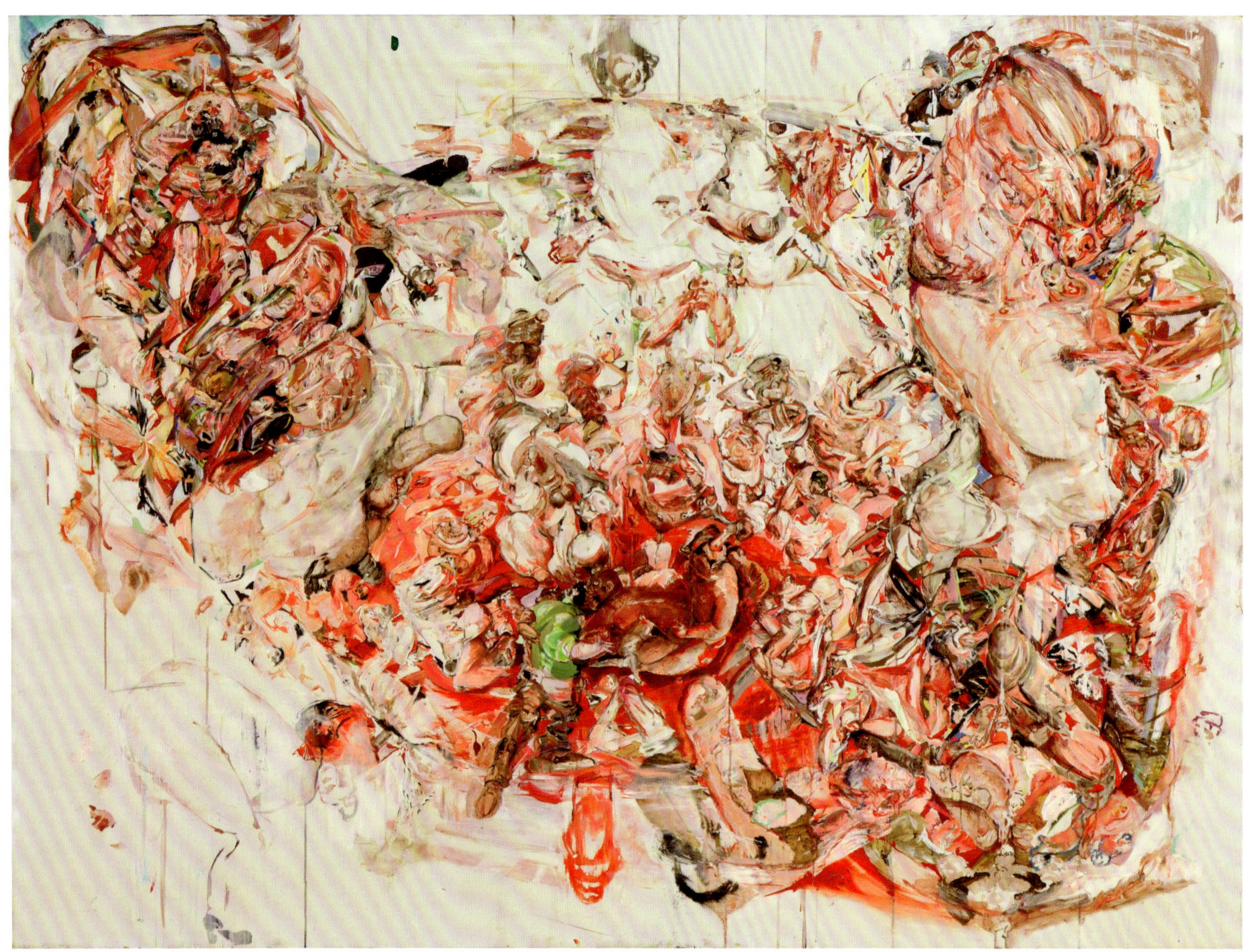

One thing that I have long tried to do in my work is to keep changing the approach to making a painting. As soon as I feel that I'm becoming too familiar with a way of doing something, I want to contradict myself and do something unpredictable. It's essential to keep surprising myself and, hopefully, the audience.

It's well known that in the mid- to late '90s, painting in oils was a very unfashionable and possibly immoral thing to do. Painting the figure was probably the worst of all. In 1996 and '97, I'd been attempting to make paintings that had all the drama and darkness of my Old Master heroes and that had a "muscularity" in the way they were made—and an emotional charge. I wanted to make content-laden images with multiple figures but did not want to deal with issues of gender, or even

the weighty problem of addressing the human figure. As a way around this problem, I used bunnies, and later other hybrid creatures, as human surrogates.

The Gang's All Here is a significant work for me because it was the first painting in a long time in which human figures appeared. The creatures in the last "pure" bunny painting (*Untitled 1997*) had undeniably human genitalia, and it became obvious that I was longing to paint humans, and that I had to do it.

I wanted to make a painting that could only be a *painting*: in other words, paint something that could not be done in any other medium. I took great liberties with space and with scale, juxtaposing areas of wide, open space with densely

The Gang's All Here, 1998, oil on linen, 52 x 76 in. (132.1 x 193 cm), acquired in 1998

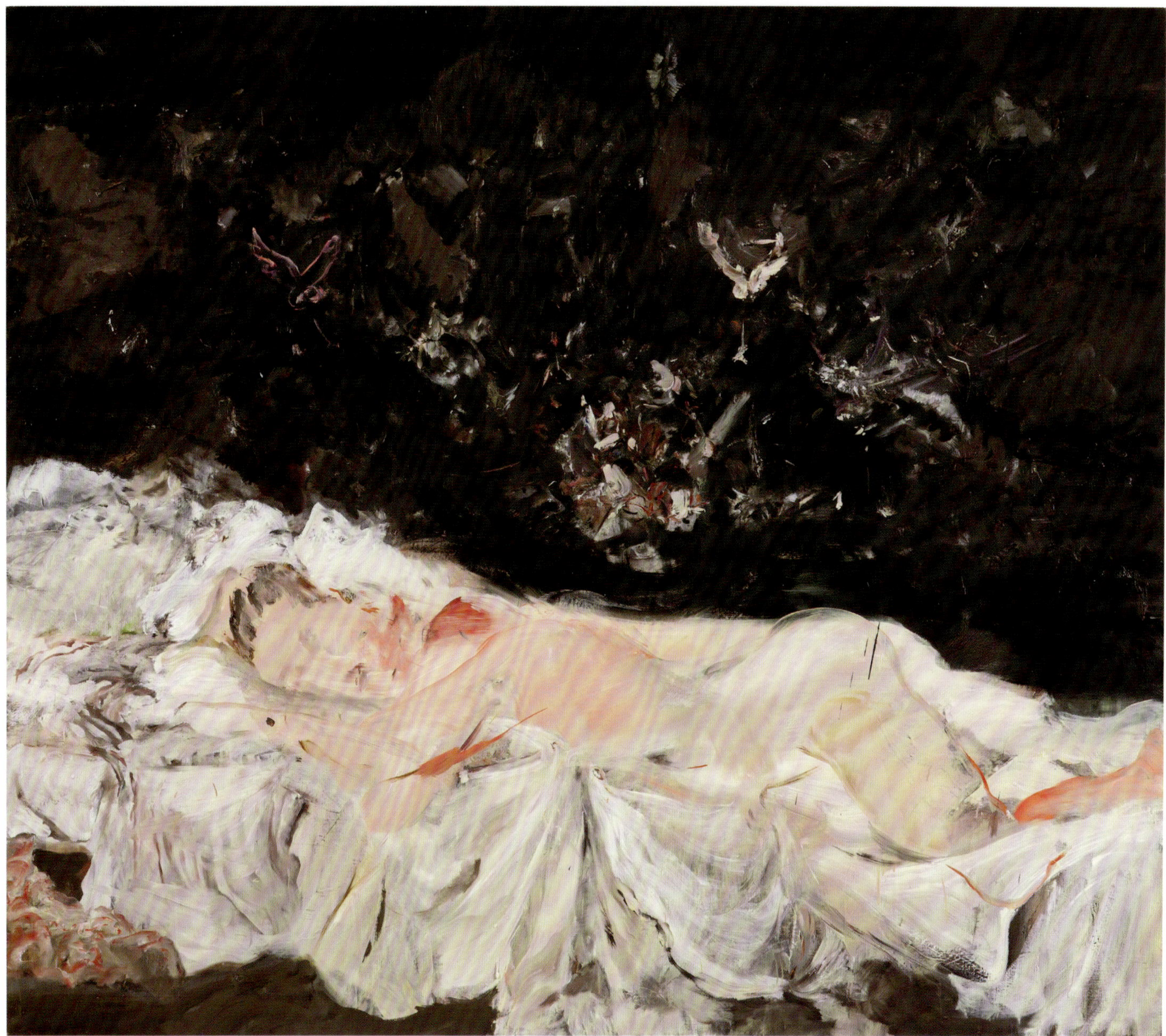

populated parts. The figures range from miniscule to giant. The image is intensely described in places, dissolving into near abstraction in others. The colours all relate to the body and flesh. I'd recently seen Twombly's scatological paintings of the '60s and was heavily influenced by that palette, as well as by the different ways of applying paint. Paint was smeared, clotted, scraped, painstakingly built up, and all but removed in an attempt to invoke a highly artificial space where anything could take place. I wanted to make paintings about desire in all its forms—paintings that could be funny and dark and dramatic and absurd; paintings that could stand up to a lot of looking.

At the time of the first *Black Painting*, I was making very colorful, crowded, chaotic paintings in which figures were suggested but never fully realized. I wanted to make something completely contradictory. I drastically reduced the palette until it was almost monochrome and attempted to paint one complete body. There's an obvious debt to Goya's *The Sleep of Reason…* and the winged genitalia are taken from more 19th-century erotica. Once I'd made the first of these paintings, I was completely seduced by the form and went on to make about six of them, all variations on this theme. While being aware that the supine female was something of a cliché, I felt that my supine females were not passive, even while sleeping, but that they had a certain anxiety and uncomfortable energy about them that made these paintings nervy and full of menace.

—Cecily Brown

Black Painting 4, 2003, oil on linen, 78 x 90 in. (198 x 228.5 cm), acquired in 2004

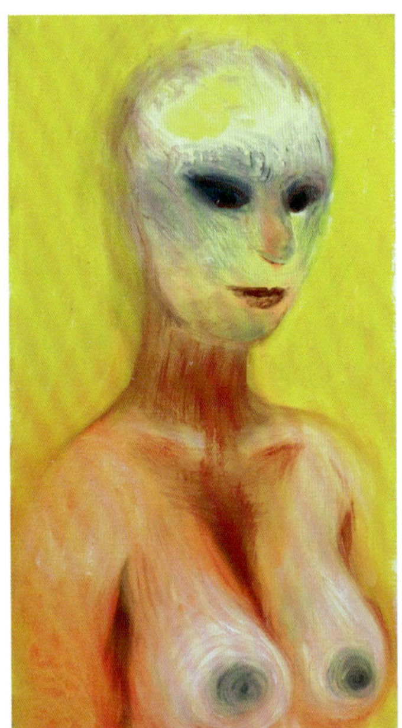
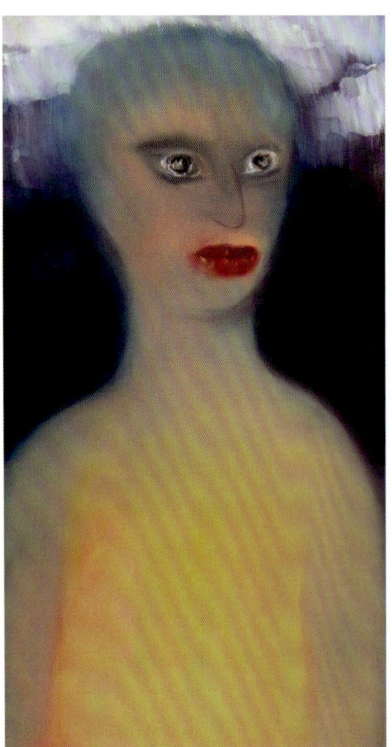
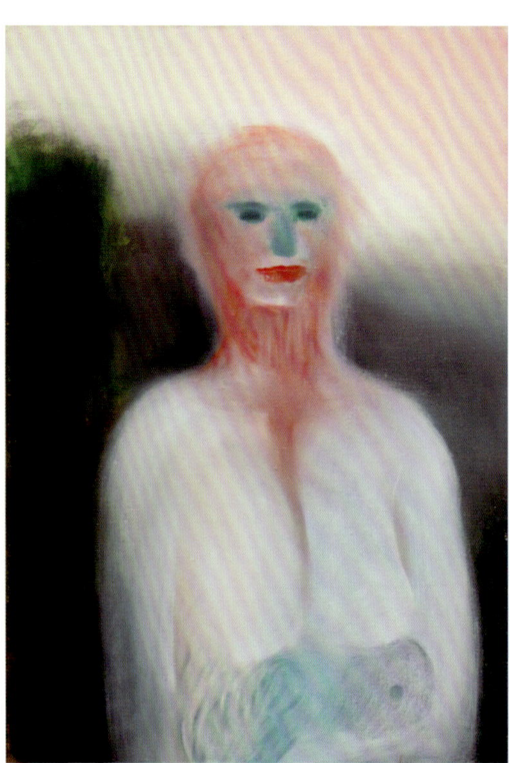

I've always drawn, even as a small child. My style wasn't necessarily childish but actually quite skilful. Drawing was just a normal thing that I did. And my mother too. She always told fairy tales and drew at the same time. Then I'd have my own personal comic.

I grew up in a house that was familiar with artists—Kokoschka, etc. It was normal. I wasn't the kind of artist who had to fight for her choices. I didn't want to go to an academy or anything. I wanted to learn all the techniques, so it was good to do an apprenticeship as a graphic artist; afterwards I made my so-called five-year plan. I thought I definitely won't become one of these artists who moans her whole life long that she isn't getting anywhere—that's completely out of the question.' In five years, I wanted to establish whether or not I would work as an artist. As far as daily life went, too, I wondered whether I could do it all by myself and be disciplined with my time. If it hadn't worked, I'd have become a designer. That would have been nice, too.

There's always a back and forth: If it's too illustrative, it's too much like shock art. Too little, and then it's art for art's sake. But if I had to choose between art for art's sake and shock art, I'd prefer art for art's sake. This constant back and forth is still something I find very exciting.

Being a woman is my public part. I think this is still less of a feminist expression and more an artistic one. That was the way it had to be: You are the being that makes things. And of course, something of yourself flows into it. I don't mean that in the biographical sense but rather, as a tool. You are the kind of tool that you are and that's why it looks like it does. I realized I had to decide. I can't be an artist, as well as have a family, and at the same time teach my husband to take part in it. I don't want any of that. It doesn't interest me enough. You have to make compromises in that case. I don't want to be Paula Modersohn-Becker. I don't want to make those kinds of compromises. I wanted to be like Camus, not even Beauvoir. Making a distinction between men and women didn't interest me. And I still find it uninteresting to differentiate between men and women. I act, to a certain degree, like a man. It doesn't matter, I'm still a woman. We had a sense of equality in Basel in the 1980s. At the beginning at the Stampa gallery, it didn't matter. Everyone did his or her work, whether man or woman. But this has to be seen in the context of the political situation in Basel after '68. It was a time of openness. At the same time, there was feminism and there was the new Left in Switzerland. But Swiss politics always took on a different, milder form.

At the beginning, the cultural situation in Basel was also interesting. Revolutionary events taking place in the world also had an impact on art. I was lucky to be a young artist at the time.

—Miriam Cahn

Left to right: *schauen/wildnis*, 2000, oil on canvas, 16 7/8 x 9 1/2 in. (43 x 24 cm), acquired in 2015
untitled, 2001, oil on canvas, 33 5/8 x 18 1/4 in. (85.5 x 46.5 cm), acquired in 2015
traum vom ende der fruchtbarkeit, 1999, oil on canvas, 32 5/8 x 22 in. (83 x 56 cm), acquired in 2015
Versehrt, 1998, oil on canvas, 67 x 34 1/2 in. (170 x 88 cm), acquired in 2013

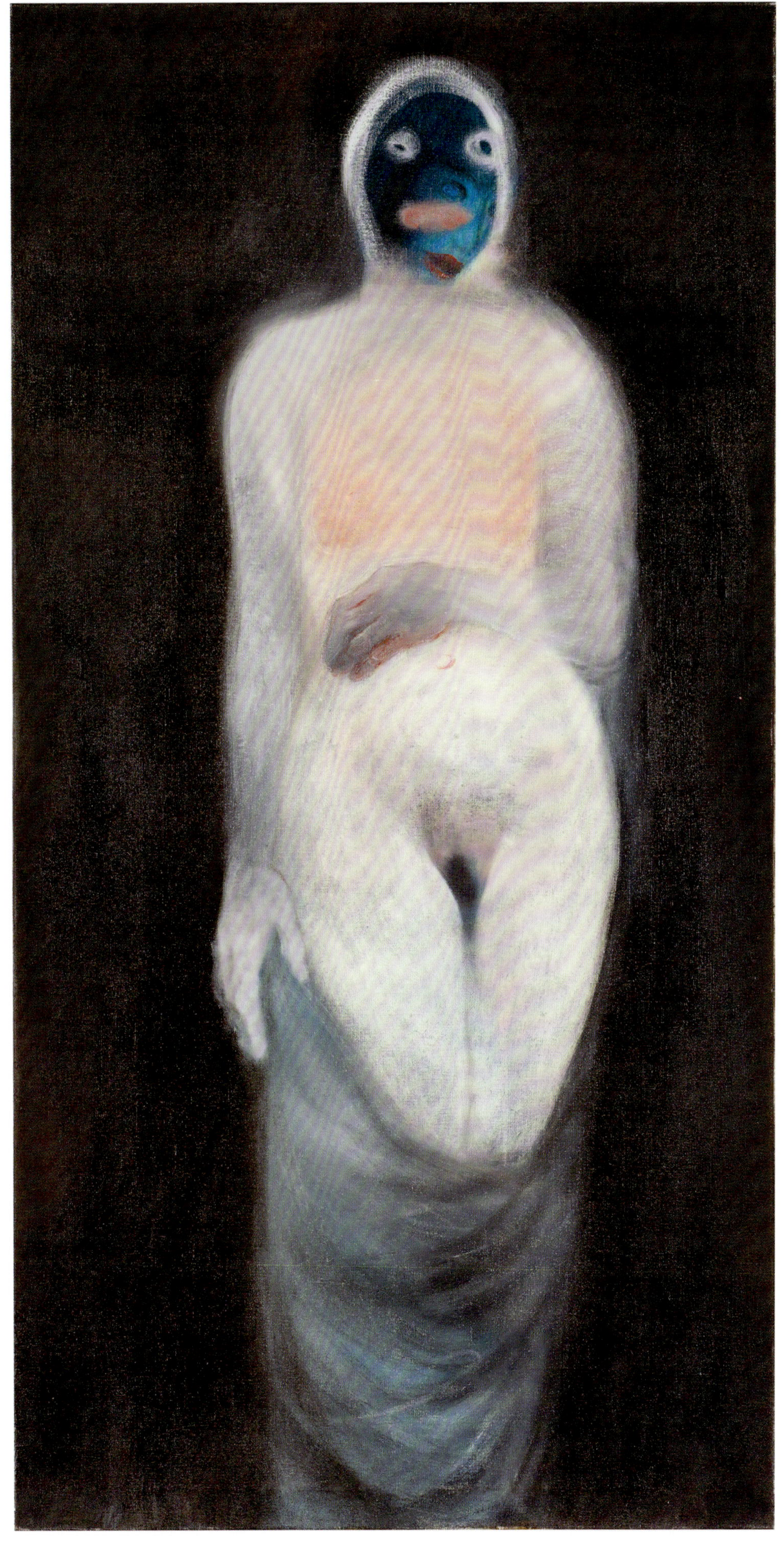

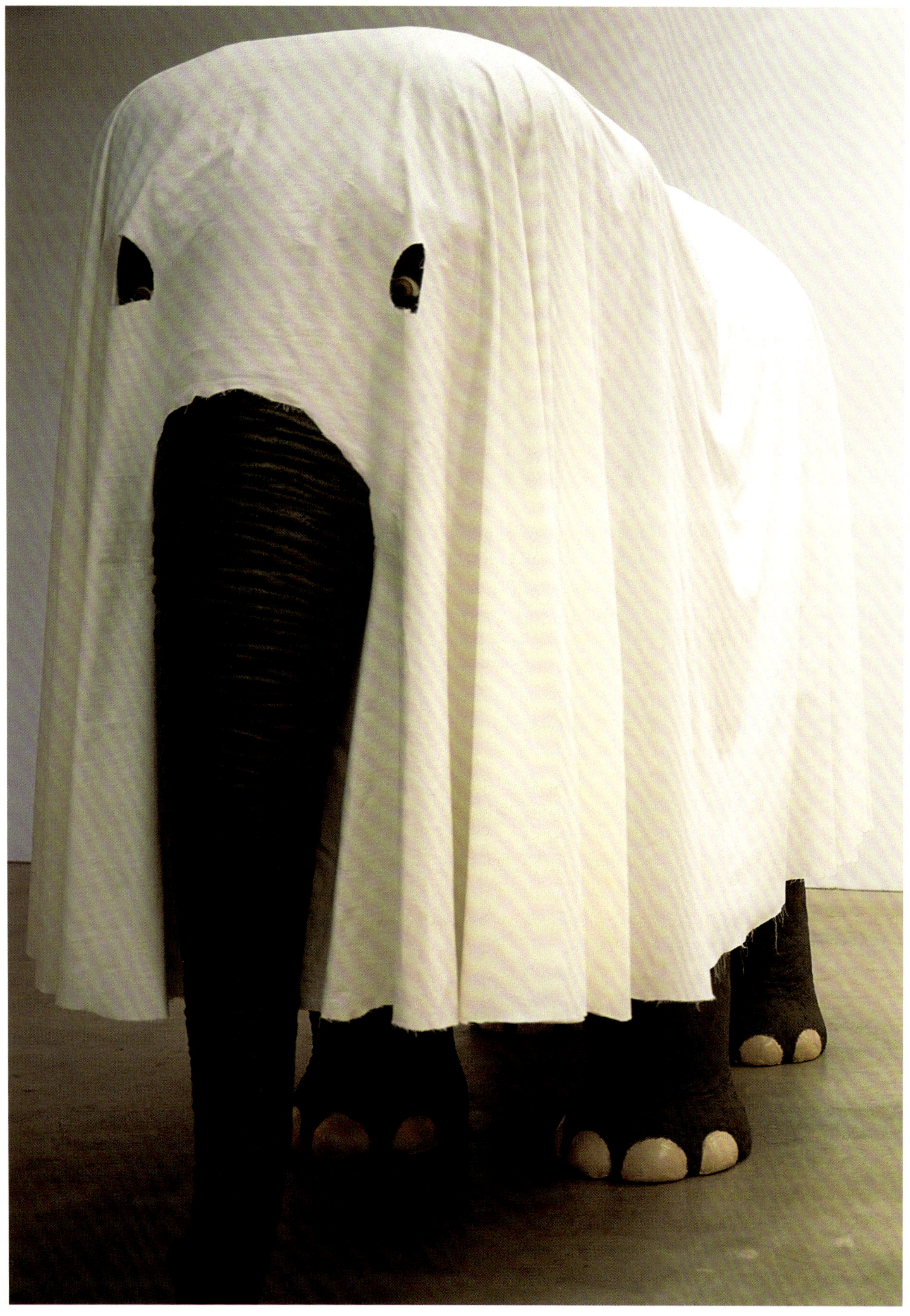

Not Afraid of Love, 2000, polyester styrene, resin, paint, and fabric, ed. 1/2, 81 x 123 x 54 in. (205.7 x 312.4 x 137.2 cm), acquired in 2000

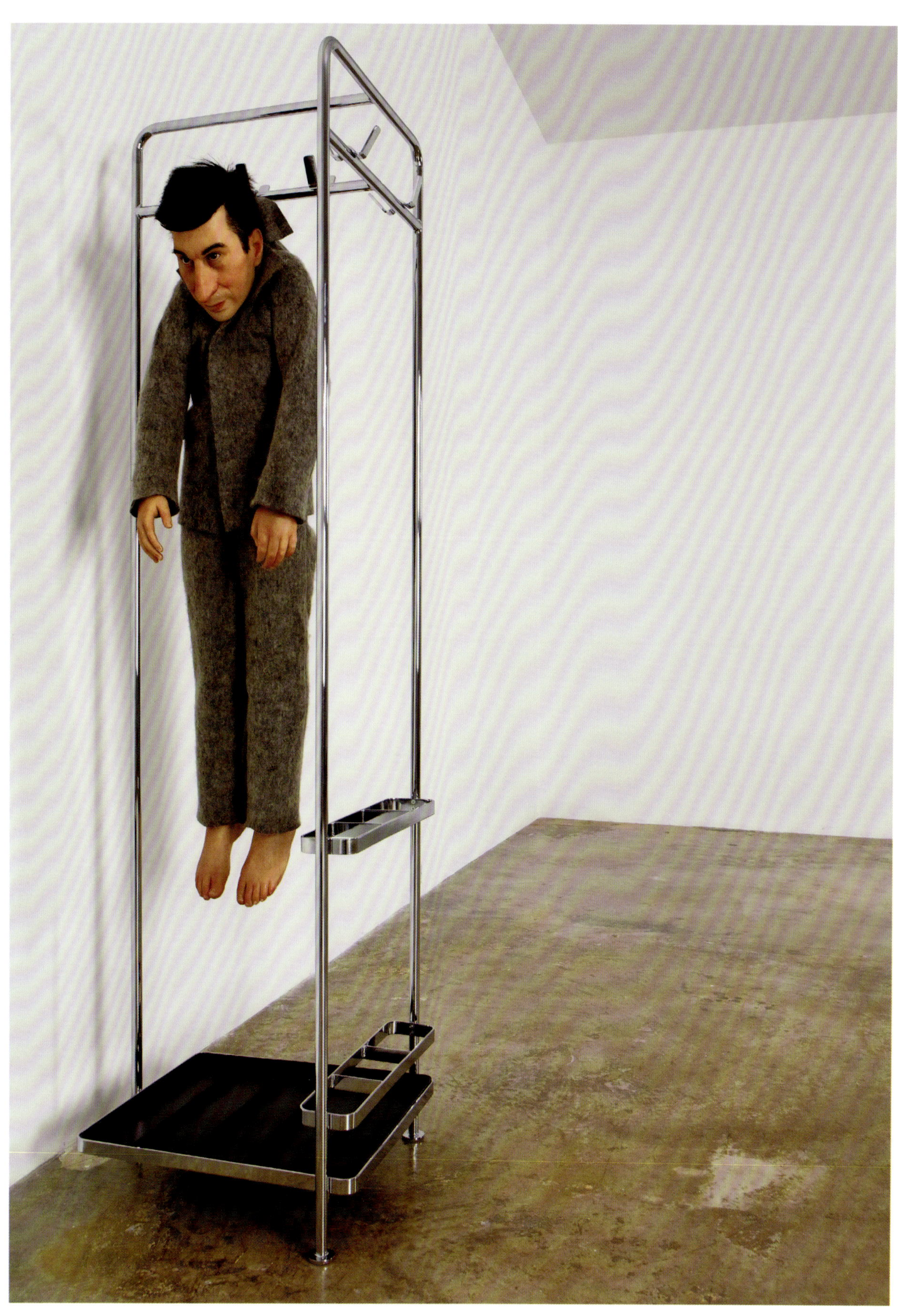

La Rivoluzione Siamo Noi, 2000, polyester resin figure, felt suit, metal, and plastic coatrack, ed. 2/3 plus AP, overall 74 5/8 x 20 1/2 x 20 3/4 in. (189.5 x 52 x 52.7 cm), acquired in 2000

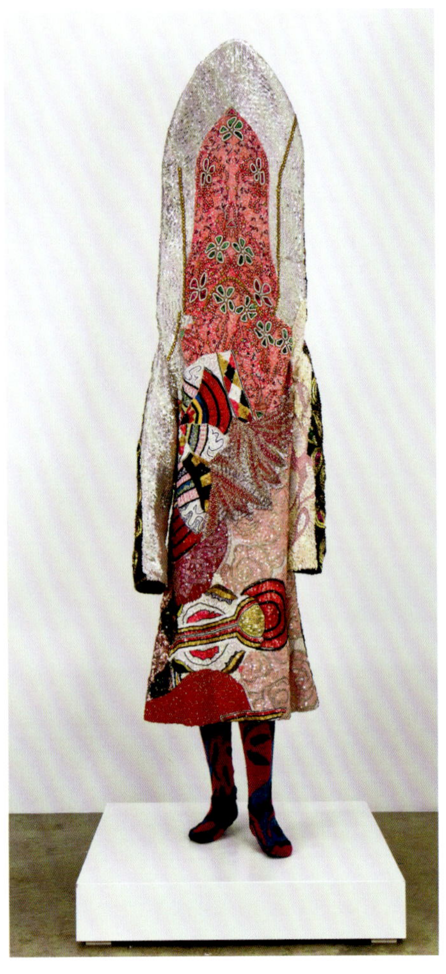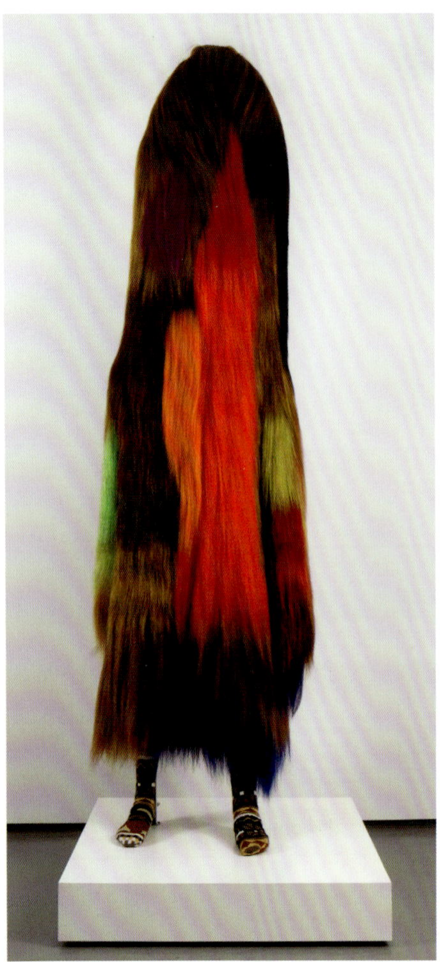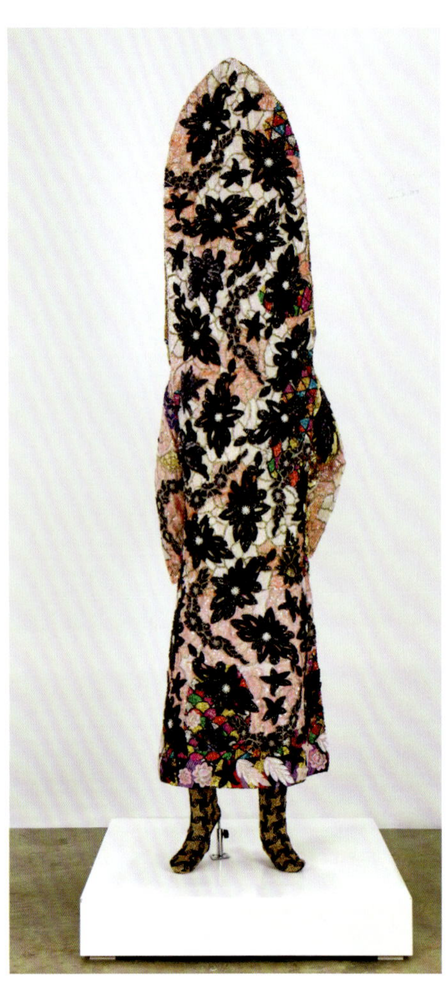

The works in the Rubell Collection are from my series of *Soundsuits*. This sculptural form is based on the scale of my body. It creates a camouflage, masking and forming a second skin that conceals race, gender, and class, forcing one to look without judgment. Three of the works in the Collection are in the shape of what I call an "A-frame." This form has many connotations that reference power, such as a bishop's mitre, a Ku Klux Klan uniform, a condom, or the head of a missile. As for the surfaces themselves, I treat them like collages, applying patterns that build on the surface. The piece that is made out of synthetic hair strips this down, using one material instead of many to create a visceral sensibility. The fourth piece, with the armature made of flowers, takes the baroque ornamental sensibility of the A-frame surfaces and brings it into an expanded dimensionality.

—Nick Cave

Left to right: *Soundsuit*, 2008, fabric, sequins, fiberglass, and metal, 100 x 25 x 14 in. (254 x 63.5 x 35.6 cm), acquired in 2008
Soundsuit, 2008, synthetic hair, fiberglass, and metal, 98 x 27 x 14 in. (248.9 x 68.6 x 35.6 cm), acquired in 2008
Soundsuit, 2006, fabric, sequins, fiberglass, and metal, 100 x 26 x 13 in. (254 x 66 x 33 cm), acquired in 2006
Soundsuit, 2008, fabric, fiberglass, and metal, 102 x 36 x 28 in. (259 x 91.5 x 71 cm), acquired in 2008

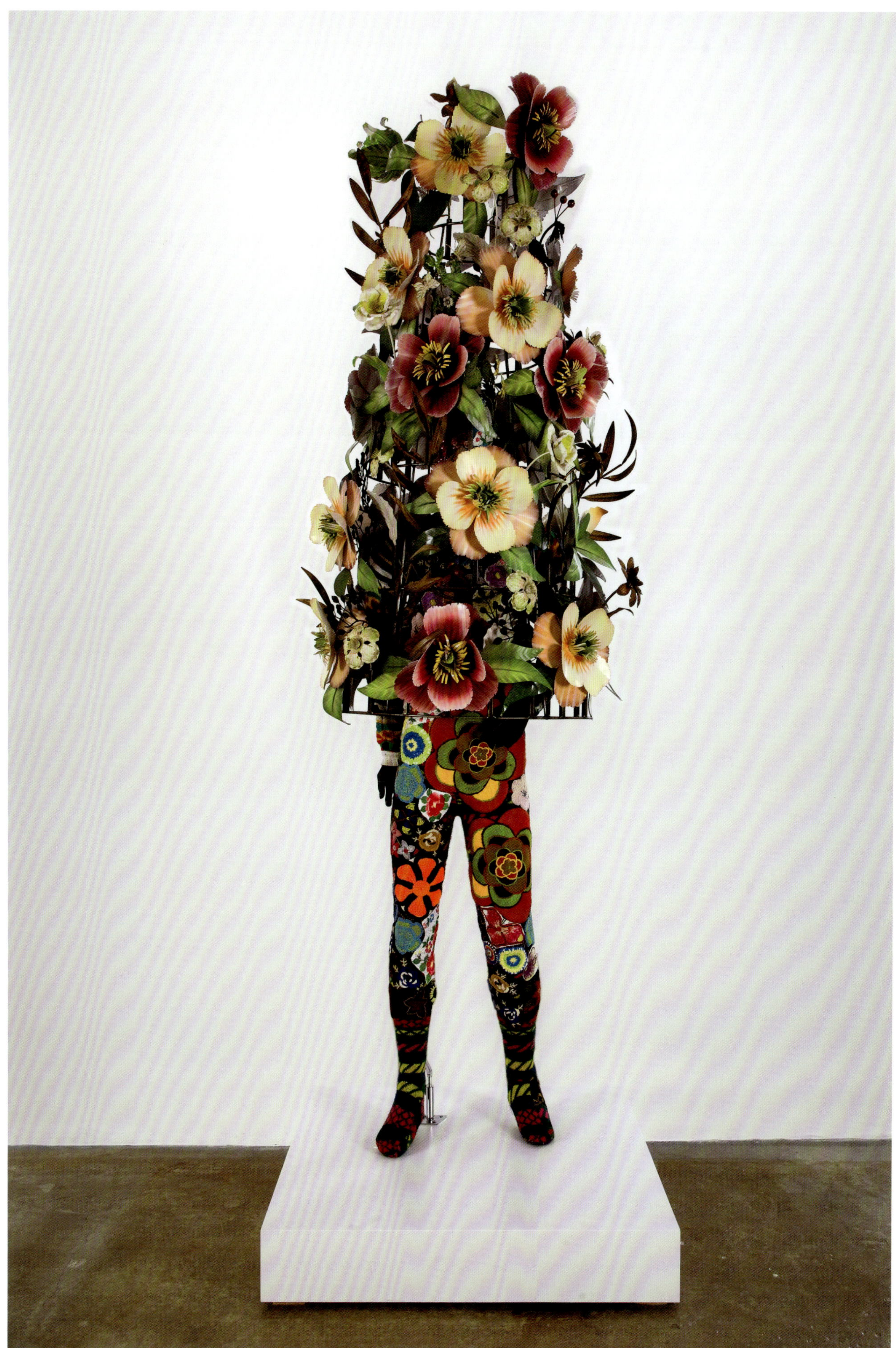

JONATHAN LYNDON CHASE

b. 1989, Philadelphia, PA / lives and works in Philadelphia, PA

2018 Artist in Residence

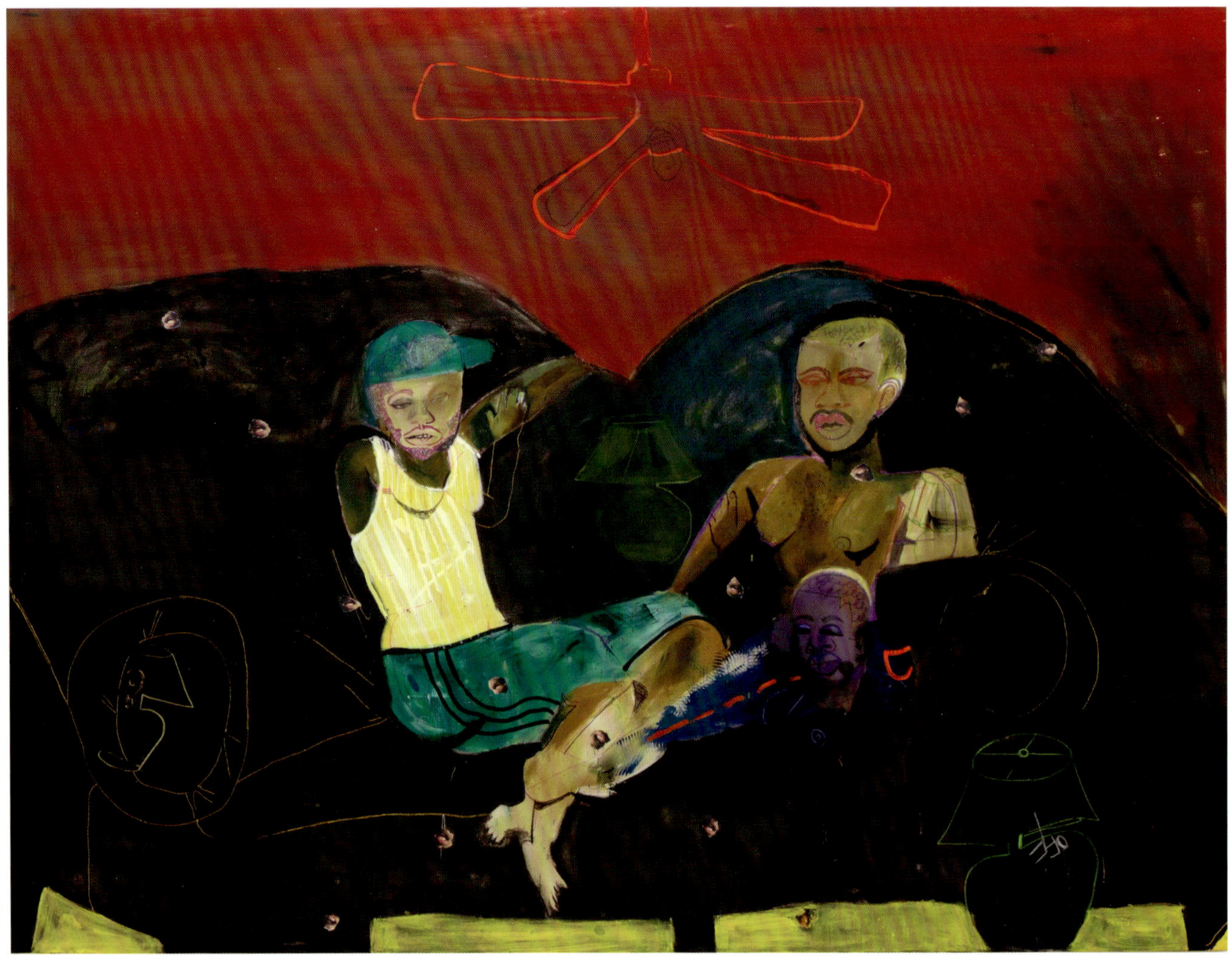

Running his thumbs under my feet
Lay on black on top of black
His feet under black
Our feet over the edge
Tender tumbling

Baby boy I know your sleepy
Rest with me
You don't need to be strong
Laying with me you're never heavy enough
to weigh me down

Heavy head
Dull with rage
Strong enough to break a couch spring

Why are you crying?
I'm not sure I'm sorry
I'm

—Jonathan Lyndon Chase

3 heads and 4 Lamps, 2018, acrylic, marker, crayon, graphite, glitter, and printer paper on canvas, 118 x 158 in. (300 x 400 cm), acquired in 2018

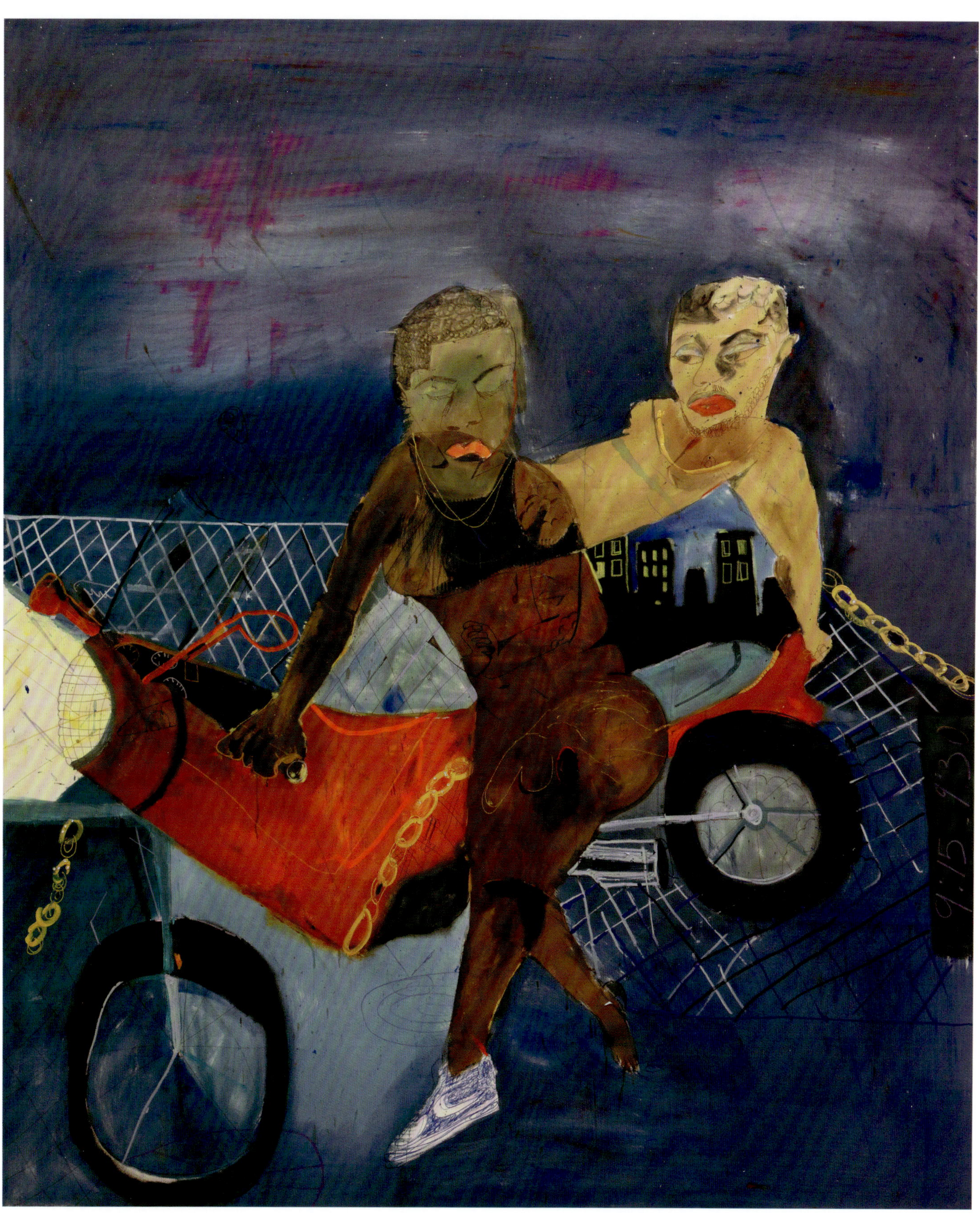

Riiiide or die boy, 2018, acrylic, marker, graphite, glitter, and plastic rhinestones on canvas, 130 x 110 in. (330 x 279 cm), acquired in 2018

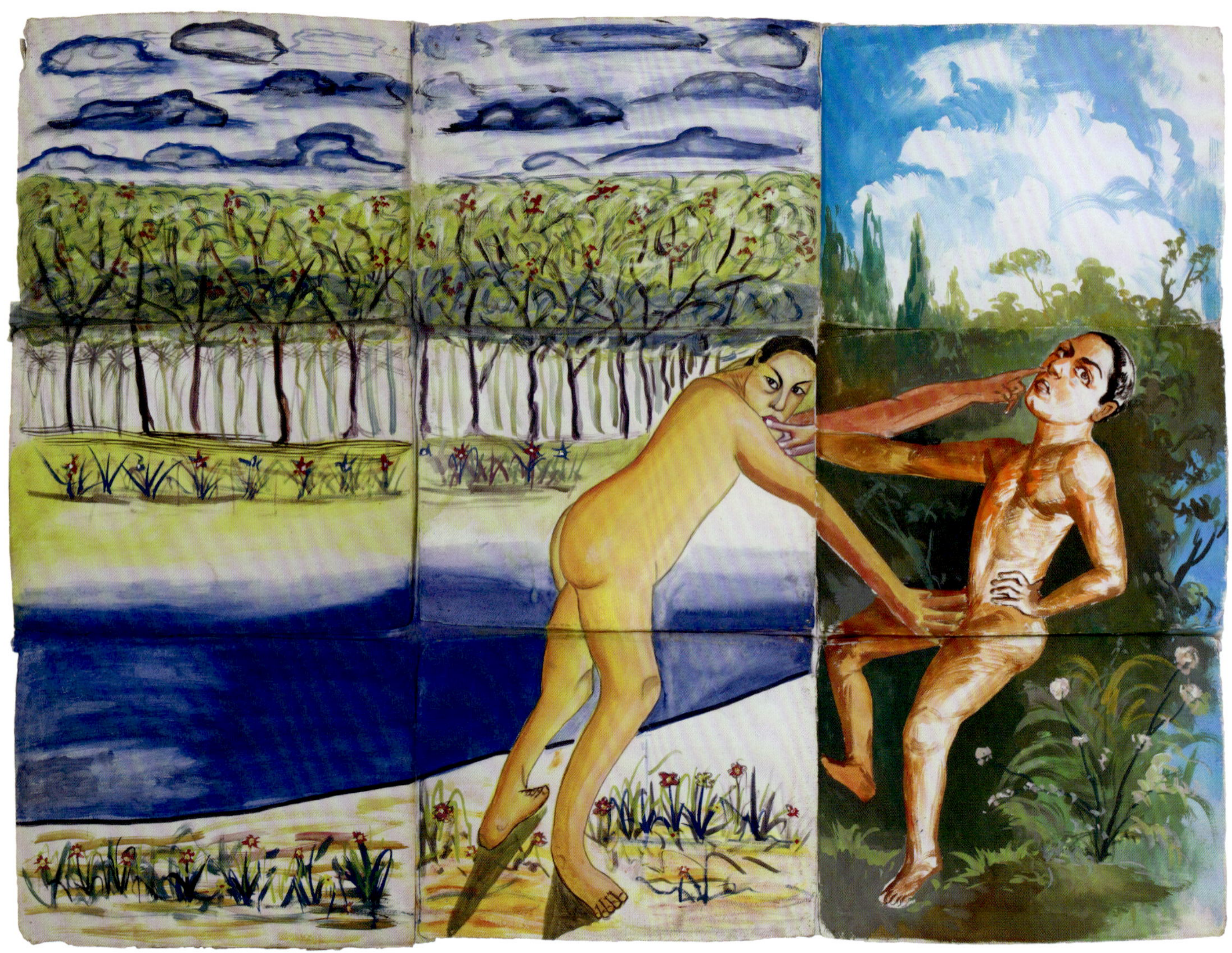

In the '70s the Rubells visited my studio in Rome. In the '80s they returned to my studio, which was by then in New York. Don said, "When we met, you had no furniture and you slept on the floor. Now you have no furniture and you sleep on the floor, but I notice that you have a TV!" The TV didn't last, but I did sleep on the floor a few more years. Two of the three large works in the Rubell Collection were made in the studios of the sign painters of India who, at that time, painted huge murals advertising Bollywood films. Through the collaborative nature of these works, I wanted to challenge the boundaries of the self and do away with any signature style or signature process. My life and work had to be nomadic and always in a state of flux, to witness and to mimic the fragmentation of the self. The paintings were on sheets of handmade paper, bound together, so that I could carry them by hand on the plane, cheaply and safely, in a pre-global planet. I was chasing an alternative narrative of modernity. I didn't—I don't—believe in progress, in formal solutions. I thought that art was the medium of the present tense, and the present was where one could embrace the experience of the great spiritual traditions without being bound to any.

—Francesco Clemente

Two Painters, 1980, gouache on handmade Pondicherry paper, joined with handwoven cotton strip, 68 x 103 in. (172.7 x 261.6 cm), acquired in 1980
Opposite page, top to bottom: *Self-Portrait (Inside/Outside)*, 1979, charcoal, dirt, and pastel on handmade Pondicherry paper joined with cotton, 64 x 164 in. (160 x 416.6 cm), acquired in 1979; *Untitled (double portrait)*, 1979, gouache on handmade Pondicherry paper, joined with handwoven cotton strip, diptych, overall 63 x 108 in. (160 x 274.3 cm), acquired in 1980

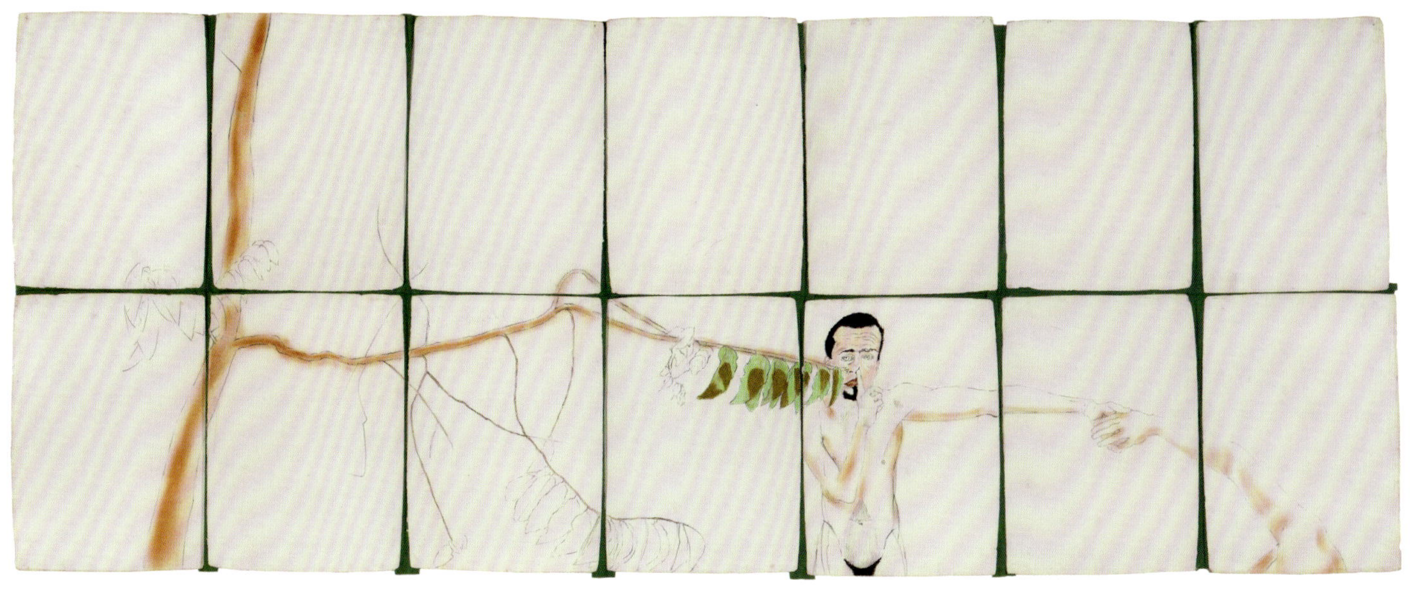

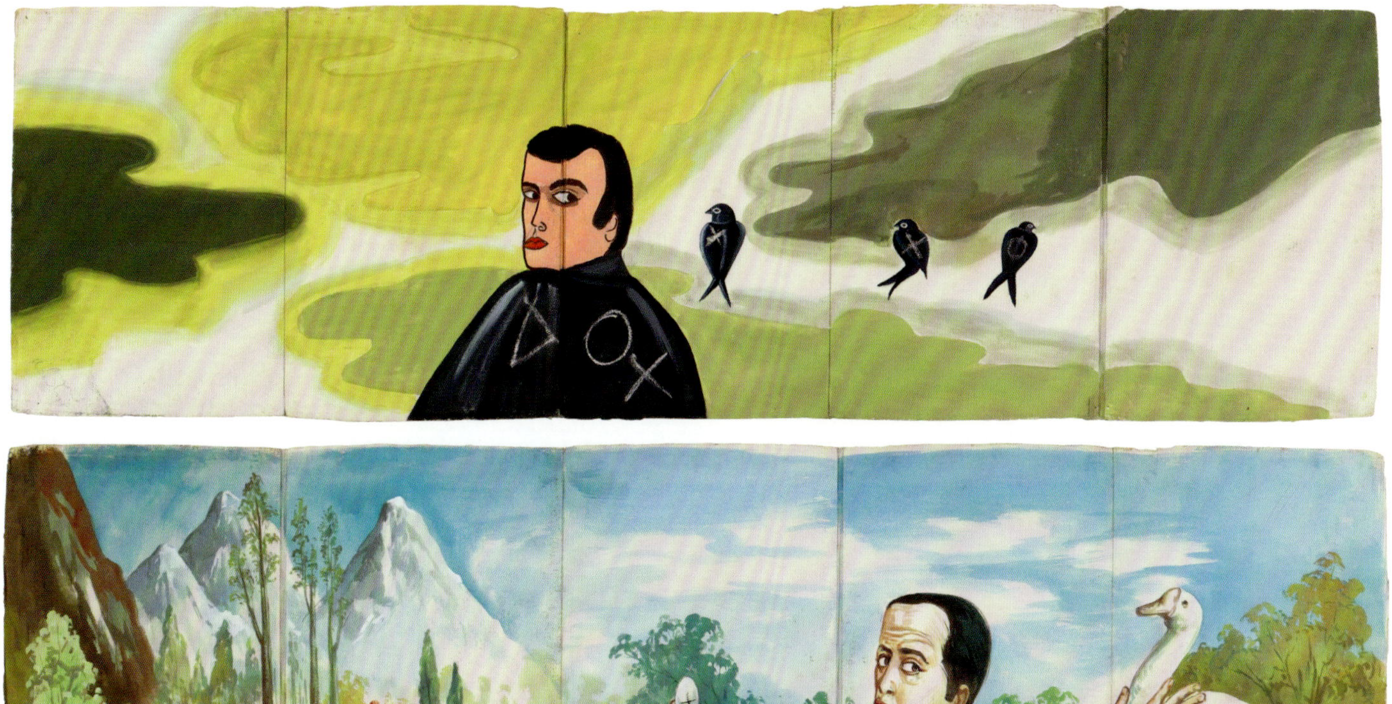

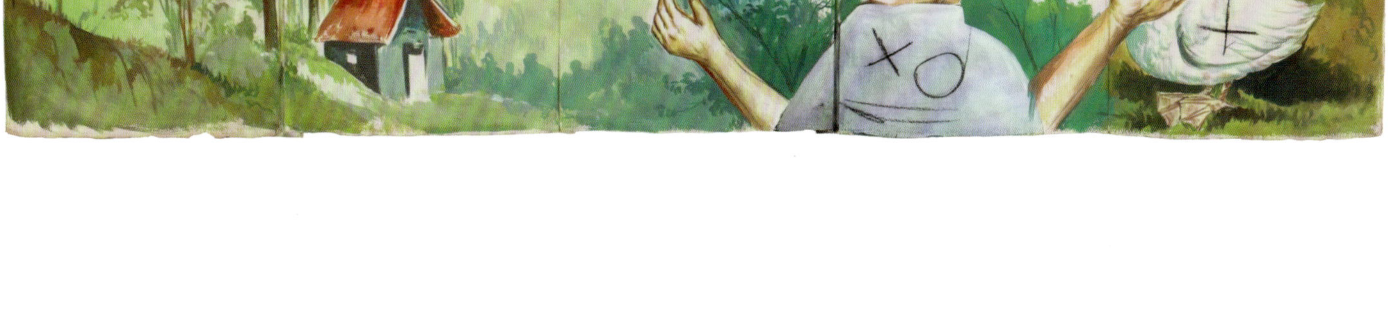

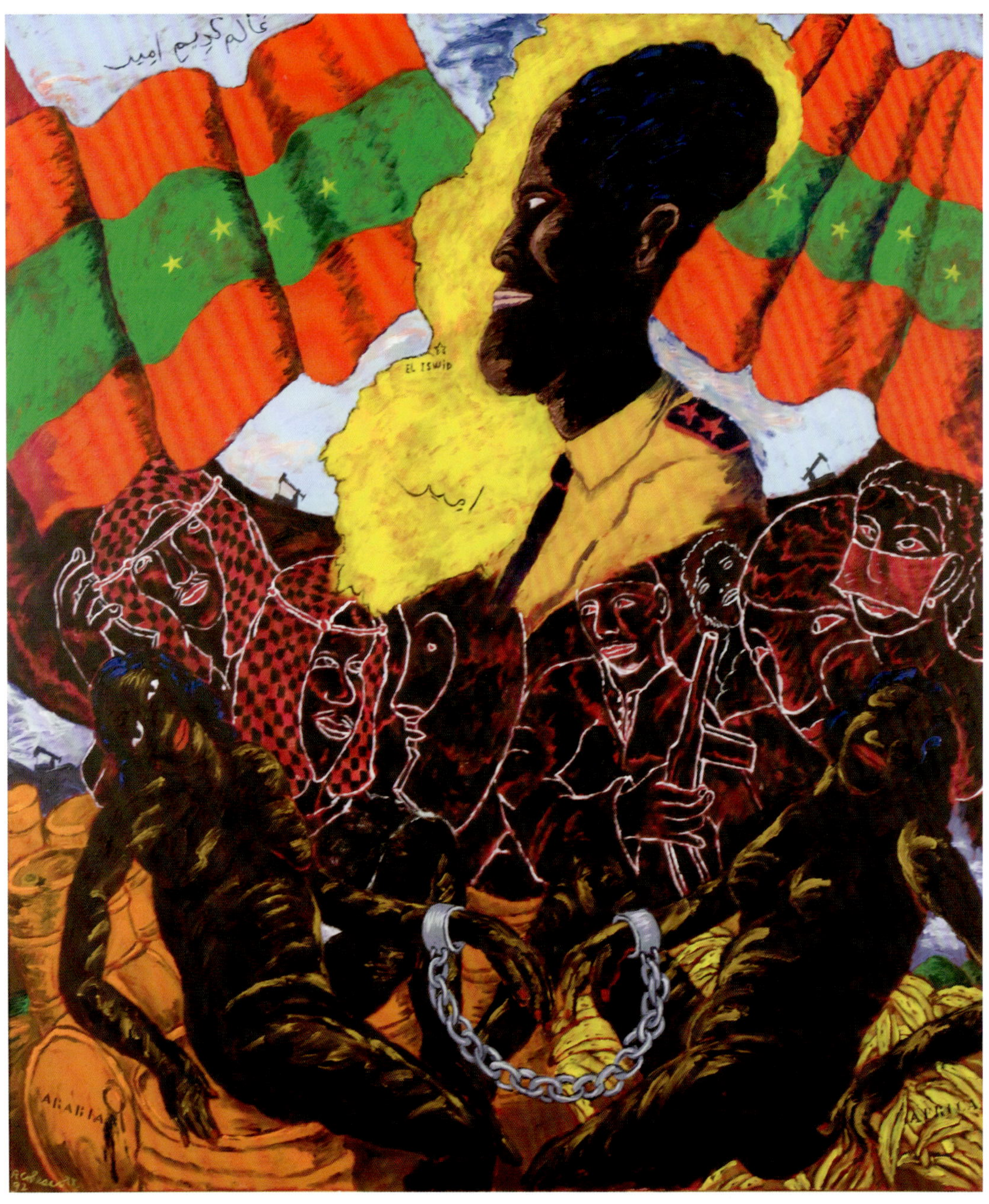

If there's one thing that Black folks have it's a sense of humor. The lyrics in blues songs are often pretty rowdy, you know, and present a rather base expression of Black arts. It's really funny. If you want to get acceptance within the community, just paint a couple of old men on mules, you know, or an old man on a mule and an old lady walking around. Some people will only be satisfied with that. And then some kind of heroic image, which is very far from the truth. The heroic image where this guy looks like a . . . looks white with a suntan, see . Any sense of exaggeration could be questioned. What I want to say about all this is, sure, I've seen all that. And I've heard it all. But at the same time, right from the very beginning when I first started showing some of these works (a response to stereotyping) I had plenty of encouragement. And I was surprised at the vigor of the responses. And it just didn't break down on racial lines. There were white people who were offended because they felt guilty because their people had created these images. And so there were white people that felt threatened by these paintings, which monumentalized these perceptions. We've already come to understand that it's about white perceptions of Black people. And they may not be pretty. And they may be stupid. We didn't make up these images, so why should we take the heat? But it's satire. It's the satire that kills the serpent, you know.

—Robert Colescott

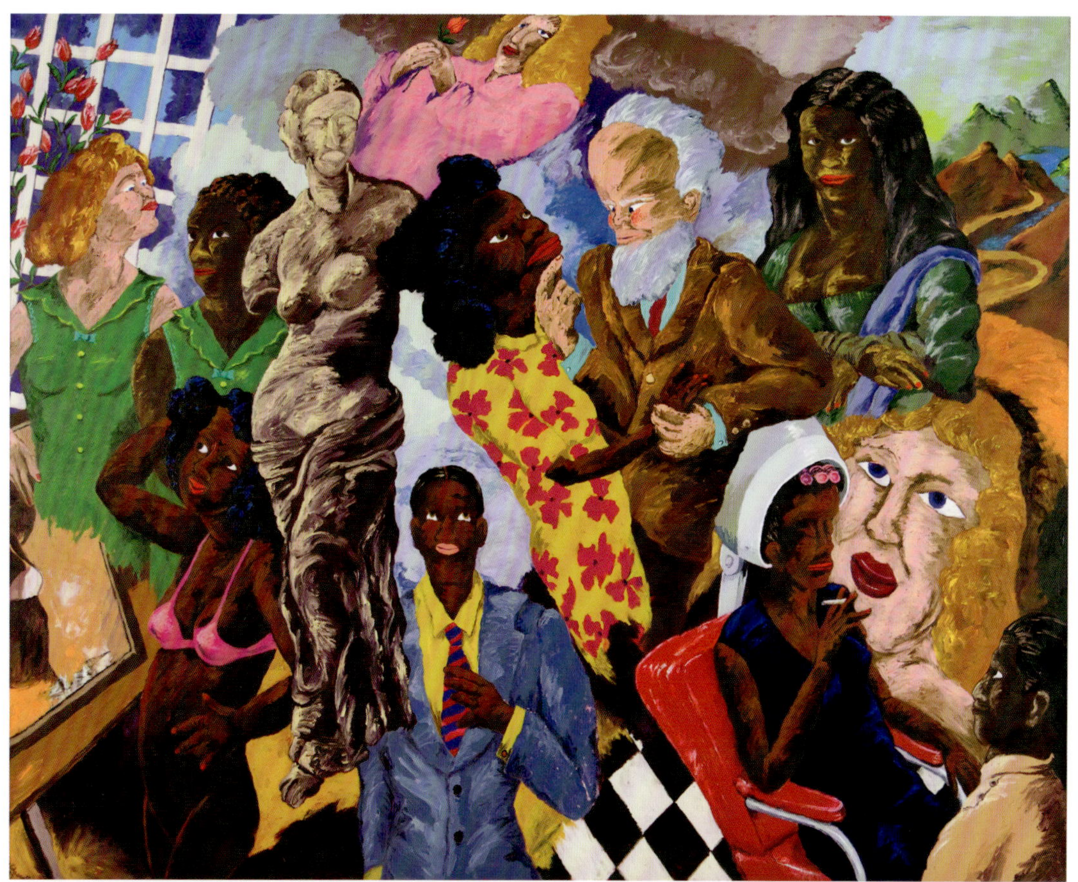

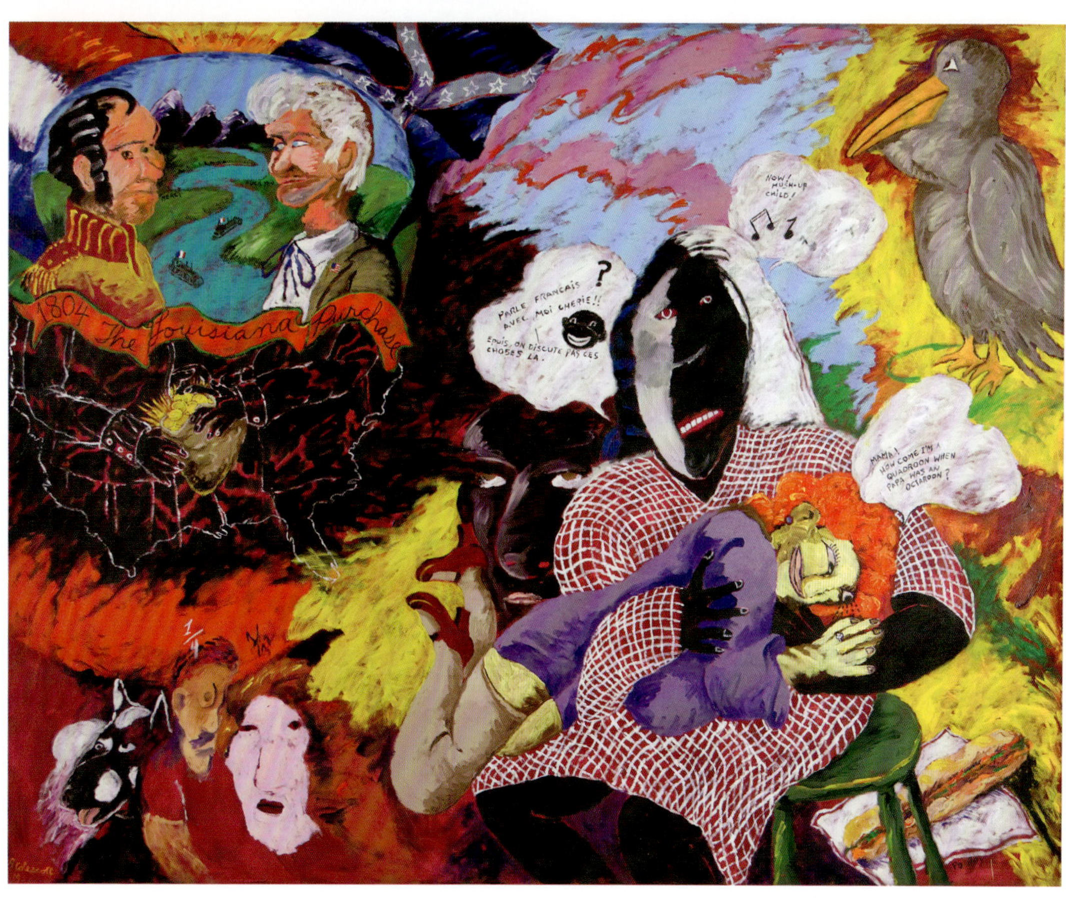

Opposite page: *Arabs: The Emir of Iswid (How Wide the Gulf?)*, 1992, acrylic on canvas, 84 x 72 in. (213.4 x 182.9 cm), acquired in 2006
Pygmalion, 1987, acrylic on canvas, 90 x 114 in. (228.6 x 289.6 cm), acquired in 2006
Sunset on the Bayou, 1993, acrylic on canvas, 90 x 114 in. (228.6 x 289.5 cm), acquired in 2006

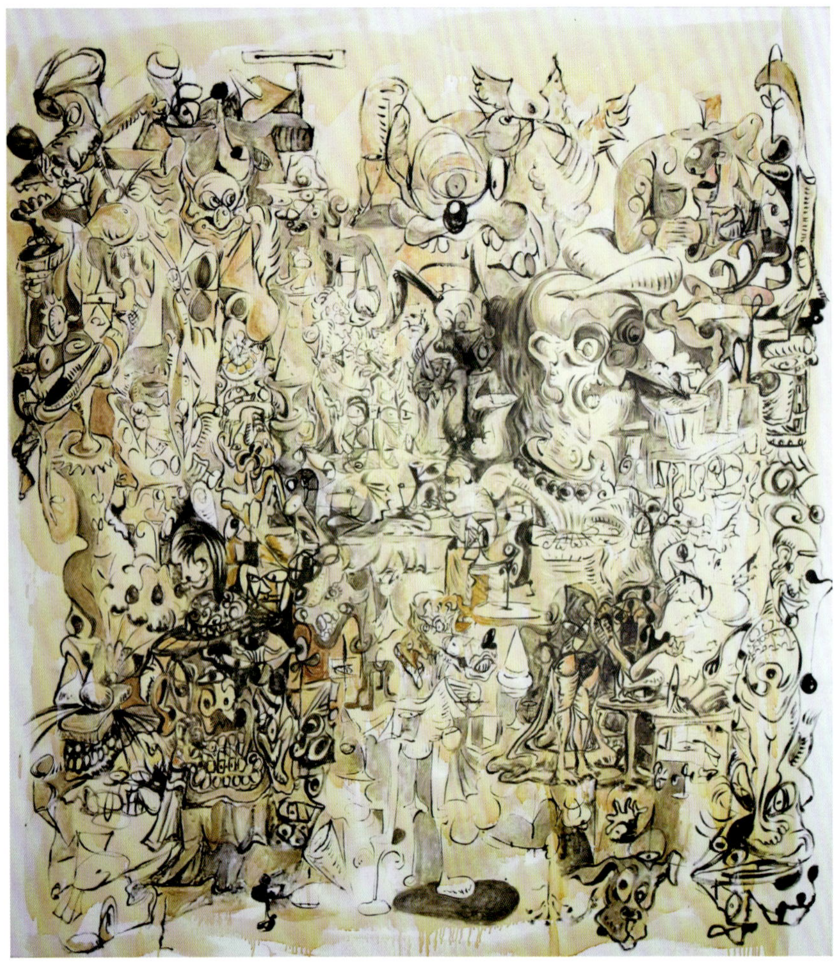

At that particular time in life [1984], as Dr. Don Rubell would know firsthand, I was not taking very good care of myself. Living in the East Village on 10th Street between 1st and Avenue A, right next to the old Turkish bathhouse; I never even made it in once. In fact, as Don also knows, I never even plugged in my refrigerator. Long nights out in the cold with buddies Keith Haring, Rammellzee, artists from the Lower East Side, JM Basquiat, and various other well-known self-abusers lent themselves to what I called and memorialized as the *Evening of Destruction*. This painting was a kind of metaphoric composition employing all the pseudo-classical elements that I was exploring after my first time in Paris and a trip to the Louvre. I was thinking of coming back to the city with my version of Delacroix's *The Death of Sardanapalus*. A kind of bedroom in the clouds, an imaginary outdoor celestial brothel with sirens and luring female figures representing torture, self-indulgence, misery, and ecstasy all at once, as it seemed life was like at that time. There was no actual narrative like in the "real" romantic classicism it was based on. That's probably why I called them "fake Old Masters," because there was no text or symbolic meaning in any of

it. There were symbols that meant essentially nothing. In fact, it was this connection I wanted to make, ironically with Malevich, in that it is what it is and nothing more. Or Frank Stella's famous statement, "it is what you see," but in my own way: it is a picture of our collective memories of classicism without the subject, academic perfection, or content. For me it was the largest painting I'd made to date, and I wanted to work it up to a finishing point to open my first one-man, double exhibition at Pat Hearn's new gallery on the Lower East Side and Barbara Gladstone's in SoHo. I wanted to prove something about the rebirth of painting, that it was not dead, and in fact, it was more alive than ever. Yet none of the academic perfection was necessary to attain in order to evoke the "memory" of those rules and regulations in art. Like a punk rock version of Mozart. In my case, I thought about "conceptual representation," a contradictory paradigm that would be a picture of a painting that seems to have existed in the history of art, yet never has.

—George Condo

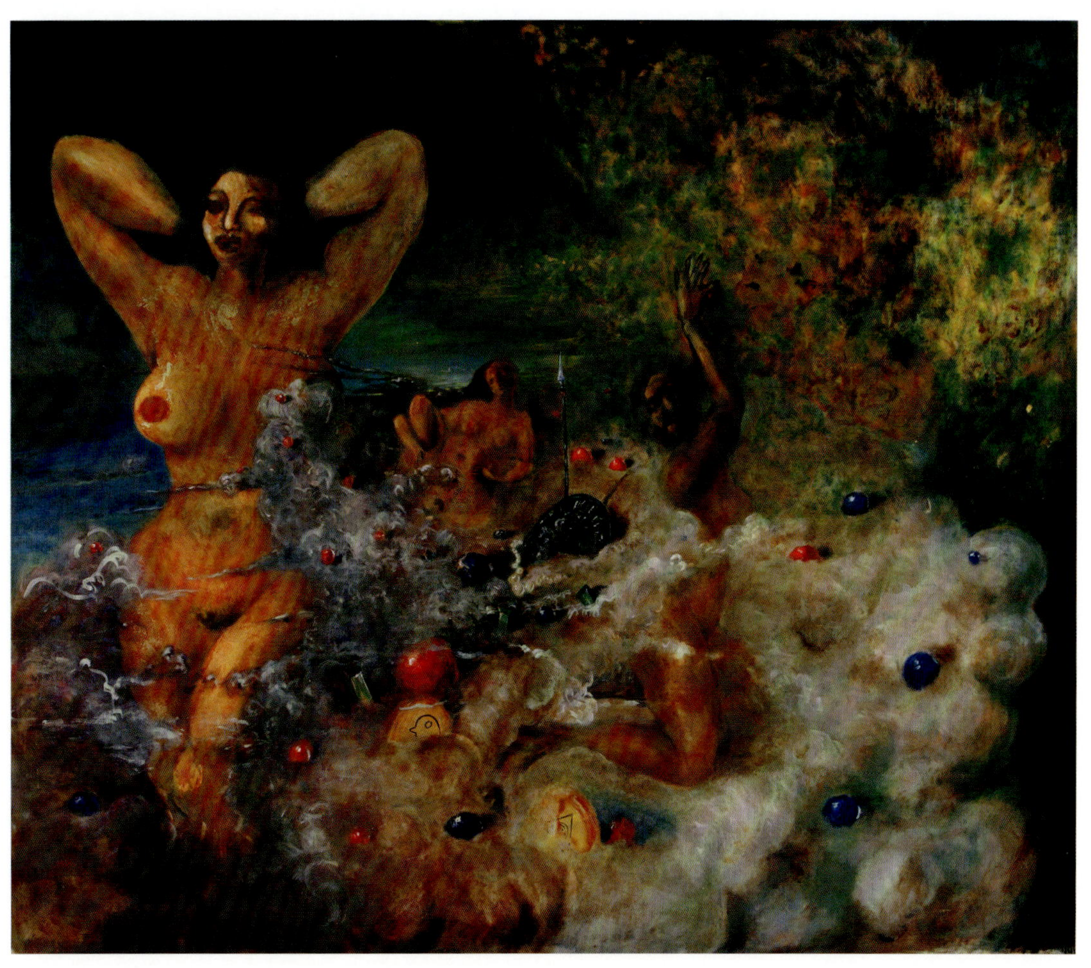

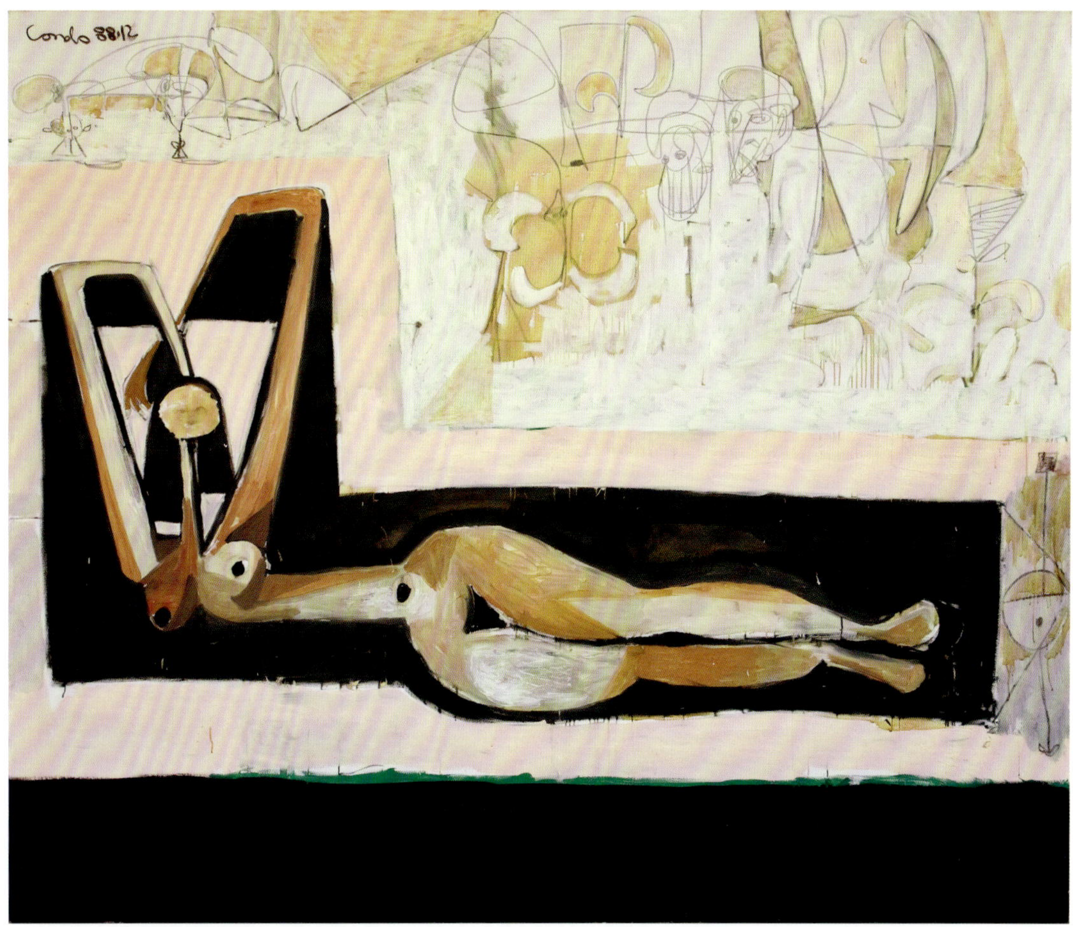
Condo 88'12

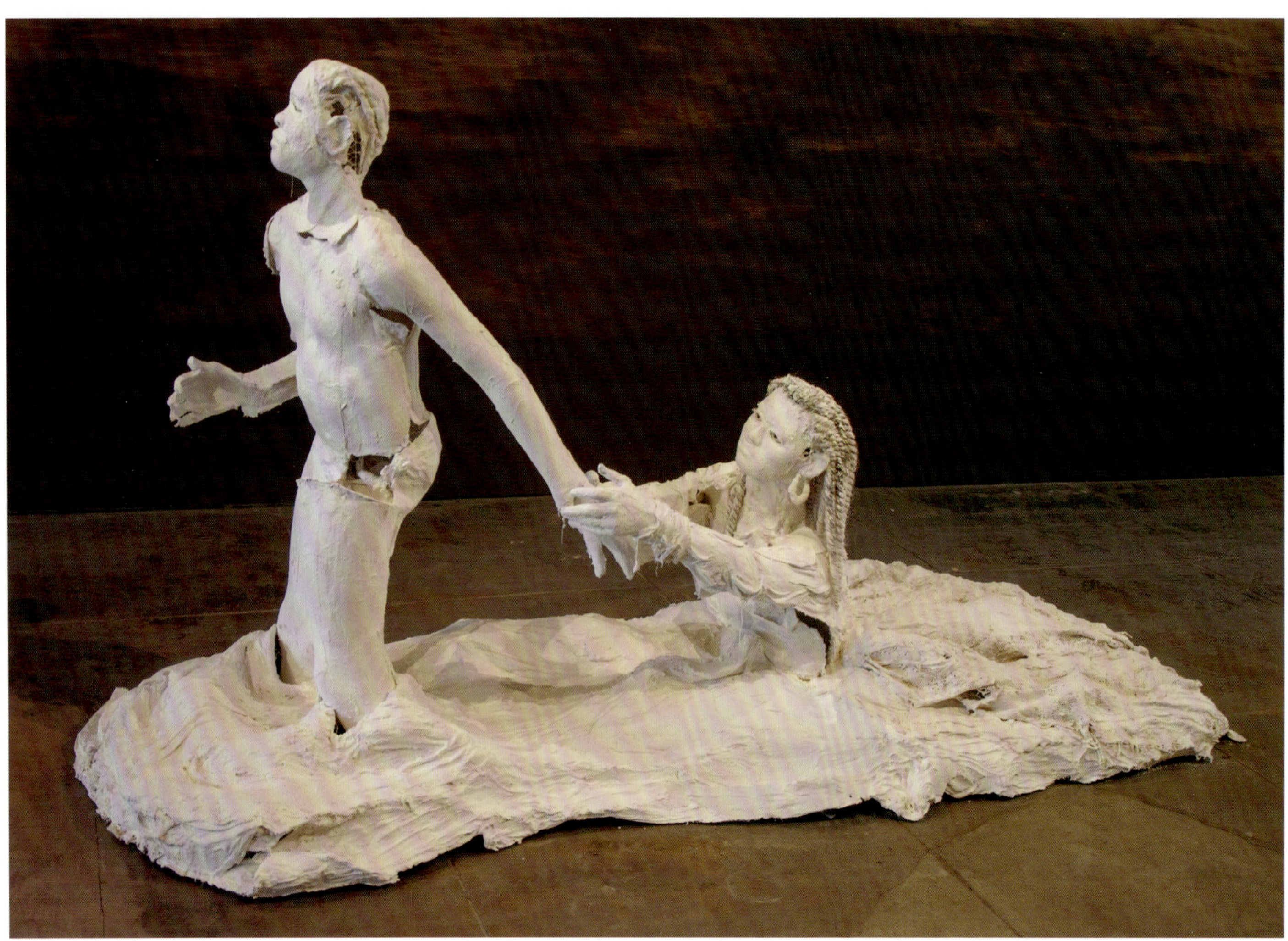

Beth and Solomon was part of a show I did called *Muddy Water* in 2018 that was based on Bessie Smith's famous tune. And as old as that tune is, the floods keep coming, right? So, again, something that keeps plaguing us now—gun violence and climate change and the effects of it. This show is really about the exodus of primarily communities of color that are not protected, that are not funded. I did a deep search into New Orleans and North Carolina and all the flooding, even flooding around the world. It's really always about a community having to leave their homes.

In the full installation of *Muddy Water*, there's a Moses figure leading everyone out through the waters, and there's Noah pulling his mother and daughter in a boat, which was based loosely on Noah's ark, and *Beth and Solomon* are part of that scene. I do dabble back into religious references, but sometimes I'll just name a piece after the people whose castings I used. These figures were cast from my best friend and her son, whose name is Solomon. He's now off to college, so when I look at it now it's also a mother watching her son become a man and walking off. She's still trying to hold on and he's reaching back for her. In my research I looked at a lot of photographs of muddy flood waters, and there is this one photograph where there's a woman

reaching, almost being left behind by this younger man, and he's trying to reach back and help her. There are so many things happening in that sculpture for me.

It's always interesting to hear everyone's perspective on what they see in a work because a lot of times people see things I don't see. A common word people use is *haunting*; that my work is haunting. I don't know how I feel about that. Is that a good thing? I don't know.

Family is related to the larger series *Game* from 2019, of which three sculptures are in the Hammer Museum. *Game* was the exhibition that I was moved to do because now, as a parent, when you drop your kids off at school, or at the mall, or anywhere in public with a lot of people, you always have this moment of *Are they going to be okay?* Seriously, I feel like it's an epidemic with the school shootings and it just was coming up all the time, and that's how I felt when I was making this work. I also felt at the time that a lot of Black men and women were being shot and killed. I was feeling like my son and I were hunted; we're game. The Black family is under attack, kids are under attack, and teachers in their schools.

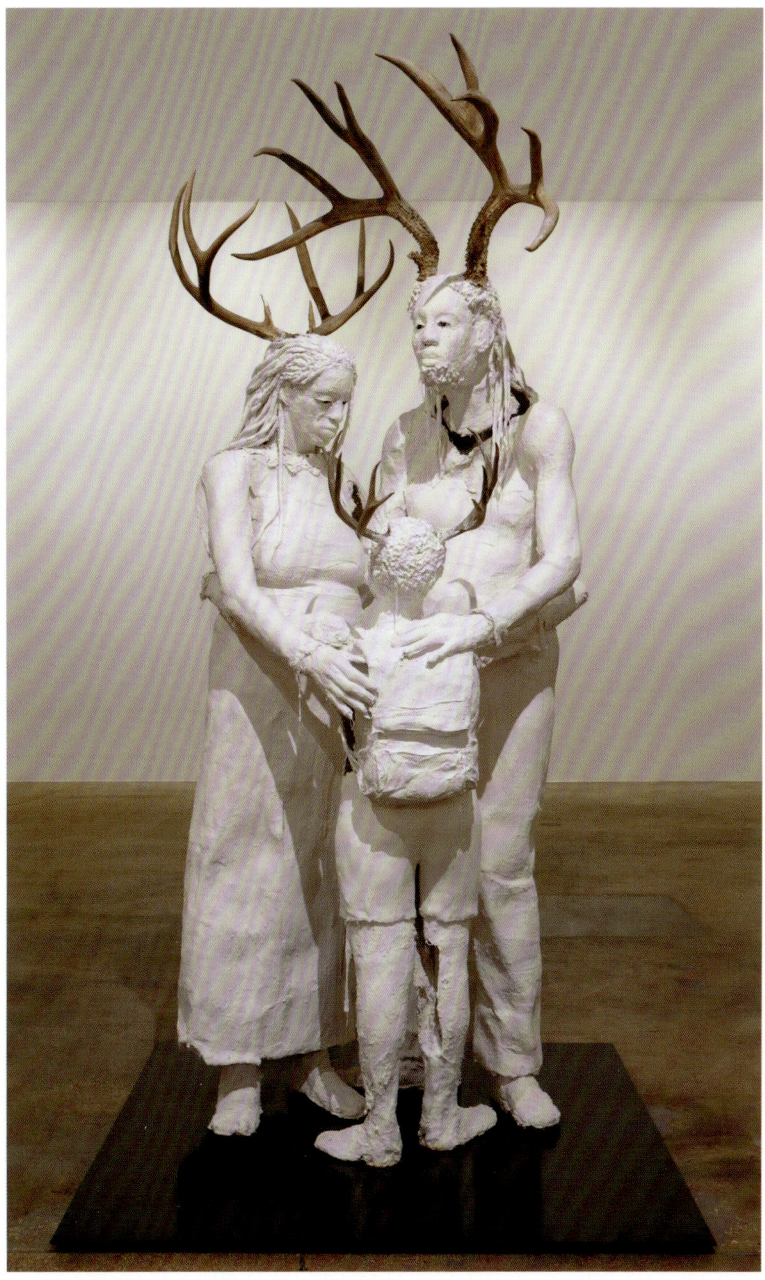

I needed to make this piece and show a visual of how I'm feeling as a parent and as an African American in this country, just always being hunted. Actually, that was the first name of the show: *The Hunted*. And then I changed it to *Game* because there are so many layers to the word *game*—in politics and the games the politicians play constantly with our children.

For casting purposes, I used my family: my husband's cousin, and her husband, and the boy is actually my son. This work was meant to be part of the whole scene of *Game*: the family dropping off the son at school, a kid playing cat's cradle, a girl going up the stairs, and a principal standing there with a gun in his back pocket. My mother had found all these horns and antlers at an estate sale, and I felt they were speaking to me. There's this mystical thing that happens when you put antlers on. They become these magical beings—transcending the pain but also providing protection over this young son. This was the whole scene I had envisioned, but I was never able to get to *Family* because my mom passed away, so they were not included in *Game*.

There's a school shooting or mass shooting every week, so I'm happy the piece is on display to have these conversations about that. It's my protest piece. Something needs to change.

—Karon Davis

Opposite page: *Beth and Solomon*, 2018, plaster strips, chicken wire, steel armature, glass eyes, burlap, 99¢-store earrings, synthetic hair, 53 x 99 x 39 in. (134.6 x 251.5 x 99 cm), acquired in 2019
Family, 2019, plaster strips, chicken wire, steel armature, glass eyes, antlers, 90 1/2 x 48 1/2 x 48 1/2 in. (230 x 123 x 123 cm), acquired in 2019

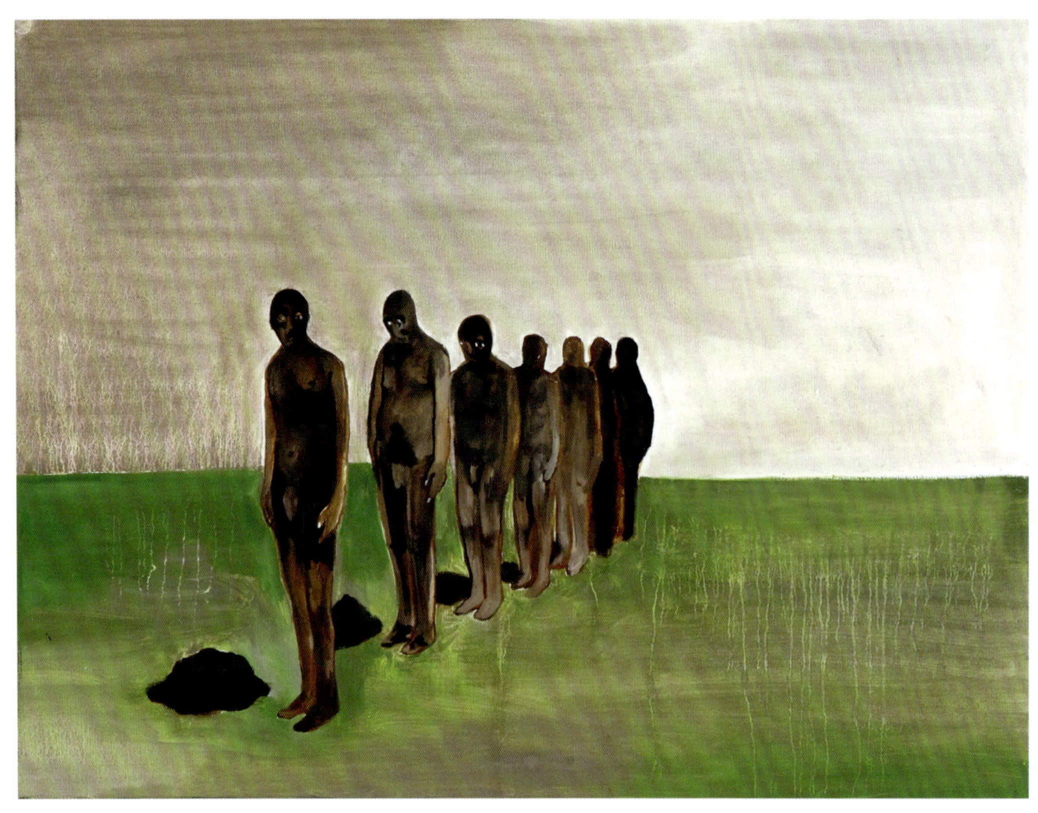

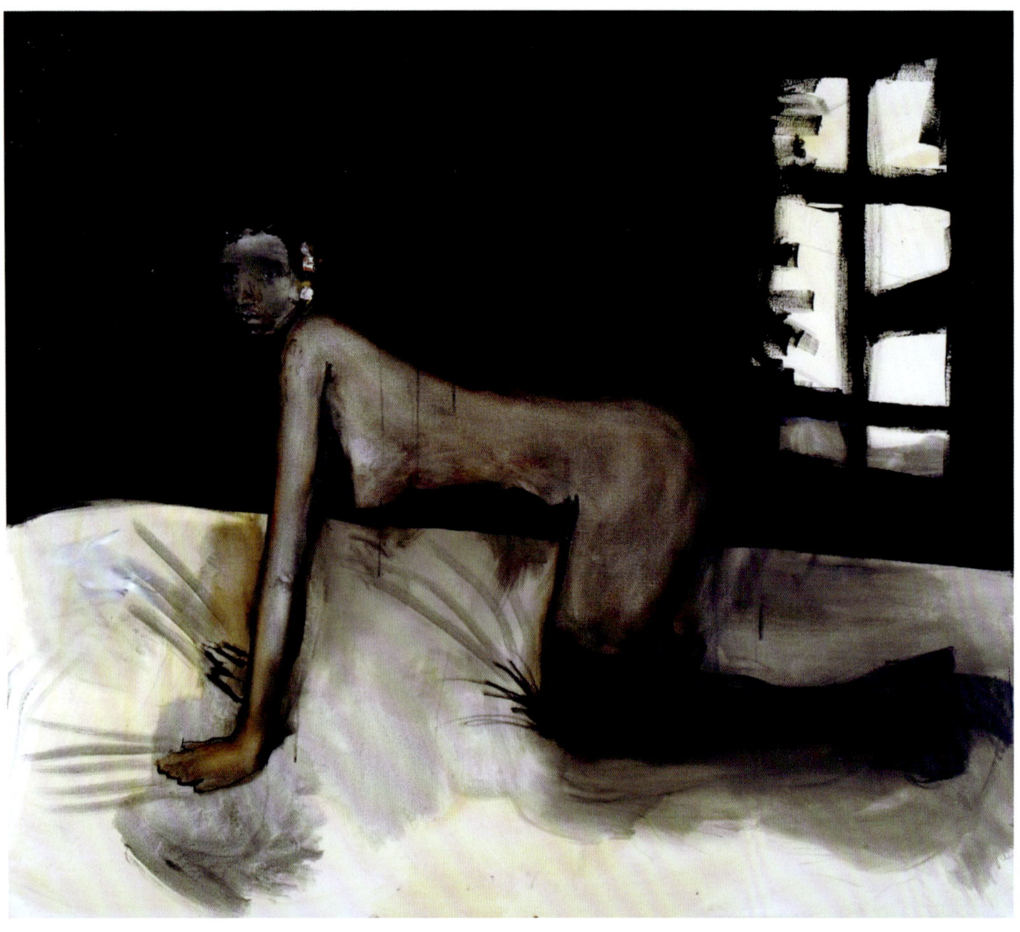

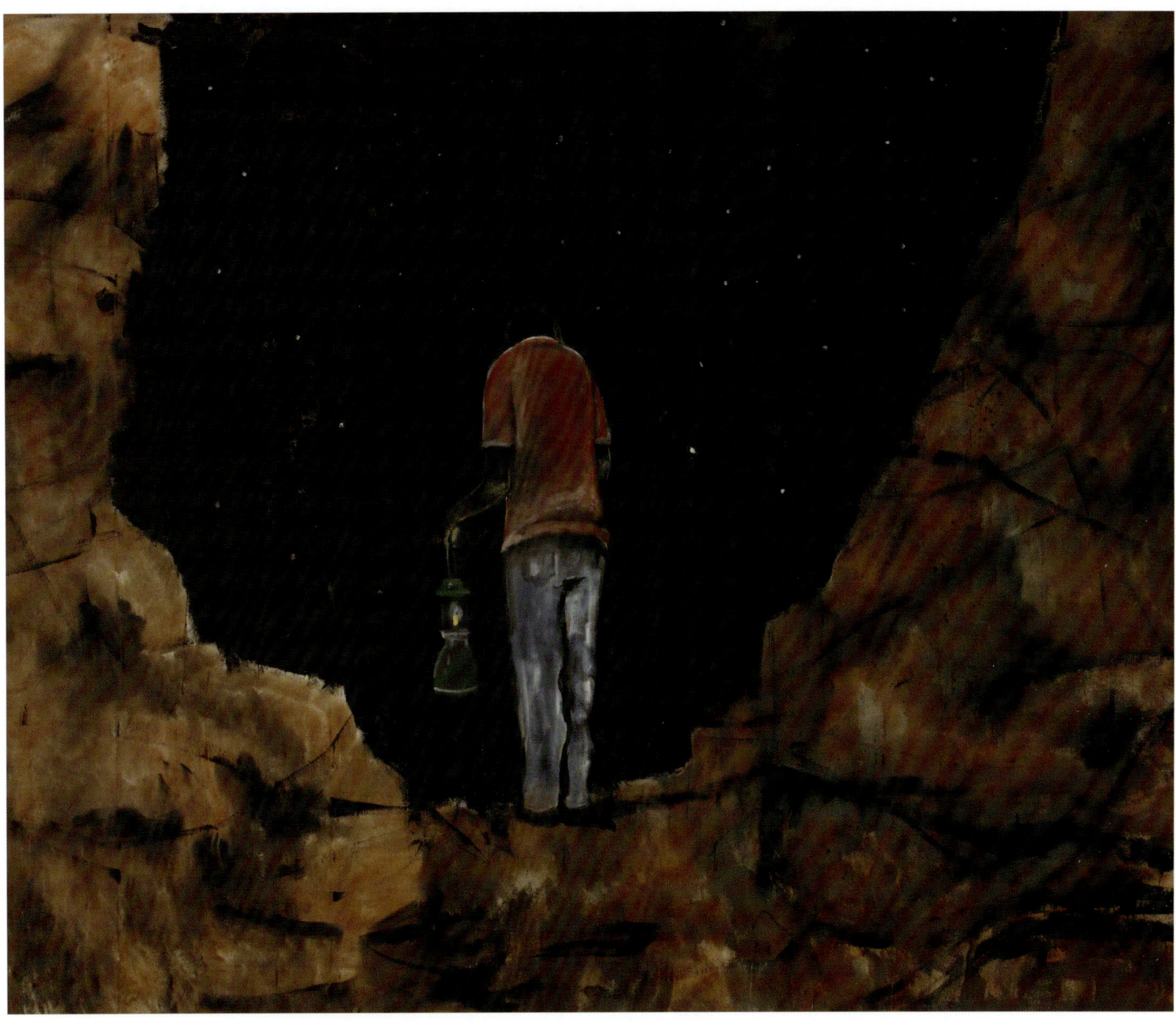

I think, like painting, spirituality makes many people very uncomfortable; spirituality is an interesting word. It is highly underrated in contemporary painting, and I feel it is the driving force behind the practice. Any attempt for me to verbalize the act of painting will ultimately fail, but, it is the spiritual nature of painting that makes it different from any other art form. The practice has a history so vast and forgotten that it can only exist in the land of the spirits.

Ultimately, I want to change the way people view art, the way people buy art, the way they make art. I've always tried to balance the tightrope of making my art accessible to those who are aware of the craft, and those who aren't convinced of art, or, more specifically, my artistic objective. I believe that concealing too much in theory is problematic and that art can function in everyday life. I strive for an artistic legacy that not only transcends Blackness but confluences and impacts all cultures.

—Noah Davis

Opposite page, top to bottom: *The Seven Prisoners of the Abyss*, 2008, oil on canvas, 30 x 40 1/4 in. (76.2 x 102.2 cm), acquired in 2008
American Sterile, 2008, oil on canvas, 52 x 60 in. (132.1 x 152.4 cm), acquired in 2008
Above: *Painting for My Dad*, 2011, oil on canvas, 76 x 91 in. (193 x 231.1 cm), acquired in 2011

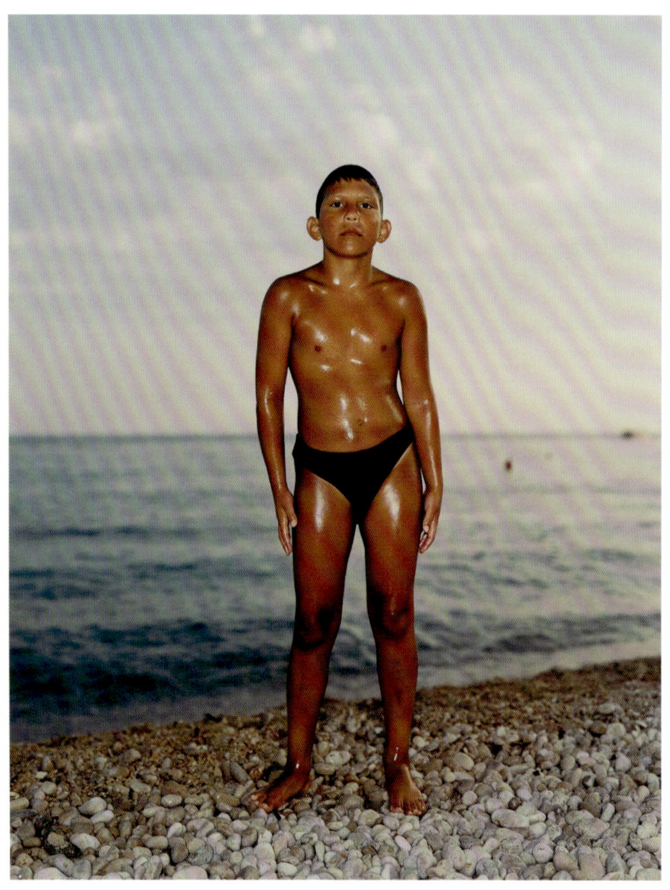

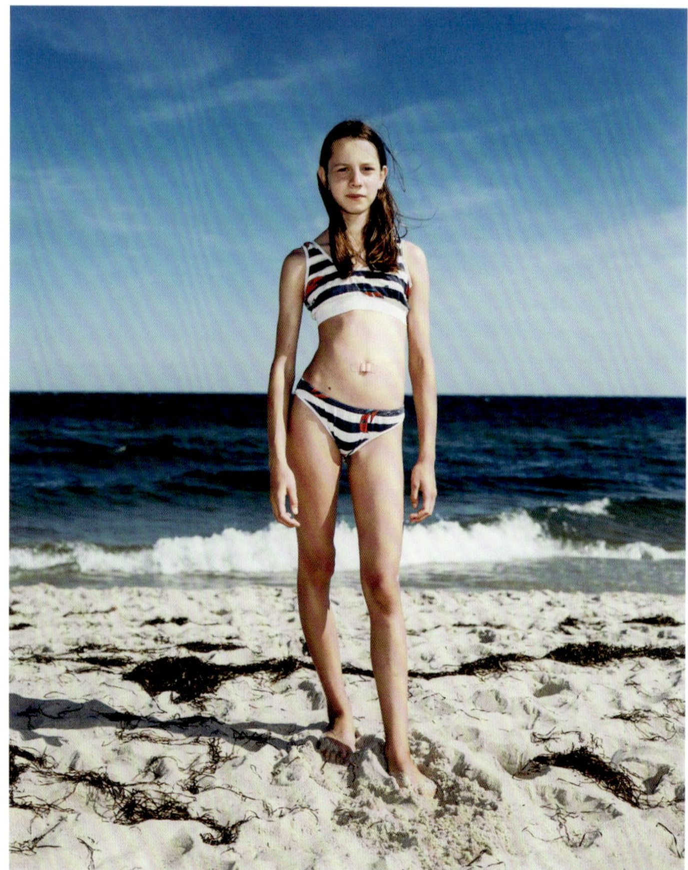

Dubrovnik, Croatia, July 13, 1996 A, 1996-1999, c-print, ed. 5/6, 60 1/4 x 50 3/4 in. (153 x 129 cm), acquired in 1999
Hel, Poland, August 12, 1998, 1998/2000, c-print, ed. 3/6, 57 1/2 x 46 in. (146.1 x 116.8 cm), acquired in 2000
Opposite page: *The Buzz Club, Liverpool, UK / Mystery World, Zaandam, NL*, 1996-1997, two-channel projection 35 mm film transferred to digital video (color, sound), 25 min. 40 sec., ed. of 2/8 AP, acquired in 2001

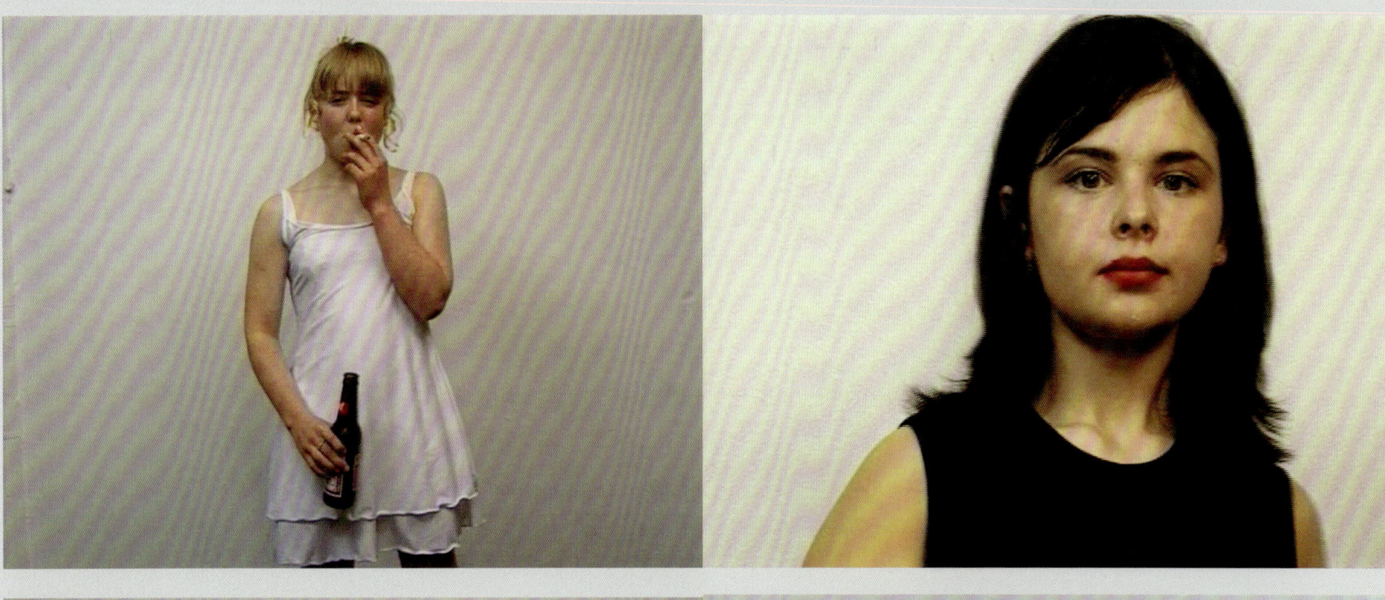

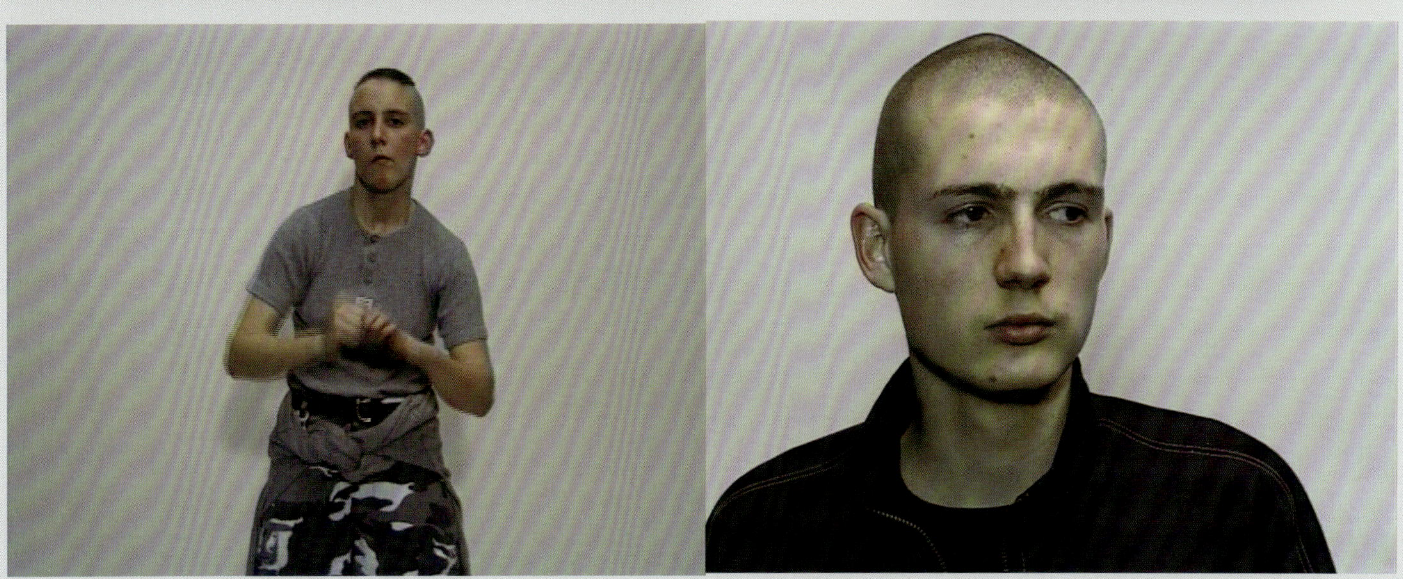

In 1994, I travelled to Liverpool because I had become interested in the idea of capturing differences between people within a given context. So I thought about making photographs of schoolchildren in their uniforms—you don't have those in the Netherlands. I liked going out at that time and because Liverpool has such a renowned music scene, I decided to spend my last evening, after work, in a club; a taxi driver dropped me off at The Buzz Club. It was November, snowing, and outside was a long line of girls waiting, wearing only skimpy dresses. The club had a 1970s interior and the DJ knew almost everyone there—he was wishing people a happy birthday and paging them over the PA. It was a world in itself. I decided I wanted to step back from all this activity and take photographs of the club's patrons in a small, improvised, white studio in the back of the club.

But when I got back to Amsterdam and looked at the contact sheets, I realized that the photographs hardly captured the strange, vibrant atmosphere in the club, and that this had a lot to do with the absence of movement and sound. So a year later I went back with a small, semi-professional video camera. I invited different club-goers to the studio and made up little scenarios for them: smoke a cigarette, dance, drink. While filming them I suddenly realized that two things came together now—the introduction of movement and sound and my interest in the portraiture of people. These were moving portraits. After filming in Liverpool as well as in the Dutch village of Zaandam, I decided to cut the film as if it showed a night out. *The Buzz Club/Mystery World* begins with the DJ welcoming everyone, the girls shy and the boys tough but insecure. During the course of the night you see the "models" getting more and more into the mood. These young club-goers chase the universal goals of going out: having fun, finding a partner (maybe just for one night), collectively losing themselves in the music and in the moment. At the same time, you, as a viewer, get the possibility of looking long and intensely at people who are so very involved in what they are doing. I hope that this involvement also hits back at the viewer when looking at the work.

—Rineke Dijkstra

2022 Artist in Residence

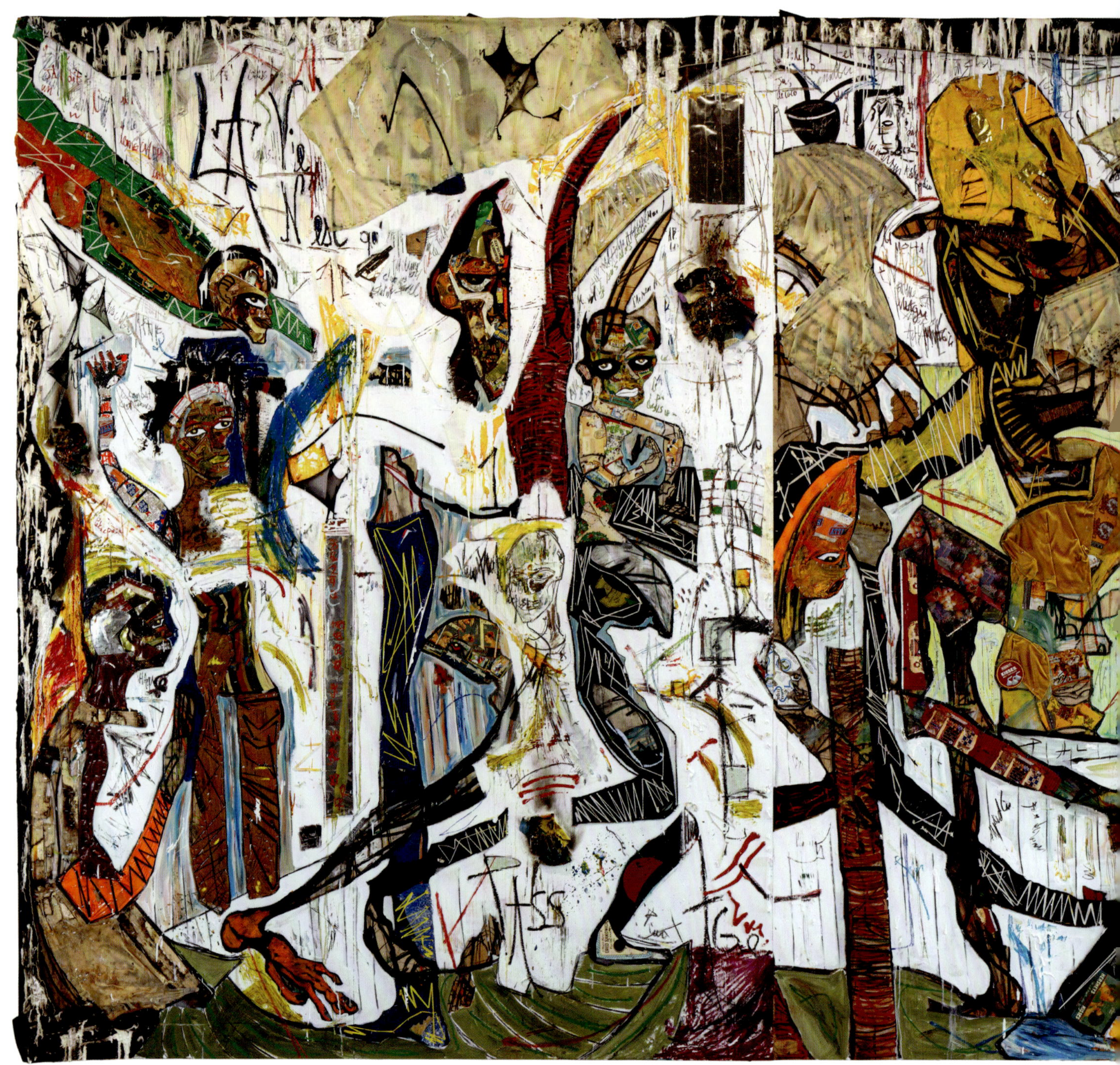

The figure in the left panel with the two black eyes is Abdoulaye, a creature I created initially as a character in a movie I wanted to make. Abdoulaye is a common name in West Africa; it's often associated with royalty. My character Abdoulaye is a child abandoned in Miami who is able to move and navigate between two worlds: the upper or real world where we all live; and the lower world—the world of death, the world where you go in time, maybe in the future, maybe in the past.

This painting shows the crossing of Abdoulaye between these two worlds; a crossing in the tradition of crossing the River Styx in Greek mythology where you're on a boat to go to hell. But here, it's a white hell, so there is nothing terrifying for Abdoulaye in this world. He's not scared, but it could definitely be a tricky world. He will have to use tricks or find clues if he wants to come back.

In the middle and right panels are the people he will encounter in his crossing. There is the wise man, there is the thinker, the jealous person, the beggar, the figure of the African revolution—the Pan African Superman. There

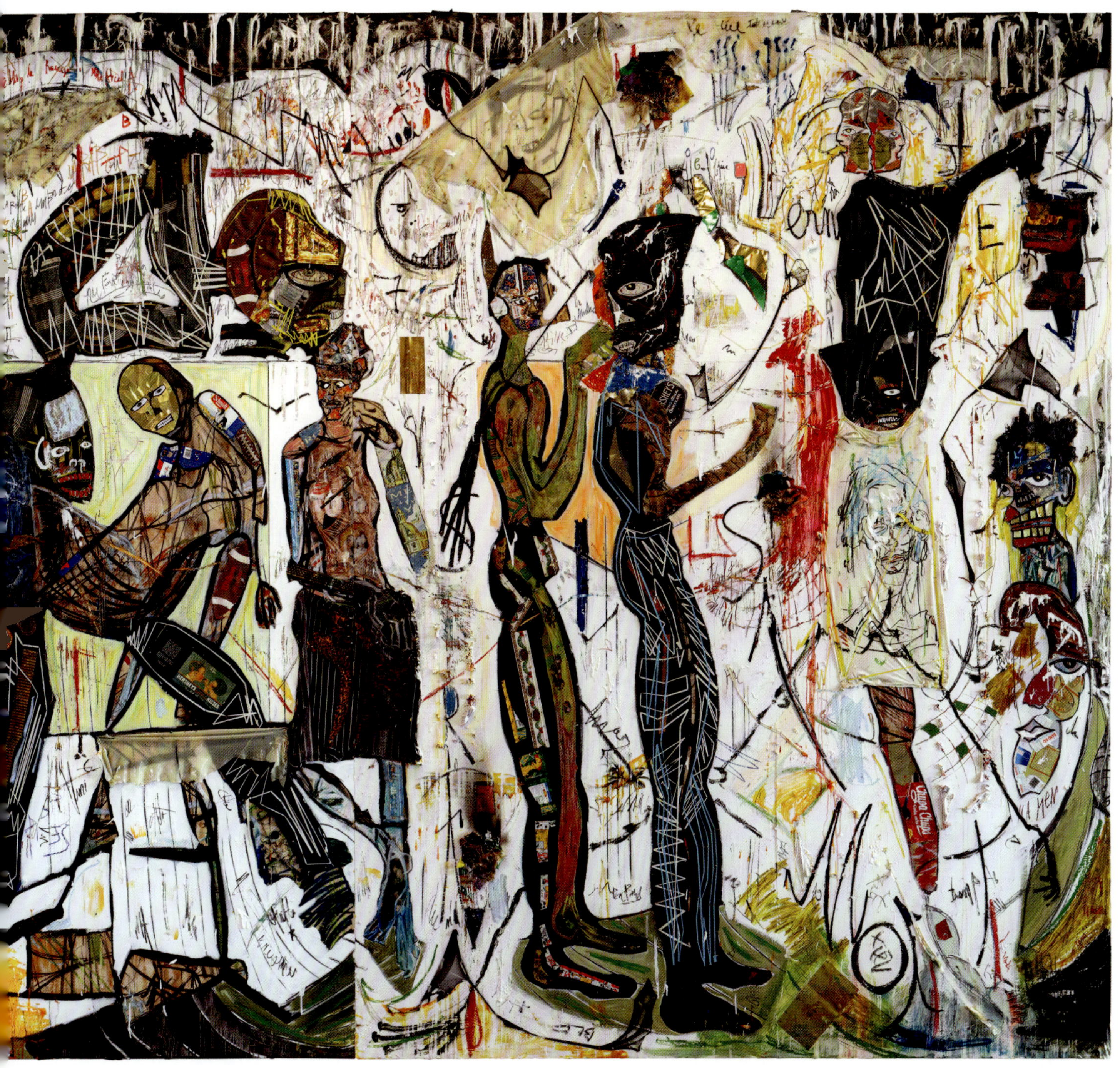

is a monster—part horse, part bird—who might be a bit dangerous, but Abdoulaye, who is fearless, is able to ride him. There is a figure of Abdoulaye when he grows up, having touched spirit, life, and death. Like in the Greek myth where Hades tells Orpheus he will be able to leave the Underworld with his beloved Eurydice, but only if he doesn't look back at her. It's the only thing Orpheus has to do, but at that moment when he is almost out, he looks back, and he loses her forever. There are also many words throughout the panels: *to all my combatants, to all my soldiers, there is a lot of revolution, there is a lot of possibility*.

—Alexandre Diop

L'Incroyable Traversée d'Abdoulaye Le Grand, Troisième de la Lignée [The Incredible Crossing of Abdoulaye the Great, Third in Line to the Throne], 2022, mixed media on wood, triptych, overall 144 x 324 in. (365.8 x 823 cm), acquired in 2022

NATHALIE DJURBERG & HANS BERG

Nathalie Djurberg: b. 1978, Lysekil, Sweden / lives and works in New York, NY
Hans Berg: b. 1978, Rättvik, Sweden / lives and works in New York, NY

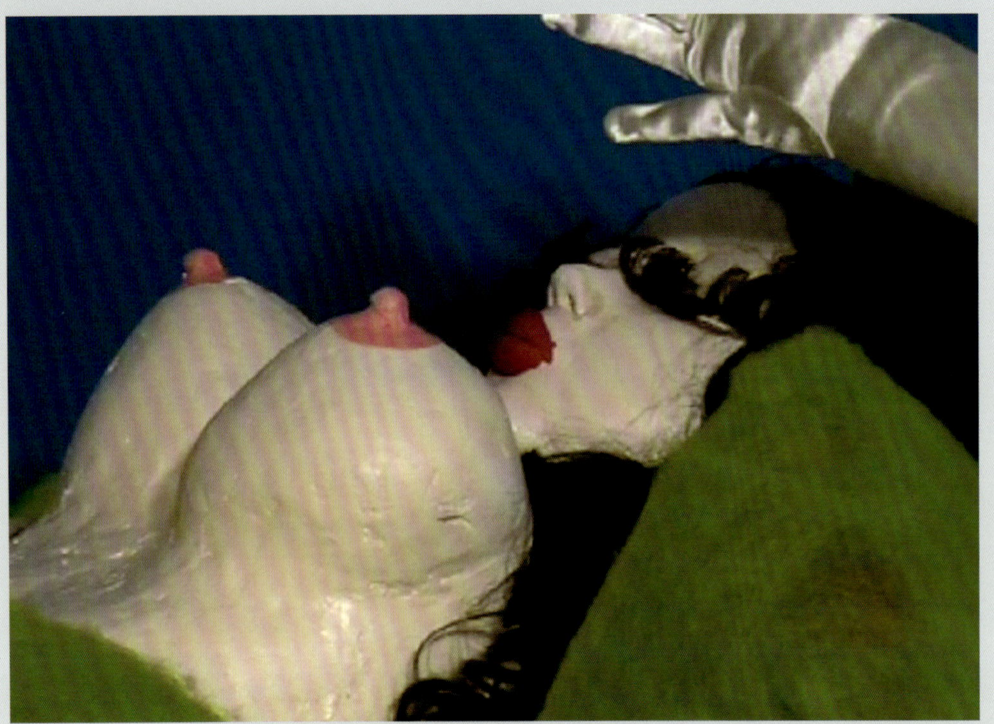

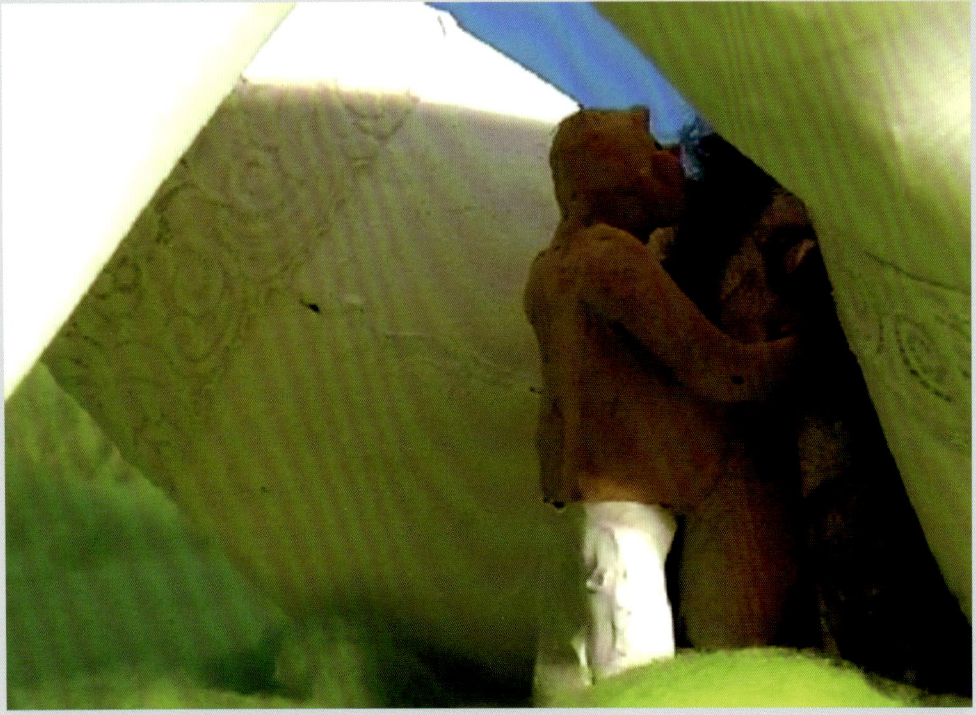

The film for us is very much about that the woman's final
weapon, or way of surviving, still comes down to her body.
For her to use it for that purpose, and be used in return.

—Nathalie Djurberg & Hans Berg

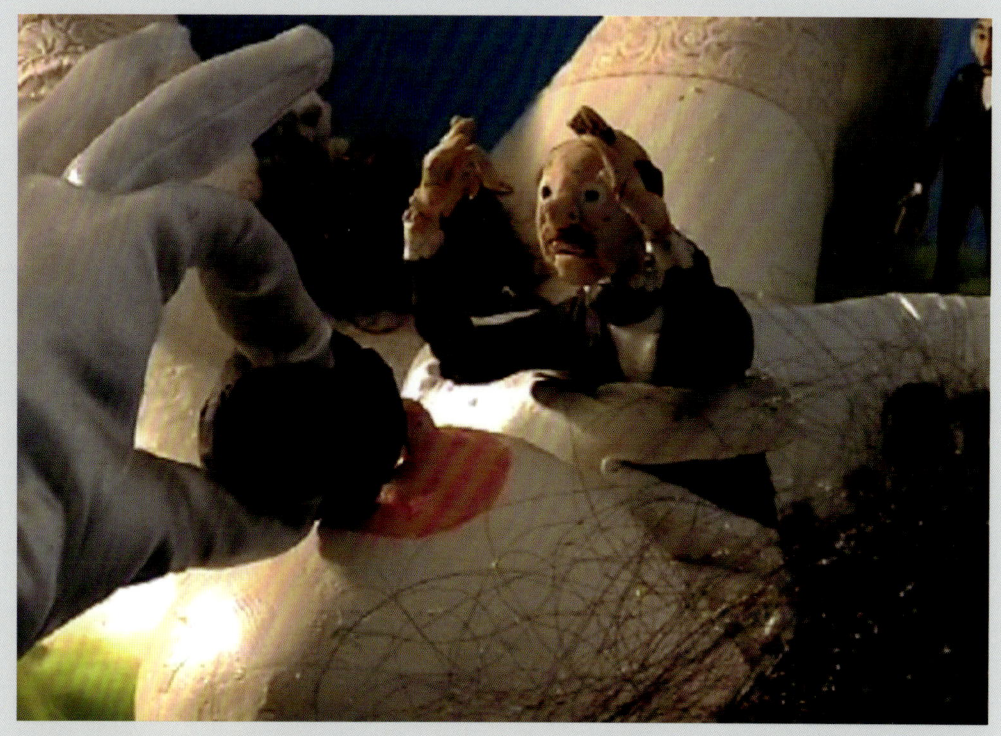

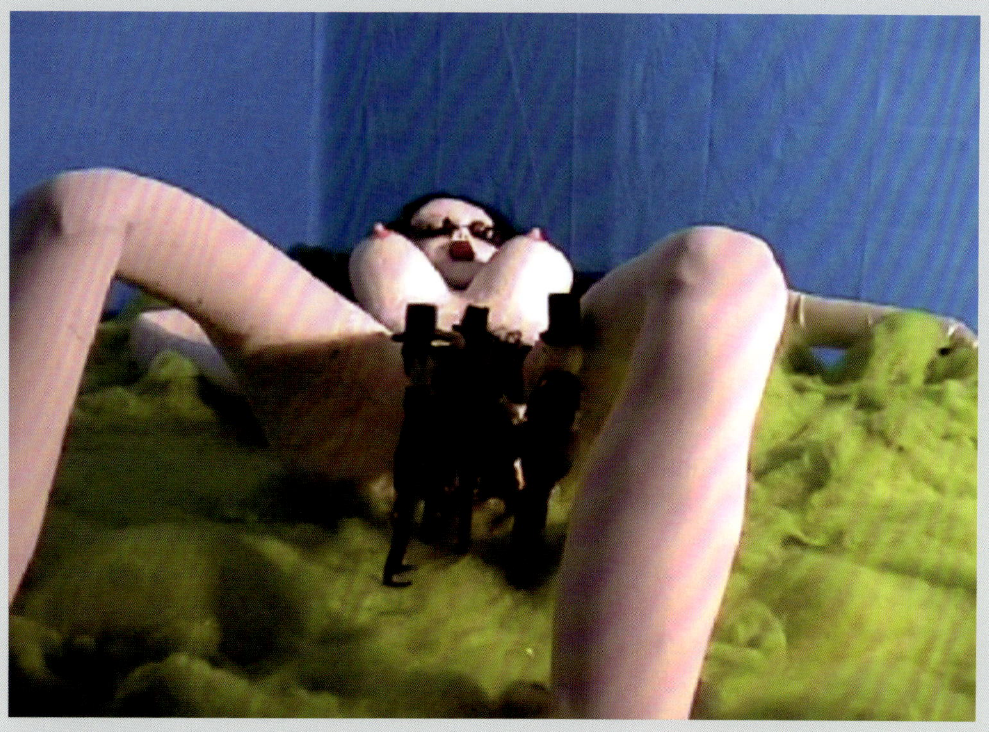

Kräsen blir utan [Easy], 2004, video (color, sound), music by Hans Berg, 3 min. 16 sec. ed. 2/4, acquired in 2006

LUCY DODD
b. 1981, Garden City, NY / lives and works in New York, NY

2014 Artist in Residence

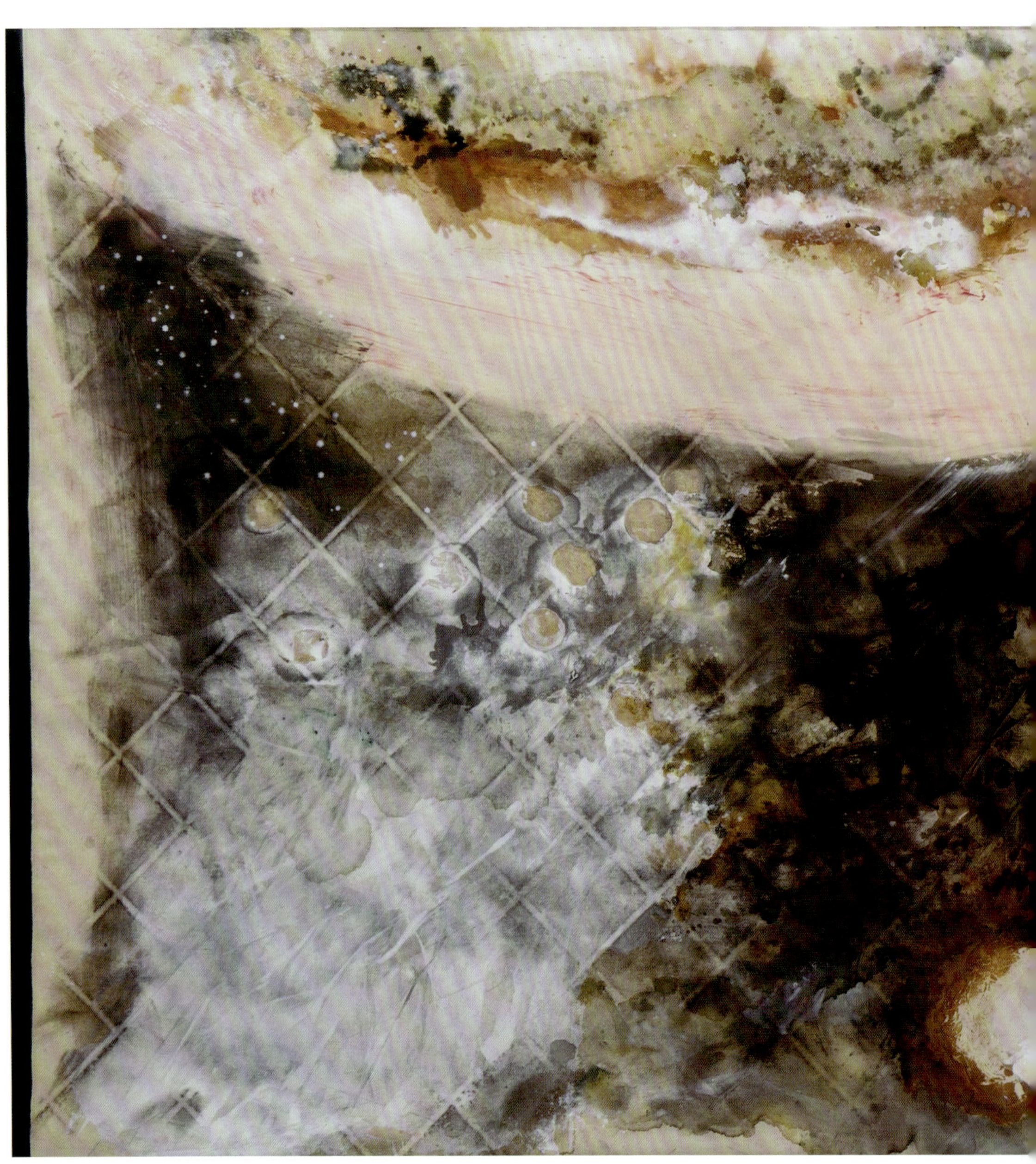

Under the 'bu blood moon is a series of 12.
Like hours they sat in a mass laying on each other
stretched on a deck on the point of Dume.
The boo of night clapped and they began under the sky of the full lunar eclipse,
the gentle blanket of white light lit them and then the red happened, the blood of the moon, the earth shadow
cast roses and the pink light appeared.
They were suspended I remember thinking wings and these were the first hovering paintings and the drips and
the leaks of the seams happened. These paintings are beyond ananda and specific of the pacific.

—Lucy Dodd

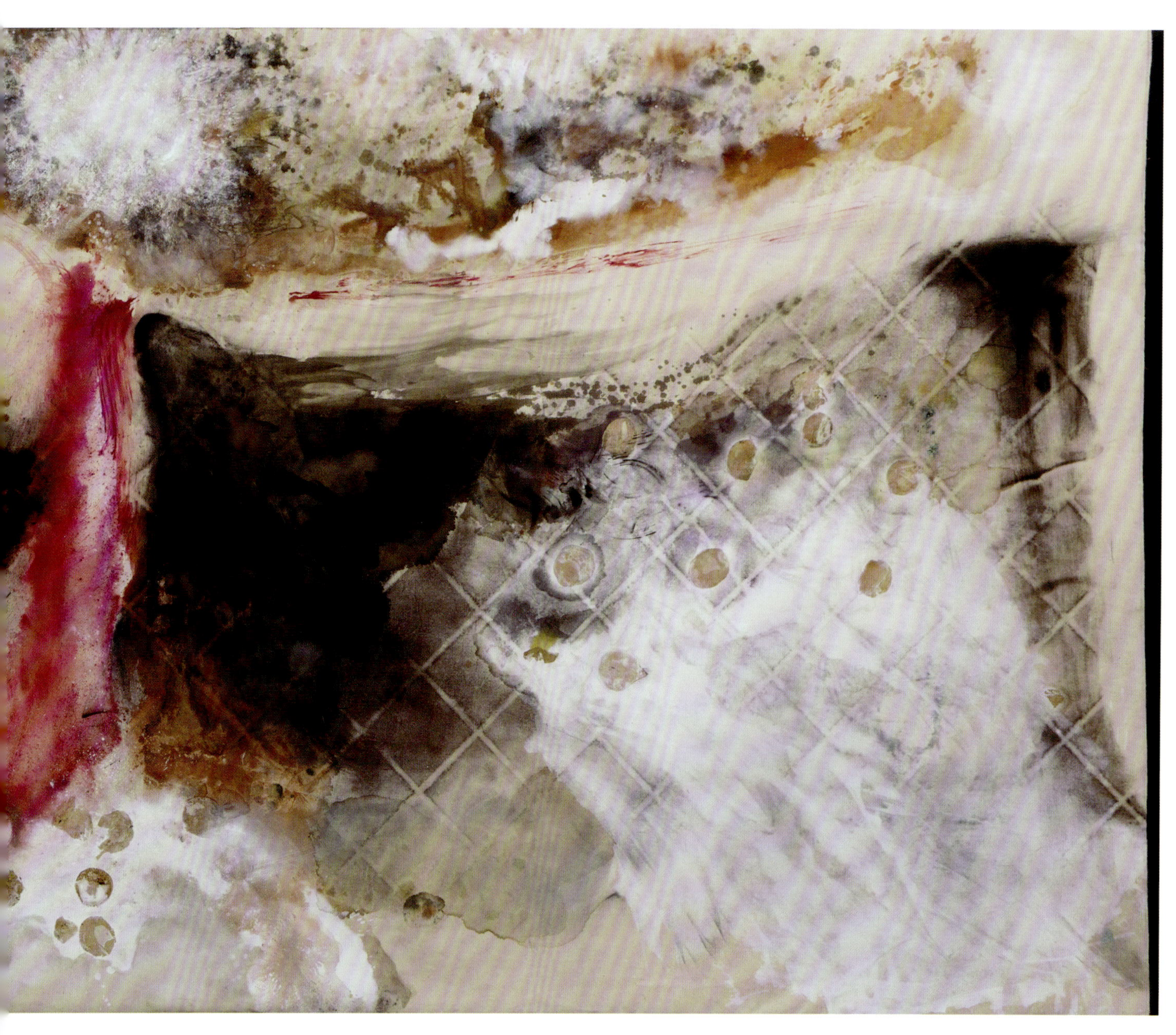

Guernika, 2014, Spanish hematite, Miami rainwater and lavender oil, cochineal, kombucha SCOBY, Rota squid ink, earth from Monasterio de Suso, Aracena, Rio Tinto, la Aldea-Bejes, and Guernika, chamomile and pomegranate from Segura de Leon, lichen from Sierra de Gata, yerba maté, Rio Tinto water, mica, spirulina, mixed pigments, and Tyrian purple on canvas, 11' 5" x 25' 6" (3.5 x 7.8 m), acquired in 2015

b. 1961, Tallahassee, FL / lives and works in San Antonio, TX

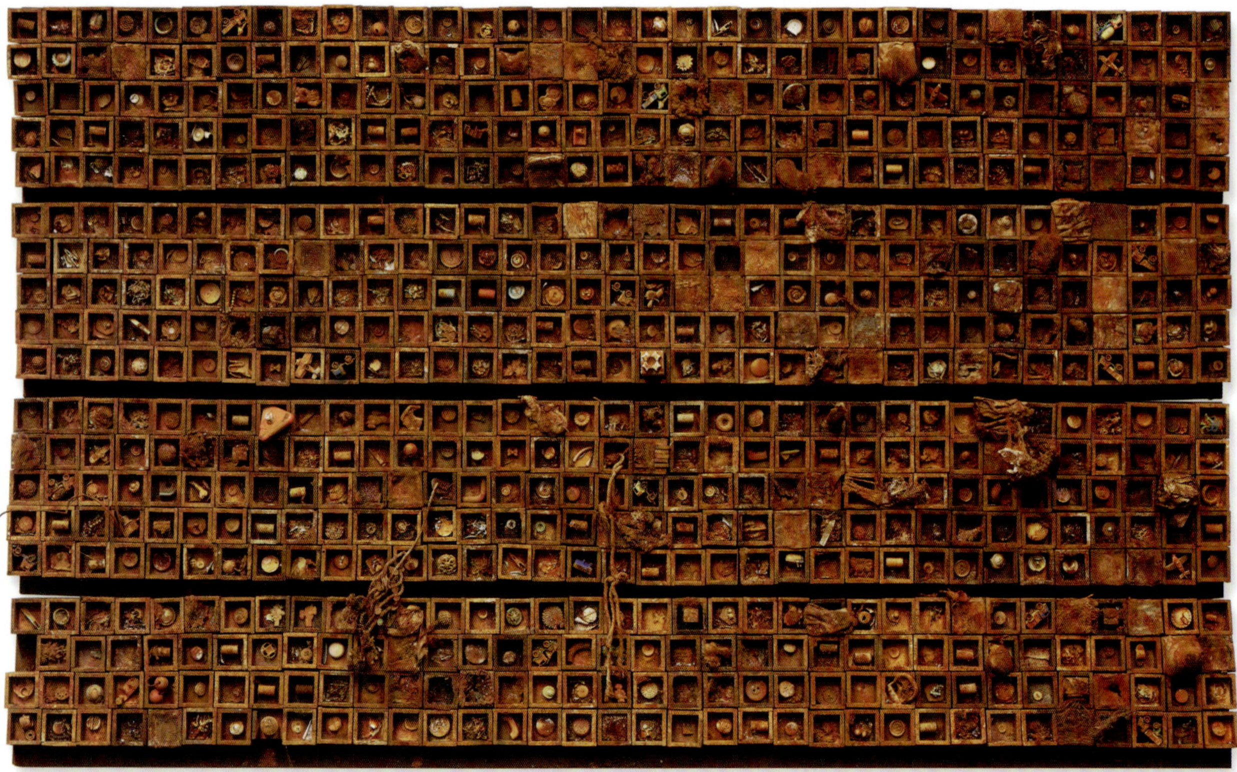

Untitled, 1998-1999, plastic toys, found objects, mixed media collage, and rust on wood, 42 x 70 x 2.25 in. (106.7 x 177.9 x 5.7 cm), acquired in 2021
Opposite page: *Untitled #25*, 1992, cotton and wax, 102 x 158 x 33 in. (259 x 401.3 x 83.8 cm), acquired in 1992

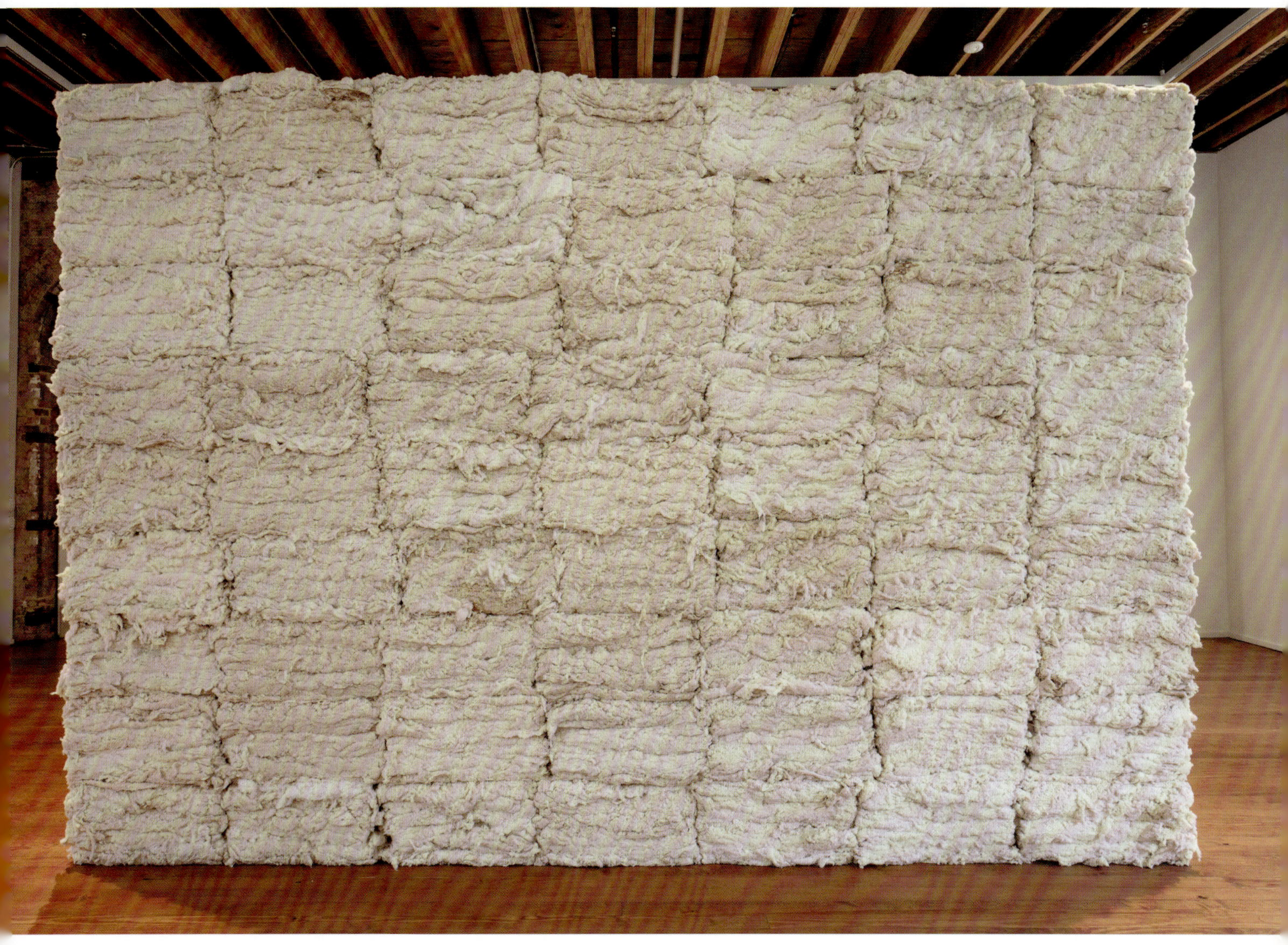

I can only say that creating the wall (*Number #25*) brought the toil and sweat of the old days. Having no vehicle and no driver's license I found myself using a dolly to transport full bales of cotton down the streets of Broadway. But that was only the beginning. The nature of the material only allowed it to be cut with scissors. Through focus, pain, and heart, *Number #25* was painstakingly realized. Of course I found in my travels years later that machines in the South are producing the very same walls of cotton…within minutes.

—Leonardo Drew

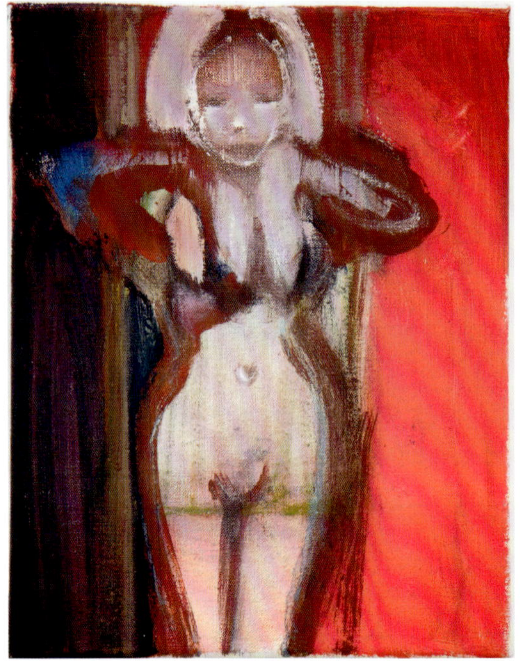

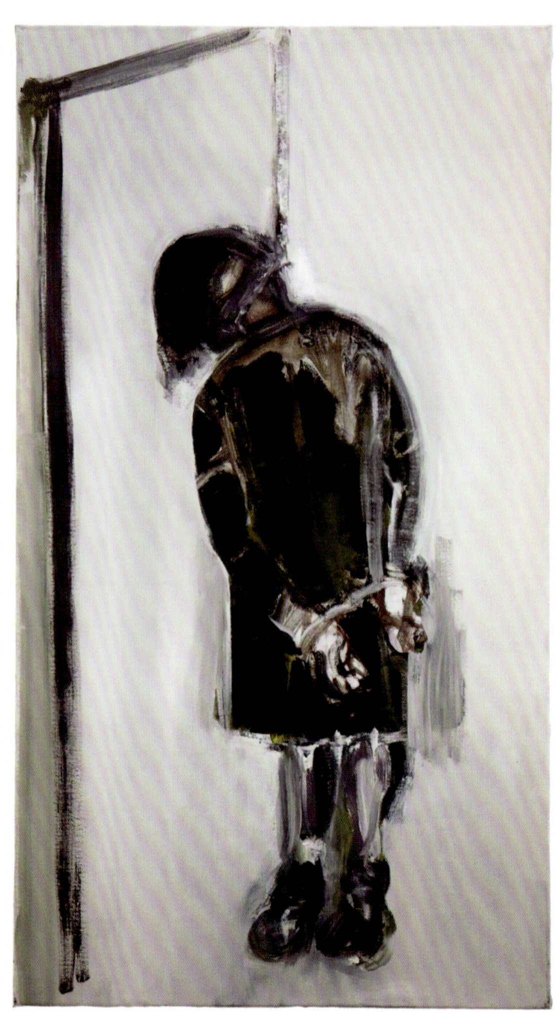

Miss January [opposite] was conceived for a solo show of mine called *Miss World*, at Galerie Paul Andriesse in Amsterdam in the year 1998.

She started out as, or rather her source was, an airbrushed, ultra smooth-skinned, high-gloss centerfold photograph for the January number of a Dutch *Playboy* magazine (date unknown, but I suspect it was the late '70s). A young, super-healthy-looking blonde that combined eroticism with winter sports. Naked but for her zipped-open, short ski jacket and socks—one foot without and one still with a bright-pink, woolen sock on. Not quite a female Santa Claus as Christmas was just over, and the December issue had just passed. But her legs, they went on forever. (In the history of Western painting, we often find that it is more sexually arousing to be half-dressed or just partly exposed than totally naked.) I was more fascinated than attracted to her. She looked like an Amazon and felt quite alien, even a bit scary to me.

Although I am a woman too, I'm small and round and more next-to-you; this was a figure to look up to. At that stage of my life I had used many different types and poses of pin-ups, porno stars, fashion models and beauty contestants in my work. She seemed to combine aspects of all of these forms of deliberate stagings of the sensous female. But this was just the start, the inspiration to make this painting. When she became a painting, all kinds of things changed. She became even taller. So tall that when you stand in front of the work, your eye level is at the point where the dark triangle starts and the legs begin to leave the torso.

She also connects to my *Magdalena* group of females that was part-modern catwalk and part-ancient mythical times. She ended up wearing a black, "gestural" (painting for painting's sake) elegant top suggesting a garment of lace. Strange to wear a sock with that maybe? Who knows what she is about. Maybe it's the mixture of sugar and spice.

—Marlene Dumas

Left to right: *The Pleasure Principal*, 1999, oil on canvas, 11 3/4 x 9 3/4 in. (28 x 24 cm), acquired in 1999
Imaginary 2, 2002, oil on canvas, 49 x 27 1/2 in. (125 x 70 cm), acquired in 2003
Miss January, 1997, oil on canvas, 110 1/4 x 39 3/8 in. (280 x 100 cm), acquired in 2000

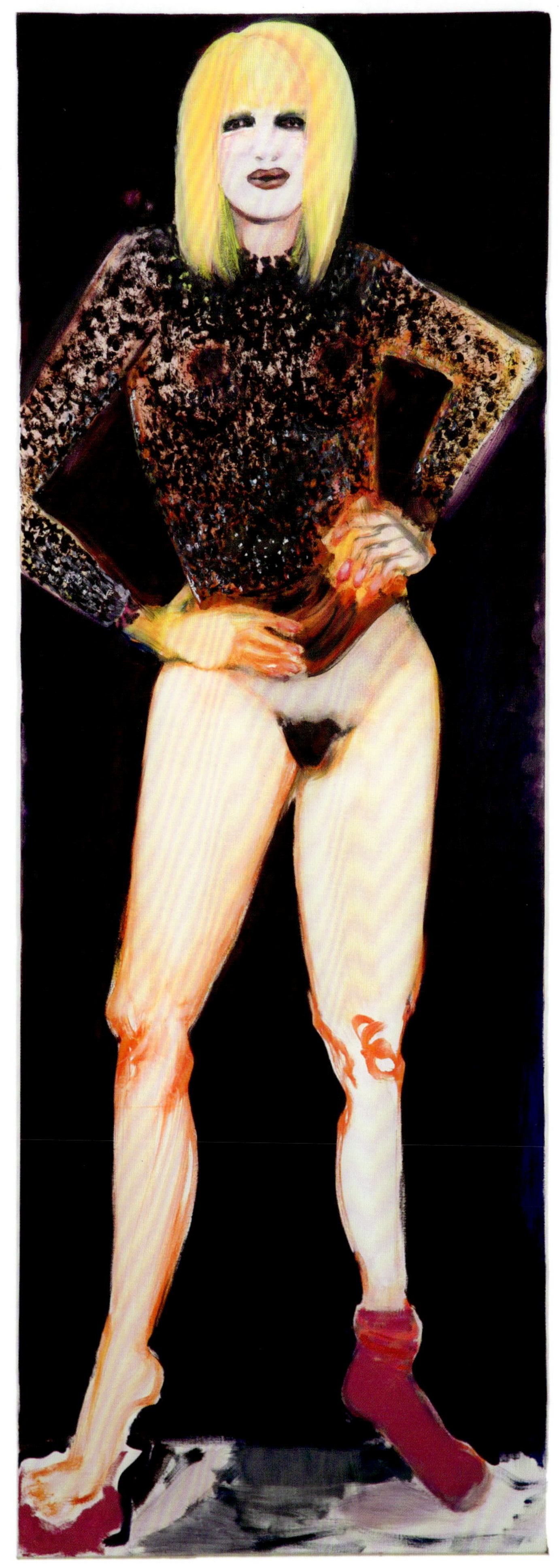

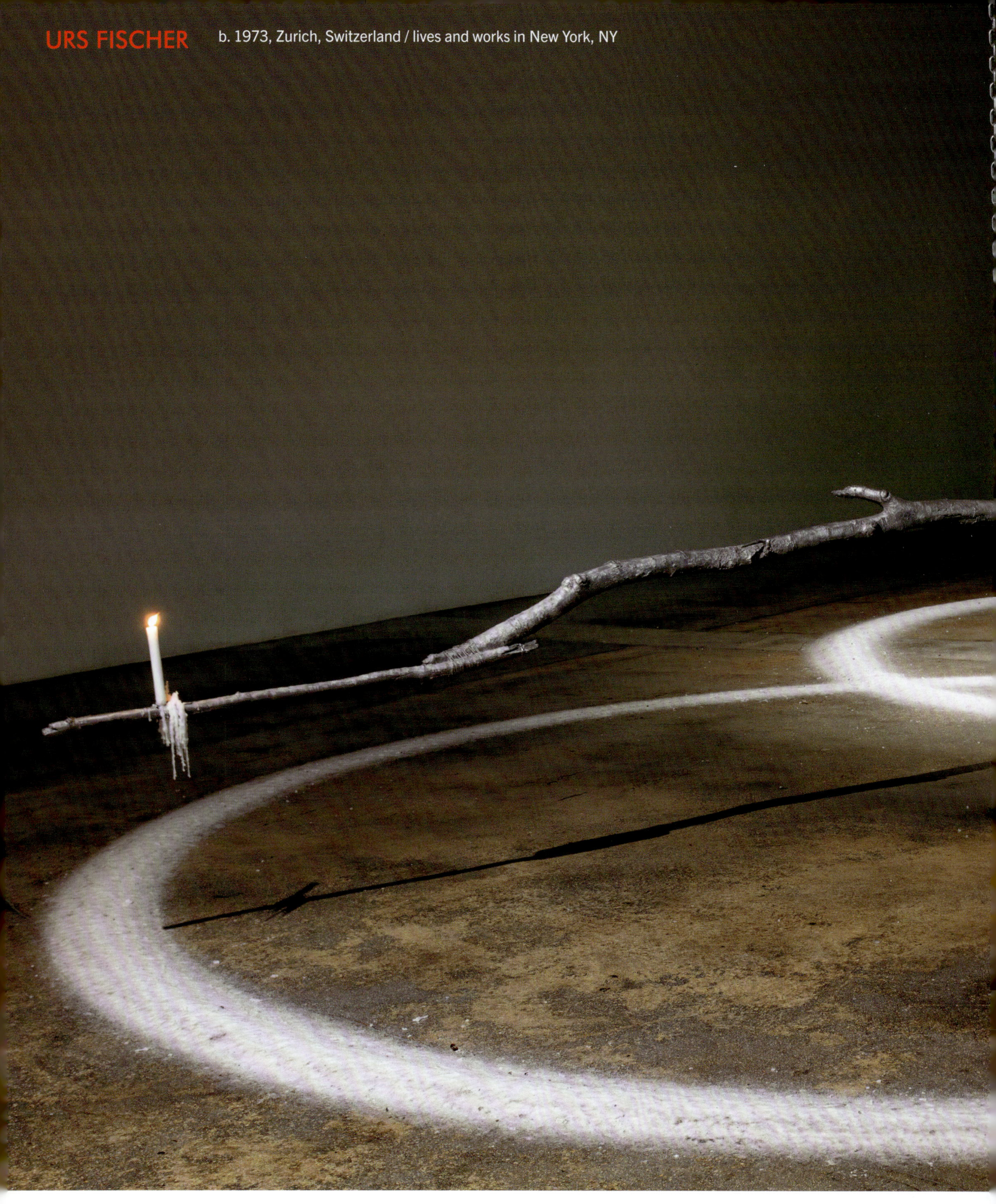

Two branches hanging at different heights move at different speeds in opposite directions. Over time, the wax from the candles drips and draws two circles on the floor that get bigger and bigger and become the form of a Venn diagram.

—Urs Fischer

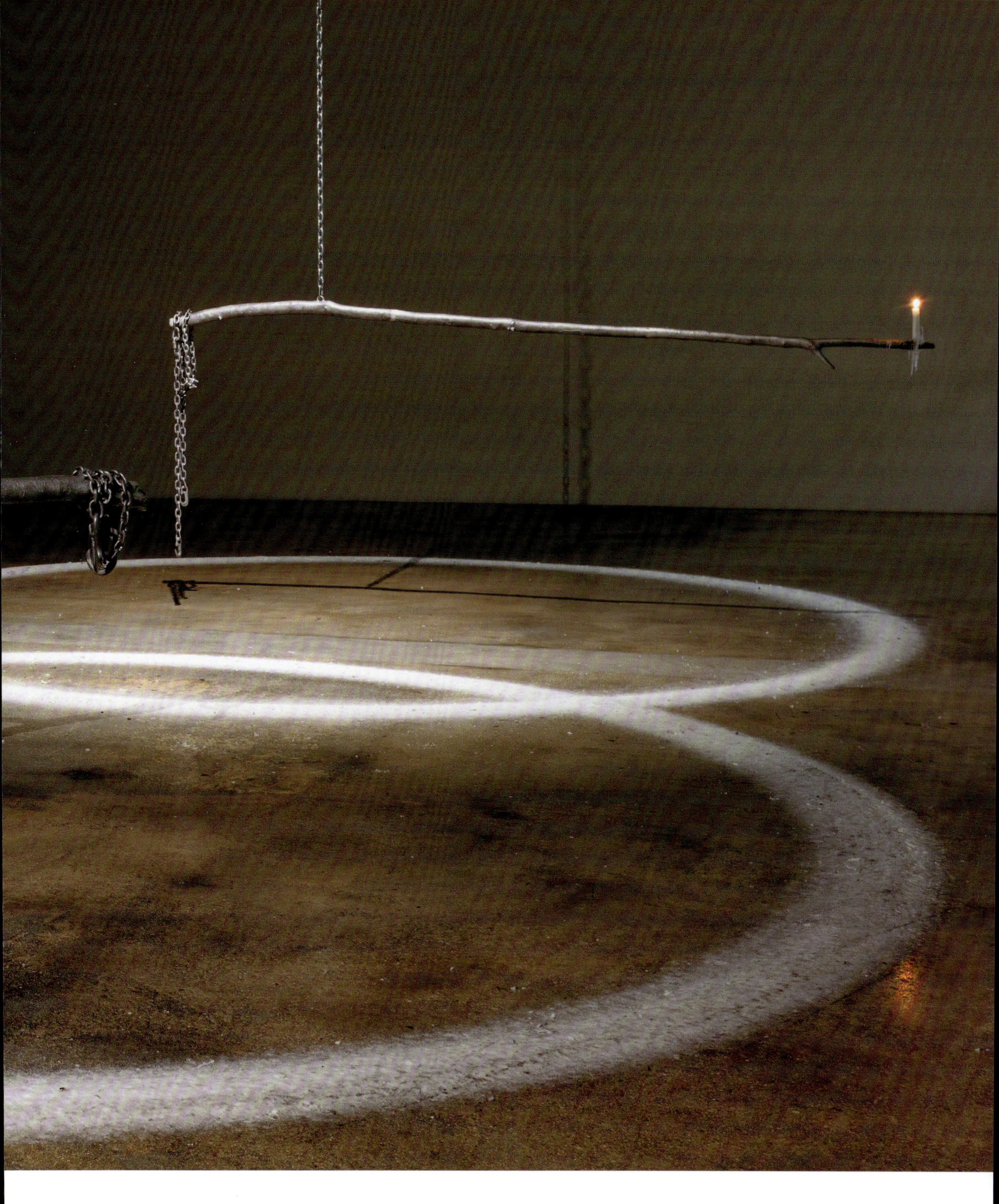

Untitled (Branches), 2005, cast aluminum, chains, candles, low-speed electric motors, control units, ed. of 2 plus 1 AP, overall 244 1/8 x 326 3/4 x 234 5/8 in. (620 x 830 x 596 cm), acquired in 2006

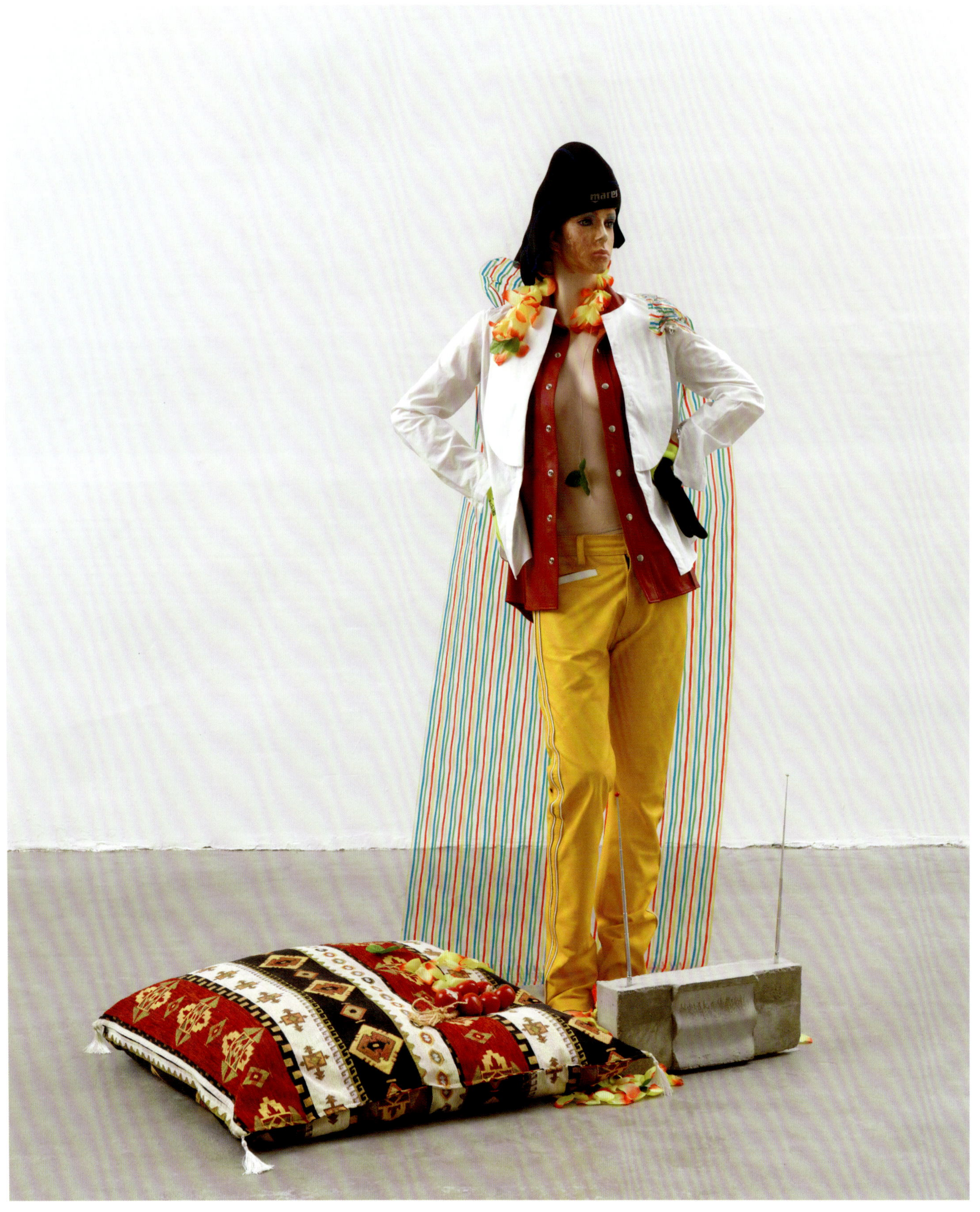

Schauspieler, 2013, mannequin, wig, glasses, lacquer, felt pen, leather gloves, ceramic figurines, metal, and acrylic glass, 72 1/4 x 18 1/2 x 10 1/2 in. (184 x 47 x 27 cm), acquired in 2015

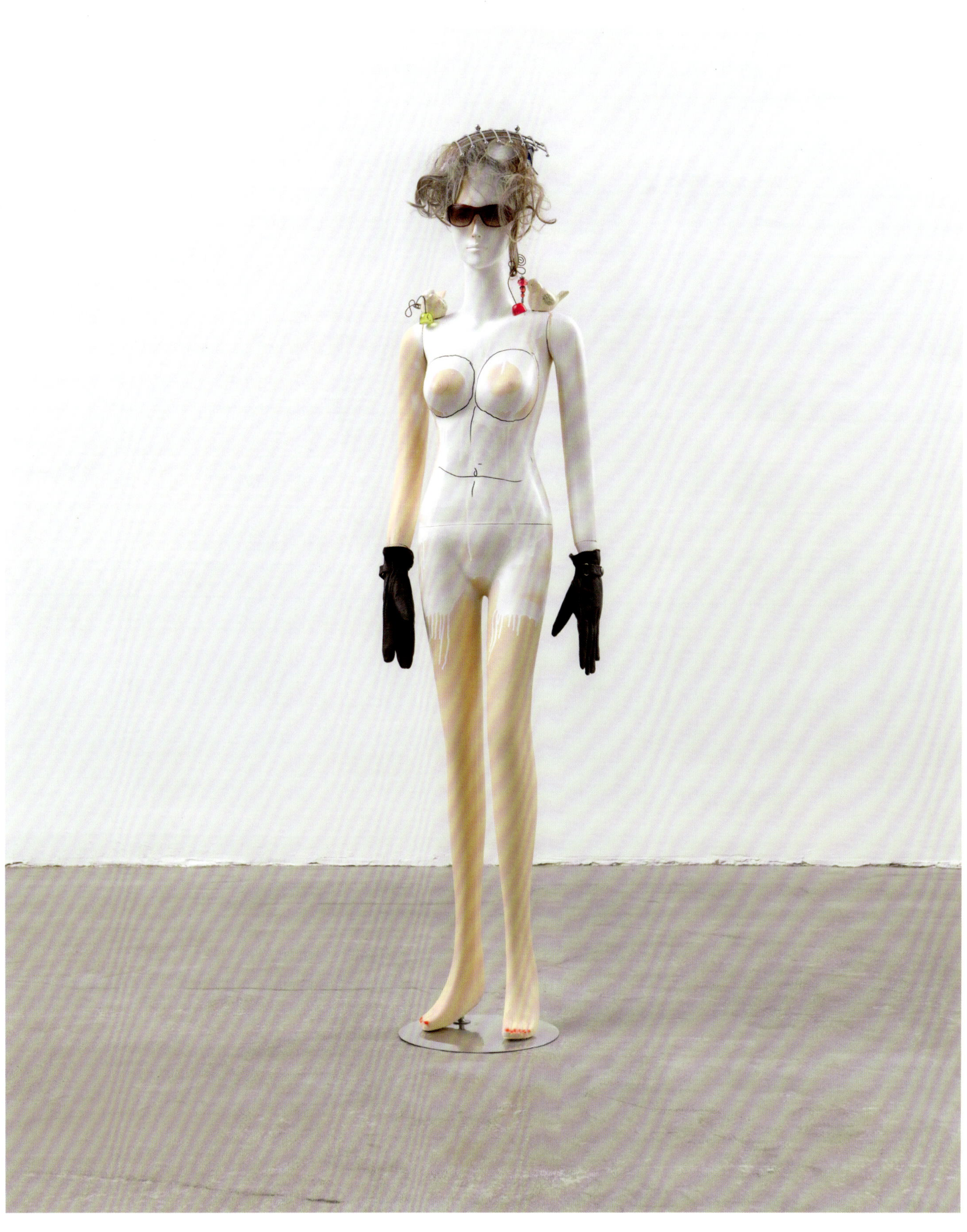

Schauspieler, 2013, mannequin, pillow, fabric, leather, plastic foil, plastic, metal, glass, concrete, antennae, 72 1/4 x 54 1/2 x 65 in. (184 x 138 x 165 cm), acquired in 2015

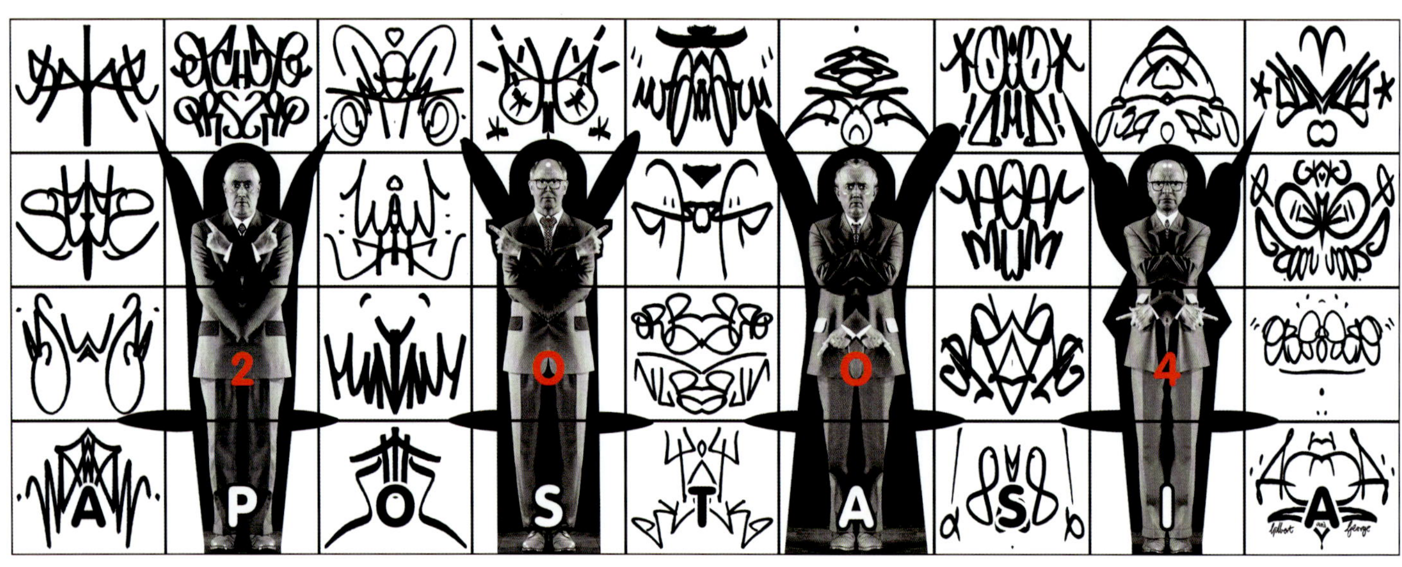

Apostasia, 2004, mixed media, each 27 3/4 x 33 1/8 in. (70.5 x 84 cm); overall 111 x 298 in. (282 x 757 cm), acquired in 2004

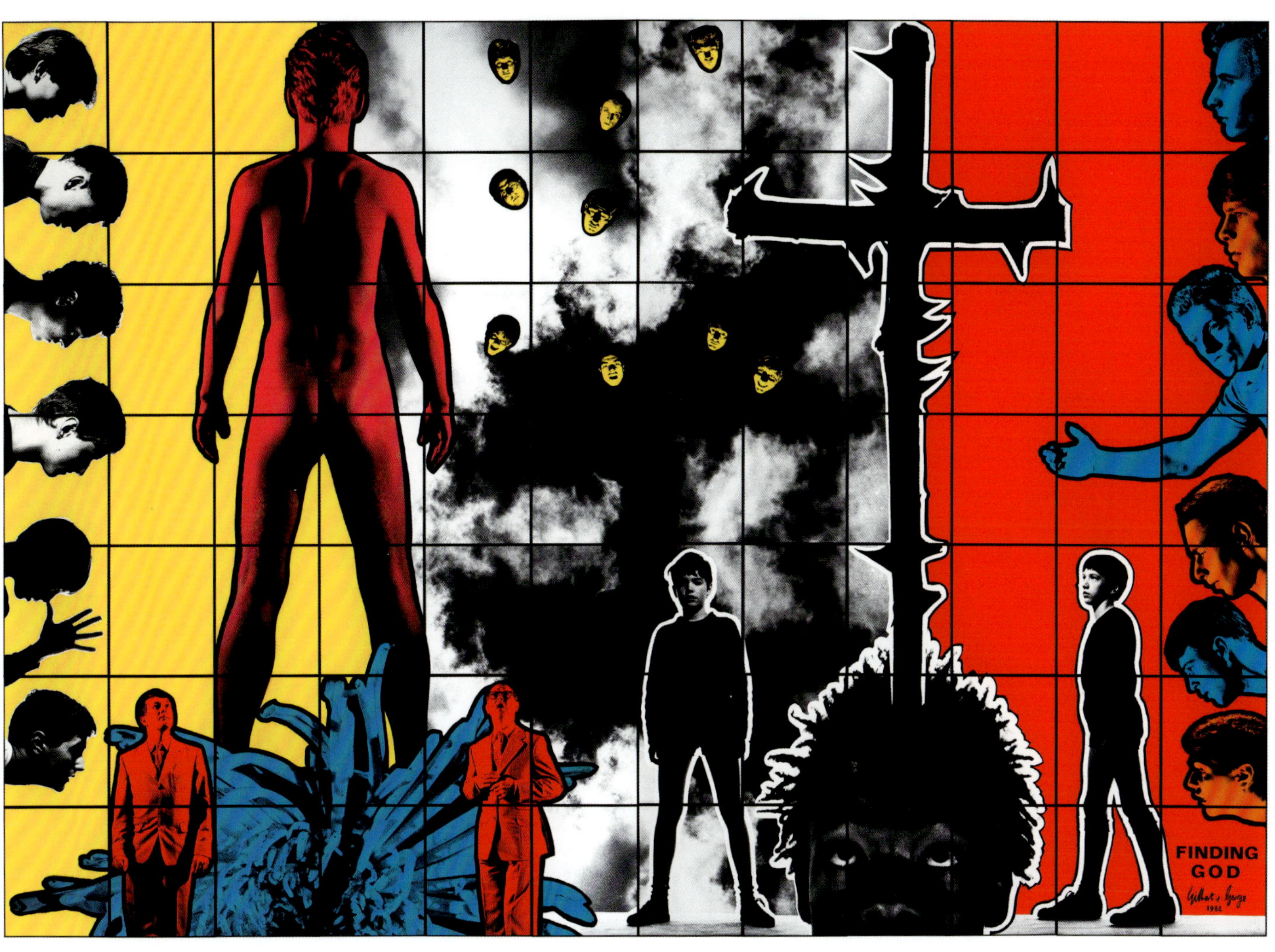

Finding God, 1982, 84 photographs hand-colored with ink and dyes and aluminum foil, mounted and framed, each 23 1/2 x 19 7/8 in. (60.5 x 50.5 cm); overall 166 x 237 in. (421.6 x 601.9 cm), acquired in 1995

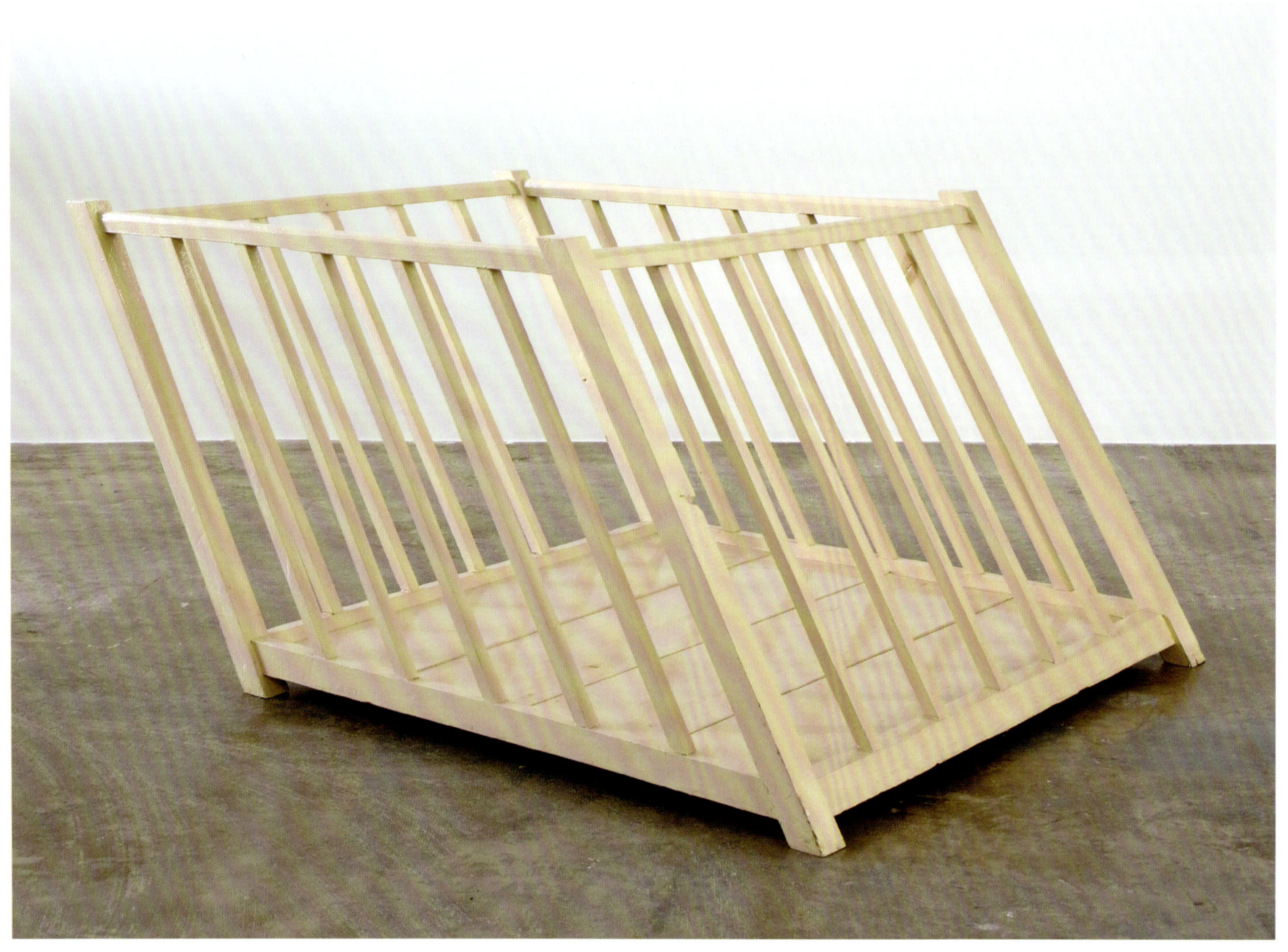

Slanted Playpen, 1987, wood and enamel paint, 23 3/4 x 50 x 36 1/4 in. (60.5 x 127 x 92 cm), acquired in 1987
Opposite page: *Untitled*, 1984, plaster, wood, wire lath, aluminum, watercolor, and semi-gloss enamel paint, 27 1/2 x 33 x 22 in. (74.2 x 83.8 x 56 cm), acquired in 1988

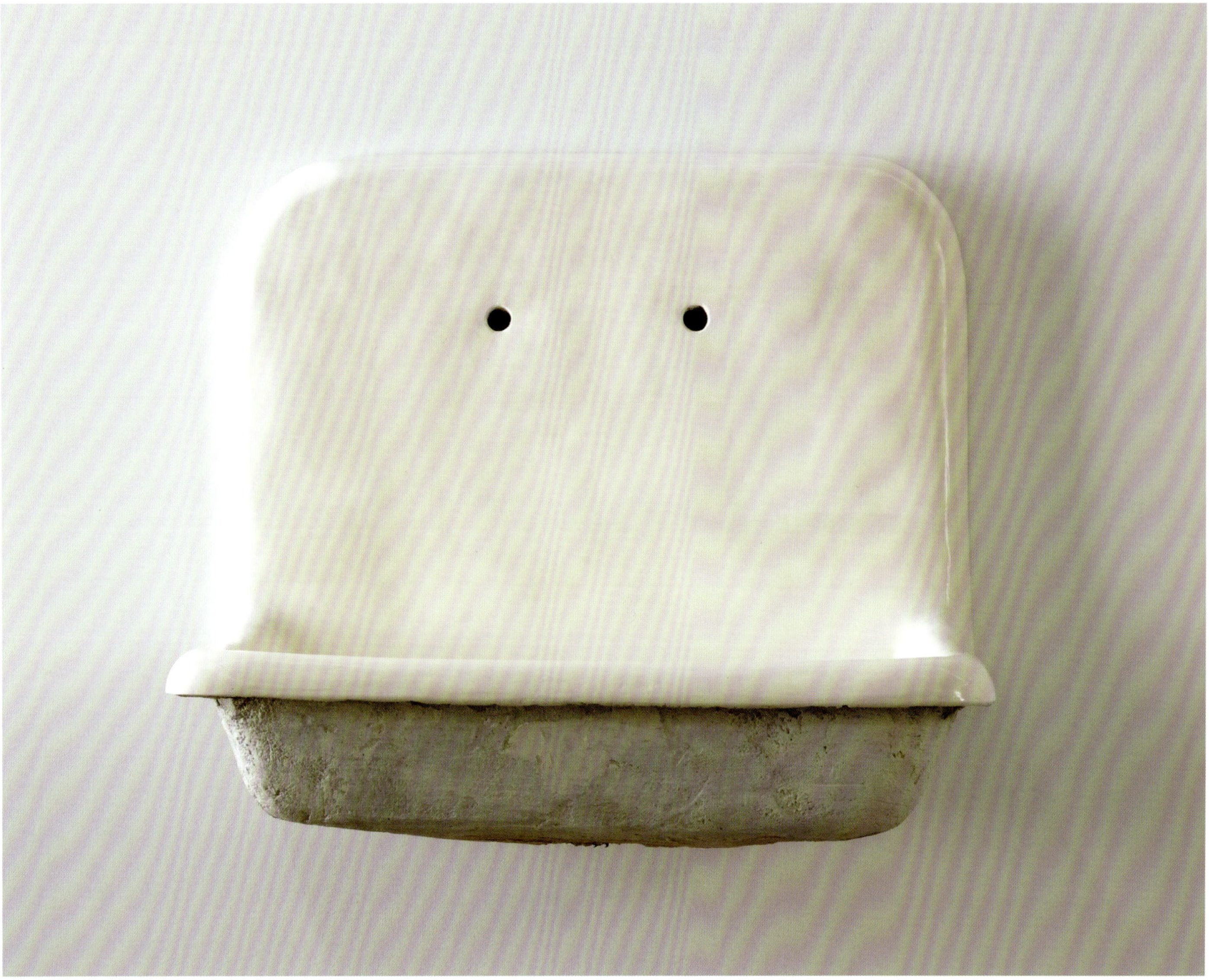

Each sculpture that I made based on the image of a sink was, at the beginning, a portrait of a sink that I knew or had lived with. This sink (*Untitled*, 1984) was based on the kitchen sink in a tenement on Spring Street where I lived from about 1978 to 1982. It was a sink that had very reduced formal qualities and I found this very useful later as I stretched and distorted the form.

Each sculpture began with a wood and metal armature. This was covered in multiple layers of wire lath and then Structo-Lite, a perlited plaster, was troweled on. When it was thoroughly dry the Structo-Lite was sanded and spackled, primed, and then painted with multiple coats of Benjamin Moore Dulamel semi-gloss white. I remember taking the painting as seriously as I took refining the forms, although almost no one noticed. I was influenced by Frank Stella and his early insistence on using paint from the can and commercial brushes. It wasn't unusual for a sink to get six or seven coats of paint to finish. The more it built up, with sanding in between, the more it looked like something other than paint.

The image of the back structure of the sink shows the board from my kitchen on which I painted *Slides of a Changing Painting* (1983). Money was nonexistent so recycling of materials was constant.

—Robert Gober

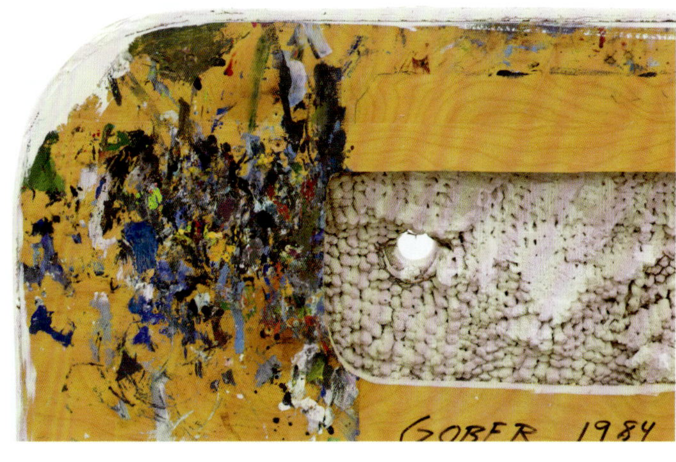

SÔNIA GOMES

b. 1948, Caetanópolis, Brazil / lives and works in Belo Horizonte, Brazil

2015 Artist in Residence

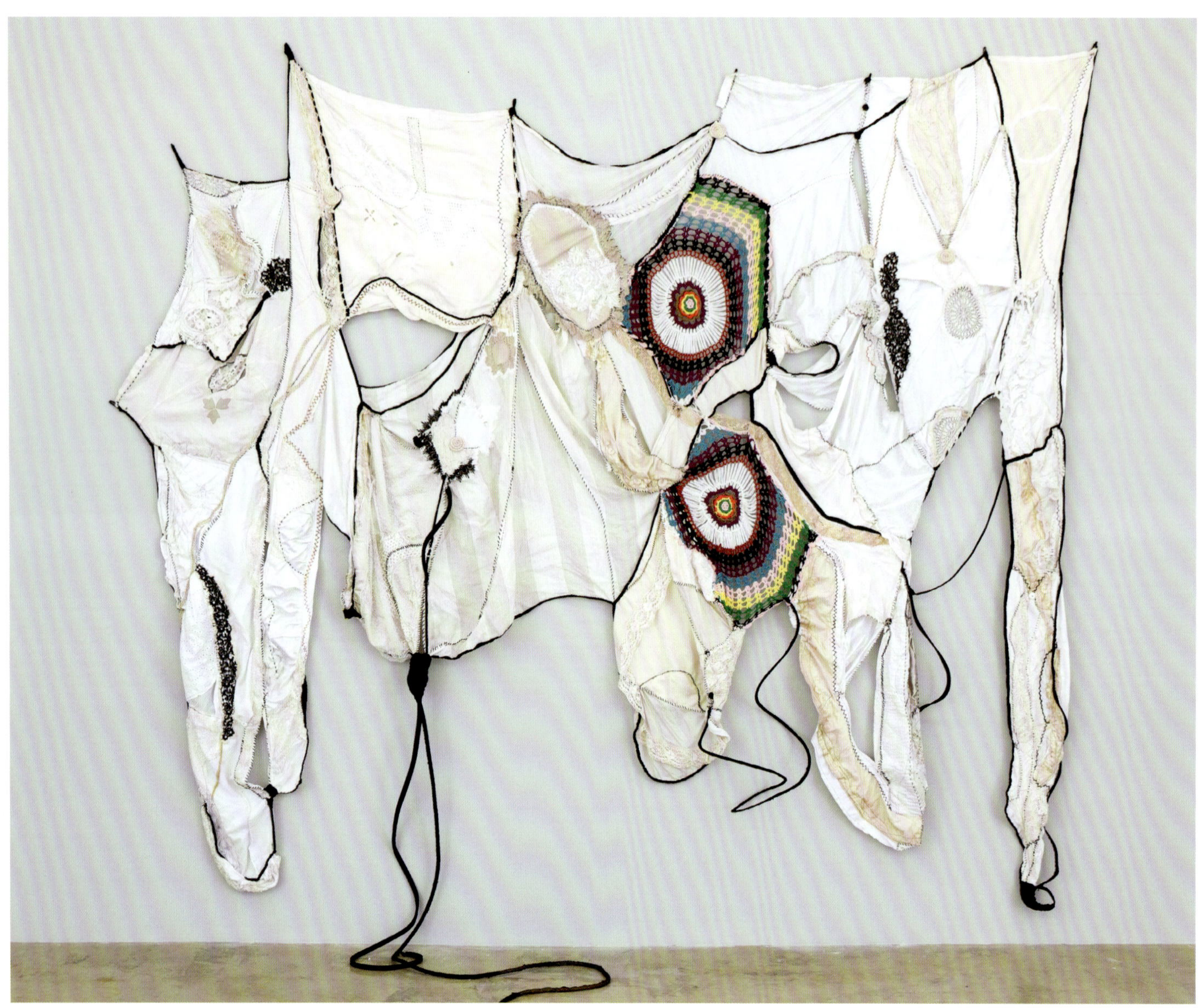

Tantas Estórias is one work from my "panos" series. The panos ("cloths") are made through the deconstruction of cloths used to dress the home (tablecloths, curtains, or some other fabric), which arrive impregnated with history and traces of time. I deconstruct to create a two-dimensional work between stitchings, holes, and knots, always looking for movement, form, and asymmetry.

A torção ("torsion") is a sculpture molded by my own body. My body is enveloped by a single line of rigid wire, which is twisted and twisted repeatedly, looking for abstract, asymmetrical shapes that emerge between tensions, and entanglements, and are filled with fabric volumes. Thus, I create the structure, permeated with solids and voids, covered with other colored fabrics, seeking a synchronism of colors and shapes, from which a three-dimensional sculpture emerges.

— Sônia Gomes

Tantas Estórias, 2015, thread, fabric, and rope, 115 x 125 x 5 in. (292.1 x 317.5 x 12.7 cm), 82 in. (208.3 cm) from rope to wall, acquired in 2015
Opposite page: *Sem Título da série Torção*, 2015, thread, fabric, rope, and wire, 80 x 123 x 14 in., acquired in 2015

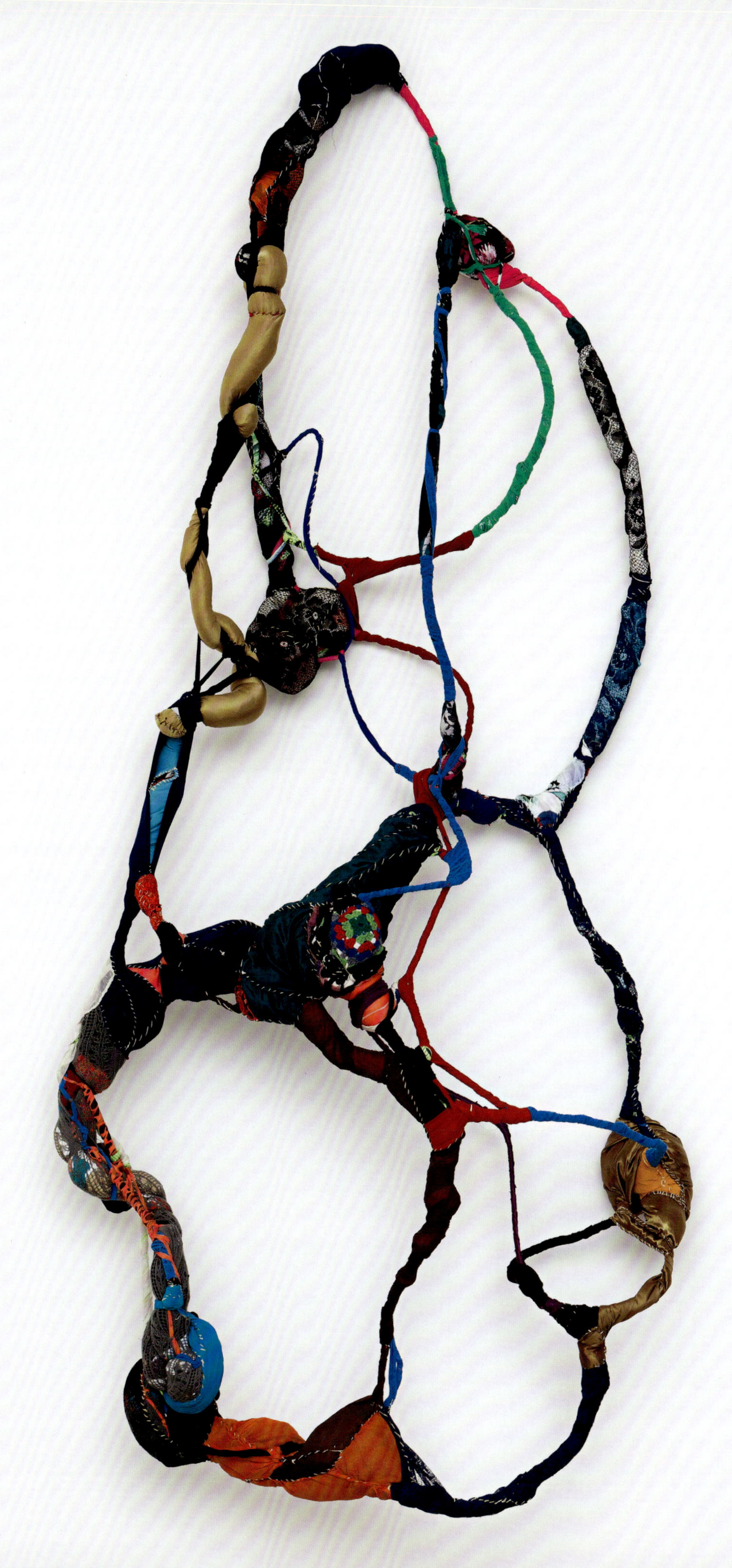

Tim Rollins: Are the works a metaphor for the relation between the individual and the crowd?

Felix Gonzalez-Torres: Perhaps between public and private, between personal and social, between the fear of loss and the joy of loving, of growing, of changing, of always becoming more, of losing oneself slowly and then being replenished all over again from scratch. I need the viewer, I need the public interaction. Without a public these works are nothing, nothing. I need the public to complete the work. I ask the public to help me, to take responsibility, to become part of my work, to join in. I tend to think of myself as a theater director who is trying to convey some ideas by reinterpreting the notion of the division of roles: author, public, and director. Your question is more puzzling to me than I had previously thought because, yes, an individual piece of paper from one of the stacks does not constitute the "piece" itself, but in fact it is a piece. At the same time, the sum of many pieces of the identical paper is the piece, but not really because there is no piece—only an ideal height of endless copies. As you know, these stacks are made up of endless copies or mass-produced prints. Yet each piece of paper gathers new meaning, to a certain extent, from its final destination, which depends on the person who takes it.

TR: You are a political person yet you're very concerned with form and you're not apologetic about it.

FGT: I love formal issues. Actually they have a very specific meaning. Forms gather meaning from the historical moment. The minimalist exercise of the object being very pure and very clean is only one way to deal with form. Carl Andre said, "My sculptures are masses and their subject is matter." But after twenty years of feminist discourse and feminist theory we have come to realize that "just looking" is not just looking but that looking is invested with identity: gender, socioeconomic status, race, sexual orientation... Looking is invested with lots of other texts.

Minimalist sculptures were never really primary structures, they were structures that were embedded with a multiplicity of meanings. Every time a viewer comes into the room these objects became something else. For me they were a coffee table, a laundry bag, a laundry box, whatever. So I think that saying that these objects are only about masses is like saying that aesthetics are not about politics. Ask a few simple questions to define aesthetics: whose aesthetics? at what historical time? under what circumstances? for what purposes? and who is deciding quality, etc? Then you realize suddenly and very quickly that aesthetic choices are politics. Believe it or not I am a big sucker for formal issues, and, yes, someone like me — the "other" — can indeed deal with formal issues. This is not a white-men-only terrain, sorry boys.

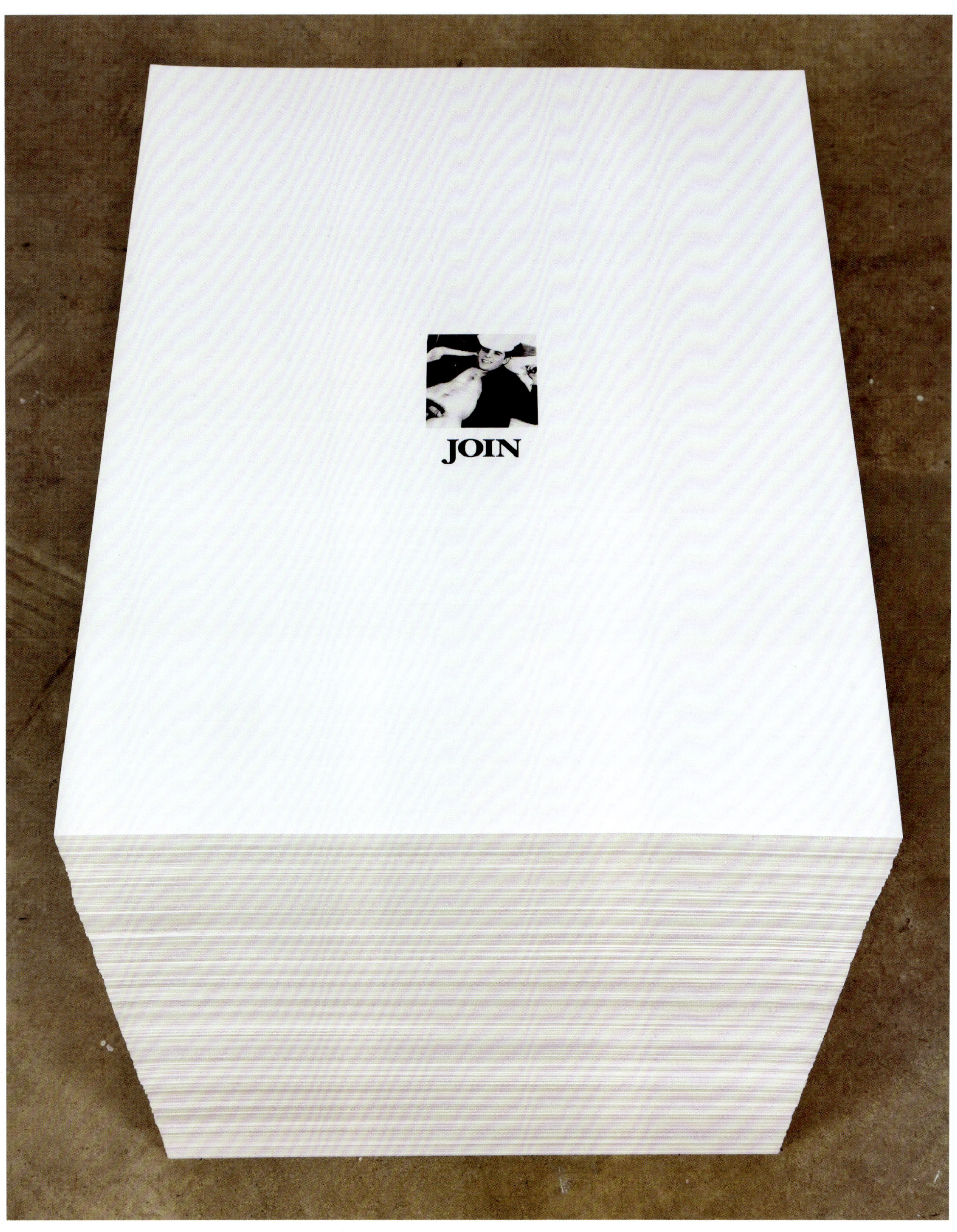

Felix Gonzalez-Torres in conjunction with Michael Jenkins
"Untitled" (Join), 1990, print on paper, endless copies, 36 inches at ideal height x 28 13/16 x 22 7/16 inches (original paper size)

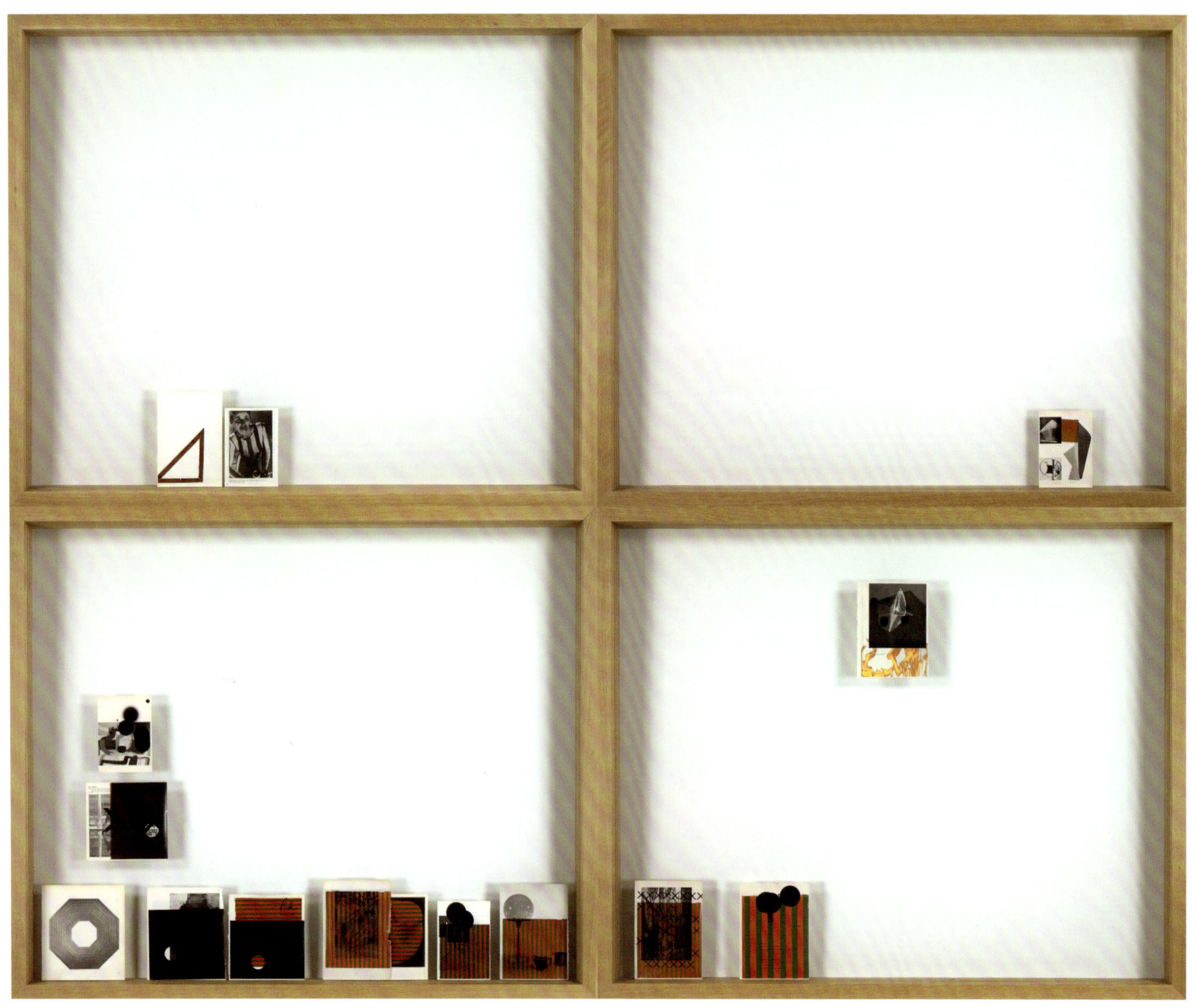

Untitled, 2005, four parts, Epson DURABrite on book pages in Plexiglas and oak frame, overall 102 x 125 1/4 x 3 1/2 in. (259 x 319 x 9 cm), acquired in 2005

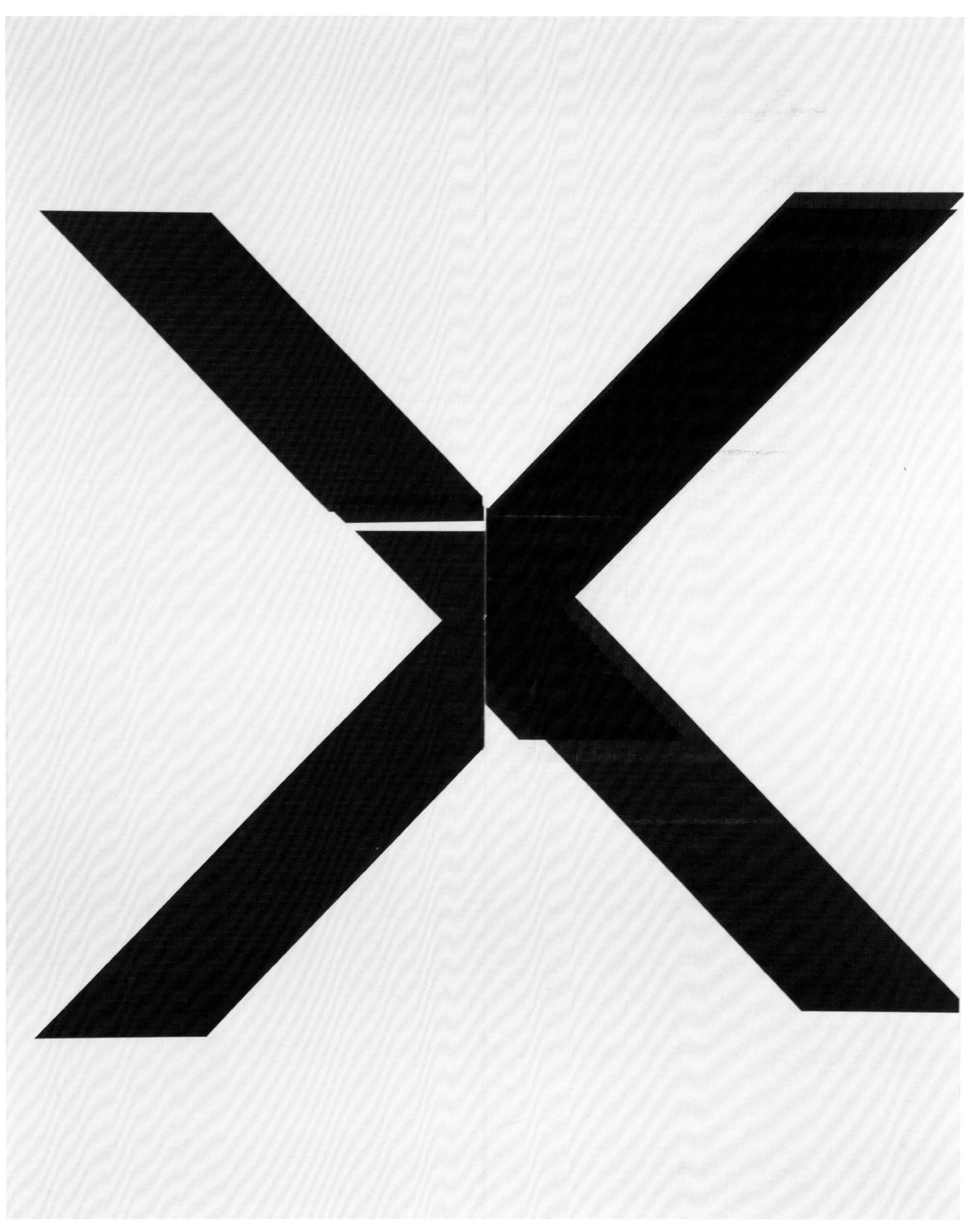

Untitled, 2007, Epson UltraChrome inkjet on linen, 84 1/4 x 69 in. (214 x 175.3 cm), acquired in 2007

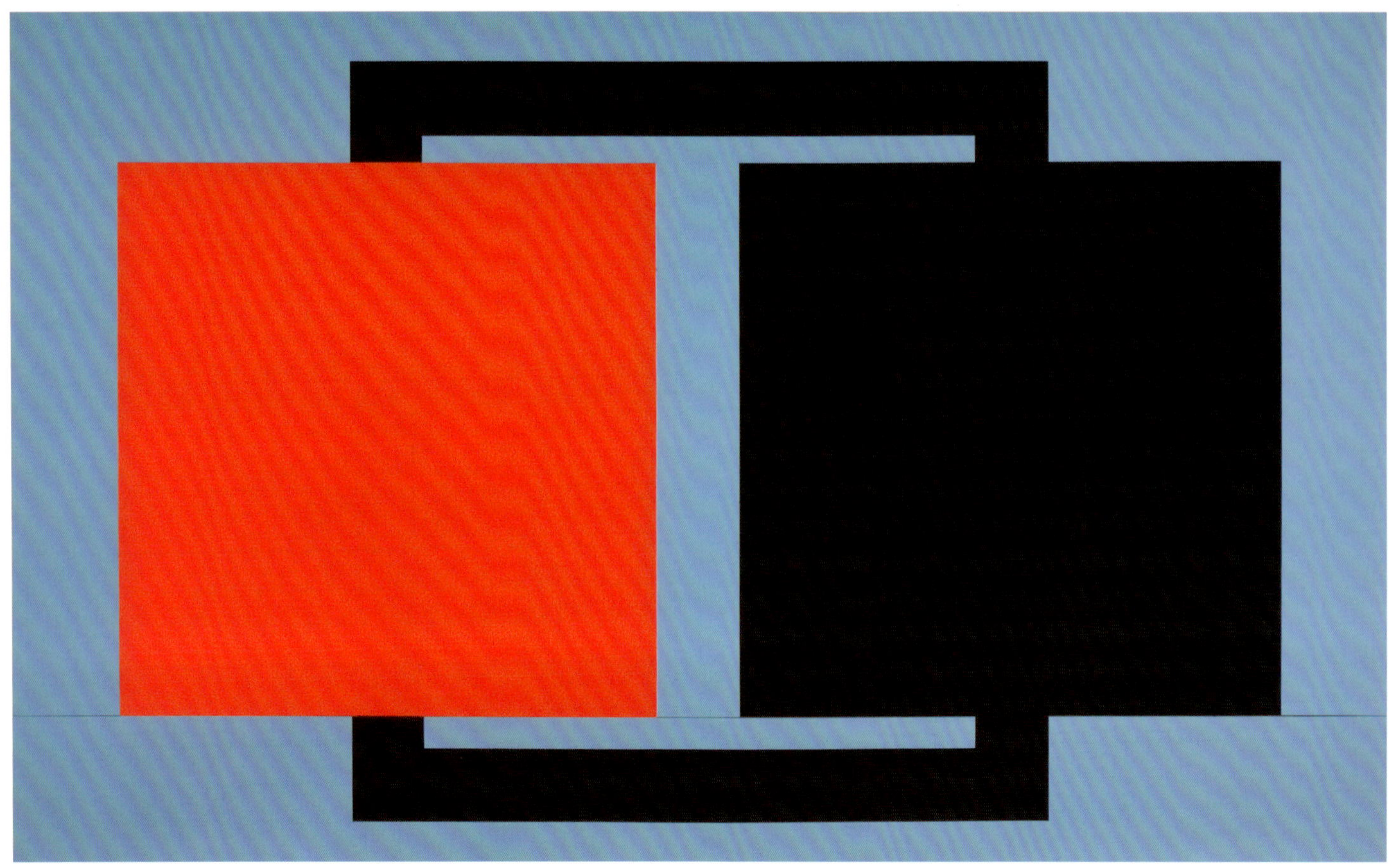

NOTES ON THE PAINTINGS, 1982

1. These are paintings of prisons, cells, and walls.

2. Here, the idealist square becomes the prison. Geometry is revealed as confinement.

3. The cell is a reminder of the apartment house, the hospital bed, the school desk
    — the isolated endpoints of industrial structure.

4. The paintings are a critique of idealist Modernism. In the "color field" is placed a jail.
    The misty space of Rothko is walled up.

5. Underground conduits connect the units. "Vital fluids" flow in and out.

6. The "stucco-texture" is a reminiscence of motel ceilings.

7. The Day-Glo paint is a signifier of "low budget mysticism." It is the afterglow of radiation.

—Peter Halley

Two Cells with Circulating Conduit, 1988, Roll-A-Tex, Day-Glo acrylic, acrylic on canvas, 81 x 134 in. (205.7 x 340.4 cm), acquired in 1988

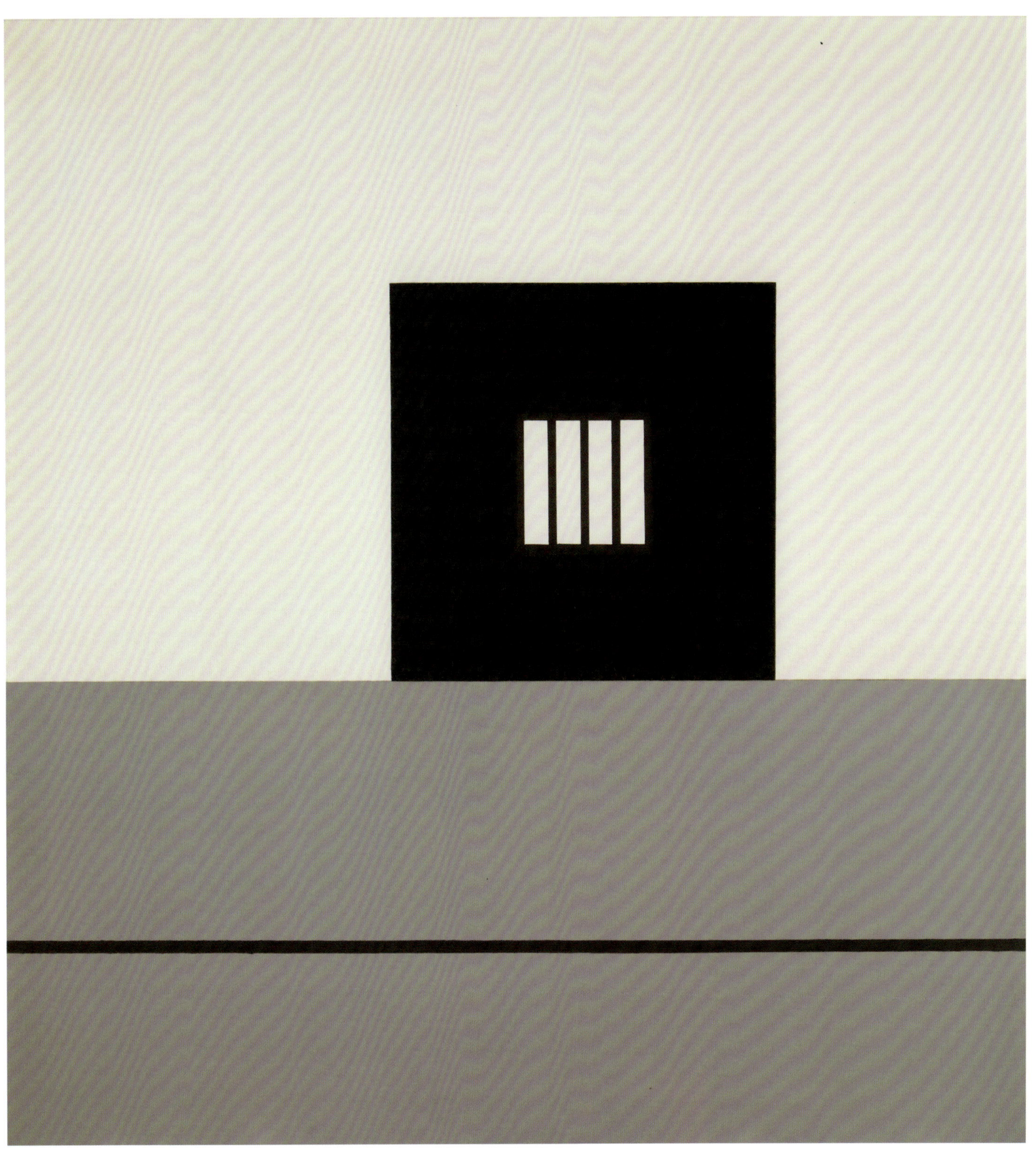

Prison with Underground Conduit, 1983, acrylic and Roll-A-Tex on canvas, 68 x 65 in. (172.7 x 165.1 cm), acquired in 1987

Sons of Watts, 2022, acrylic, enamel, metal leaf, and CDs on acrylic and wood, 102 1/2 x 78 x 39 inches (260.4 x 198.1 x 99.1 cm), acquired in 2022

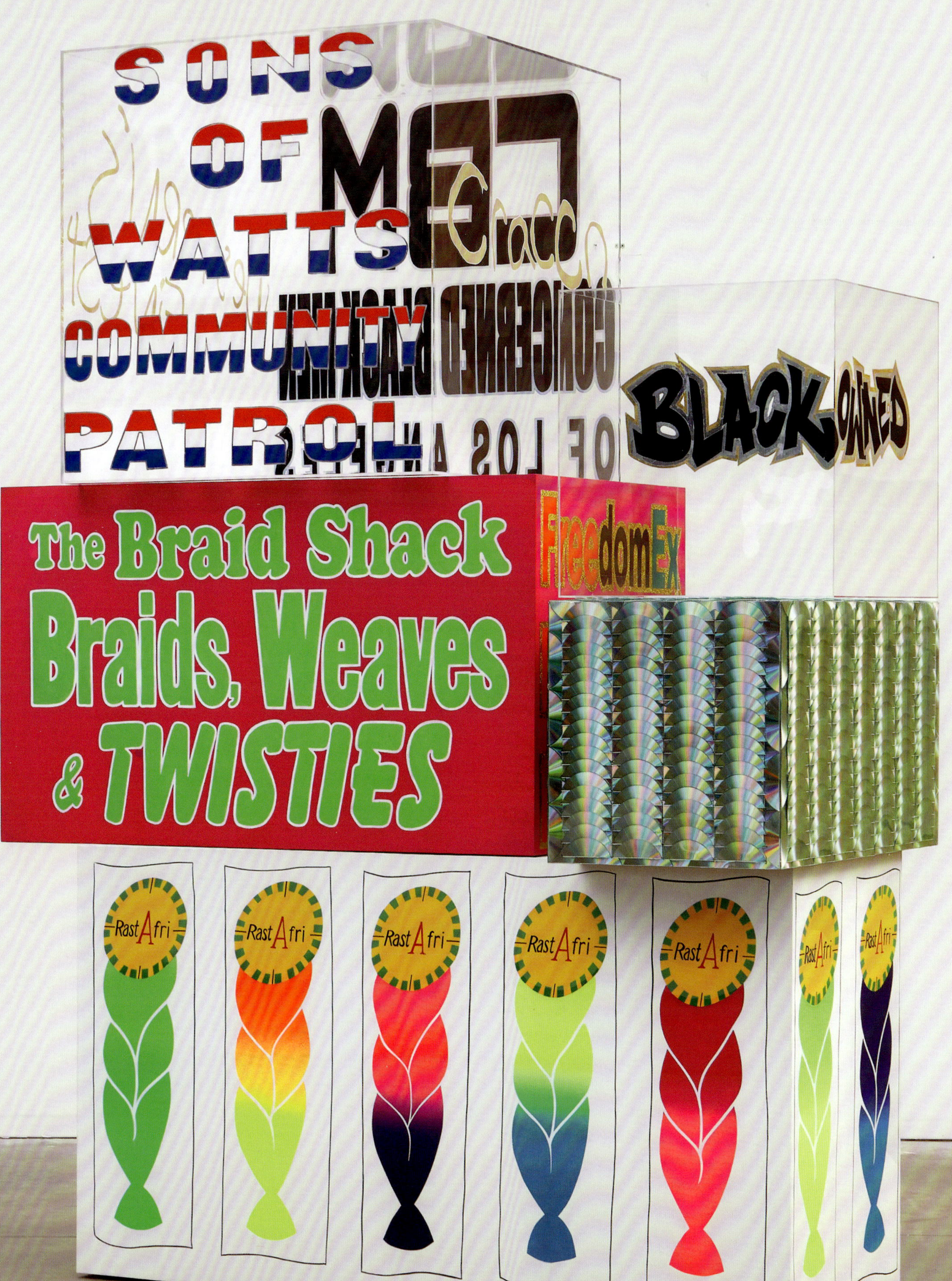
SONS OF WATTS
OF MEN
CBM
Gracc
CONCERNED BLACK MEN
COMMUNITY
PATROL
OF LOS ANGELES
BLACK OWNED
The Braid Shack
Braids, Weaves
& TWISTIES
FreedomEx
RastAfri
RastAfri
RastAfri
RastAfri
RastAfri
RastAfri
RastAfri

Esquire (or John Henry), 1990, steel, rock, human hair, and tin, 45 x 9 x 5 in. (114.3 x 22 x 13 cm), acquired in 1991

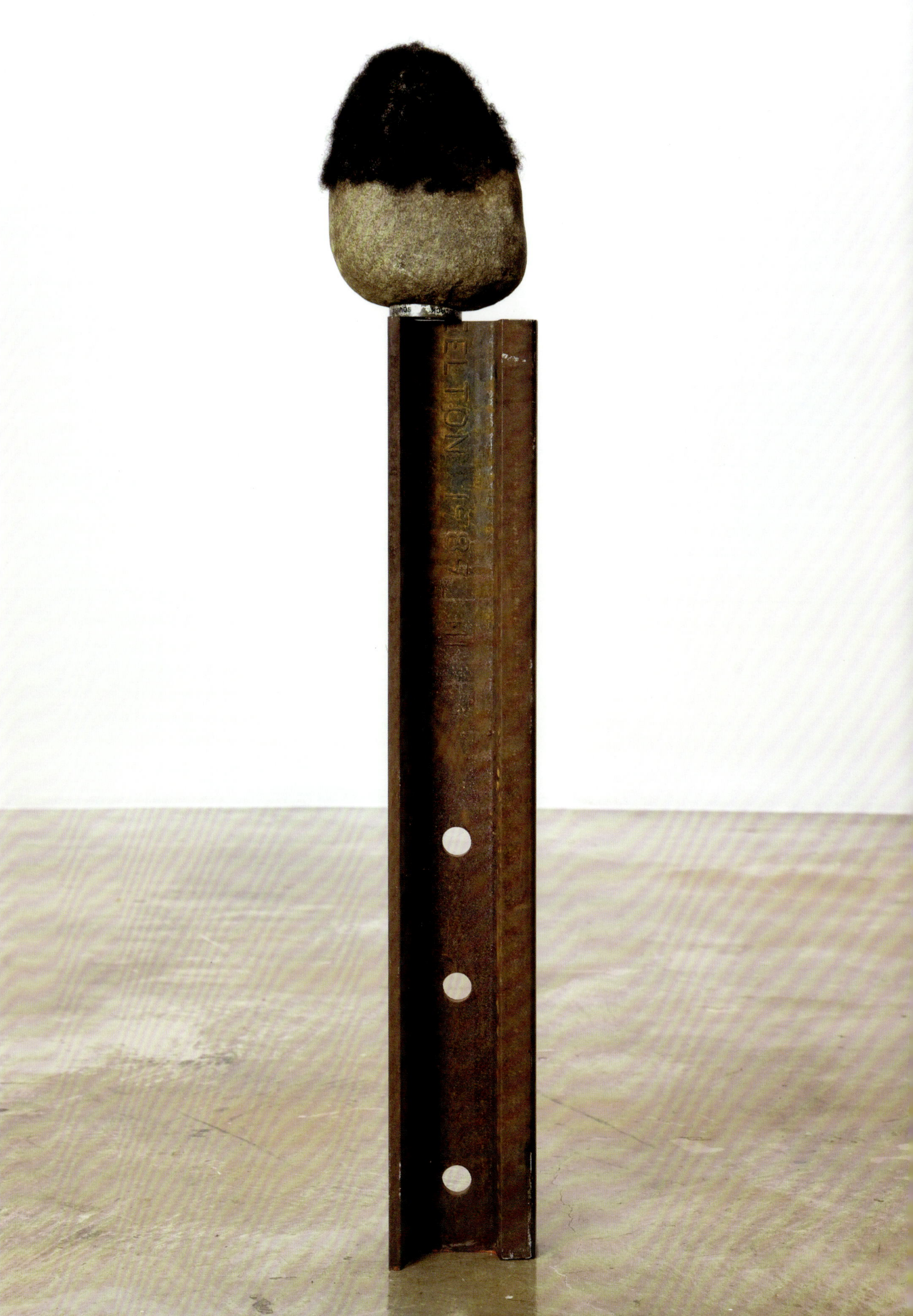

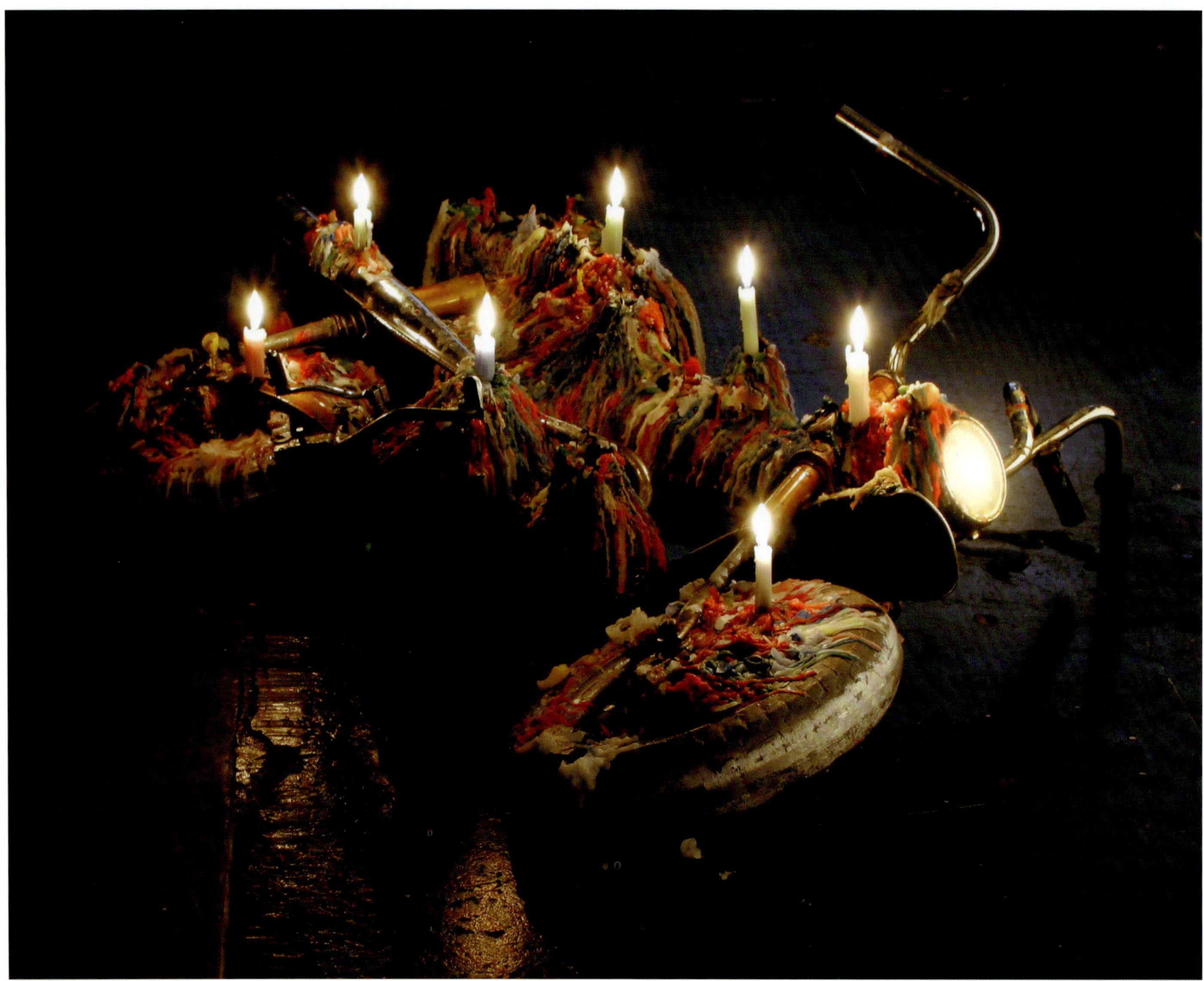

In *Honda*, the candles are a way of keeping the static sculpture alive, of not giving in to the monument but somehow maintaining the creative process, of keeping it all fluid, rolling, open. By handing over the essential creative gesture—whoever places the candles really makes the piece—I hoped to throw it open; there is no particular end and no particular destination. At the same time, by virtue of the meaning and function of those materials, the piece inevitably becomes a strange kind of monument; all that molten wax, all that fluidity, hardens into the floor and locks the moment in time, locks the bike in place, buries it. The flames are very much alive; but strangely, the more life there is to the flame, the more dead the bike becomes.

We live on I-95, the undulating ribbon of connectivity that forms the mangled spine of our disproportioned city. We could read the highway signs here as gargantuan haiku of officialdom, spanning the lanes with their hard, modernist ambition—black text on color field—floating abstract messages against a relentless shimmering sky. Strange emblems of control, rude and confrontational.

Perhaps surprisingly, I see *Right* as a weirdly positive piece. Its physicality is of the order of bombastic sculpture, yet materially it is all skin and text and glow. It only stands because it is bent and twisted. Its inherent strength is pulled from its apparent failure; a fumbled origami, it becomes strong in collapse.

—Mark Handforth

Honda, 2002, metal, aluminum, and candles, 25 3/8 x 56 1/4 x 45 1/8 in. (64.4 x 142.9 x 114.6 cm), acquired in 2003
Opposite page: *Right*, 2005, aluminum and vinyl, 116 x 148 x 82 in. (294.7 x 376 x 208.3 cm), acquired in 2006

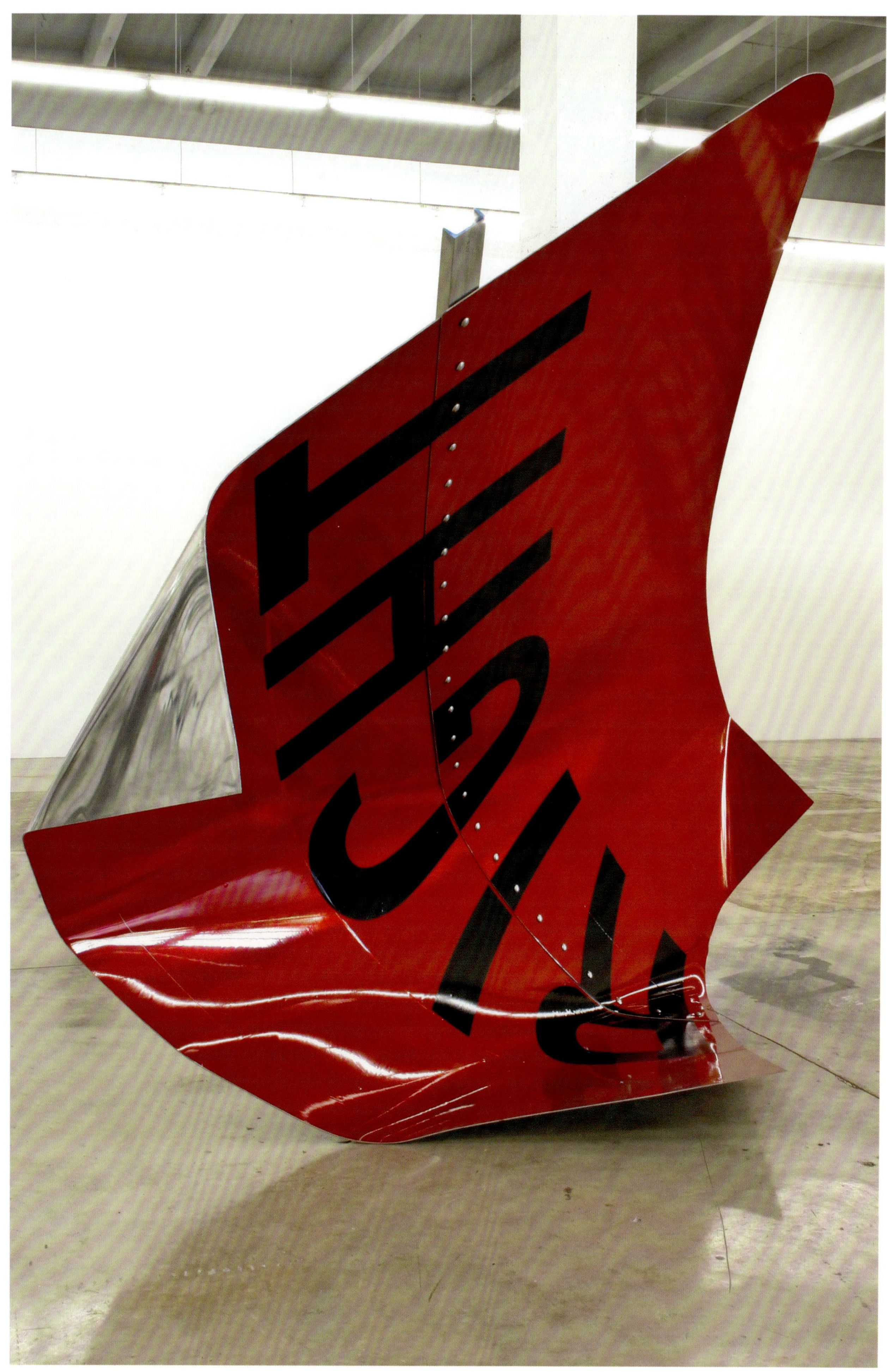

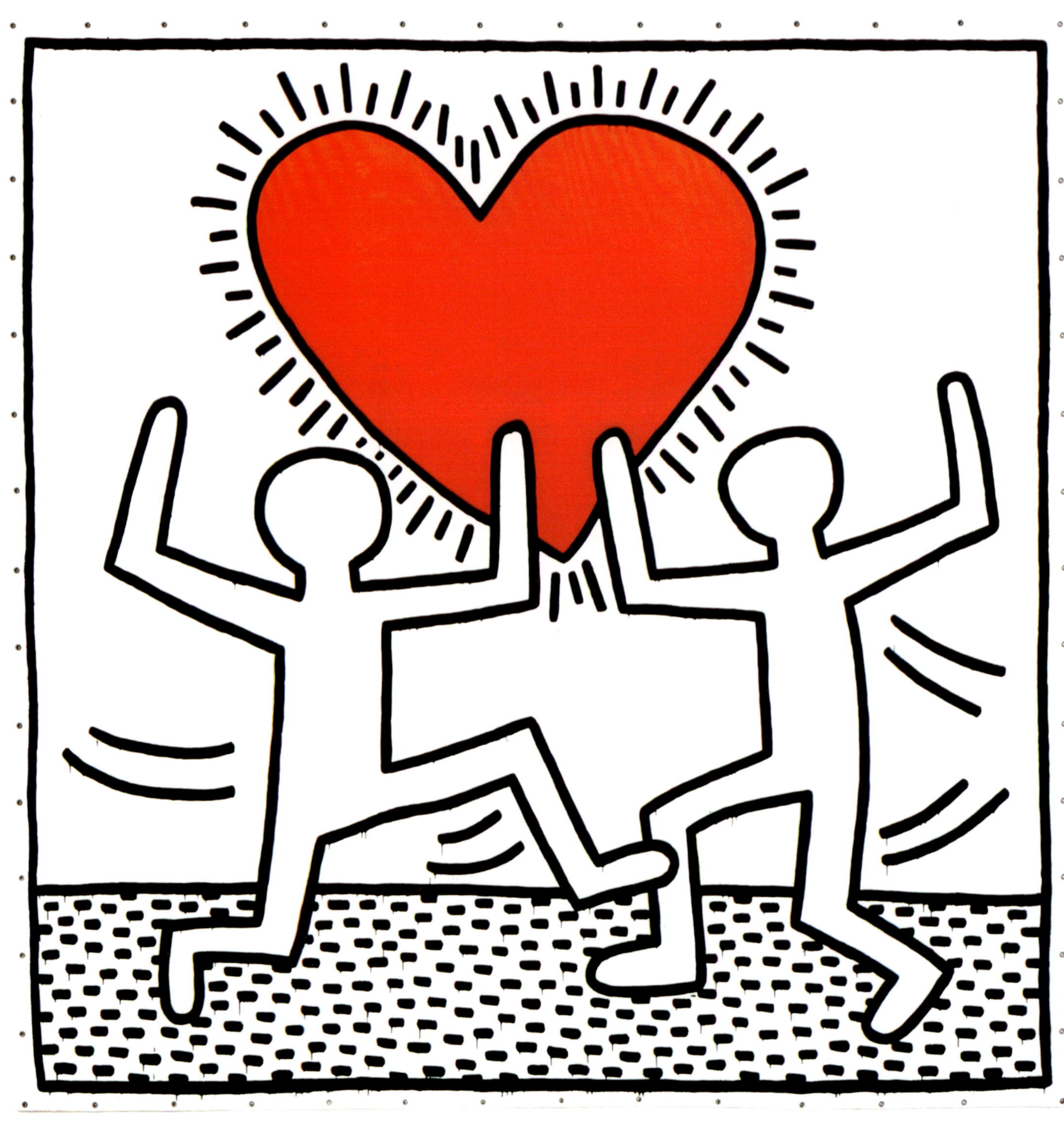

Untitled, 1982, acrylic on vinyl tarpaulin, 180 x 180 in. (4570 x 4570 cm), acquired in 1982
Opposite page: *Statue of Liberty* (In collaboration with LA II), 1982, acrylic and enamel on fiberglass with light bulb, 95 x 35 x 14 in. (241.3 x 88.9 x 35.6 cm), acquired in 1982

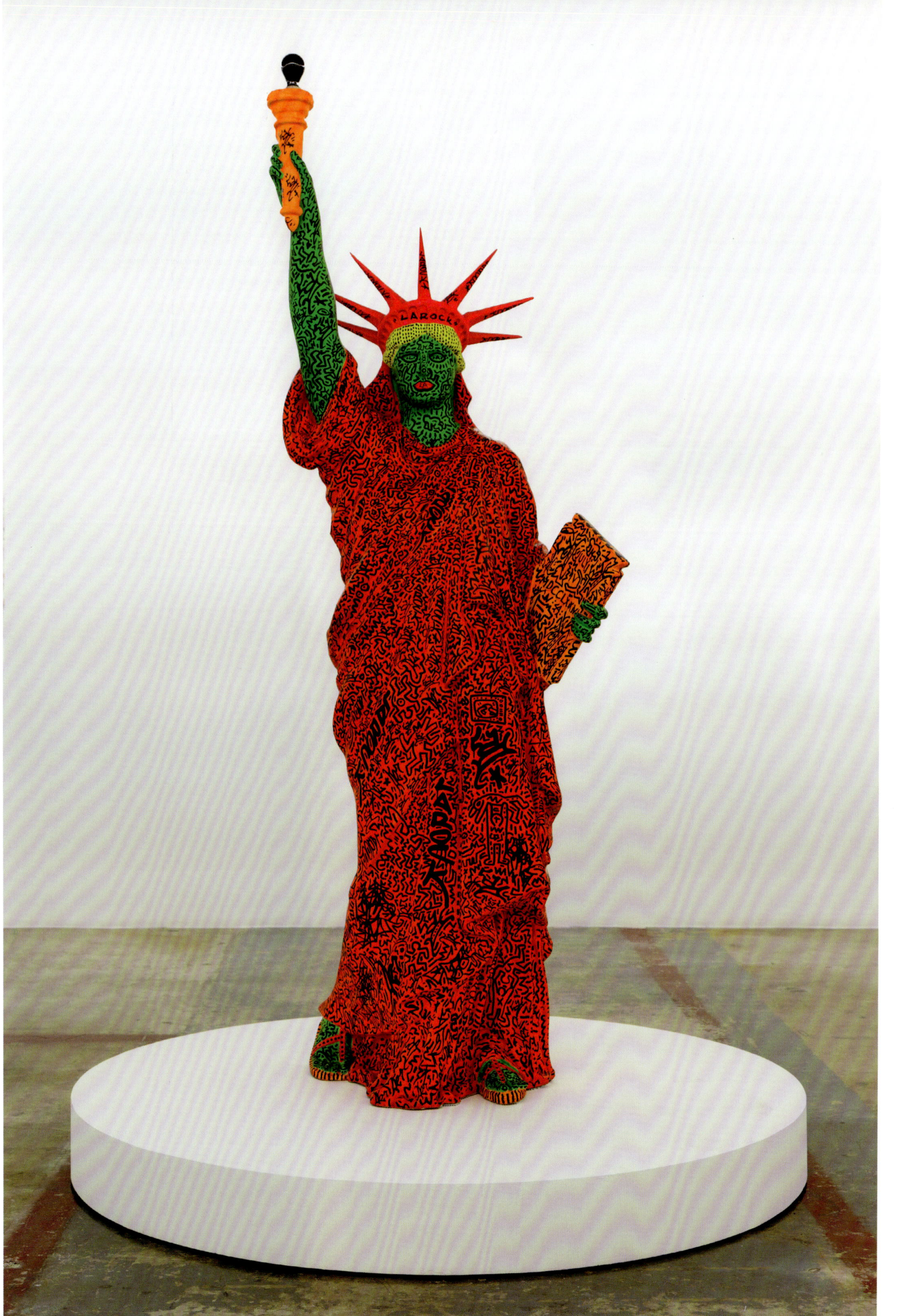

20 DRAWINGS
OCT. 3, 1989 K. Haring
⊕

BÉBERT, ROTTERDAM

20 DRAWINGS
OCT. 3, 1989

These drawings were created one afternoon in October in my studio in New York City. As usual, they were created instantaneously, without a pre-determined plan or concept. The materials were very simple — handmade Dutch linen paper, brush, and Sumi inks which I got in Japan.

All the drawings generate from what happens in the first drawing. I just "let" it happen. Each drawing builds on the previous drawings and advances the "story". It's very difficult (and against the basic principal of their existence) to explain the "meaning" of my drawings. In this case, however, there may be a clue. During the first 2 hours or so I was listening to Marvin Gaye's classic album "What's Going On?" over and over. In it, pessimistly he questions the future of the planet. The remaining time was spent listening to Bob Marley's songs of oppression and peoples' struggle for freedom. Sometimes music is a "backround" for drawing, but sometimes it becomes an essential part of the creation of the work.

These drawings are about the Earth we inherited and the dismal task of trying to save it — against all odds.

K. Haring JAN. 27-1990 N.Y.C.

This book is dedicated to the memory of Steve Rubell — not because of the content, but because these drawings were created with the same energy and intensity with which he lived his life.

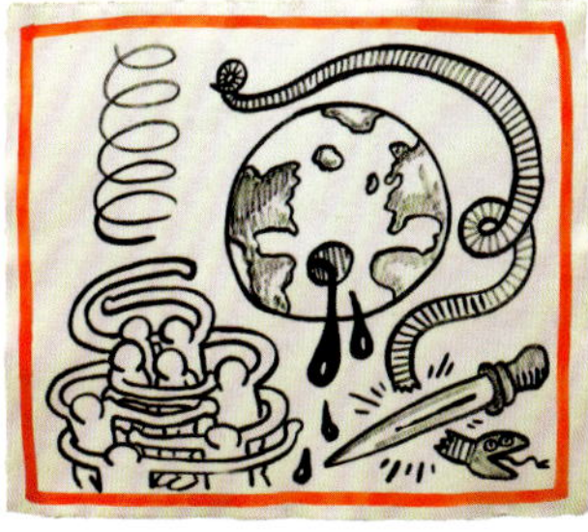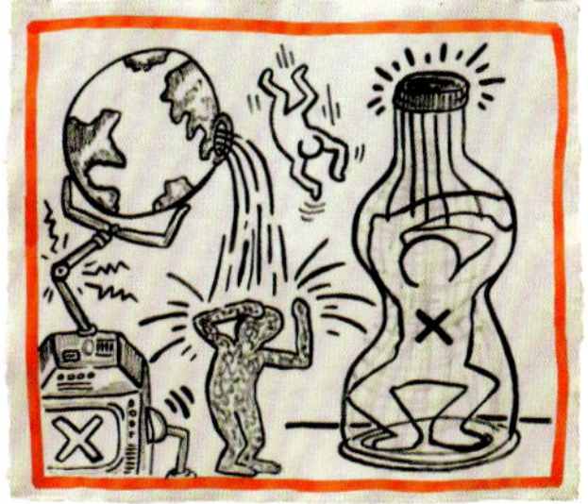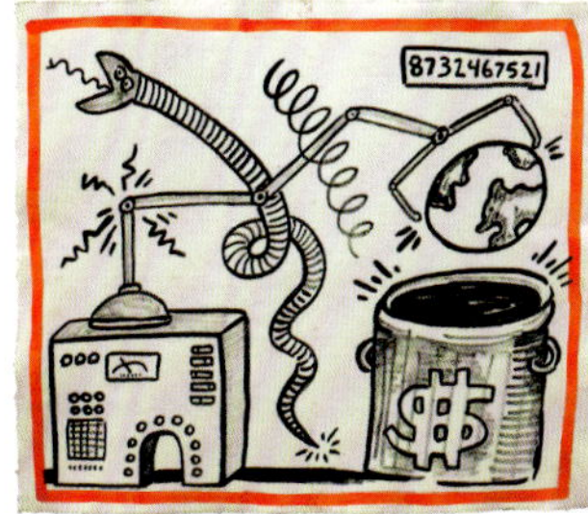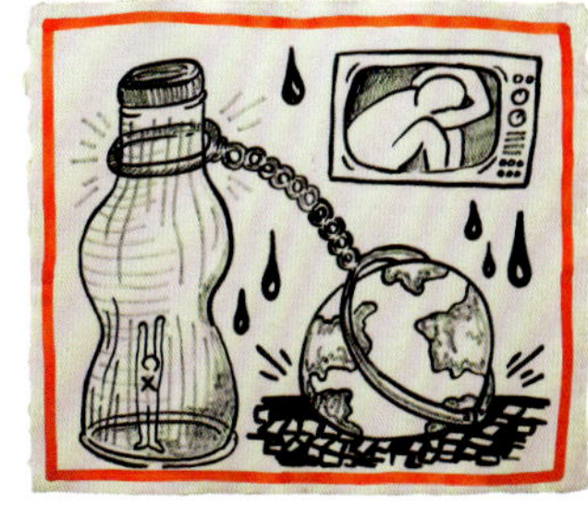
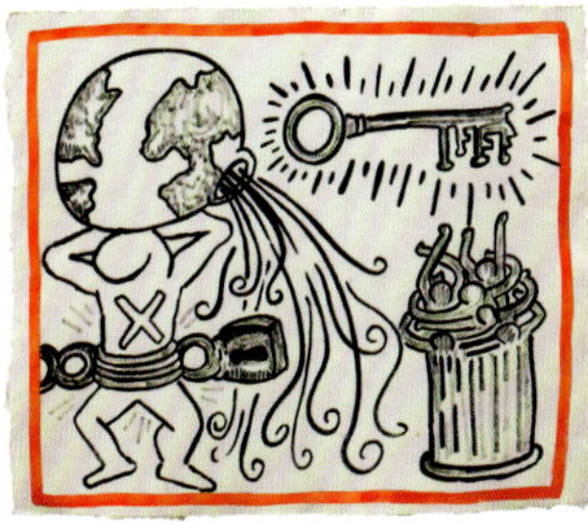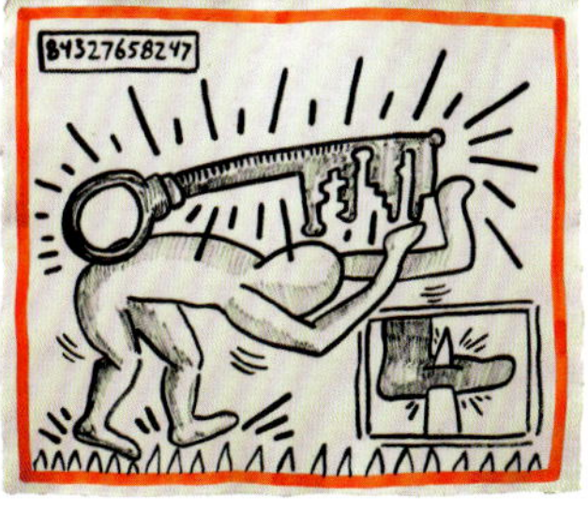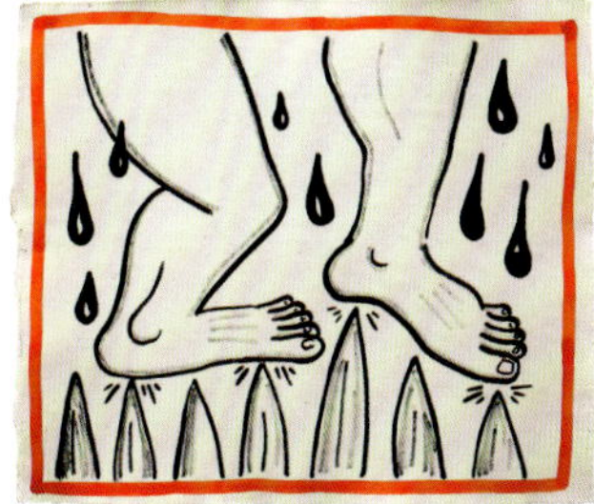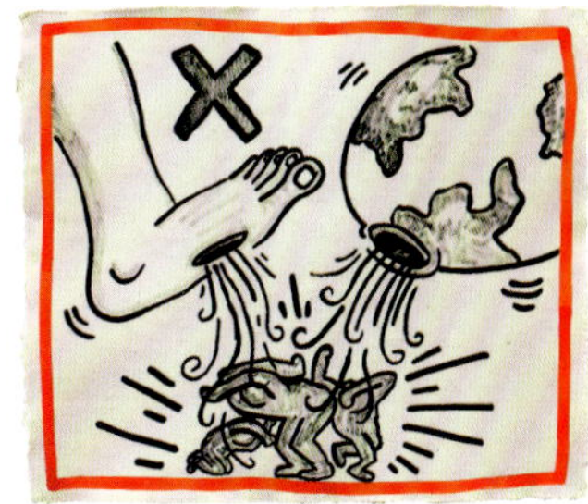
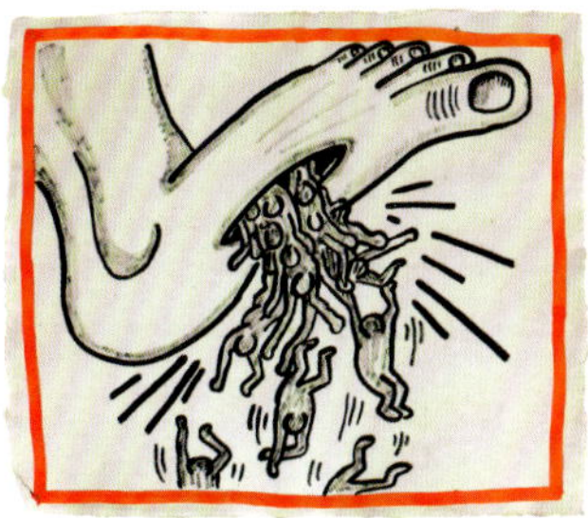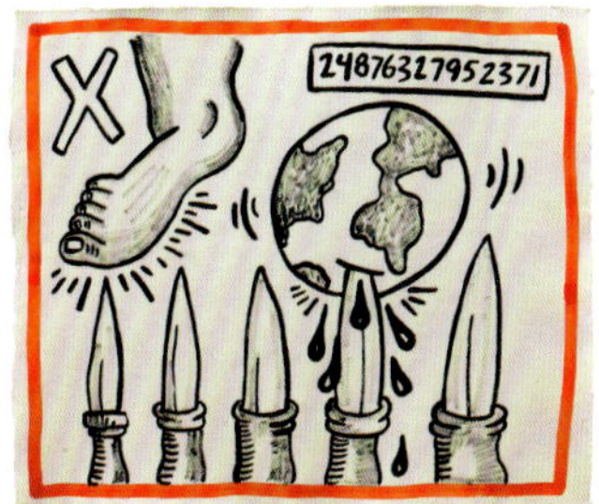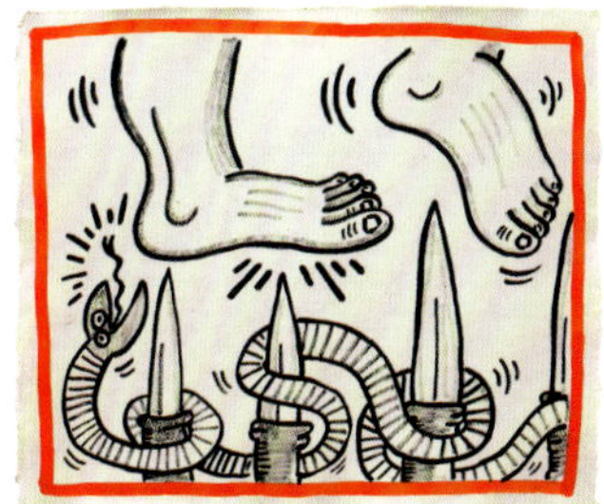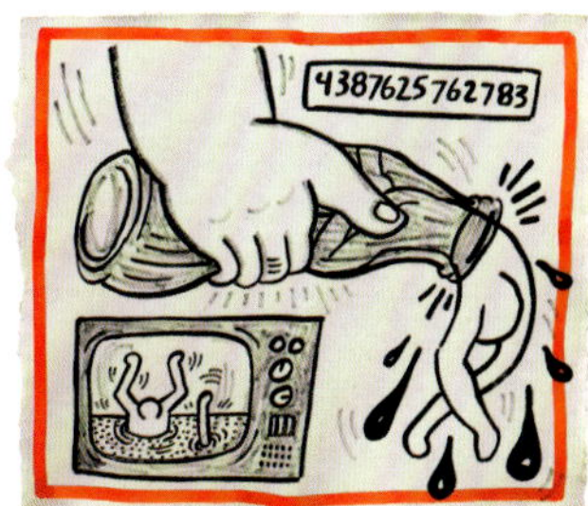
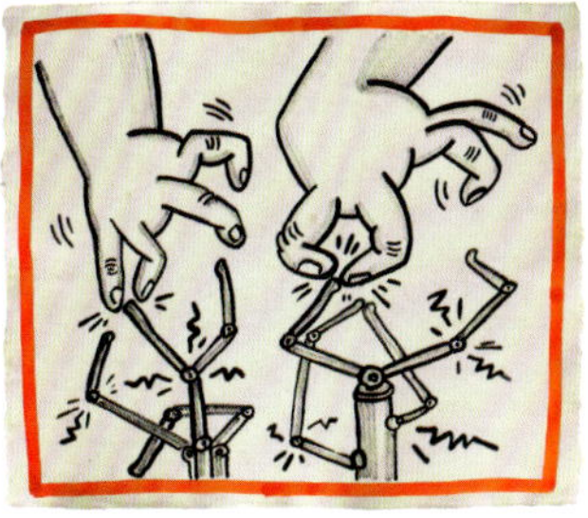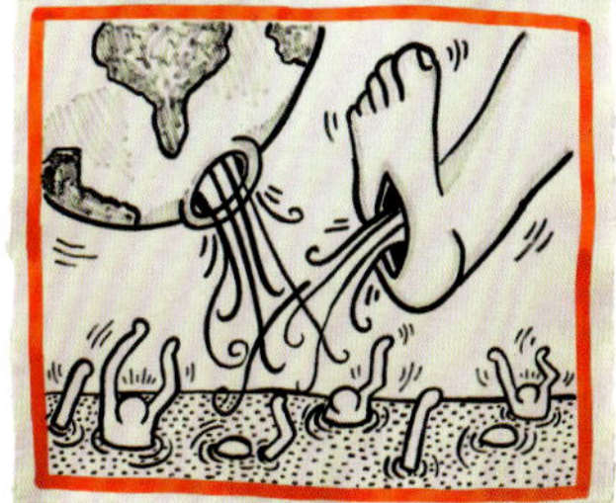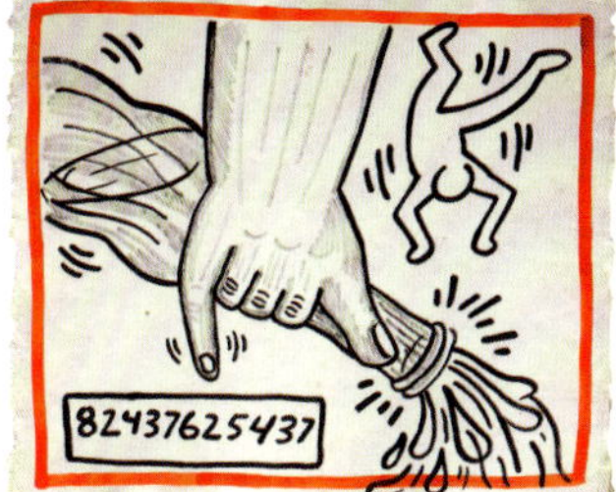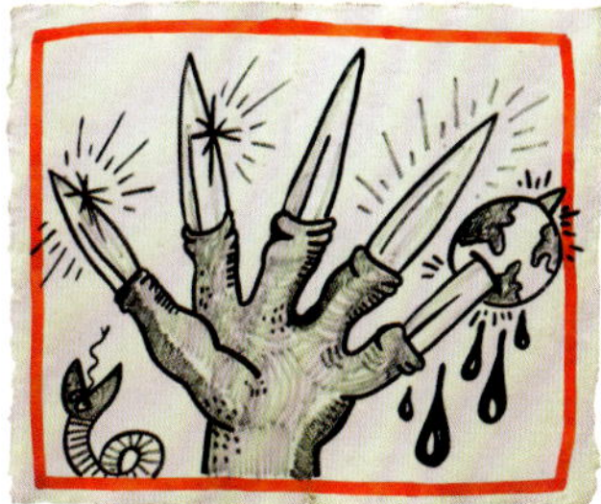
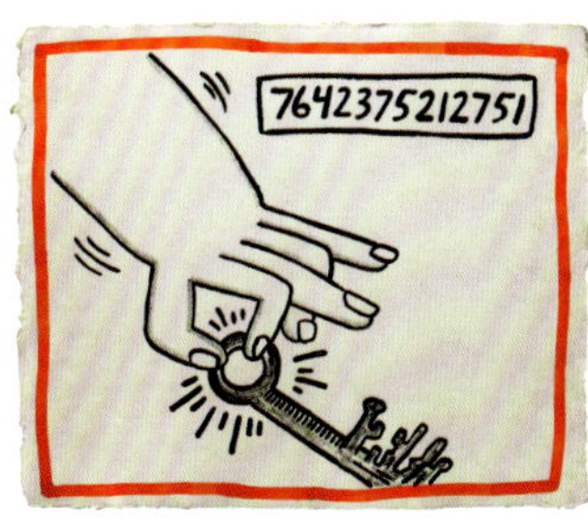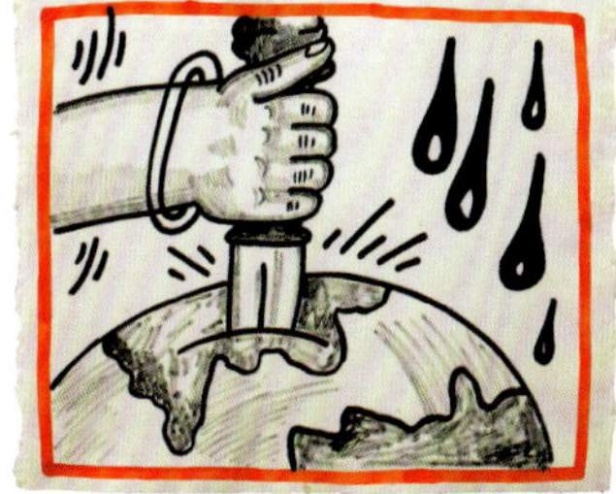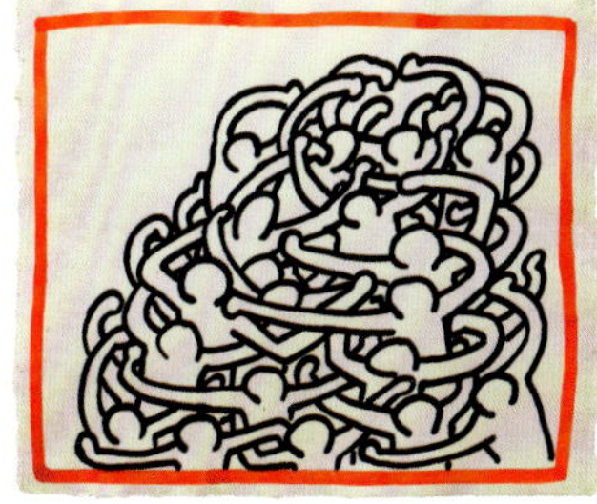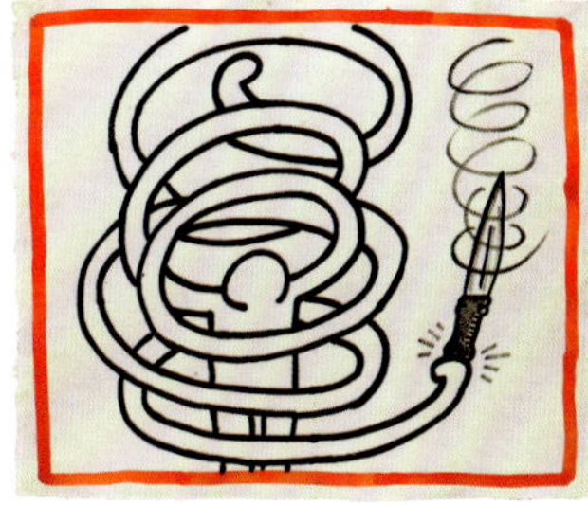

Against All Odds, 1989, sumi ink and gouache on handmade linen paper, twenty sheets, each 25 x 30 in. (63.5 x 76 cm), acquired in 1989

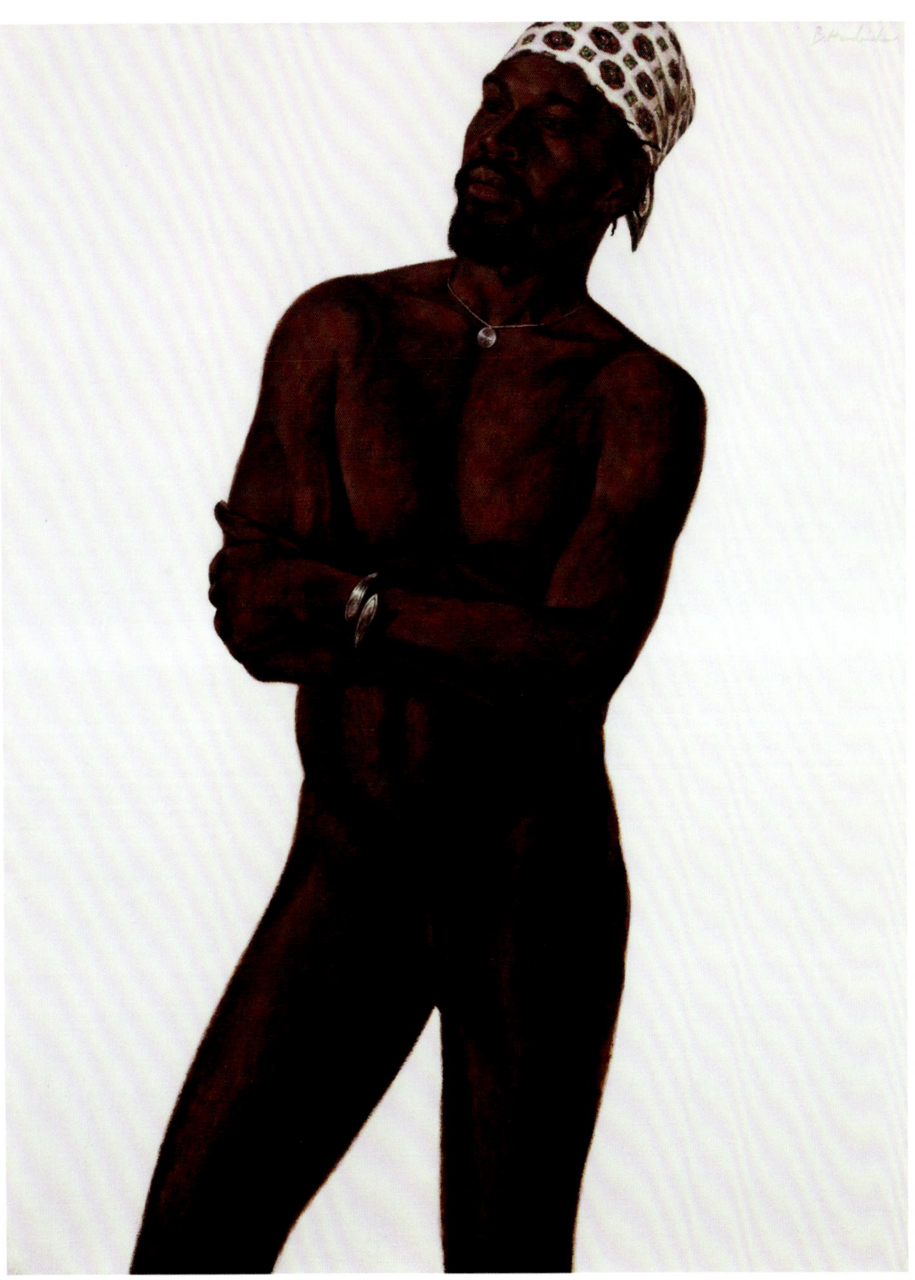

When I first met Eddie, he was a model for local art classes and arts organizations. Upon hiring him, I learned he was a jack-of-all-trades in addition to being a Connecticut State relay champion. I'm not sure this fact was known by the group of young men he was drinking and smoking with one Saturday evening. They challenged him to a race after their testosterone and booze made them push Eddie's buttons. The summer sun was giving off its last light of the day when they squared off at the starting line in the valley of the long dirt drive. When "Go!" was shouted, the four racers could be heard making their way up the dusty road. One of the racers fell midway through the sprint and was left in a cloud of dust as the remaining three made their way to the finish line at the top of the hill. Eddie was well out in front and very much over the finish line when James and Bobbie finally crossed the line. Eddie was there waiting and laughing at them when they staggered to the end. Bobbie didn't take losing well, whereupon calling Eddie a "jive niggah," Eddie's retort was "I may be a jive niggah, but I can beat you slow motherfuckers any day of the week and twice on Sundays!"

Fast Eddie Jive Niggah, 1975, oil and acrylic on linen, 48 1/2 x 36 1/2 in. (123.2 x 92.7 cm), acquired in 2008

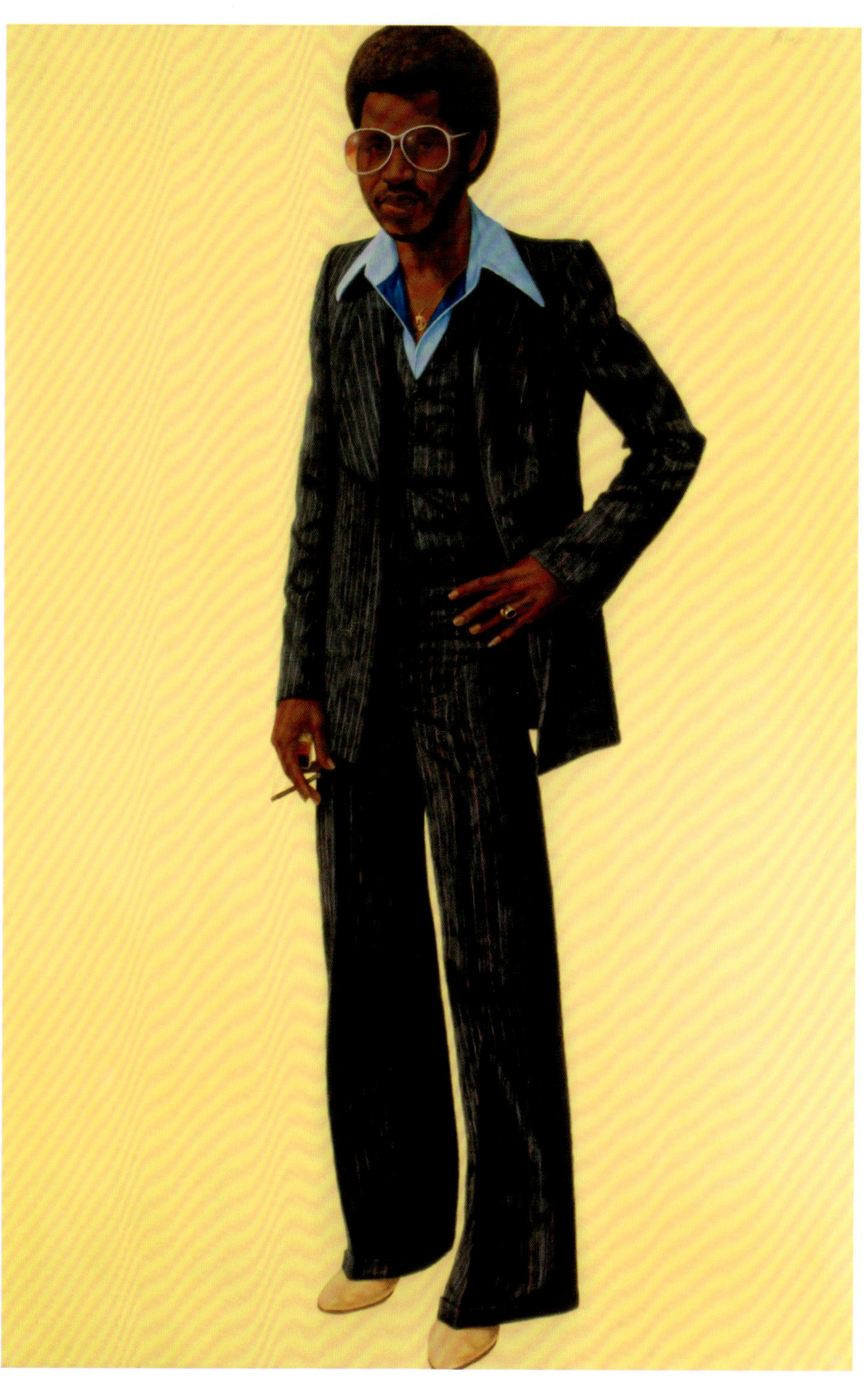

When I was in Paris, France, in 1978, there was a bevy of long, lean, suited French–African men on the streets of Pigalle wearing graceful, tailored, high-vented "vines" (a colloquial name for suits from my Philadelphia neighborhood).

Noir was the one of two portraits I crafted from photographs I took. The other painting is in the collection of the Yale University Art Gallery. It is a double portrait from 1978 titled *APB's (Afro-Parisian Brothers)*. *APB's* featured one of the male subjects (also the solo subject of *Noir*) in a plain fabric garment. This work, *Noir*, shows that same suited man in a blue pinstripe suit. All I can say is that the pinstriped pattern took a lot out of me. I avoided painting pinstripes for many years after.

—Barkley L. Hendricks

Noir, 1978, oil and acrylic on canvas, 72 x 48 in. (182.9 x 121.9 cm), acquired in 2008

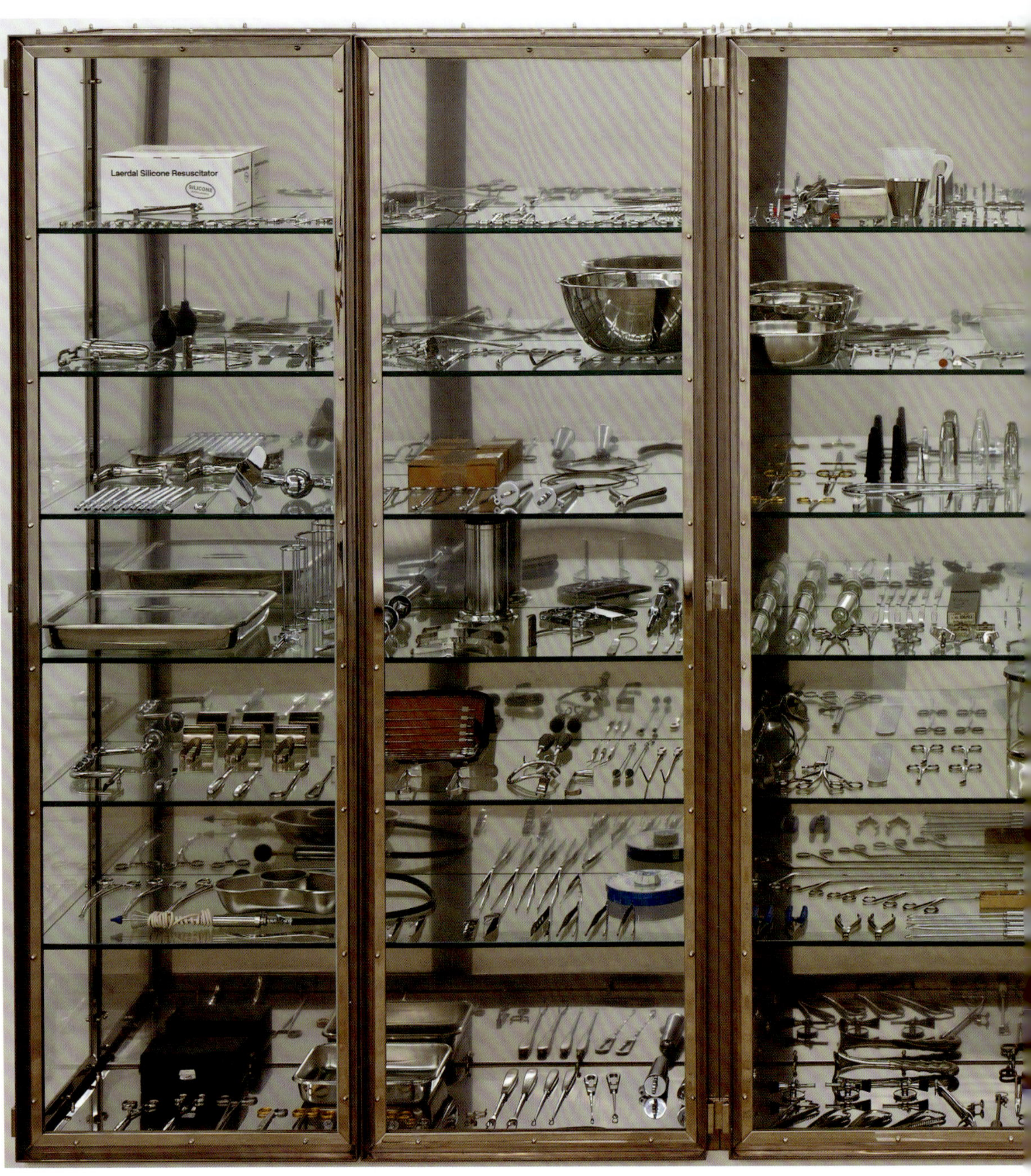

Mirta D'Argenzio: What is it about medical objects that you find most interesting?

Damien Hirst: I just think that they do everything that art is supposed to do. They are phenomenal objects because they have to have this confidence and this belief. They are the best quality. They are brilliantly designed, for all the right reasons, and they have got the greatest colours. Even test tubes are fantastic objects. They are like Shaker furniture, those Shaker designs, a great combination of aesthetics and function. All medical tools and surgical implements and all that kind of stuff, they are all designed with the same rigour as Shaker furniture.

MD'A: The associations tend to funnel inwards. But I take it that you would never want somebody looking at the image of medical objects arranged in your cabinets and thinking about death.

DH: I don't really think of them as death. Maybe I have kind of overdone it. I don't know, but I just keep finding something else medical that I can make art with. Do you remember *Dead Ringers*, that film? Have you seen that film, with the red clothing and the gloves and all those gynecological instruments that they made? I think I got my first idea to do them from that, those instrument cabinets, but I don't know. There is that funny thing of it being in an art gallery, of taking

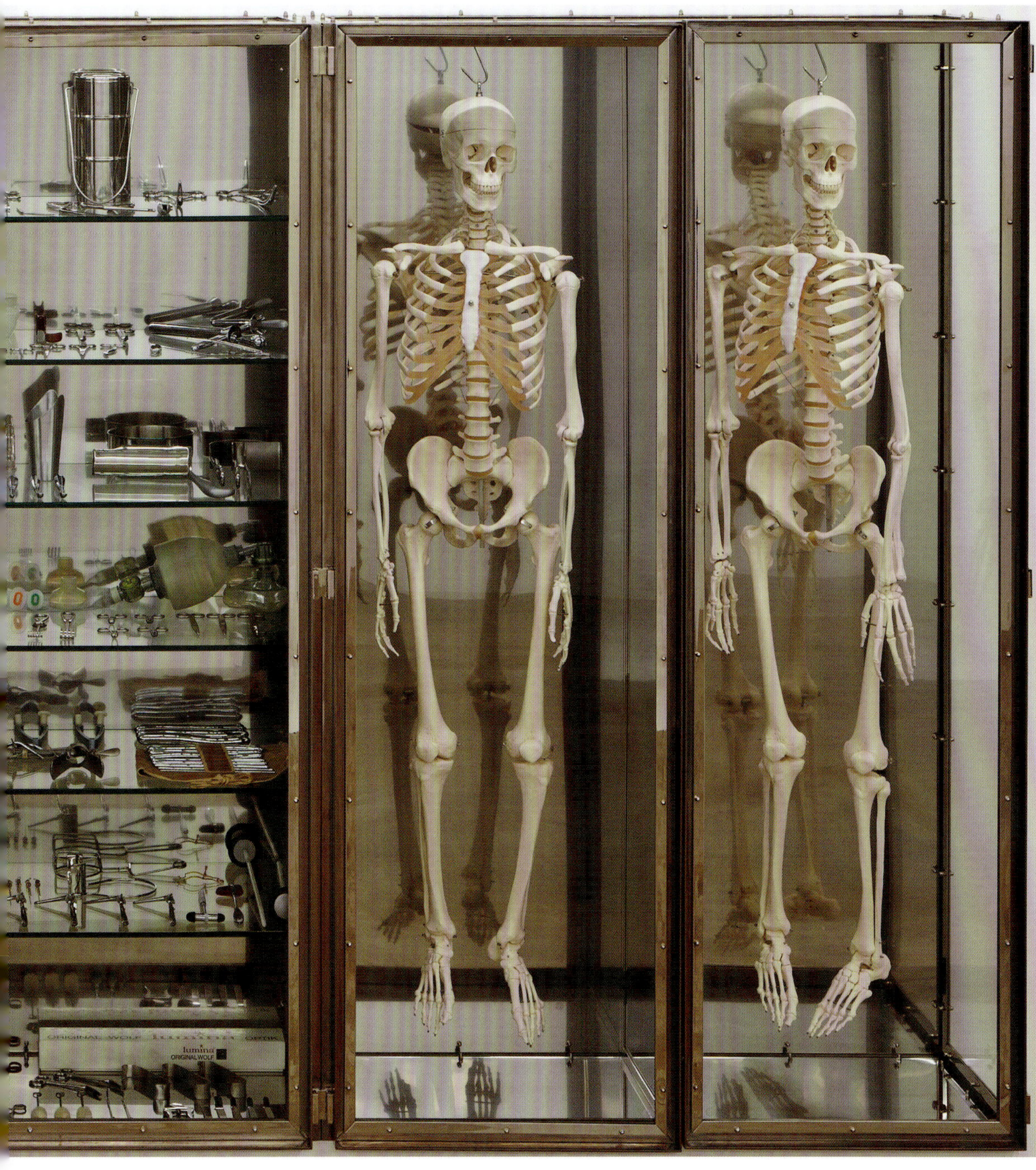

them and putting them in an art gallery. There is something just really sexy about them. You can't resist it. You see it and think "I am going to do that again." Those medical waste cabinets that I made, you just think that it is glorious trash. A syringe is a phenomenal thing; it is a brilliant object. I can definitely understand heroin addicts...

MD'A: You mean like in *Naked* (1994) and *Still* (1994)?

DH: It is almost like once you do one of those medical things, then you have to do them all because you have to get it out of your system. When I said I would probably stop doing the butterfly paintings and things like that, I don't think that I'll stop doing the medical stuff. It is kind of like a Morandi as well. It is something that you play with, the way that they all sit together with those amazing shapes, with all those personalities. I would rather arrange medical objects than do paintings I think, than do abstract paintings. Scissors are fantastic, especially medical scissors. All those different ones, and then the cross in it as well, always having that cross.

Dance Naked, 1997, stainless steel, glass, surgical equipment and, plastic skeletons, 77 x 149 x 19 in. (195.6 x 378.5 x 48.3 cm), acquired in 1998

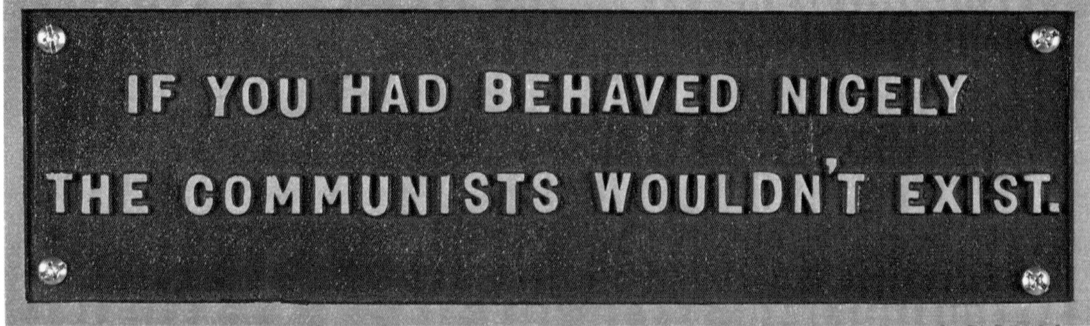

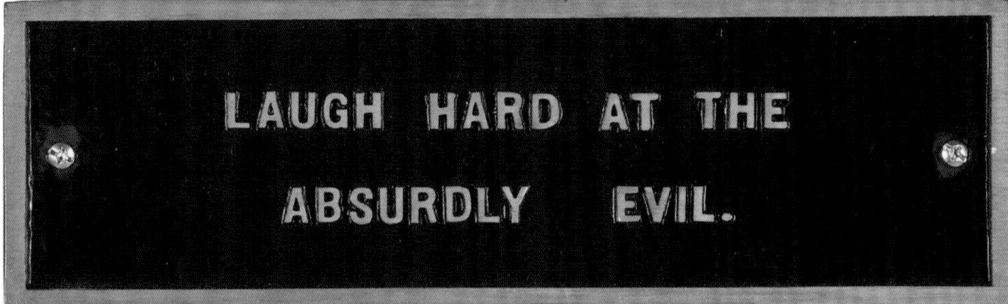

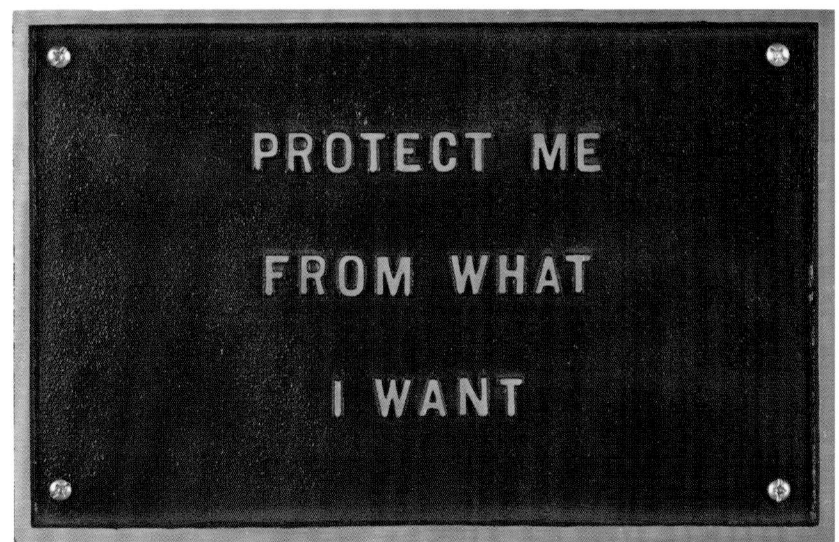

If You Had Behaved..., 1983-1985, aluminum plaque, 3 x 10 in. (7.6 x 25.4 cm), acquired in 1985
Laugh Hard at the..., 1983-1985, aluminum plaque, 3 x 10 in. (7.6 x 25.4 cm), acquired in 1985
Protect Me..., 1983-1985, aluminum plaque, "6 x 10 in. (15.2 x 25.4 cm), acquired in 1985

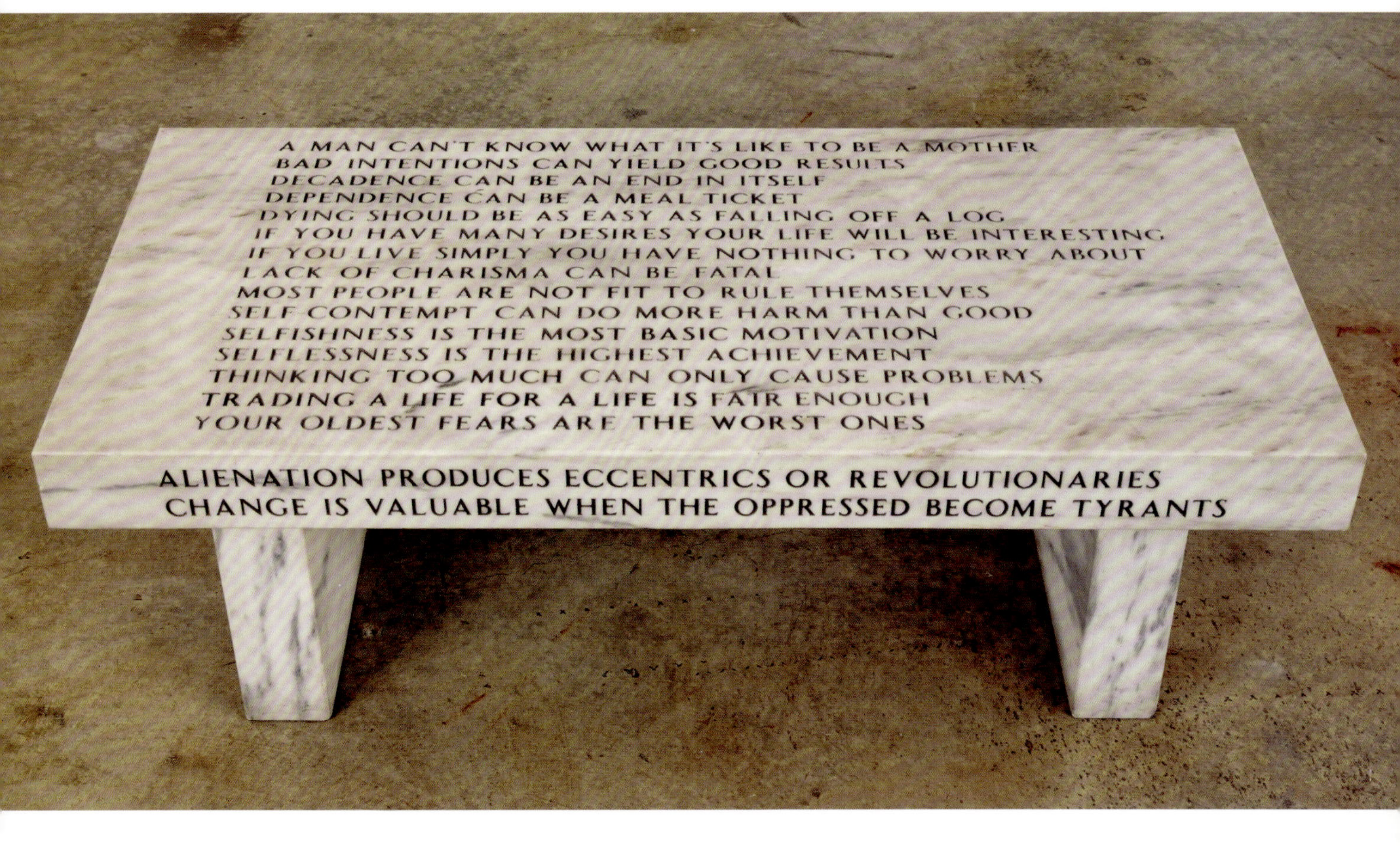

Truisms "A man can't know…", 1987, Danby Royal JH 399 marble, ed. 1/3, 17 1/4 x 54 x 24 7/8 in. (43.8 x 137.2 x 63.2 cm), acquired in 1988

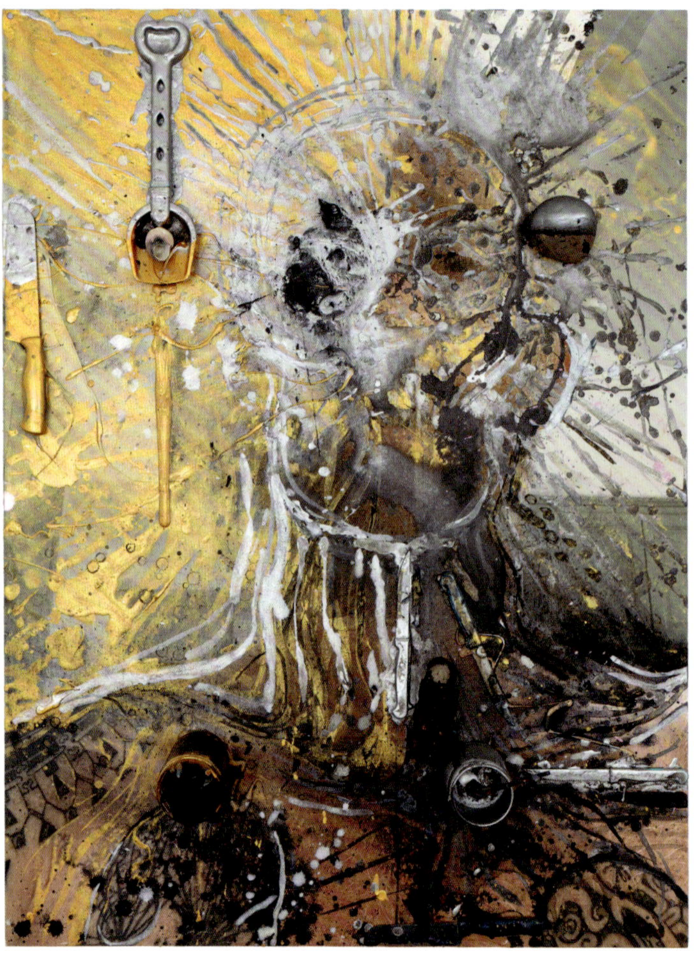

I'd probably been in L.A. a year and a half, two years maybe, when I met Don and Mera Rubell. I had the chance at that moment to reinvent myself artistically and as a person. I periodically go through periods where I lose everything in my life and I have to rebuild again—like a phoenix. In this case, I was taking all these European, archetypal, sculptural, historical touchstones, and I was fusing them into this new experience of being in L.A. and being under this different sense of space and pressure and relationship to history. It was almost like I could play with those ideas, those sculptural notions, with a renewed energy and a renewed focus.

I believe looking at them now—and you have to remember I haven't seen most of these in more than 15 years—I think that I was also beginning to express what was going on inside me. I mean, it's a great moment, the act of making the sculpture. There's an emotional relationship between the artist and the material. That's what struck me really strongly about this group: how tactile it is, how vulnerable it feels, and that you can't look at anything without seeing what's inside it. I don't think I had done that before. So, for me, what's really beautiful about placing the new vortex vision painting (*Untitled*, 2021), with these sculptures from 15 to 20 years ago is that the painting is me post-recovery. But it's the same face; I mean it's literally the same face because that's a photo of me underneath.

I had just worked with a dear artist friend that had a lot of trauma that had gone unresolved, a lot of sexual trauma, a lot of violence, and he didn't have the means to deal with it like I did. When he died, I actually took a selfie of myself crying to record that moment for my own sanity. I'd just come out of recovery about a year, and when he died I felt that we were so united. It was like my twin died and I, somehow, was

Above: *Untitled*, 2021, acrylic, plastic, glass, and mixed media on wood, 48 x 36 x 12 in. (121.9 x 36 x 12 in.), acquired in 2021
Opposite page: Installation view, Rubell Museum, 2021; On the wall: *Untitled*, 2021; On the floor, left to right: *Standing Boy*, 2006; *Squatting Man*, 2006; *Untitled*, 2006; *Sunrise*, 2006; *Untitled (60 Thomson)*, 2009; *Box Figure, Sitting Nude*, 2006

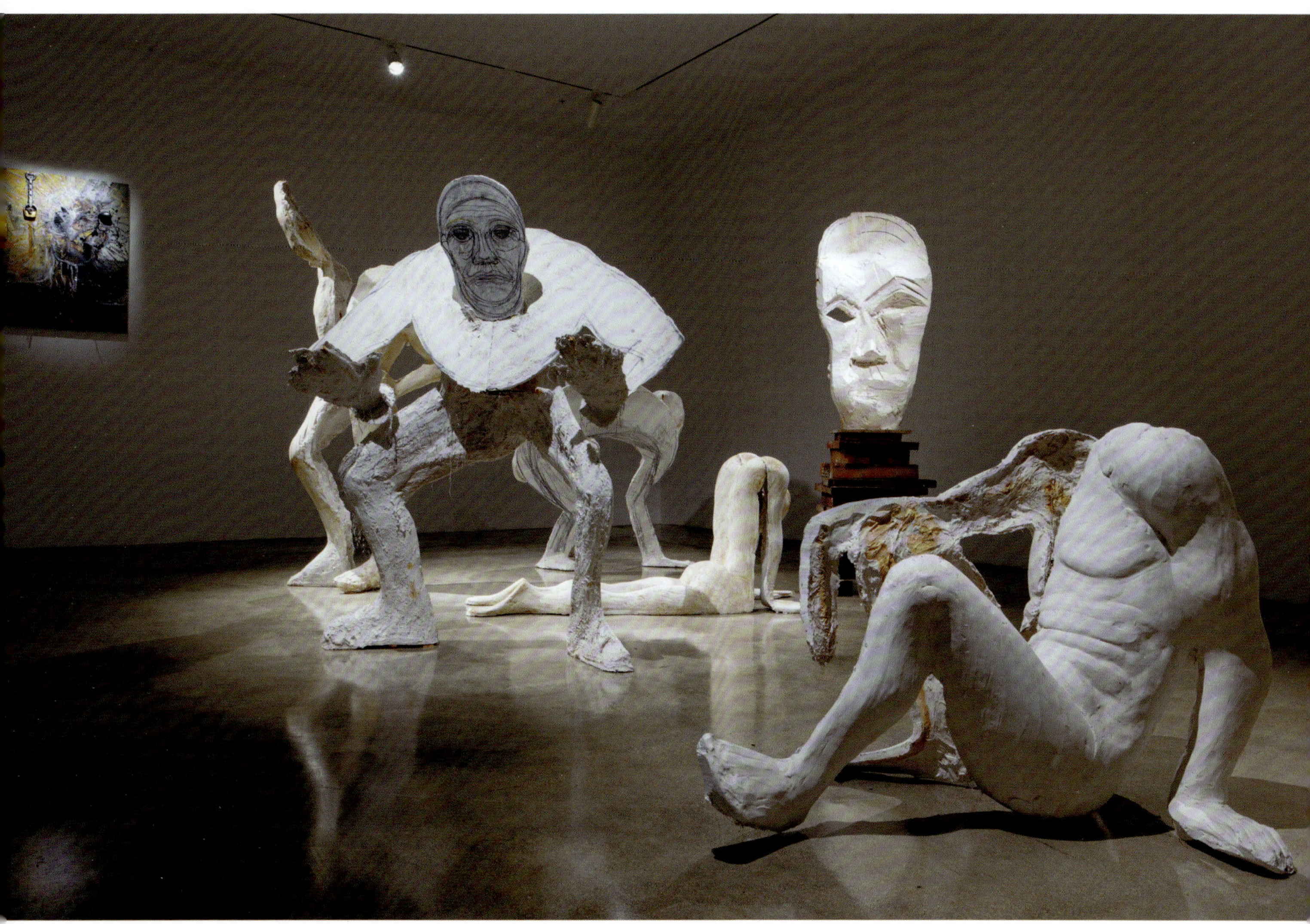

being asked to record this moment to make my decision to survive all of this, right? We always had this childhood thing; he always used to joke that he'd come to Malibu and we'd play in the sand. I planned on just having a photograph and living with the photograph to remind me of losing him, and then I started painting on top of it. In this painting the internal is on the outside, so this is an intensely personal painting.

When I started doing these, that was when I started on the journey to get to where I am now. Of course, Don and Mera show up right at the key moment as they've always done in my life. I'm in my underwear, I've got an outdoor studio, and they immediately saw this, and they were the only people who understood this painting. They were the only people who even noticed that the painting existed at the time. No one ever mentions that this piece is in this room; they're not ready to make that link yet. I would say I am. I'm ready. And Don and Mera being Don and Mera, and almost knowing me from a DNA standpoint, are ready.

What's so interesting is that when a work contains an emotional intensity, for most people, it's too much. If you listen to a song, you've got three minutes to listen to that song and it eases you in. But a work of art hits you in seconds. Art just hits you. You don't even really know what you're taking on. You don't even really know what's happening to you when you look at a work of art. I was just in Milan and I went to see Michelangelo's *Rondanini Pietà*. I'm planning a show in Italy, so they let me in to be alone with that sculpture. I assumed it would be a kind of majestic, formal experience, and instead I walked in and it was just heartbreaking. This is Michelangelo's last sculpture, he worked on it right up until he died, and you can see he's carving with such urgency. He refutes his own legacy of being this virtuoso, right? It's no longer the David—you can barely make out the faces. It's all highly Gothic. I just saw that and was incredibly moved by it in a way I wouldn't anticipate. I've always had that kind of interest. Sculpture is an emotionally visceral affair: you have to walk around them.

—Thomas Houseago

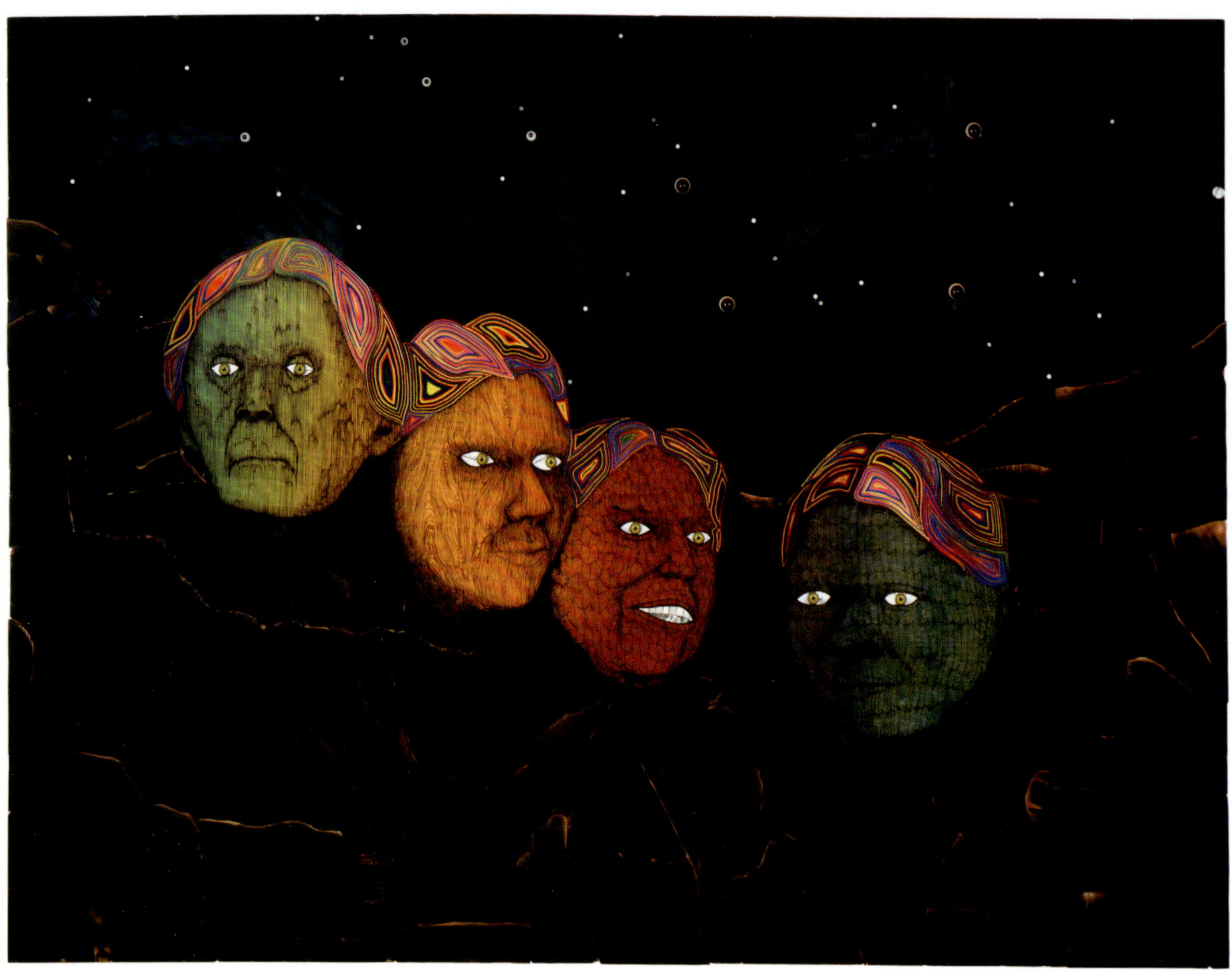

This painting, made by an impassioned and feverishly working young artist, is about the "Great White Fathers" of the country. It was conceived while reading autobiographies by Eleanor Roosevelt [third from left] and Ulysses Grant, *The Journals of Lewis and Clark*, and *April, 1865* by Jay Winik. The confluence of these texts animated me to look at Mt. Rushmore as a structure to rethink the parentage of this country. The women I envisioned as idealized pillars would likely be different if I were to create such a painting today. In the place of Susan B. Anthony [far left] I likely would have chosen Sojourner Truth, Shirley Chisholm, Billie Jean King, Elaine Brown, Angela Davis, the list goes on. But in truth, the only visages that belong in the rock face are those formed by time and the elements. The Black Hills are the center of the universe for the Lakota Sioux, and the monument is a desecration.

Mt. Rushmore, 2006, scorched wood, dyed panel, faux brick, Sculpey, yarn, panther eye, abalone shell, mother-of-pearl, and tooled leather on panel, 96 x 144 x 6 in. (243.8 x 365.7 x 15.2 cm), acquired in 2006
Opposite page: *Chariot (The Day After The End of Days)*, 2005-2006, Polish hay cart, scrap wood, T1-11 plywood, fluorescent lights with colored lenses, bronze, twenty state flags, wool, scorched wood, buttons, rope, abalone shell, mother of pearl, Powell Peralta skateboard, bucket, purple resin, Black Panther Party's Ten-Point Program, 120 x 312 x 72 in. (304.8 x 792.5 x 182.9 cm), acquired in 2006

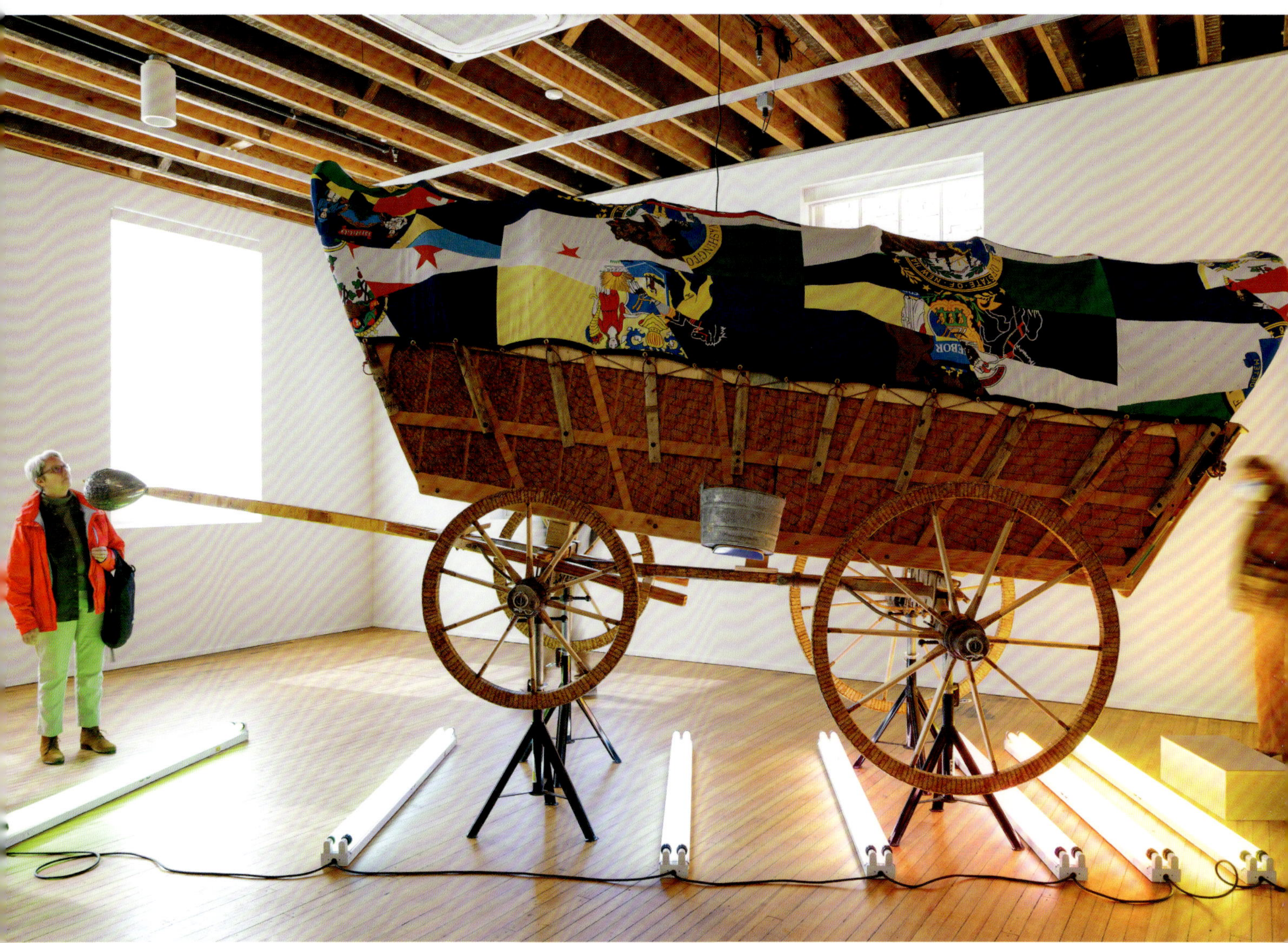

Chariot (The Day After the End of Days) was the successor to my first post-grad sculpture *Sepulcher (Viking Burial Ship),* 2004. *Sepulcher* is a burial vessel depicting the death of my working methods at that time, as well as a diagrammatic representation of the formalisms I wanted to employ making MY sculpture, which I continue to apply in my practice today.

In *Chariot*, I was interested in the collective understanding of the covered wagon from a historical and utilitarian sense. The covered wagon was a farm tool, became a travelling tool, as well as, I would argue, a military tool. The first wheeled vehicle to cross the continental divide was a "four-pounder" cannon. I think of the covered wagon as an extension of the cannon, as occupation (or invasion) is a military method.

This moment in the history of westward expansion could be simplified as rapacious, murderous, poisonous, and contagious. I wanted to look through and beyond this dark view and consider the motivations of many who left the East in search of something better. In many cases, these people met a life that was much worse than the one they were leaving or fleeing and were confronted with the hardness of their surroundings and the ugliness of their character. The ones who flourished often did so with violent methods and were aided by disease. In this darkness there is an image of the dream, which became a night terror.

Chariot was envisioned as a sculpture and a functioning vehicle. I built the wagon so it could be pulled (with some adjustments) by horses to the Whitney Museum where it was to be exhibited. As the wagon passed through the museum doors, and once put on display as you see here, it would be transformed into sculpture. I wanted this "functional" sculpture to be considered through our contemporary understanding of the readymade.

—Matthew Day Jackson

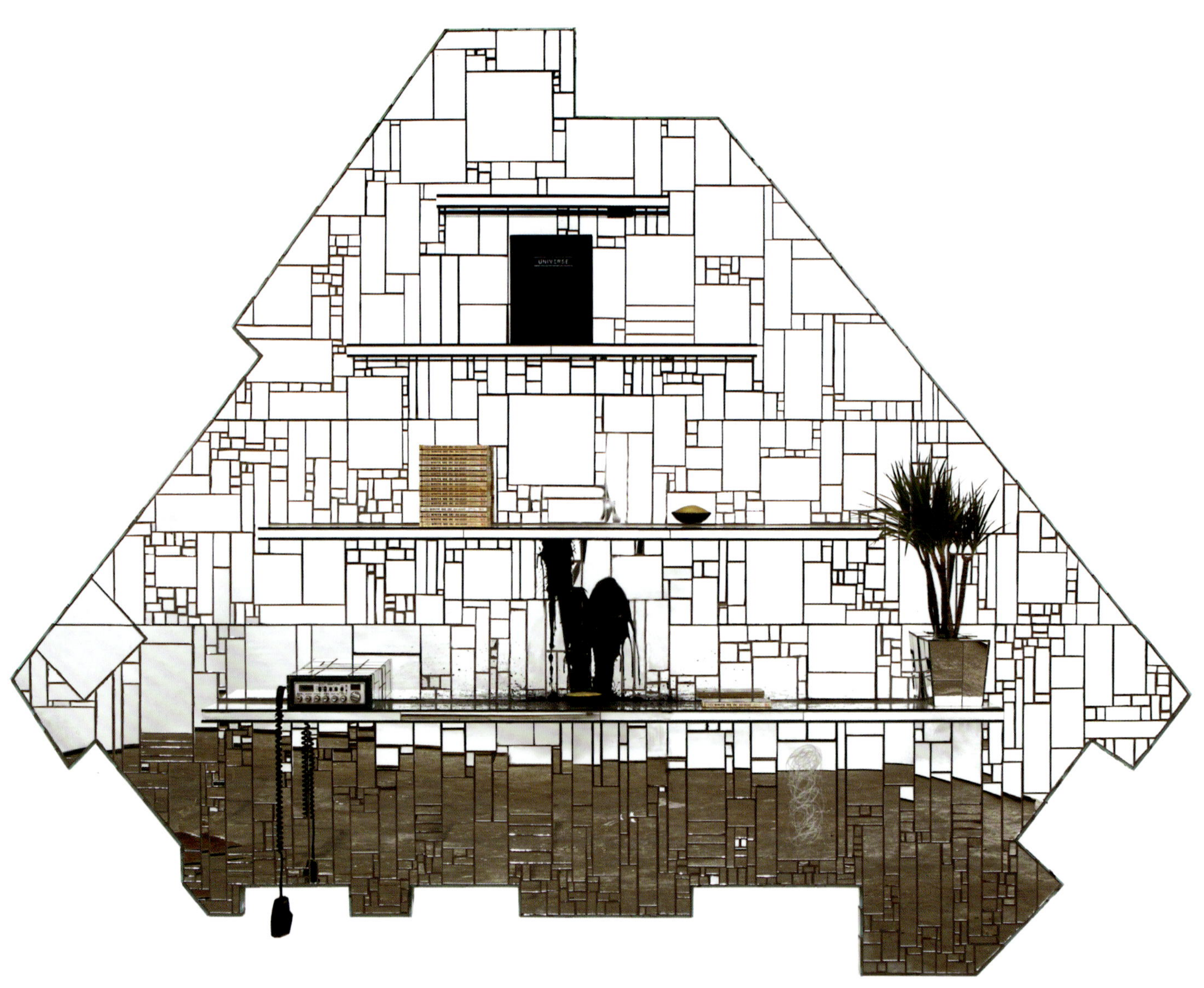

The Shuttle, 2011 mirrored tile, black soap, wax, books, shea butter, oyster shells, plant, and CB radio, 96 1/2 x 125 x 11 3/4 in. (245.1 x 317.5 x 29.8 cm), acquired in 2011
Opposite page: *After Medium*, 2011, branded red oak flooring, black soap, wax, and paint, 132 x 168 x 2 3/4 in. (335.3 x 426.7 x 7 cm), acquired in 2011

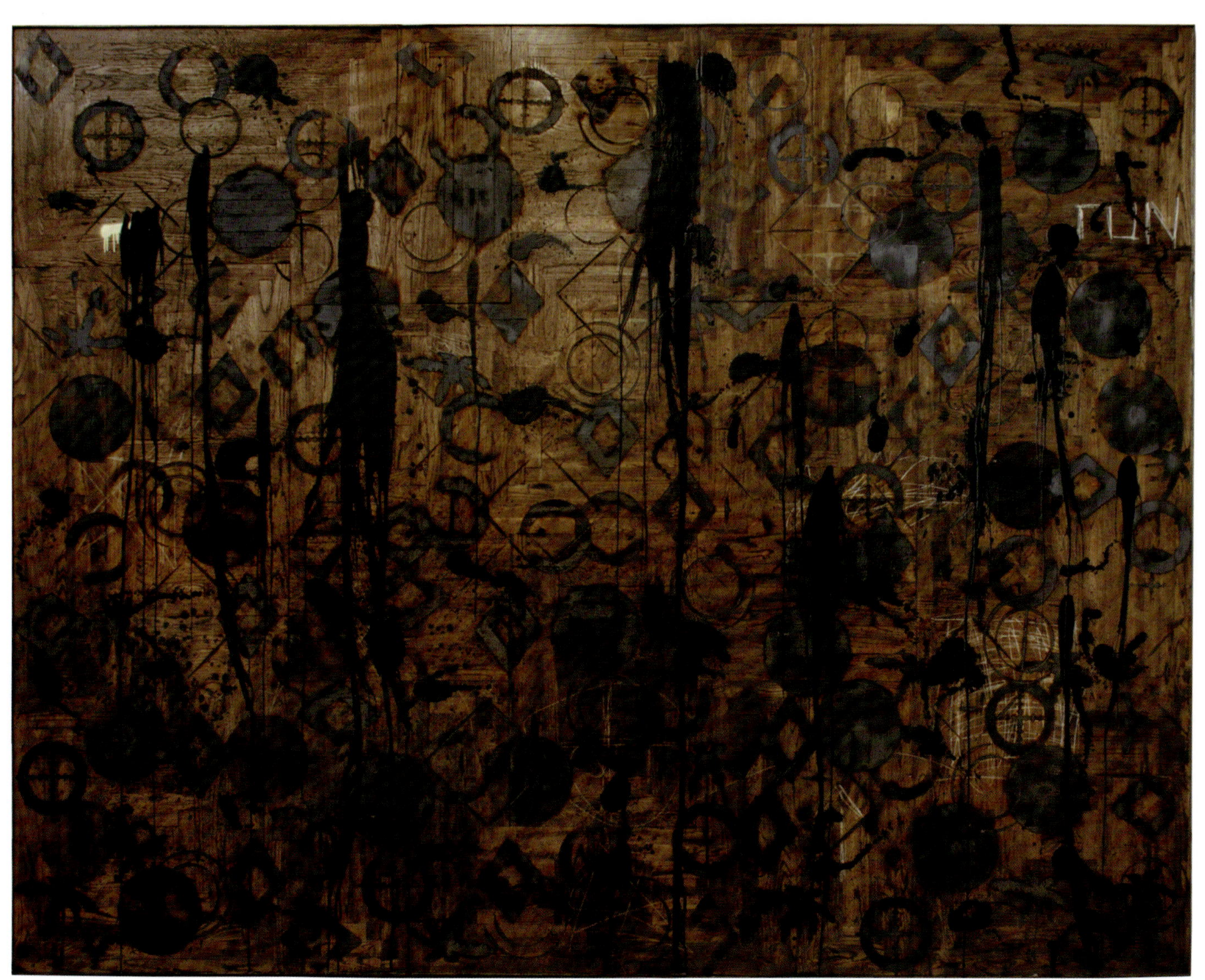

Young American artist seeks audience to enjoy poly-conscious attempts at post-medium condition production.

Must enjoy race mongering, disparate disconnected thoughts, and sunsets (really). Familiarity with the work of Sun Ra, Joseph Beuys, Rosalind Krauss, Richard Pryor, Hans Haacke, Carl Andre, and interest in spelunking in the death of identity a plus. I'm looking for an audience with a good attention span that is willing to stay with me through the good and the bad. I enjoy creating movies, producing sculptures, painting, and making photographs. My interests are costuming, Sam Greenlee novels, Godard films and masturbation. Ability to hold conversation using only rap lyrics and a sense of humor a must.

—Rashid Johnson

the ape in me

the ape in me
method: back to the old brains, to the senso-motoric
to before spoken language
to before perception
to before memory
to before the obtrusiveness of objects
to before euclid where the straight lines meet at the
vanishing point
not thinking while painting.

untangling the assimilation, porously swamping it,
a bath sponge: capturing the rapid, fluid world of
images, the rags of memory.

i invent a pictorial language, an equivalent to the
rigid, binding reality, to the remaining 20% of
perception that suffices not to run against corners,
to recognize a few objects: the déjà-vu, the smile of
the third month, the rest discarded. my pictorial
reality is charged with passion, a language tied to
the body, to dynamic movement. colorful streaks
and blots in tangled relation, swiftly spontaneous,
blindly immeasurable, an irreproducible space for
action. inner images surface and sink, current
perception controls the motorics, the blots and
colors that form movement, a system right within
itself, not conforming with the binding reality.
no on-sight painting.
viewing and painting are split, the eye and the hand
asynchronous. blots flying out of the body, executed
simultaneously on vertical surfaces.
my painting is bound to me, to the moment, to the
supple hand, the sharp eye, the good legwork, to un-
controlled drifting, to the unit of time and feeding.
to the moment of happiness; it is not a binding
language, nor a traffic signal to make sure there is
no crash when the troglodytes are on the road, and
not a symbol, means nothing, there is no convention
to discover behind it.

it is asocial, an end in itself, a flow undisturbed
by reflection, an adroit move of the limbs, halted at
the right moment.
the often practiced subsided. induce the random
event, detect it without delay and use it as an
element to go forward.

leave open the constellations of blots, reject and use,
center and decenter, leave visible the painting
process, no retouching, risk not recipe. non finito.

unadorned, all-at-sea painting, is what i strive for.
to the reptilian reflex
to the brain stem
to the acte gratuit
to before the rem sleep, in the "temporal lobes of
the monotreme," my painting is action and passion:
a dynamic space.
the image a fluid shadow, becoming an eeg of
creaturbility, if it succeeds in penetrating the
billowing oceanic all-over waves. where the old
proteus counts to five.
to before the cutting out, sending in and winning.
to before rules
to before the ego-shift
where my ego is the world and vice versa where it
paints, the s(ubconscious) m(ind), the limbic system
no metaphysics
no doctrine
no occultism
no shamans
no philosophy
no scheme
a blot is a blot is a blot, a smart or a stupid one,
nothing else.

assimilation: from a biological perspective, assimilation is the integration of external elements into the
developing or mature structures of an organism.

senso-motoric: the first stage of intelligence,
sensual and motoric functions are linked, practical
intelligence.

on-sight painting: a type of painting that depicts
objects so that they can easily be recognized as such,
according to the agreed rules of reality.

ego-shift: is what i call the moment at the end of
primitive thinking at the age of seven when teachers
start drilling rules and drive out the fairy-tale age.

—Martha Jungwirth

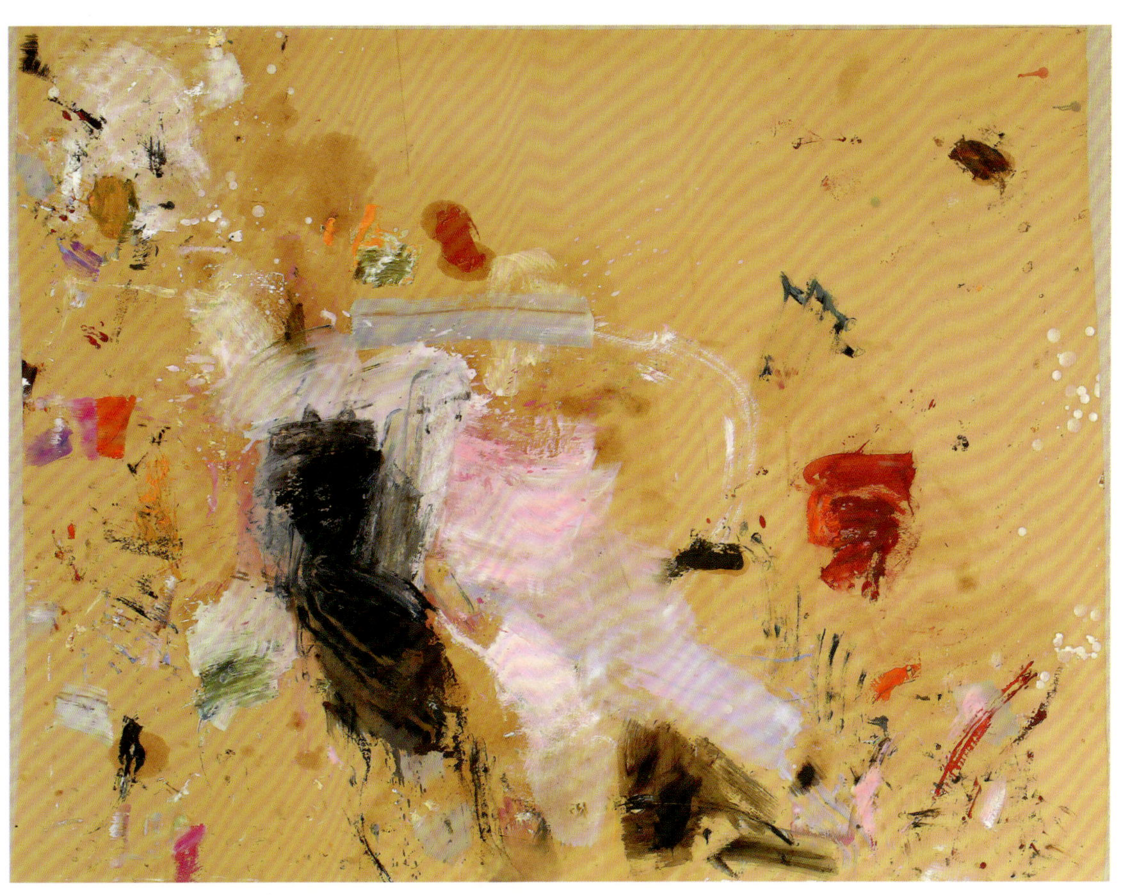

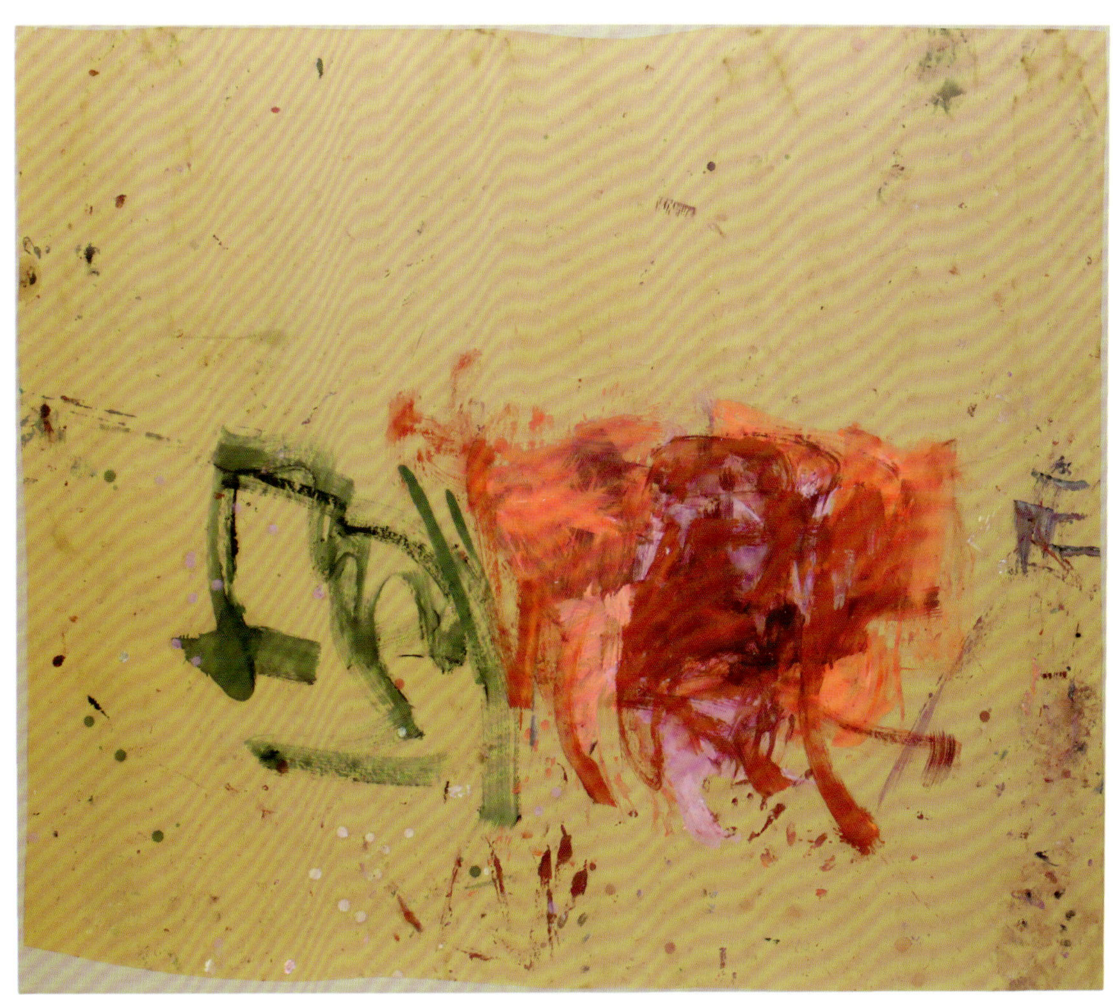

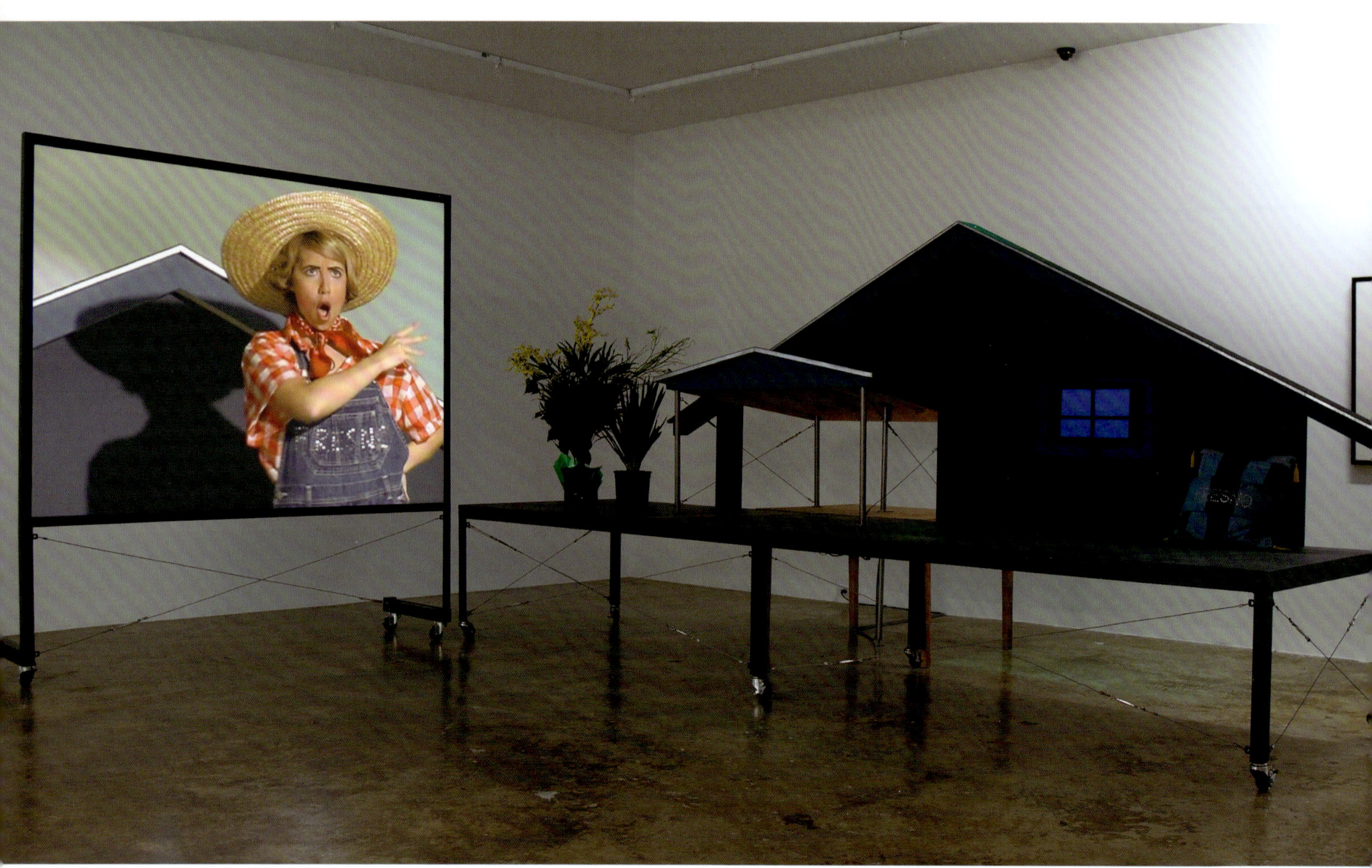

In the 1980s, when some artists self-consciously began to produce works that embraced their status as commodities, there arose, simultaneously, the desire in other artists to make works that escaped such commodification. The argument was advanced that an artwork could function analogously to the gift, an object outside of the system of exchange. This is what initially led to my interest in homemade craft items: that is, objects already existing in popular usage that are constructed specifically to be given away. This is not to say that I believe craft gifts themselves harbor utopian sentiments; all things have a price. The hidden burden of the gift is that it calls for payback, but the price is unspecified, repressed. The uncanny aura of the craft item is linked to time. Crafts are the literal embodiment of the Puritan work ethic. They seem to announce that work is its own reward. This is conveyed by the long, labor-intensive hours required to construct them by hand. They speak the language of the wage earner in which there is a one-to-one relationship between time spent and worth. The equation is not between time and money; it's a more obscure relationship drawn between time and commitment, one that results in a kind of emotional usury. The gift operates within an economy of guilt; an endless feeling of indebtedness attends it because of its mysterious worth. And the highly loaded nature of these objects is intensified by their material nature: by the seeming contradiction that their emotional weight far exceeds the worth of the cheap and lowly materials from which they are constructed. However, it isn't proper to speak of the "junk" status of the craft item; it is in bad taste to comment on the financial worth of a gift. The fine art "junk sculpture" could be said to have value *in spite of* its material, while the craft item could be said, like the icon, to have value *beyond* its material.

—Mike Kelley

Extracurricular Activity Projective Reconstruction #9 (Fresno), 2005, installation: wood, paint, metal, tar paper, silk plants, plastic, fabric, photographs, screen, speakers, and DVDs, video (color, sound), dimensions variable, (Farm Girl) 4 min. 22 sec., (Bray's Burgers) 1 min. 33 sec., acquired in 2005
Opposite page: *Untitled*, 1990, stuffed animals on afghans, 6 x 48 x 287 1/2 in. (15.2 x 121.9 x 730.3 cm), acquired in 1991

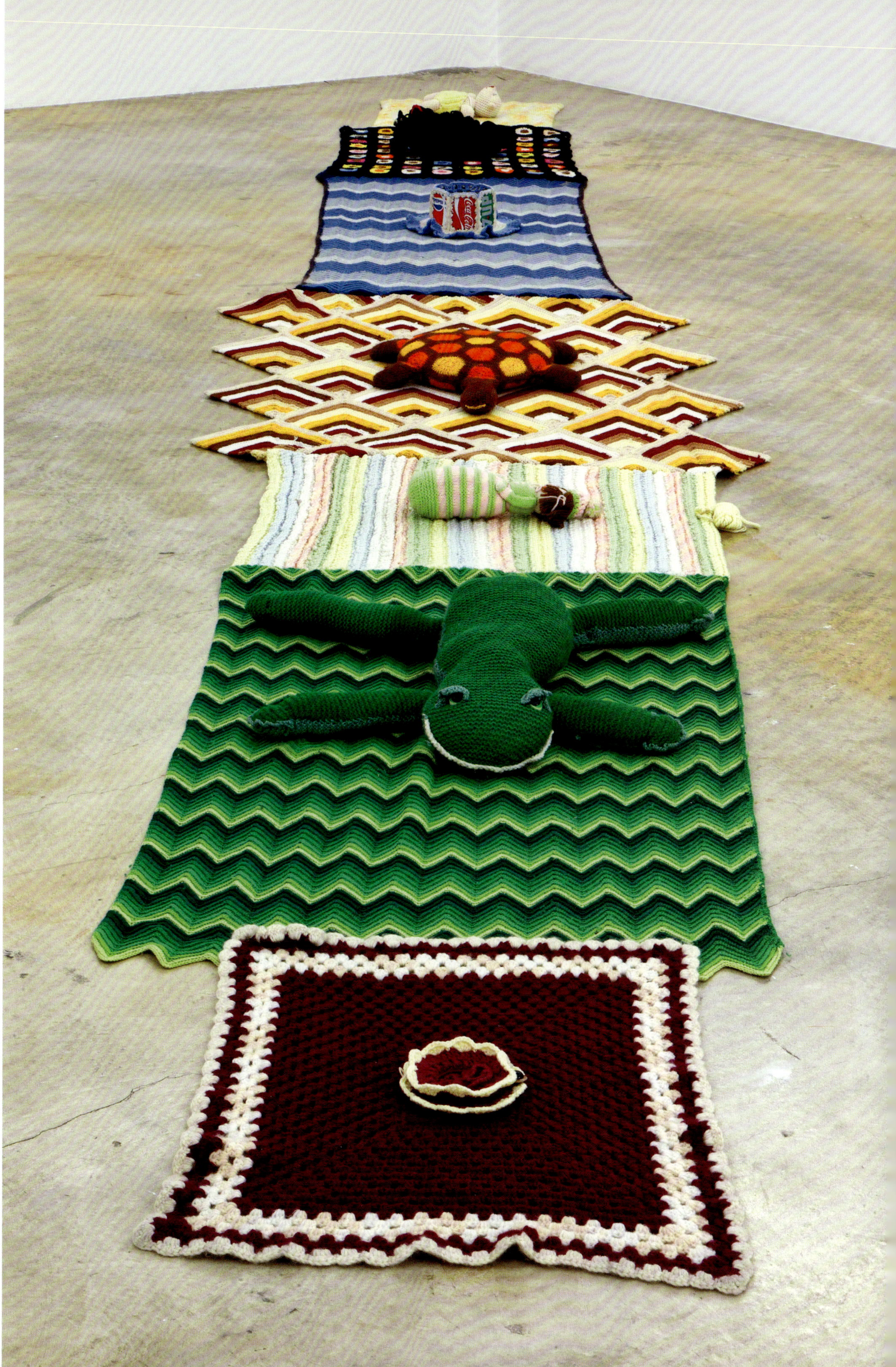

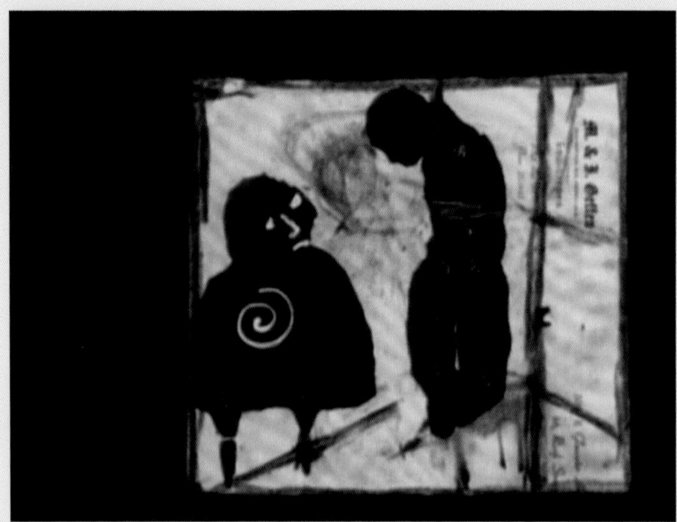
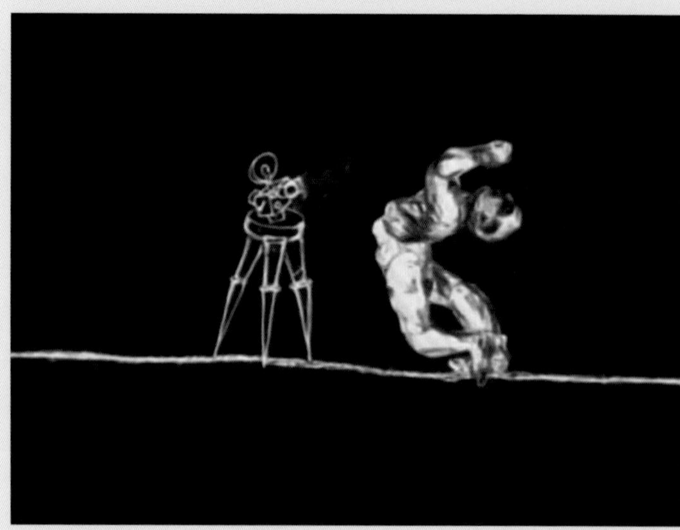

Carolyn Christov-Bakargiev: Early in 1996, the Truth and Reconciliation Commission began as a series of public hearings broadcast on national television. Agents and victims of human rights violations perpetrated under apartheid testified before a national forum. Perpetrators of abuse were offered possible amnesty in exchange for testimony. The main objective was to create a context through which national healing was made possible. The video projection *Ubu Tells the Truth* (1997) and the play *Ubu and the Truth Commission* (1997) layer South African realities with Alfred Jarry's grotesque portrayal, in his *Ubu plays* of the 1890s, of the way in which arbitrary power engenders madness. The installation seems more open-ended: less clear who the "bad guys" and "good guys' are.

William Kentridge: When I made the series of eight etchings *Ubu Tells the Truth* (1996-97), which initiated the play and installation in the following year, I wanted to draw a version of the character Ubu that was different from Jarry's. I first had the idea of a schematic drawing of Ubu, in Jarry's style, with a moustache and a pointed head, wearing a robe with a huge spiral on it, but I didn't want a pastiche. I had the idea of someone in front of this figure drawn in a different style. I would draw this other figure as a naked man. Then I wondered whether to base this figure on the naked figures in Eadweard Muybridge's *Animal Locomotion* (1887), who were often in ridiculous, bombastic poses. Finally, I decided I might as well enact those poses myself. I placed the camera, with a self-timer, on one side of the studio, and I performed Ubu in front of the blackboard. I was not thinking of those images as myself at all; they were the poses that Ubu needed.

When I made the video installation, I assumed that people who had seen the play would have no interest in the installation because there's no new material. In the

play he shows a different kind of anarchy, madness, and illogicality to the installation, but it needs the hour and a half of the play's duration for that to be extricated. The video demonstrates that anarchy through the very impossibility of connecting the fragments of the piece. What is the significance of a cat that suddenly becomes a radio? In the play it's easier to understand: you see it as the drunken thoughts of Ubu. Here you almost have to become Ubu yourself to understand that this is a world where successive waves of violence or craziness follow each other. If you're watching something that's eight minutes long as you do in the video installation, this kind of extreme open-endedness is fine. If you're watching for an hour and a half, you keep on wanting a structure that makes sense.

CCB: How do all the machines of communication depicted in your work fit into this?

WK: They often indicate what needs to be heard or seen, outside of oneself. I draw megaphones because they're so beautifully painted in Beckmann or because they appear, for example, in photographs of Italian Futurist concertos for factory workers. I feel I'm part of earlier heroic attempts at connecting the world with art.

CCB: There is also the image of the camera in your drawings, which transforms into a police helicopter or a surveillance eye.

WK: There's a range of associations around the camera as an instrument of control, scrutiny, recording, and memory. It's a rich emblem. But I couldn't tell you if, in the film *Ubu Tells the Truth* when Ubu turns into a camera, he is photographing himself. Is it some god-like body or conscience photographing him to judge him? All I can say is

Ubu Tells the Truth, 1997, 16 mm animated film transfered to DVD, ed. 4 of 4 plus 2 AP, duration: 8 min., acquired in 1998

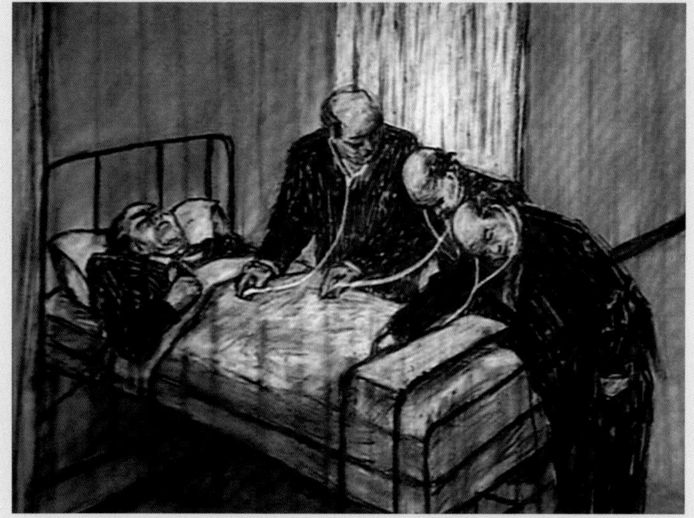 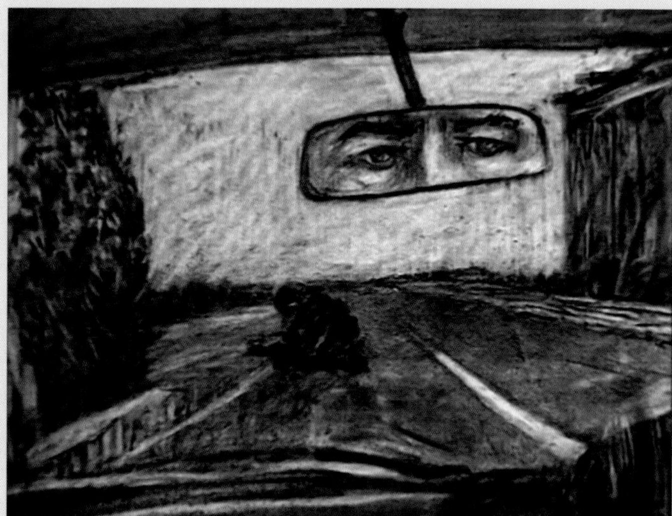

that during a Truth and Reconciliation Commission hearing of one of the South African police, part of the evidence presented was home movies of murders, which the police had filmed themselves. Were those policemen filming this out of a crazed sadism? Were they doing it thinking that, if they were charged, they could prove that others were also involved? Were they perversely acting as documentary photographers? That ambiguity is echoed in what the image might be doing in the film. The story of how those police came to have those home movies somehow confirms the figure of Ubu turning into a camera.

CCB: Although stemming from the Truth and Reconciliation Commission, guilt does not seem to enter the Ubu works. On the other hand, the character Soho Eckstein in *History of the Main Complaint* (1996) explores his personal responsibility in horrific events. Lying in a coma in hospital he relives two incidents: first he is driving and witnesses a man being beaten in the middle of the road; next he is driving when a man suddenly runs in front of his car and is killed.

Is recognition of one's indirect guilt enough?

WK: I don't know; that's a moral or ethical question. The film asks how you map the effects of guilt. For me the film was about trying to be as accurate as possible.

CCB: In some ways ethics is the object of your art—or maybe its subject.

WK: I hate the idea that my work has a clear, moral high ground from which it judges and surveys. To put it blandly, my work is about a process of drawing that tries to find a way through the space between what we know and what we see.

The drawings attempt to map things that normally one just talks about. For example, if you have a notion of two rooms, one room full of secrets, the other an empty room of truths—how can you draw these two spaces? We have a certain sense of ourselves that derives from our surface, our skin. So much of the history of Western art consists of representations of the surface, yet there's this whole other side of us, our interior. We hope that the engineering inside us will work, day after day, year after year.

CCB: Your work explores the borders between these states: between memory and amnesia, drawing and erasure. The process of re-drawing and erasure means that each drawing is poised in a state of uncertainty. Each stage of the drawing carries with it the visual memory of its recent past. This suggests a view of knowledge as constantly negotiated between the present and memory, as if forgetting and remembering were not distinct moments, but overlapping. Does that have a political implication?

WK: I think it has more to do with the personal, psychological structure of my way of working in the world. It's a position I would defend as a polemic for a kind of uncertainty.

CCB: What are the political implications of the cultural and moral relativism you seem to be describing?

WK: I don't think it's relativism. To say that one needs art, or politics, that incorporate ambiguity and contradiction is not to say that one then stops recognizing and condemning things as evil. However, it might stop one being so utterly convinced of the certainty of one's own solutions. There needs to be a strong understanding of fallibility and how the very act of certainty or authoritativeness can bring disasters.

History of the Main Complaint, 1996, 16 mm animated film transfered to DVD, ed. 9 of 10 plus 2 AP, duration: 5 min. 50 sec., acquired in 1998

Götz Adriani: Both the book *Die Hermanns-Schlacht* [*The Battle of Hermann*; 1977/1979], composed of numerous woodcuts of once popular portraits, and the painting *Wege* [*Paths*, 1977/1979] are about redefining historical as well as literary legacies, by alluding to a forest that the German Romantics declared a national symbol. This Romantic view begins with the portrait of Arminius (on the left in *Wege*, on the first page in *Die Hermanns-Schlacht*), who was born around 17 BC and was given the name "Hermann of the Cherusci" in the 17th century. In the year 9 AD, Arminius, who was originally in Roman service, entered the history books with his victory in the Teutoburg Forest over three Roman legions under the command of Publius Quinctilius Varus, who had been sent from Syria to Germany. The rest of the portraits are dedicated to Arminius, and they portray intellectual greats who, like Kleist and Grabbe, have used the Hermannsschlacht in their work, or relied on a patriotism that can be traced to the Germanic struggle for independence against the Roman occupying power.

Tacitus called Arminius the "liberator of Germania" and, starting with him, your wide-reaching genealogy stems both from those who turned the Germanic liberation struggle in the face of the Napoleonic armies into a vehicle for their own ideas of liberty and those who subsequently made it into a nationalistic legacy to suit their own fatal, morally bankrupt needs. You take aim at a *furor teutonicus* ["Teutonic Fury"] already cannibalized by Nazi forerunners, that extends to Schlageter, Horst Wessel, and Heidegger. Your woodcut Valhalla of German literati, philosophers, and politicians, the military men and entrepreneurs who in some way thought about the battle in the Teutoburg Forest, ranges from Klopstock, Kant, Schleiermacher, and Fichte up to Holderlin, Mérike, and Uhland, from Eichendorff and Jean Paul to Herwegh, Rilke, and George. It extends from Queen Luise to Clausewitz, Blücher, and Moltke, from Bismarck and Roon to Krupp and Schlieffen. Of course, all of these illustrious names can't hide the fact that such a relatively young nation as Germany had difficulties in developing a civic self-image that would help forge a specifically German national identity. Instead of exploring this self-critically, many have been content with either making reference to it, or complaining of its supposed absence. Especially Hermann's Battle and the Nibelungen have been used as patriotic myths, and people have looked to Hoffmann von Fallersleben's *Das Lied der Deutschen* ["The Song of the Germans"] as a source for meaningful patriotic feelings. Yet, ultimately, at the end of the road towards a belated national

consciousness, which, in your woodcuts, is marked by often tortuous dead ends and false steps, the racial ideology and destructive mania of the slogan "Volk ohne Raum" ["People without space"] even went as far as genocide. Are the woodcuts meant to level the hierarchies among those who have used history and its names so scandalously? Or was your gathering of heroes, so deeply rooted in the political and cultural traditions of 19th-century Germany, an original reaction to Andy Warhol's standardized portrait sequences of celebrities and the (exclusively male) historical personages that Gerhard Richter took from the Brockhaus Encyclopedia, then a sign of good breeding in households across West Germany, for his 1971 portrait series *48 Portraits*? Your woodcut portraits, marked by woodgrain and growth rings, make up an uncouth compendium of travesties surrounding the cliché of the German forest, and they've been presented in the Galerie Helen van der Meij in Amsterdam [25.11-23.12.1977] and, under the title Wege der Weltweisheit — die Hermannsschlacht [Ways of World Wisdom — The Battle of Hermann], at Galerie Maier-Hahn in Diisseldorf [12. 5-6.6.1978]. I wonder if you see both celebration and arrogance in the work?

Anselm Kiefer: It would have seemed too easy for me to just paint a few portraits from the lexicon. Also, it's not just the "good guys" and the "bad guys" who should be juxtaposed with one another. I was more concerned with the gradual transition to perversion. Earlier, I talked about Germans having a hard time finding an identity. They have no great, unequivocal mythologies like the French, the English, and the Americans. Hermann's Battle isn't enough. For example, German fraternities were initially liberal-minded organizations that then atrophied into reactionary unions. The line from the German national anthem "From the Meuse to the Neman" was initially intended as the description of a space free from the arbitrary will of the many princes that ruled over the separate German lands. But it didn't take long for it to take on a different meaning as a call for expansion and more Lebensraum ["living space"]. This is the transition that interests me. You speak of celebration and arrogance. Celebration, yes, as far as there's something to celebrate in Hélderlin, Grabbe, and others. Arrogance, too, because, knowing that there's no such thing as true, objective history, I perceive it as a field of rubble that I can use as material to set up my story, which can never be the conclusive one.

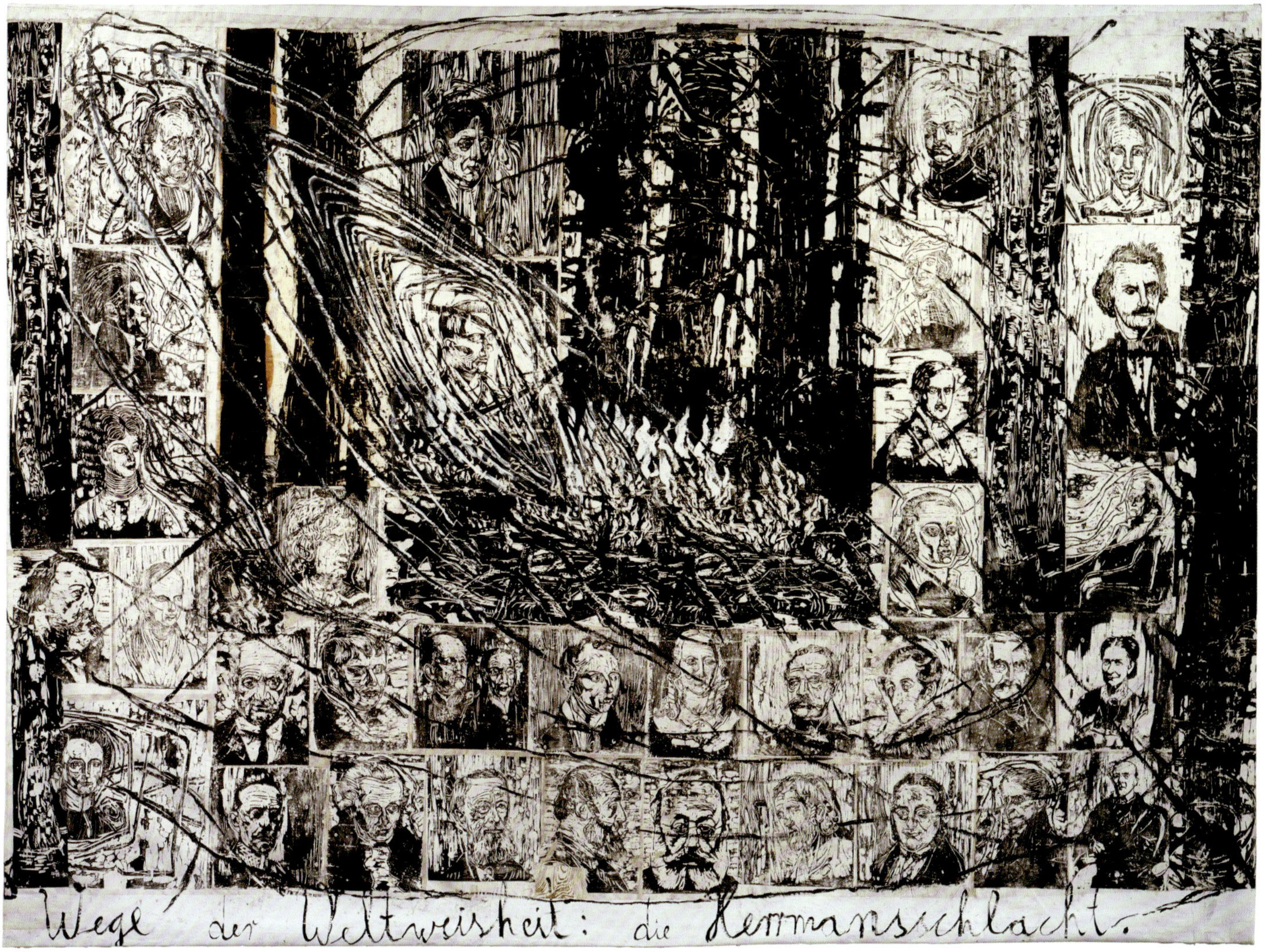

Wege der Weltweisheit: die Hermannsschlacht.

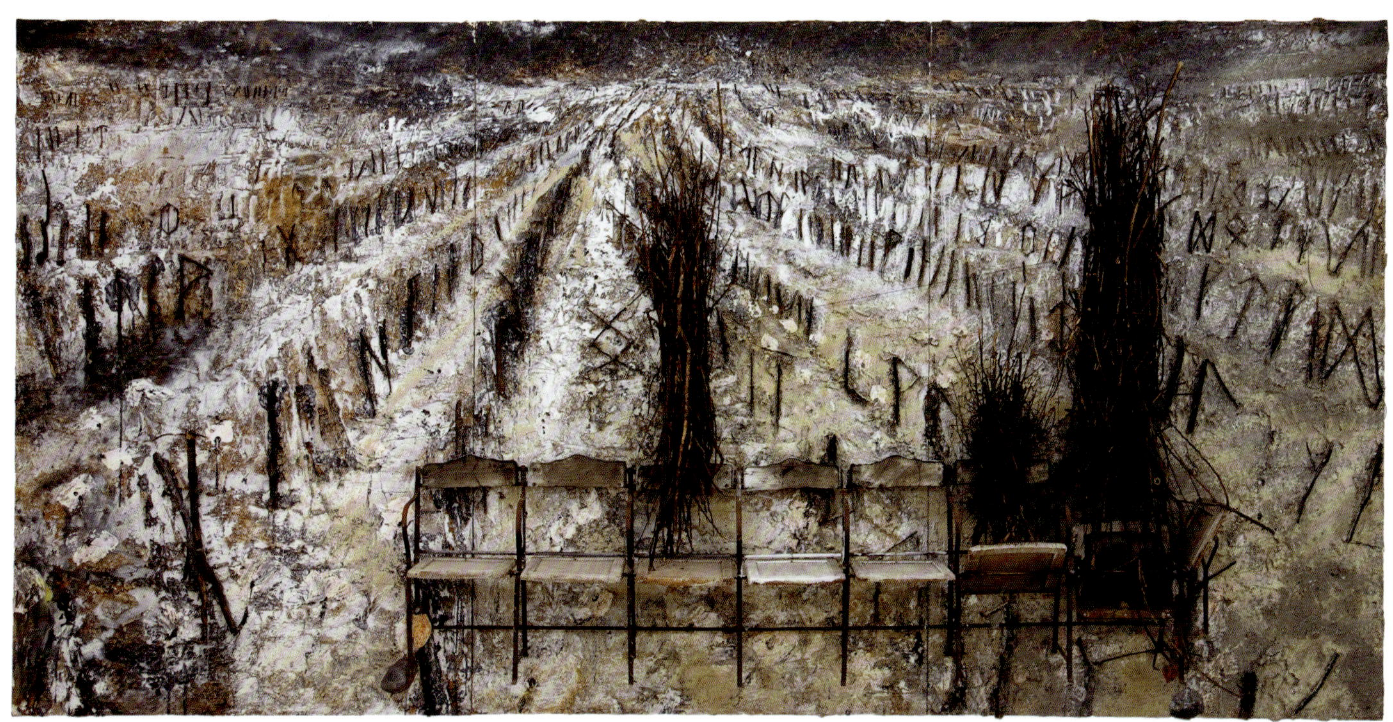

BASIL KINCAID
b. 1986, St. Louis, MO / lives and works between the United States and Ghana

2023 Artist in Residence

When I received confirmation that I would be doing the residency, the first thing I did was look back over my old work. My earliest quilts were abstract and heavily focused on drapery, texture, and movement. These 2023 quilts have even more of that three dimensionality— the flowing movement and drapery— within the composition, which elicits the original application of the quilt as an object that lives on the bed. If you sleep with a quilt, you wake up and it's disheveled. I just fell in love with those naturally occurring shapes. With this residency, I set out to expand on all the lessons I have learned quilt making.

A throughline in my quilt-making is this sensation of musicality. In middle school I used to make beats on the computer, and the way that those layered little clips of sound appear in the program somehow resemble the background and pulse of the quilt; you see those little blips of color. If you imagine a timeline going across the quilt, as you progress left to right, first the yellow swath would sound, then the blue patch would sound, then the green would sing— like the fabric is playing this beat. I've become fascinated with this relationship between quilt-making, especially improvisational quilt-making, and jazz. Miles Davis developed a way of making jazz called modal jazz, where each player had a framework that they would improvise in, and that was their mode. When you layered the modes, it created the composition. That's what I do within the quilt. When we're making patterns and the patchwork, it's a rhythm we're creating: I'll have one person working on one type of rhythm, another person working on another rhythm, and I'll be working on yet another. When it comes together, you get these big sheets of quilt that have an orchestral nature to them.

With the piece *The Fields We Lay and Turn with Horns* (2023), I wanted to pay homage to the quilters that have come before me and to my family lineage of quilting and farming. The navy and brown striations in the middle ground remind me of my grandparents scorching the fields to revitalize the soil and prepare for the next season. There are also a couple of references to me and my brother: the farmhouse in the upper right-hand corner with the little yard, and in the foreground where a woman is lying in the field breastfeeding two babies. The affectionate and devoted environment my parents created for us through the active practice of their love is the greatest privilege of all and I wanted that to be the focal point. I incorporated the moose because the male moose is a solitary animal and a symbol of tenacity and power. As an artist, there's an element of solitude you have to overcome, which builds your character. There's a playful nature to the movement in the work, yet this piece feels the most serious. With farming, with art, with any pursuit of passion, there's an element of toil involved at some point. To make a quilt of this scale, the amount of work and collective energy that went into it is enormous. People may think of it as a labor of love, but the labor is the love.

Courtship of Fireflies (2023) is the first piece I started on during the residency. I was initially thinking about this sensation of offering. When you're in a relationship, there's the physical dance of it, but then there's also the spiritual dance, the making of the love as a creative collaboration, this kind of back and forth. The figures are bringing something to each other in a type of energetic, generous exchange where both people give freely of themselves and both benefit. The jittery, electric linework with the yellow and the seafoam green is a new element I'm incorporating where I'm depicting the energy rising. I'm playing with drawing, breaking reality, which is fun for me. I love the movement of it, the flowing drapery of it, and its spirited and flirtatious title embodying the joy of it all.

The figures are cut from hand-woven Ghanaian kente cloth that we embroidered with symbols: one means "go with God" or "trust God," and the other is a golden stool. In Ghanaian lore, a golden stool descended from the heavens. They say the stool landed in the Ashanti region and that is why Ghana has so much gold, but I look at it too as a symbol of prosperity. The first time I went to Ghana, I thought I was going to learn how to make art, but I was really learning how to be a person. Even in an area where we had less than I had ever known, people were so generous and so kind. There was this kind of unity, that we're in this together, recognizing each other's experience. Within this work the golden stool represents the cultivation of character, understanding wealth as an internal wellspring.

The last symbol is two crossing swords. I create board games and I've always been fascinated by the physical, mental, and spiritual strategy of martial arts. I've been thinking about how I can cultivate that mentality within my art-making process. The Japanese text *Hagakure: The Book of the Samurai* talks about doing everything with seriousness and discipline. I value that, and the swords represent that seriousness. I live my life from this framework of play, but it's playing with a purpose.

—Basil Kincaid

The Fields We Lay and Turn with Horns, 2023, corduroy, kente cloth, Ghanaian wax block fabric, cotton, wool, fur, polyester, sequins, embroidery floss, selected materials from previous performance works, curtains, 180 x 240 x 6 in. (457.2 x 609.6 x 15.2 cm), acquired in 2023
Courtship of Fireflies, 2023, kente cloth, Ghanaian wax block fabric, cotton, wool, fur, polyester, embroidery floss, tweed, yarn, velvet, curtains, 96 x 168 in. (243.8 x 426.7 cm), acquired in 2023

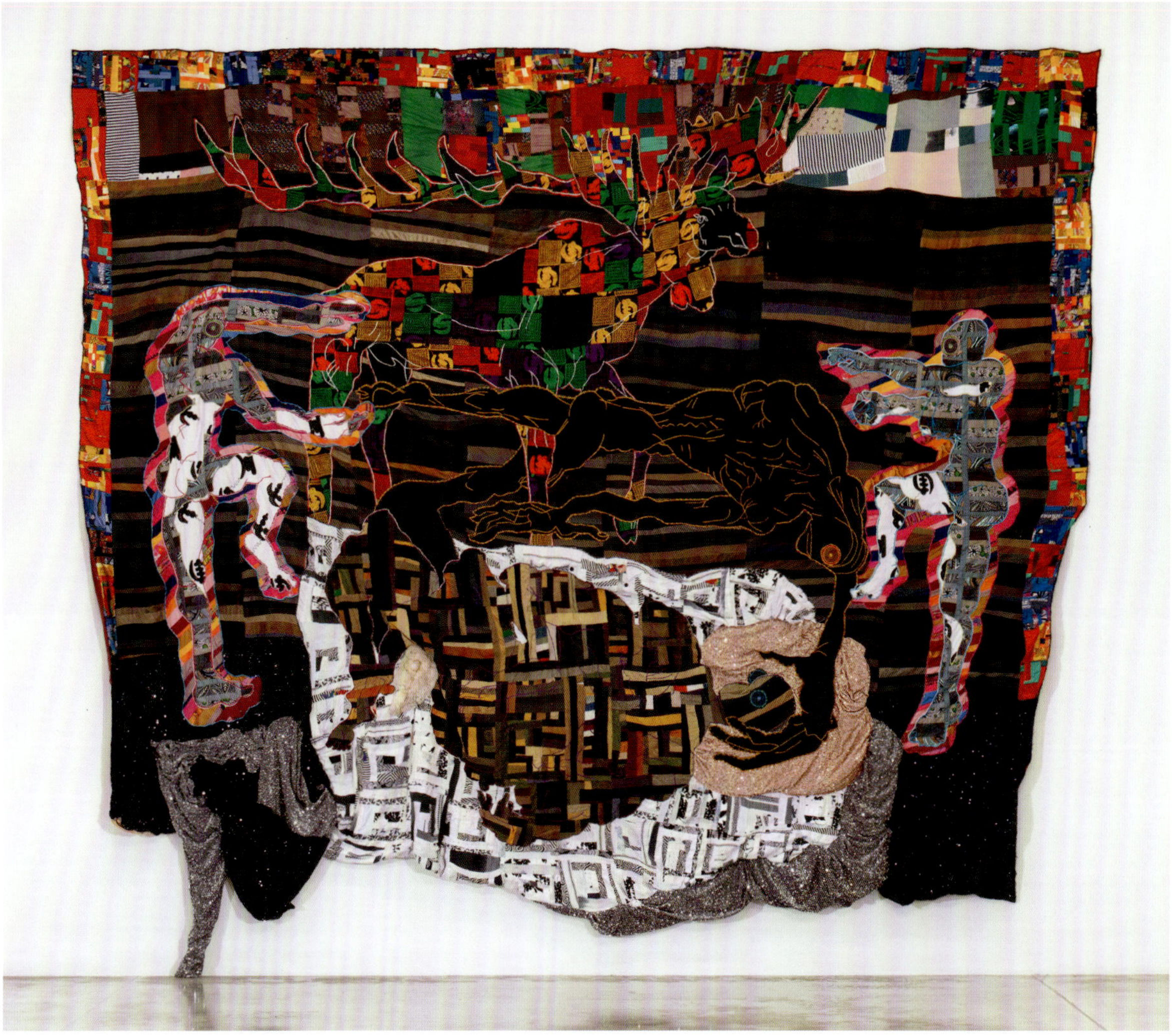

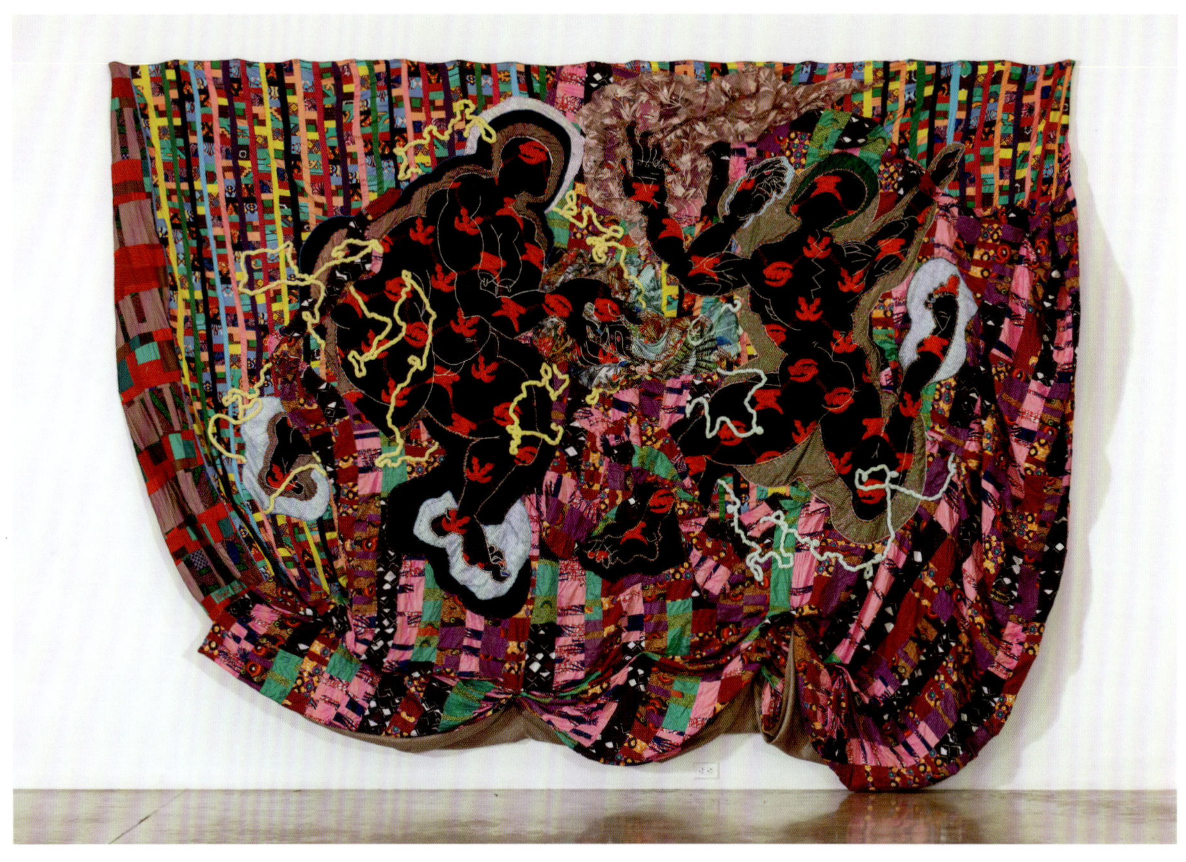

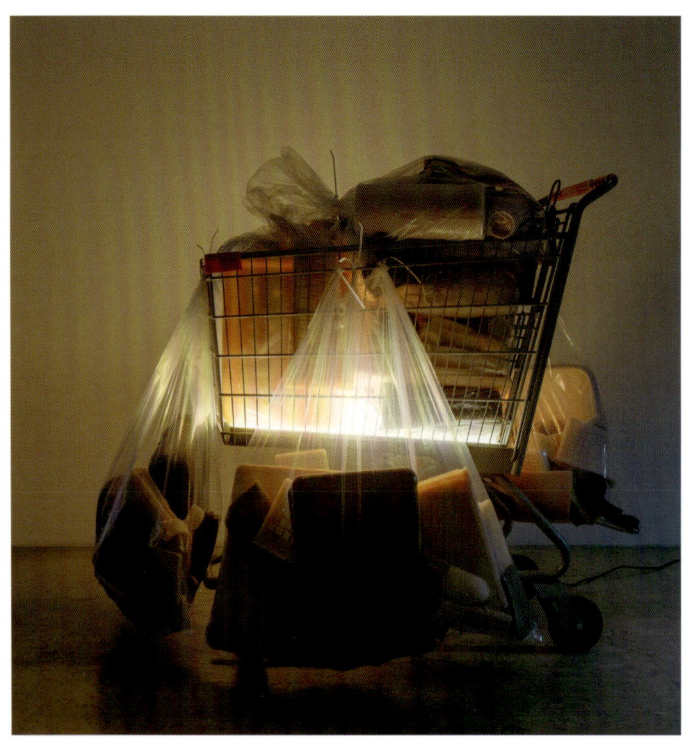 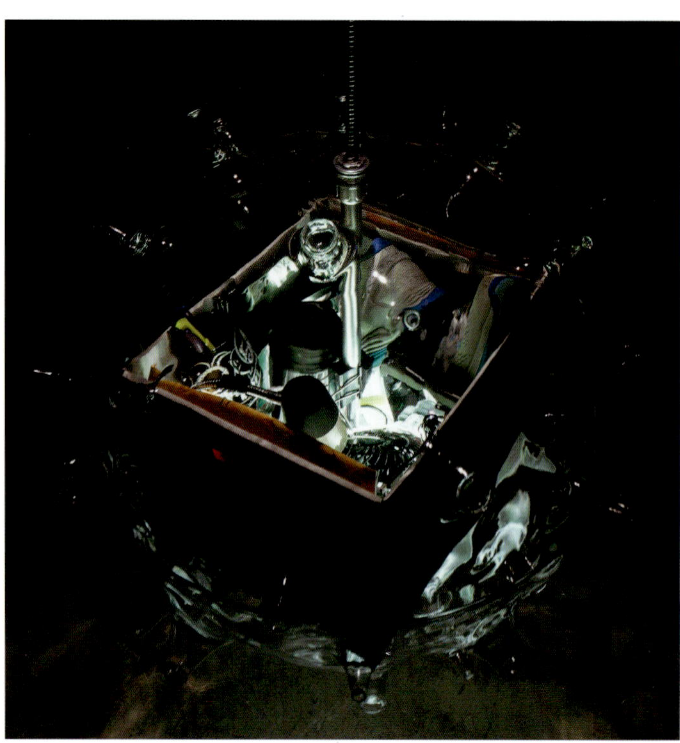

Fast forward 10 or 20 years from our present—half a generation. Another American presidential election is scheduled for fall 2031. Baggy skater pants are back in style in the suburbs. And increasingly intelligent software has turned out the lights on a hundred million jobs. Most of the middle class will never work again. Considered too old, too expensive, too obsolete, and too set in their ways for the faster-paced time in which they find themselves, the majority of people in middle age, born in the 1970s and '80s, have no future prospects for professional employment. Lawyer, accountant, banker, administrator, manager, secretary— these now expendable careers have been starved to near-death, following professions like taxi driver, truck driver, train conductor, and factory worker into automated oblivion. What is to be done with the hundreds of millions of people who will never "earn" another paycheck? What is to be done with you?

And what will you do? Will you prowl the streets scavenging pennies and nickels from discarded plastic and glass? Will you Airbnb your body out to strangers in order to make rent? Your mind has left the real economy, but your body still needs to eat food and spend its days somewhere. In a sharing economy, people subscribe instead of owning, so Suburbia's growing homeless population can't sleep in their cars anymore.

Income inequality scales exponentially and unemployment escalates up the asymptote along with it. The money version of Moore's Law. Twenty-first-century economic crises come equipped standard with a jobless recovery and more effective, efficient automation. Every recession from here on out will close with an ever more brutally competitive round of musical chairs around a diminishing number of lower and lower-paid employment possibilities. If you're left standing at the end without a job, it's your own fault, right?

In its heyday, middle-class status in the "developed" world was a kind of sanctified protection racket. In exchange for giving over most of your waking life to mind/body drudgery, a reasonably salaried job offered shelter from the market's harsher elements. As the fairytales about a trickle-down future for you and your great-grandchildren expire and evaporate, instead of financial security, disposable income, material comfort, and leisure, you're left holding a go-bag filled with desperation, debt, and fear. Plush carpeting replaced with dirty discarded cardboard.

Among the "disruptors" in Silicon Valley's upper echelons, the nameless, faceless millions whose livelihoods are being fast-tracked for the abattoir are often seen as necessary casualties of progress. Unavoidable victims. On the other side of automation's promise, the public is told that there will be new jobs for the next generation. That a whole new ecosystem of sustainable employment will bubble up around the new sharing economy. Prior to World War I—before the mass adoption of the horseless carriage—millions of horses toiled in the shit-filled streets of the world's great cities and on the bloody battlefields of the West. After the war, in less than a generation, they were replaced by internal combustion engines. Where did all the horses go?

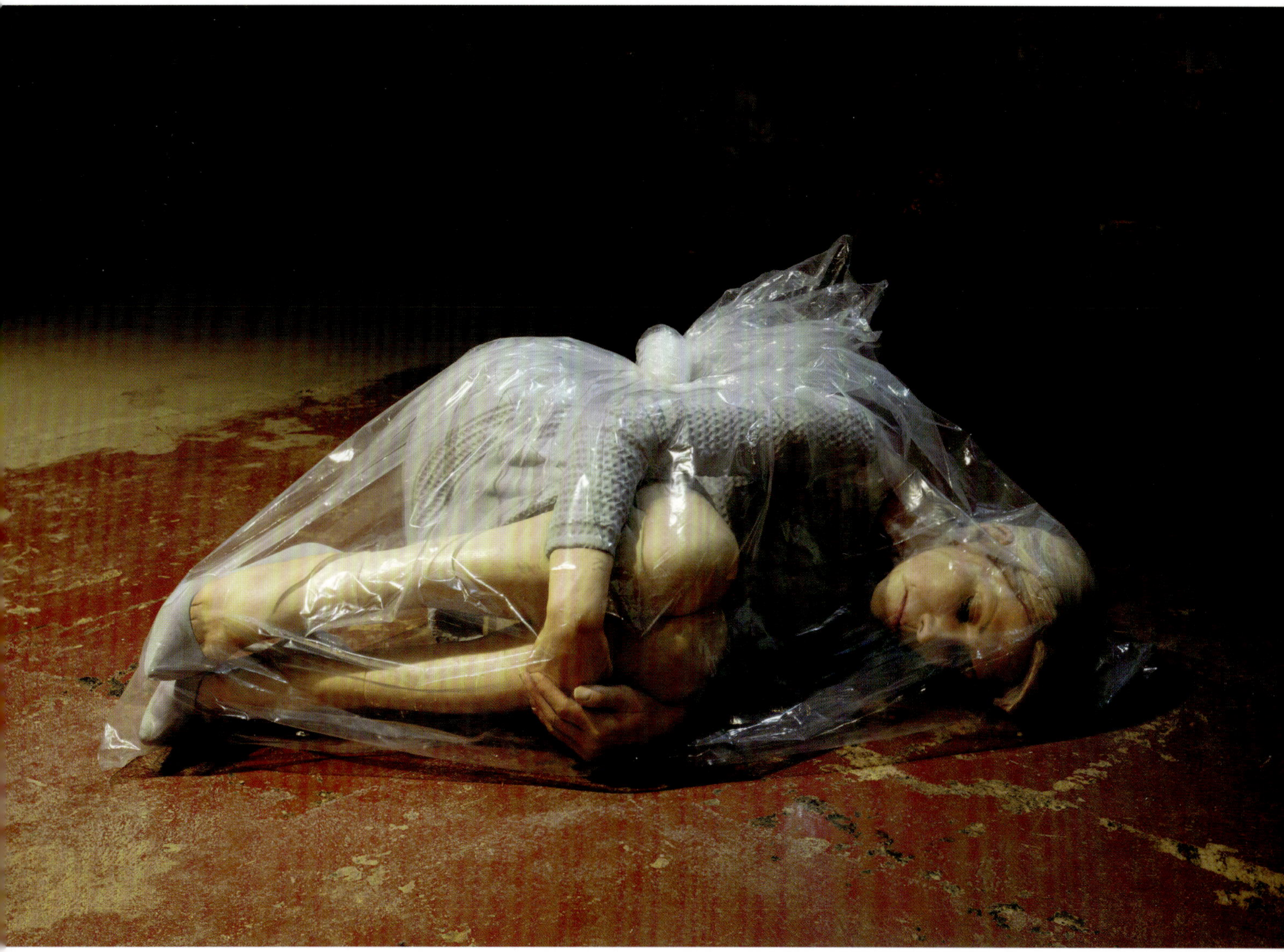

Surprise—this is your going-away party! We bought you this personal-sized little cake in gratitude for your years/life of hard work and service. Your brain is no longer required here. Sure, you're 55, but you can retrain. And start over with an unpaid internship. It'll be fine.
XOXO KIT.

Capitalism doesn't care about you. Economic systems don't have feelings. In a society designed around planned obsolescence, the inevitable fate of goods and services and the people who provide them is to become waste. The same economic alchemy that transmutes a human being into a product—into "human capital"—also turns them into sentient garbage. The other side of consumption's cheap coin is disposal. Desired, acquired, used, used up, discarded, forgotten—this is the lifecycle of expendable labor inside a runaway free market.

The first step towards a cure is diagnosing the disease. You are not your job. You are not your career. You are a human being.

—Josh Kline

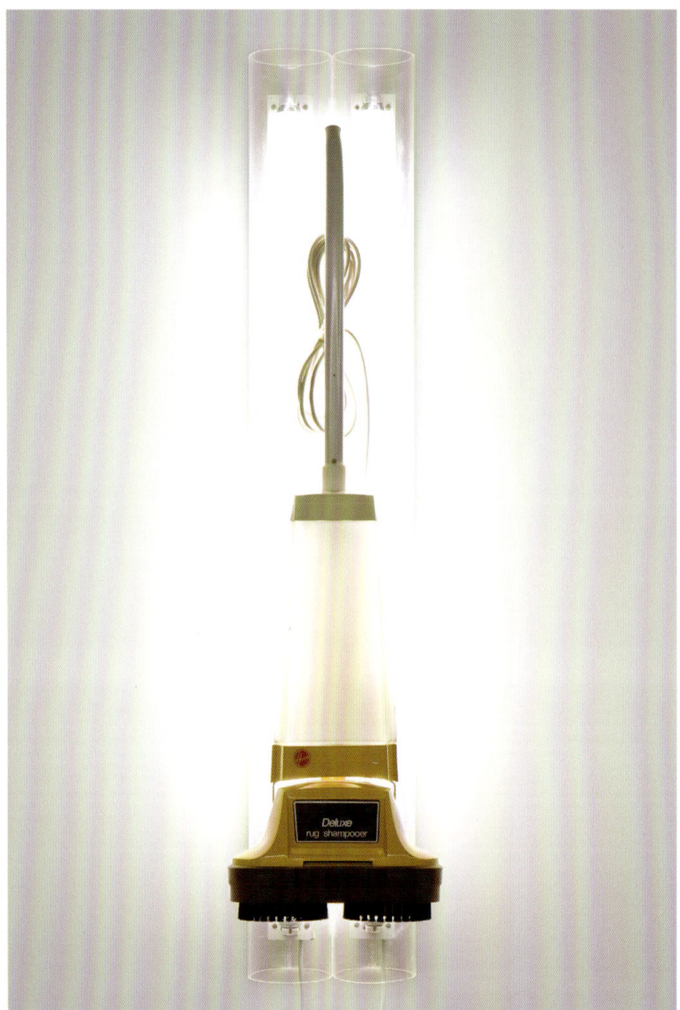

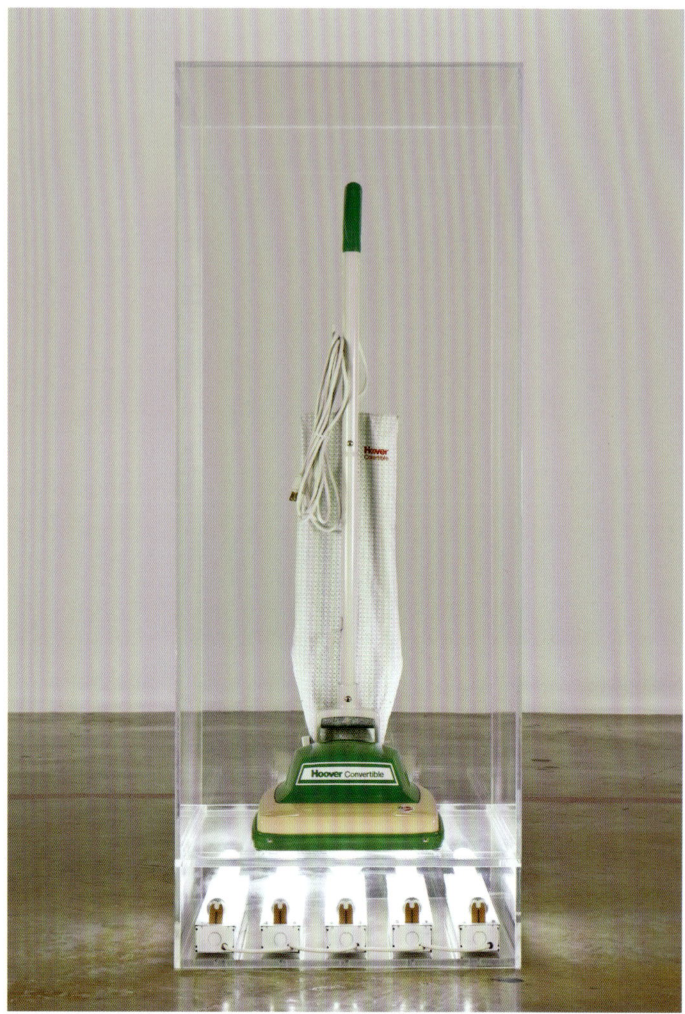

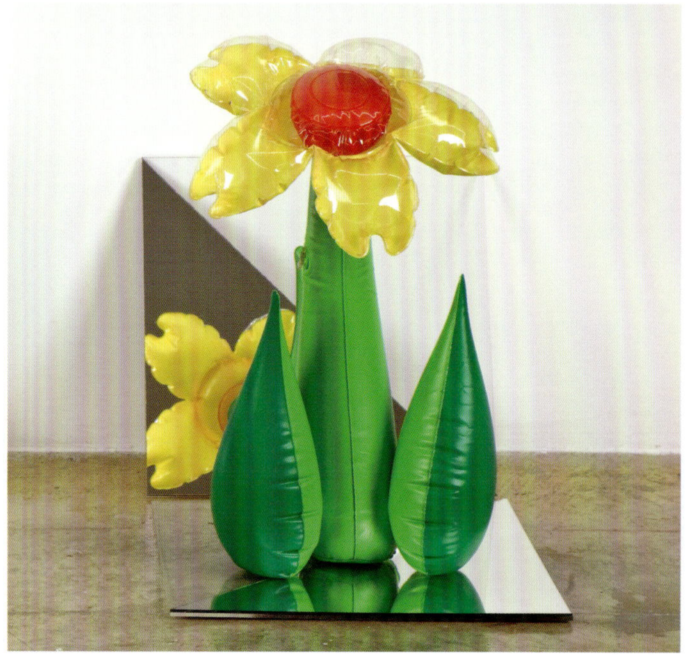

When I was a young artist in New York, the Rubells were one of the most important collectors of young, contemporary work. I knew that the Rubells always had a party for the Whitney Biennial, and in 1979 I went to their home for the party, but it was the wrong evening. They were kind enough to invite me in, so the following day I sent them *Inflatable Flower (Tall Yellow)*. The Rubells were fantastic, and I was thrilled they eventually got more involved with my work. They acquired *New Hoover Deluxe Rug Shampooer* and continued to be supportive with future bodies of my work.

—Jeff Koons

Clockwise from top left:
New Hoover Deluxe Rug Shampooer, 1979, rug shampooer, acrylic, and fluorescent lights, 53 x 10 x 13 in. (134.6 x 25.4 x 33 cm), acquired in 1980
New Hoover Convertible, 1980, vacuum cleaner, Plexiglas, and florescent lights, 56 x 22 1/2 x 22 1/2 in. (142.2 x 57.2 x 57.2 cm), acquired in 1987
Inflatable Flower (Tall Yellow), 1979, vinyl, mirrors, and acrylic, 16 x 12 x 19 in. (40.6 x 30.5 x 48.3 cm), acquired in 1979
Opposite page: *Three Ball 50/50 Tank (Dr. J Silver Series)*, 1985, glass, steel, distilled water, and three basketballs, ed. 1/2, 60 3/4 x 48 3/4 x 13 1/4 in. (154.3 x 123.8 x 33.6 cm), acquired in 1995

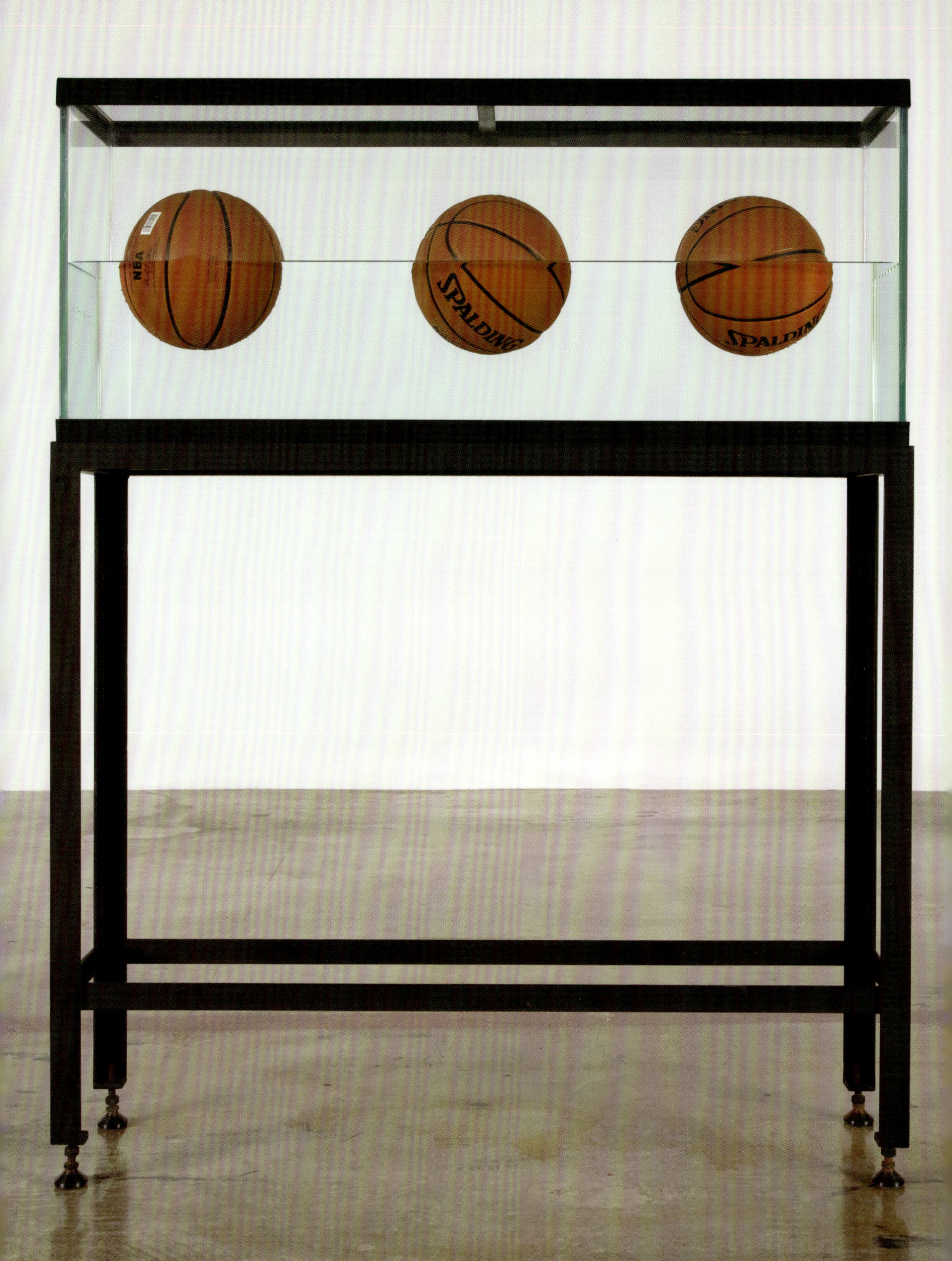

NBA
SPALDING
SPALDING
SPALDING

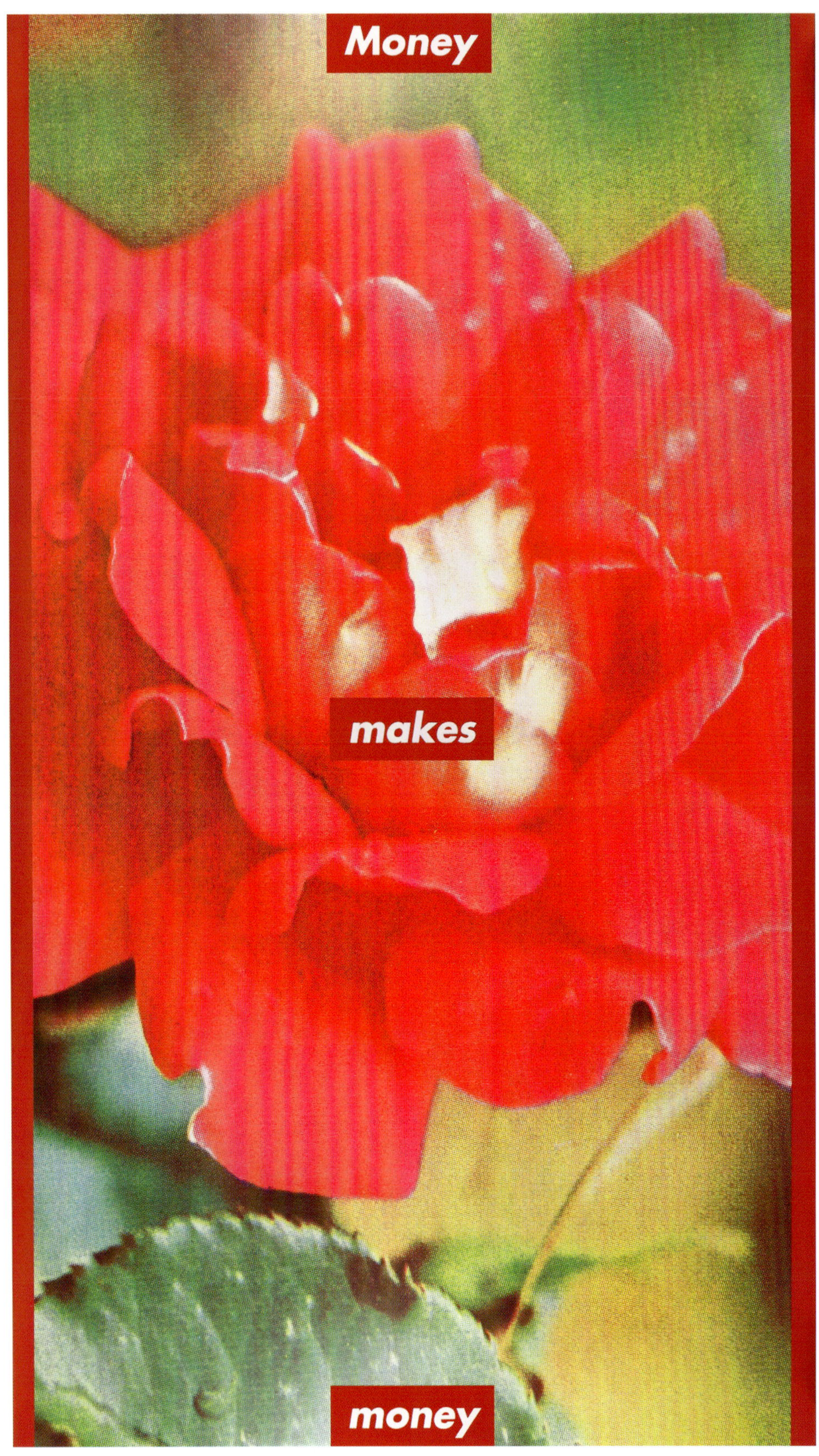

Untitled (Money Makes Money), 2001, screen print on vinyl, 155 x 90 1/2 in. (394 x 230 cm), acquired in 2006

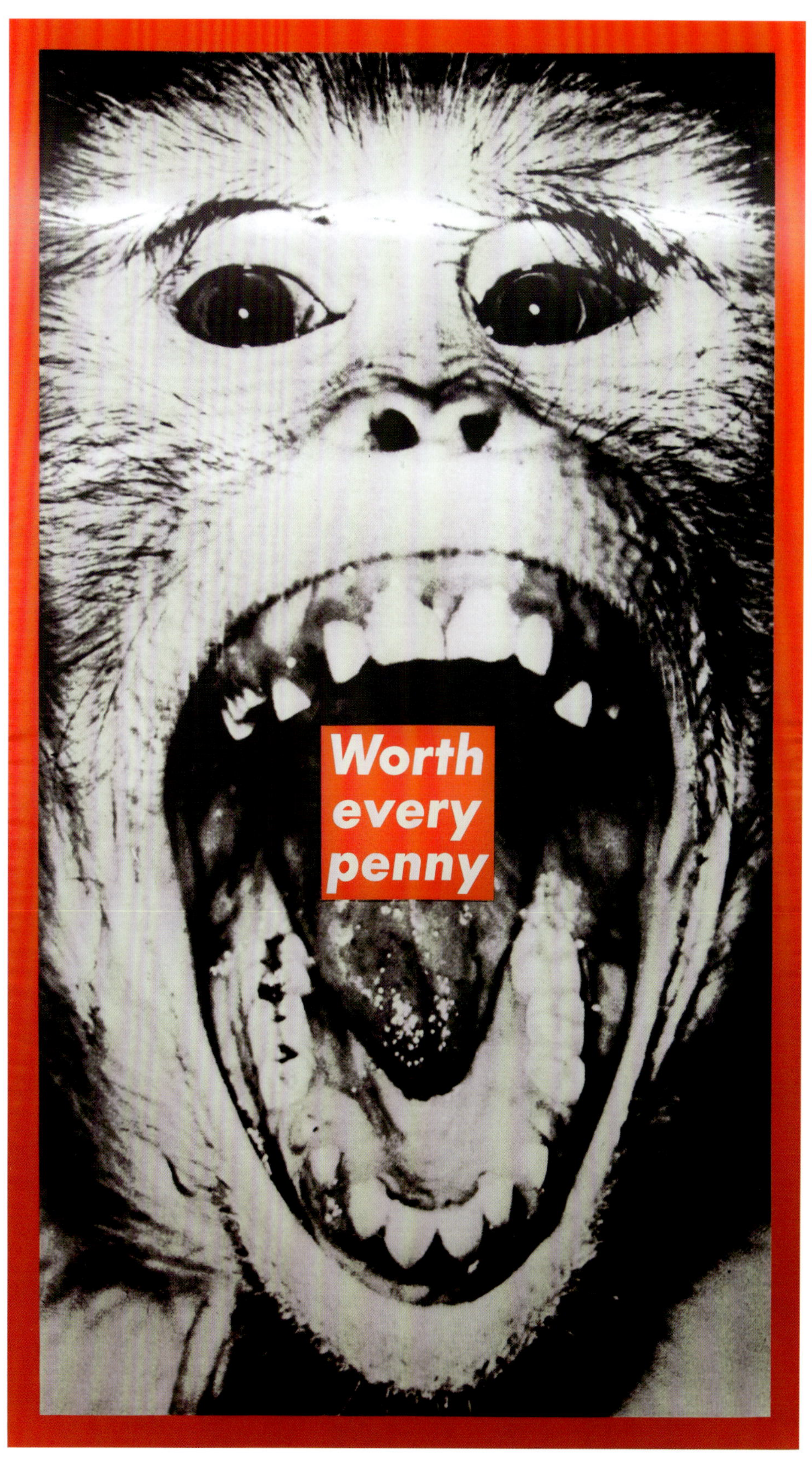

Untitled (Worth Every Penny), 1987, screen print on vinyl, 181 3/4 x 110 1/4 in. (461.5 x 280 cm), acquired in 2005

From the end of 1965 to the beginning of 1966, I stayed in Milan, devising my plans for an outdoor installation to present at the 33rd Venice Biennale, which was to begin in June. Lucio Fontana was most supportive of me during this time, allowing me access to his studio in Milan and assisting in my project even to the point of helping me with financing. In return, I presented him with a *Compulsion Suitcase* covered with phalluses.

Concerning the Venice Biennale of 1966, some have reported that I attempted to participate without an invitation and was sent away, but that is not how it was. It is true that I was not officially invited, but I had spoken directly with the chairman of the committee and received his permission to go ahead with my installation.

Narcissus Garden was an environmental piece consisting of 1500 plastic, mirror balls covering a section of green lawn. The chairman himself had helped me install the reflective spheres, so it was hardly a "guerrilla" operation. I stood among the mirror balls in a formal gold kimono with silver obi and handed out copies of the statement Sir Herbert Read had provided for my exhibition two years earlier.

As a comment on commercialism in the art world, I was selling the mirror balls for 1,200 lira (about $2) each, an audience-participation performance that shocked the authorities. They made me stop, telling me it was inappropriate to sell my artworks as if they were "hot dogs or ice cream cones." But the installation remained.

Nearly 30 years later, in 1993, Akira Tatehata became the Japanese commissioner for the 45th Venice Biennale, and I was officially invited to represent Japan. This was, of course, a moving and meaningful experience for me, but the 1966 Biennale will always remain closer to my heart, if only because back then I had to do everything on my own.

And so my artistic expression has developed, evolved, and propagated, just as it continues to do today. I feel as if I am driving an endless highway, all the way to my death. It is like drinking thousands of cups of coffee cranked out of automatic dispensing machines. And until I reach the end of my life I will, through no choice of my own, aspire to all sorts of feelings and visions, while at the same time fleeing them and seeking obliteration.

I cannot cease to be; nor can I escape death. There are times when consciousness of continuous existence drives me quite mad. Before and after creating a work I fall ill, menaced by obsessions that crawl through my body—although I cannot say whether they come from inside or outside of me.

I fluctuate between feelings of reality and unreality. I am neither a Christian nor a Buddhist. Nor do I possess great self-control. I find myself stranded in a strangely mechanised and standardised, homogenous environment. I feel this most keenly in highly civilised America, and especially in New York.

Psychological and physical frictions abound in the rifts between human beings and the enigmatic, civilised jungle they inhabit. I am deeply interested in trying to understand the relationships between people, society, and nature; and my work is forged from accumulations of these frictions.

—Yayoi Kusama

Narcissus Garden, 1966-, 700 stainless steel spheres, 34 cms diameter each (for floor presentation only); dimensions variable, acquired in 2019

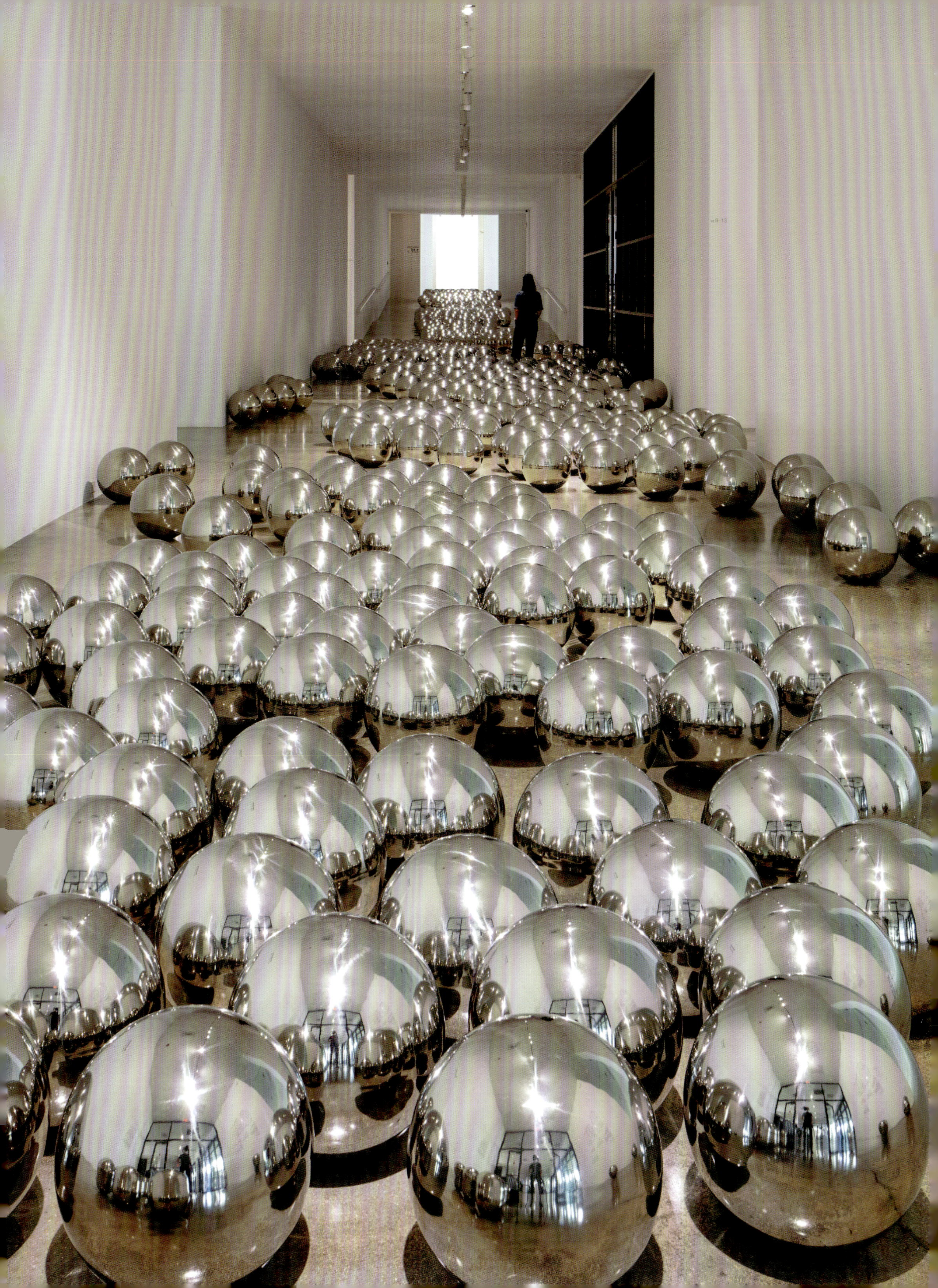

YAYOI KUSAMA

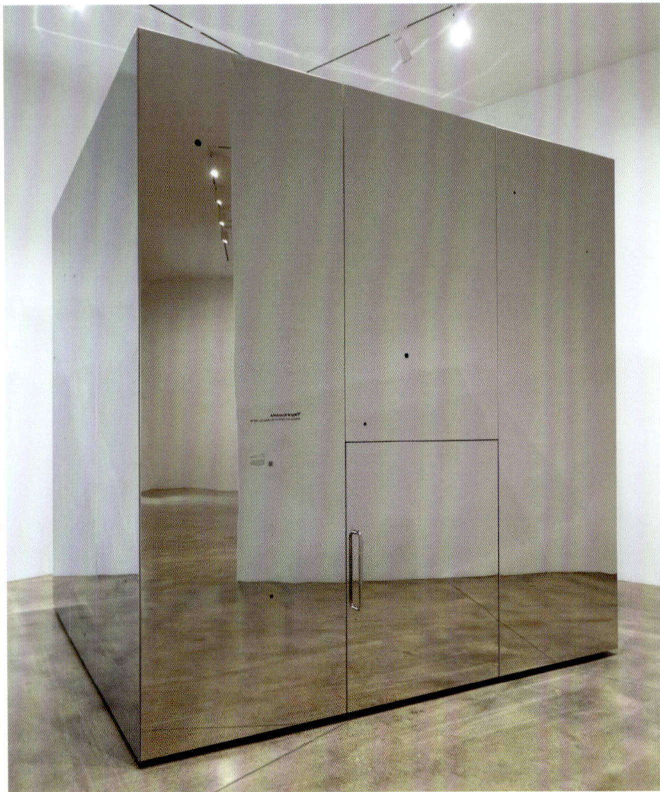

Where the Lights in My Heart Go, 2016, mirror-polished stainless steel with glass mirror, 137 3/4 x 137 3/4 x 137 3/4 in. (3.5 x 3.5 x 3.5 m), acquired in 2017

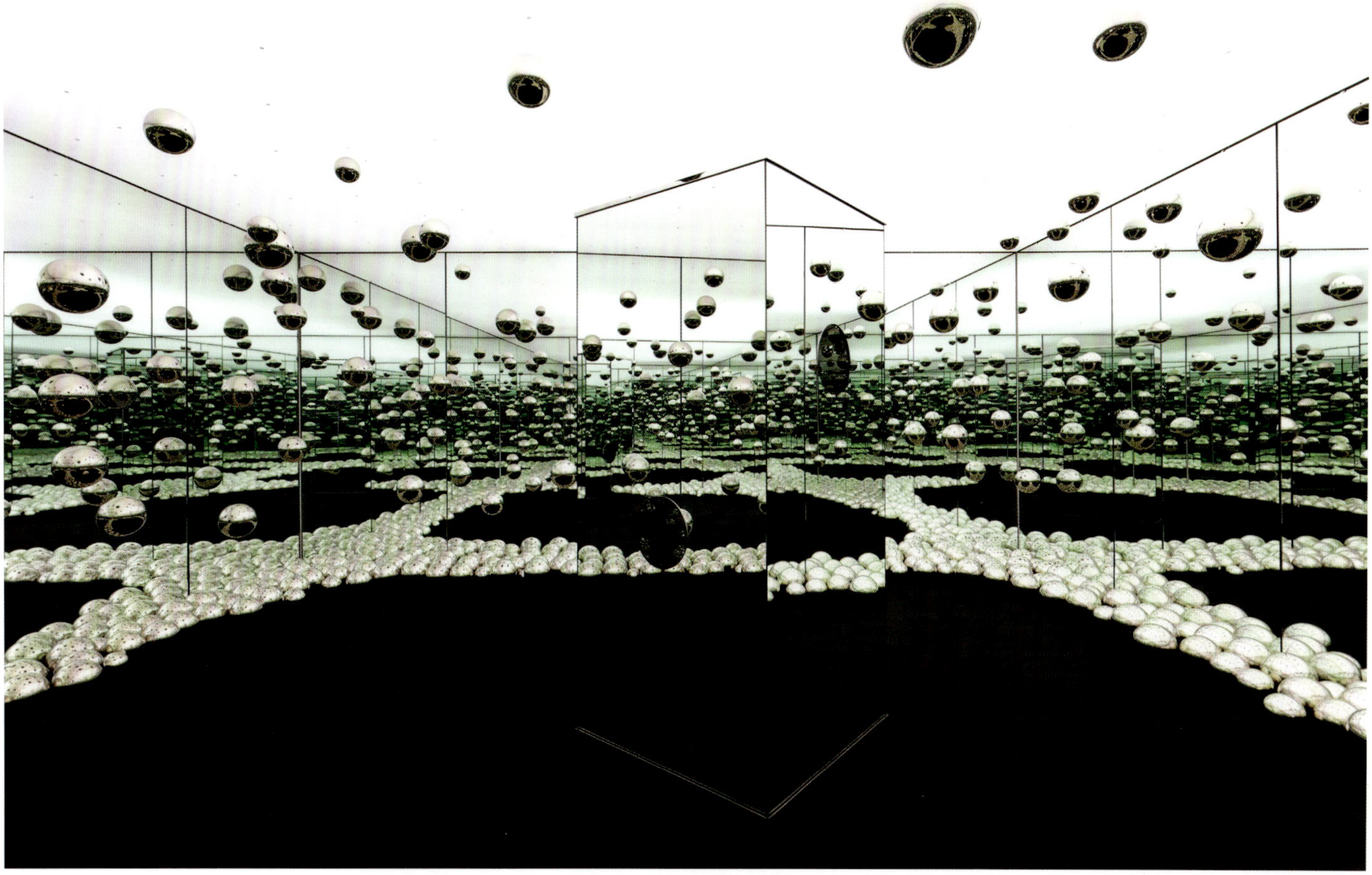

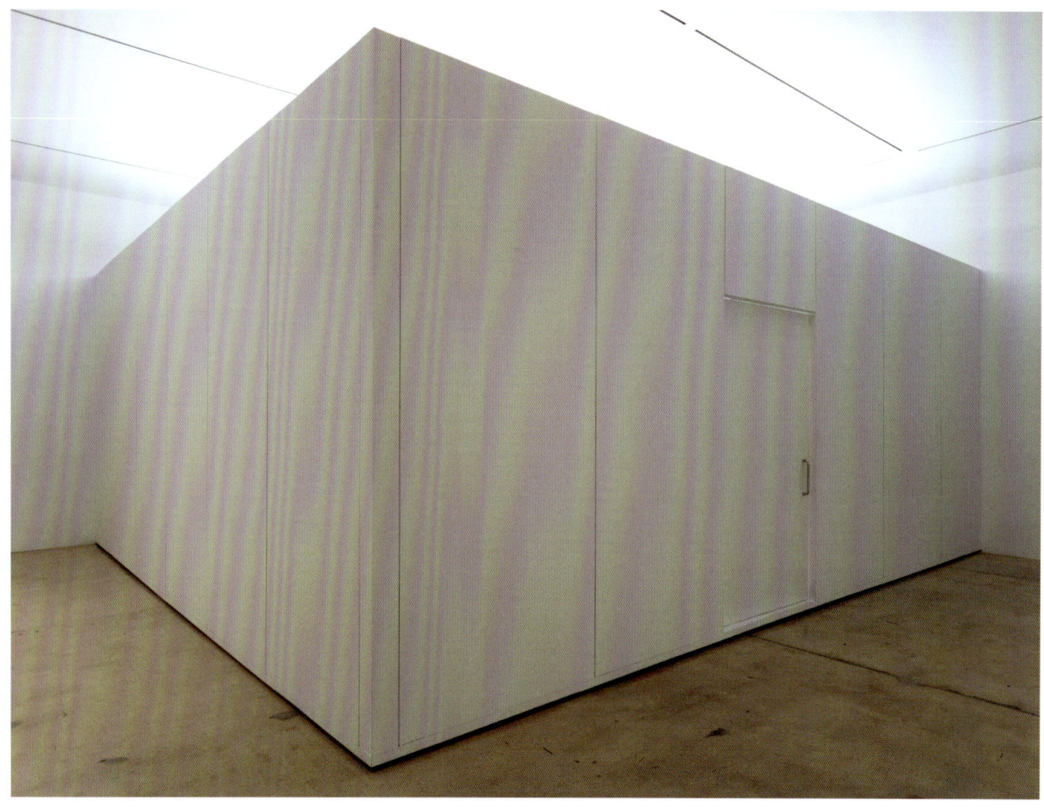

INFINITY MIRRORED ROOM - LET'S SURVIVE FOREVER, 2017, wood, metal, glass mirrors, LED lighting system, monofilament, stainless steel balls, and carpet, ed. 2/3 plus 1 ap, 123 x 246 x 245 1/4 in. (312.4 x 624.8 x 622.9 cm), acquired in 2017

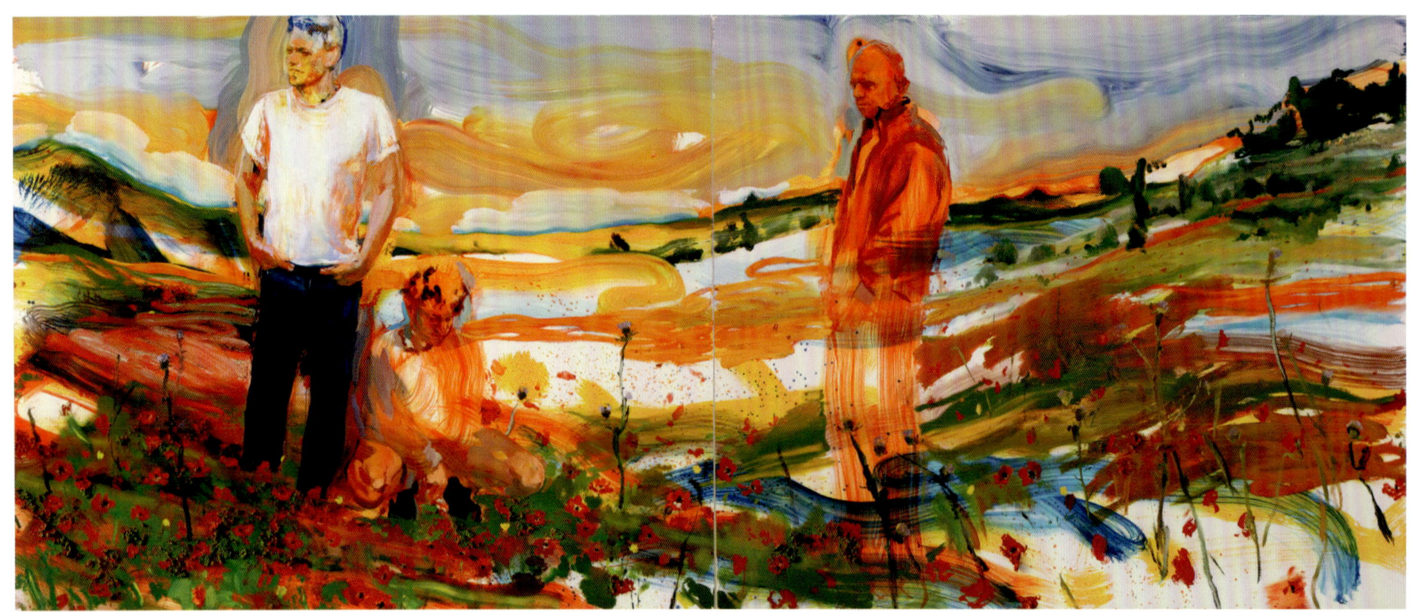

Made after my sister passed away from cancer right before the pandemic in February 2020, *Brothers* depicts me and my two brothers hiking in the Manasseh Hills that surround the valley where I grew up in Israel. We were all at home for the shiva, a traditional Jewish mourning period of seven days, and went on a hike together as we would do in normal times, when we came across this very beautiful field of anemones, common in Israel during that time of year. To me, the flowers are a representation of my sister's presence in the painting. They symbolise both the flowers that we brought to her grave but also serve as metaphor for both vitality and life as well as mourning and death. This was a very difficult time, and I wanted to convey that not only in the imagery itself but also through the turbulent visual language. I was thinking a lot about Edvard Munch's landscapes when I was making this piece and the ways a landscape can capture a psychological and emotional state.

Lovers is part of a body of work depicting couples, each attempting to represent a different emotional state inherent to being in a relationship. This painting describes a bird's-eye view of a naked couple embracing in bed. I wanted to capture the moment after a fight or an intense conversation during which a lot is said, and a lot of feelings are cycled through. To me, this is a loving embrace but also an embrace in which the couple holds onto each other to form an anchor in a turbulent moment. I was thinking of the bed below the couple, which is really just a collection of lines and smears of color, as the residue or the aftermath of that emotional intensity.

Lovers 2 was one of the first paintings I made when I got back to my studio during the pandemic, around May 2020, and because I couldn't really work from observation or have access to models, I was using source material I created when I was an undergraduate student. The painting depicts me and a former partner of mine and is based on small graphite drawings I made from a video of us together. The space in this piece is almost abstract, made of expressive mark making. The bodies come in and out of focus, revealing sweeping brushstrokes that connect the figures with their environment. Through the movement and chromatic color, I wanted to embody the physicality and eroticism of the subject matter.

—Doron Langberg

Brothers, 2021, oil on linen, 80 x 192 in. (203.2 x 487.7 cm), acquired in 2022
Opposite page, top to bottom: *Lovers*, 2022, oil on linen, 80 x 96 in. (203.2 x 243.8 cm), acquired in 2022
Lovers 2, 2020, oil on linen, 80 x 96 in. (203.2 x 243.8 cm), acquired in 2020

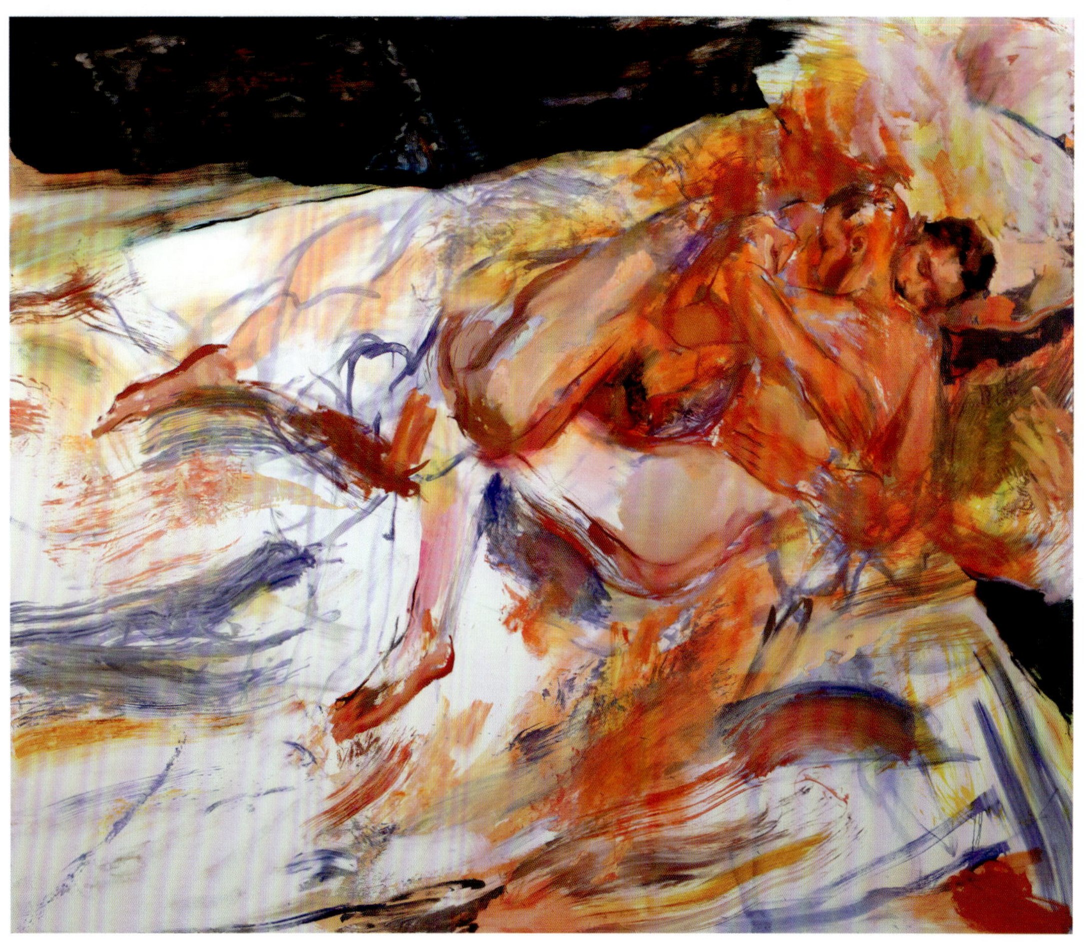

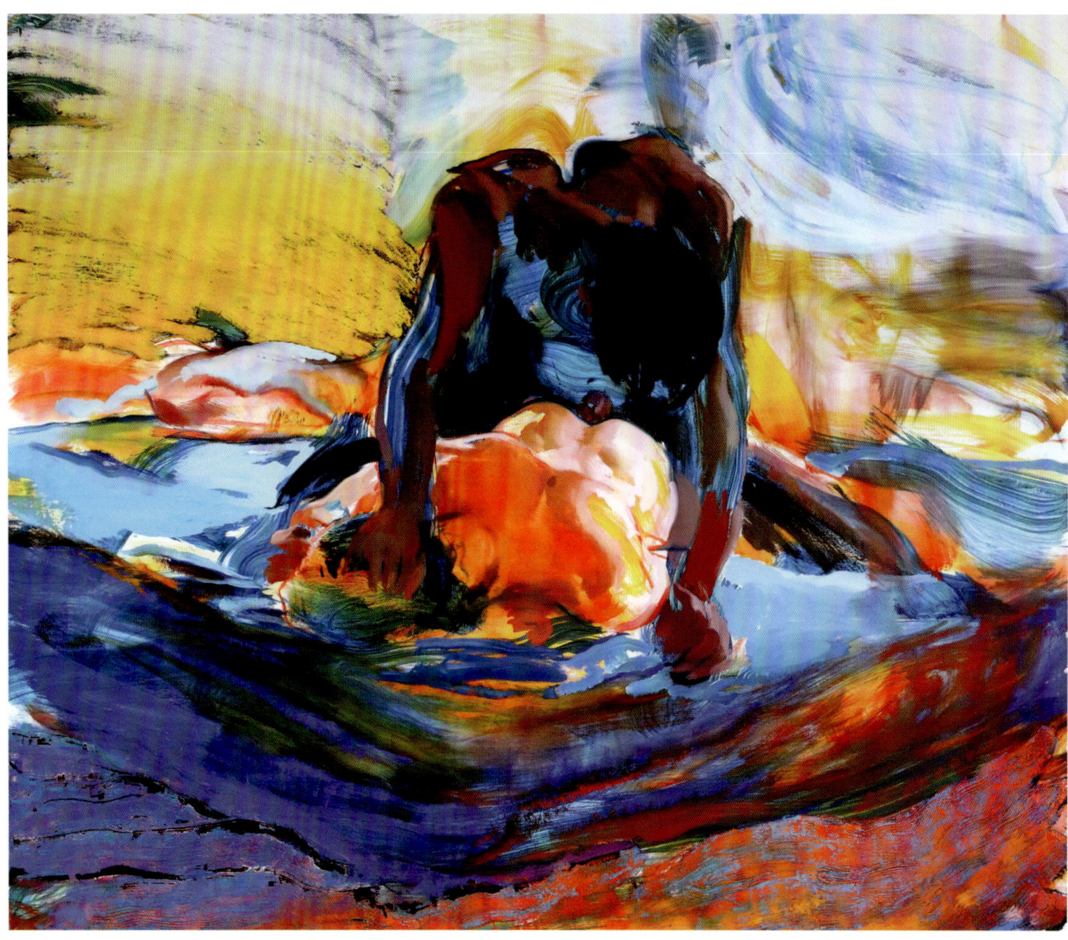

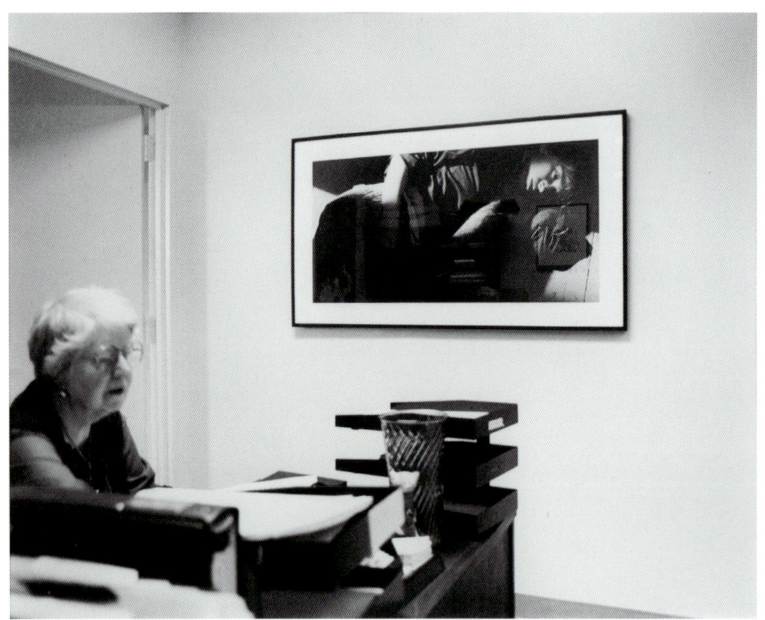

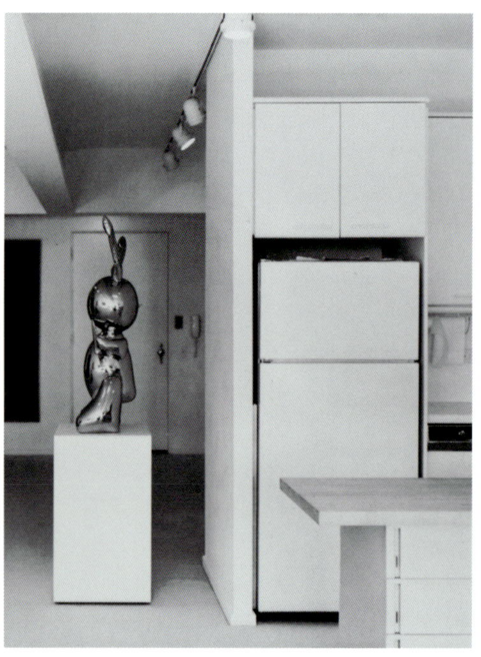

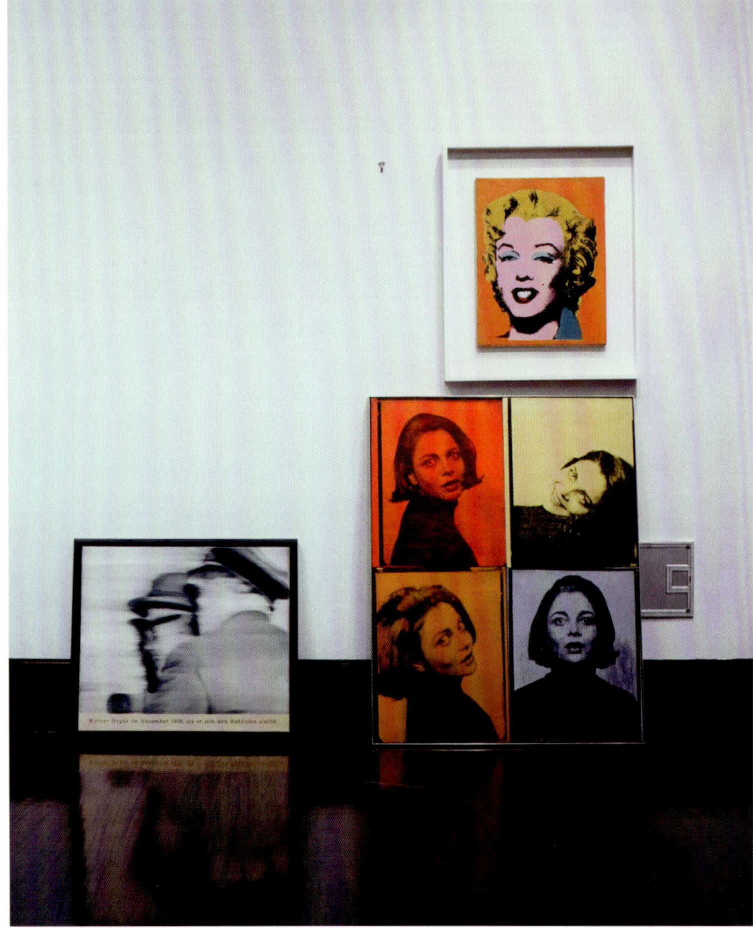

Clockwise from top left:
Arranged by Carl Lobell at Weil, Gosthal & Manges, 1982, black-and-white photograph, ed. 1/5, 13 1/2 x 17 1/2 in. (34.2 x 44 cm), acquired in 2008
Foreground, 1994, black-and-white photograph, ed. of 10 plus AP 1/2, 5 x 3 3/4 in. (13 x 9.5 cm), acquired in 2008
Life After 1945 (Faces), 2006-2007, cibachrome mounted on aluminum and wood, ed. 4/5, 40 x 33 1/2 in. (101.5 x 85 cm), acquired in 2008
Opposite page:
Arranged by Mera and Donald Rubell, New York City, 1982, black-and-white photograph, ed. 4/5, 17 3/4 x 19 in. (45 x 48.4 cm), acquired in 2006

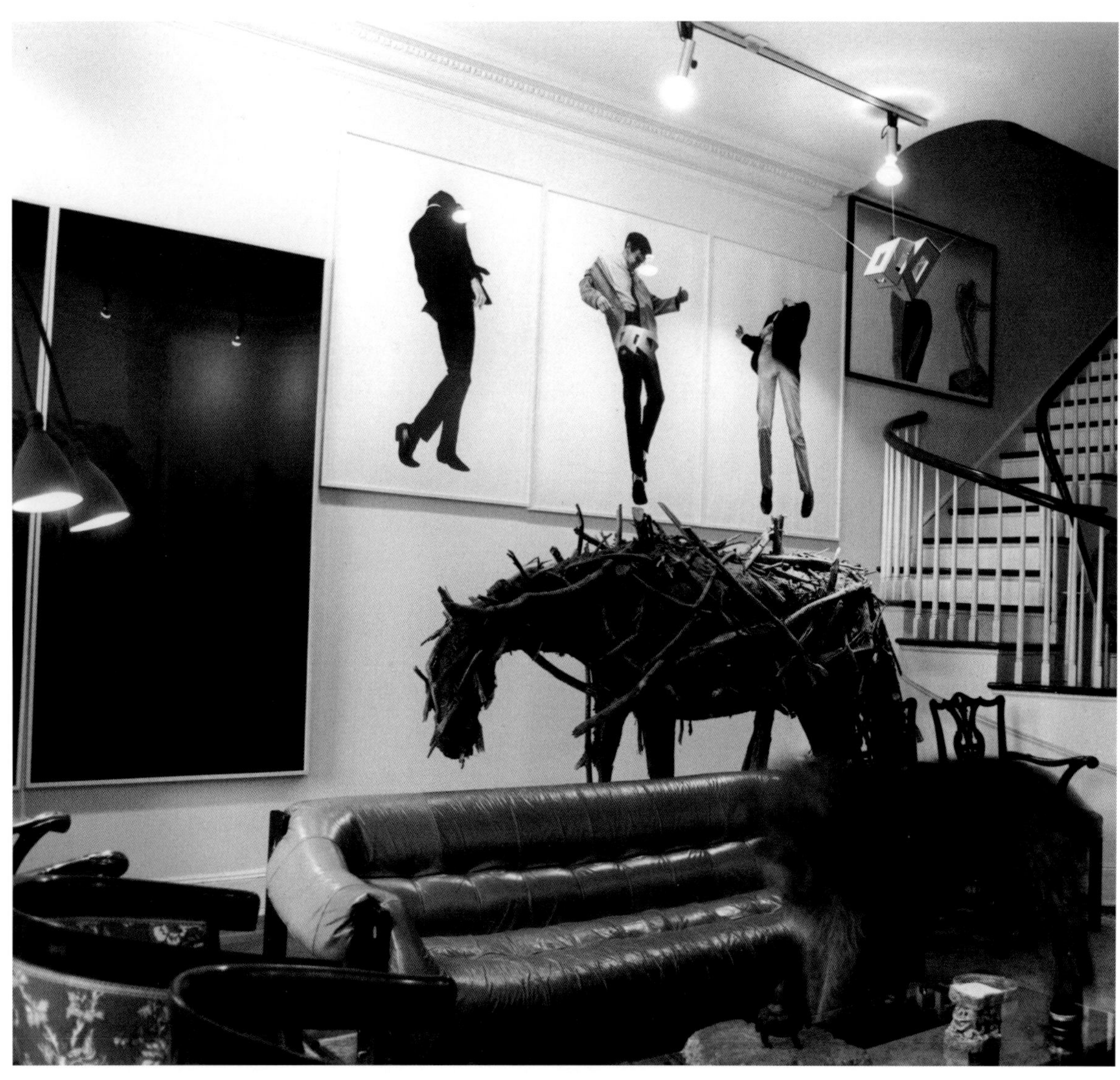

Louise Lawler: When Metro asked me to do a show in 1982, they already had an image. They represented a group of artists whose work often dealt with issues of appropriation and was often spoken of and written about together. A gallery generates meaning through the type of work it chooses to show. I self-consciously made work that "looked like" Metro Pictures. The first thing you saw when you entered my show, *Arrangements of Pictures*, was an arrangement of works the gallery had on hand by "gallery artists" Robert Longo, Cindy Sherman, Jack Goldstein, Laurie Simmons, and James Welling. A wall label titled it "Arranged by Louise Lawler." It was for sale as a work with a price determined by adding up the prices of the individual pieces, plus a percentage for me. I went to the collectors to whom Metro had sold work and photographed the Metro artists' works in those contexts. I printed the resulting images a "normal" picture size and titled them "arrangements," too—for example, *Arranged by Barbara and Eugene Schwartz, New York City*. The Metro situation at that time formed that work, and it also formed a way of working for me.

Douglas Crimp: Having this sort of information is very clarifying; it isn't reductive.

LL: The problem is that you say what's easiest to say or what you can be most articulate about, which neglects other aspects of the work, because you can't talk about everything. It's a matter of focusing, and focusing the meaning of the work limits its reception for the viewer. It's like the phrase I printed on one of my drinking glasses, "It's something like putting words in your mouth." Then again, if I were to do a book of very accurate captions giving all the pertinent information about the situation in which the work initially appeared, it would seem fetishizing. That would limit the work's meaning in another way. Of course, there's also what else is out there, which is part of how the work is received, too. The work can never be determined just by what I do or say. Its comprehension is facilitated by the work of other artists and critics and just by what's going on at the time.

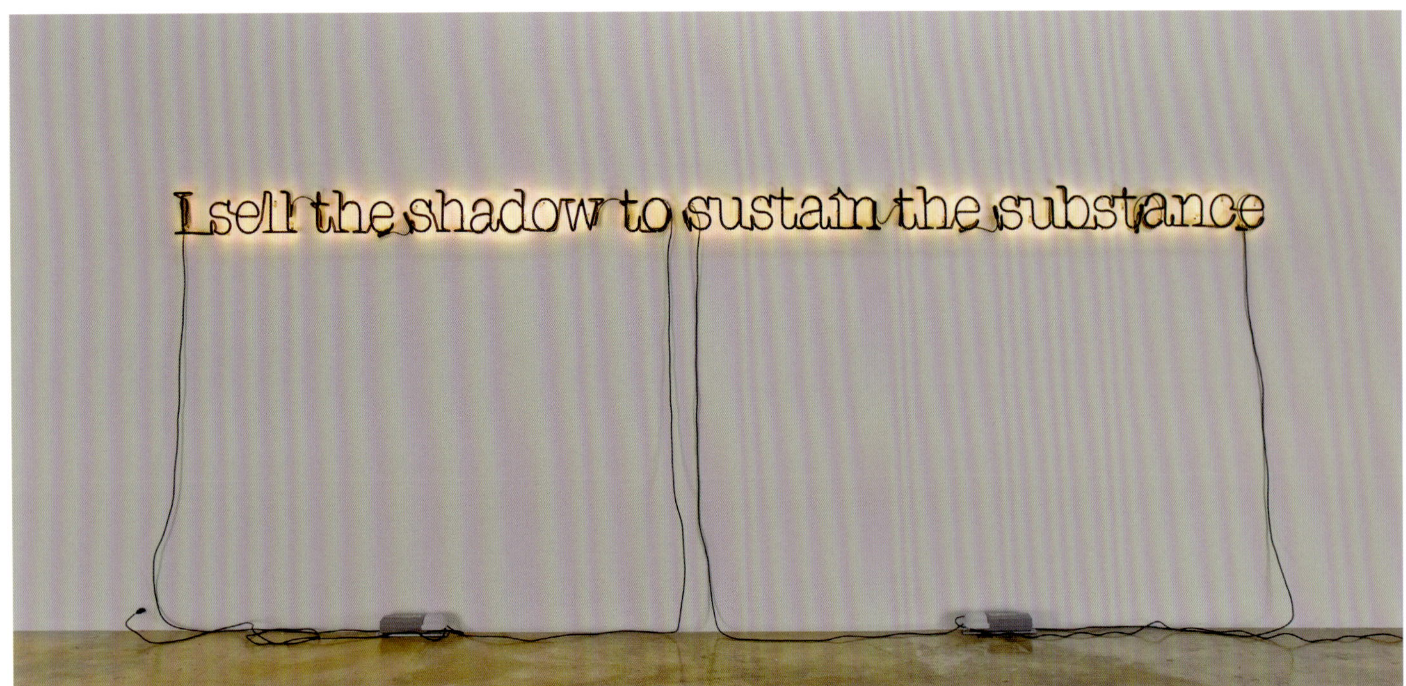

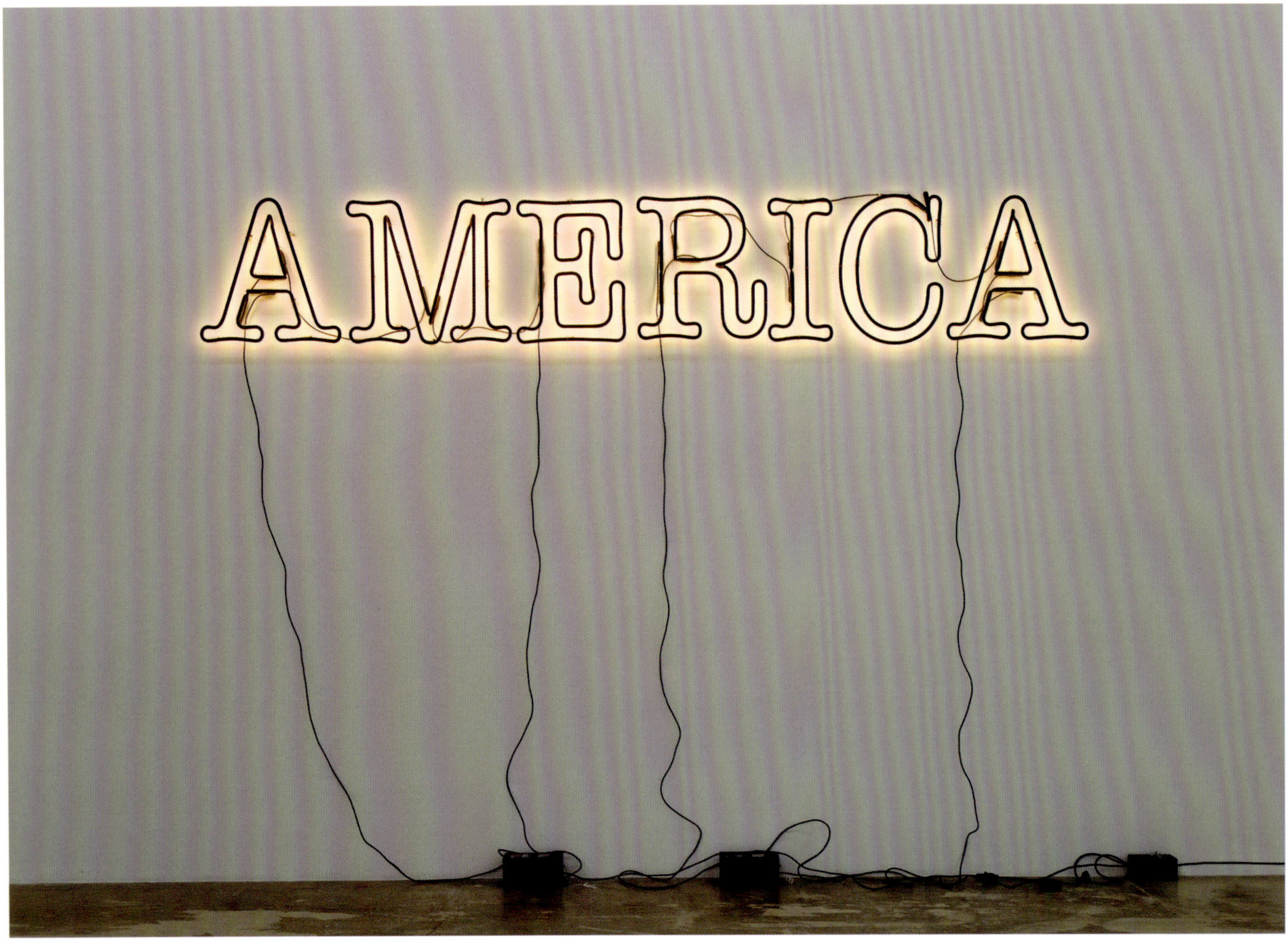

Untitled (I Sell the Shadow to Sustain the Substance), 2006, neon and paint, ed. 3/3, 7 1/2 x 192 1/2 in. (19 x 489 cm), acquired in 2006
America, 2008, neon sign and paint, ed. of 1 plus AP, 24 x 168 in. (61 x 426.7 cm), acquired in 2008

UNTITLED | GLENN LIGON

A IS FOR AFROPESSIMISM

A dyspeptic variation on Afrocentrism, Afrofuturism, Afronauts and various other "Afro" words.

B IS FOR BLACK

A child of the civil rights movement, my mother believed that as Black people we would use our natural talents and abilities to rise above adversity. Paradoxically, she also believed that Blackness consisted of habits, not nature, and most of those that she associated with it were negative. In response to the "grown acting" of my childhood years she used to say, "Roll your eyes at me again and I will knock the Black off you." For years I imagined that Blackness was like the shell of a hard-boiled egg, which, if tapped frequently and methodically, could be peeled away; or that Blackness could be scraped off like the surface of burnt toast.

C IS FOR COCOROSIE

My mother attributed some of my bad habits to "following what white people do," which only added to my general confusion about racial identity. Nowadays, following white people's behavior is not an option because there is so little of it left to emulate. The breadth of this scarcity was made clear to me when I read a recent article in *The New York Times* about the band CocoRosie ("Twisted Sisters," July 6, 2008). Bianca, one of the sisters who make up the group, explained that their mom was ashamed of the looks she had inherited from her Syrian Orthodox mother and Native American father. "Our mom's a seriously beautiful woman; she looks like Cher after the surgery, but growing up, she was ashamed of who she was," Bianca said. "Nowadays, who would want to be white? But back then, in farm country, anything other than button-nosed blonde didn't fly."

While I applaud the sentiment behind this white flight, I note that it occurs at a moment of increasing Black misery and hopelessness. It would seem that not all forms of disappearance are created equal.

D IS FOR DISNEY

A more radical instance of *disidentification* was Sun Ra's retreat from the category of "human." After all, better to be from Saturn than to be from pre-civil-rights-era Birmingham. What Ra did not give up, ironically, was his love of Disney. Ra's 1989 album, *Second Star to the Right*, is composed of freewheeling versions of Disney classics such as "Some Day My Prince Will Come" and "Zip-a-Dee-Doo-Dah." While some jazz musicians have been drawn to popular music in general, Ra—with his sense of self-invention and the fantastic—

perhaps found a particular resonance in the *gesamtkunstwerk* that Walt Disney created at his theme parks.

E IS FOR ELMO

And better to be an alien than unemployed. Actors such as Michael Dorn and Tim Russ as Worf and Tuvok in *Star Trek*, Joe Morton as the Brother in *Brother from Another Planet*, Ahmed Best as the voice of Jar Jar Binks, James Earl Jones as the voice of Darth Vader, and Kevin Clash as Elmo have excelled in giving voice to the non-human.

F IS FOR "I BELIEVE I CAN FLY"

Rising above the confines of the terrestrial reminded me of another act of levitation I witnessed at the opening of *Frequency*, an exhibition at the Studio Museum in Harlem in 2005. Standing in front of Rodney McMillian's *Untitled* (2004), an abject piece of canvas with strokes of latex paint and charcoal that started on the floor and traveled eight feet up the wall, I thought, 'The children believe they can fly.' This is not to say that I haven't flown too, but the effortless, Michael Jordan-like virtuosity of the piece and its dialogue with the work of artists such as Marcel Duchamp and David Hammons left me speechless.

G IS FOR GREEN

Richard Green burst into seventh grade French class to ask what *Voulez-vous coucher avec moi ce soir?* meant. Richard was what my Uncle Tossy called "a complicated Negro." Streetwise yet slightly 'country,' athletic, yet bookish, Richard was an anomaly in the overly liberal, predominantly white private high school we attended. My more wicked classmates would sing Kermit the Frog's theme song, "It's Not Easy Bein' Green," whenever he walked into the student lounge. Richard's outburst in French class became legendary, although I knew he was simply asking about lyrics from the LaBelle song "Lady Marmalade." Embarrassed for him and for my people, I told my classmates that I didn't know what all that mess was about.

H IS FOR HAPPENS TO BE BLACK

Obama, it is said, is a presidential candidate that "happens to be Black." This is despite the fact that he is biracial and chose to call himself an African American. I happens to be Black too, though I don't know how it happened. Because I never felt I was in a position to choose my racial identity, it never occurred to me that Blackness was something that could happen to you, like being mugged, or winning the lottery. I thought one was just Black and that was that.

I IS FOR INVISIBLE MAN

I first read Ellison's novel in high school. The density of the text mirrored what I thought about Black people: that we were a deep people. It was reading that book that made me think I wanted to be a writer, although when it was first published not everyone was happy with its depiction of Black life. One critic claimed, Black people "need Ralph Ellison's *Invisible Man* like we need a hole in the head or a stab in the neck." Still, that novel was a crucial catalyst for the use of text in my paintings.

J IS FOR JERRY LEWIS

Every Labor Day I would watch his muscular dystrophy telethon. I wondered what it would be like to have someone raise money for *my* cause. What that cause would be, I wasn't sure. Brooding Negro Syndrome, perhaps?

K IS FOR KRAZY KAT

I, too, used to mistake bricks for love.

L IS FOR LIGON!

My mother worked as a therapist's aide at Bronx Psychiatric Center, a large mental health facility in the Northeast Bronx. Sometimes, after school, I would meet her at work to go to the lunch counter at Woolworth's for grilled cheese sandwiches and ice cream sundaes. Since the hospital was an outpatient facility, half of the people we ran into on the walk to Woolworth's were being treated at the hospital. I would play a game with my mother called "Patient or Employee," the object of which was to guess whether the person who shouted "Ligon!" at my mother as we passed on the street was a mental patient or a co-worker. I was never very good at this game.

M IS FOR THE MANY THINGS SHE GAVE ME

International Children's Day, a United Nations-sponsored holiday celebrating the rights of children, was a holiday that my brother and I took very seriously. Every year on Children's Day I would ask my mother what presents she had bought for me. "When you are a parent, every day is Children's Day," she would reply, rolling her eyes.

N IS FOR NEGRO SUNSHINE

"Rose Johnson and Melanctha Herbert had been friends now for some years. Rose had lately married Sam Johnson, a decent, honest kindly fellow, a deck hand on a coasting steamer.

Melanctha Herbert had not yet been really married.

Rose Johnson was a real Black, tall, well built, sullen, stupid, childlike, good looking negress. She laughed when she was happy and grumbled and was sullen with everything that troubled.

Rose Johnson was a real Black negress but she had been brought up quite like their own child by white folks.

Rose laughed when she was happy but she had not the wide, abandoned laughter that makes the warm broad glow of negro sunshine. Rose was never joyous with the earth-born, boundless joy of negroes. Hers was just ordinary, any sort of woman laughter."

Three Lives, Gertrude Stein

O IS FOR OPRAH

Oprah Winfrey believed her ancestors were Zulus, but they turned out to be from Liberia. "Oprah, of course, wants to be Zulu. She's announced to the world she's Zulu," said scholar Henry Louis Gates, who helped her trace her lineage. "Oprah is not Zulu. None of us are Zulu. There is no African American who comes from the Zulu people."

("Fascinating look into history, race and DNA," *Oakland Tribune*, January 31, 2006)

P IS FOR PROUD

James Brown's "Say it Loud" was released in 1968. When it came on the radio I could sing the "Say it Loud" part but I could only whisper, "I'm Black and I'm proud."

Q IS FOR QUESTIONS AND ANSWERS

I gave a lecture at Princeton where, as an aside during a lull in the question-and-answer period, I said that Black people were going to disappear. Afterwards at the wine and cheese reception, an elderly woman came up to me to thank me for the talk. "When you said you thought Black people were going to disappear I knew exactly what you mean," she said, her face full of sympathy. "I mean you're just not interesting to us any more. Now there are Chinese people and Mexicans..."

R IS FOR RACE

Childhood crushes: Race Bannon on *Jonny Quest*, and Racer X on *Speed Racer*. Every Saturday morning I would wake up at 6 a.m. to wait for my cartoon paramours to appear in black-and-white on the old console TV we had in the living room of our apartment.

S IS FOR SHADOWS

I first saw Warhol's *Shadow* paintings at the Heiner Friedrich Gallery in 1979. I remember thinking that it was an awfully big room in which to show paintings of nothing. Although I never met Andy Warhol, I saw him once on the street in SoHo. He was thin, ghostly, and almost transparent. To make a career out of being fascinated with one's own disappearance is quite a feat. I realized that if disappearance could be a subject matter, I could be an artist.

T IS FOR TYRONE

My brother Tyrone was a year older than I and although we didn't look alike, people would often ask if we were twins. When we were in elementary school, my mother used to give me his secondhand clothes to wear. She stopped doing that when I told her that wearing hand-me-downs made me feel like "I was not myself."

U IS THE UNITED STATES OF AFRICA

The U.S.A. is where Uhura, the communications officer on *Star Trek*, was from. Recently I read that Nichelle Nichols, the actress that played Uhura, wanted to quit the show after the first season, but Martin Luther King Jr. persuaded her to stay on because she was a "role model." Although I was proud to see a Black person on TV, Uhura annoyed me. In the future, couldn't Black people do more than just operate the switchboard?

V IS FOR VULCAN

A planet where they had learnt to suppress emotions. I was obsessed with Vulcans and when I went to *Star Trek* conventions as a teenager I bought all the Vulcan paraphernalia I could find. I tried to imagine being a Vulcan, although I knew it meant that I would have to give up my Richard Pryor and Parliament-Funkadelic LPs and that was too much of a sacrifice. Also, there wasn't a Black Vulcan until 1995 when the character Tuvok was introduced on *Star Trek: Voyager*; by that time I had moved on to wanting to be Jeff Koons.

W IS FOR WHITE

Q. You've seen the evolution from Negro to Black to African American? What is the best thing for Blacks to call themselves?

A. White.

Sociologist Kenneth B. Clark being interviewed for *The New York Times*. ("An Integrationist to This Day, Believing All Else Has Failed," May 7, 1995)

X IS FOR X

When I was in my twenties, I met a member of the Nation of Islam who told me that since Black people took the last names of their masters, we all had slave names. That was why, he explained, Malcolm Little had changed his name to Malcolm X. I considered changing my last name to *X* for a week or so, but decided that it would involve too much paperwork and it would upset my mom.

Y IS FOR "YOU FEEL ME?"

You feel me?

Z IS FOR ZULUS

I remember when being called a "Zulu" was an insult. When I was very young, Black people didn't want anything to do with Africa. Ironically, this was after a period earlier in the century when Black people organized themselves around leaving America and going back to Africa. In the late sixties, Black people rediscovered Africa again, although it was still a mythologized Africa, an Africa where everyone knew our name. Nowadays everybody wants to be a Zulu, though we don't necessarily want to live in Africa. Being a descendant of a Zulu is enough. Zulu is beautiful. Now *that's* change you can believe in.

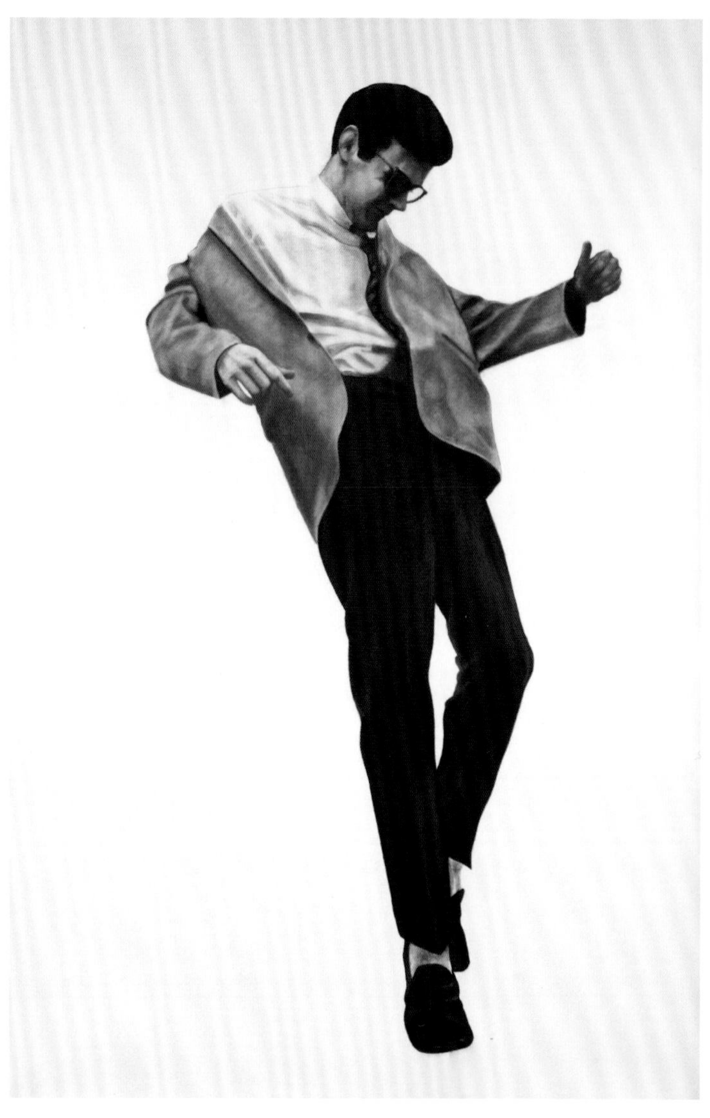

The title of this work, *Men Trapped in Ice*, comes from a dream I had of men with their feet frozen in ice. They could only move from the ankles up and squirmed and writhed in torment. This work was the second triptych that I made in the very early stages of my practice. I was soon to focus all my attention on the *Men in the Cities* series, so this was the first work that I created once I had figured out what my main investigation would be. It would set the tone for the explosion that became the *Men in the Cities* series, which included both men and women. I soon stopped playing in bands and doing performances in order to hunker down to this journey. What is significant about this seminal work is that the three drawings are all based on photographs I took of my friends— not appropriated images. Two of the men are punk/no wave musicians. The clothes they have on were our uniforms, our "no wave" urban uniforms. Men wore skinny ties, stovepipe pants, and women wore skirts and black dresses. It was stuff that we found at thrift shops. These figures are not the "yuppies" that they have been confused with recently. They are much more rock 'n' roll, film noir, violent. The triptych is designed in an almost rhythmic pattern, like chord changes in a song. It's less like Muybridge—sequential—and more about rotation. In that sense I think of them as abstract calligraphy, in a way. I think that informed me. I also love this dichotomy

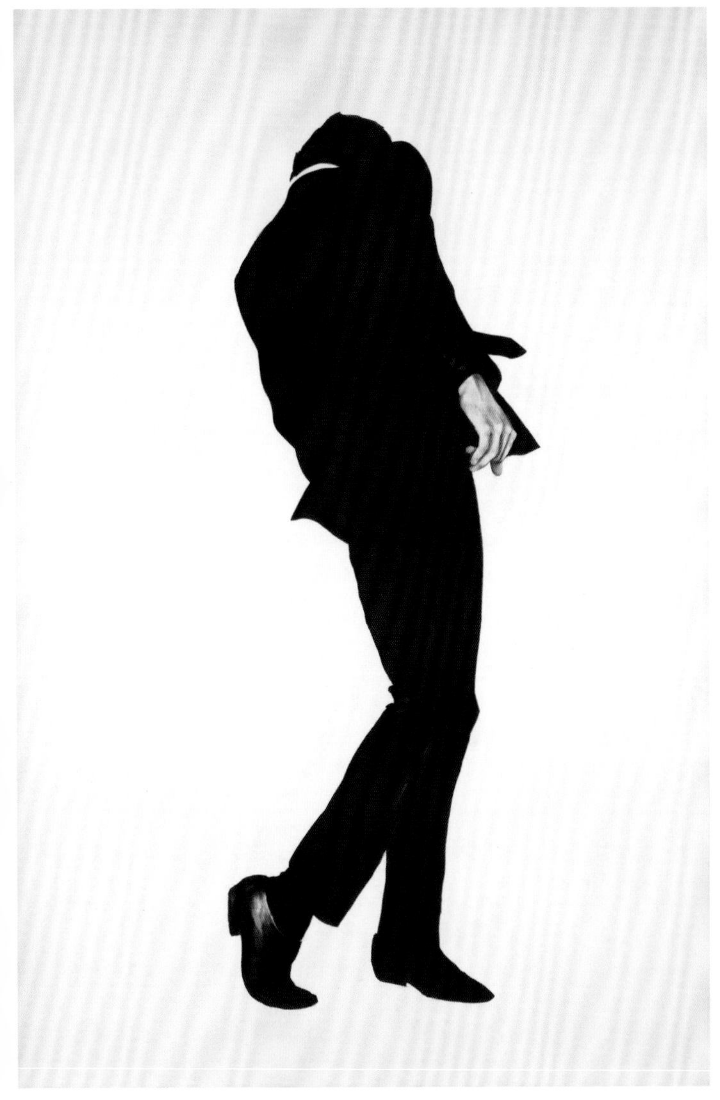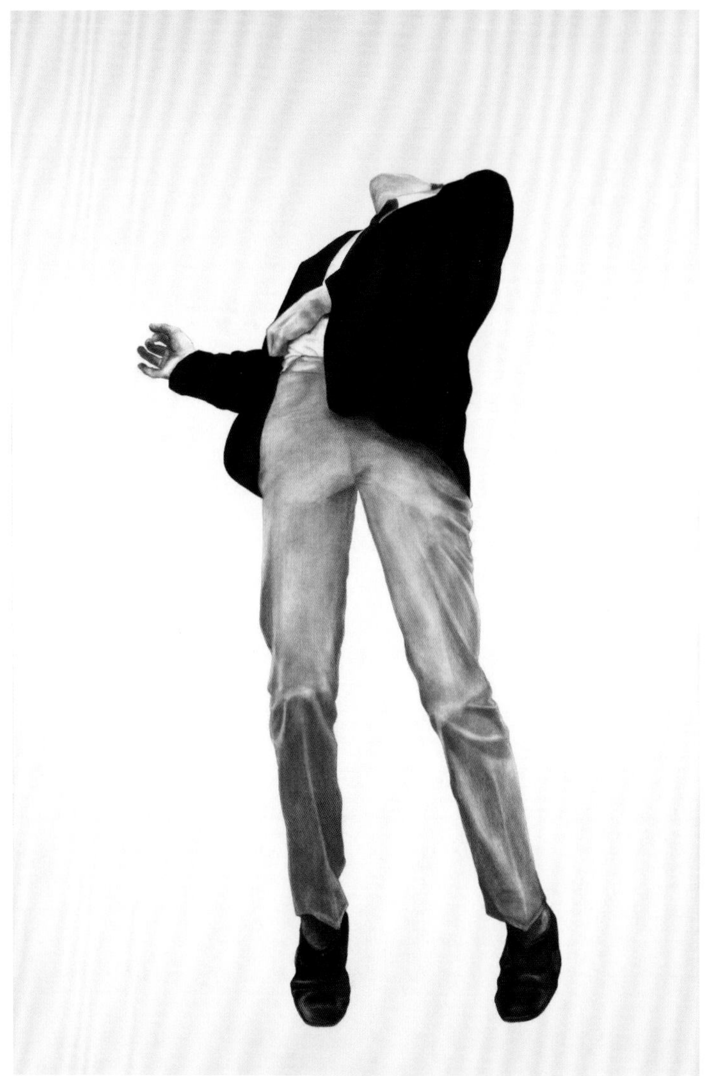

of *are they dying or are they dancing?* The duality became increasingly more interesting once I gained a grasp of what I was doing.

In creating these works, I would make plans and sketches almost like music notations, which I would follow to take the photographs that served as source images to the large-scale drawings. In the beginning I was throwing everything at the models—tennis balls, film canisters—to get them to move in a spastic, psychotic manner. I wanted to capture the image of a gesture that existed between gestures; the split seconds. Some of the photographs I took during these shoots, I recently published as a series of photographs. In some of the photographs you can actually see the film canisters or tennis balls that I threw at them. Eventually the drawings in the *Men in the Cities* series became significantly larger—as tall as 9-by-5 feet—and I presented them in groups of three-to-ten drawings of men and women. When the Rubells bought this work it marked a crucial moment for me as a young artist; it gave me the vote of confidence that I was on to something important.

—Robert Longo

Men Trapped in Ice, 1979, charcoal and graphite on paper, triptych; each 60 x 40 in. (152.4 x 101.6 cm), acquired in 1980

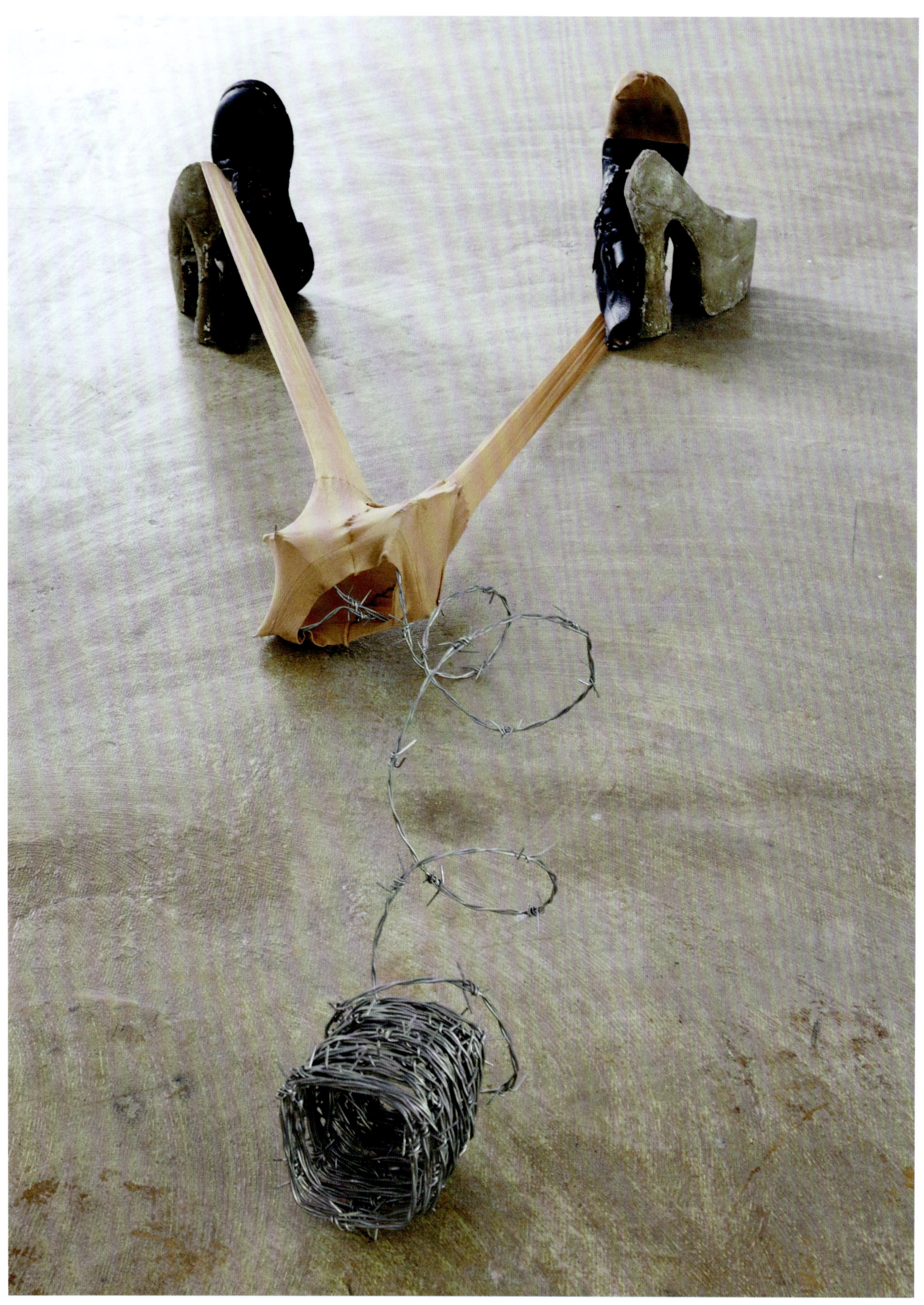

Testosterone and Martydom, 2005, barbed wire, nylon, concrete, leather, rubber, and cotton, 12 x 70 x 35 in. (30.5 x 177.8 x 88.9 cm), acquired in 2005
Opposite page: *Prière de Toucher*, 2000, c-print, ed. 4/6 plus 2 aps, 109 5/8 x 73 1/4 in. (278.4 x 186 cm), acquired in 2014

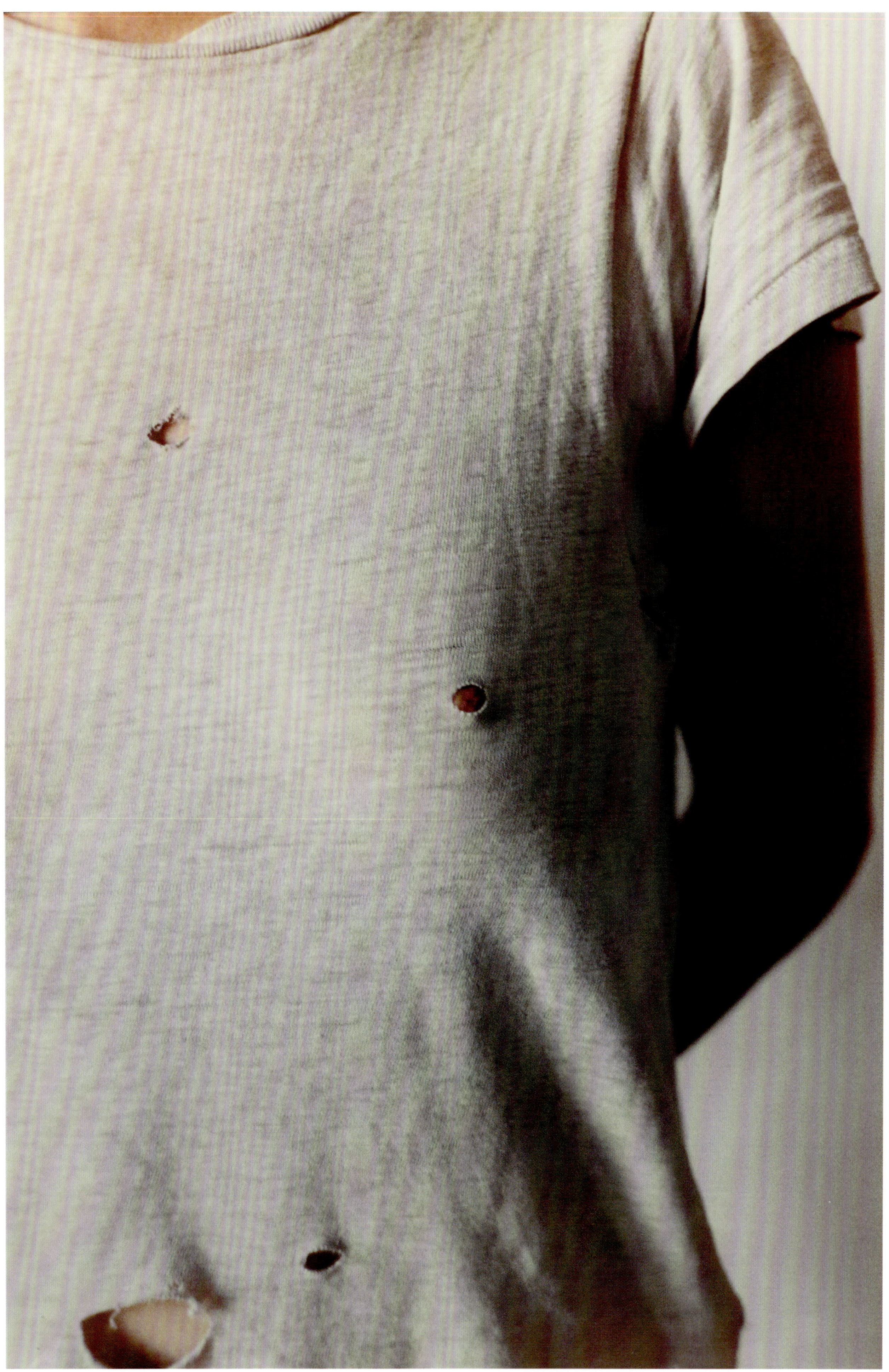

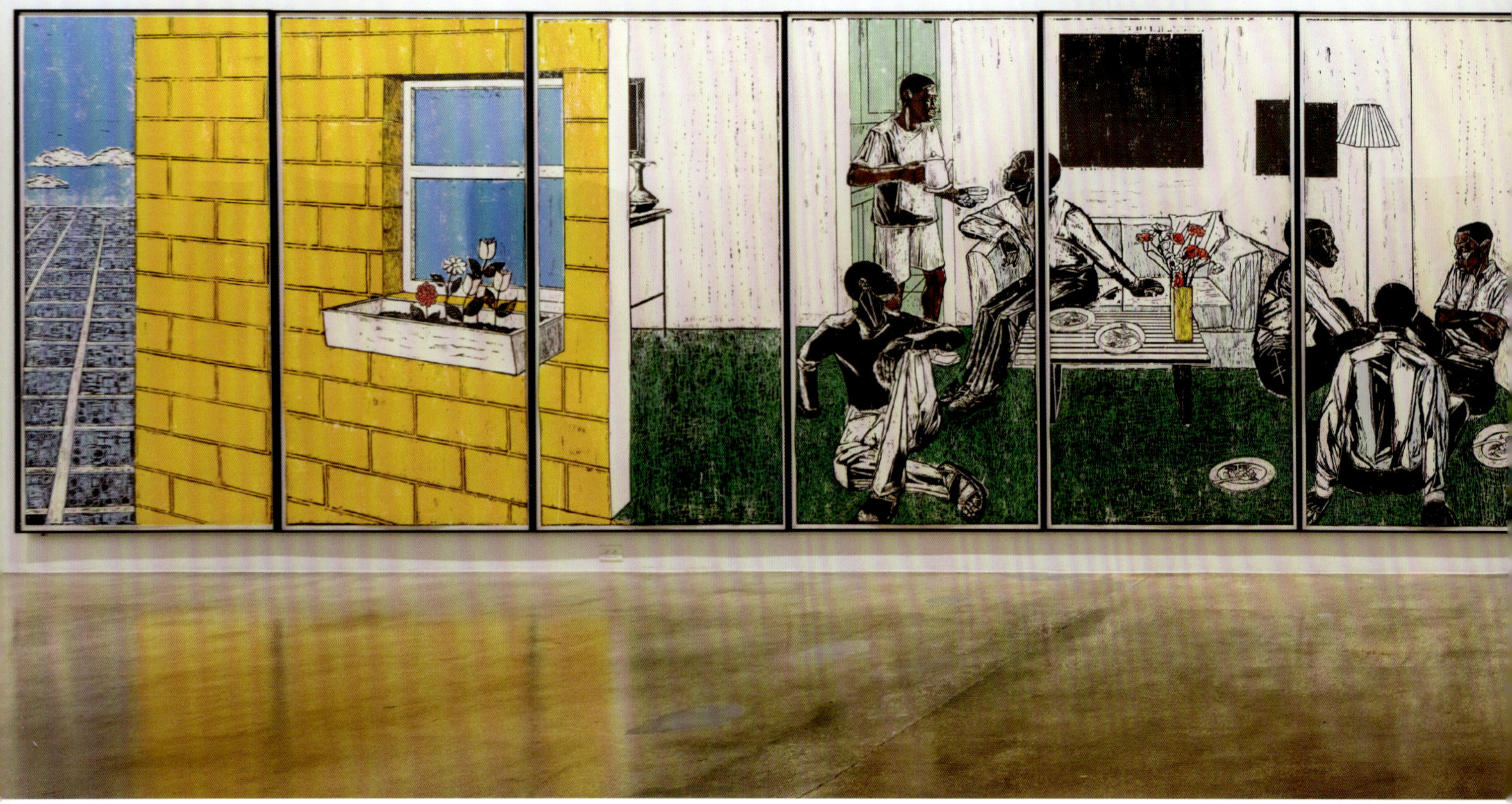

None of us works in isolation. Nothing we do is disconnected from the social, political, economic, and cultural histories that trail behind us. The value of what we produce is determined by comparison with and in contrast to what our fellow citizens find engaging. I am convinced that we would never have heard of Bearden had he not abandoned abstraction for the representational collages with which he has become synonymous.

Of course, I hope someday that it can be said that I showed another way to the summit of achievement in painting. To be sure, the mode of Black figure representation I employ is a clear departure from most popular treatments of the Black body. I am trying to establish a phenomenal presence that is unequivocally Black and beautiful. It is my conviction that the most instrumental, insurgent painting for this moment must be of figures, and those figures must be Black, unapologetically so.

—Kerry James Marshall

Untitled, 1998-1999, eight-color unique woodcuts, ed. 1/4, twelve panels, overall 98 1/2 x 608 1/2 in. (250 x 1545.6 cm), acquired in 1999
Vignette #10, 2007, acrylic on fiberglass, 74 x 110 in. (188 x 279.4 cm), acquired in 2007

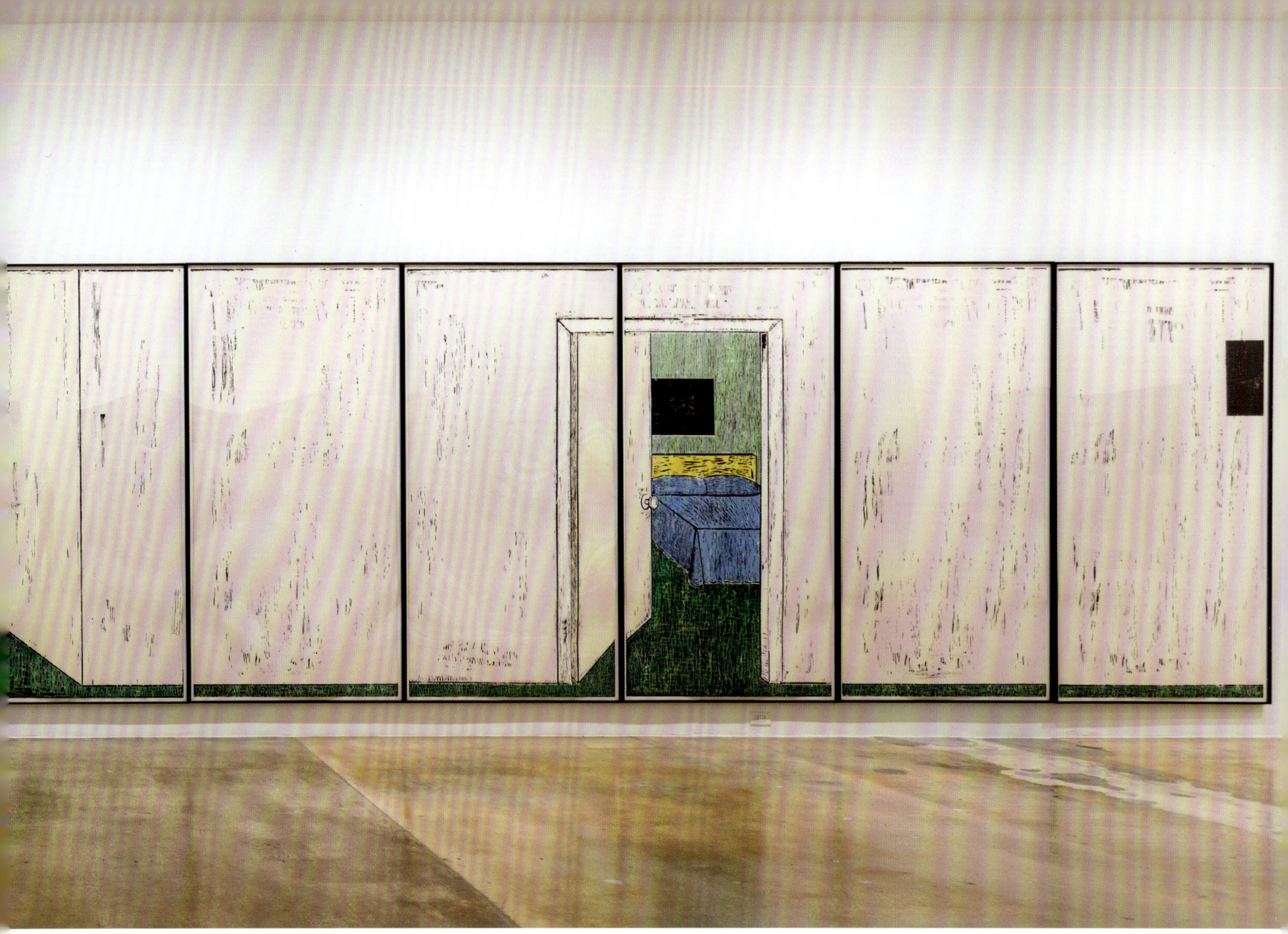

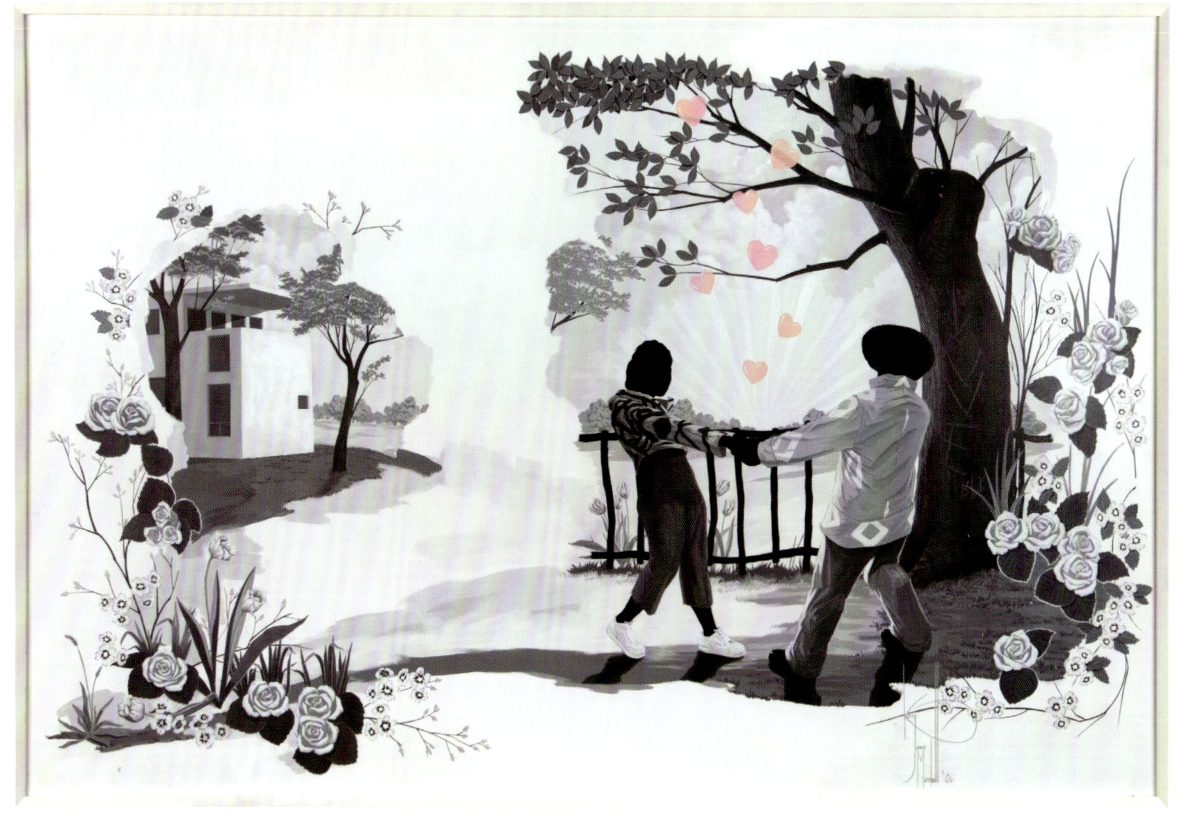

b. 1945, Salt Lake City, UT / lives and works in Los Angeles, CA

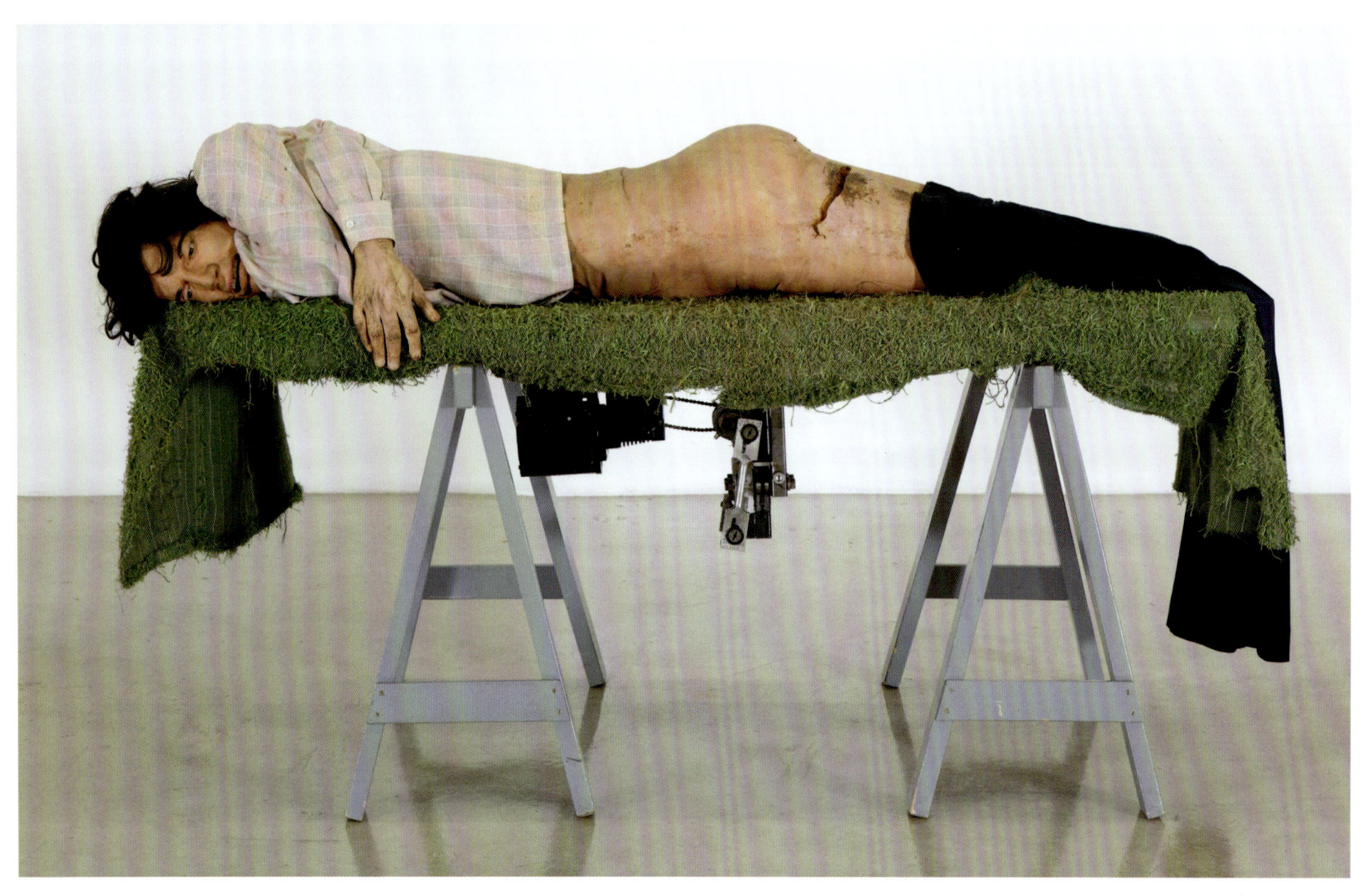

MoCA Man, 1992, latex rubber, urethane foam, clothing, wig, wood, motor, artificial turf, and sawhorses, 36 x 72 x 36 in. (91.4 x 182.9 x 91.4 cm), acquired in 1995

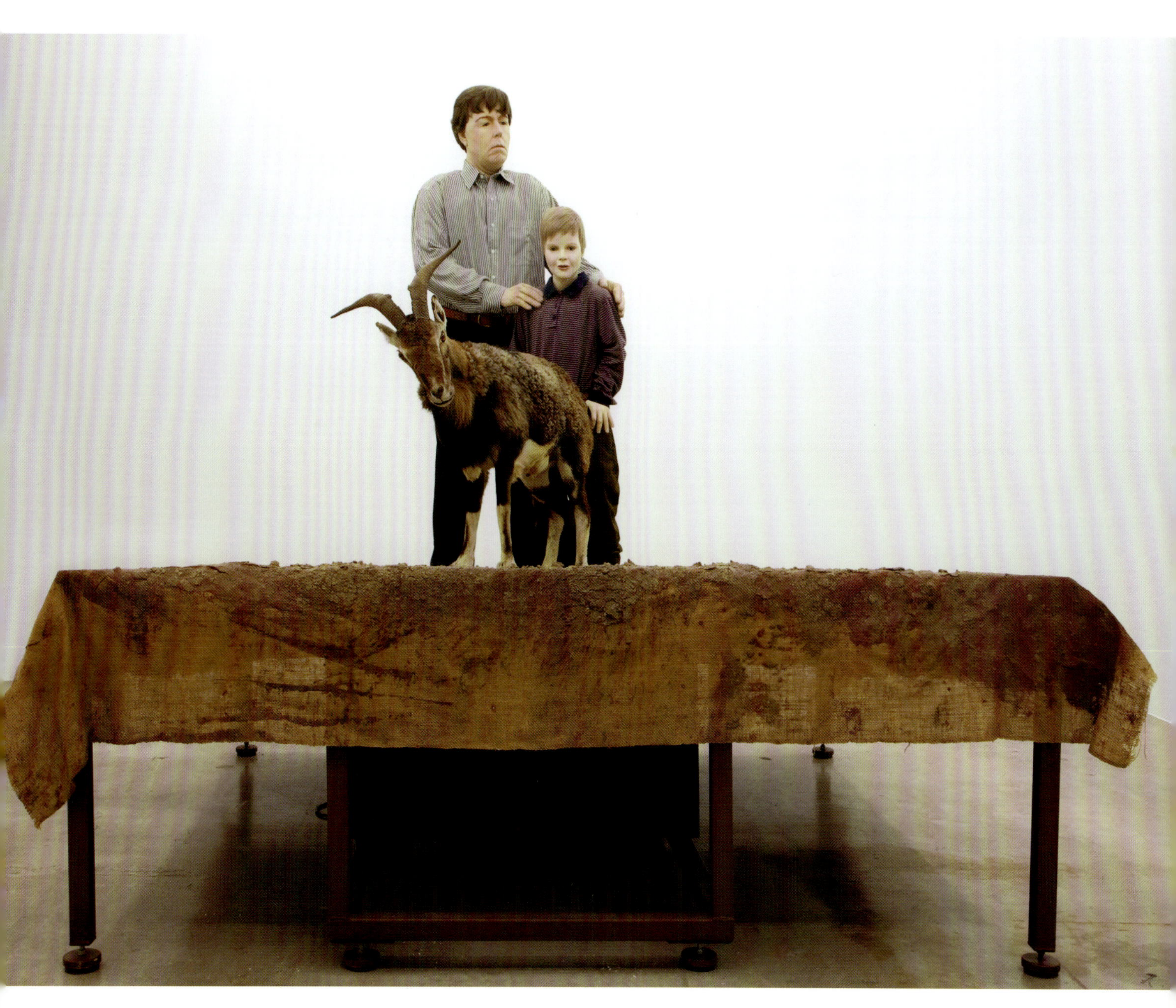

Cultural Gothic, 1992-1993, metal, wood, pneumatic cylinder, compressor, programmed controller, burlap with foam, acrylic, dirt, fiberglass, clothing, wigs, and stuffed goat, 96 x 94 x 94 in. (241 x 235 x 235 cm), acquired in 1993

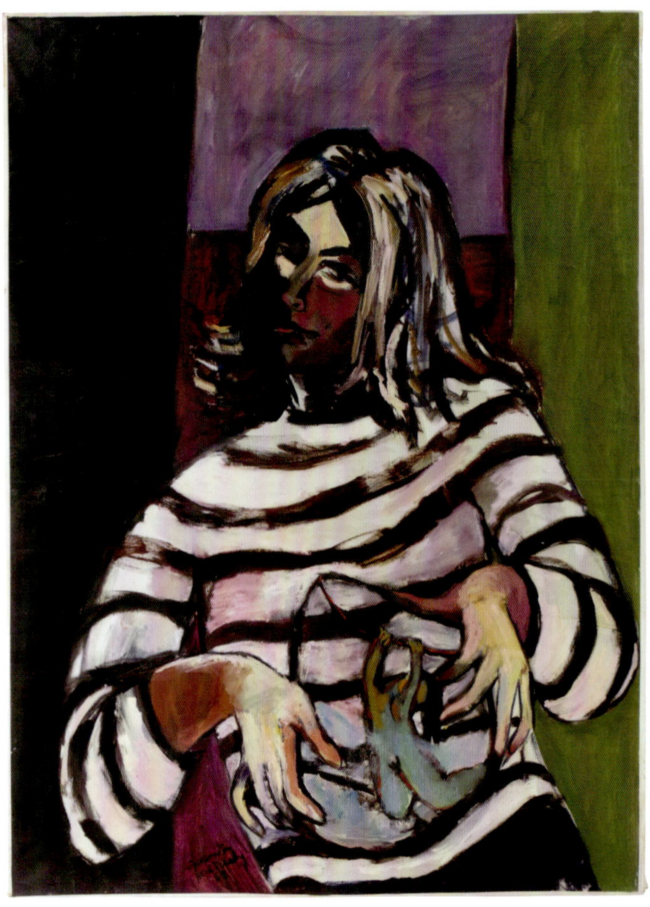

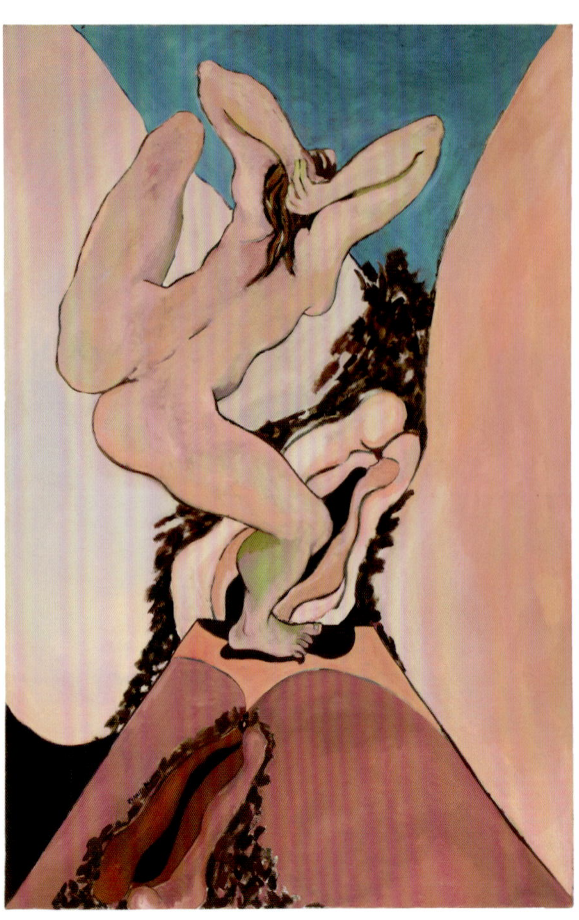

Self (1968) is a self-portrait and the figure in the fishbowl is me, really. I didn't try to paint me exactly, but the hand in the fishbowl, just for me, said that I was in something, trying to hold on and still live, with just enough water for the day. Look at Matisse's fishbowls—they are different but very beautiful.

I always painted men and women, and when I started thinking about painting women, the vagina was big to me. I wanted to impress how real and important it is: the center of woman is the center of her potential womanhood, physically as well as emotionally. From there, she could hopefully have a child. It's complicated—I had lost the ability to have children because of medical sterilization. I had the imagery to paint women, but I don't know how I was open enough to be able to do it. *On the Edge* (1970s) is a very large vagina. I was showing in SoHo in New York, and it was really when SoHo was just starting to have gallery stuff. Many people walked in. They were so aghast, like they didn't know what they were looking at. And on top of that, if they looked, they didn't know if they should. I remember some men came to the door and asked if they had to pay to come in.

I always envisioned *Woman's Psyche* (1968) as a four- or more-panel piece. Even when I was a very young student, I started making triptychs and things like that. I felt like I was never finished with the story; I just wanted another story, so I just kept adding panels. With *Woman's Psyche*, I really had no idea at first what I was going to have at the end. It made sense that I would have the woman being me of course, an arm outstretched and pulling against what looks like a black phallic form. On the far-right panel of this piece, I was wringing the neck of this chicken-creature because they controlled something. I wanted to physically rip out what I couldn't stand. The animals depicted in the piece became very real to me. Some were really loving, some were hateful. Animals, when you depict them, can be more brutal and more loving than humans. The woman in the central panel I was thinking was quite beautiful. I loved the look of the red coming around underneath her nose. I found out after from a physician—because I didn't know this and I don't know who does—that a lot of women also bleed from the nose during their menstrual cycle. So, I had depicted a lot of blood every place, and many people, particularly women, were shocked. I remember one woman came in and said, "How can you do this? How can you have these bleeding people? Don't you realize I have a daughter who's going to come in here?" I just looked and thought, *Don't come in if you don't want to. I didn't ask you.* But I said instead, "This is life you're looking at. When you're looking at all this blood, these are going to be your children if you're lucky." I never understood people so horrified over

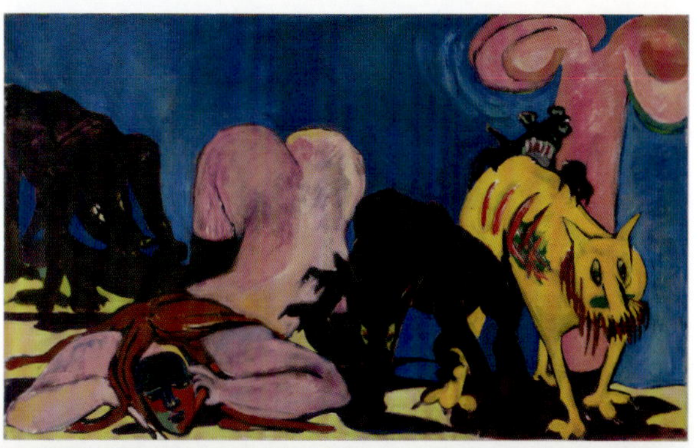

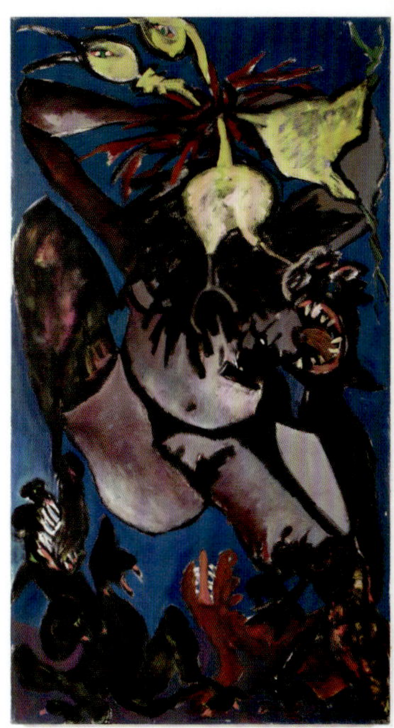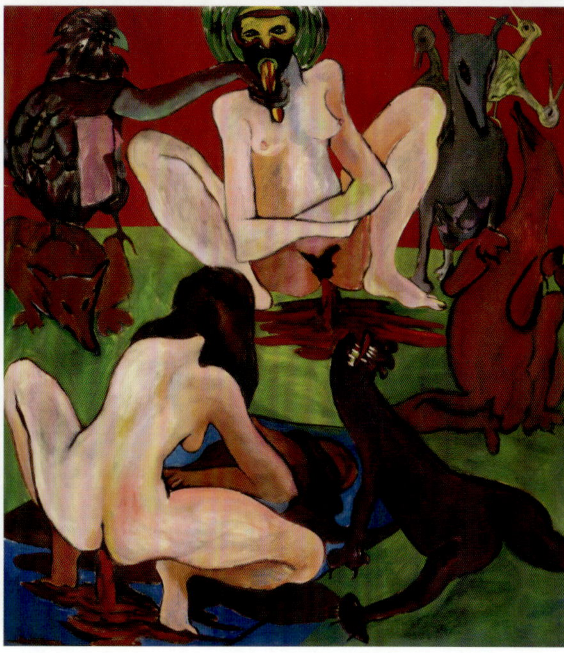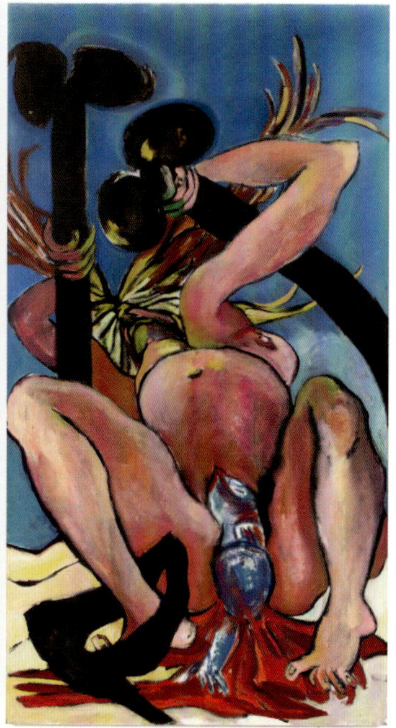

blood. I mean, it's both life and death. When I was very young, I had a lot of hemorrhaging going on, so blood was only too real for me, and it was just a part of my life, so I did it. There was a beauty of being so free in my mind at the time. I wanted to paint stories about women.

Things were raw and people were coming right up to the work to see it. A woman who was a feminist, and who was always going around doing reviews and who had classes in a few places, was told by some of her students that she should come see my show. I was in the gallery when she came in—I didn't know who she was—and she said to my friends who were in the gallery with me, "Who's the artist here? Is she crazy? There's something really disturbing about the work. Does she need a shrink, or what?" Well, I was standing right there and it was a gift given from heaven. I just went over and said, "Excuse me, I'm Juanita McNeely. I thought maybe you'd want to meet me." And that was it. I never got a review after that. A lot of people thought it was crazy; that didn't stop me. I think there's a certain amount of power in it. I didn't have a gallery director; it was a co-op gallery and so I was

on my own. The males that came into the gallery were really insulting. You're listening to their comments and you think you're going to kill them.

You realize you don't ever want to go to another opening because it did away with my illusion of what the safety line was for me. That's when you realize if you have a gallery director, they are protection for you. It was so wonderful when James Fuentes came to me; I was bowled over. No one had ever come to me and said, "I like your work. I think I'd like to show it." I've been very blessed with James and everyone else who has given me the love and support I needed. I'm very fortunate I now have a husband and partner that is everything a person, a man, an artist should be, so I'm very blessed. When we got married it was 1982. We already knew who we were and we're certainly still together and still enjoy the time with each other. You go for a long time where you're trying to say something, and if they don't want to let you say it, you just keep going.

—Juanita McNeely

Left to right: *Self*, 1968, oil on linen, 48 x 36 in. (121.9 x 91.4 cm), acquired in 2022
On the Edge, 1970s, oil on linen, 90 x 59 1/2 in. (228.6 x 151.1 cm), acquired in 2022
Woman's Psyche, 1968, oil on linen, 146 x 126 in. (370.8 x 320 cm) overall, acquired in 2022

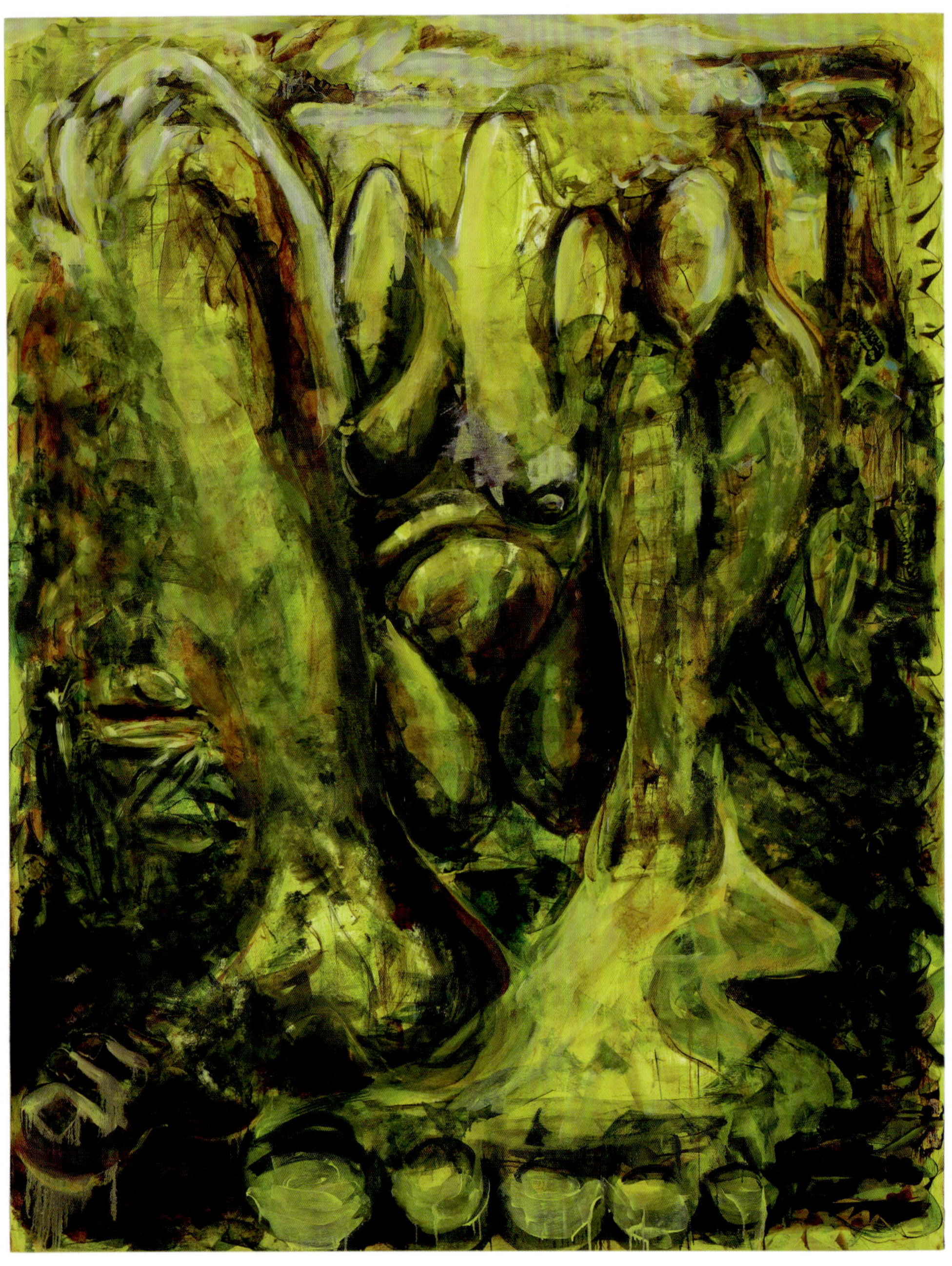

My goal with all the work, large and small, is to create a slowness. The act of mark making is fast, so to create a space that is slow is challenging for me. Is it one figure moving? Multiple figures huddled together? How do you create a different sense of time? I am also invested in how time can be embattled within a painting. How can I create a sense of time?

With each painting I made for the Rubell Museum, I tried to use the figures to break up space differently— either to create an extreme, crammed feeling or a loose, sweaty movement.

—Jo Messer

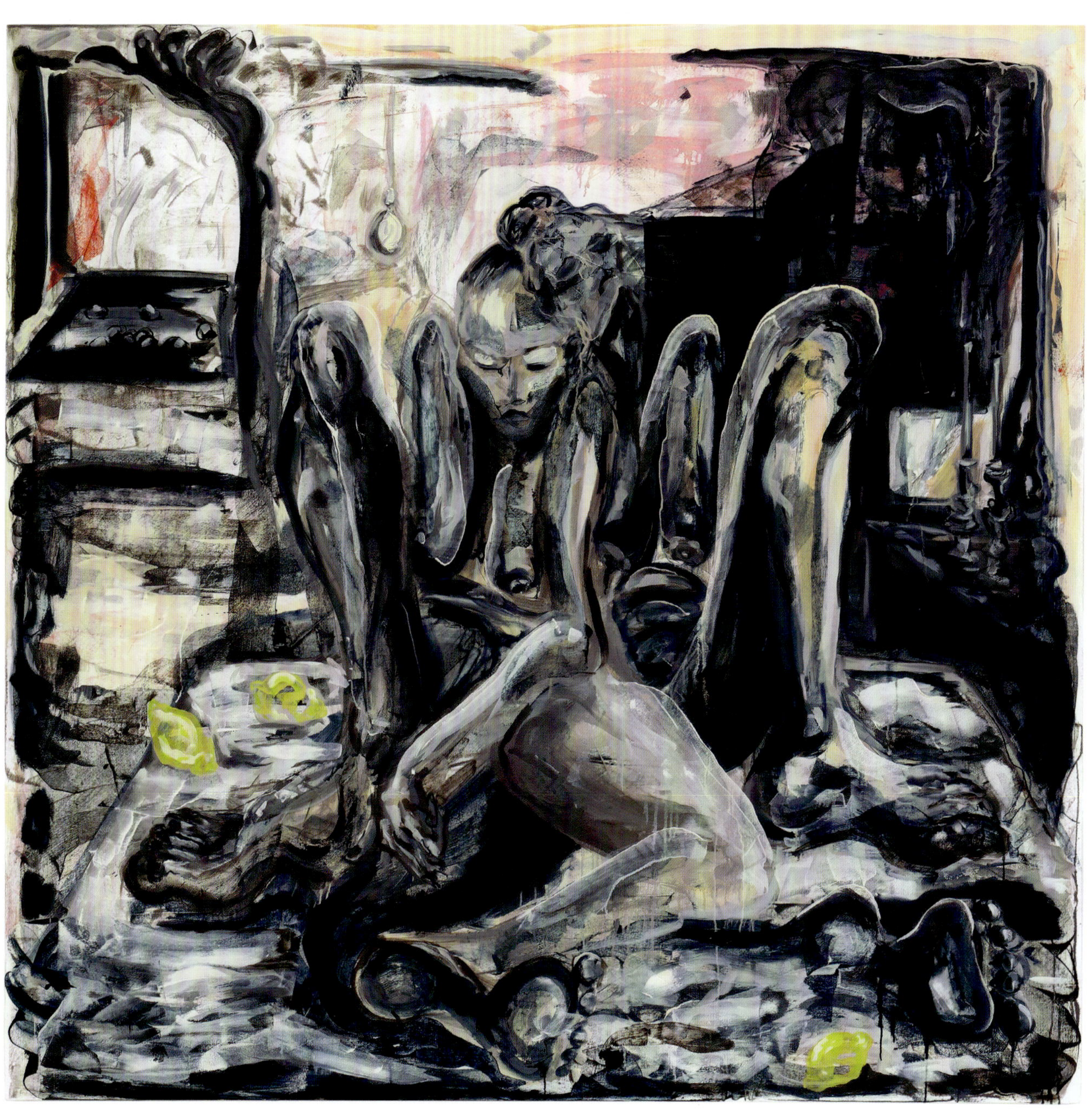

Opposite page: *She is afraid of nothing, especially not the sun*, 2022, oil on canvas, 92 x 72 in (233.7 x 182.9 cm), acquired in 2022
Walk-in through the back, 2022, oil on canvas, 65 x 67 in (165.1 x 170.2 cm), acquired in 2022

I've taken to designing a lot of my stuff using Google SketchUp, so it really allows you to kind of foresee what something will look like. You can adjust proportions very quickly and get measurements, and fairly complex angles; things that used to take weeks to do can be done very quickly. But the odd, kind of deflating aspect of it is that once something is built it looks very much like the sketch, which is a good thing, but you have a feeling that the materialized object is almost an aftereffect of the virtual sketch.

My objects that I made for the ruin [*A Refusal to Accept Limits*] aren't really life-sized, but they have a kind of quasi-convincing life-sized feel because you can walk between them. You can actually pass under the arch, although compared to a real Romanesque arch it's quite small, and the obelisk is quite small. They're all going back to the kind of minimal, sculptural definition of a monument—they're all bigger than a person so they still function as monuments even though they're very much reduced. That all has to do with some sense of being present in the installation and being able to walk through it, but then it's qualified by this whole virtual design sensibility.

If anything, there's an appeal to Classicism, but it's a kind of qualified one— through the gilding—where it does refer to the Roman Empire, but it does by way of, say, a middle-class Italian restaurant that has fake neoclassical décor. Or Las Vegas, so it's like a chain of references that's happening in the piece. Some of the objects are littered with things that suggest debris, and one model for that, that I had in my head, was teenagers having a beer party in the ruins and leaving everything behind, and this kind of tourism, or some kind of residual use of an artifact that is a ruin, or different kinds of ruins.

When I was in junior high I was into Roman history, and then hadn't thought about it much until I started listening in the studio to this series of podcasts called *The History of Rome*, and now it's got me reading Roman histories. It's interesting to go back and look at what kind of function architecture played, and how closely it was linked to this imperial aspect of Roman culture, and how sometimes Roman emperors would erect whole cities. There was always this kind of tension between the ambitions of a given figure who would

want to immortalize himself through public works projects and what the economy could sustain. It was always this matter of striking a delicate balance between taxing the provincial population and building things. There was one emperor who said, "The point is to shear the sheep, not to skin it." So you know, get as much as you can from your tax base without killing it.

I did a couple pieces in the '80s where I used real gold, and I just put acrylic matte medium over it. Real gold doesn't tarnish, but imitation leaf does. So I had done these couple of gold pieces, and then what got me started working with gold again was a show Walead Beshty and Bob Nickas did at PS1 called *The Gold Standard*, and Bob remembered those works and asked if I would do a new piece. So I agreed, but I was kind of dreading it because working with the leaf is so labor intensive. Gold leaf is much softer than the fake composite leaf, so if you breathe on a sheet of real gold leaf the wrong way, it crumples up into a little ball and you can't use it. The imitation leaf has a lot more tensile strength. The price of gold had changed significantly since the '80s, so for what I wanted to do I realized I could only afford the imitation. We did a couple of pieces with those, and then as soon as I made the work for the PS1 show I realized I could do something much better and much more interesting. I started kind of gearing up in the studio, and at the time I was working at Columbia, so there were a lot of Columbia grads who wanted work. We had this kind of high-intensive production going on during that period. It took us a while to figure out the right way to apply the leaf, although with the ruin, I didn't produce that myself. That was done in Portugal by Icon Art Services, which is now defunct. But I think there's, like, a whole culture of gold leafing in Portugal, so they had access to these craftsmen and they used actual architectural imitation leaf; it doesn't come in these little sheets like I used, it comes in these big rolls. I wasn't there when the leafing was done in Portugal, but I think those guys really knew what they were doing. They had real "leafers" in there. The imitation aspect of it has come to inflect the work, but originally I did use real gold.

—John Miller

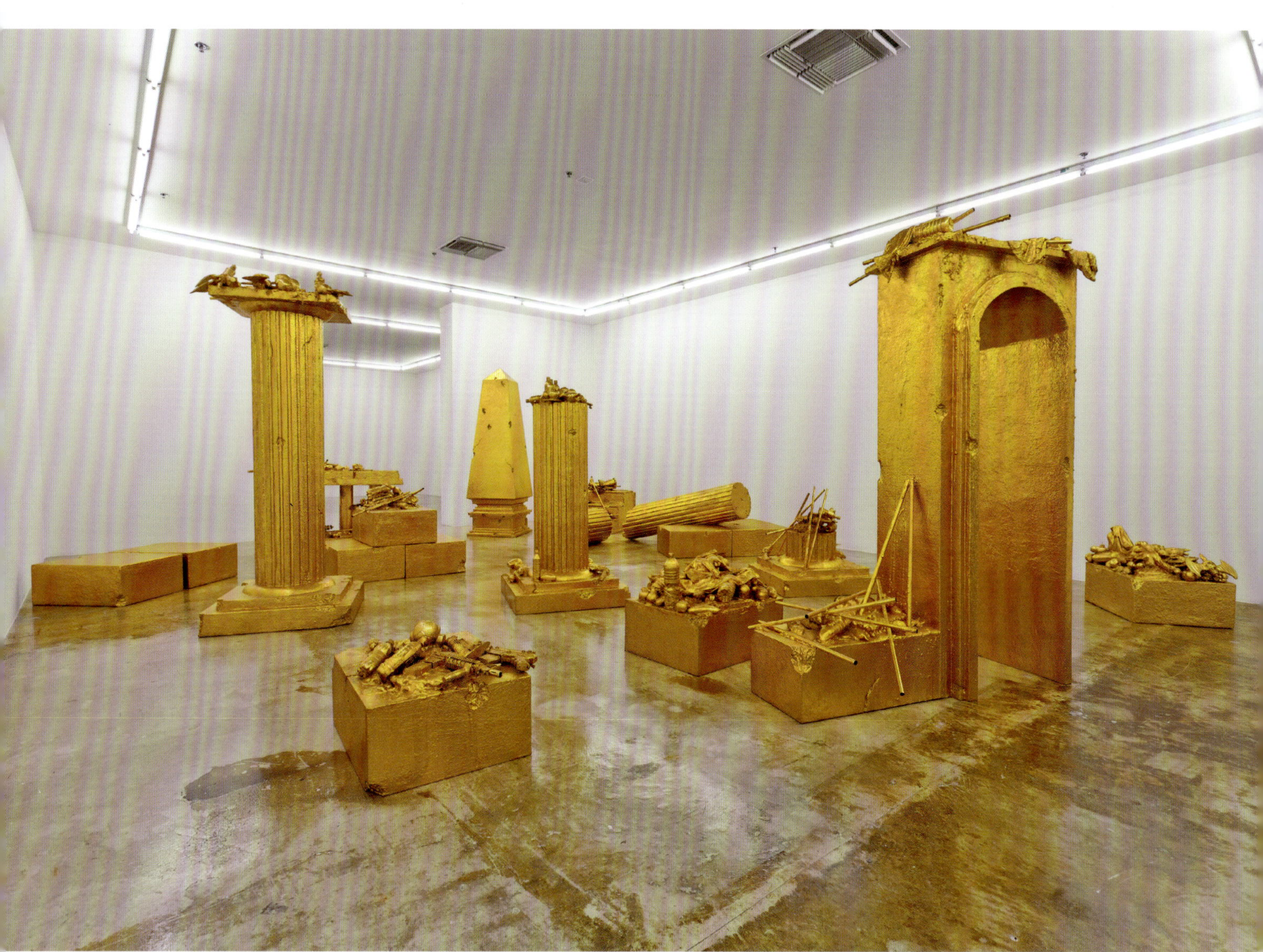

Dear ****

I don't know how far you ultimately want to go into the matter; nevertheless, a few lines here on the vitrines: It is not only about evoking, depicting, keeping, conserving and illustrating memories, pasts, *history* but — apart from positioning and locating in terms of scale and proportions in actual space — using the transitory vehicle of the vitrine to make clear — clear as glass, as it were (*vitre* / pane of glass) — the relevant Here and Now of a museum or other (art) context and bringing it to consciousness. And this in the truest sense of the word. Free standing, they no longer have any contact with the ground of facts, and this makes them stand out even more. "Where am I?" is the name of the game. And "in what form and in what (art-specific) way is the appropriateness of means ensured?" — in a place like a museum, which has long since turned out to be the explicit place of placelessness of art.

In the wall vitrines, this theme (with its reference to the normally hidden machinery of a theater stage) is half shifted behind the frontally glazed viewing sides. There, it becomes perfectly obvious that it is by no means a matter of course how and that something hangs on a wall and is more less firmly anchored in an architecture and how what lies behind helps determine what hangs in front and vice versa. The problem of plinth — vitrine — museum as traditional settings and instruments of auratic elevation and as tried and tested tools for drawing aesthetic boundaries naturally also plays a part in this here, too.

Footstool. At first sight subordinate, the psychology of its unmistakable model-character wavers, as we know, between self-abnegation and delusions of grandeur. Some spontaneous associations: *Support — Subservience — Ordinariness — Proportionality; Unobtrusiveness — Inconspicuousness[1] — Social Work; Office Holder — Placeholder — Proxy — Joker — Salon Rebel. The artist as Rabble Rouser — Illuminator — Visionary — Revolutionary — Missionary? As Artist — Jester — Trickster, as a Fool? Disturbing, Destroying, eternal Child?*

So much on the subject of footstools. Lowest step. Try stepping up onto one, dear ****! You'll be astonished how far you can see from there, so much closer to Heaven.

—Reinhard Mucha

1 "He has always been at particular pains to show that great is small and small great. The divining rod of his intuition reacts in the realms of all things inconspicuous, generally devalued, ignored by history and finds precisely here the highest significances."
(Siegfried Kracauer, 1926, in the Frankfurter Zeitung, on the methodology of Walter Benjamin)
Translation from German by J. W. Gabriel and Fiona Elliott

On the floor: *Freiheit for Berlin*, 2008, solid wood, float glass (display case); oil paint print on bituminized feltbase (found object) on blockboard (pedestal); wood (three footstools, found objects); aluminum (nine folding rulers); binding wire, 71.89 x 30.31 x 20.47 in. (182.6 x 77 x 52 cm), acquired in 2014
On the wall: *Minden*, 2013, aluminum, float glass, alkyd enamel painted on reverse of glass; rails with so-called diamonds, billiard cloth, cushion rubber (carom billiards table, split found object); rests of different oil paints, resin and dispersion paints, plywood (floorboard from an artist's studio, split found object); canvas, felt, plywood, blockboard, 66 3/4 x 166 1/8 x 19 5/8 in. (169.8 x 422 x 49.8 cm), acquired in 2014

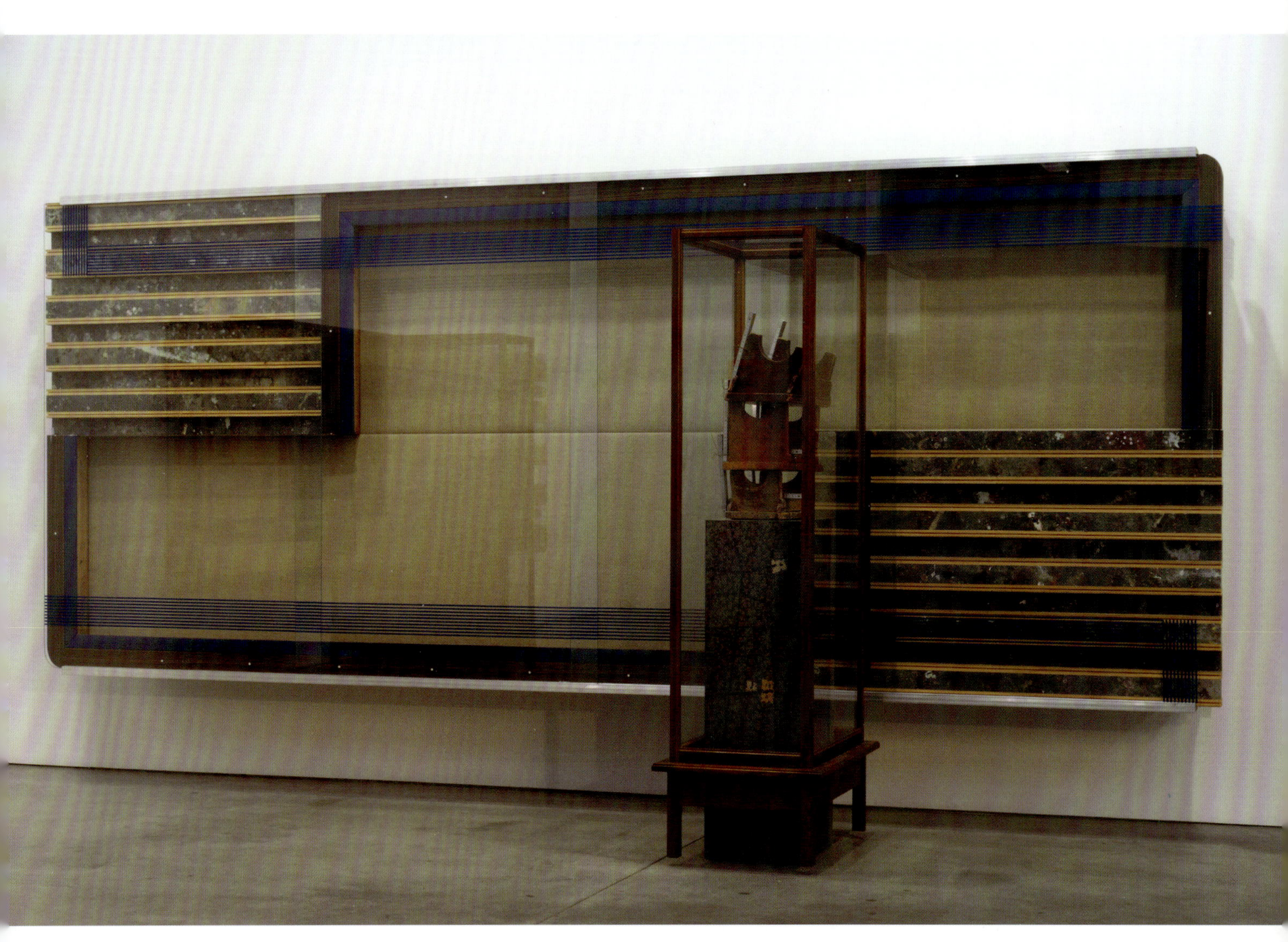

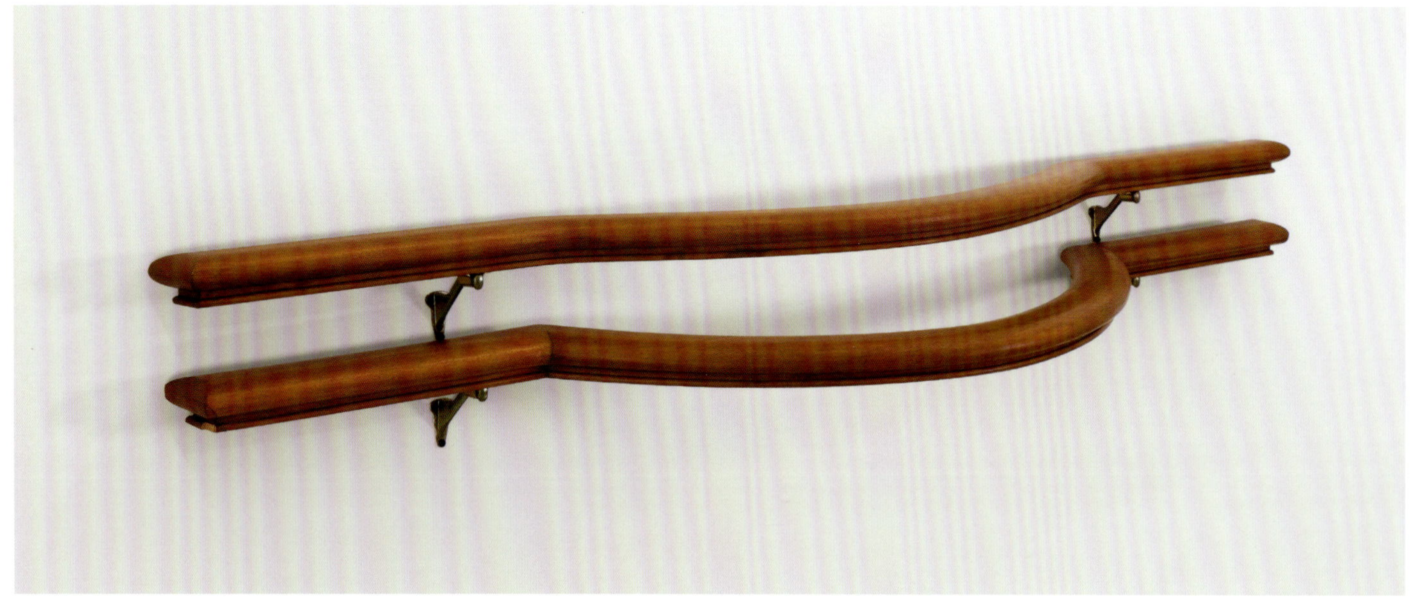

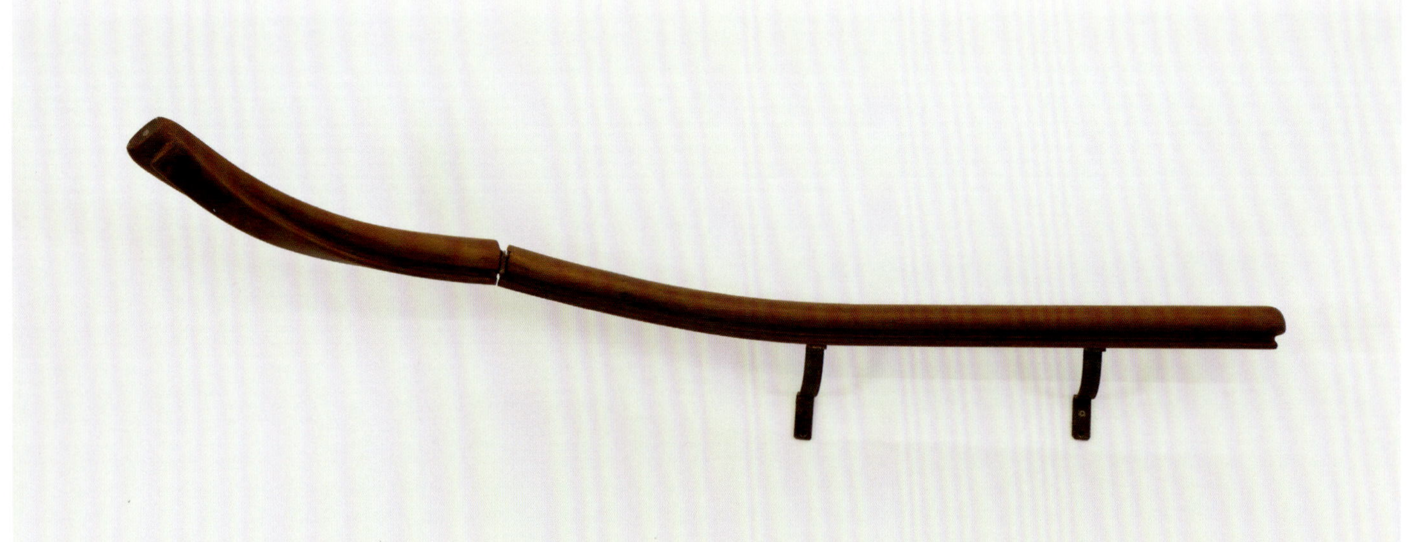

The dwarf is a constant image of the Baroque period. You find it in a lot of Italian painting, even Japanese movies. The dwarf was the only person who could criticize the court. Because of his physical distortion, he was allowed to distort or exaggerate reality. One of the dwarves painted by Velázquez was bought because he had a disease that made him laugh constantly. So they would take him out after dinner and his laughter was so contagious that everyone would laugh, and then they'd get bored and send him home.

Perhaps the more successful things I have made have always been about something other than what you're actually looking at. And this other, this reference, this impossibility of representation that you try to describe is a boundary which confronts the sculpture. When I made the dwarf, I was not so interested in the physical presence of the dwarf. It was more a reference to the question of strangeness than the problem of size.

—Juan Muñoz

Double Banister, 1987, wood and metal, top 4 1/2 x 79 x 10 (11.4 x 200 x 25.4); bottom 4 1/2 x 79 x 14 in. (11.4 x 79 x 35.5 cm), acquired in 1987
A Banister After, 1987, wood and metal, 16 x 57 x 18 in. (40.6 x 144.7 x 45.7 cm), acquired in 1988
Opposite page: *Enano con Tres Columnas [Dwarf with Three Columns]*, 1988, terra-cotta, overall 92 1/2 x 59 x 78 3/4 in. (235 x 150 x 200 cm), acquired in 1988

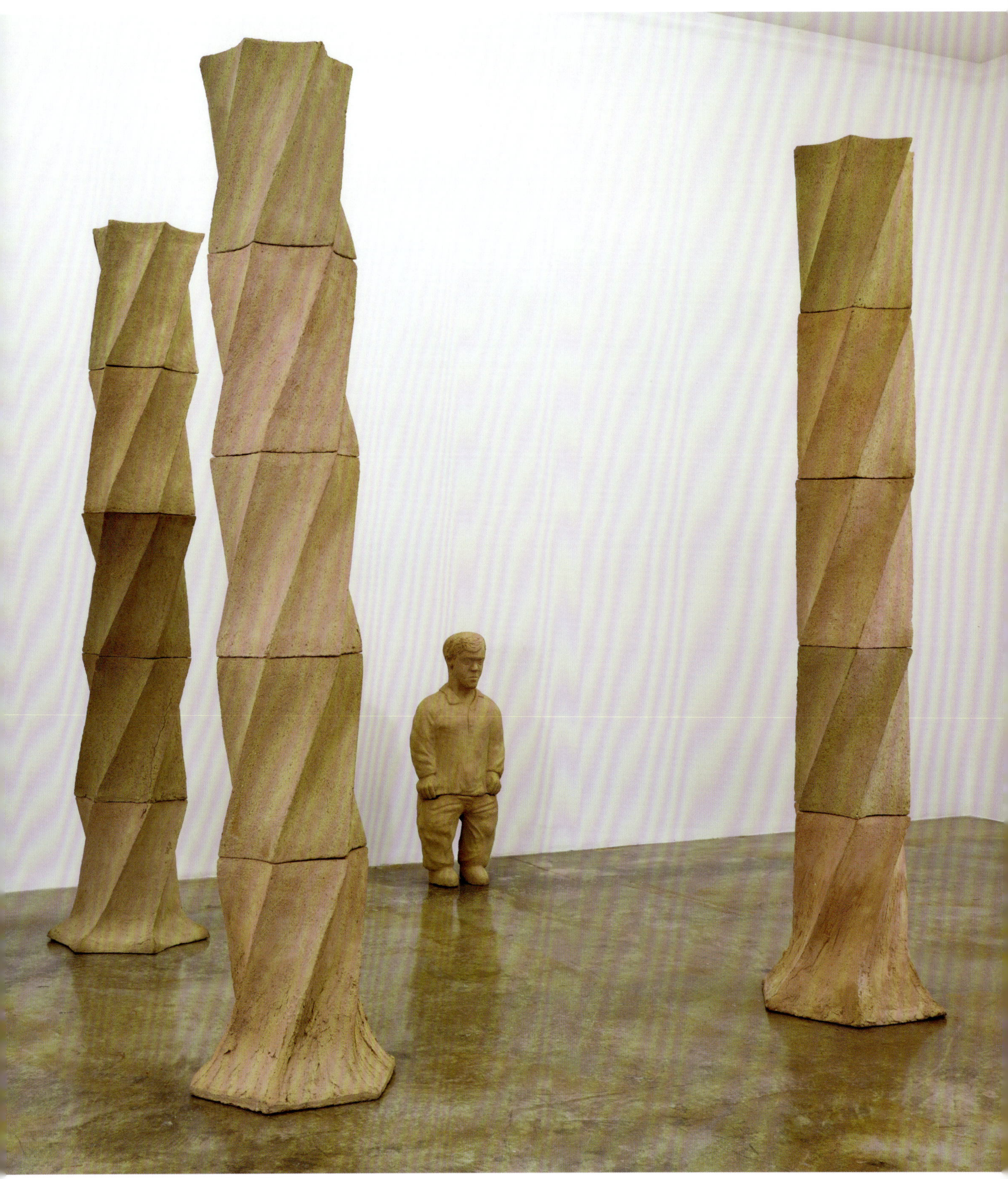

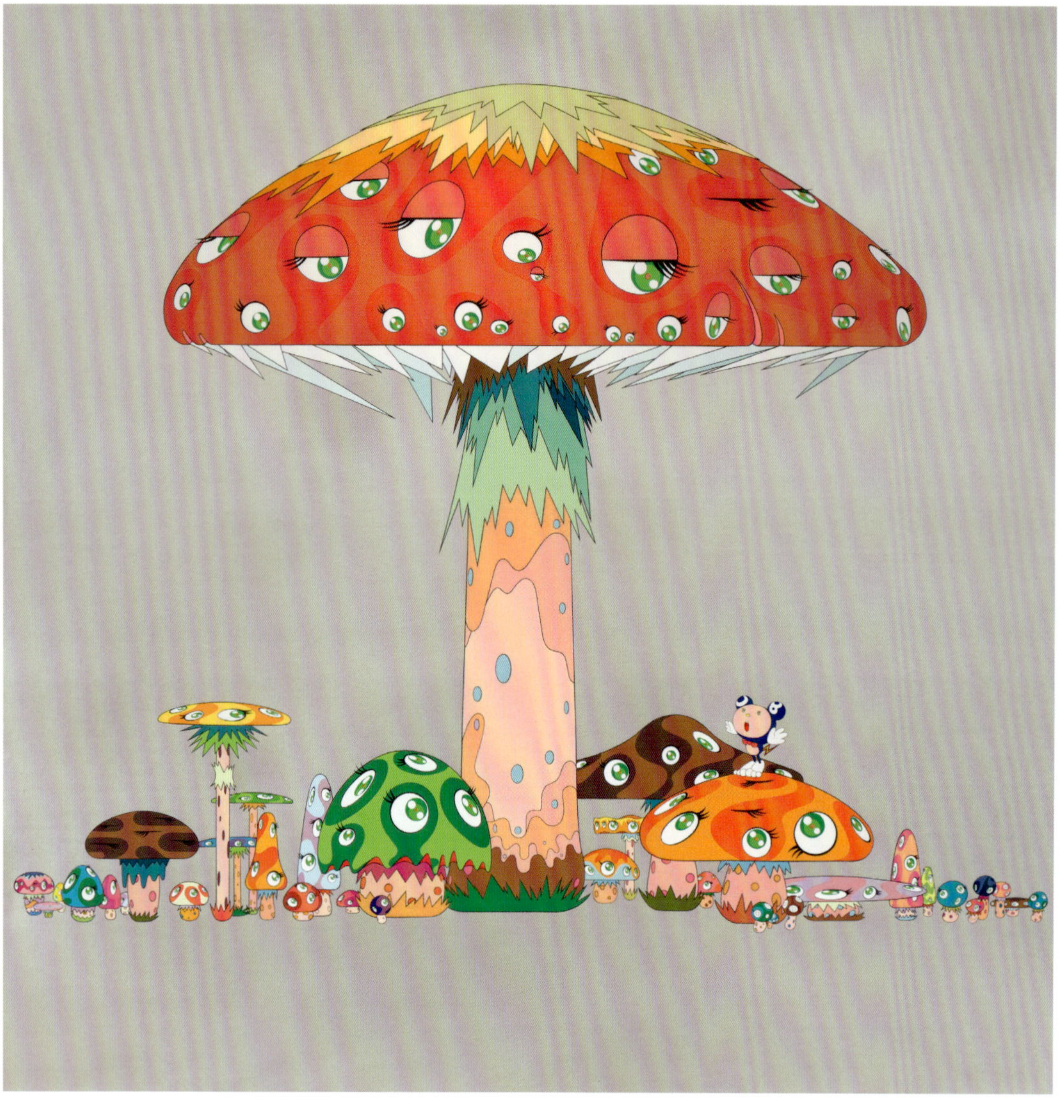

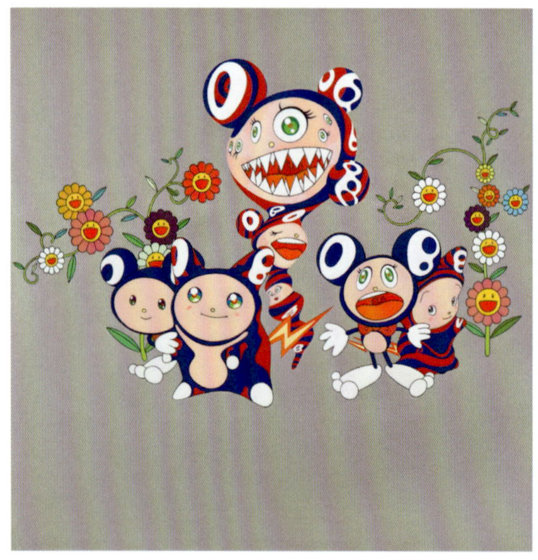

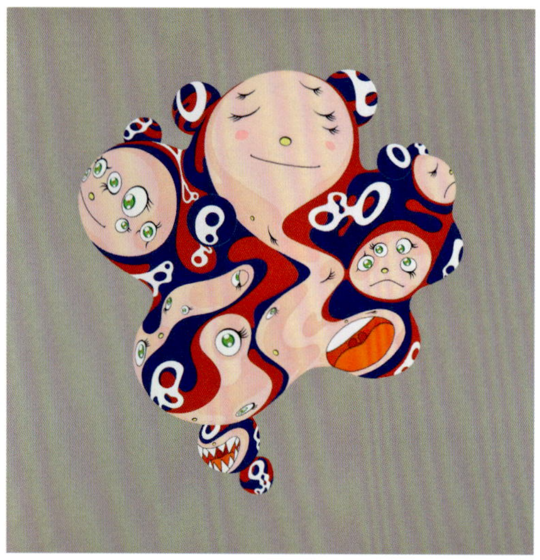

Clockwise from top left: *DOB In the Strange Forest*, 1999, acrylic on canvas, 71 x 71 x 2 1/4 in., acquired in 1999
Mr. DOB All Stars (Oh My The Mr. DOB), 1998, acrylic on canvas mounted on board, 15 3/4 x 15 3/4 in. (40 x 40 cm), acquired in 1998
Four Monks Sleeping, 1998, acrylic on canvas mounted on board, 15 3/4 x 15 3/4 in. (40 x 40 cm), acquired in 1998
Opposite page, on the floor: *DOB in The Strange Forest (White DOB)*, 1999, FRP, resin, fiberglass, acrylic, and iron, diameter 120 x 50 in. (304.8 x 127 cm),
acquired in 1999; On the wall: *PO+KU Surrealism (Blue)*, 1999, acrylic on canvas mounted on board, quadriptych; each 110 1/4 x 55 1/8 in. (140 x 280 cm);
overall 110 1/4 x 220 1/2 in. (280 x 560 cm), acquired in 1999

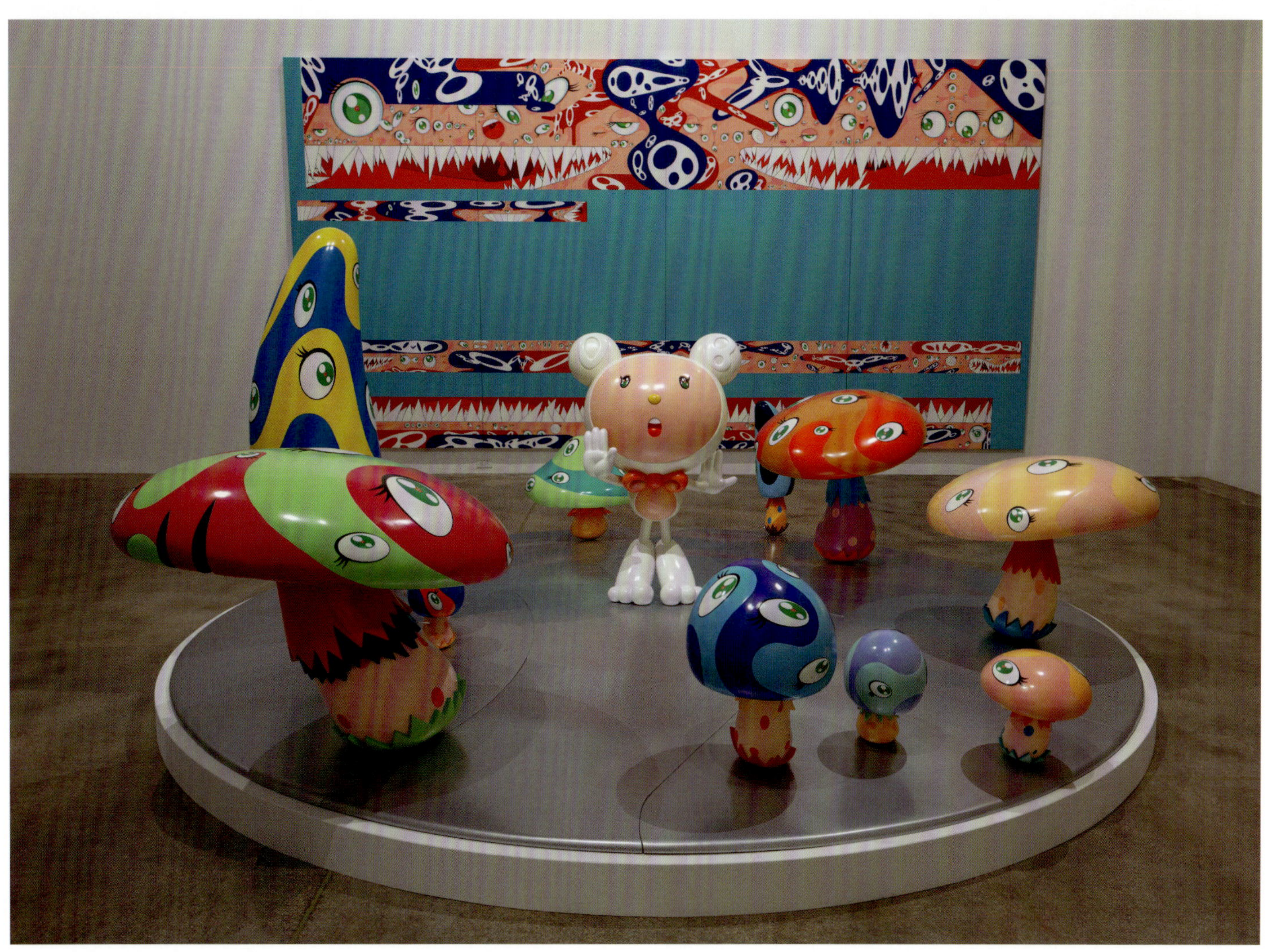

The two works seen here both feature Mr. DOB, one of my most well-known characters. In the painting, DOB has shifted his shape to the point that he is almost unrecognizable, but he also can be seen in his original form in the sculpture as the character with the bowtie and the letters D and B written on either ear. His round face in the middle forms the letter O, thus "D-O-B."

The history behind Mr. DOB is quite long, but it begins in the early 1990s with the words *art movement* which had become a hot trend in the Japanese art scene. As was often the case at the time, many Japanese artists were choosing to simply mimic trends from Western contemporary art, and, in one period, they began making English word art pieces in the style of artists like Barbara Krueger and Jenny Holzer. It got to the point where I couldn't tolerate it anymore, and so to parody the situation I thought up a nonsense phrase, "Dobojite Dobojtie Oshamanbe," and used it in a signboard and performance piece. The word *Dobojite* is an accented pronunciation of the Japanese word *doshite* ("why") and comes from the dialect of one of the characters in the manga "Inakappe Taisho" (The Country General). *Oshamanbe* is a pun, derived from the name of a town in Hokkaido, that became a popular catchphrase for the comedian Toru Yuri. So as you can see, the combination of these two phrases has no literal meaning whatsoever.

At the same time I came up with this phrase, there was another trend that interested me: the abundance of companies who had decided to create mascot characters (Sega Entertainment's Sonic the Hedgehog being a good example). I decided to try and create my own character and with the assistance of some talented people around me, we came up with a design. For the name of the character, I took the first three letters from "Dobojite Dobojite Oshamanbe," D-O-B, and thus, Mr. DOB was born.

In later paintings and sculptures, Mr. DOB would cease to take on one set shape and began appearing in many different forms. Sometimes he is small and cute; at other times, as in *PO + KU Surrealism (Blue)*, he is rendered like a monster with multiple eyeballs and countless sharp teeth. I have come to believe that the numerous emotional and spiritual states portrayed in these works are a kind of self-portrait.

The sculpture *Dob in the Strange Forest (White DOB)* is one of my earliest sculptural works and shows DOB lost in a forest of many colored mushrooms. Before working on this piece, I had already made several "figure" sculptures, but this was the first time I had tried to convert motifs from my paintings into three-dimensional shapes. In that sense, it was a new and exciting challenge for me. —Takashi Murakami

2012 Artist in Residence

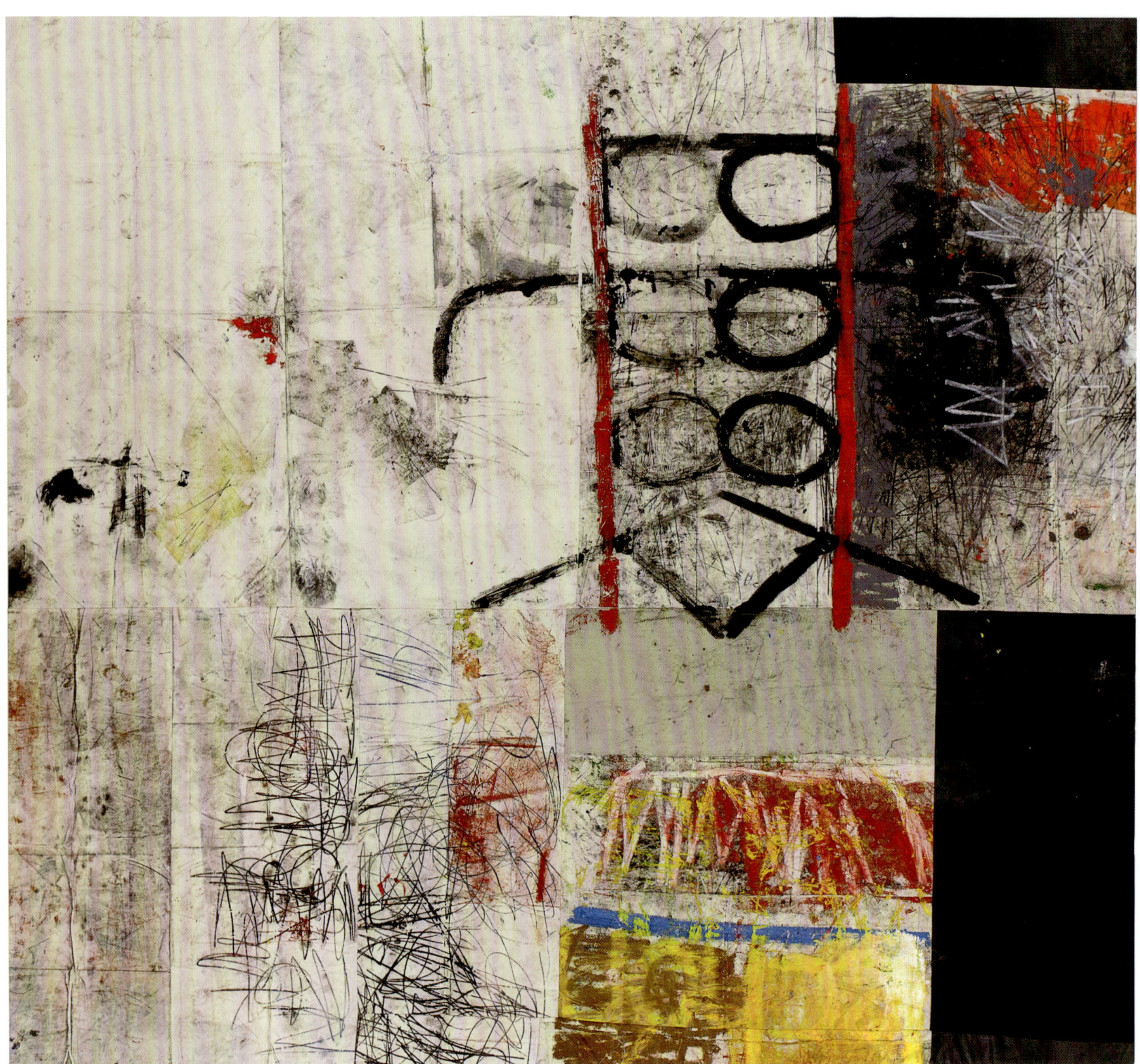

In the summer of 2012, when the museum was closed before the "work" exhibition, I was invited by the Rubell family to treat the space—the entire main room—as a studio. I felt like it was important for the work; it was necessary for me to live in the space and that the work be born out of the space. So, I moved into the Collection for six weeks and from scratch I made all the work. I did some preparation in London, but every single piece in the show was constructed and produced at the Collection.

My paintings are produced by working on different canvases individually. Parts are rendered in oil paint, other sections are marked through a printing process. There are all these sections that go through different processes. There's a point where I begin to lay all these different pieces down on the floor, and then they get stitched together using a sewing machine. They go through an editing process—some parts of the canvas respond better to each other—and I leave those and remove the others and add more. It's almost like quilting. Printing and quilting. Mark making. Dyeing. Fragmentation happens in all of the paintings. Fragments from one canvas are taken to form a bigger picture. *Work 6* and *Work 7* happen as residues of everything else that occurs. These are the leftover canvasses. To a certain extent they didn't have a use or a function. They get—I wouldn't say recycled— but turned into these abstract, somewhat minimal paintings. All the mark making on the surface are things that happen. You leave them around the studio or you leave them on the floor of the space, you walk

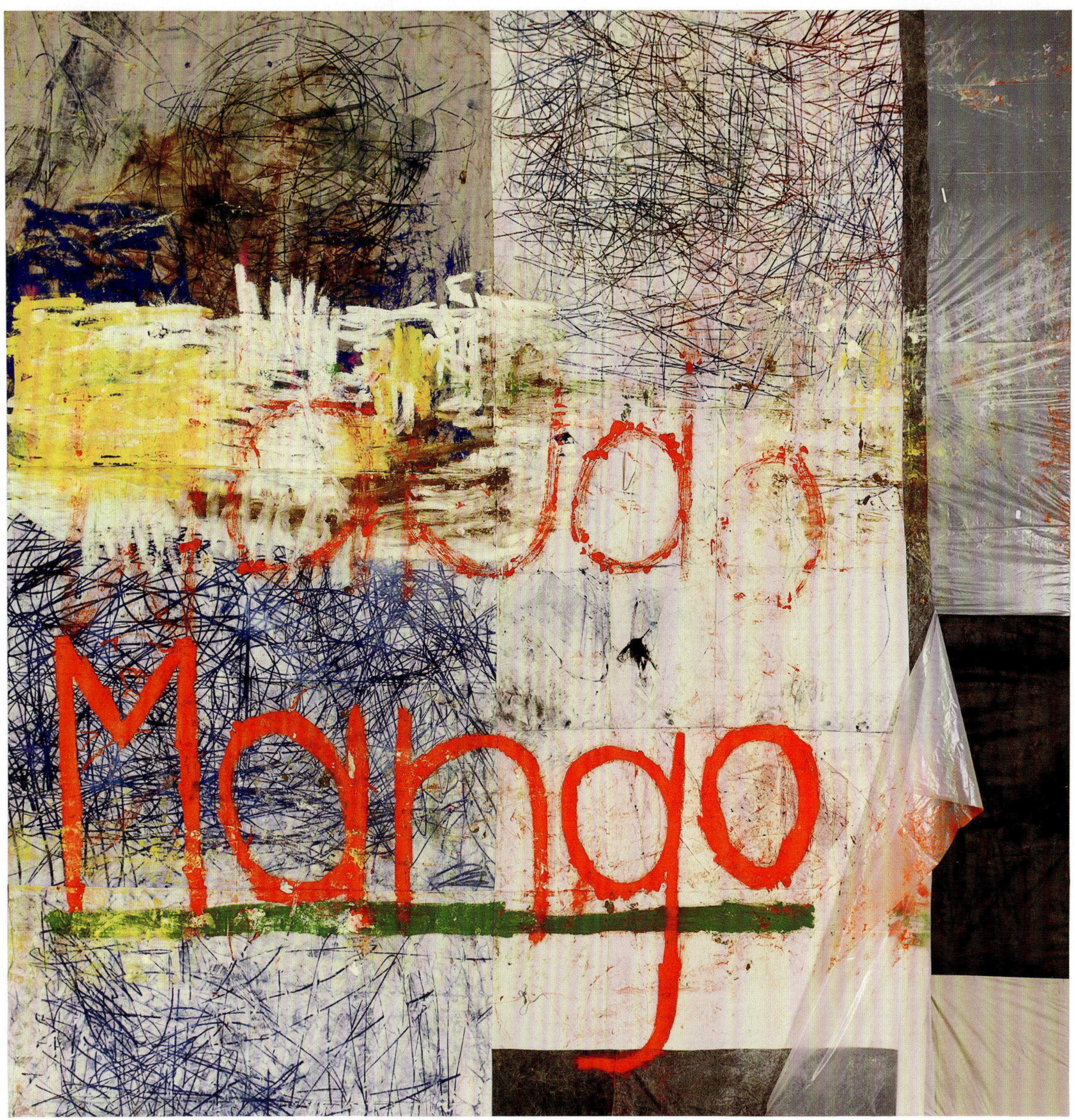

around on them, and they begin to accumulate pollution. They are the byproduct of most of my production time here at the Collection making the rest of the work. So the space, which was in the end a clean white cube, was a studio full of canvases and things on the floor.

To simplify things, what motivates me to write certain words like *yoga*, *chorizo*, or *mango* is that for a number of years now I've been interested in certain cultural currency shifts. Let's take yoga, for example. Centuries ago, there was no such thing as yoga in the Western social domain. Yoga was primarily practiced by men in Hindu and Buddhist societies. In the last couple of decades or so it has become a business, and it gets franchised around the world. What's also interesting to me is how mostly the female population dominates this industry. I'm interested in this mutation. Then because of my own kind of fascination with this practice, I began to do projects in and around the idea of performance. So the paintings become, just like the *work* paintings, an archive of all these activities that I carry out within my practice.

—Oscar Murillo

Opposite page: *Untitled (yoga)*, 2012, oil paint and dirt on canvas, 188 x 207 x 2 in. (477.5 x 525.8 x 5 cm), acquired in 2012
Untitled (mango), 2012, oil paint, plastic, and dirt on canvas, 185 x 184 x 2 in. (470 x 467.4 x 5 cm), acquired in 2012

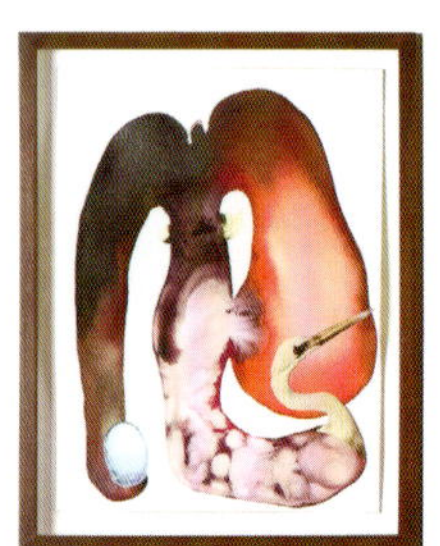 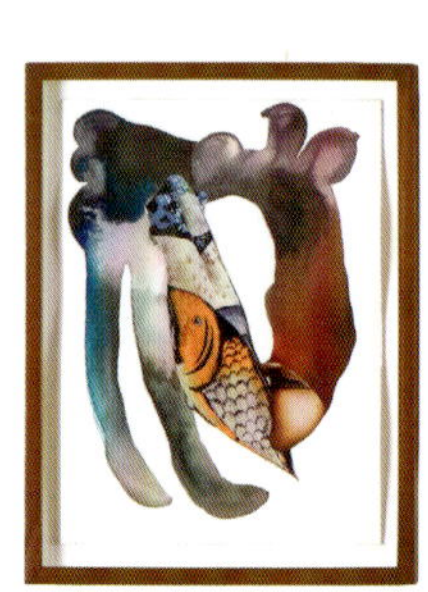 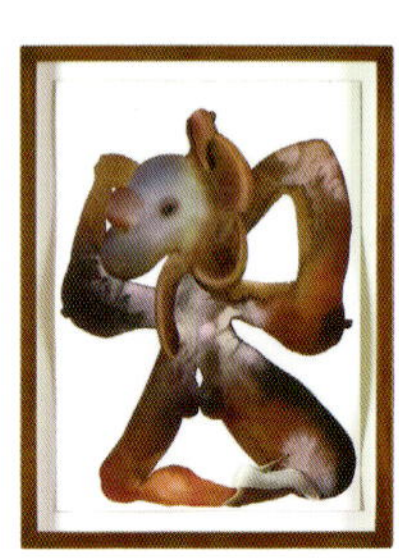 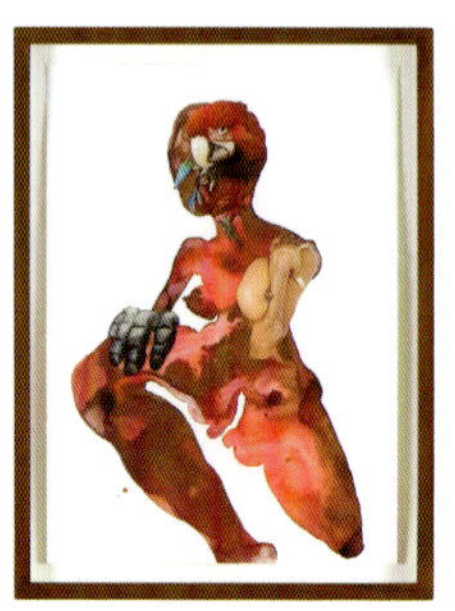 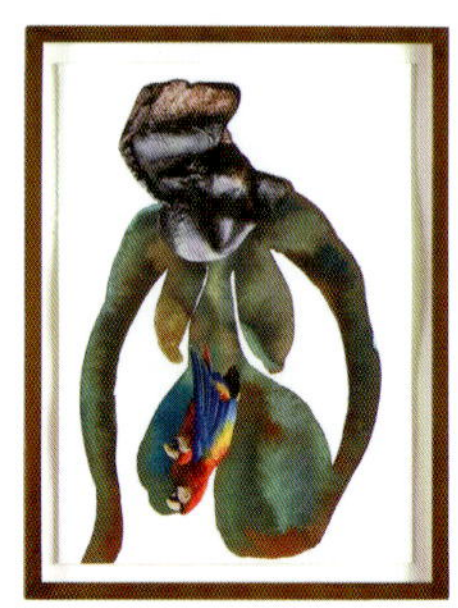 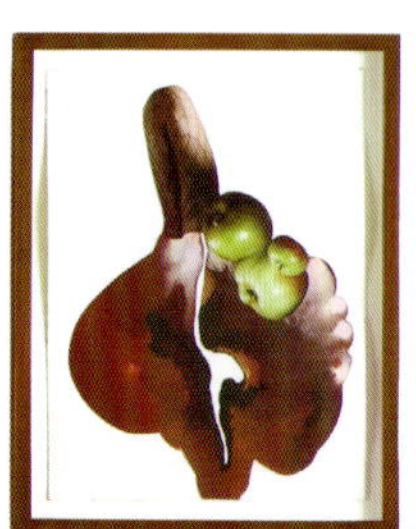

The Evolution of Mud Mama from Beginning to Start, 2008, six watercolors, gold leaf, and collage on paper, acquired in 2008
Opposite page: *Non, je ne regrette rien*, 2007, ink, acrylic, glitter, cloth, paper collage, plastic, plant material, and mixed media on Mylar, 54 1/2 x 92 1/2 in. (138.4 x 233.7 cm), acquired in 2008

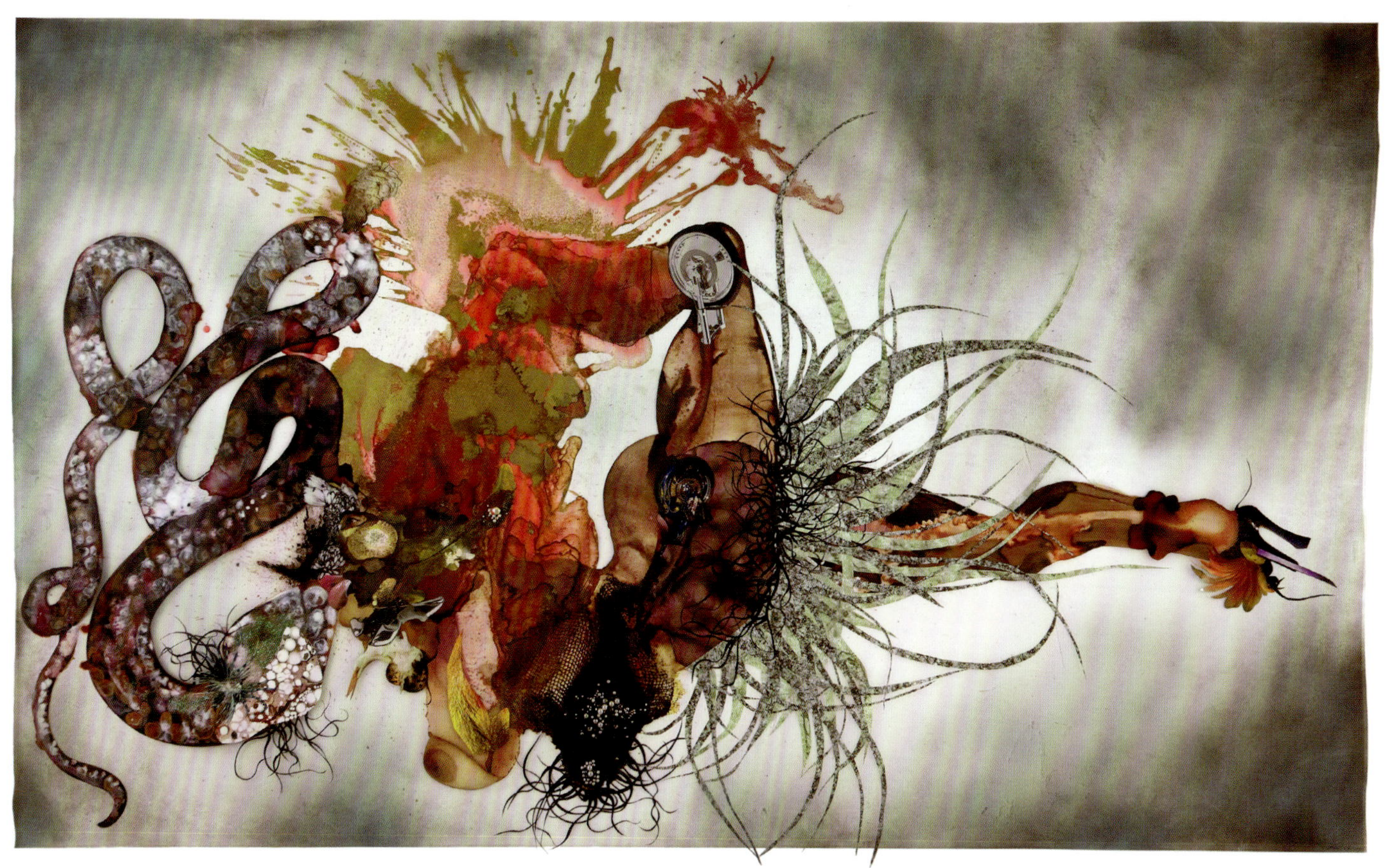

The entire body of work I was making at that point was of these characters suspended in between dimensions, between reality and dreams, between being specimens and spirits. The femaleness of the figure is apparent, but it's not clear what in Heaven's name any of these figures are. That includes other works that I did for that particular exhibition; my first show at Victoria Miro was called *Yo.n.I* or *Yoni*. This figure is bent over in this very acrobatic, balletic position. It's almost an impossible, painful position for the body. I think, to be quite honest, the work was being done when I had these issues—immigration and travel problems. One of the things I was expressing, either overtly or not, was that I have no regrets, everything is fine, that I'm able to make work, and that even though I couldn't be at my show in London, it didn't take anything away from the experience of creating these creatures and collages.

There's a lot of serpents. There's dragons, and vaginas, and foliage. There's a lot of references to the exotic impression, the aftertaste of Josephine Baker in visual culture. But really I think the title specifically for this piece is more about that I don't regret coming this far. I don't regret leaving home when I was young to go pursue my dreams because that's what I'm doing.

—Wangechi Mutu

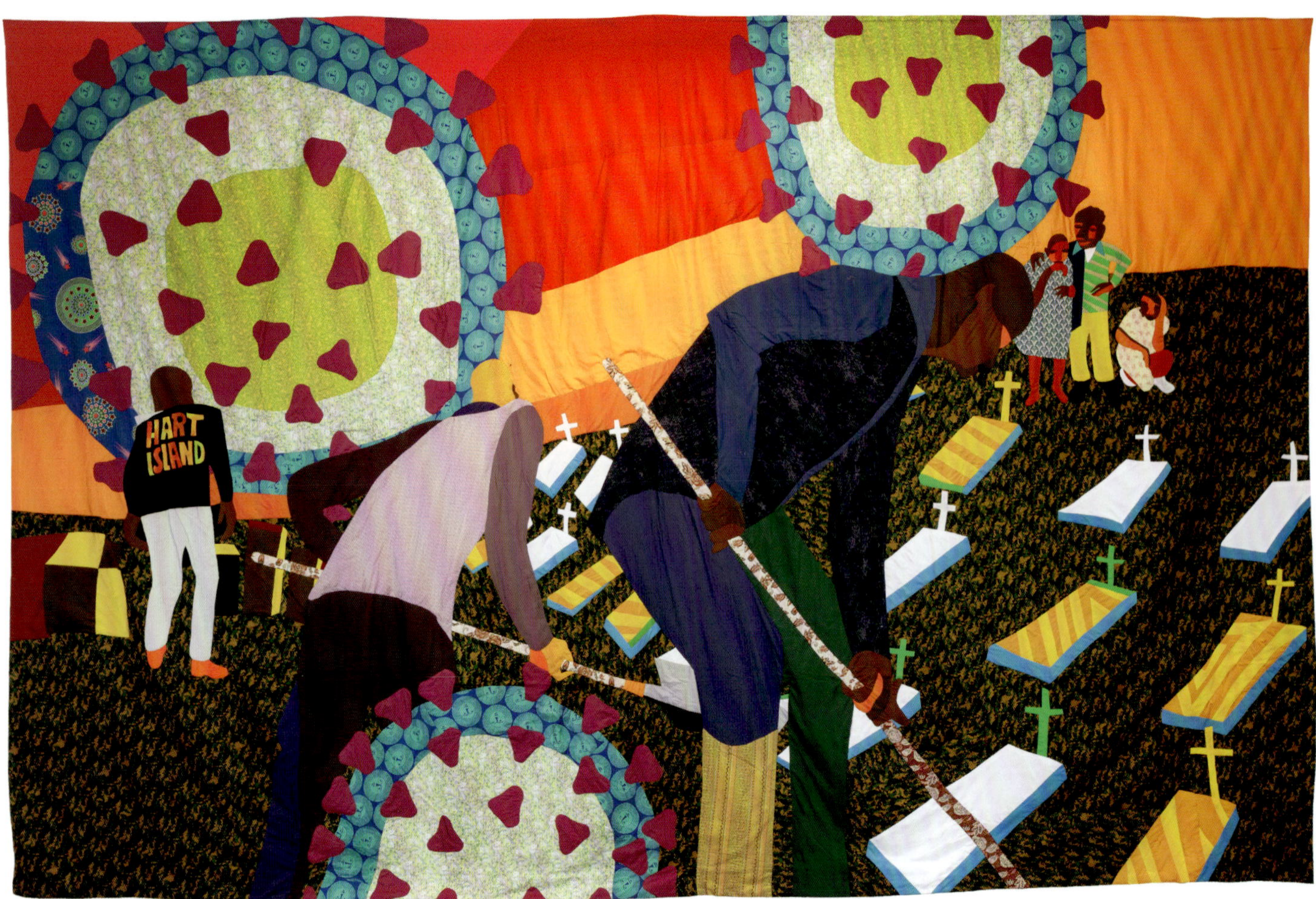

Part of a series considering the four classical elements (air, earth, fire, water) and their relation to Black lives and histories, in *Earth* I am working through the proximity of the African diaspora to death and to death work. During the opening year of the COVID crisis I watched as African Americans died at significantly higher rates than other races. As bodies piled up in morgues and hospitals, Black workers were employed to deal with the surplus of the dead. This history echoes throughout the history of the United States, going back at least as far as the yellow fever epidemic of 1793, in which African Americans provided the majority of the labor in both taking care of the ill and handling the bodies. The resonances and proximities to death and death work also echo the theses in Orlando Patterson's *Slavery and Social Death*, as well as in Joseph Roach's work *Cities of the Dead*. The workers on Hart Island, burying the dead in New York City's Potter's Field, felt like an epic representation of doormen to the land of death and being forgotten.

There is, of course, a history of holding death in quilts and tapestries that I am interested in, as with the death and commemorative quilts of Gee's Bend, the scraps of fabric each have their own histories and memories and come together to bring those memories forward. Many of the scraps of these fabrics I gave to folks who were sewing masks in the early days of the pandemic.

I was also interested in the consistent visualization techniques of the media trying to depict the invisible and silent threat of COVID. Abstractions of the structure of the virus abounded. In so many ways the crisis of COVID was and continues to be a literalization of the tension between what is seen and cannot be seen. Where breath or microscopic viruses or racial and class disparities are invisible but absolutely affect our lives, there are still folks that deny the importance or even existence of these factors. The virus floats like a sun over the entire dystopian scene.

Earth, 2020, appliqué fabric, 183 x 285 in. (464.8 x 724 cm), acquired in 2020

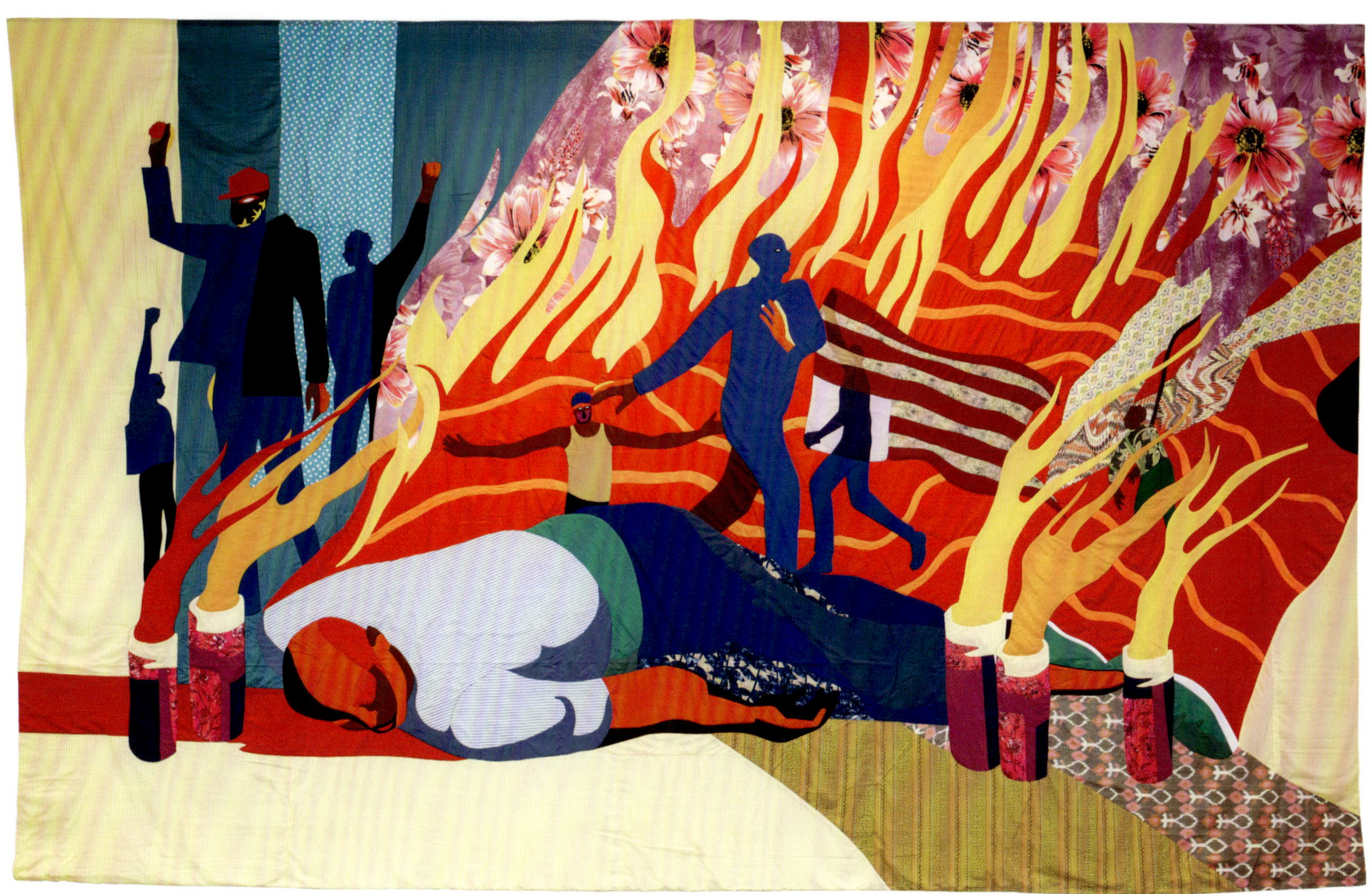

In *Fire*, I am thinking about recent histories of protest and rebellion in urban centers and the place of fire in that history, specifically the burning of buildings and structures within Black communities.

The question of "Why are 'they' burning down their own neighborhoods?" has dogged the narratives of protests and rebellion in desperate communities thirsting for change for generations. The obvious answer is that oppressed people rarely feel an ownership of the spaces that they inhabit, and this lack of ownership is re-enforced by hegemonic and ontological strictures surrounding these "underclasses." Fire, burning, and destruction of property often serve as a reminder of the inversion of value experienced by various populations, a rebellion against capitalist structures that value property over people. During the protests in Ferguson, or concerning the murder of George Floyd, there were numerous inversions referenced in the protests: the elevation of Black bodies and

images of Black death as a focus of community power and outrage, the destruction of neighborhood institutions as a way of signifying how these institutions do not serve us. Fire for me is often an externalization of internal pain, similar to the self-harm of teenagers; things are not right on the inside (in the values and mores of our societies), and we want to demonstrate that outside (in the very architecture we live in). There is also some reference to the gospel song and James Baldwin text, *The Fire Next Time*, which implies a reckoning for the injustices and pains of today.

—Christopher Myers

Fire, 2020, appliqué fabric, 178 x 293 in. (452.1 x 744.2 cm), acquired in 2020

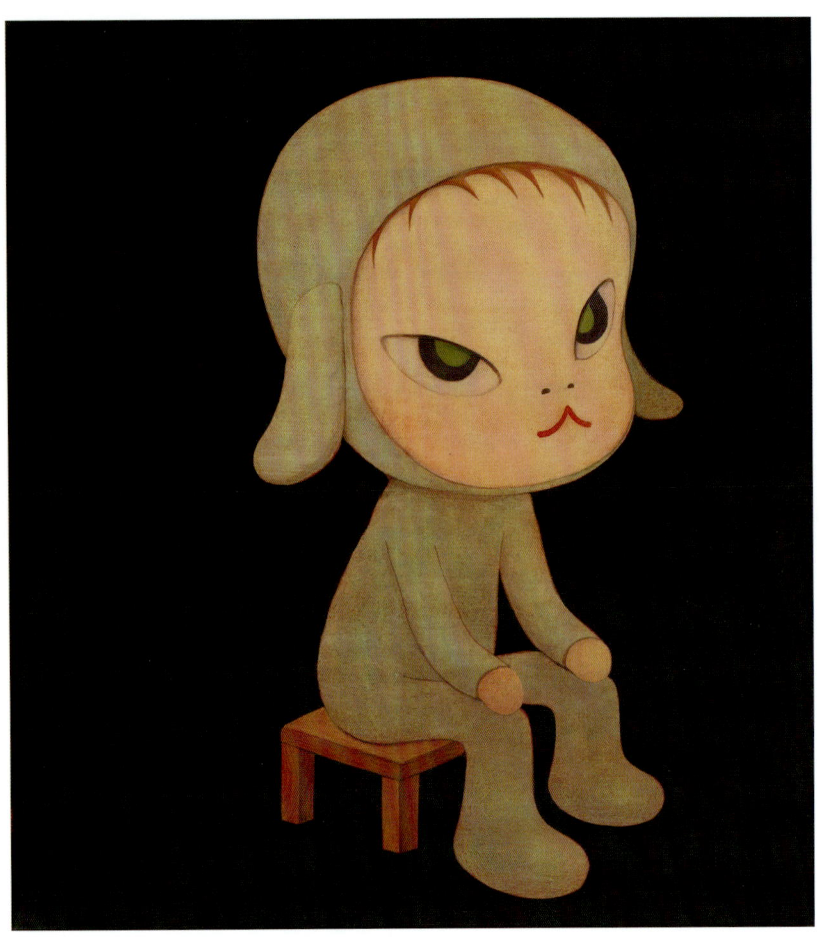

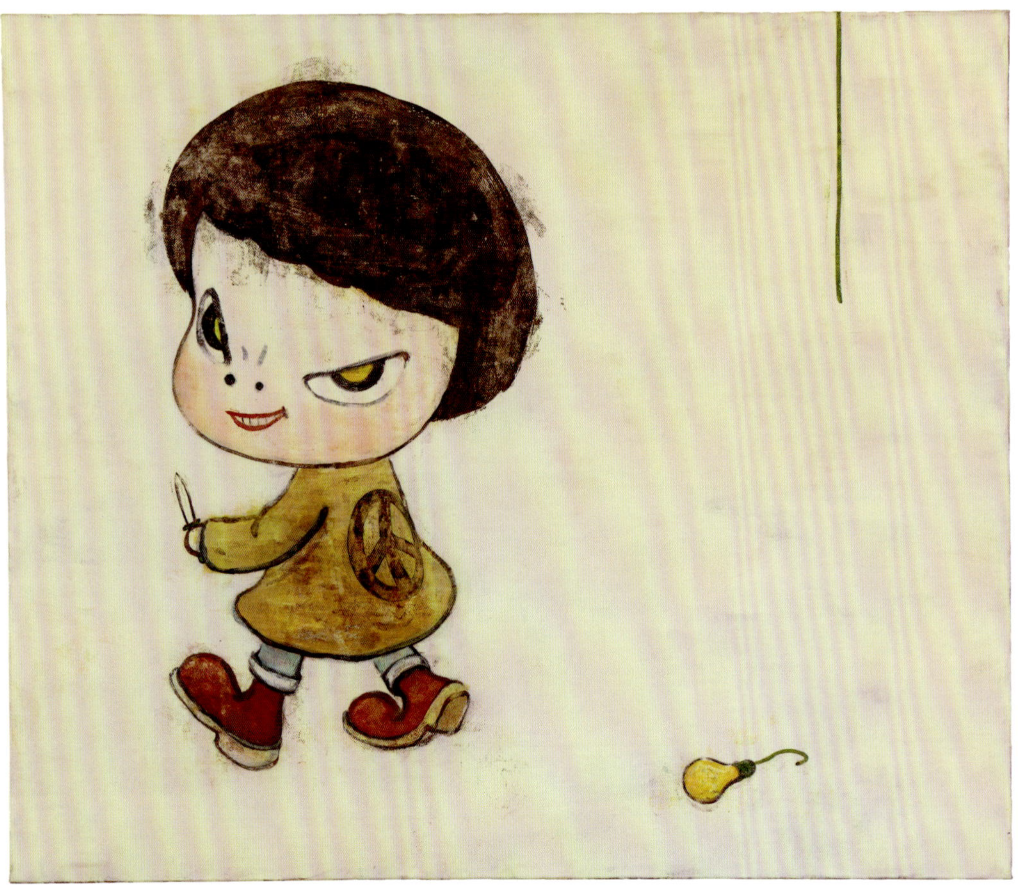

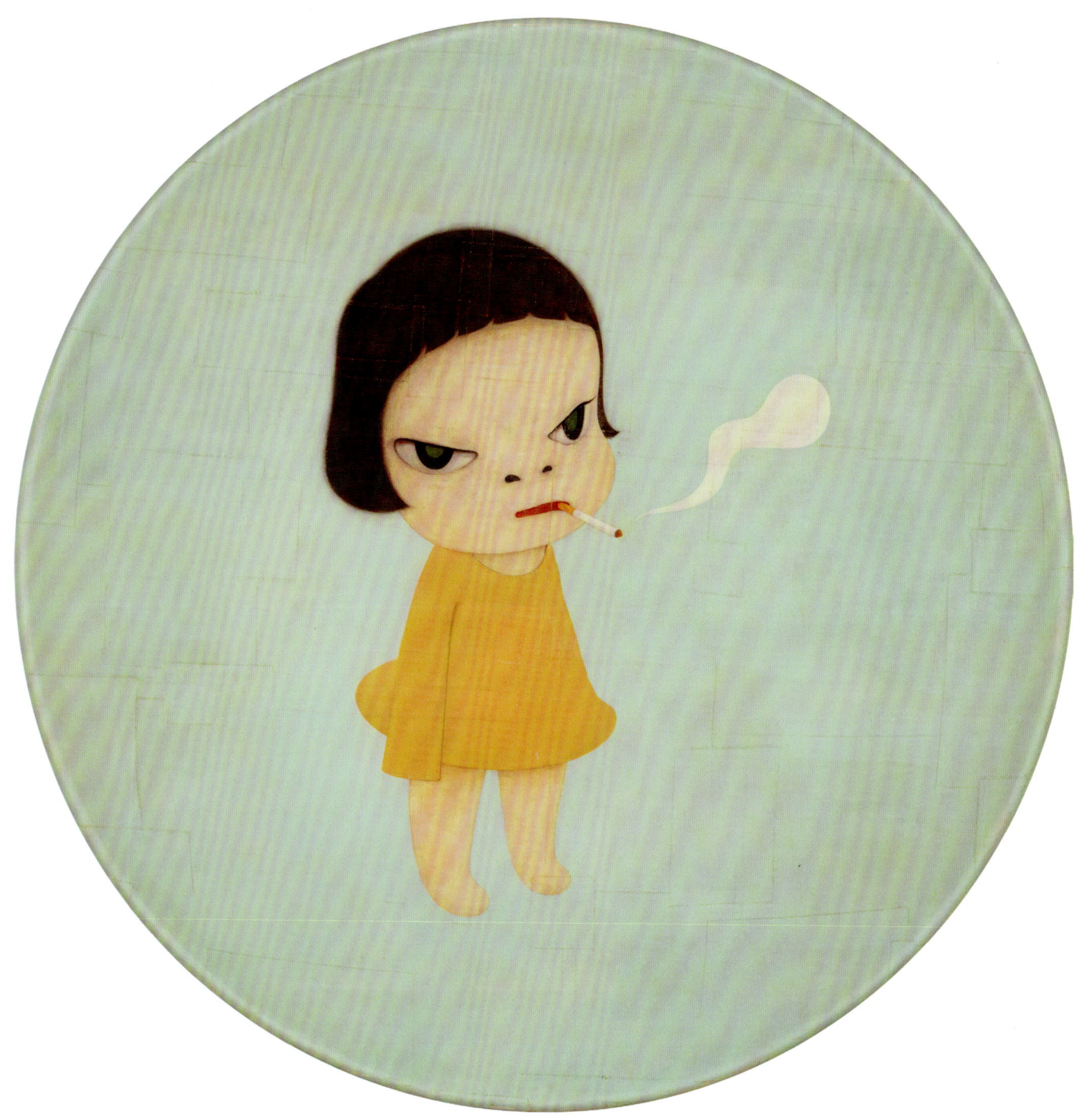

From the expanding watchtower of my frontal lobe,
My thoughts race beyond the dream mountains to the
wide-open wilderness,
Where a wafer moon gently melts.

In the midst of the milk-white fog,
A dog spins around and around.

Boarding a plane on the pier of my heart,

A transfusion line flies off,
Sightseeing its way towards that dog.

If the gathered past becomes the present,
Then perhaps the fragment of the imploding now that is the
dog,
is me, is you, as well.

—Yoshitomo Nara

Opposite page, top to bottom: *Hyper Enough (to the City)*, 1996, acrylic on canvas, 49 x 59 in. (125 x 150 cm), acquired in 1997
Sleepless Night (Sitting), 1997, acrylic on canvas, 47 1/8 x 43 1/8 in. (119.7 x 109.5 cm), acquired in 1997
Above: *Too Young To Die*, 2001, acrylic on cotton mounted on fiber reinforced plastics, Diameter: 70 3/4 in. (180 cm), acquired in 2002

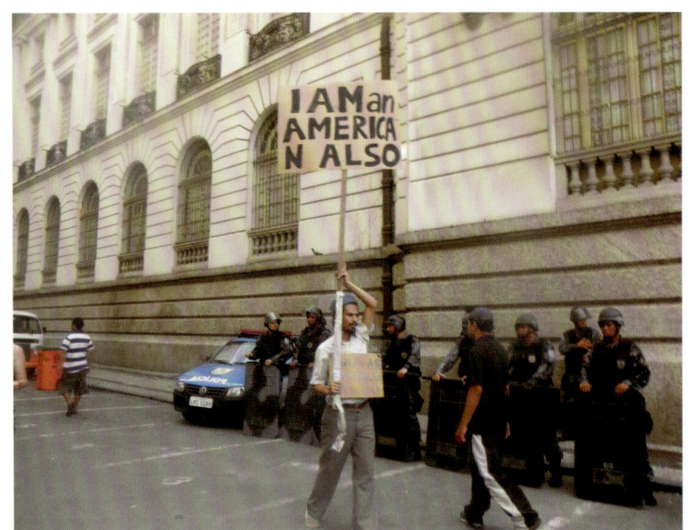

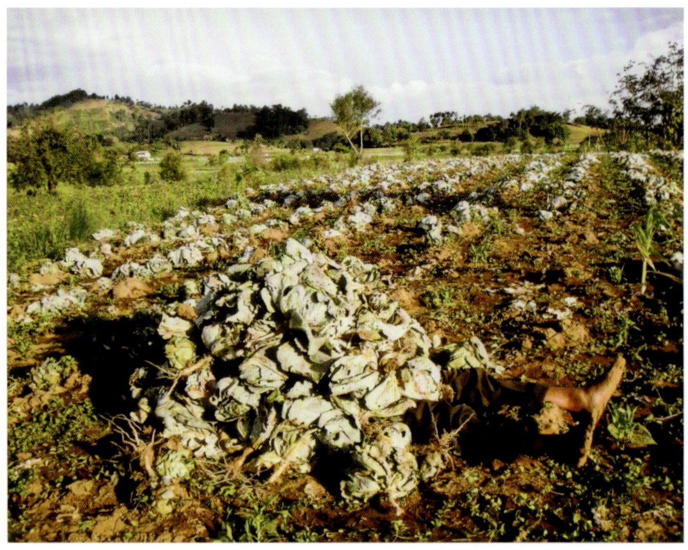

I AM an AMERICAN ALSO. Much eludes this announcement, demonstration, protest, manifesto. I, Paulo Sergio Mohamed Nazareth Cassiano de Jesus da Cruz Brugre Borun da Silva, was born in Nak Borun / Watu Valley [Minas Gerais], central region of Pindorama [Brazil] in southern Abya Yala. I am Afro-Borun by my mother— the path from Africa goes through the quilombos that settled between the mountains of the Atlantic Forest and the banks of the river. Before carrying Américo Vespúcio, I carry the waters of the Watu being carried by the Ererres, Boruns, and Egunguns from Africa. But when America comes into existence on Earth, I become an American too. Until the conflict is resolved and Kuarahy [the Sun God] removes America from Abya Yala, I still carry the many stories that occur on this side of Pacha Mama: I am American too. I am an Afro American on the Euro American scale; I am Latin American on the Anglo American scale [Anglo-Saxo-American] and the balance follows¬—Afro Latino Americano / Afro Anglo Americano [Afro Anglo-Saxo-Americano] as opposed to Euro Latino Americano / Euro Anglo Americano [Euro Anglo Saxo Americano]. I'm an American like any other born in the Americas, and if we create drawers and subcategories, we must have a place for whites in the filing cabinet of racialization.

__ cabbage field — I let the body lie down / fall on the countryside of the ancient continent. Yes, Abya Yala is as old as the other corners of the world. Young Luzia here in the south next to my house is about 12,000 years old. She certainly climbed Morro do Palmital many times in Santa Luzia / Minais Gerais to look afar and to know where to go. The bones of the prediluvian beings that Peter Lund searched for in the middle of the 19th century can still be seen at the base of the hill, not very far from where the contemporary flying machines rest. I let my body fall on the countryside of America as well as along the south and north of the entire continent. Many times fallen on the land, I go to sleep, and between sleep and death I can travel in time where I see so many other fallen bodies throughout history that create the concept of America and forge contemporary borders. A fallen or lying down body reminds me of the stories of the construction of the power of the State, which dismembered bodies of rebels and insurgents throughout all the earth to serve as an example to other possible insurgents throughout colonial history, republic, dictatorships, and pseudo democracies / DEMOCRACIES. A body fallen on the countryside tells many stories: of the sugar plantations in Brazil, Cuba, Haiti, and cotton plantations in the United States in the 1700s and 1800s, oil in Venezuela, and soybeans, cattle, chicken, bananas, oranges, coffee in many corners. The bodies continue falling this morning of this day/month/year, which is now in the 21st century, and I continue with a brutal hope that this century will end with a colossal diversity of risen / erect / and standing bodies still alive rewriting the history of the Americas.

Left to right: *Untitled, from the News from the Americas series*, 2011/2012, color photograph, ed. 1 AP, 8 x 10 in. (18 x 24 cm), acquired in 2015
Untitled, 2011/2012, color photograph, ed. 1 AP, 26 1/2 x 35 in. (67.5 x 90 cm), acquired in 2015
Untitled from the For Sale Series, 2011, color photograph, ed. 1 AP, 35 x 27 in. (90 x 67.5 cm), acquired in 2015

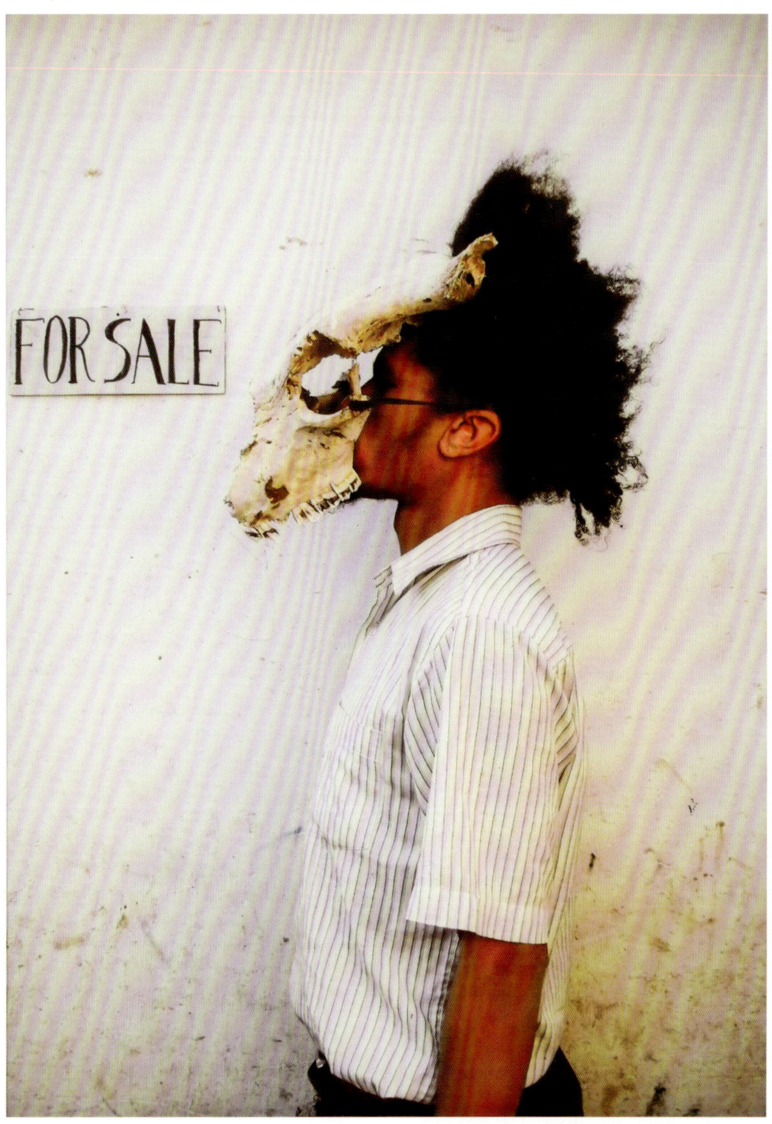

When NAZARETH CASSIANO DE JESUS was kidnapped and forcibly sent to the Psychiatric Colony of Barbacena / Minas Gerais, my mother, ANA GONCALVES DA SILVA, could not grab her and prevent her physical disappearance. My mother was between three-to-eight months old, and the Great War in Europe was ending, but here the war continued. NAZARETH was deprived of her own name and was given a number. She remained inside the asylum, which treated people as merchandise, for about 20 years. For many years, the institution sold the bodies of deceased patients to the principal medical schools in Brazil, where to this day black bodies only enter as objects of study. The university where I studied bought about 543 bodies. Perhaps among them was the mother of my mother, who disappeared from the hospital in 1964, the year of the beginning of the Brazilian Civilian Military Dictatorship.

To look through cracks, locks, and pinholes can leave us feeling safe or imprisoned, depending on where we are. The mother of my mother was on the inside, she saw the world through a pinhole. FOR SALE has many sides from which it can be seen. It is a game between today, yesterday, and tomorrow. It can be the black body (Native American and Black African) enslaved and up for sale. It can also be the perpetuation of that image for sale, the vicious circle that must be broken. The racialized body continues to be a product for sale and pseudoscientific studies. When I put the bull's head over mine, I know that today the majority of cattle that eat the grass of America do not have their origins there. To dominate the Native people, the white invaders killed the bison and their native ancestors of the earth and introduced private property using the European cattle to trample the earth and mark the space of the white man. I think of Álvar Núñez Cabeza de Vaca, known as Cabeza de Vaca, who originally landed somewhere in Florida and from there went west to what is today Texas eventually completing a circle going south, passing through the old Mexico City, and returning to the Caribbean gulf. Later, on a second voyage, he came to the South of America, which today forms, in part, Brazil, Argentina, and Paraguay. When I put the FOR SALE bull's head over mine, a lot is happening inside. I see that all the black racialized and enslaved bodies in the United States and all of the Americas had ancestors dehumanized and carried south before being taken north as merchandise.

—Paulo Nazareth

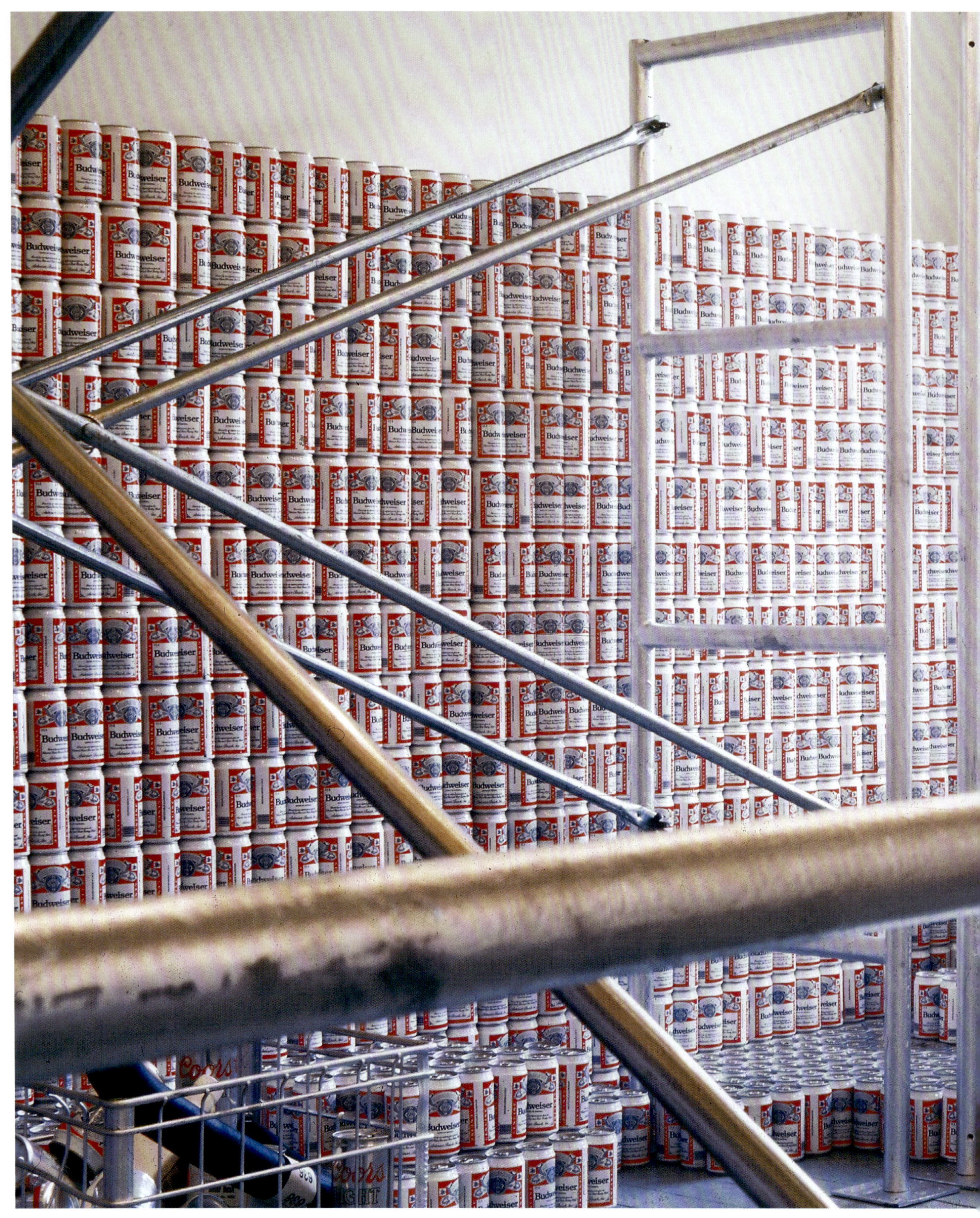

This Piece Has No Title Yet, 1989, installation: beer cans, flags, steel scaffolding, paint, and mixed media; installation view, 1989, Mattress Factory, Pittsburgh, PA, acquired in 1996

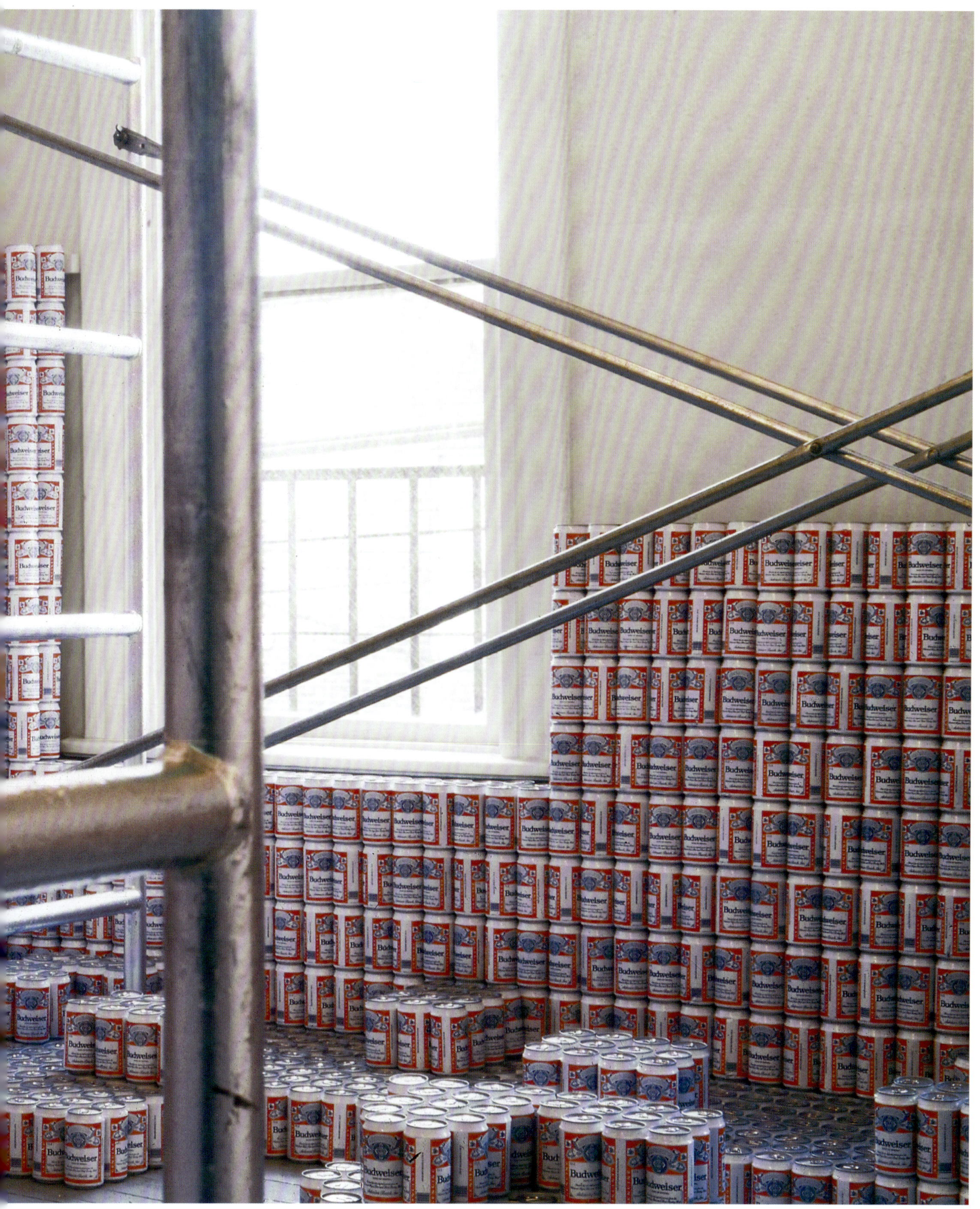

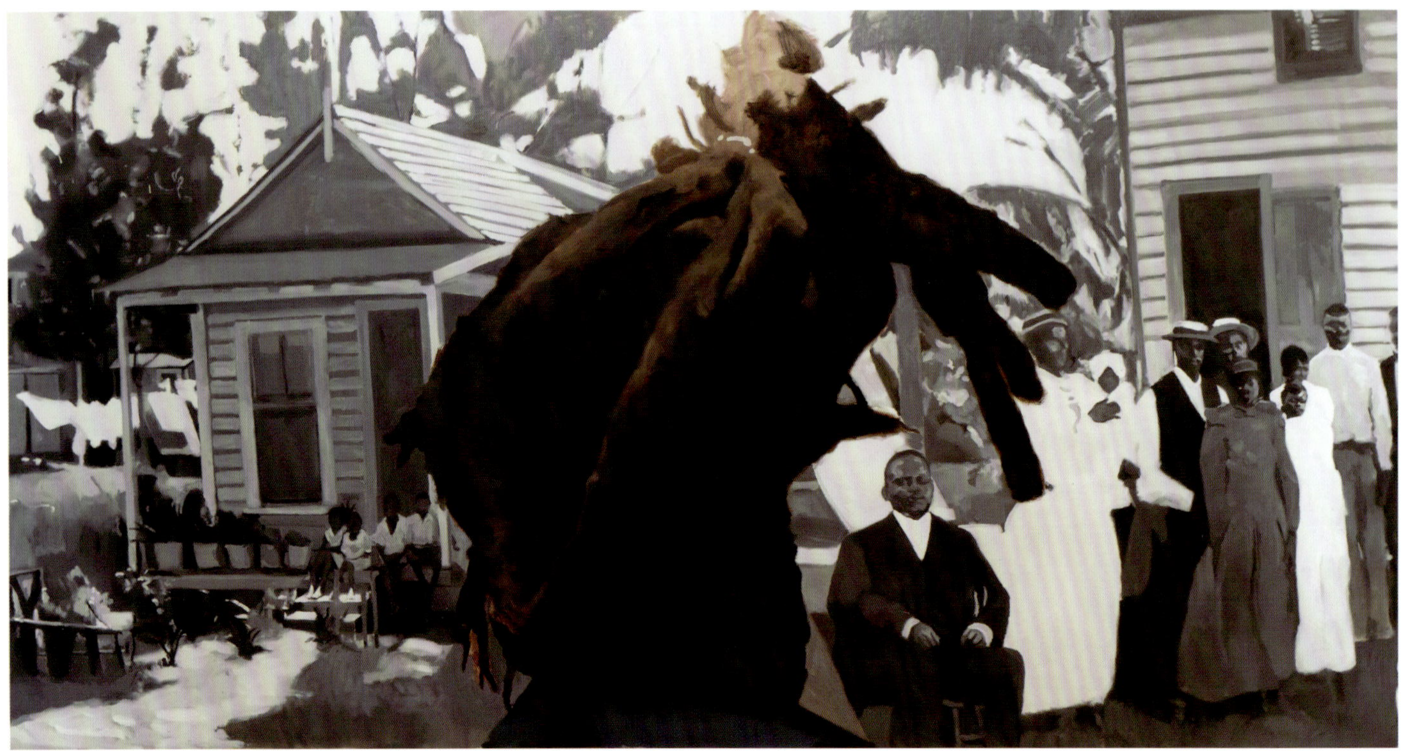

This painting creates a thread of different people in different parts of Miami across time. Two separate black-and-white images depict historic people—children sitting on the porch of their homes in Overtown on the left, and wealthy pioneer Bahamians in Coconut Grove on the right. In the foreground, a modern man stands in with his back to viewers of the painting.

The title *As I am* is derived from a phrase commonly used in churches: "come as you are." Being that Overtown was established in 1897, it went through a variety of changes over the course of time. People of the African diaspora were responsible for the cultural development of the community, but outside groups deliberately used tactics to reduce it. The modern man in the foreground represents a beautiful culture of the present that can only be fully understood by those who live it.

As I Am, 2021, oil on canvas, 108 x 210 in. (274.3 x 533.4 cm), acquired in 2021

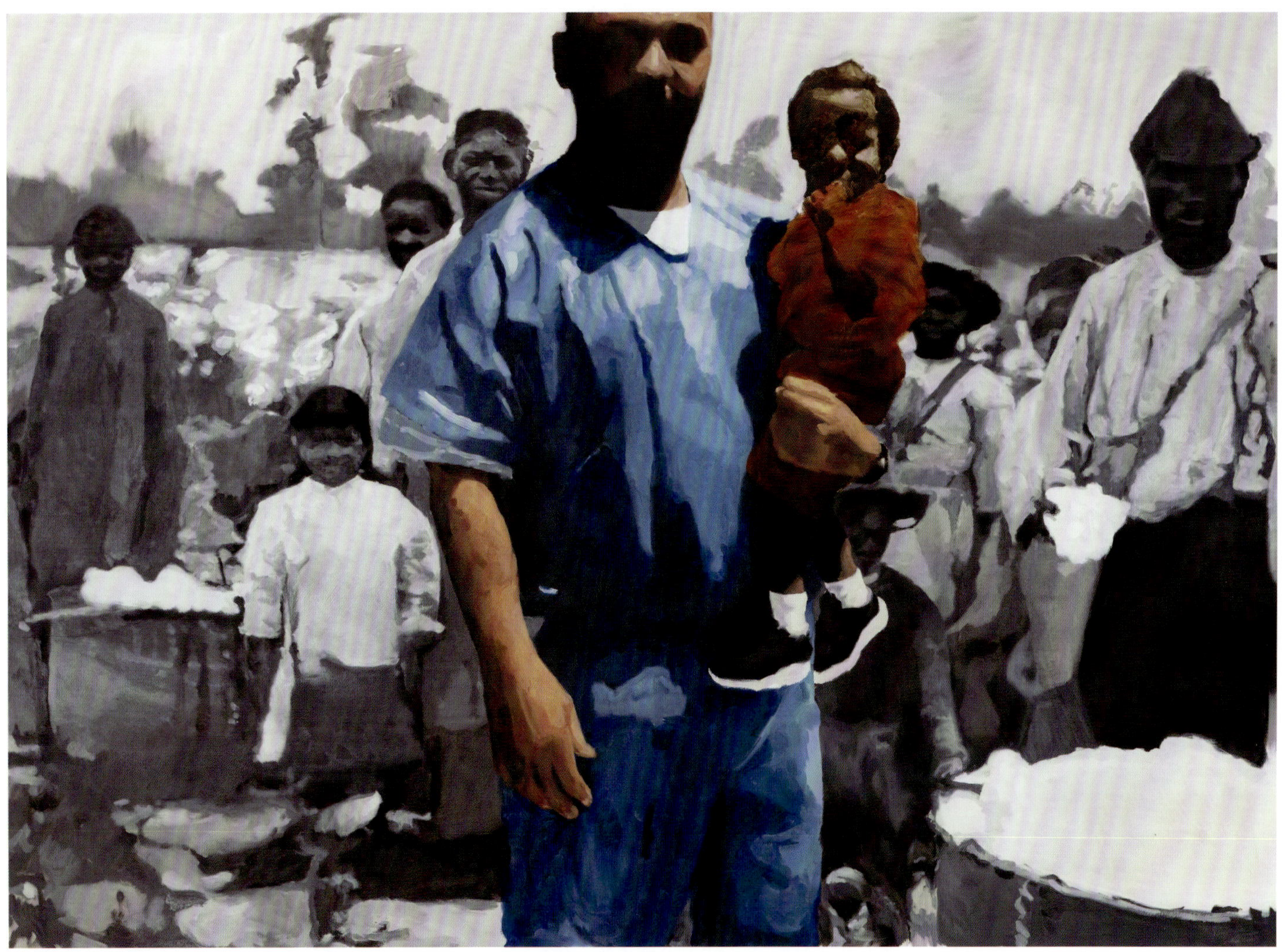

The 13th Amendment in the Constitution states, "Neither slavery nor involuntary servitude, except as a punishment for crime whereof the party shall have been duly convicted, shall exist within the United States, or any place subject to their jurisdiction." This is my father when he was serving a 25-year prison sentence, holding my second cousin, and our ancestors. This painting not only reflects the commonalities between the prison industrial complex and slavery in America, but it also represents the resilience of existing and thriving despite cycles of displacement, extraction, and violence. That being said, these conditions are not essential to who we are and do not wholly represent our entirety.

—Reginald O'Neal

My Father, Lil Pat, and Our Ancestors, 2021, oil on canvas, 120 x 168 in. (304.8 x 426.7 cm), acquired in 2021

Russell Ferguson: When you began making portraits, were you consciously setting out to represent a community rather than individual people?

Catherine Opie: Yeah, I thought of it as a community. My investment in the community is very important to the work. In fact, I probably wouldn't have done the work if I hadn't felt that I didn't like the way my community was being represented in the world. I'm really interested in the structure of communities. I grew up in Sandusky, Ohio, and when I was 13 moved to Rancho Bernardo in California, which is a master-planned community. I left there at 18 to go to San Francisco. The underlying basis of all my work has been about the structure of urban and suburban space, and about how communities begin to form. I'm curious about the way family begins to be defined within community. In a suburban community the family is defined by the individual house. In the gay and lesbian SM community, family is defined by those members who get together on holidays, and who are close friends. My work is always close to home. It's always about my surroundings and the way that I wander through the world.

RF: On one level, your standardised portrait formats evoke early 20th century photography—social survey photographers like August Sander—but because you don't have the environmental clues in the background, it's a much more iconic presentation. Your portraits all have brightly coloured backgrounds, for example.

CO: To photograph the people in their environments would have been too much like documentary for me. I was thinking about Hans Holbein and the way that he used colour behind his subjects. Formally, it can bring out all these different shapes within the body, to make it pop. It is a way to take the people out of their environments and isolate them, because the art is really what they're doing with their bodies. It's also to make the focus really on the person. And then the body of work as a whole brings it back to documentary by the way that it's kind of narrowed down, and by the repetition within the different formats of the portraits.

Another reason I wanted to do the portraits that way was that I was getting really tired of the various magazines that were coming out about body modification, where nobody cared about the people, and also nobody had any formal concerns. It was all just to document it in very basic ways, like the nipple with the ring going through it, the penis with whatever, and the representation of it was just all fragmented. It was all about the body, but I wanted it to be about the person as well.

RF: Do you give your subjects a lot of latitude in how they present themselves in the portraits? To what extent are they directed by you?

CO: Clothing, a lot of latitude. They wear whatever. Unless it's a drag queen, and then we talk about the outfit. Once they are in the studio, though, they are so completely manipulated by me. Even though I don't believe that there is a true essence of a person, I do believe there is something that they see within themselves that I end up capturing.

Top left to bottom right:
Justin Bond, 1993, chromogenic print, ed. of 8 AP 1/2, 20 x 16 in. (50.8 x 40.6 cm), acquired in 2006
Mike, 1993, chromogenic print, ed. 1/8, 20 x 15 in. (50.8 x 38 cm), acquired in 2007
Jo, 1993, chromogenic print, ed. 6/8, 20 x 16 in. (50.8 x 40.6 cm), acquired in 2006
Mike and Sky, 1993, chromogenic print, ed. 1/8 , 20 x 16 in. (50.8 x 40.6 cm), acquired in 2006
Crystal Mason, 1994, chromogenic print, ed. 4/8, 20 x 15 in. (50.8 x 38.1 cm), acquired in 2007
Mitch, 1994, chromogenic print, ed. 2/8, 20 x 16 in. (50.8 x 40.6 cm), acquired in 2006

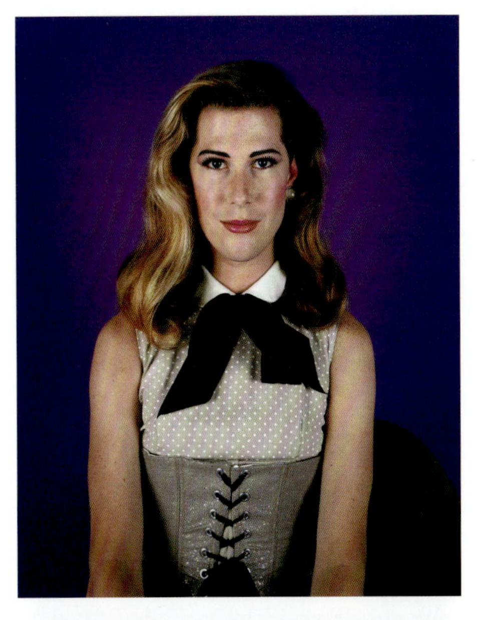
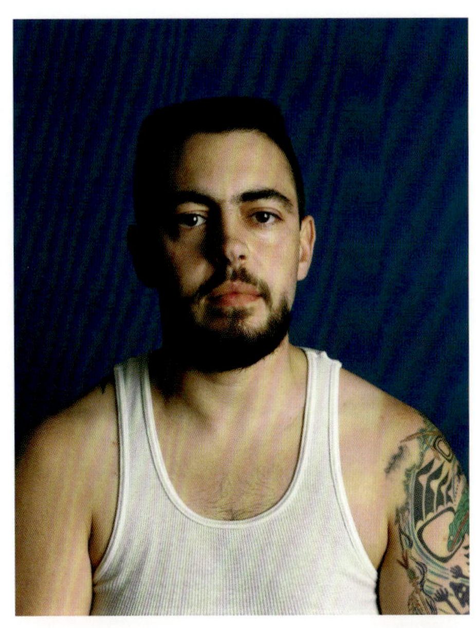
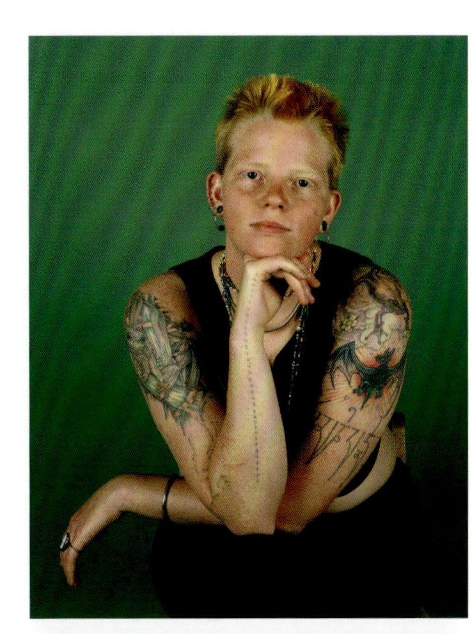
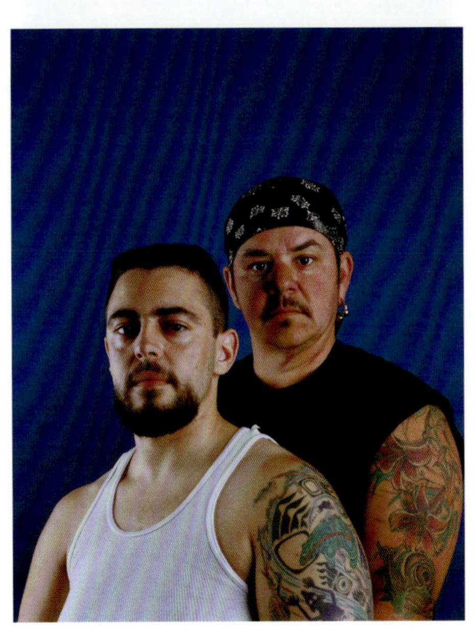
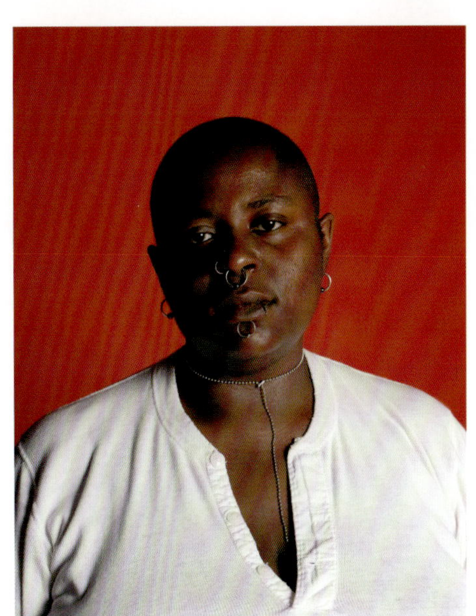
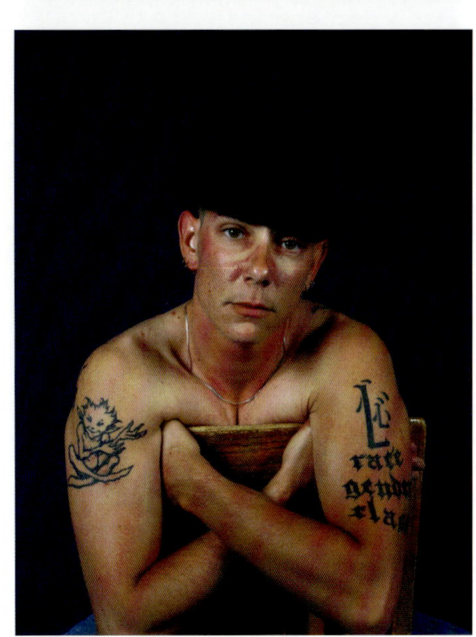

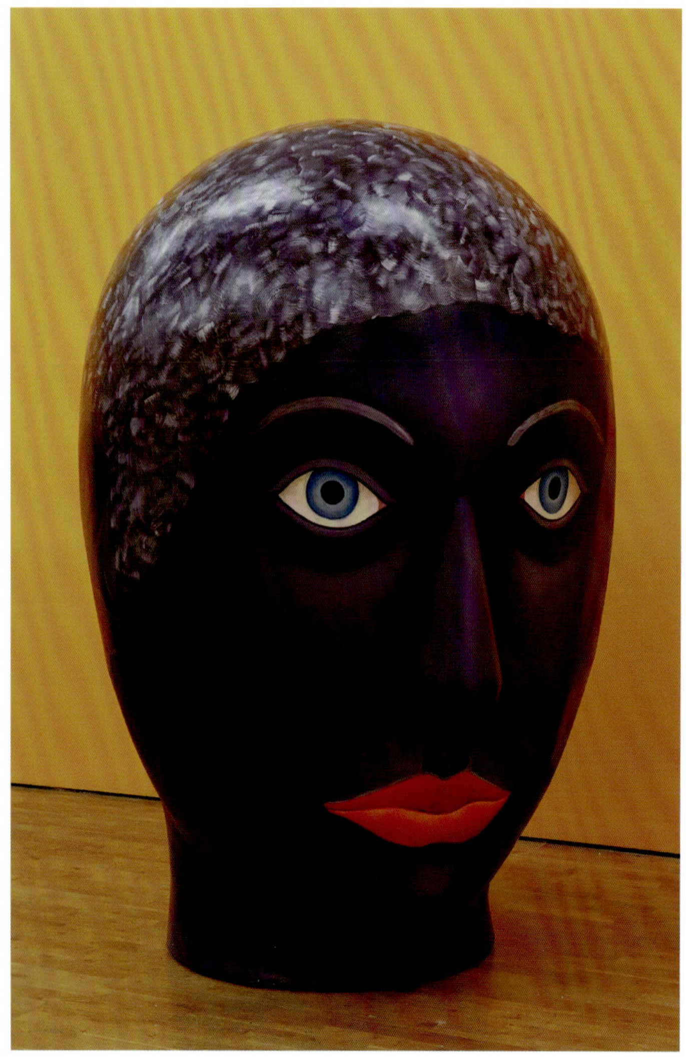

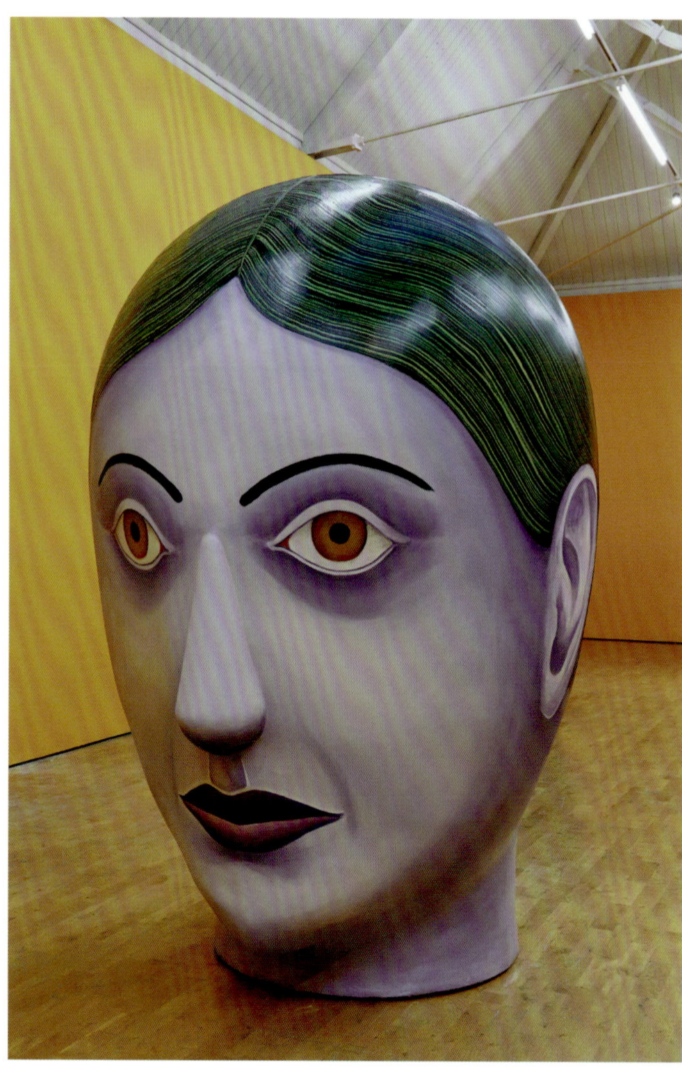

I'm interested in adopting and recasting the classical themes and genres of painting—portraiture, still life, and landscape, amongst others. My portraits don't depict real sitters, but their format references the subjects and styles of historical painting. The patterned clothing and fixed expression of the subject in *Portrait with One Butterfly* references the extravagant costumes of 18th century portrait paintings. The idea of including the butterfly—an allusion to metamorphosis, camouflage, and changeability—started after looking at Otto Marseus van Schrieck's intricate paintings of flowers and butterflies. The dust of the pastel itself recalls the pigmentation of butterfly wings.

The two *Speaker* sculptures emerged from my ongoing interest in masks, make-up, and the Rococo style. They have a direct affinity to my pastel portraits, where coloration, facial expression, and elements of the natural world play a key role. Their imposing scale and bright colors reference polychrome – the decorative practice, first established in ancient Greece, of painting sculpture and architecture in a variety of colors. In this case, the process mirrors the application of makeup as I hand-painted their smooth surfaces.

—Nicolas Party

Left to right:
Speaker (TBC), 2017, wood, metal mesh frame, gypsum plaster, acrylic and oil paint, 55.1 x 55.1 x 78.7 in. (140 x 140 x 200 cm), acquired in 2017
Speaker (TBC), 2017, wood, metal mesh frame, gypsum plaster, acrylic and oil paint, 55.1 x 55.1 x 78.7 in. (140 x 140 x 200 cm), acquired in 2017
Portrait with One Butterfly, 2019, pastel on canvas, 45 1/2 x 43 3/4 x 2 1/2 in.(116.2 x 111.2 x 6.9 cm), acquired in 2019

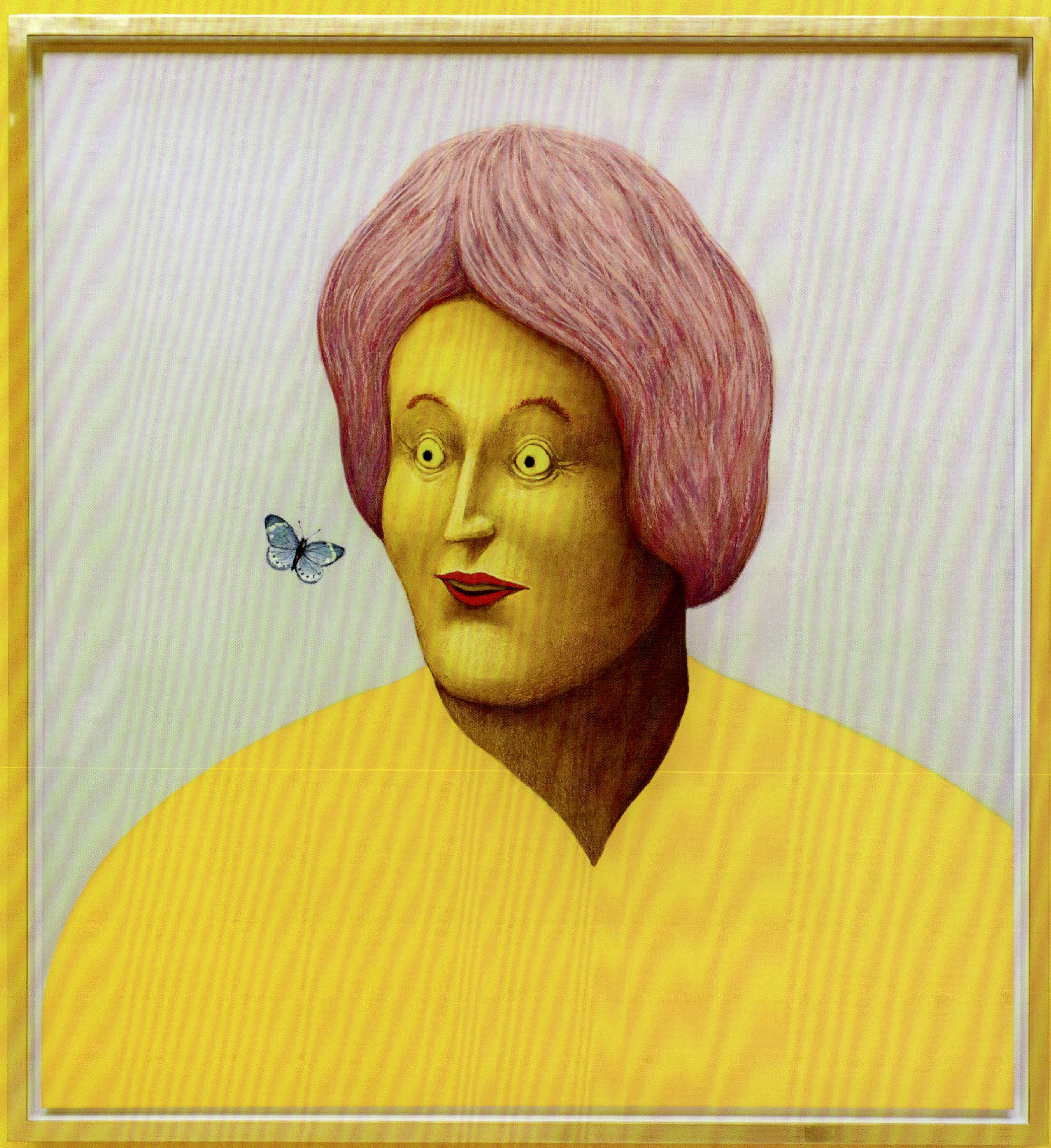

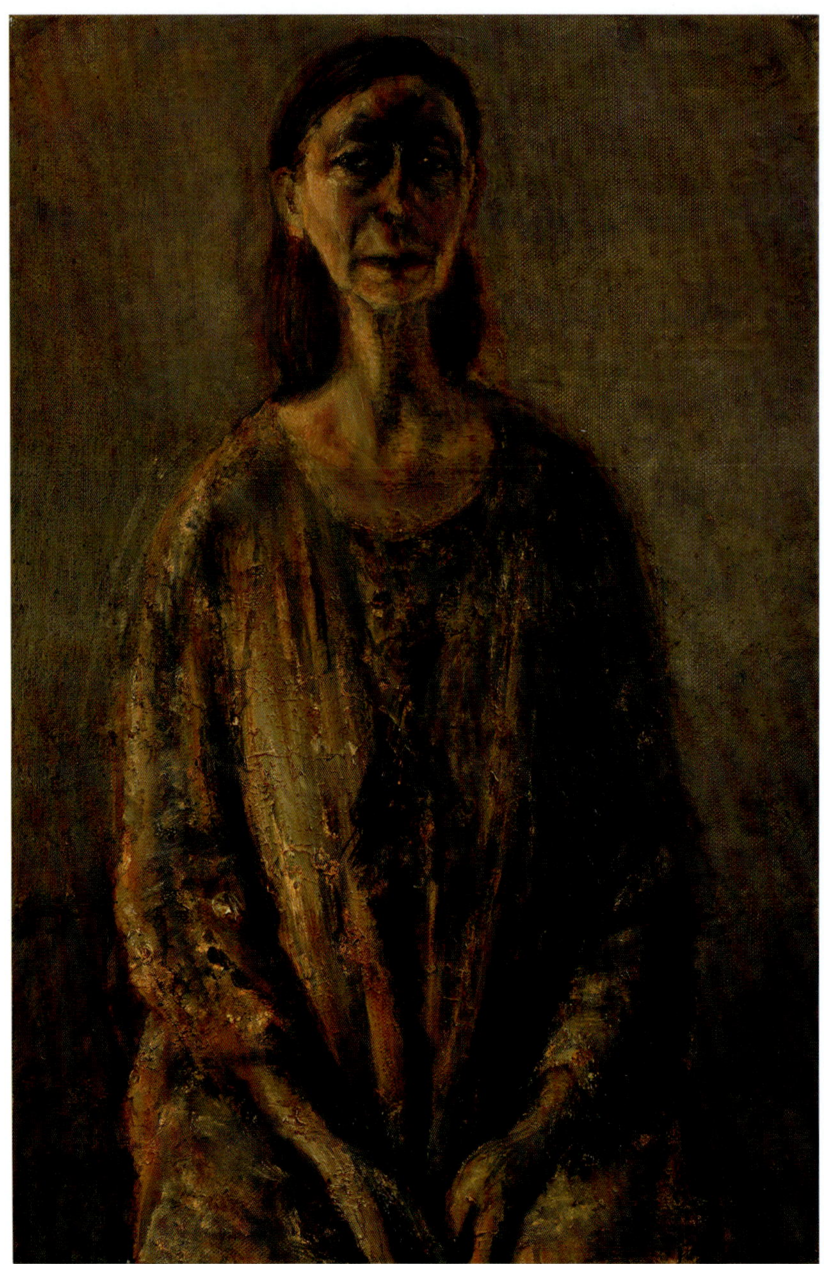

When I made *Self-Portrait, August-September*, I had recently moved to Victoria Miro gallery. I was exhilarated by the change. I felt energised and understood and empowered, suddenly. For years I had worked with hardly any recognition; now I felt seen.

Even though my hands are resting in my lap, I have a powerful Sphinx-like presence. My gaze is enigmatic but direct. I repeatedly wipe my paintbrush and palette knife onto my dress and, over time, the resulting texture becomes like clay, moulding my form. I have almost turned into a sculpture.

In *Kate in White*, my younger sister Kate seems to glow mysteriously. The light doesn't come from a natural source. It appears to emanate from her. She is quietly contained, her hands folded in her lap and her eyes are lowered. She is inhabiting her own inner world. The melancholy of her expression is offset by the peaceful golden aura that surrounds her.

When this painting was made, our mother was dying. She was admitted into hospital in the autumn of 2014, suffering from dementia. She died in February 2015. Kate is thinking about our mother, and how our lives are changed by her loss.

—Celia Paul

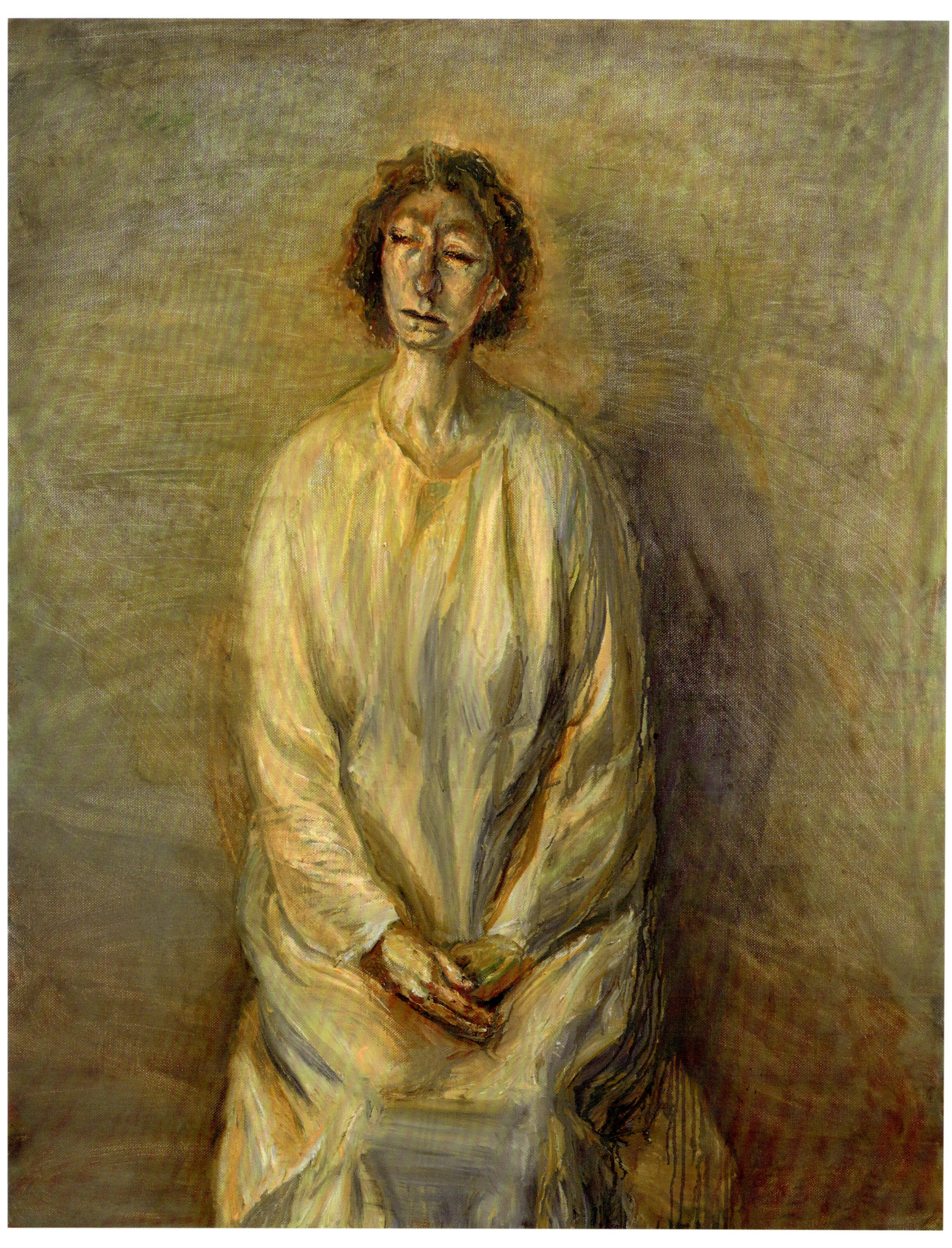

Opposite Page: *Self-Portrait August-September*, 2014, oil on canvas, 36 x 24 in. (91.4 x 61 cm), acquired in 2015
Kate in White, 2014-2015, oil on canvas, 40 x 50 in. (101.6 x 127 cm), acquired in 2015

The group of works called *Apocalypse Ballet* in the Rubell Collection were all made for my show at Barbara Weiss in Berlin in 2006, and were shown later that year at Chicago's Renaissance Society. Another work from the same series is now in a museum in Maastricht, the Bonnefanten Museum. It's a coherent group. I started working with papier-mâché mannequins in 2003 or 2004. They were originally meant to be like store mannequins for *The Crystal Frontier*, the master-narrative I was working with at the time. My idea was to make mannequins to showcase the clothing and the everyday products, the utilitarian objects, that members of this autonomous commune in the desert in New Mexico—a female commune—were making. Everything I was making was connected to this story. The first group of mannequins I made was for a one-person show at Statements at Art Basel in 2004. The display was set up like a market stand where I asked my friend Ligia Dias—who is the same person who made the clothes for the sculptures that are at the Rubell Collection—to collaborate. She made a really amazing fashion collection to dress these women; it's heavily influenced by Russian Constructivism and avant-garde design. The papier-mâché mannequins I made were mostly lying down on the floor in a star formation, and they were meant as display systems for the clothes but also as a representation of the commune members. After this group, I made a single figure holding a neon ring. I came up with the idea after watching a Busby Berkeley film called *The Gang's All Here*, where the dancers in the final sequence are holding neon hoops as props. A little after this I made the figures for Barbara, the "Ballet" ones. Those were a strange mixture of ballet dancers and the lights; I like how almost robotic the neon inserts made them, the contrast between a very handmade, childlike material—papier-mâché—together with the neon, which is so modern and industrial. This group of work was a very big step for me.

The postures of the figures were based on dance moves. Most of them I gleaned from books and magazines—books about avant-garde dance, fashion magazines, things relating to the Bauhaus and Russian Constructivism. The figure with the neon dress, where the neon is really the clothing she is wearing, was very much inspired by Rodchenko.

—Mai-Thu Perret

Clockwise from top left: *Apocalypse Ballet (2 White Rings)*, 2006, papier-mâché, wire mesh, acrylic, gouache, wig, viscose dress by Ligia Dias, leather belt, snow-white neon, and steel, 70 x 63 x 25 1/2 in. (177.8 x 160 x 64.8 cm), acquired in 2006
Apocalypse Ballet (3 White Rings), 2006, papier-mâché, wire mesh, acrylic, gouache, wig, viscose dress by Ligia Dias, leather belt, snow-white neon, and steel, 65 x 46 x 33 in. (165 x 116.8 x 83.8 cm), acquired in 2006
Apocalypse Ballet (Neon Dress), 2006, papier-mâché, wire mesh, acrylic, gouache, wig, white neon, and steel, 67 1/2 x 63 1/2 x 30 in. (166.3 x 161.3 x 76.2 cm), acquired in 2006
Apocalypse Ballet (Pink Ring), 2006, papier-mâché, wire mesh, acrylic, gouache, wig, viscose dress by Ligia Dias, leather belt, pink neon, and steel, 82 x 53 x 39 3/8 in. (208.3 x 134.6 x 100 cm), acquired in 2006

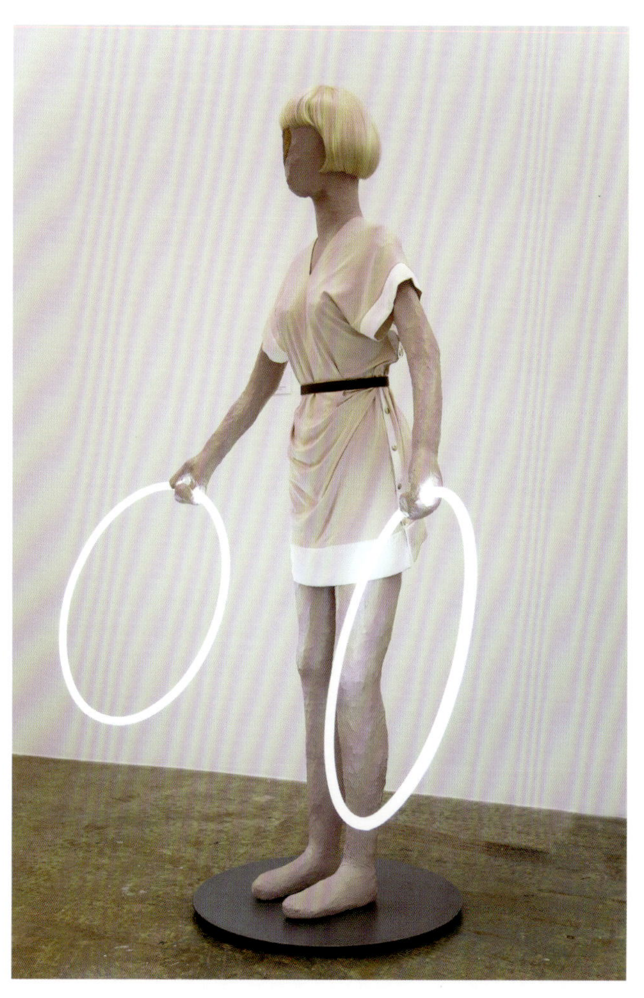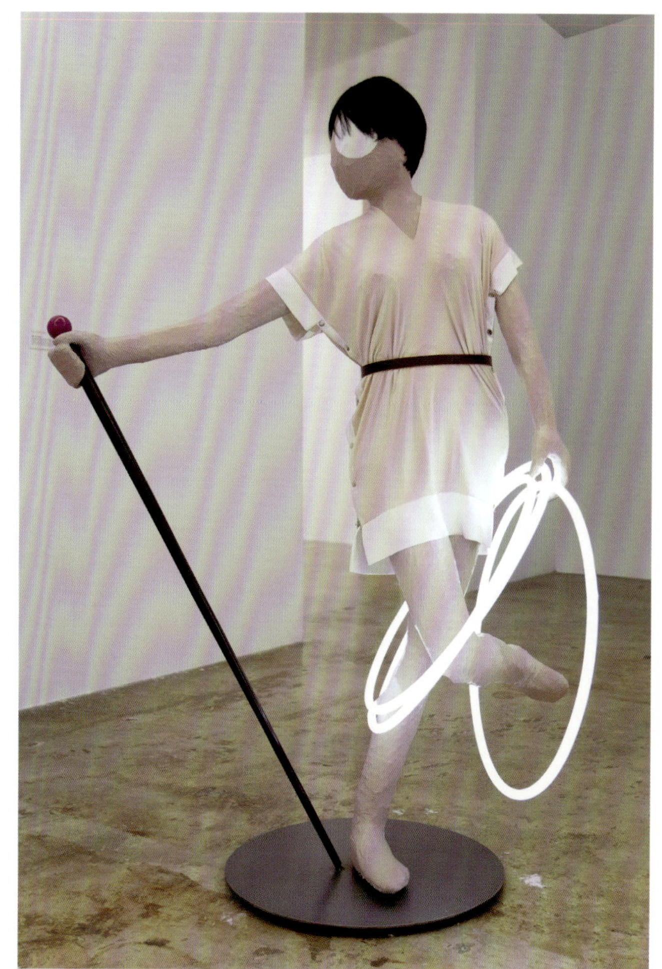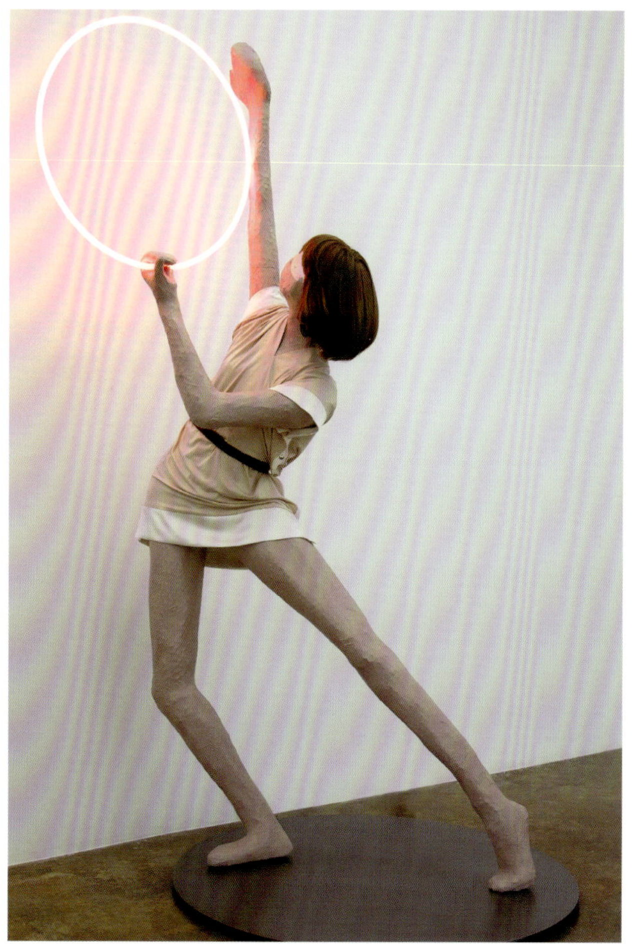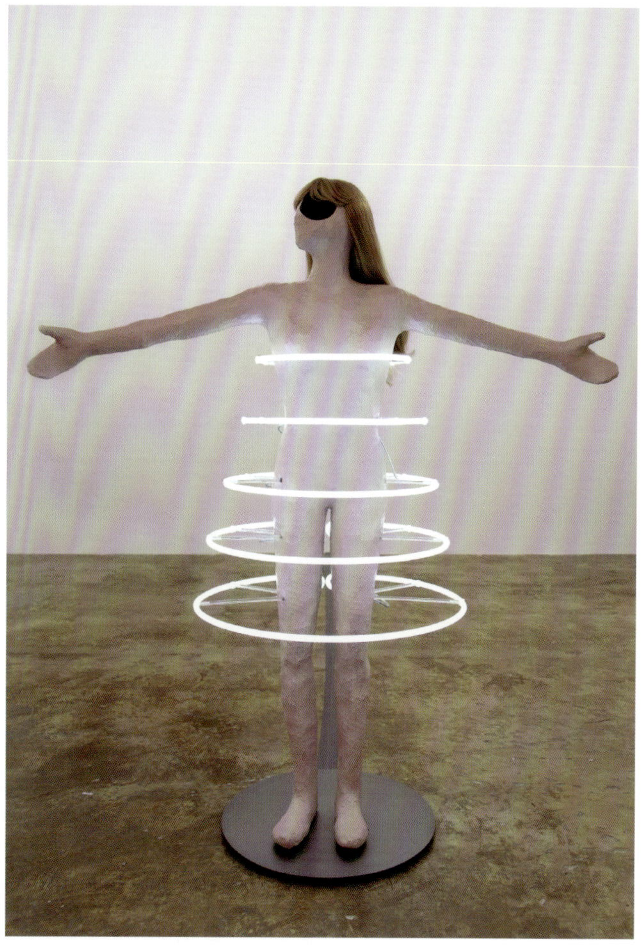

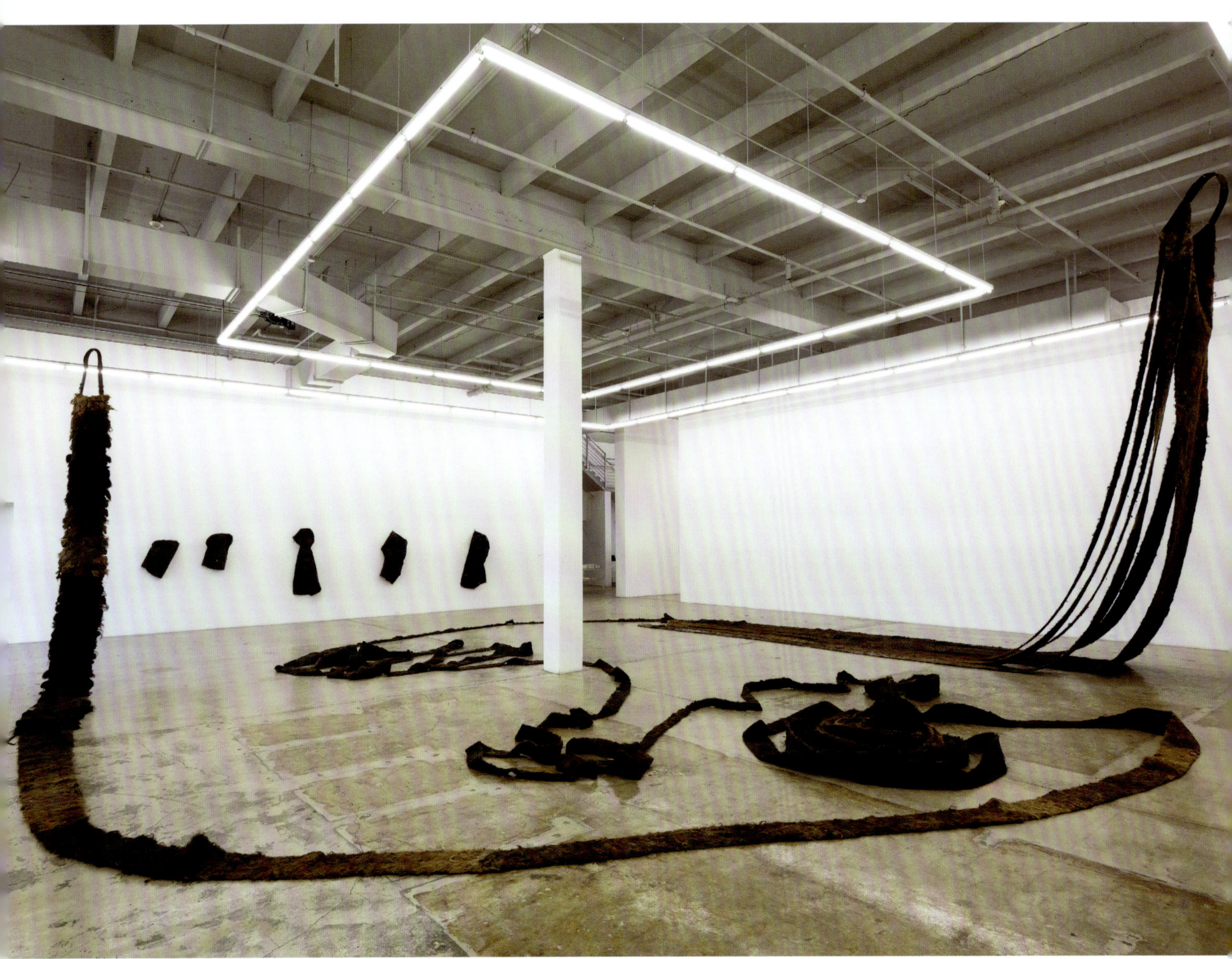

Liz Munsell: Can you walk us through your process of creating *Catedral* (1990-2003), which took over a decade to complete, and was originally displayed in the Bienal do Mercosul in 2003? To make it, you wove together hundreds of miles of individual hair strands. How are the physically laborious, durational aspects of such a process felt in the work? Is this durational experience related at all to your past work in performance?

Solange Pessoa: *Catedral* was one of these works that started in a simple way and then became gradually more complex. I had no idea what it was going to become. Originally it was a piece that was nicknamed *trança* ("braid"), as a reference to Tunga, in which I integrated hair taken from myself, my siblings, and close friends. Simultaneously, I was working on another piece that somehow recalled the structure of the Brasília Cathedral, designed by Oscar Niemeyer, and its

verticality that curved in contact with the floor, hence the name *Catedral*. The structure was penetrable; it was one in which bodies could enter. In both pieces, the verticality was already very accentuated. The material, albeit unusual, was natural. I never thought it was going to be something too absurd or transgressive. Here in Minas Gerais, human hair was often used in representations of saints and for ex-votos (religious offerings). Building these structures was a natural process, even though the context was conservative and resistant to these experiences. When they were exhibited publicly, people told me they had dreamt about the works, and things like that.

Experience with psychoanalysis in the 1990s helped me understand pulsations and processes. The most difficult element for me was not the hair but the horses. They were pulling everything into perpetual movement. These animals

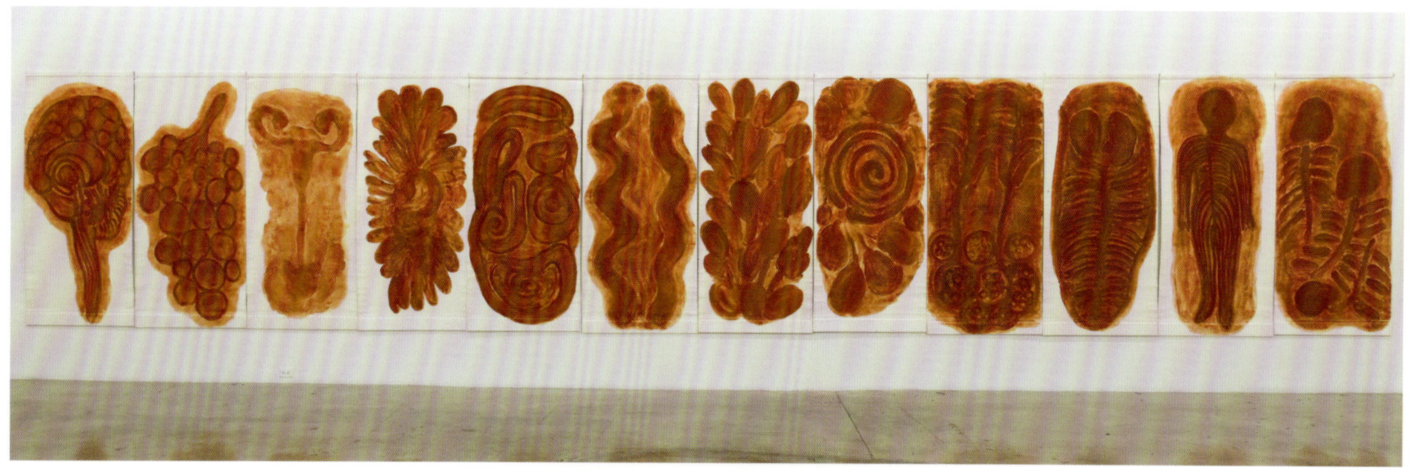

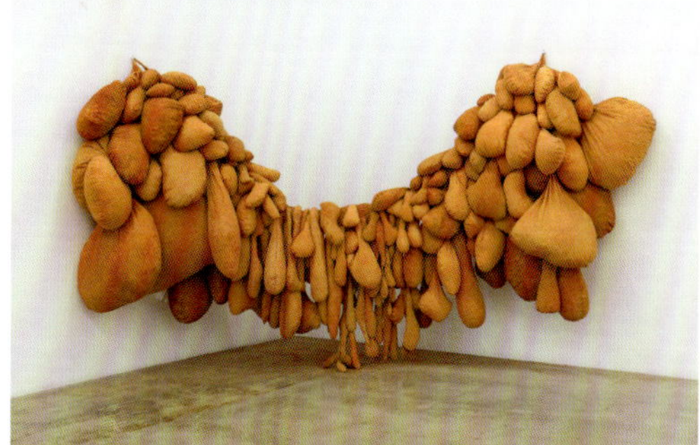

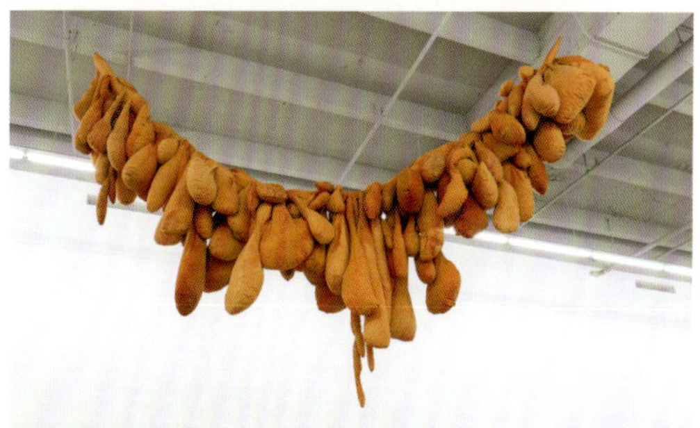

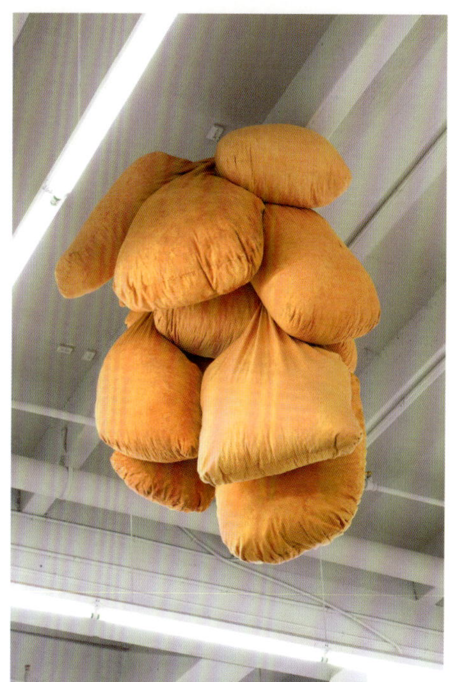

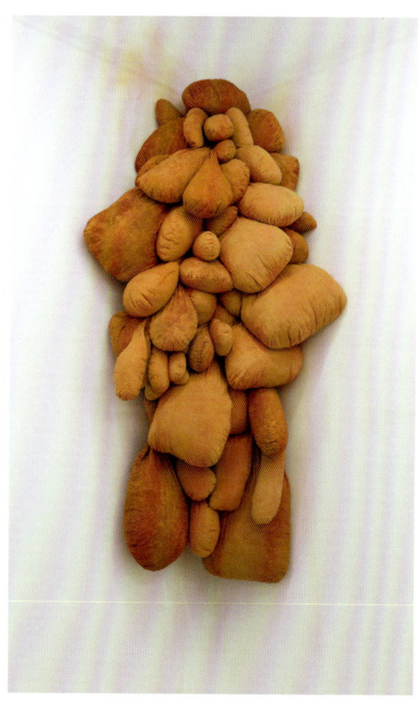

were hidden in the sculptures. The leather pieces, the framework, were all derived from harnesses used for riding. I introduced other materials related to hair, such as skin and blood. But even before working with hair, I had worked with chicken and bird feathers—another epidermal material —in my first sculptures from 1990. Some of these materials reappeared many years after that.

At the end of the 1990s, there was an accident in the collective studio where I worked and stored my artworks. All my production from the 1990s was lost in a fire. They were already ephemeral. From then on, I started to think again and again about those sculptures and had the urge to rebuild them. Everything became maximized: verticality, matter, transcendence, scale. There was a large degree of uneasiness and a rush of facts and images that just flowed. The materialization of these flows was not easy at all. It took me many years to be able to materialize these movements into drawings, videos, and installations. There are many things around *Catedral*: animals, magical apparitions, buried memories, temporalities. The "live sculptures" recorded in video and attached to the installation (I like to call them that rather than "performances") activate the imagination by expanding it.

Opposite page: *Catedral*, 1990-2015, hair, leather, fabric, and digital video, dimensions variable, acquired in 2015
Above, top to bottom: *Untitled*, 2011-2012, clay on vinyl, twelve panels, each 78 3/4 x 35 1/2 in. (200 x 90 cm), acquired in 2015
4 Hammocks, 1999-2003, thread, fabric, clay, and cotton, dimensions variable, acquired in 2015

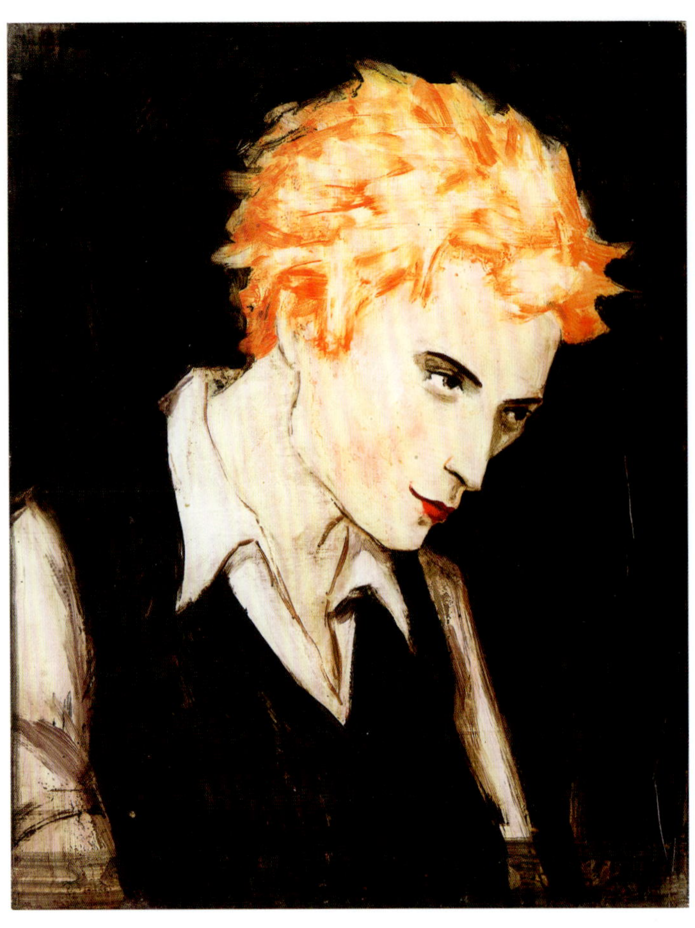

I suppose these painting were made around the same time and had some similar reasons that led me to do them.

The *Sex Pistols* paintings began after an afternoon I spent at Gavin's gallery. I wasn't feeling well and was looking through Gavin's books and found one on the Sex Pistols…and then I started listening to their music. I was moved by the intensity of the belief in what they were doing…that it was a very personal feeling of alienation they were expressing that simultaneously reflected and merged with the general feeling around them—that's powerful. I was also very interested in the personal relationship between John Lydon and Sid Vicious. both the paintings are of them in America…two friends hurled out to touring the middle of America…so, so young…their relationship seemed like it had an unironic love that I was very interested in. And I guess I was feeling like if I worked with people in my professional life showing art that I really believed in and connected to, it would just add to the integrity and atmosphere of the work, hence the painting of Burkhard, who was one of my first art dealers.

When I was first showing, I was conscious that my work could be misperceived as "light," and I wanted to have some dealers with a lot of attitude…and so Burkhard and Gavin… The way I was painting these at this time was pretty spare (sepia underpainting with some thicker color over it), and in general this was the time when I was finding subjects in my own time or close to as inspirational and heroic as the ones I had been painting before, like Napoleon, characters from Proust, King Ludwig. I was beginning to have an eye for my time.

—Elizabeth Peyton

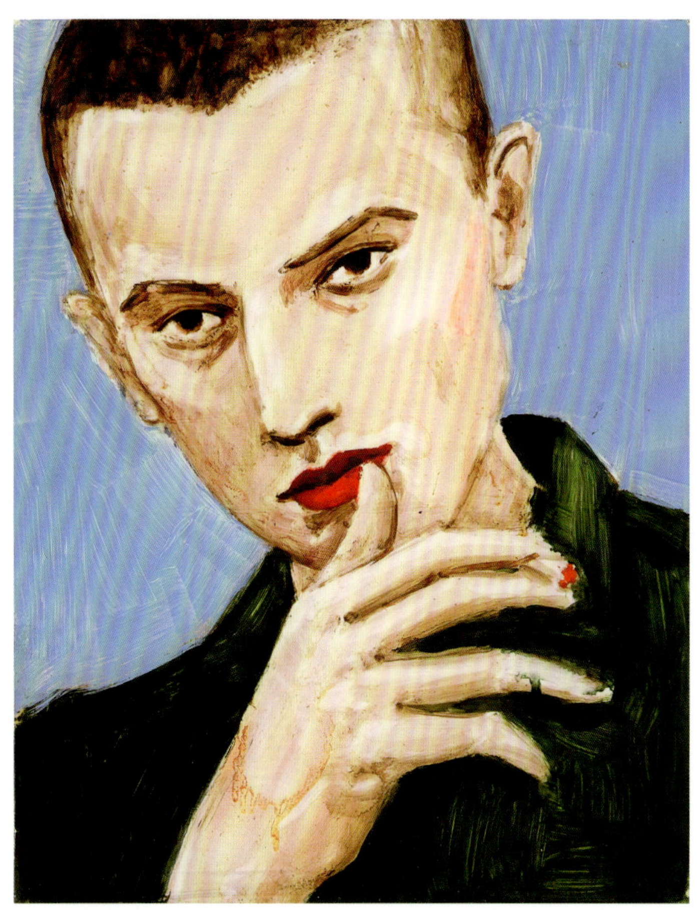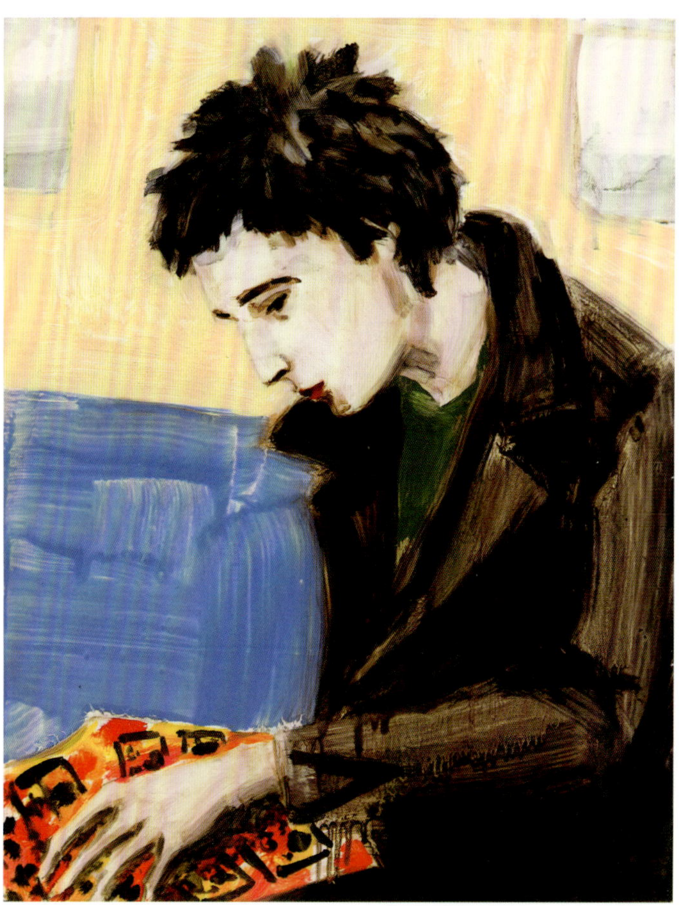

Left to right: *John Lydon*, 1995, oil on board, 14 x 11 in. (35.6 x 27.9 cm), acquired in 1997
Burkhard Riemschneider, 1995, oil on board, 14 x 11 in. (35.6 x 27.9 cm), acquired in 1997
John Beverly Ritchie (Sid), 1995, oil on board, 14 x 11 in. (35.6 x 27.9 cm), acquired in 1997

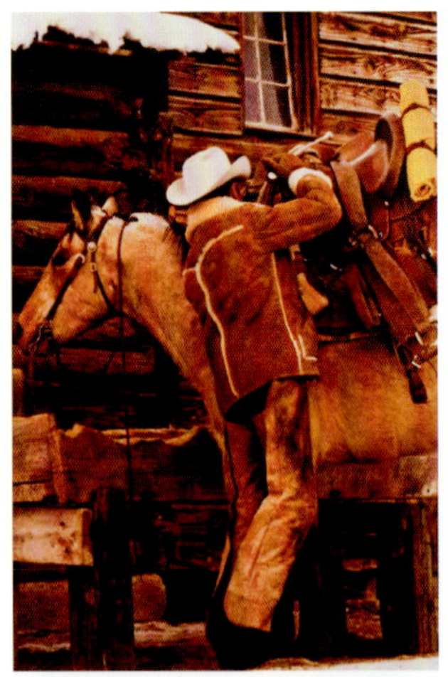
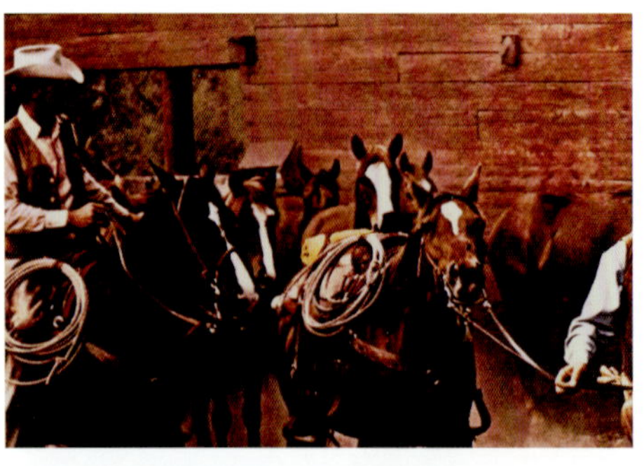
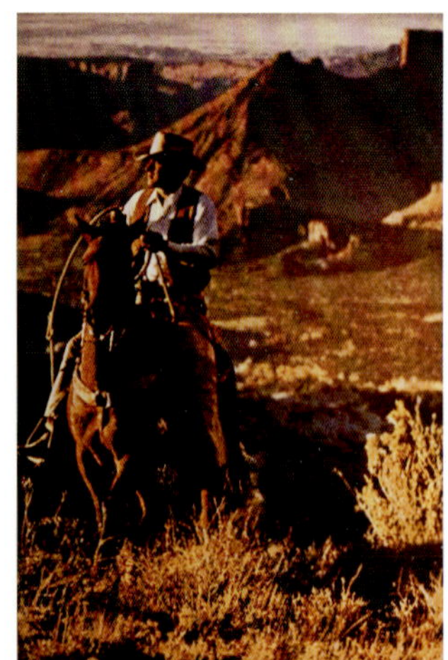
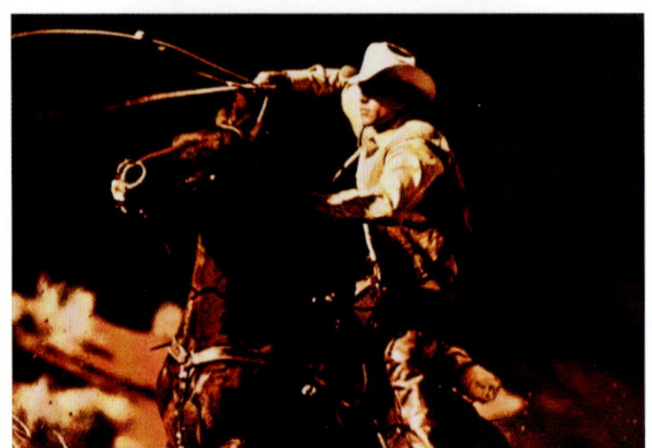
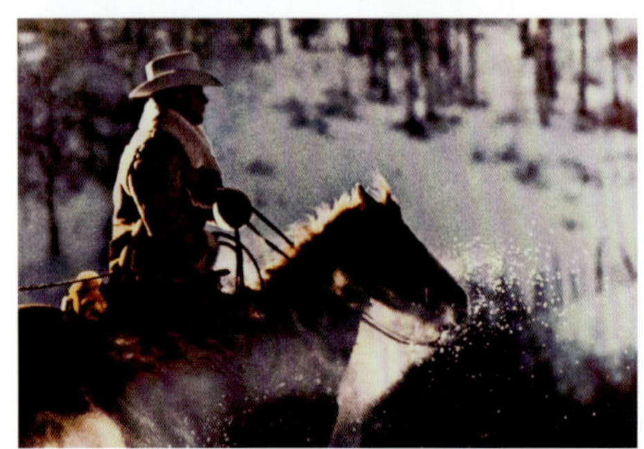
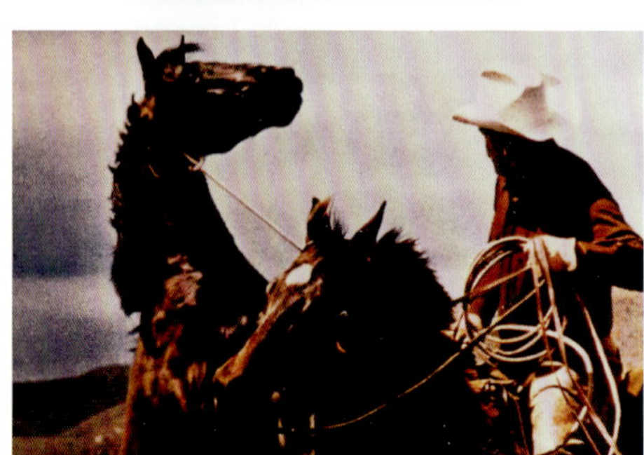

Most of all I remember the Rubells' parties after the Whitney biennials.

And seeing all the art from my generation on their walls. They were the first to do anything like that. Early '80s. Stuff that had been made only a couple of years before. Up-to-date doesn't begin to describe it. I don't know how they got there. But they did. And they did it together. That was another thing that stood out—they were forward and fierce in their choices, but their decisions were tempered by four romantic eyes.

Anyway, it was the first time I'd ever seen anything of mine hung on someone else's wall. *Untitled, (man's hand with cigarette)*. They got it. And in more ways than one. It was in their living room and there were tons of people shouting at each other. It was loud. The place was packed. You could hardly move. Good times. Drinking and smoking. (There were plenty of hands with cigarettes.)

I was still an outsider but that evening I felt, if only for a moment, part of another family.

One other thing...
It was the first time I'd seen or met Robert Mapplethorpe.
He was decked out.
Motorcycle gear.
Leather jacket and fucking chaps!
He didn't say a word. He just looked and looked and he looked.
I looked too.
I couldn't help it.
This was like the second biennial party. Around 1985? '86?
I'd just done my first *Untitled (Girlfriend)*.

Seeing Robert that night made think... maybe I should go back to the drawing board...
I did.
I started drawing cartoons and jokes.
Don and Mera bought those too.

—Richard Prince

Untitled (cowboy), 1987, Ektacolor photographs, ed. 2/2, six individual artworks, each 20 x 24 in. (50.8 x 61 cm), acquired in 1987
Opposite page: *New England Nurse*, 2002, inkjet and acrylic on canvas, 79 3/8 x 52 1/4 in. (201.9 x 132.7 cm), acquired in 2004

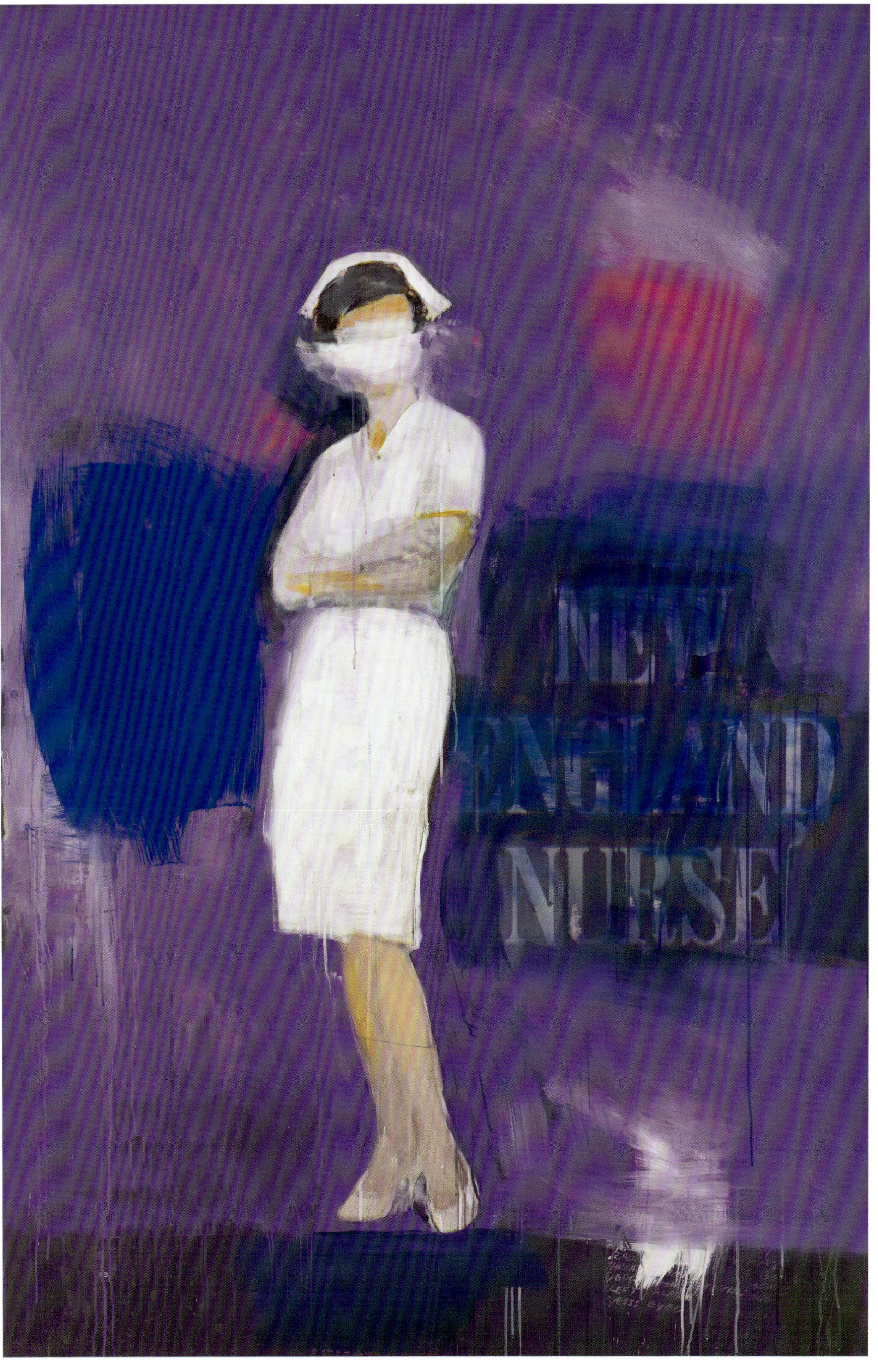

NEW
ENGLAND
NURSE

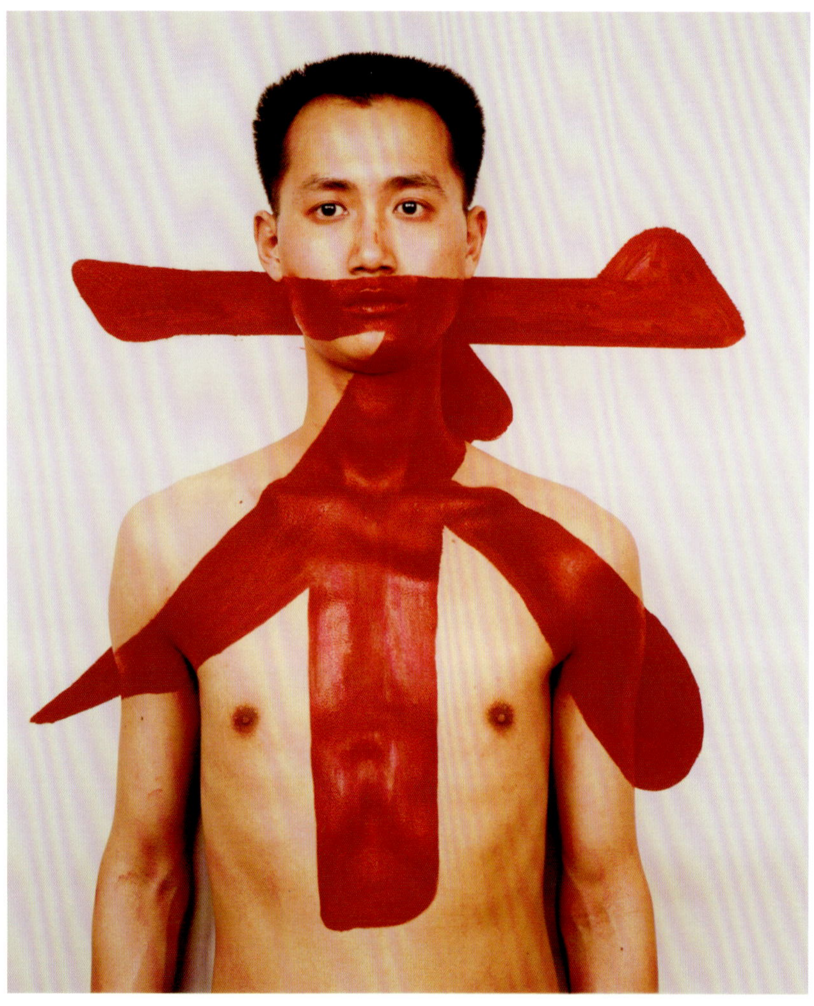

The *Tattoo* series discusses the questionable relationship between a figure and its background. Keeping an appropriate relationship between the two is one of the preconditions of the traditional portrait game. Now, because of some shared characteristics of the two—being pierced through by the same object, or attempting to become the same Chinese character—the supposed distance between them disappears; the volume of the main body disappears, the weight of the person disappears, the smell of flesh disappears, all that is left is a two-dimensional plane that anybody can write or draw on endlessly. This person does not have the power to resist, because he has become an image only.

In *Tattoo-2*, a red Chinese character was painted on the body and the wall; the meaning of the character is "No!" It covers and erases the boundary between body and wall.

In *Memorial for Revolutionary Speech,* I picked all sorts of revolutionary speeches and slogans from China's long history, from the Daze Village Uprising in the third century BCE until recently. Revolutions and uprisings have always happened periodically in China's history, and this periodic shock became part of China's history. Every time

a revolution happened new aphorisms came up, and these monumentalized the ideals and desires of that age.

I carved these characters onto the surface of a cement board and made an ink rubbing of the characters on the surface of this layer. Then I again put cement on top and waited until it was thoroughly dry before carving out a second layer of characters, which was a slogan of the next revolution, and again made a rubbing. This process was repeated until the "memorial stone" became a cement cube. On the surface it looks very much like a modern minimalistic sculpture, but it has 20 layers. On the surface you cannot see the characters, but on the side you can horizontally observe the traces of repeated pouring of cement and ink rubbings, as if it were the layers in an archeological pit.

Since with every carving I applied the style of calligraphy used at the time of the corresponding revolution, the entire set of rubbings produced through the whole process also forms a history of calligraphy. Together with the history of revolutionary concepts they constitute a double history.

—Qiu Zhijie

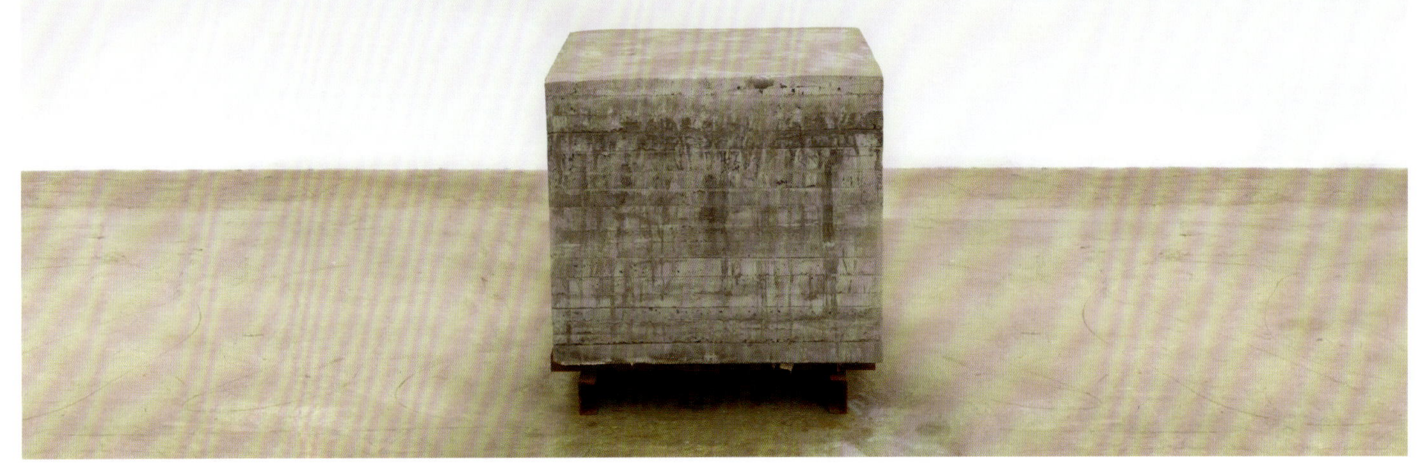

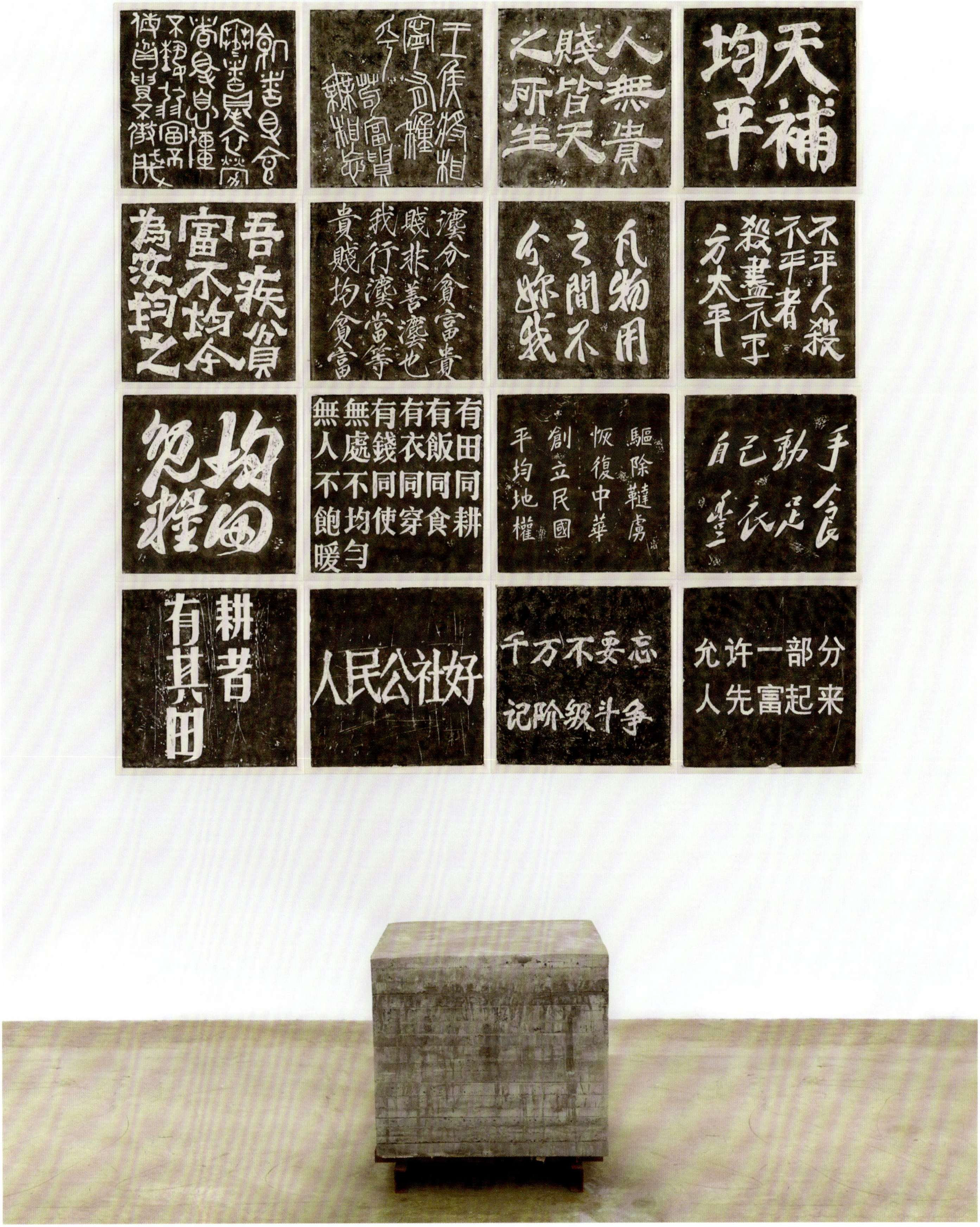

Opposite page: *Tattoo-2*, 1994, chromogenic print mounted on aluminium board, 73 1/4 x 62 3/4 in. (186 x 159.5 cm), acquired in 2011
Memorial for Revolutionary Speech, 2007, sixteen ink rubbings and cement cube, ed. AP, ink rubbing: 31 1/2 x 31 1/2 in. (80 x 80 cm), cement cube: 31 1/2 x 31 1/2 x 31 1/2 in. (80 x 80 x 80 cm), acquired in 2011

2021 Artist in Residence

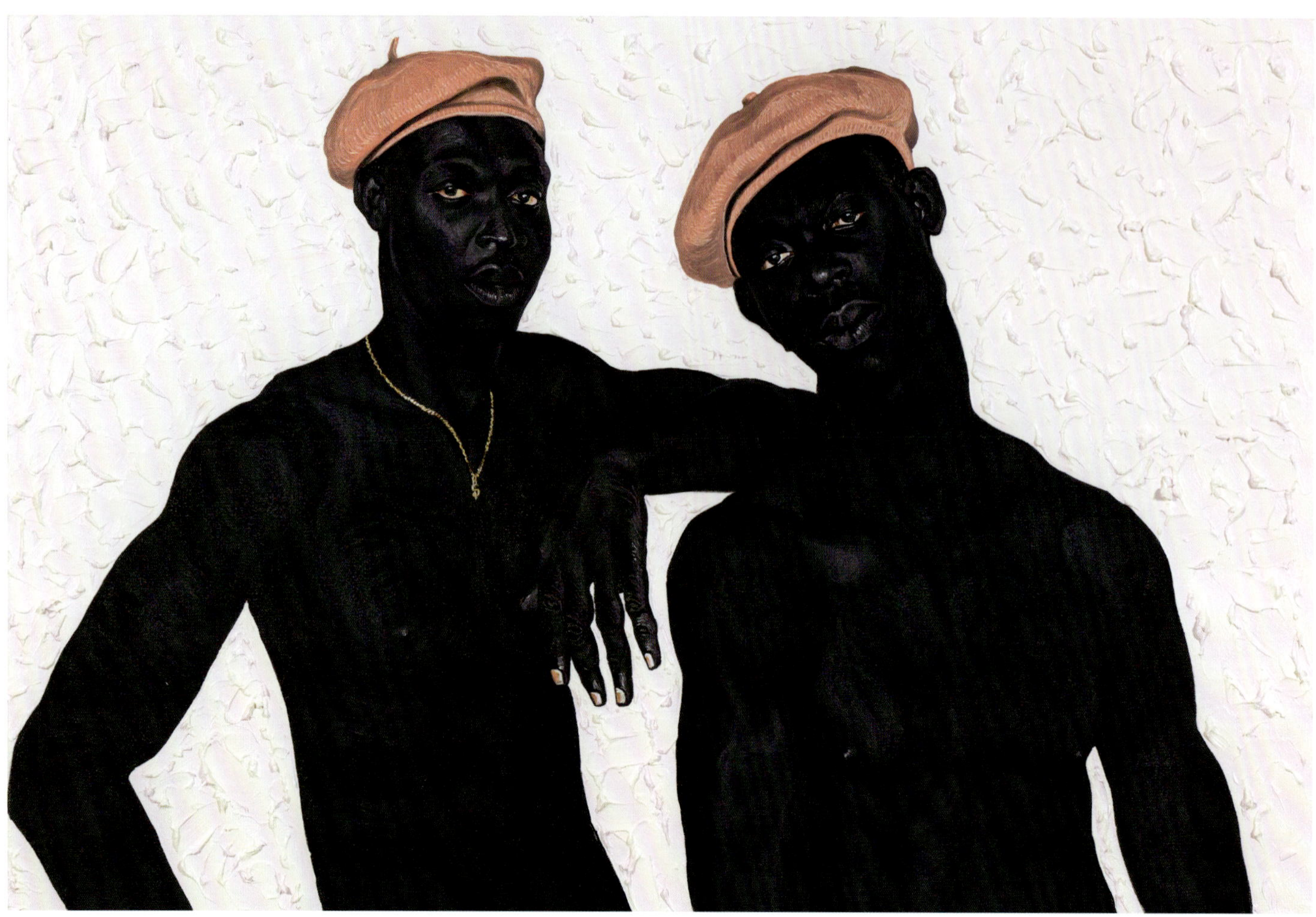

The idea to paint twins came about when I was in my home country of Ghana. In Ghana, we have a yearly festival for twins because we believe they are sent by the gods, who are our ancestors, to bless us or to benefit the family that gave birth to the twins. It's mostly a cultural thing for us—the belief that we have in twins and the mystery surrounding them. I thought it would be a great idea to talk about it here in the States so that people have an idea of how we think about twins in Ghana and how important it is for us to have a set of twins in a community or in a family. Twins exist in the States of course, but they aren't celebrated as we do in my country.

The paintings of the twins and the cowboys are always about identity—that is the most important thing for me. Identity and

the essence of the subject. Identity is important because I find myself in different places, and I'm aware of how I'm treated by different people. First and foremost, this is my experience in the U.S. as a Black person: how people stare at me wherever I go and then the gaze they give me.

In most of my paintings the eye is my focal point to draw the viewer in. I like the figures or the subject to stare back at you, so you have the experience of being looked at too. This is a way to talk about the gaze and the attention we get as Black people when we walk around.

—Otis Kwame Kye Quaicoe

Oko and Akwete in Beret, 2021, oil on canvas, 40 x 60 in. (101.6 x 152.4 cm), acquired in 2021
Opposite page, clockwise from top left: *Moses Adomah*, 2021, oil on canvas, 144 x 108 in. (365.8 x 274.3 cm), acquired in 2021
David Theodore, 2021, oil on canvas, 144 x 108 in. (365.8 x 274.3 cm), acquired in 2021
Rainyanni (Cowgirl), 2021, oil on canvas, 144 x 108 in. (365.8 x 274.3 cm), acquired in 2021

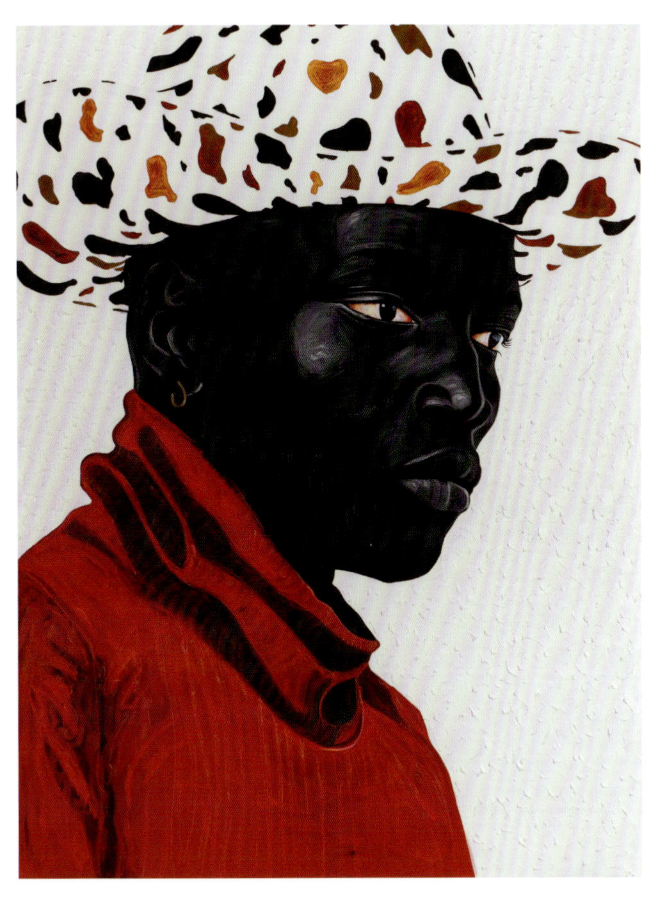
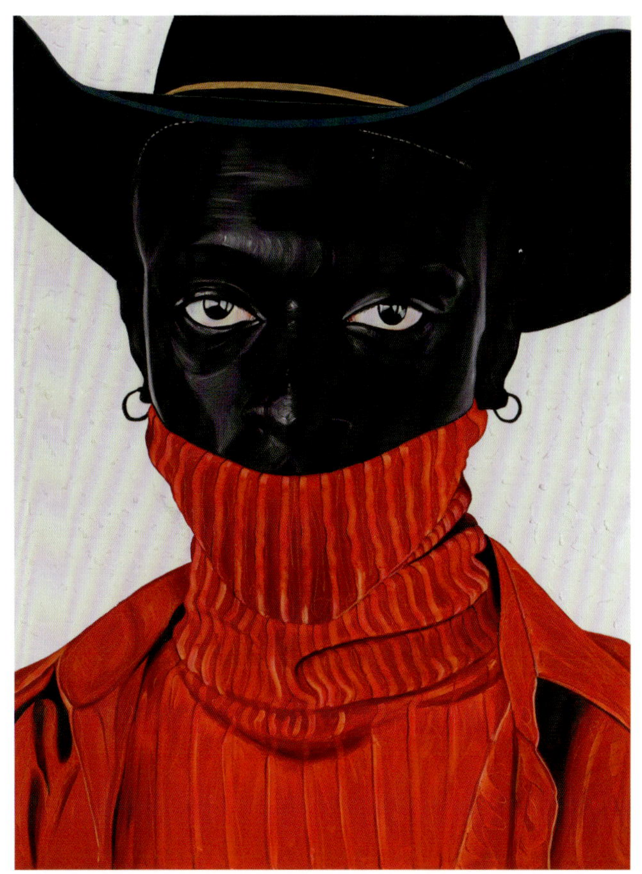
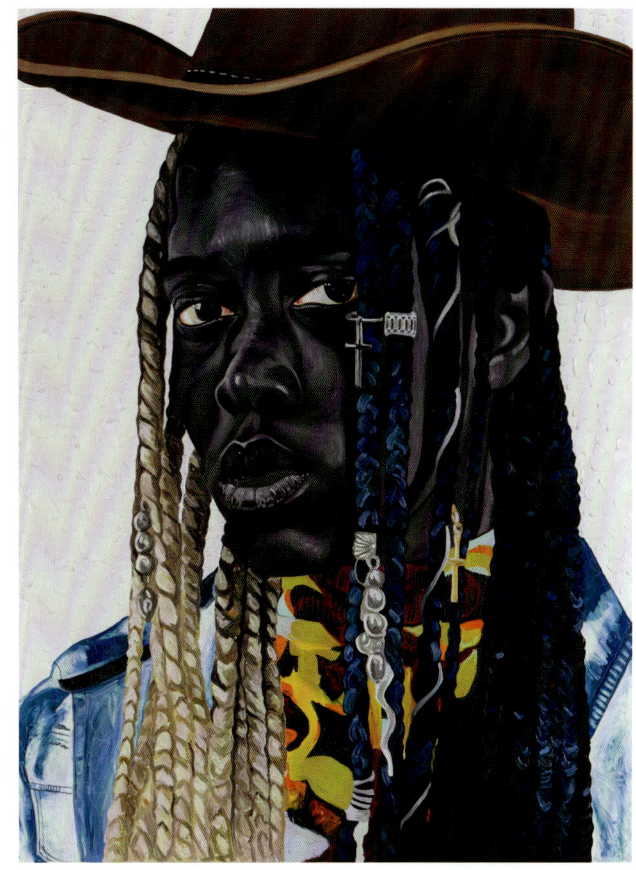

My aim is to paint portraits depicting the experience of living within a body, rather than the experience looking at one. Bodies are occupied by space in my work, collapsing and expanding as they run into shifting contexts. Because we are regularly defined by context, perception remains central to the language of my art. So often, we project a sense of solidity onto other people, while experiencing a multitude within ourselves. I try to articulate this feeling—of possessing alternate selves—within my work, shifting between fragmentation and cohesion.

...Tha Color of Tha Sky (Magic Hour) was a painting that I made shortly after I finished my MFA at Yale and a residency, that following summer, at Skowhegan. I made this piece in a small garage behind my house—my first studio following grad school. In this piece, I was newly exploring certain compositional, physical, and digital techniques—particularly, the use of Adobe Illustrator. So, this piece really represents the intersection of beta-testing the vocabulary of my work in graduate school, and figuring out the language of my painting on the other side of that. This is why there's so much in this piece that references earlier works, and other elements are referenced and refined in some of my later works.

There's this splitting composition, which is mimicked in other paintings like *Yew've Got Yer Gud Things, n' I've Got Mine (Split)* (2018). This work also replicated the grass technique and sky pattern, which I replicated for a third time, in a painting called *For Whom Tha Sunsets Free* (2019). It's an iterative process of making, and although I don't use sketches, each of my paintings includes a mental "sketching process," which I'll re-deploy later on. *...Tha Color of Tha Sky (Magic Hour)* was one of those paintings for me, and it became a very important reference point throughout my practice.

You can see in the clouds that I've rendered a digital perspectival plane, and this was one of the first times that I moved from freehand to creating that effect in Illustrator. At that time, I would project these digital stencils onto the canvas and physically trace what I had created on the computer. Today, I print my stencils on a vinyl plotter, but in 2017 I was still using the projector, tape, and an X-Acto knife.

I was also beginning to experiment more with various physical tools, to play with texture. You can see that I used a comb to render the hair on the figure on the right, and the checkered pattern on the body was also done with painter's tape.

Another concept that remains central to my practice is the idea of building an image on top of previous decisions. I call this a "zig-zagging" process, where I constantly observe what I've done, and re-think those gestures or marks. It's a negotiation between intention and chance.

For example, in the lower right quadrant, you can see that I built a form from a "messier" brushstroke. I utilized the plane on top of it to add definition back into that abstracted form. In the central face, you can also see that I built texture on top of that checkered pattern, which I rendered more loosely. There's a conversation going on here between the decisions that I made at different points in my process. I like for this dialogue to remain evident. It's a way of showing my work or demonstrating the history of my thinking over the course of completing a particular piece.

Although the complexity of pattern making has been refined in my work, many elements remain more freehand, and that's evident in this work, which exemplifies a more experimental period of my practice. There are only a few visual elements that I'll repeat in my work, and all of them are depicted in *...Tha Color of Tha Sky (Magic Hour)*. Again, this has to do with my interest in the idea of building an image, or a visual plane, but this also has to do with my practice of creating a visual glossary containing personal points of reference.

As far as the composition, I was exploring what I refer to as a bound, inner landscape. There's physical tension and clustering in the central right, but there's also this breaking out or expansion into the space of the canvas on the left where I've rendered the "washier" figures. I'm toggling between opacity, and more of a stained, water color effect, in terms of my paint application, while also exploring themes of limitation and fragmentation as well as expansiveness and wholeness.

This painting actually takes its title from an even earlier unstretched work, which is unusual because I almost never repeat titles. The composition similarly reached across a horizontal plane and laid the groundwork for what I was able to explore and achieve in this piece. The title, "Tha Color of Tha Sky," is taken from a poem by the South African writer Keorapetse Kgositsile. It's a mis-remembered quote, spelled out phonetically, as is the case with many of my titles, because the translation of language relates to the theme of uncovering meaning in my work, as well as the experience of hearing and reinterpreting language as something embodied.

The title reflects the literal landscape, but also that process of making. In this case, the reference has to do with a sort of revelatory experience, or at least a moment of clarity, where the image shines through. Sometimes clarity of image happens immediately and sometimes it's a building process that begins with more chaotic or gestural brush strokes, as is the case here.

—Christina Quarles

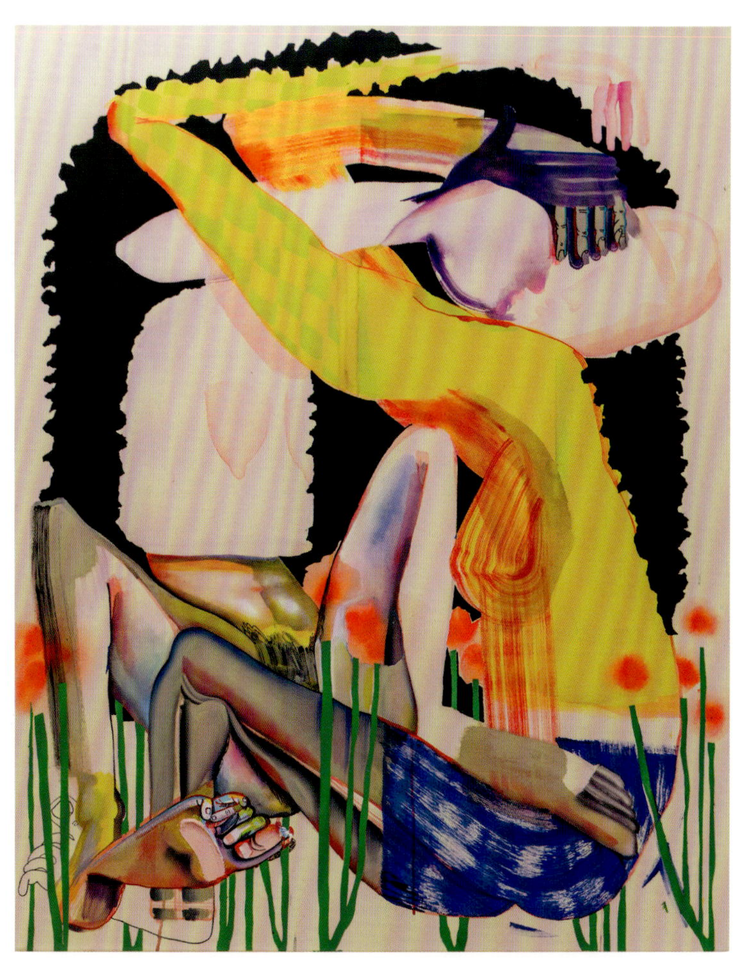

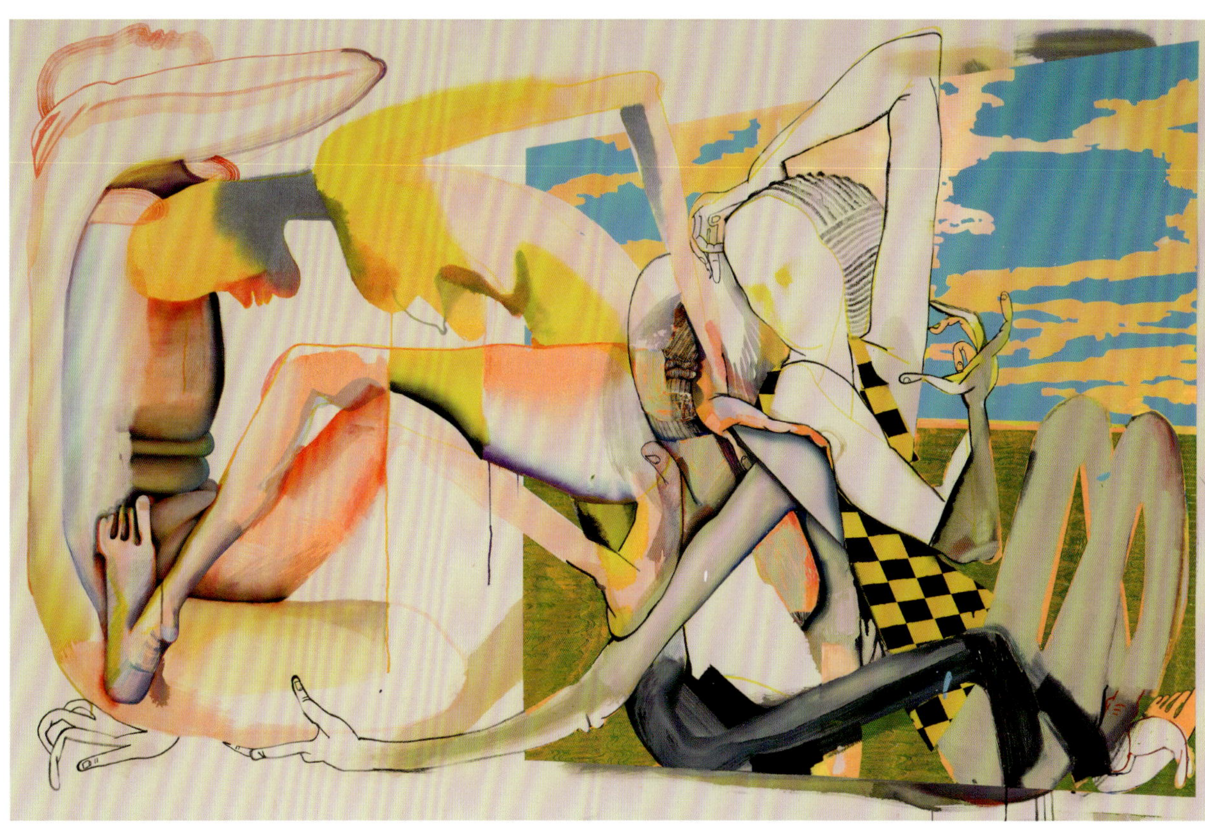

Hedge Yer Bets (Baby, I'm a Maze), 2017, acrylic on canvas, 60 x 48 in. (152.4 x 121.9 cm), acquired in 2017
...Tha Color of Tha Sky (Magic Hour), 2017, acrylic on canvas, 55 x 80 in. (139.7 x 203.2 cm), acquired in 2017

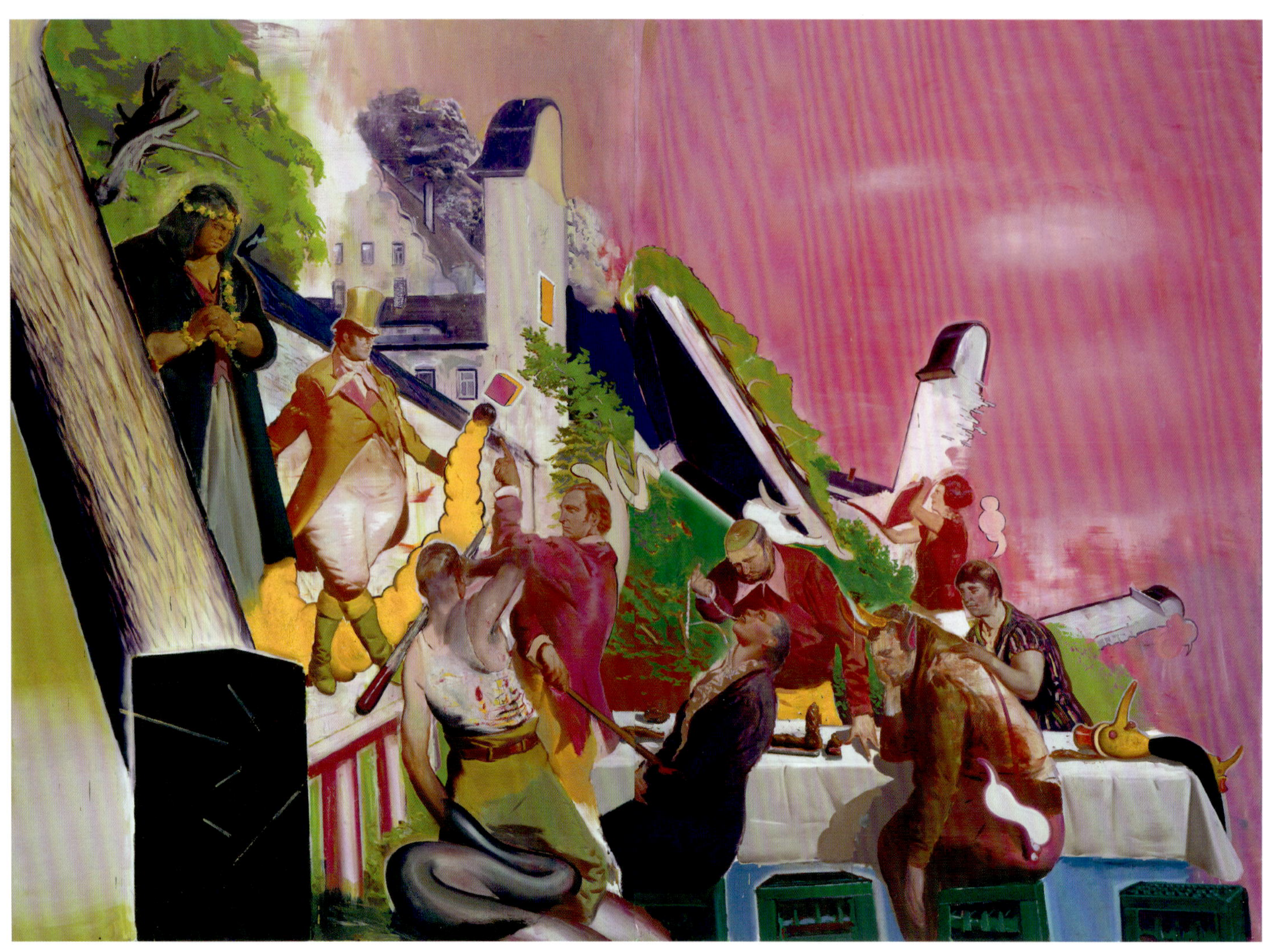

Vorführung- I remember as if it were yesterday, in my studio. Today I see the tower as a subtle reference to my hometown, Aschersleben. In the work you recognize individuals, always in pairs, intertwined in questionable exchanges. In the middle, the old question arises: is he pulling the rope of pearls out of her throat or threading it in? The two figures to the left are painters engaged in a collegial duel. To the right the devil is being consoled, his performance canceled.

All four of the paintings are still dear to me and, I have to say, well chosen.

—Neo Rauch

Vorführung, 2006, oil on canvas, diptych, overall 118 1/2 x 165 3/8 in. (300 x 420 cm), acquired in 2006
Opposite page, clockwise from top left: *Das Neue*, 2003, oil on canvas, 90 x 117 in. (210 x 300 cm), acquired in 2003
Demos, 2004, oil on canvas, 118 1/2 x 82 3/4 in. (300 x 210 cm), acquired in 2004
Diktat, 2004, oil on canvas, 106 3/4 x 82 3/4 in. (270 x 210 cm), acquired in 2004

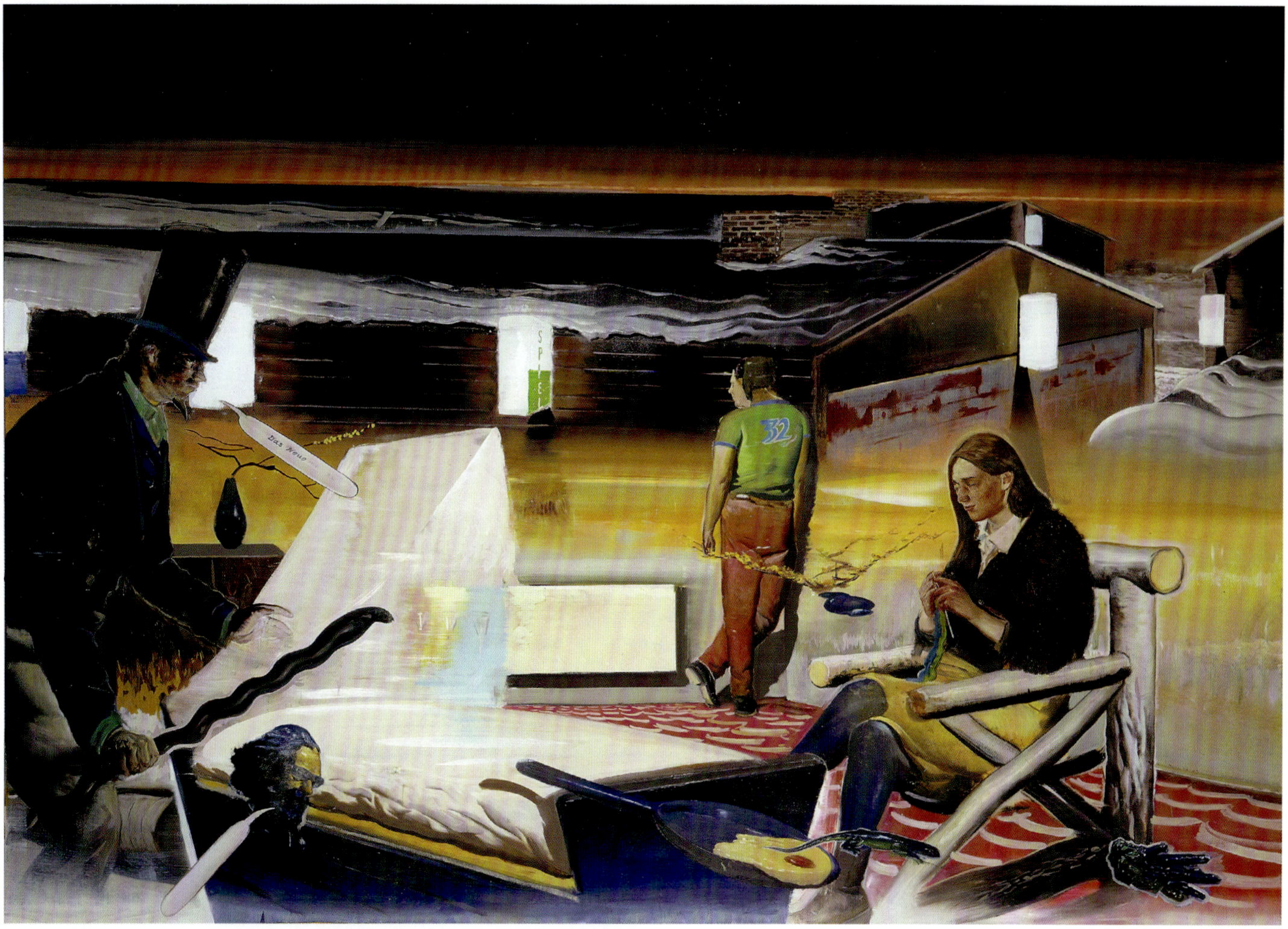

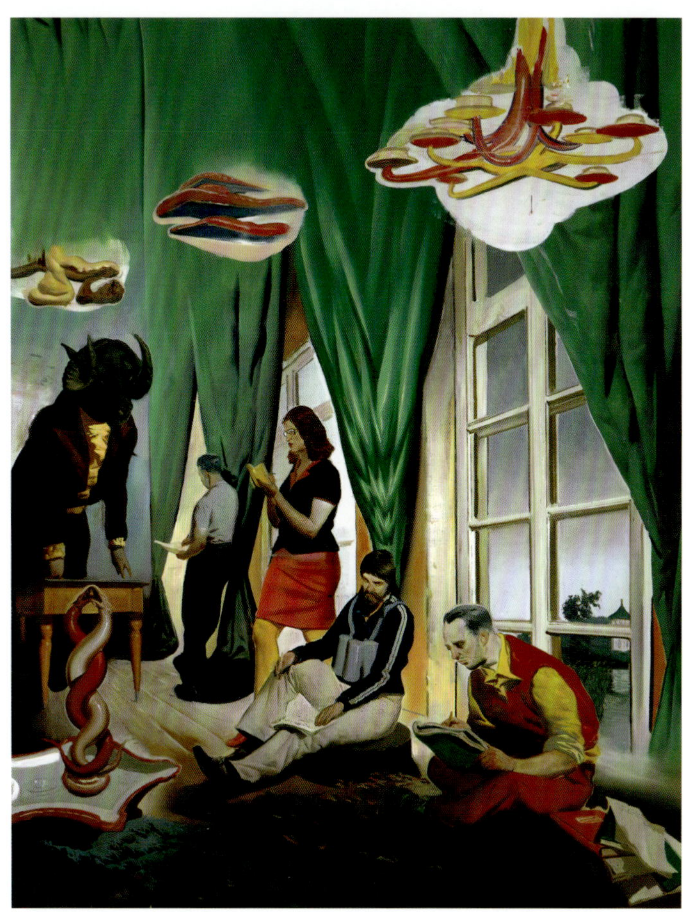

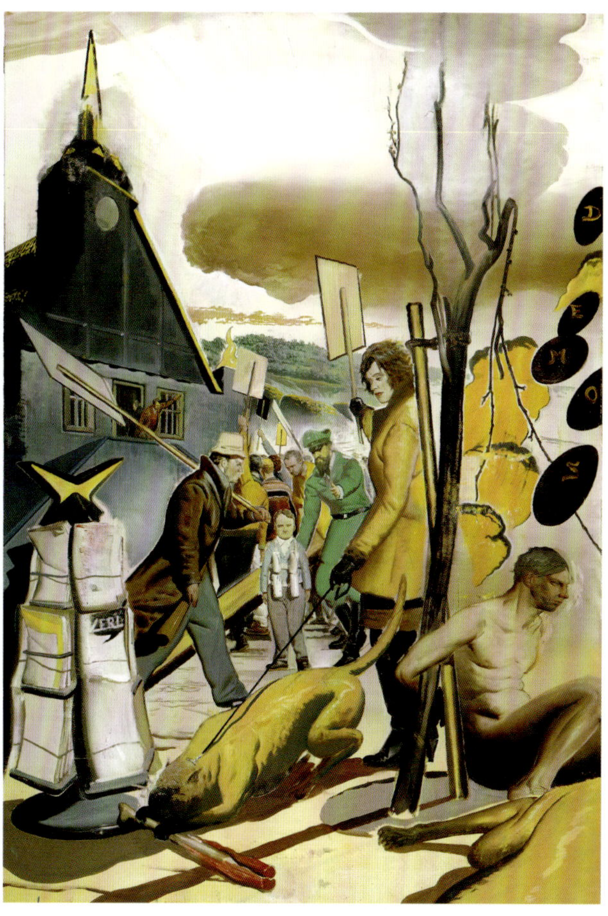

Oh! Charley, Charley, Charley… is a group figurative sculpture I made in 1992. It was inspired by Brancusi's sculpture *The Kiss*.

The Kiss beautifully demonstrates how two become one in physical love. Its two separate figurative forms are joined in embrace by arms that cross the sculpture, creating a temporal visualization of past and future unity. The two lovers are carved from one block, and I think they will return into this single object, their mutual attraction generating a profound primitive or cosmic unity.

Oh! Charley, Charley, Charley… also found its inspiration in sexual attraction, but from a different trajectory. When looked at from the other side of the coin, Brancusi's cosmic sexuality flips to reveal that your lover is simply a projection of your self! Is there no "other" out there?

The physicist John Wheeler pondered the question of why all electrons have the same mass or weight. It's a ridiculously specific number, and every electron in the universe shares this specificity in a manner both improbable and imponderable. Wheeler once called up the brilliant Richard Feynman, who at the time was his graduate student at Princeton, in the middle of the night: "Feynman, I know why all electrons have the same weight!" "Why?" Feynman asked. "Because there is only one electron in the universe, and it's flying through space and time, creating a knot in its world line that appears in cross section as an electron when moving forward in time and as a positron when moving backward in time!" "But professor," Feynman answered, "there are more electrons than positrons." "Oh well, they must be hidden in protons or something," said Wheeler.

The one-electron universe is as beautiful in its simplicity as the one-person world is frighteningly lonely in its implication. Or is it?

—Charles Ray

Oh! Charley, Charley, Charley…, 1992, painted fiberglass and synthetic hair, 72 x 180 x 180 in. (182.9 x 457.2 x 457.2 cm), acquired in 1992

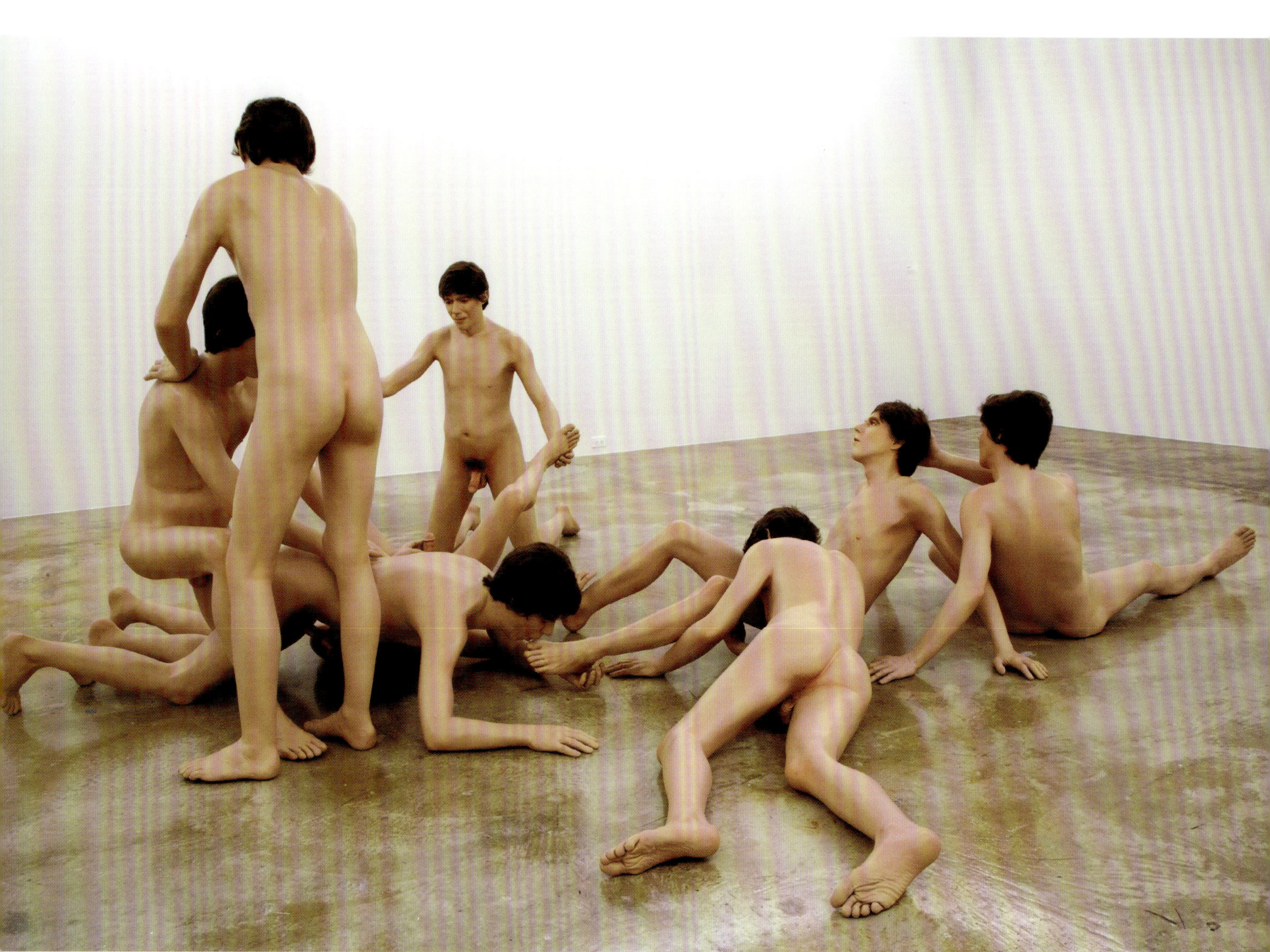

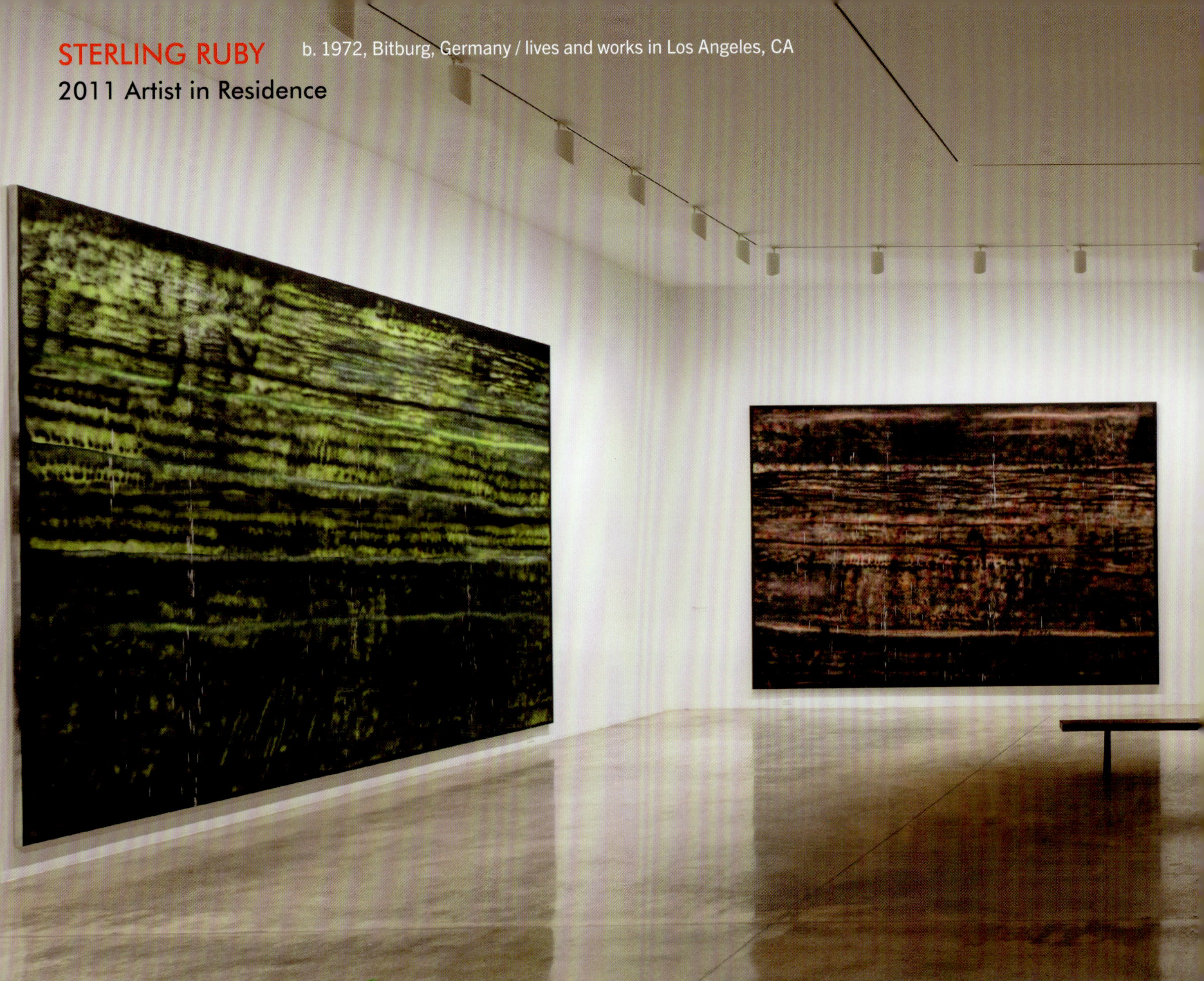

I always imagined the *SP*s (Spray Paintings) filling a room, creating a continuous horizon line that traveled between walls. I started making these works back in 2011 using just spray paint. I live in Los Angeles, where there are incredible sunrises and sunsets that completely transform the urban landscape into a meditative plane. While driving to and from my studio each day I would often witness these fleeting, almost electric scenes. This time in my car was contemplative, and I wanted to conjure these transient, vivid moments in a way that prolonged the experience of their witnessing.

Around this time, Don and Mera were visiting my studio frequently during their trips to Los Angeles. They saw works in progress and watched the different stages of formation; we established a dialogue as different pieces developed and bodies of work grew. Our conversations were (and continue to be) generative and meaningful, and we formed a genuine friendship that has endured for more than 10 years now. This continued while I was putting together a show in Beijing, during which time Don and Mera visited and came to the local foundry I was working with. Over the years, we've met each other's families and spent time together in many different

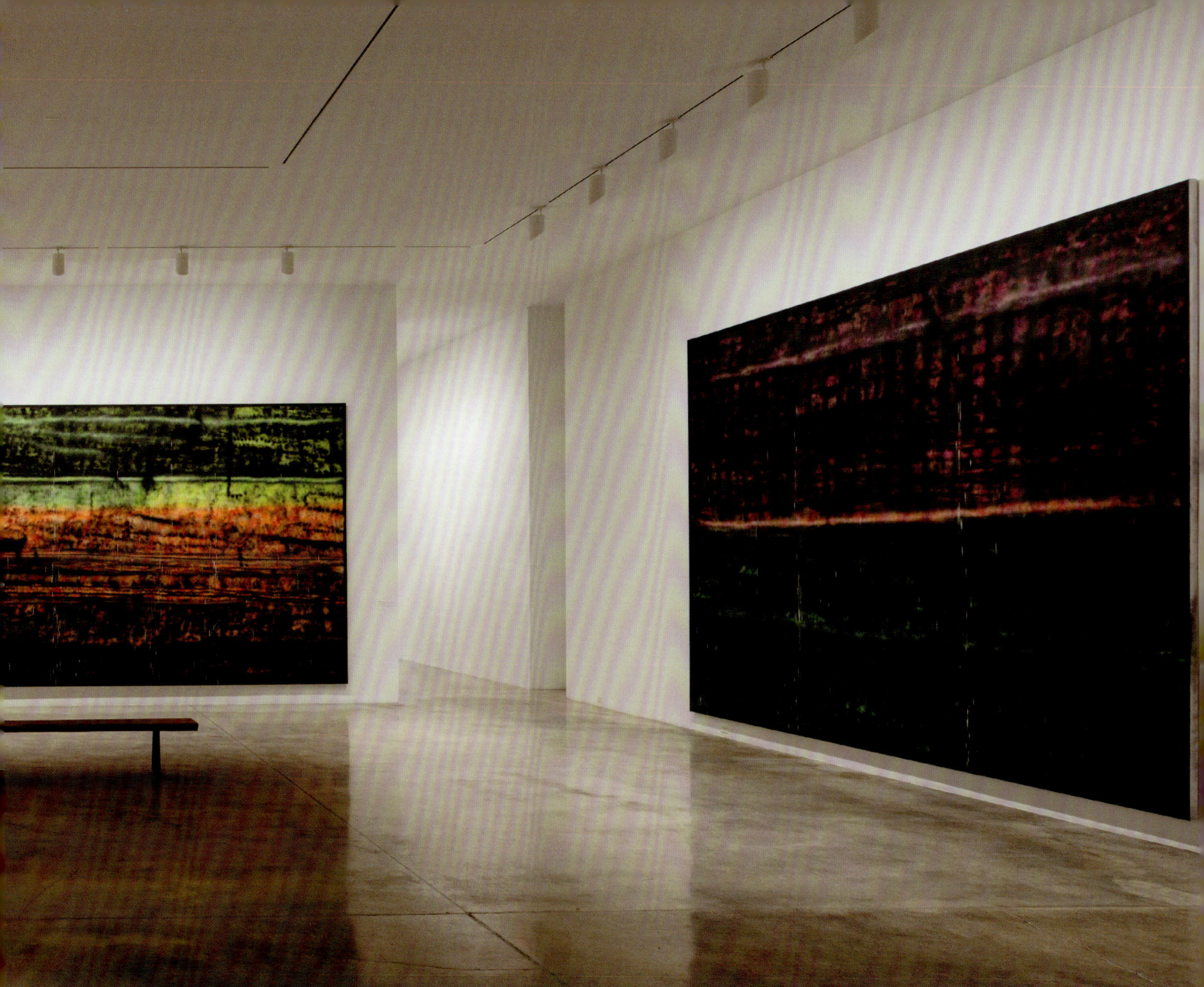

places. As an artist, it's incredibly rare to find a relationship that is based on a long-term dialogue and engagement, one where there is a mutual sense of exchange and support.

While the *SP* works progressed, we often spoke about which room in the Rubell Museum would be best to install these pieces. Don and Mera asked about which areas of the space excited me the most, and I (slightly brazenly) suggested that I could make a suite of *SP*s to fill the largest room. It was a privilege to be included in these conversations and to be given the opportunity to fulfill my early instinct to create a whole environment in which these pieces could occupy an entire span of vision.

From this point forward, this area in the Rubell Museum became a sort of residency program where artists would take over the room where the suite of *SP*s was originally installed. Giving artists the freedom to respond to the architecture of the museum and occupy a whole space on their own is an incredible gift.

—Sterling Ruby

Installation view, Rubell Museum, 2021, left to right: *SP170*; *SP177*; *SP173*; *SP171*, 2011, spray paint on canvas, 145 x 214 x 2 in. (368.3 x 541 x 5.1 cm) and 160 x 235 x 2 in. (406.4 x 596.9 x 5.1 cm), acquired in 2011

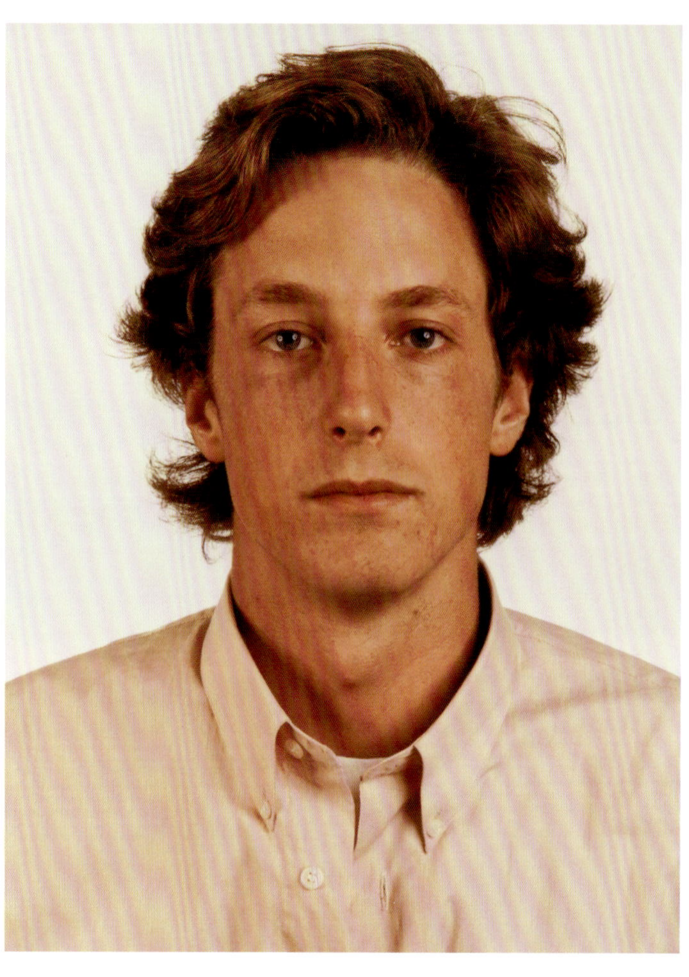

Photographs aren't depictions, they're just images. With the portrait photographs, I worked on the basis that a photograph can't represent a person or a character, that a person has too many layers to be depicted in a photograph. A photograph of a person is just one of a million possible photographs of that person. I don't believe in the psychologizing portrait photography that my colleagues do, trying to capture the character with a lot of light and shade. That's absolutely suspect to me. I can only show the surface. Whatever goes beyond that is more or less chance. I can't control it and don't want to speculate about it either. The fact that the portraits have taken on the character of passport photographs has to do with the model of the passport photograph. The person is identified by society via the passport photograph. My generation didn't grow up with painting, but with other media, with magazines, television, with a lot of sources of photographic depiction. If a young person decides to be an artist today, he won't necessarily decide to paint. Our image models are the images in the media. For that reason, my images are not depictions of reality but show a kind of second reality, the image of the image. If I make a portrait I don't believe I'm making a depiction of a person, but I have so many other portraits in my head that my portrait tends instead to come close to the image that I've already seen.

—Thomas Ruff

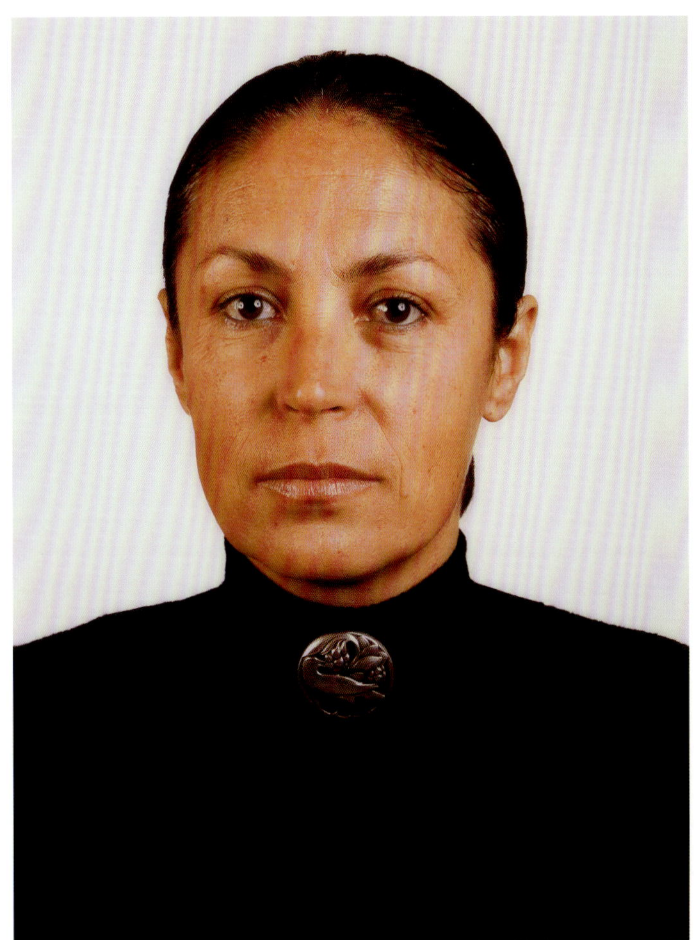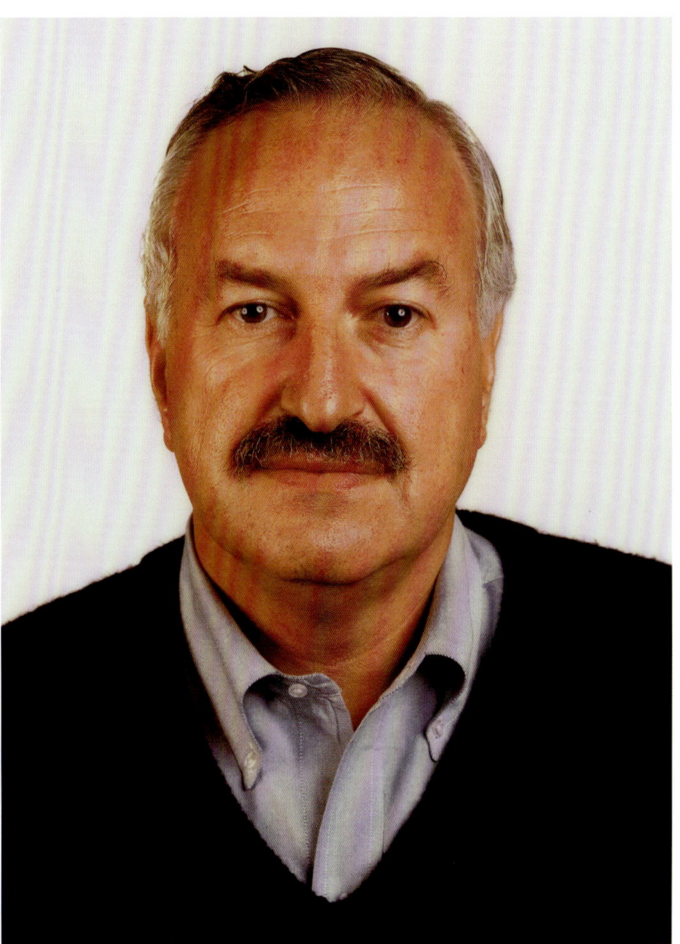

Left to right: *Portrait (Jason Rubell)*, 1989, chromogenic print with Diasec and wooden frame, ed. 3/4, 82 5/8 x 63 in. (210 x 160 cm), acquired in 1998
Portrait (Mrs. Rubell), 1988, chromogenic print with Diasec and wooden frame, 82 5/8 x 63 in. (210 x 160 cm), acquired in 1989
Portrait (Mr. Rubell), 1988, chromogenic print with Diasec and wooden frame, 82 5/8 x 63 in. (210 x 160 cm), acquired in 1989

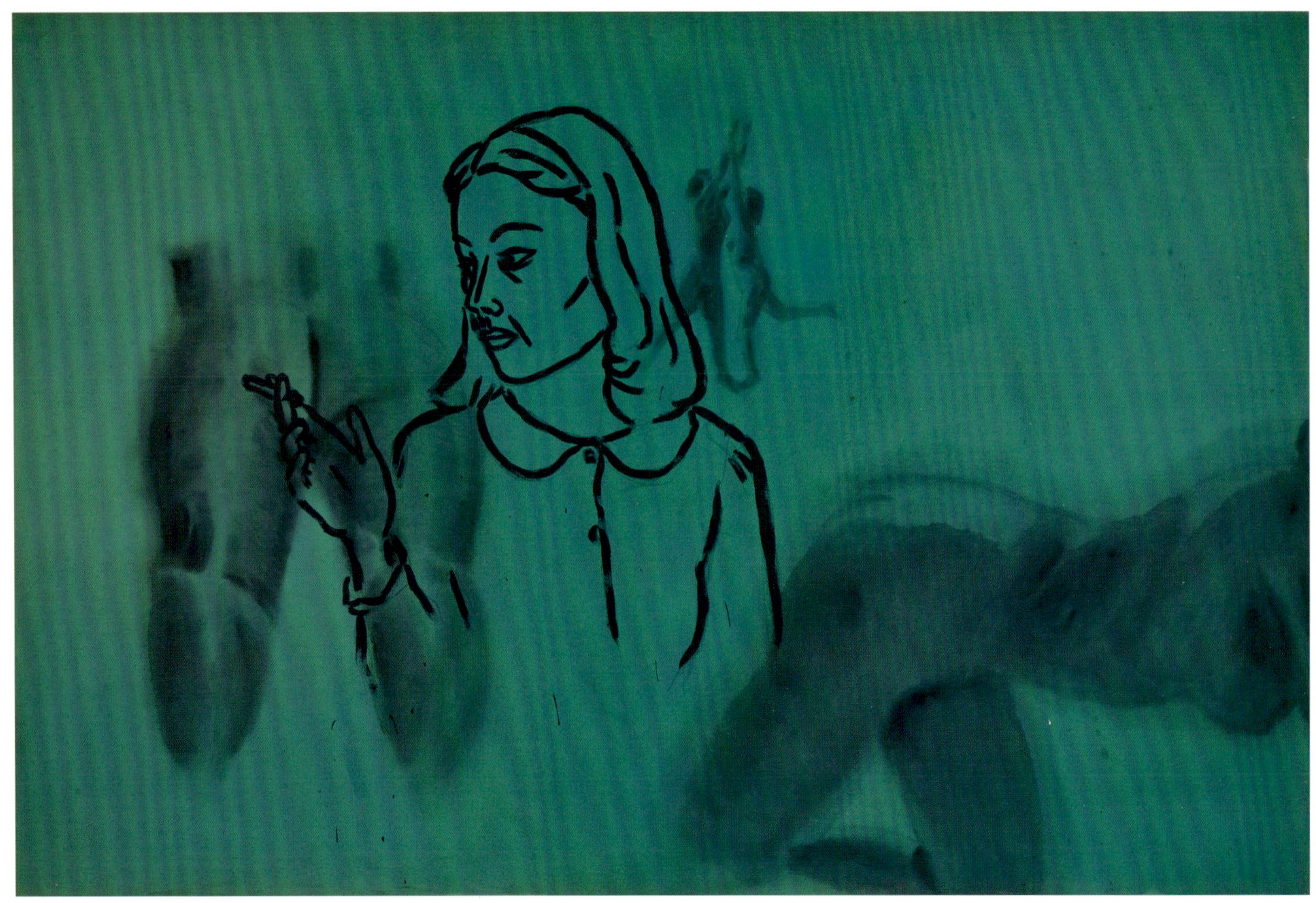

Rainy Night in the Rubber City—what does that title mean? I don't know, it's too long ago, but I can imagine that there was something *noir*-ish about it that appealed to me. It's a painting *drenched* in sensibility. The specific color of green—Veronese Green, or Emerald—is more or less the color of absinthe, at least as I imagined it then. The painting is likewise drenched in the color, saturated with it. A romantic image, a night soaked in absinthe and god knows what else. Two women dancing, a third one smoking, seeming to disregard the others, but somehow not entirely unaware of the viewer's involvement. That's its charm: to be both aware and unaware. The painting speaks back across time, the way art can. Not just to the early 1980s, to which it seems to have very little connection, but much further back, perhaps to the '20s or '30s. I can imagine the painting hanging companionably next to one by Charles Demuth, or even Florine Stettheimer—any one of that circle. It would be interesting to do the experiment.

—David Salle

Rainy Night in the Rubber City, 1980, acrylic and conté crayon on canvas, 58 x 88 in. (147.3 x 223.5 cm), acquired in 1980
Opposite page, top to bottom:
The Cruelty of the Father, 1987, oil and acrylic on canvas with chair, diptych, overall 98 x 196 in. (249 x 497.8 cm), acquired in 1998
Michael Rips, 1998, oil and acrylic on canvas and linen, five panels, overall 72 x 144 in. (182.8 x 365.7 cm), acquired in 1999

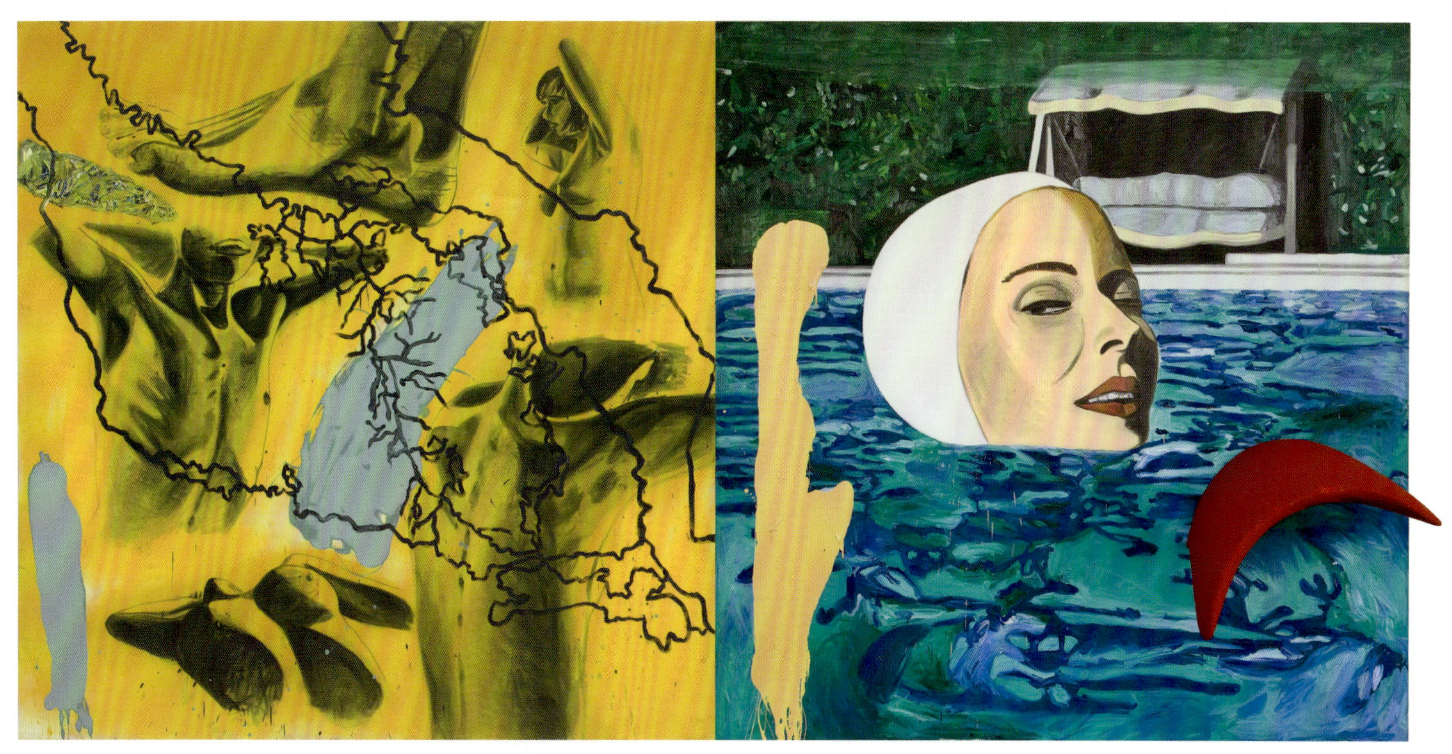

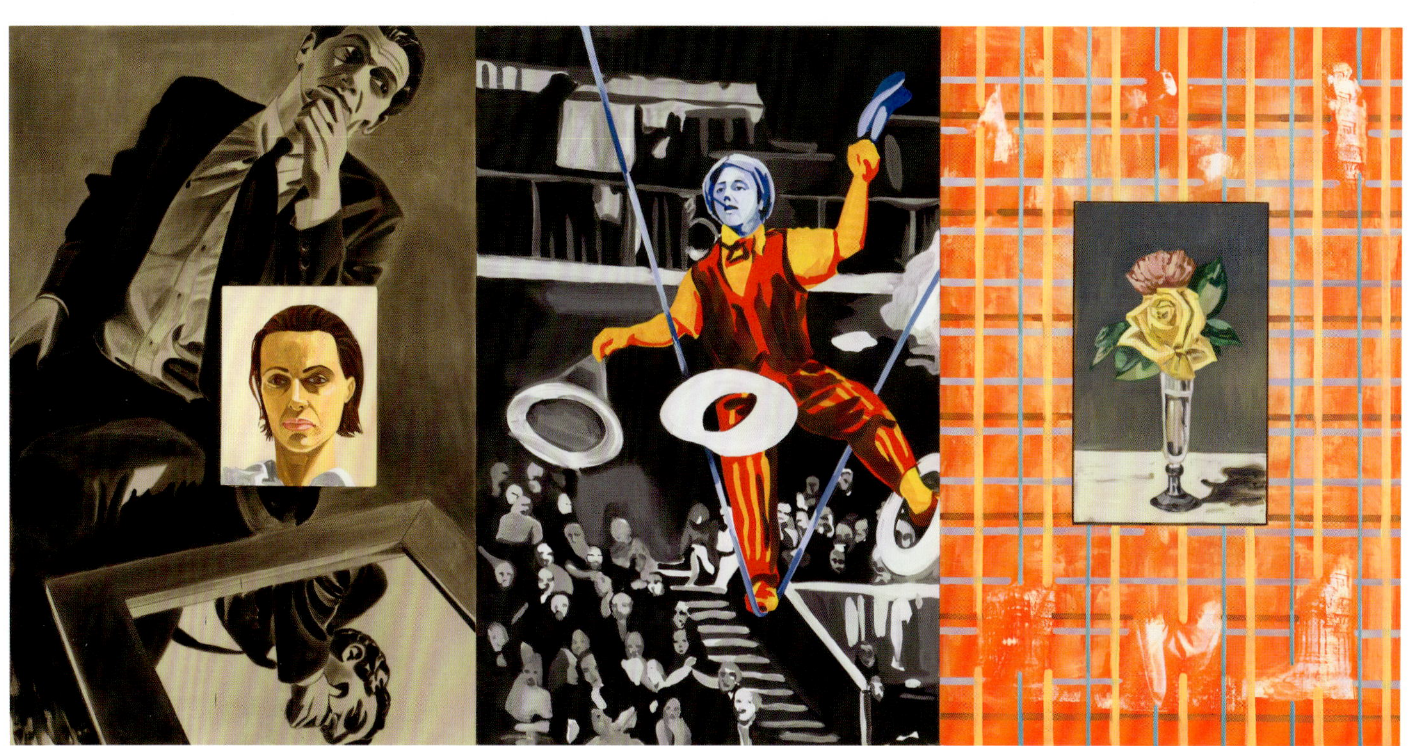

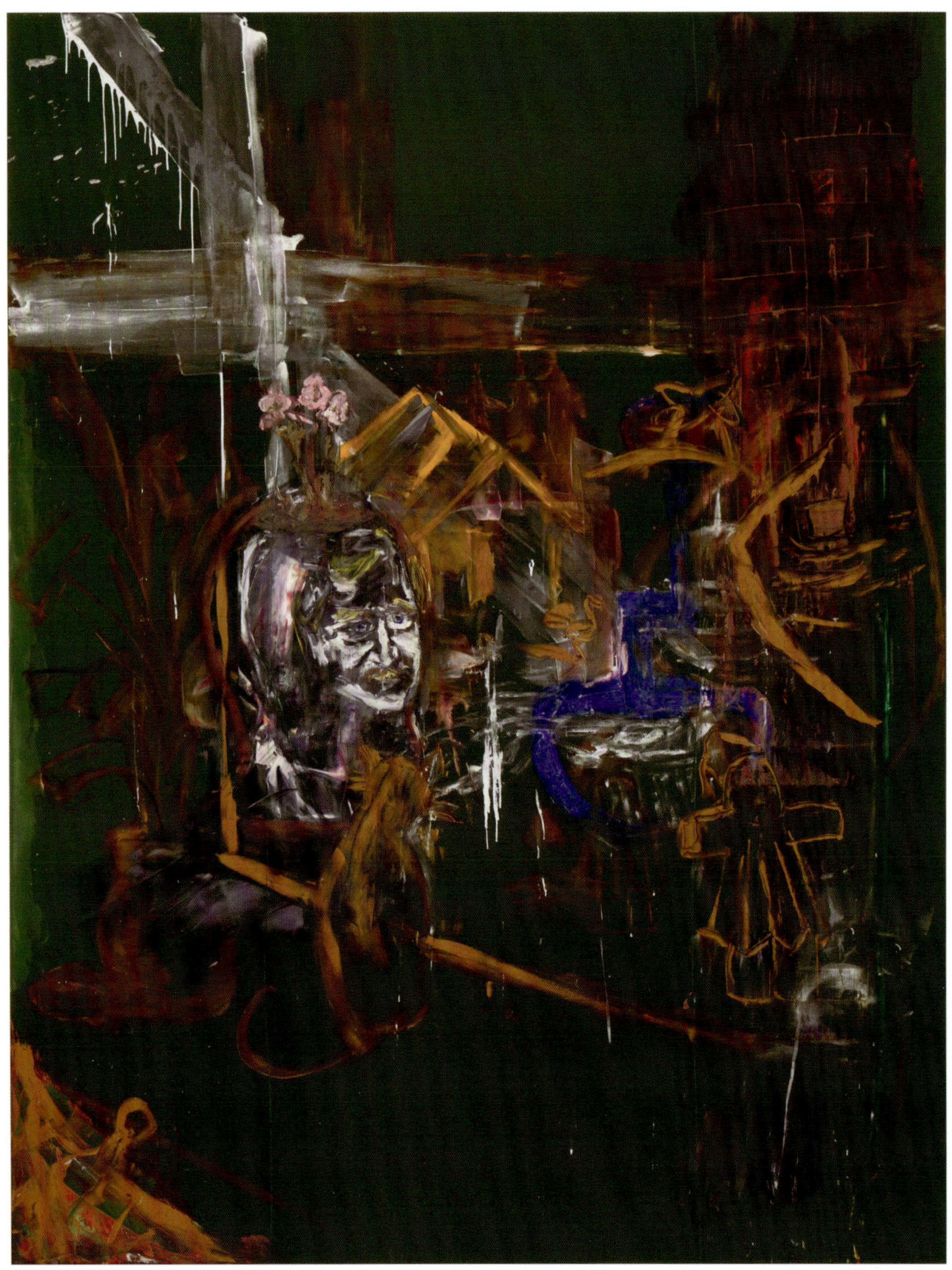

Only through the work can there be a recognition, a harmony of intention and revelation, artist and viewer communing. Making art is the only way some kinds of people mediate the world. It is the way they fit into the world. The work is ultimately a physical fact, a microcosm of the world for the artist, a handbook for others. It can only be constructed out of displaced love; the curiosity to know something (through the making) that is seemingly unknowable. Out of the acceptance of the finite terms (possibilities) of painting one achieves a self-respect. Through making objects one learns things about life that cannot be learned (or communicated) in any other way. It gets made out of the need for a direct, concrete truth

that stays intact, available, as long as the work exists. It is a way of transgressing death. It reassures others of a stability, a sameness, a quality that is a recognition of a shared humanness and thought.

The materiality of a work of art is important only as long as it imparts a quality of being, meaning, feeling, a recognition. It is appropriate only as long as it is true; it is modern only so long as it is true. Deeper than conversation, it has its own dignity.

Authorship and ownership of an idea or work are not identical. The artist creates a symbiotic relationship of author and sign,

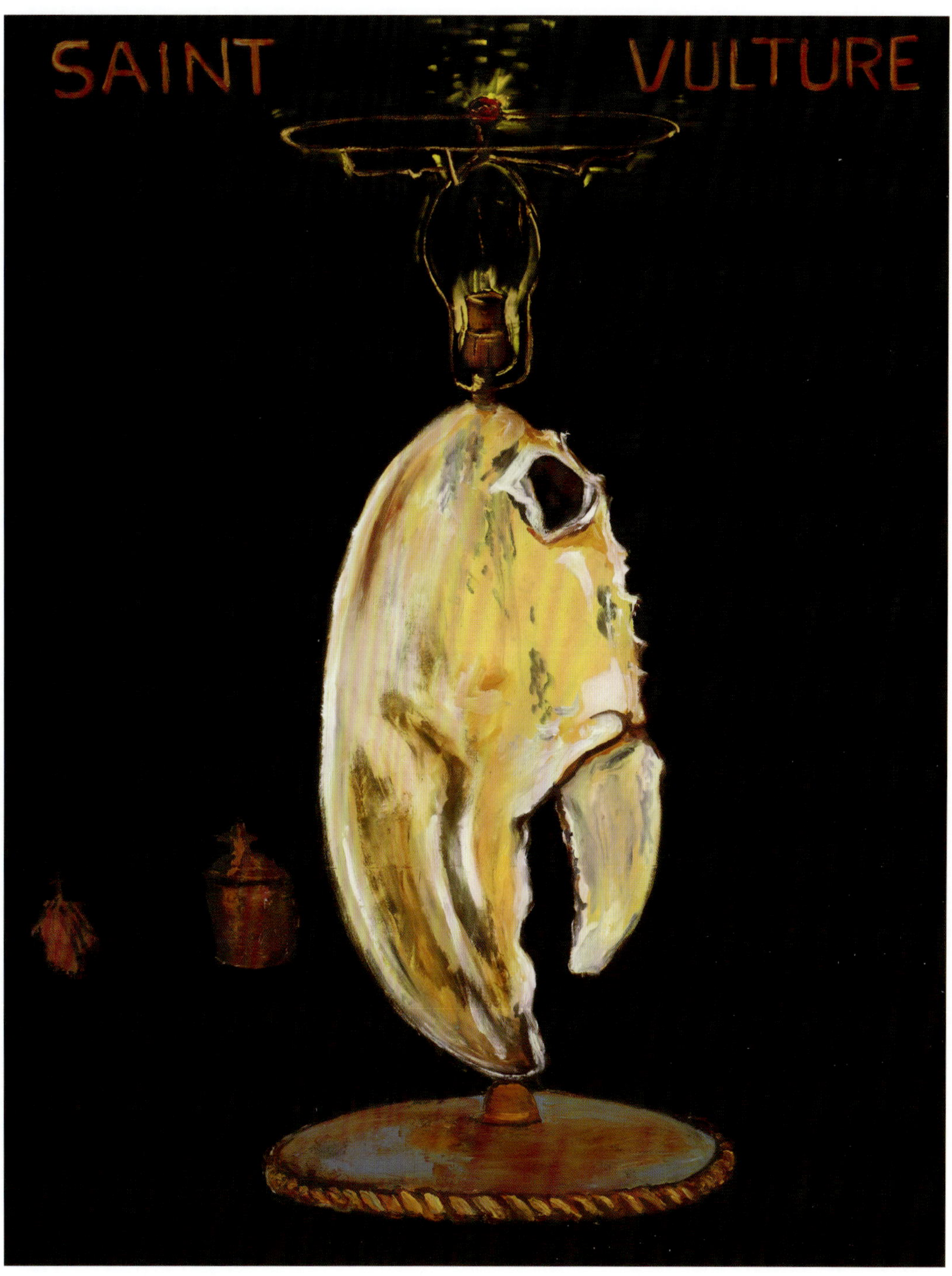

handmade, a gift to others to align himself with them in a common truth; a clearer realization of the world we live in, an individual attempt to cut out the static, the shit.

All components of the work are parts of a desire to transform the spirit; prior meanings, existing meanings, and newly attached meanings, all necessary to create in the work an accumulative meaning whose configuration is something no one has ever seen before. This doesn't mean you can't recognize it when you see it.

What artists can give to others, how they are of use in this life, is in their discovery of a point of convergence where the physical fact denotes a state of consciousness.

This is how art is generative.

—Julian Schnabel

Opposite page: *Sad Vase*, 1983, oil on velvet, 108 x 84 in. (274.3 x 213.4 cm), acquired in 2013
Saint Vulture, 1983, oil on velvet, 108 x 84 in. (274.3 x 213.4 cm), acquired in 1984

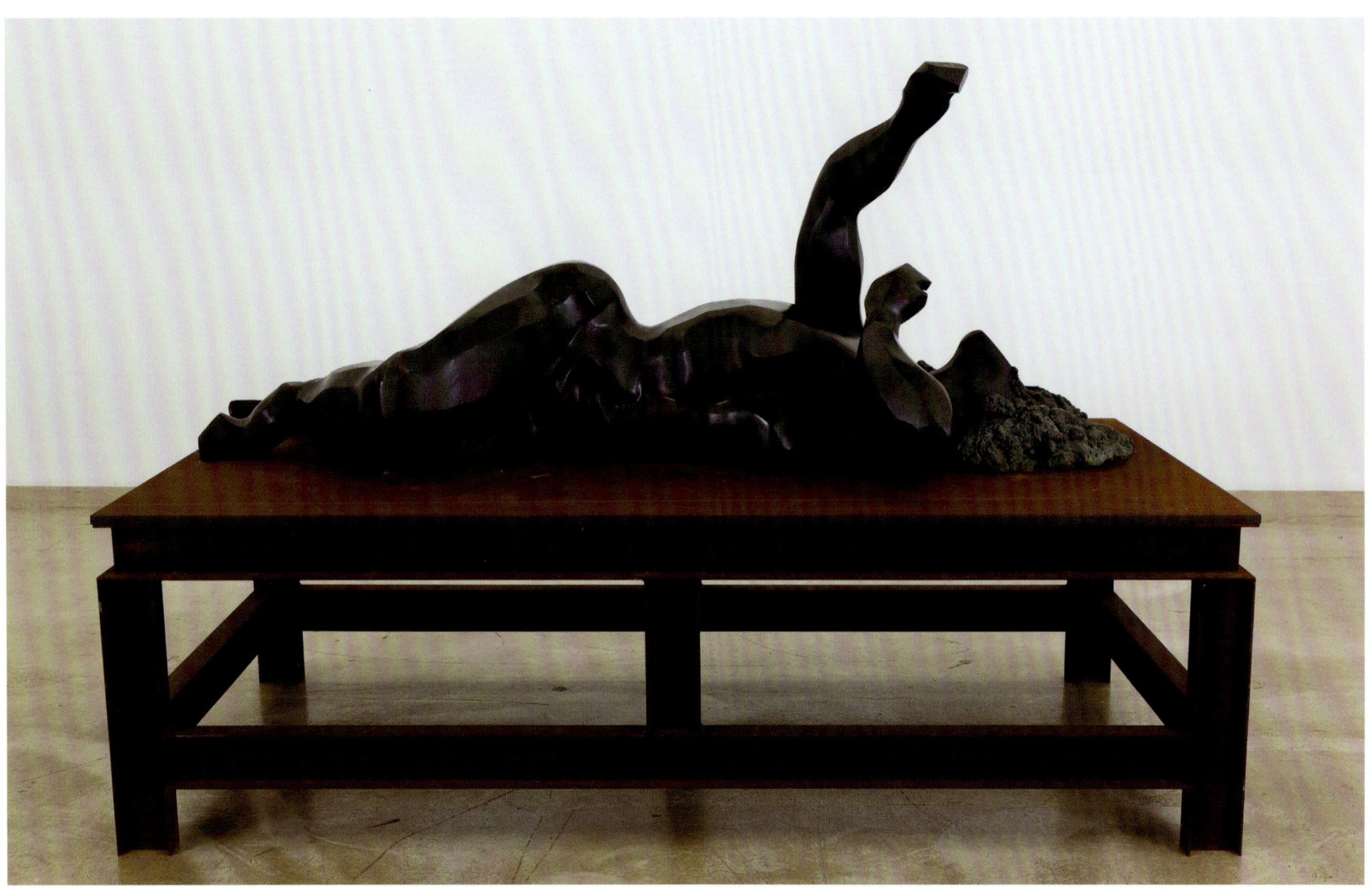

James Lingwood: How did you proceed with the sculptures of women? How did you arrive at the form for the large reclining figures?

Thomas Schütte: Initially there were about 120 rough ceramic sketches. These are essential to find out what might work and what might not work on a larger scale. They help make sure you don't get too lost in this mountain of material. Sometimes they have everything already, sometimes they need a few cosmetic changes.

JL: Are the successes and the failures equally interesting? Is that why you decided to show them all together?

TS: Yes, yes, the failure is part of the work, perhaps the major part. The process to find a form and a physical expression is interesting by itself. For me, it's become essential to live through this process for months and sometimes years because the general attitude today—let's call it the 'Milli Vanilli' problem—it's just completely obsolete and very, very sad. Nice face, no voice, sells good.

JL: There is a very long tradition of the reclining woman in Western art, with all sorts of implications of dominance and passivity. Where did the idea of working within what might be considered a fairly contaminated or corrupted tradition come from?

TS: Of course it's contaminated, but is it any less contaminated than the endless Duchamp spiral of today? The idea of making reclining figures has been there for quite a while in my head, but I didn't feel strong enough to take it on.

JL: It's been latent in your mind for a while? What stopped you from developing the idea earlier?

TS: Because it could seem to be pretty much a dead-end, repeating old historical mistakes—a kind of "mission impossible." Basically, I was afraid. Actually, there is still a lot of fear about what this will lead to, but I see some light at the end of the tunnel.

JL: How relevant were the modern masters of the nude? Did they liberate you or did they create a kind of block?

TS: The more I work on the figures, the more I know and the more these artists have my respect. Actually, it was only after I had completed all four figures that I went to Paris to look at Rodin and Maillol and Picasso and so on again, but with very different eyes this time. But I'm not interested in quotations in any direct way. The artist's work is more than the editing or re-editing of historical achievements. Working with the material has a certain slowness to it, just making the shapes by hand. From my point of view this way of working is more or less completely forgotten and needs to be revitalised.

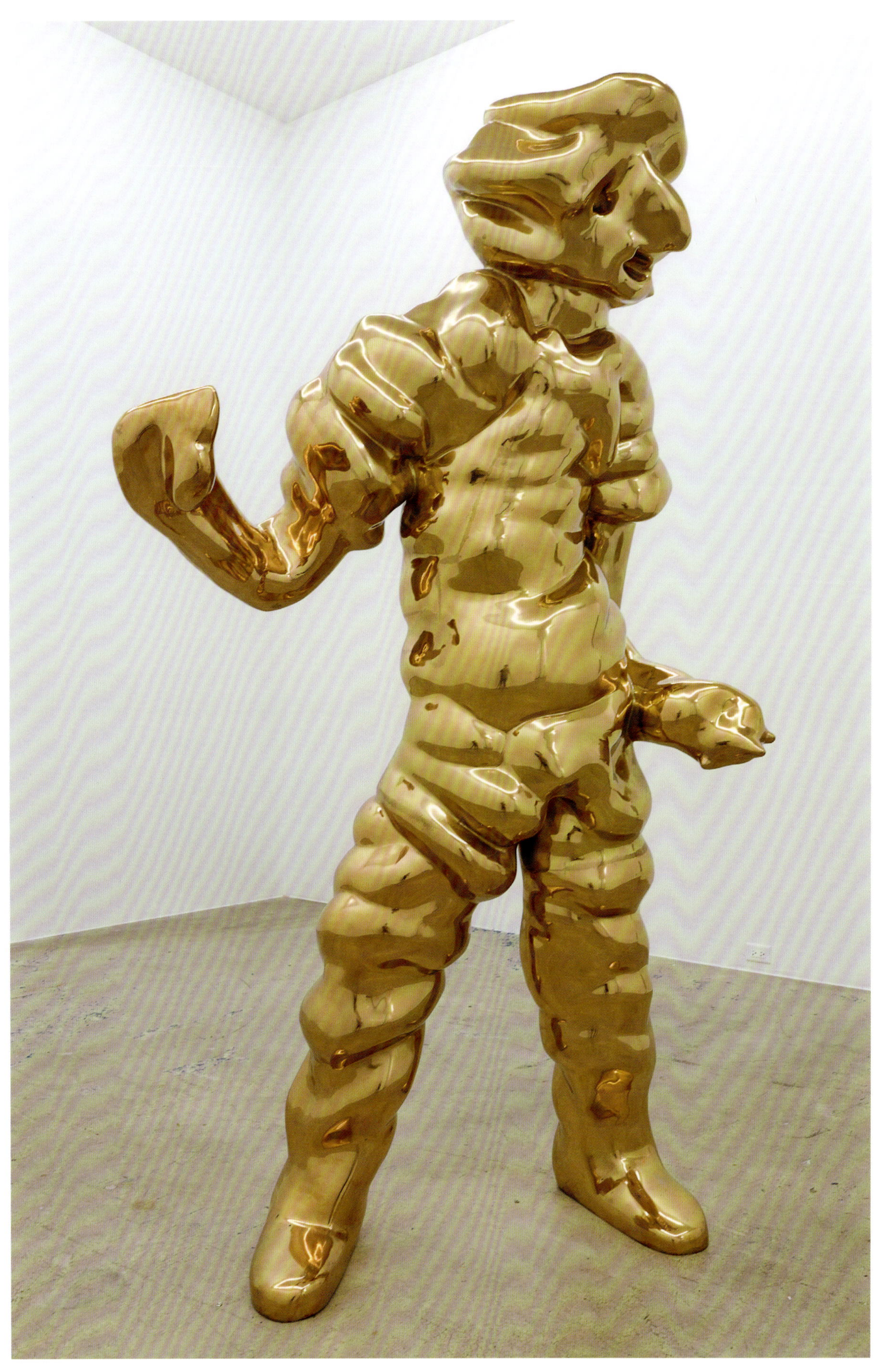

Opposite page: *Bronzefrau Nr. 15*, 2004, patinated bronze and steel, 86 x 99 x 49 in. (218.4 x 251.5 x 124.5 cm), acquired in 2004
Großer Geist Nr. 2, 2003, polished bronze, 96 x 56 x 34 in. (243.8 x 142.2 x 86.4 cm), acquired in 2005

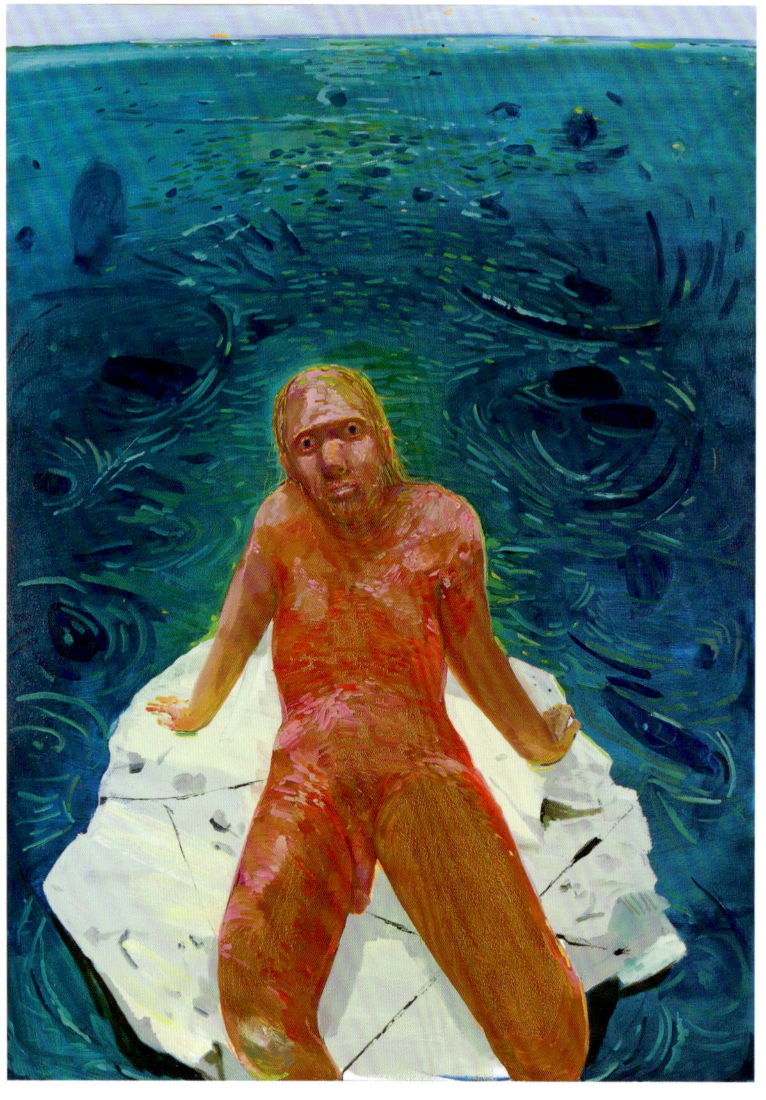

Frank was somebody I invented, but I proposed to paint him from observation. He was the last subject and the last audience, and I was the last painter. It was like starting from ground zero. "Imagine as a possible subject the last man on earth from observation." He was a hybrid of information I found in narratives and people I know. In one of the paintings he has my friend Pat's eyes; in another he is part proboscis monkey. He was like a ball of Play-Doh rolled on the floor, picking up different attributes as the paintings went on. I called him Frank after Frankenstein and also as an allusion to the word *frank*; he also just looked like a Frank.

I invented his parts; in *Frank on a Rock*, his penis is either stuck to or slightly tucked under his thigh, or I just put it in the wrong spot. It is placed closer to where female genitals would be. I guess that could be a kind of anatomical mishap similar to a man painting a woman's breasts super-far apart. But I don't mind him sitting on his own penis—it's possible. In this painting, Frank is extremely sunburnt and sitting on an ice floe. I wanted the color to have a grating, physical effect and the depiction of his skin to be painful, as it is scaly and scraped down to the canvas.

—Dana Schutz

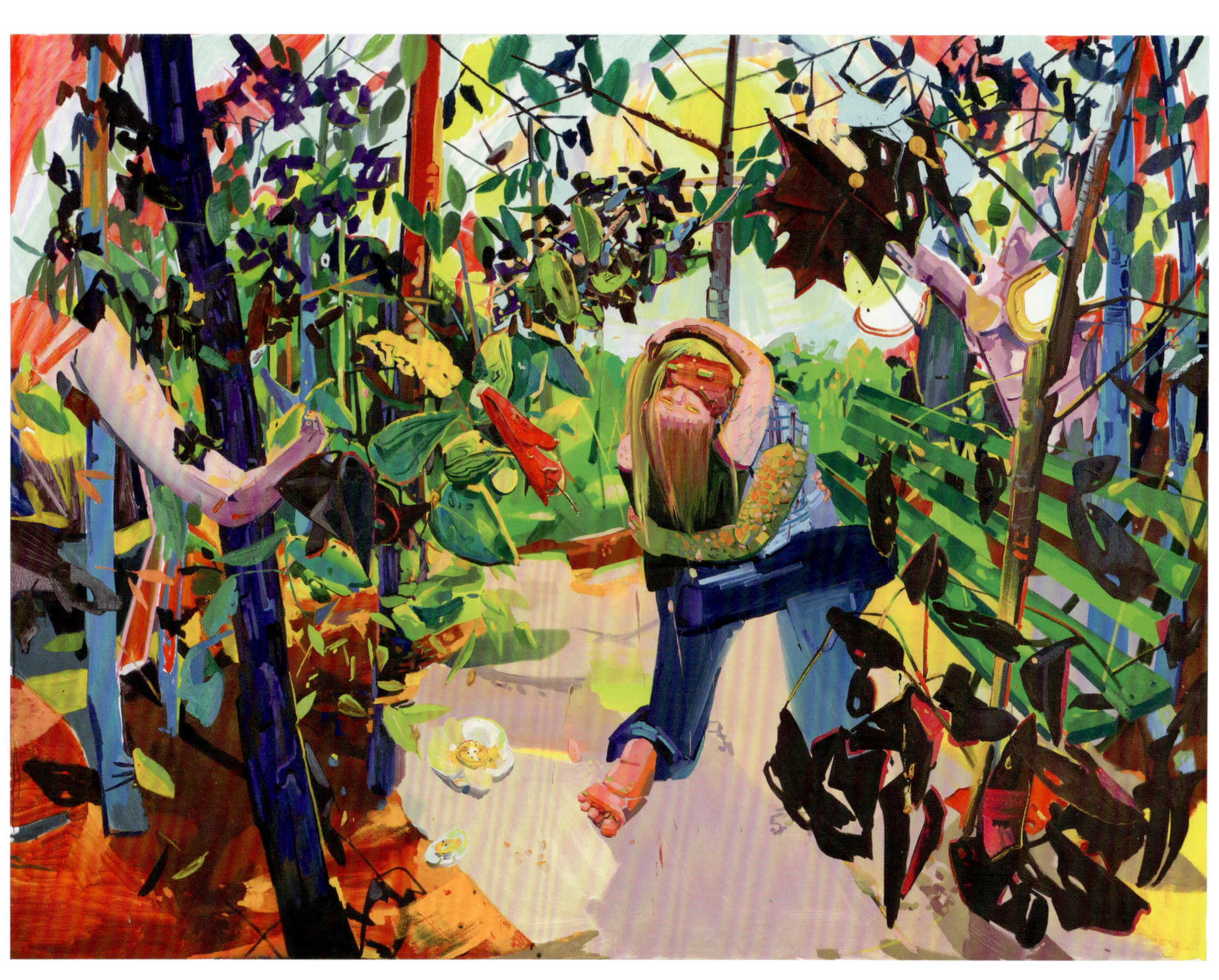

Opposite page: *Frank on a Rock*, 2002, oil on canvas, 66 1/4 x 47 3/4 x 2 1/4 in. (168.3 x 121.3 x 5.7 cm), acquired in 2003
Lovers, 2003, oil on canvas, 84 x 120 in. (213.4 x 304.8 cm), acquired in 2003

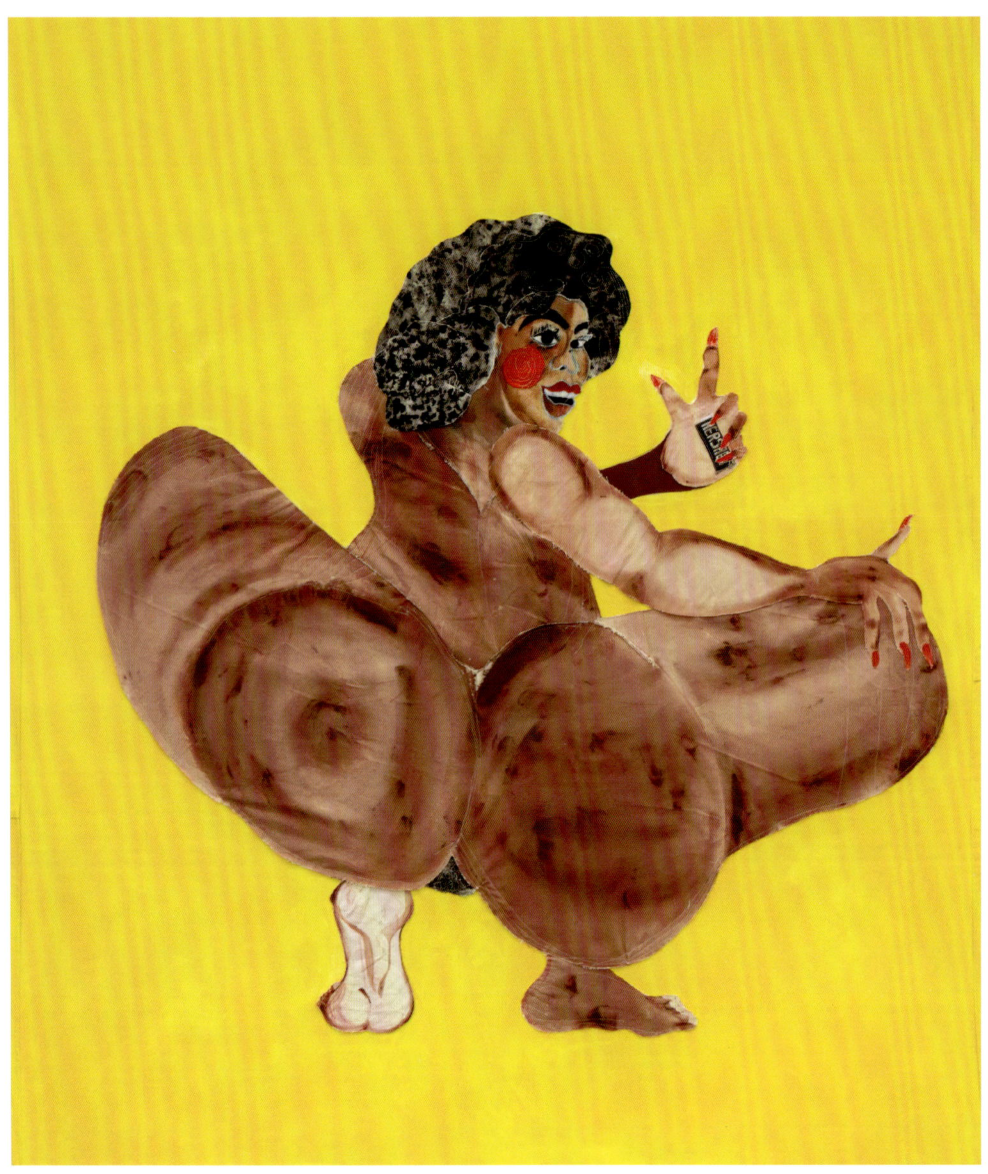

Milk Chocolate (2017) depicts an exuberant, brown-skinned Black woman holding a Hershey's Milk Chocolate candy bar. The protagonist of this painting looks coquettishly over her shoulder directly at the painting's viewer, confronting their gaze confidently. Ultimately, this work is entirely about confidence—confidence and defiance. *Milk Chocolate* is an anomaly in the *Bodega Run* series it occupies, a series that investigates the social and political significance of the New York City corner stores known colloquially as *bodegas*. *Milk Chocolate* is the only work from *Bodega Run* depicting a nude in a liminal space rather than an environment. The reason for this is that *Milk Chocolate* speaks to one of the many subtexts in the project: the relationship between objectification and communication as it pertains to the Black body. Within a historical context, the Black American body in particular has been rendered an object through its commodification within the institution of American chattel slavery, the consequences of which have contributed to the reality of mass incarceration, economic exploitation, and cultural appropriation. *Milk*

Chocolate conflates the image of the nude Black female body with the iconic American treat—a Hershey's bar—as a means to acknowledge the reality of Black objectification while asserting that such historical reality can be changed in this contemporary moment through the Black individual's reclamation of their image and personhood.

Two Girls (2019) shows two female figures standing side by side in an embrace. The piece was made for the occasion of my 2021 solo exhibition at the Baltimore Museum of Art, in response to a work in the museum's permanent collection: Henri Matisse's sculpture *Two Women* (1907-08), originally titled *Two Negresses*.

The BMA has the largest public collection of Matisse work in the world. When preparing for my exhibition at the BMA, I wanted to make an artwork that spoke simultaneously to my intentions as an artist and to the institution's history. This desire led me to look through the many works by Matisse in

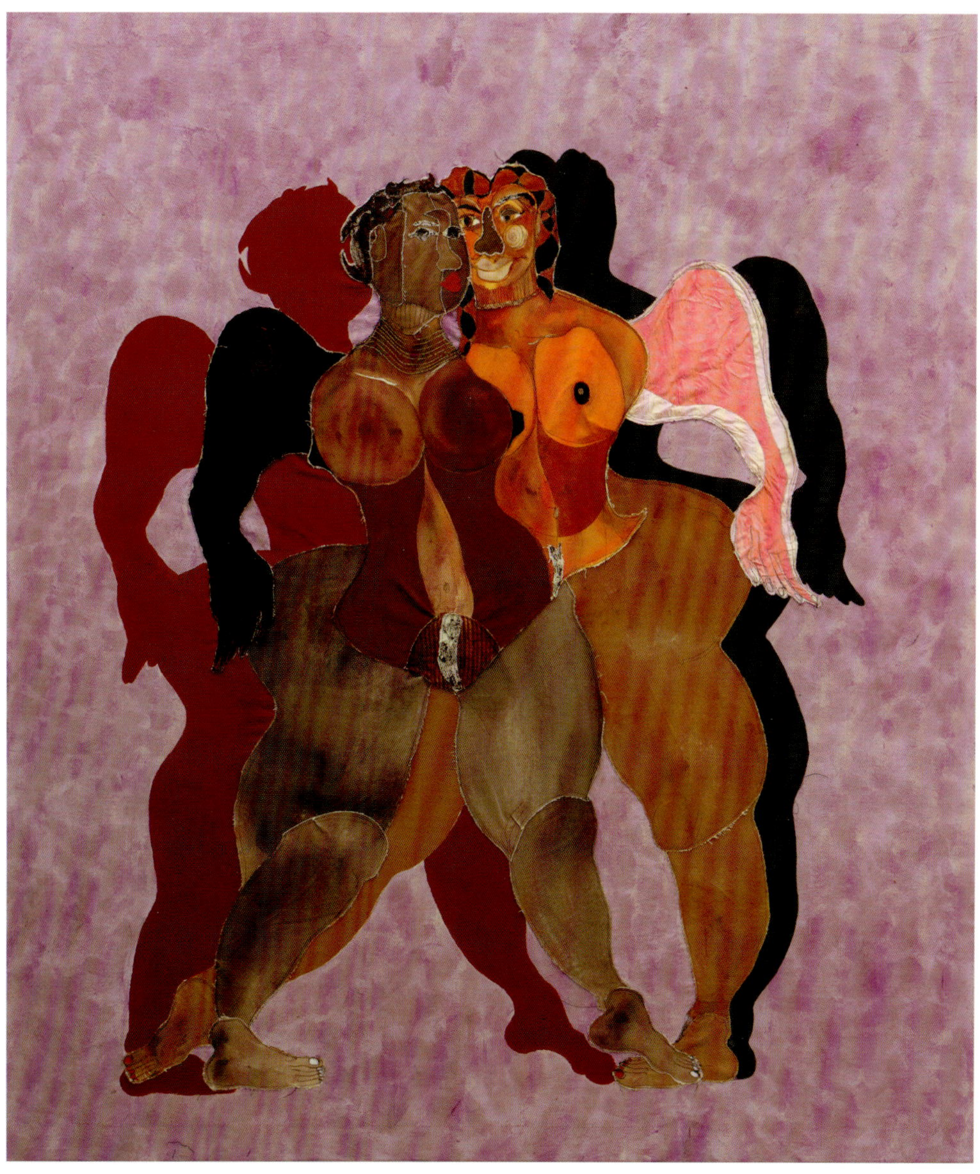

the museum's collection. His sculpture *Two Women* stood out to me the most, given its original title, *Two Negresses*, which plainly identified the work's subjects as two Black women. As my practice is firmly dedicated to investigating the iconographic significance of the Black female body in Western culture, I wanted to respond to this work using my own aesthetic language as a means to interject a Black and feminine voice into the dialogue already embedded in the work. The original sculpture was based on a photograph titled *Young Tuareg Girls*, from a 19th-century Orientalist French erotic magazine. The source image for the sculpture was fetishistic in nature. I believe Matisse's intention, by further immortalizing the image in bronze, was to complicate it, yet his intentions still feel short. The original gaze was still maintained despite Matisse's efforts to bring an individuality

into each figure's form and representation. More than anything, the diminutive scale of the sculpture mirrored the scale of a reproduced image and still left the viewer larger and able to both physically and visually consume the subject. In my reinterpretation of the work, both women confidently face the viewer and dwarf them in their larger-than-life scale. The subjects of the work embrace and uplift one another, showing both solidarity and affection to the other. They stand conspicuously not for the edification of the viewer, but for their own desire.

—Tschabalala Self

Milk Chocolate, 2017, acrylic, watercolor, flashe (vinyl emulsion paint), crayon, colored pencil, oil pastel, pencil, hand-colored photocopy, thread, hand-painted canvas on canvas, 96 x 84 in. (243.8 x 213.4 cm), acquired in 2017
Opposite page: *Two Girls*, 2019, fabric, thread, acrylic, hand-painted canvas on canvas, 96 x 84 in. (243.8 x 213.4 cm), acquired in 2019

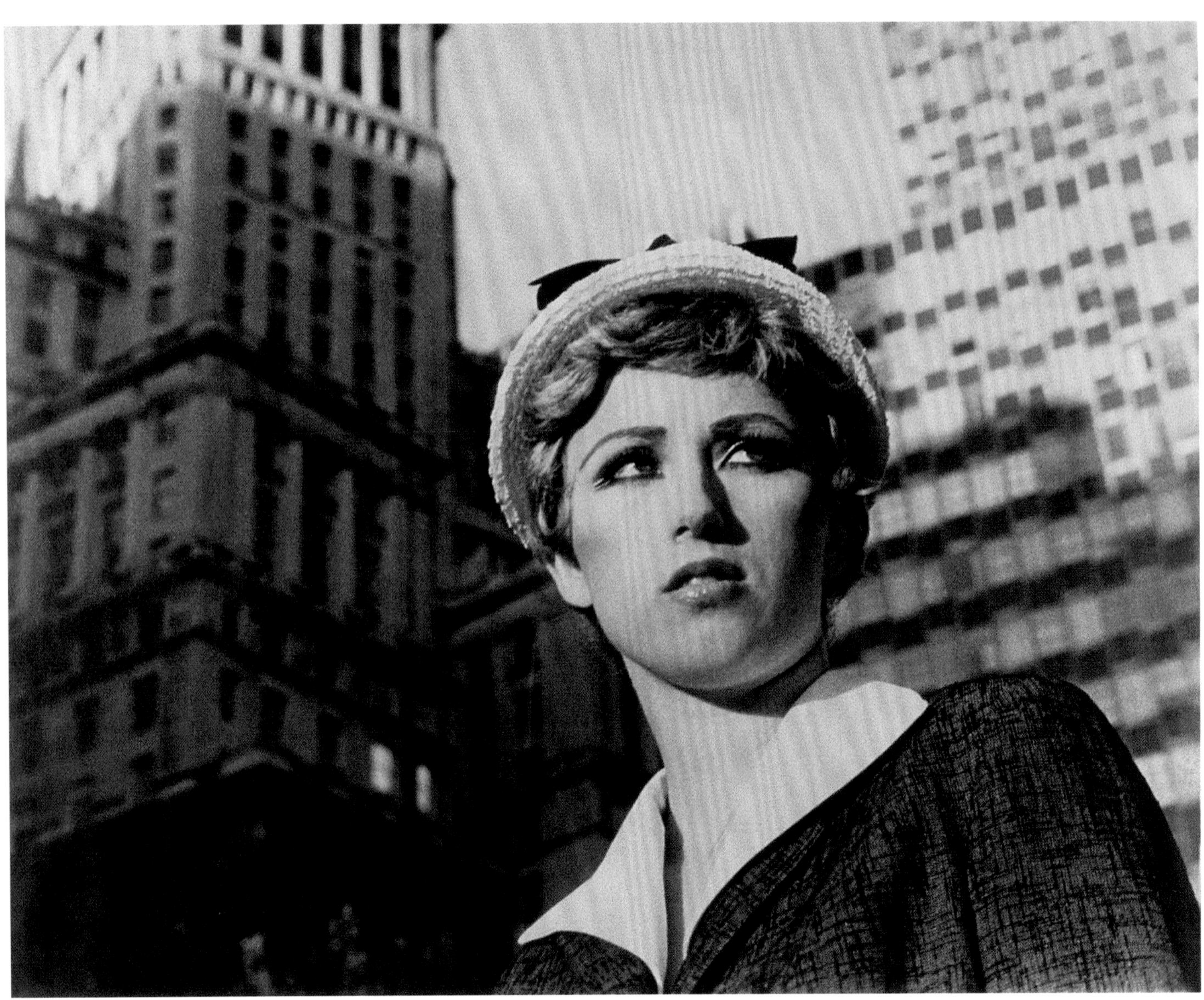

When I made this photo, I'd already shot several of the other *Film Stills* images from that year and, since I always worked where I lived, every nook and cranny of my loft had been pretty much utilized, so I was ready to head to real locations.

I'd made lists of what kinds of backgrounds I thought I could find in the city. I forget if I'd actually done any scouting—it's possible. But the idea was that my boyfriend at the time, Robert Longo, would drive his van around downtown where we lived, and I would have costumes and makeup in the back and transform into characters once I spotted a good location, once I decided upon the character for that location. Which I guess also meant thinking about what would be happening there: is she an office worker coming out of a building, or is it her first day on the job in a strange city, or is she running away from something, on her way to a mysterious assignation?

Of course, as always (even then), I wanted to leave it ambiguous.

So this was the character in the suit. We shot her way downtown near Battery Park, I believe in front of the Customs House or nearby. I'd give the camera to Robert and then tell him where to stand, guiding/directing him.

In those days, since I couldn't really afford the luxury of shooting a lot of film, I would just shoot maybe six to seven shots per character. As soon as I thought we'd gotten enough, I'd move onto the next character, so each contact sheet had about four or five different characters/locations on it.

—Cindy Sherman

Untitled Film Still (#21), 1978, gelatin silver print, ed. 2/3, 30 x 40 in. (76.2 x 101.6 cm), acquired in 1978
Opposite page: *Untitled (#207)*, 1989, color photograph, ed. 2/6, 65 x 49 in. (165.1 x 124.5 cm), acquired in 1990

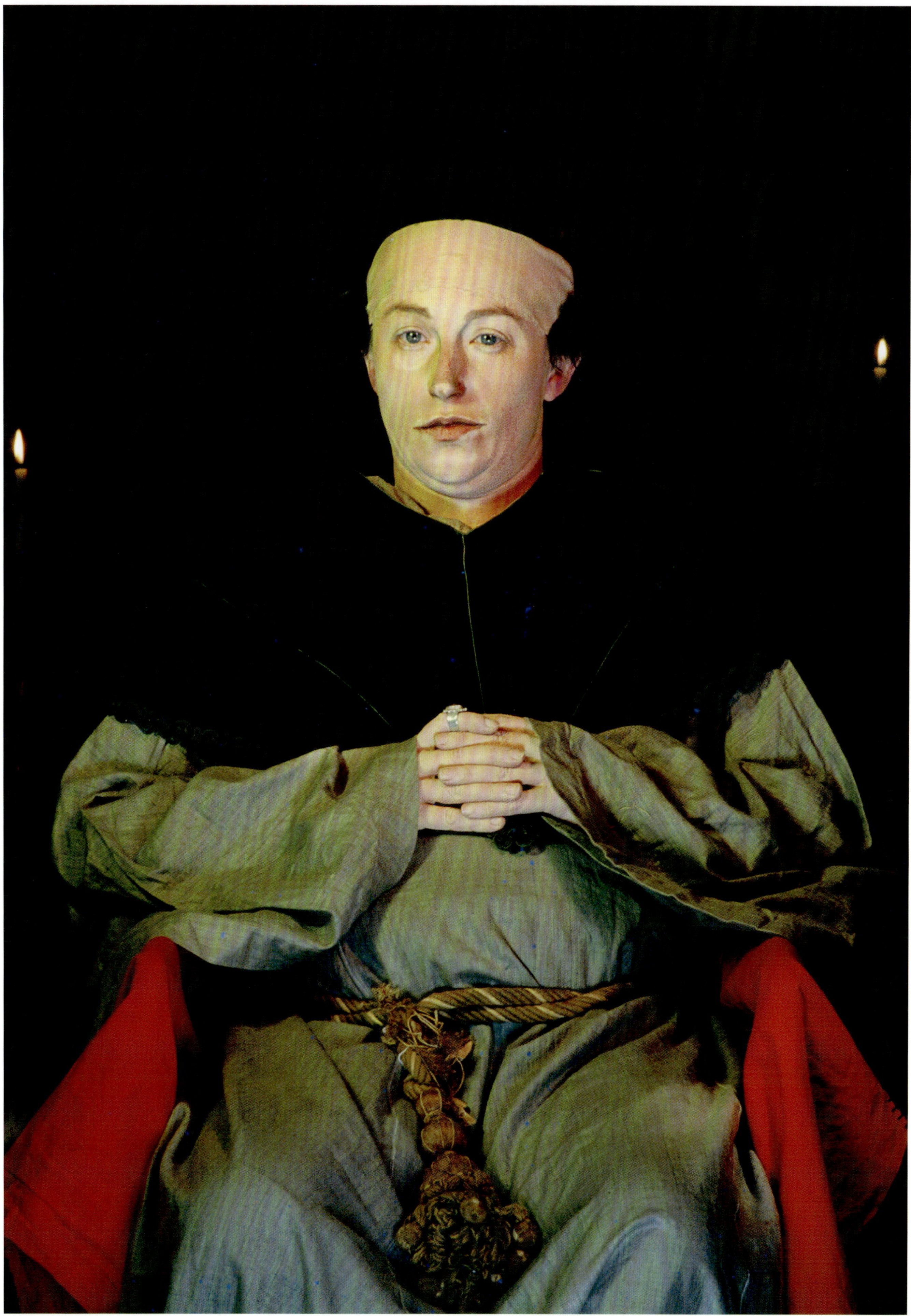

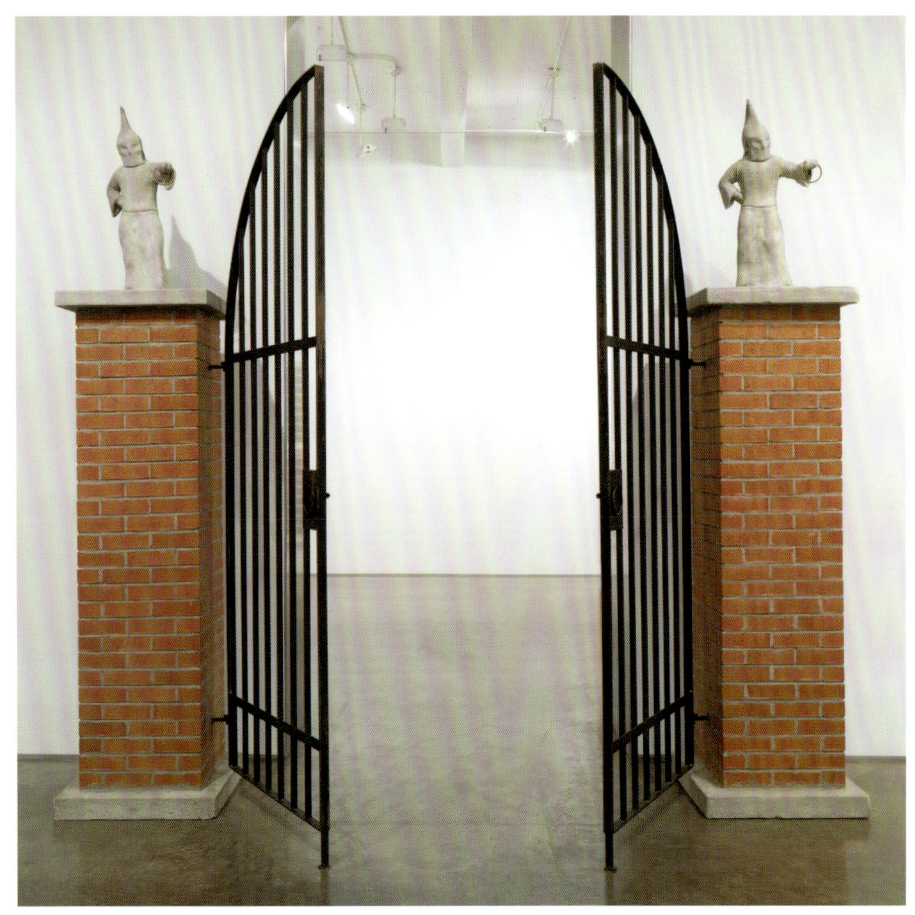

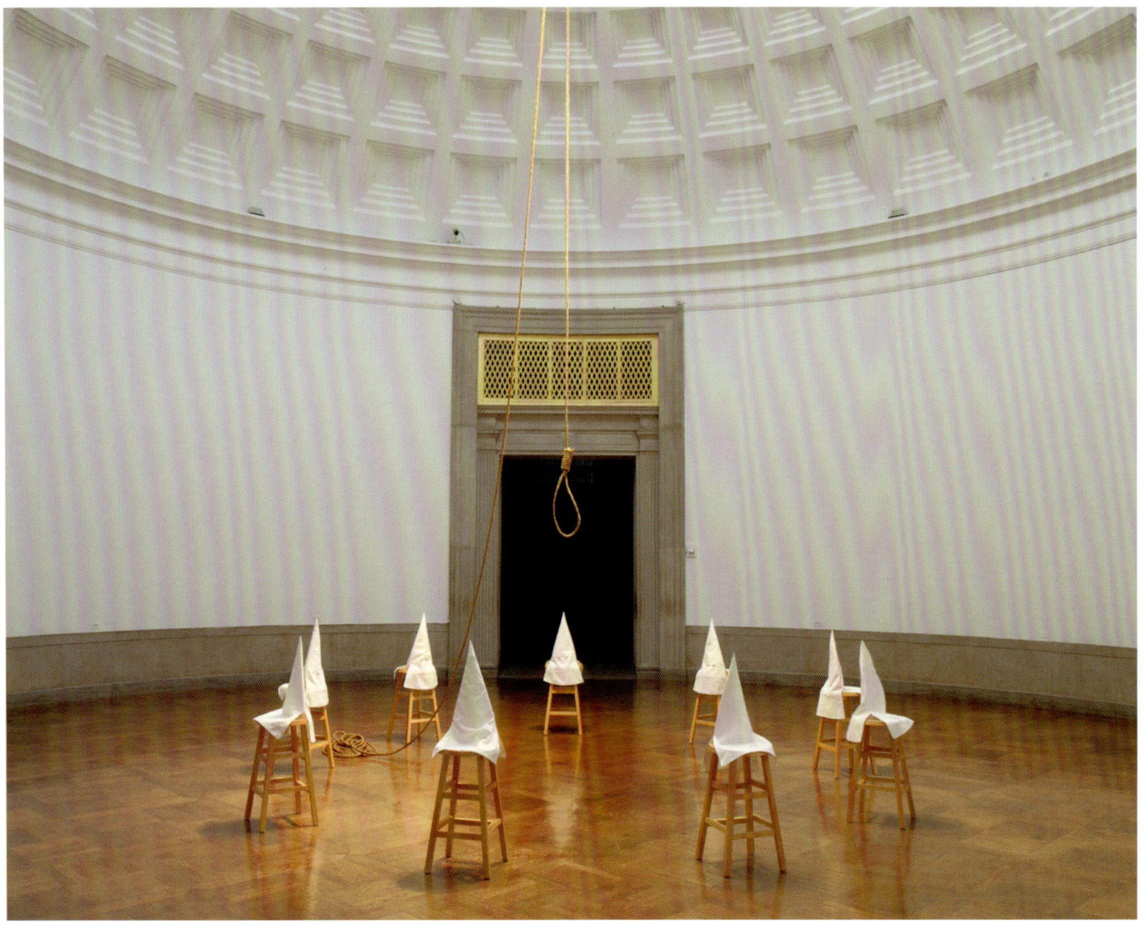

The original little Klansman came about when I was driving toward the Lincoln Tunnel going into Manhattan, there was this plant nursery and they had this really big collection of lawn ornaments. And in this collection, they had hundreds of these little lawn jockeys. I thought, *What the fuck*? I was in traffic and I practically wrecked the car, but I pulled over and I got out of my car to look around. There were all these cast jockeys, and all their faces and hands were painted. There was red for Native American; black, like boot black, for a Black figure; white, like stark, bright white; and then yellow for an Asian character. Nothing else about them was altered at all—they were all the same exact figures, just painted racially. I said to the person there, "What the fuck are you doing with these?" And he said he couldn't keep them on the shelf long enough, that people that own property around there were buying them. I'm sitting there thinking, *Jesus Christ, that's amazing*. And then I said, "Well, what the fuck. I'll buy one too!"

So I bought one because this is too rich an object not to own, and then I kept it in the corner of my studio. I have this way of collecting items like that, and they can sit around sometimes for years. This little jockey went back and forth with me from L.A. to New York, back to L.A. Everywhere I went, the jockey came, and it was really heavy because it's cast concrete. One day, I'm sitting in the studio and I'm smoking a cigarette, and I'm looking at this jockey and I thought that if I ever had a house or some property or something, what would I do? I certainly wouldn't put one of these offensive, racist jockeys out there, but I think I would tie my horse to a little Klansman. So I got all of this clay and started sculpting the Klan suit around the thing, kind of just on a whim. And as I'm looking at it, I'm thinking that this would make a great piece. Then it morphed into that. I had him cast because I wanted him to feel just like one of those original lawn jockeys. It was concurrent with a lot of the other work I was doing, like *Six-X* (1989). I was trying to push the envelope of race and racism and what goes into teaching these kinds of hateful thoughts, where it comes from and to whom it's directed. I was really on this education sprint.

Klan Gate (1992) came about when I was thinking about Anytown U.S.A—sort of like Mayberry, that perfect American town where people leave their doors unlocked and are safe from people who look like me. I was shifting it to institutions and how those iconic, institutional buildings like banks, post offices, and town squares formed the center of how the "perfect town U.S.A." was perceived. For me, it wasn't just an isolated one-to-one type of racism, it was more institutional. It was something that represented something bigger. I was thinking of people with McMansions and how every Ivy League school has a gate of some sort. I wanted those two scary gargoyles at the top of those pillars on either side of the gates. *Klan Gate* is more about the institution and the idea of a guarded, gated community and those that are on the inside, as opposed to those on the outside.

Duck, Duck, Noose (1992) is the same family, the same body of work. *Duck, Duck* really came out of that children's game Duck, Duck, Goose. I loved that game when I was little, where somebody goes around tapping you on the head and you get up and chase them around the ring. That catch-me-if-you-can game. I was always pretty fast, so I'd catch the person before they sat down.

When I was working on the piece, that was one of the most powerful images that stood out for me. It goes beyond the schoolroom. It goes into that field-of-play area where hateful games also shape the way that children play, because a lot of those games that we played are actually quite horrible. They were homophobic and racist and sexist. Kids are not always aware of their language. They say things without thinking. They are taught to communicate in a way and it goes unquestioned. I think kids become comfortable in hate speech at a very early age, and *Duck, Duck* taps into that because there's this playfulness to the kind of economy that is circled around the game of Duck, Duck, Goose. It's an interesting thing, the way we construct hate in that way. When I first came up with *Duck, Duck*, I was making the piece and the title came to me because it was this circle, and then I thought to put the noose in the middle. That's the playful thing grafted onto this insidious core: Here they are in this sick, twisted school game, and they're hanging somebody.

As the piece travels with *30 Americans* it's gotten a response. I still get emails and texts and things. Sometimes it's heartfelt, like some older person would say, "I saw your piece in *30 Americans* and it really moved me." Or, "I couldn't bring myself to be in that room with that piece." We have endless notes and emails and exchanges just on that piece alone as it travels. Museum guards that refuse to be in the room with *Duck, Duck*. Guards that refuse to pass through *Klan Gate*.

I think it doesn't help us to cover those things up, and that's the point. These are things that you have to talk about openly, those painful things. Art is not just looking at flowers in a vase. Sometimes art can reach into those places that you fear the most or are the most uncomfortable with.

—Gary Simmons

SHELL SNOWDEN BUTLER

SHELL IS MY DAUGHTER AND THE SUBJECT MATTER OF THE SERIES "SHELL; GLIMPSES."

MY PAINTING IS EXPRESSIONISM. IT IS OFTEN REFERRED TO AS PASSIONATE AND POWERFUL. IT IS DIRECT, WITH AN EMPHASIS ON SHELL, WHICH IS DIRECT, AND REFLECTS A HUMAN STRUGGLE TO ENDURE- ORGANIC SHAPES.

MY PAINTING IS A PERSONAL FORM OF COMMUNICATION, WHICH DEPICTS AN EMOTIONAL REACTION WITH A STRONG SENSE OF DESIGN AND COMPOSITION.

THIS SERIES SHOWS AN EXPERIENCE, WHICH IS DEEPER THAN APPEARANCE. THE SURFACE IS RICH WITH TACTILE AND VISUAL TEXTURE. THE BRUSHWORK IS SENSUAL AND VIGOROUS, WHICH AIDS IN THE PORTRAYAL OF SHELL'S ENERGY. SOME AREAS PROPEL FROM THE SURFACE, IMPASTO, REMINISCENT OF BAS RELIEF SCULPTURE MAKING USE OF GESTURAL BRUSHWORK.

IMPASTO. THE LUSH USE OF PAINT DEFINES THE ESSENCE OF SHELL AND GIVES A DEPTH OF SPIRIT - A CELEBRATION OF JOY OF A DAUGHTER. THE EMPHASIS IS ON EMOTION DISCIPLINED BY A STRONG SENSE OF DESIGN, WHICH ATTEMPTS TO SHOW DIFFERENT PERSPECTIVES OF SHELL'S LIFE EXPERIENCES.

I OFTEN USE RED TO DEPICT SHELL'S STRENGTH OF CHARACTER: A BALANCE BETWEEN STRENGTH AND FEMININITY. SHELL'S FRONTAL POSITION AND ITS MOVEMENT CREATES A "LIVE" CONNECTION AND COMMUNICATION BETWEEN VIEWER AND SUBJECT MATTER, ADDING A SENSE OF LIFE. THE WORKS HERE ARE PART OF A VERY LARGE SERIES ON CANVAS AND PAPER.

SHELL IS MY DAUGHTER AND THE GRANDDAUGHTER OF DR. GEORGE W. SNOWDEN AND MRS. JESSIE BURNS SNOWDEN. THEY HELPED TO SHAPE HER STRENGTH OF CHARACTER AND FORM HER GIVING PERSONALITY.

SHE RECEIVED HER BACHELOR'S DEGREE FROM SYRACUSE UNIVERSITY, DEAN'S LIST, AND ENTERED DEVRY UNIVERSITY.

MY BRUSHWORK EXEMPLIFIES SHELL'S ZEST FOR LIFE, HER EFFORTS TO "GRAB LIFE BY THE HORNS," HER ABILITY TO GET RIGHT UP AFTER LIFE'S UPHEAVALS.

STRENGTH AND FEMININITY.

- SYLVIA SNOWDEN, WASHINGTON, D.C., SEPTEMBER 2022

Shell; Glimpses #20, 2010-2012, acrylic on canvas, 72 x 48 in. (182.9 x 121.9 cm), acquired in 2022

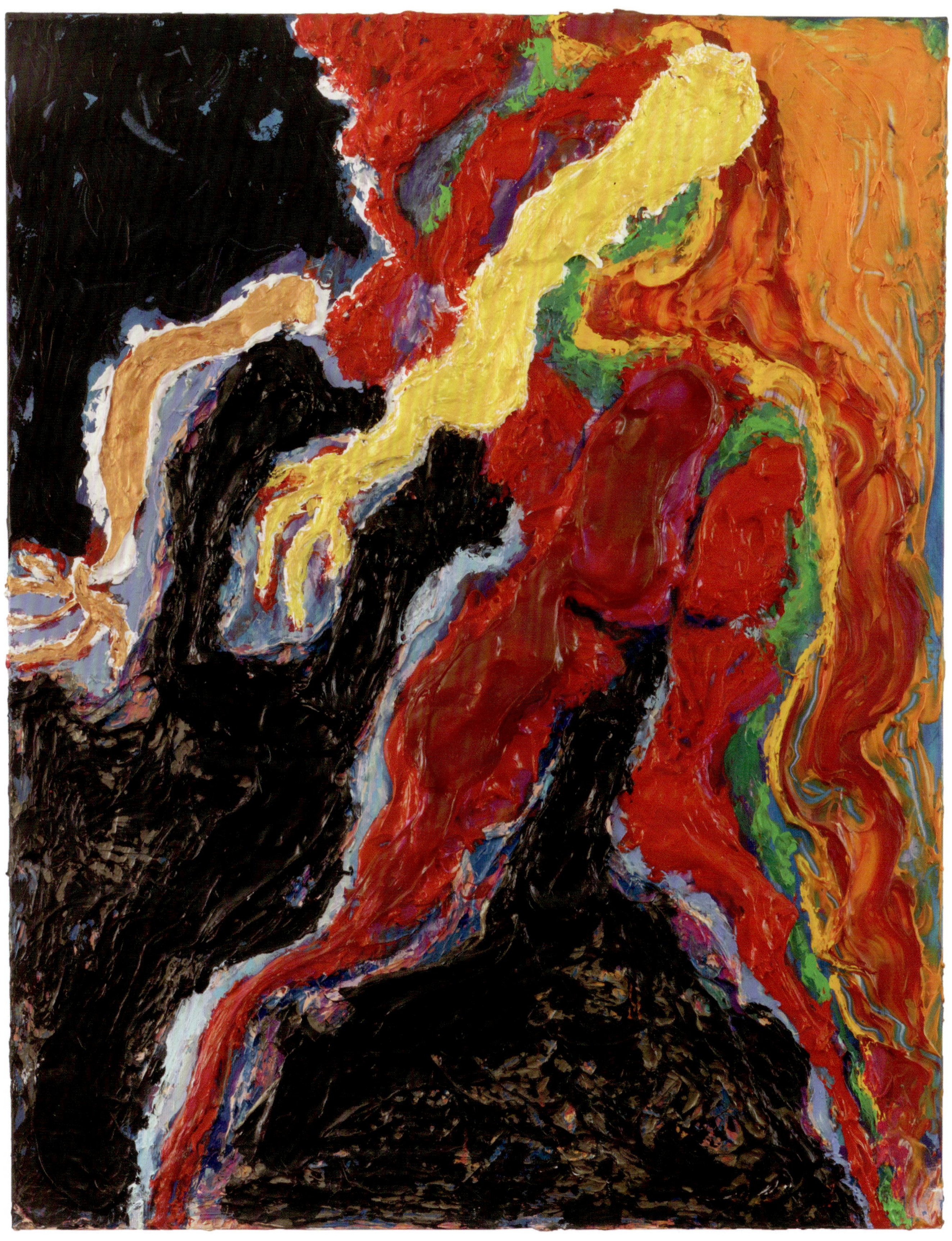

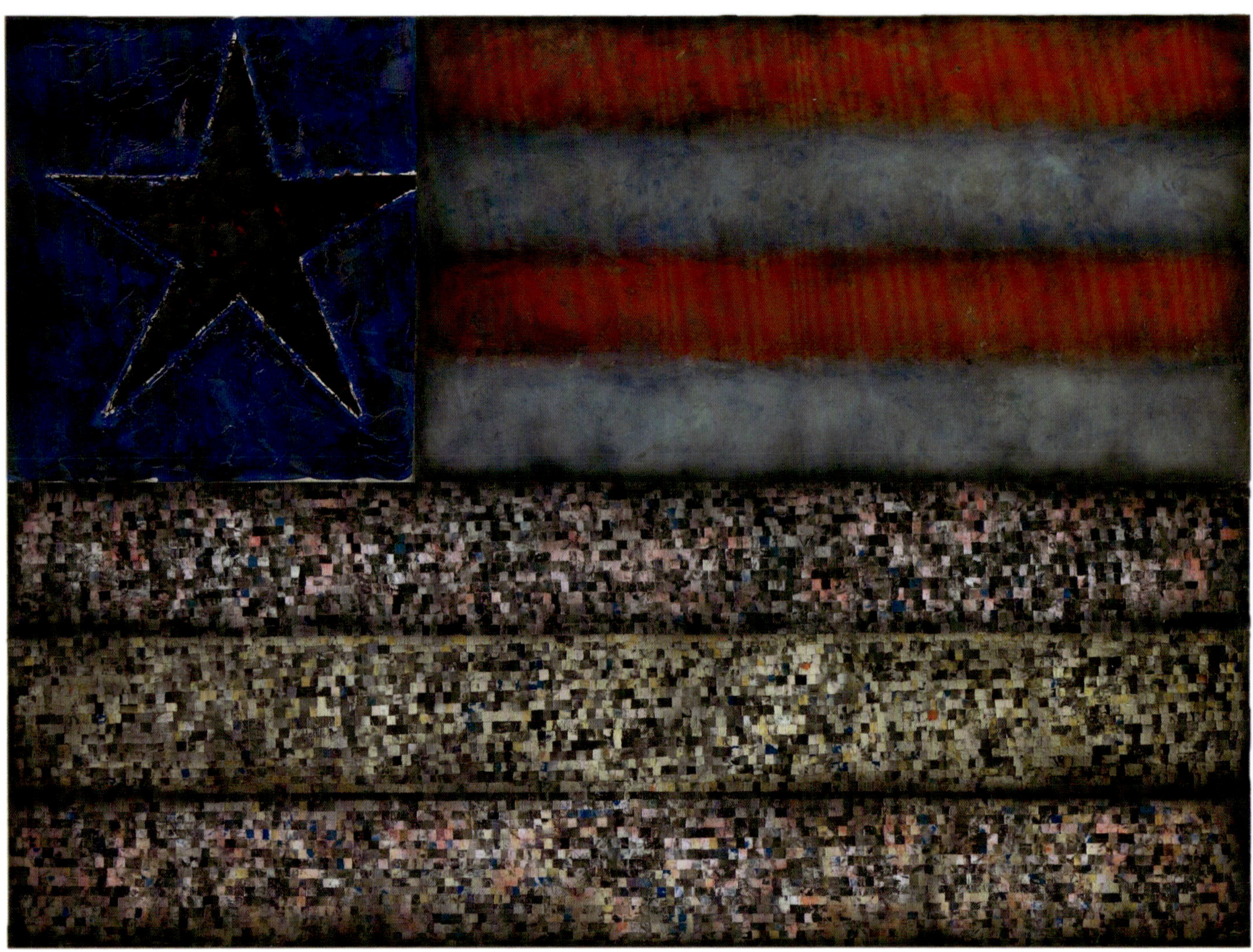

Both paintings center around the idea of hope but also around the idea of gloom or even doom. *Big Black Rainbow (Smoky Eyes)* [opposite] is a work from my rainbow series. Basically, the series began from trying to gather my feelings around the killing of Trayvon Martin that happened several years ago. I just felt this impending sense of despair, and I was trying to search for my own correlation to sort out this idea of hope and to figure out how to pick up the puzzle pieces. For me, as an African American in the U.S., are there any signs of hope? How do we move forward?

A lot of people see the work and for some people it resonates. They ask why there is black in the rainbow and why it looks unique. In the painting itself, there is this inclusion of blackness into the spectrum and an insertion of black on the initial band of the rainbow. There are a lot of shadows and dark recessive spaces as an indication that beyond the hope and fleeting happiness, another rainstorm is always around the corner.

Dark days bring new hope (never forget) is from my *Flag* series. The series is a postmodern idea of how we might take

these symbols, our relationship to these icons, and splice new meanings into them. The title of the piece is about the idea of claiming space and holding on to that proximity to the flag to interpret it on my own. In the painting the flag is very dark; It's a gloomy flag because there's a lot of darkness and trauma we as a nation are perpetually working through.

As an American, but also a Black American in this country, I've always grappled with my relationship and proximity to the flag. Something I think artists have historically challenged is, who gets the right to be patriotic and who doesn't? I think about artists like David Hammons, who created his vision of the pan-African flag as a sort of Black icon. As much as I admire Hammons' interpretation of the flag within the context and time it was made, I always felt like that it centered itself around this otherness, this sense of removing ourselves or positioning ourselves away from the American dichotomy.

I feel that instead of fleeing from our relationship to the American flag, we need to hunker down and claim more of that space but hold true to our historical truths. I really like that position. I, too, am patriotic. This is my home. I can not

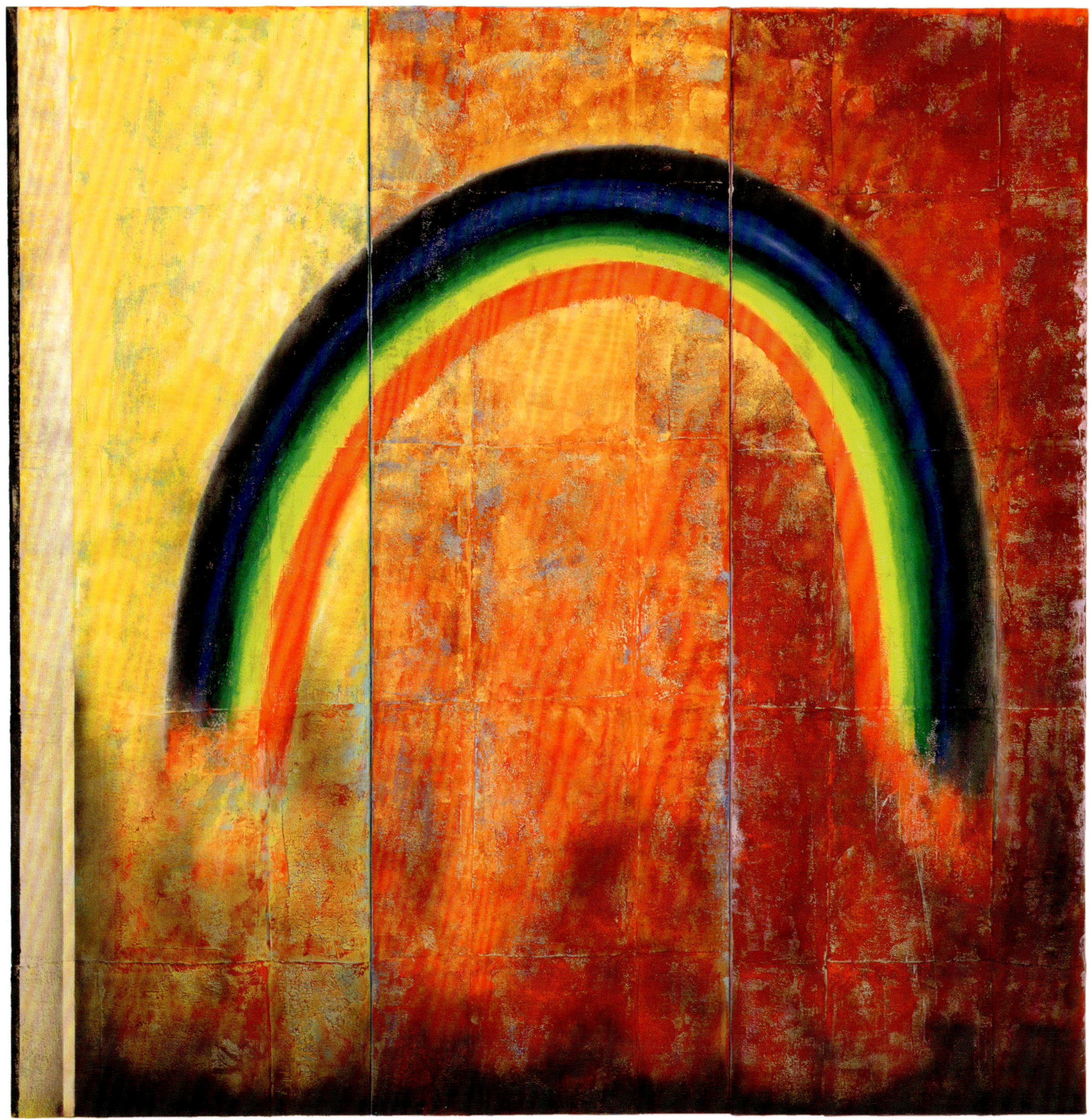

be erased. I, too, am AMERICAN. There's enough room for us here to ruminate collectively.

My granddad was a war vet. I always think about the history of African Americans who have fought for this country. That history—that legacy of them coming home and seeing a country that didn't give a shit about them at all— that's a deep wound. I want to honor those Black Americans who fought for this country. America is all I know. I can't claim another country. For better or for worse, as fucked up as it is, I just have to sit with it and find what it means to me. I feel like that's what a lot of other Black folks in this country have been trying to figure out.

—Vaughn Spann

Opposite page: *Dark days bring new hope (never forget)*, 2020, polymer paint, pulp, mixed media, terry cloth, canvas on aluminum stretcher bars, 160 x 220 in. (406.4 x 558.8 cm), acquired in 2021
Big Black Rainbow (Smoky Eyes), 2019, polymer paint, terry cloth on aluminum stretcher bars, 180 x 180 in. (457 x 457 cm), acquired in 2019

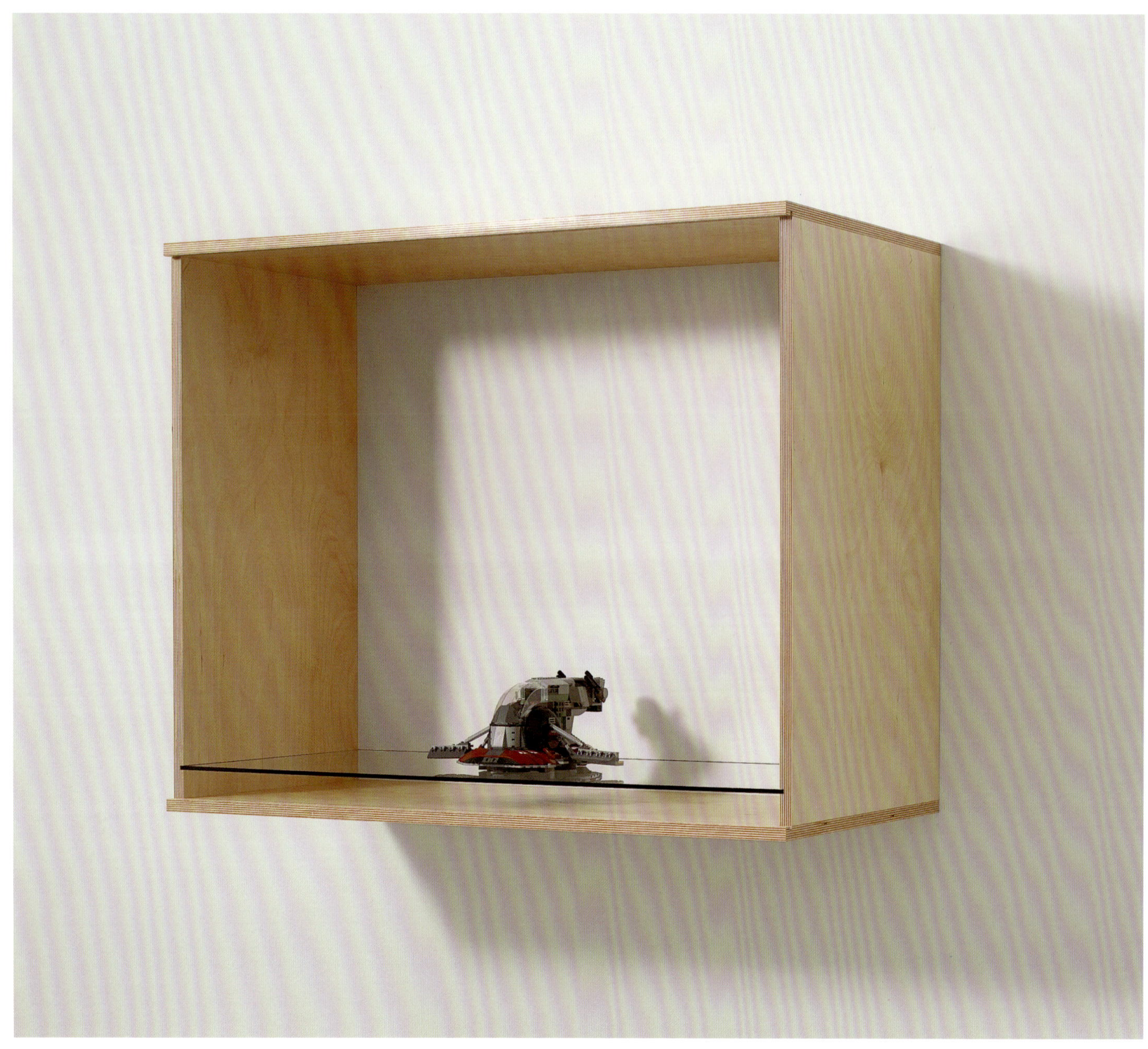

Peter Schwenger: Do you remember what impelled you the very first time you put an object on a shelf, on any kind of shelf? Is that a moment in time that you can recall?

Haim Steinbach: So many things led me to it. For one, In my parents' home in Upstate New York, there was a shelf about 10 inches above the kitchen table, which was pushed against the wall. On that shelf was everything from a small calendar to knickknacks and a flower vase. There were also other little objects there, like the figure of an Israeli boy wearing the typical Israeli hat—a *kova tembel*, which means "silly hat"— and a napkin holder with a lozenge-shaped piece of wood on it. Some things were exchanged for others from time to time. Every time I sat at that kitchen table I would look at that shelf and I would ask, What are these objects doing here? I would

question the decorative details, the cultural associations, the functional reasons for these things to be there.

And so in 1975, as I was turning from painting to sculpture, I made a simple shelf and put a few plastic miniature objects on it. In a way I was just doing what people ordinarily do with the objects that they like. But, at the same time, I was asking myself, What am I doing? What does it mean to be doing this as an artist? This eventually led to my first installations. By 1979, this practice became my work's structuring device. I was placing objects on shelves, on prefabricated shelves or ones I made. Nothing was manipulated to interfere with the function of the shelf or the function of the objects. They sat the way you would normally see them on a table or any piece of furniture. Whatever the objects were—food containers,

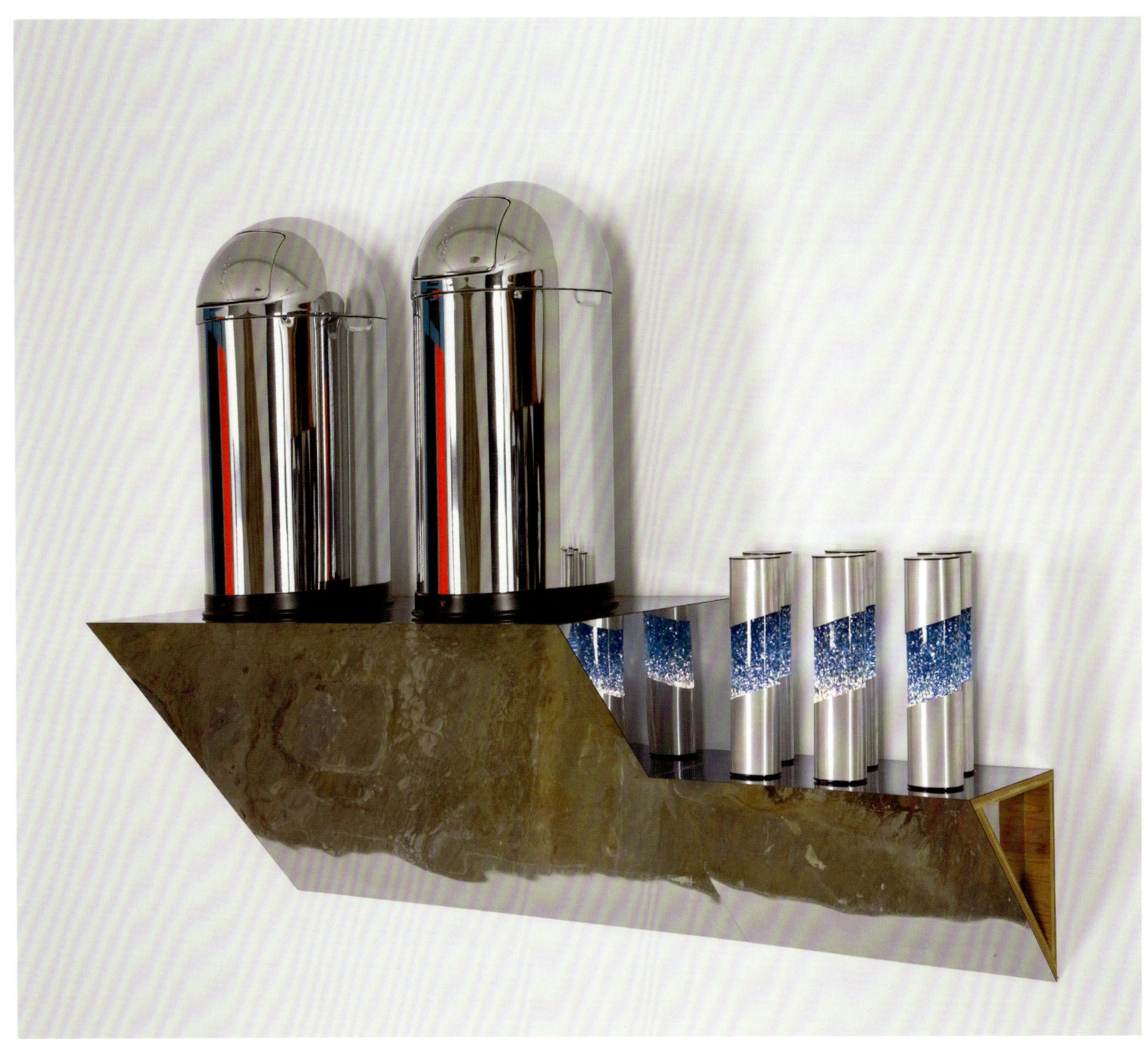

plastic or wooden figurines, etcetera—their design and form was inherent to them. I didn't design that representation, I was just presenting.

PS: But you do choose the objects, and you arrange them. You once said that the objects on a shelf are arranged the way words are arranged in a sentence.

HS: We communicate through objects just as we communicate through language. We see objects, we have feelings about them, and we feel them when we touch them. We know what material they're made of. Sometimes we are not sure: Is this glass or plastic? We touch it, or even lick it. So when you arrange objects, you're talking, you're putting them in a certain way that's part of a conversation. And that's a language; the ordering functions like language in that it allows us to communicate and to get things done. The way I arrange objects in one line is like the way that we arrange words in a sentence.

Opposite page: *slave I*, 2011, Scandinavian birch plywood, plastic laminate and glass box; plastic Lego "Slave 1," 32 1/2 x 40 1/2 x 20 1/2 in. (82.6 x 102.9 x 52.1 cm), acquired in 2011
ultra lite #2, 1988, chrome laminated wood shelf, chromed metal trash cans, glass, metal, wax, and colored oil Gem Lites, 55 x 78 x 21 in. (139.5 x 198 x 53.5 cm), acquired in 1988

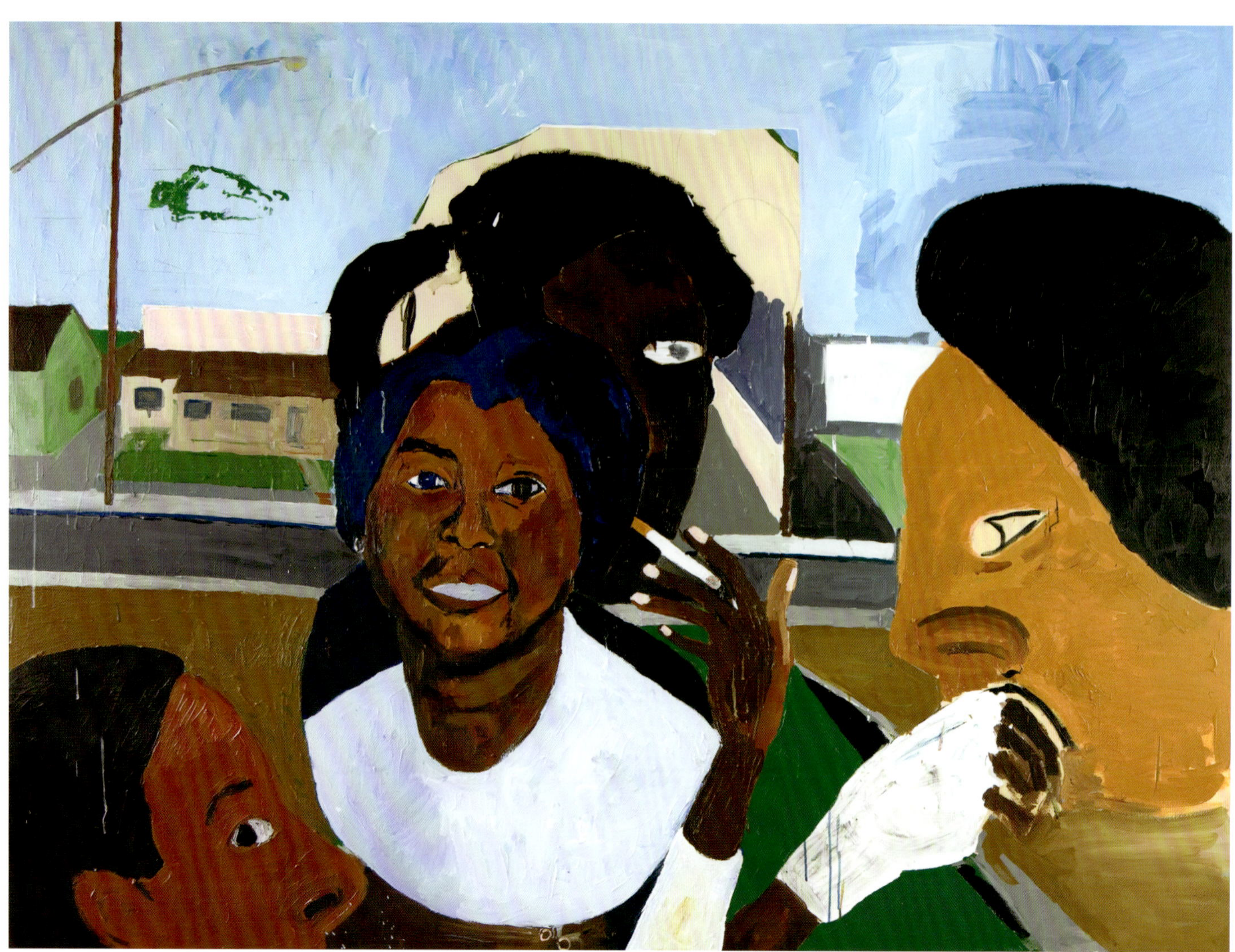

ms. or leah was a neighbor i had had growing up and i thought ms leah was alright. she was from louisiana not too educated and far from dumb. anyway, she was my mom's friend and a neighbor who i found always cordial, pleasant and lets say sincere. that image was taken from her obituary. i 'd visit miss leah on occasion after my mom died and would keep her up to date on things and she seemed to get a kick out of my "success" for lack of a better word.

Lusiana Georgescu was a girlfriend of mine who I've painted and continue to paint. this particular painting was done in her backyard in santa cruz one summer.

fuck that previous shit I wrote it was really Bigger Thomas and not me. Love Pam. That painting is of a cousin of mine by the name of Alister who was just visiting me and I had him sit for that/this portrait, but the title is the name of an old friend that I went to high school with and the only person from my graduating class that I know who majored subject-wise in art. And behind that sitter Alister Gaston was a joseph beuys postcard [original grafic serie1./Koln/Nr.16 Koln offset/ edition staeck.69 heidelberg1.Postfach 471] that she sent to me in 1978 from Germany. my old friend Pam

i think we should smell/spell luciana with an s, lusiana my bad. so, i've been out but i'm back! how in the hell is Big Don? Tell em he's my frickin idol! that gyno! now you think i'm some kind of freak huh — caroline but if you only knew, when i asked Big "D" what was his occupation you should have heard him, it was classic and since then well he's become the man. i must admit i, fuck i'm trippin but really though … i wish i could say what i wanted to say w/ out someone thinking and winking. right now i'm happy i'm alive. anyway, about #3, its title is oh henry right well, that painting is of a person duh … but caroline that day i was walking and walking's good as long as there are no landmines, anyway, i was walking and i saw this man staring up i don't remember if he had his hand out but to me even if he did what i saw was no bum but simply a being and instantly it was a more spiritual THANG! the underground kang, so it ain't and never was about me henry. it was just a sweet moment underneath "oh hennery" is a candy bar u know that so the moment was sweet even though i wish i could have helped my bro … sorry. there's a story there somewhere i g ya tee ya. you know how they say, "angels are among us" well maybe that's whats i'm talking about, however, i'm not sure. cut the cake   —Henry Taylor

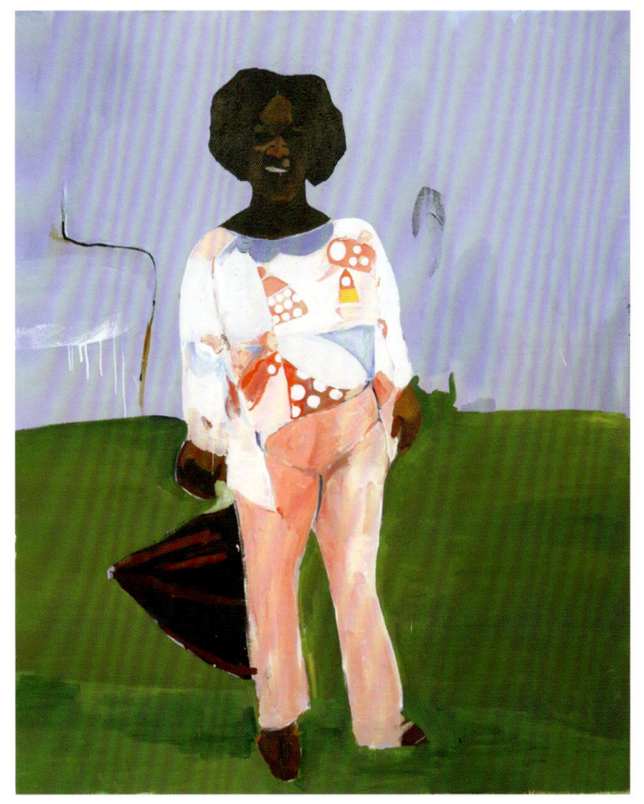

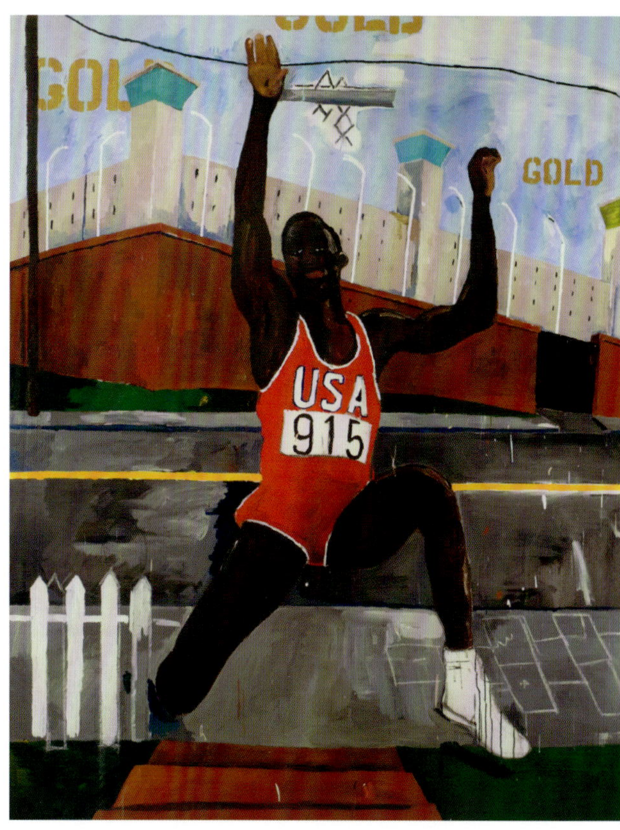

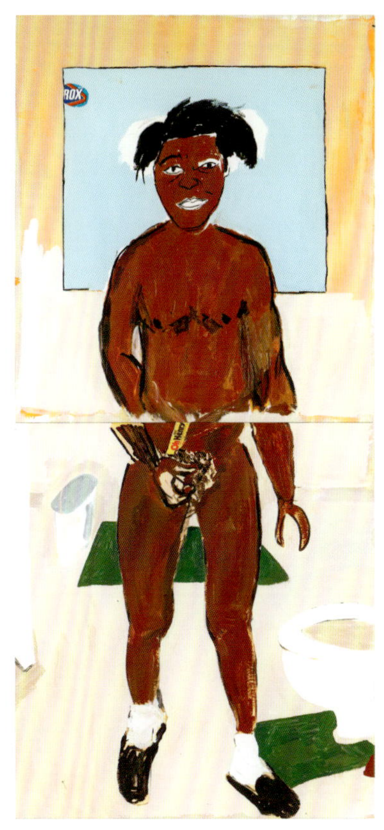

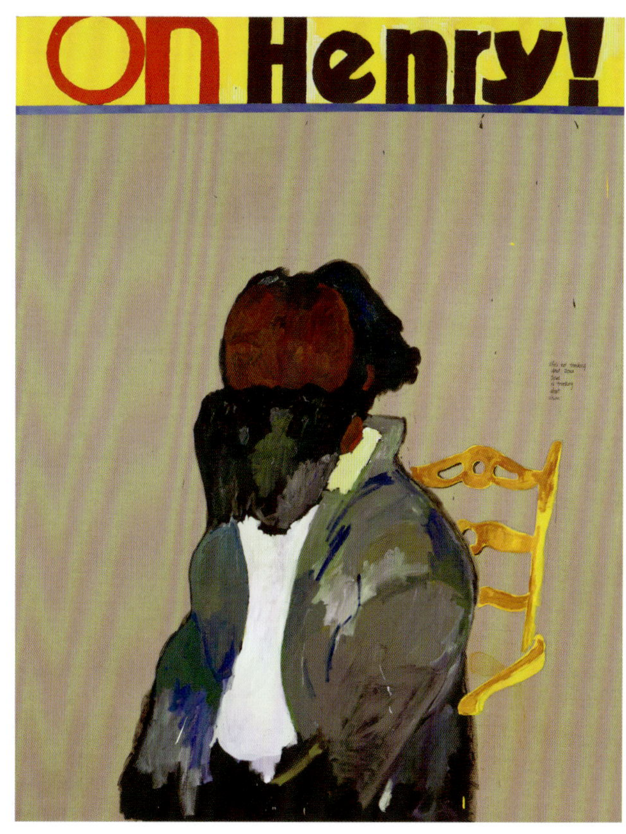

Opposite page: *Miss Leah*, 2008, acrylic on canvas, 68 3/4 x 92 1/4 in. (161.9 x 235 cm), acquired in 2008
Above, clockwise from top left: *Watts County*, 2004, acrylic on canvas, 76 x 61 1/2 in. (193 x 156.2 cm), acquired in 2005
The Long Jump by Carl Lewis, 2010, acrylic on canvas, 87 1/2 x 77 in. (222.3 x 195.6 cm), acquired in 2012
Oh Henry, 2004, acrylic on canvas, candy bar wrapper, 96 x 48 in. (243.8 x 121.92 cm), acquired in 2022
Oh Henry, 2006, acrylic on canvas, 96 x 76 in. (243.8 x 193 cm), acquired in 2006

I had been making a lot of images that looked like ads for a series called *Unbranded*, and they were speaking to issues related to the exploitation of primarily the Black male body in popular culture, but also in history—looking at slavery and commodity culture in general. In the midst of that, I was doing a talk somewhere or maybe showing some of my work, and someone gave me an ad for a 2001 Toyota Rav4 that had an African American male's mouth smiling with bright white teeth. In the middle was a gold tooth in the shape of the Toyota Rav4. The person who gave me the ad said, "You should do something with this." It almost seemed like the truth was better than fiction. I had been trying to make work to speak to these issues, but they were actually still very present and maybe more potent in real life. I realized that with any ad, the moment you remove the text and the logos all you're left with is the photograph, and basically the photograph tells us what's really for sale. I had been talking about the ways that Black bodies were used to sell things, and then here we have Japanese cars being sold through gold teeth as kind of a value system that's attributed to African American men.

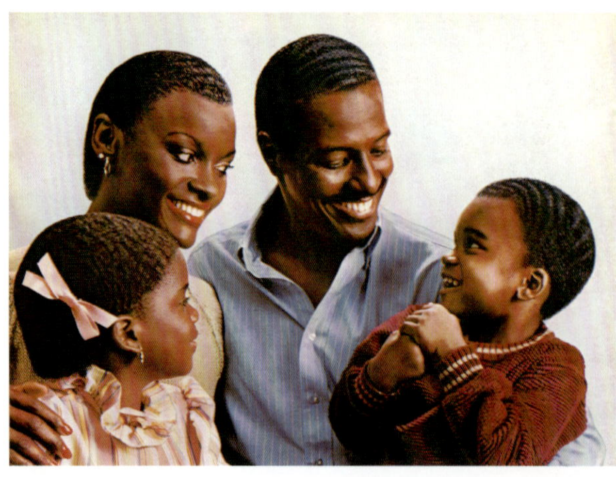

I wanted to look at how real ads could tell stories about the way we learn identity and culture, etc. I think about advertisement as a form of social conditioning and almost brainwashing, and that it's where we learn what our values are in our society. You look at most ads and the actual image has nothing to do with the product. It's only the myths and generalizations that we have that bring to light this kind of logic that makes an ad work. I started this series that ultimately became *Unbranded: Reflections in Black by Corporate America*. I removed the text from two ads for every year from 1968 to 2008, and I really wanted to track Blackness in the corporate eye over the course of 40 years. I chose 1968 because it was the symbolic end of the Civil Rights Movement, when Martin Luther King and RFK were assassinated. I chose 2008 pretty randomly, but it ultimately wound up being the year that the U.S. elected its first president of African decent. That means it's bookended by these two historic events. The fact that most of the people who were making the ads for Black people to consume—then and now—were white men on Madison Avenue, basically, I found fascinating. So, the values that are created, are they "Black" values? Or are they just generic American—some people might call it "white"—values that are being projected onto the African American community? By "unbranding" advertisements, I can literally expose what Roland Barthes referred to as *what-goes-without-saying* in their images, and hopefully encourage viewers to look harder and think deeper about the empire of signs that have become second nature to our experience of life in the modern world.
—Hank WIllis Thomas

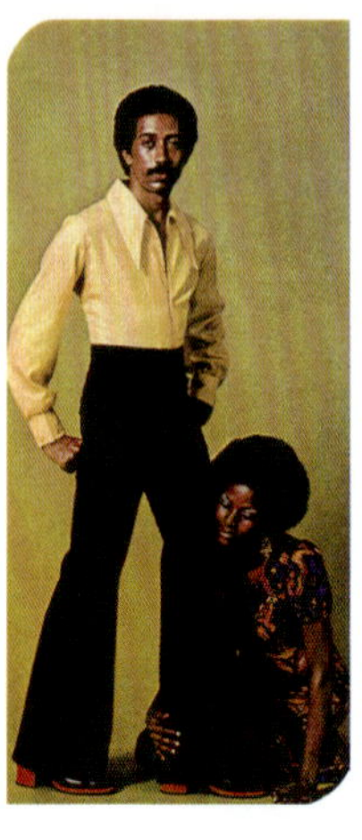

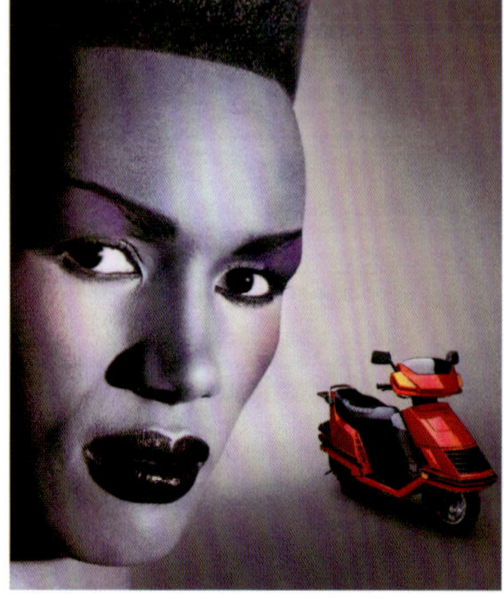

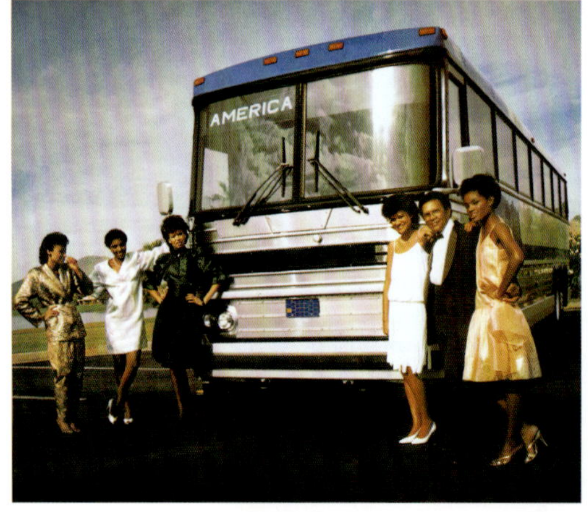

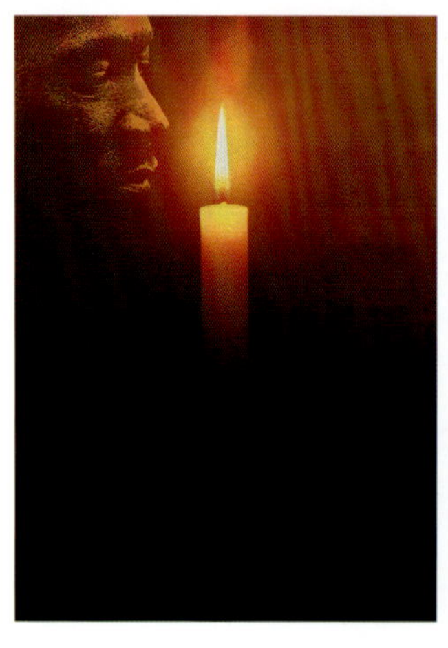

Unbranded (detail), 2006-2007, eighty-two Lambda photographs, dimensions variable, acquired in 2007

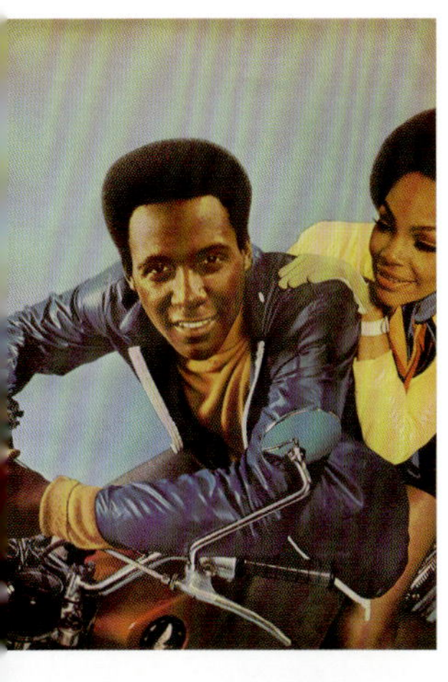
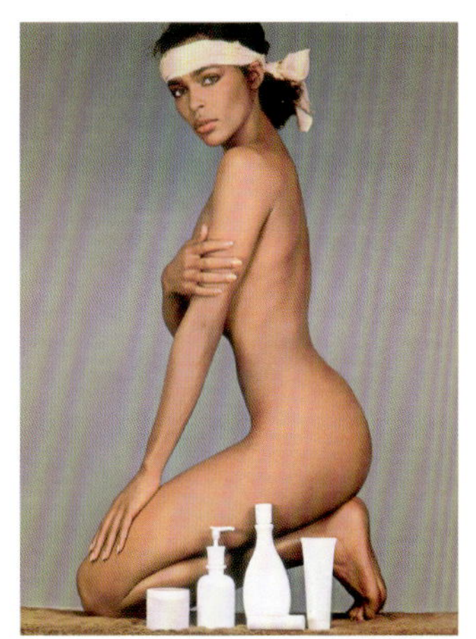
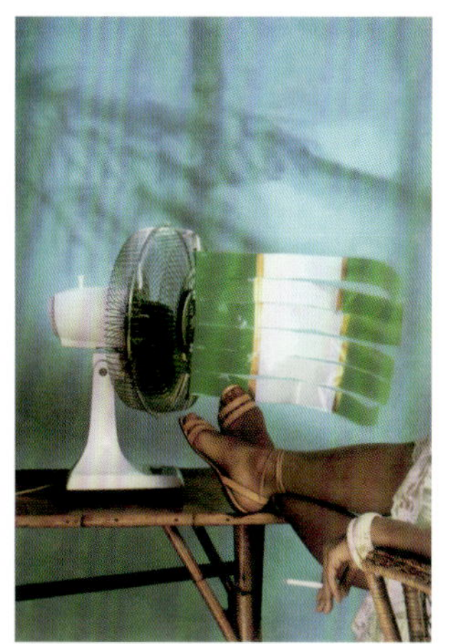
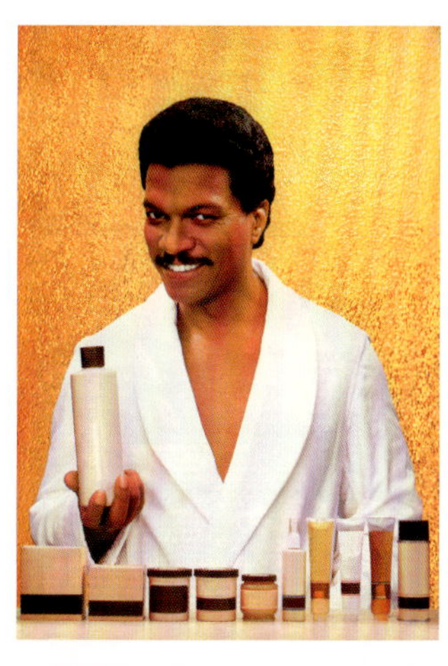
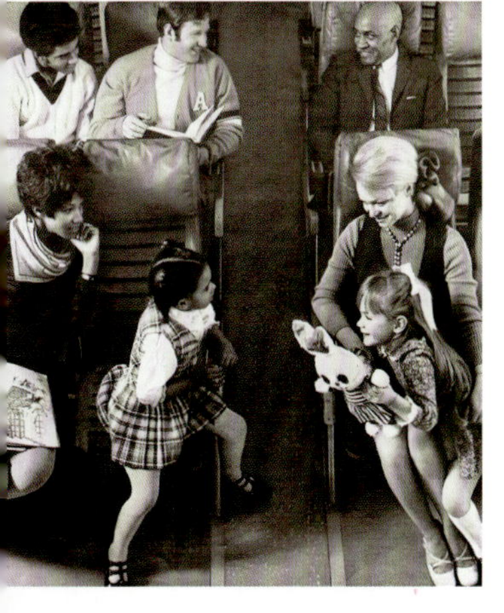
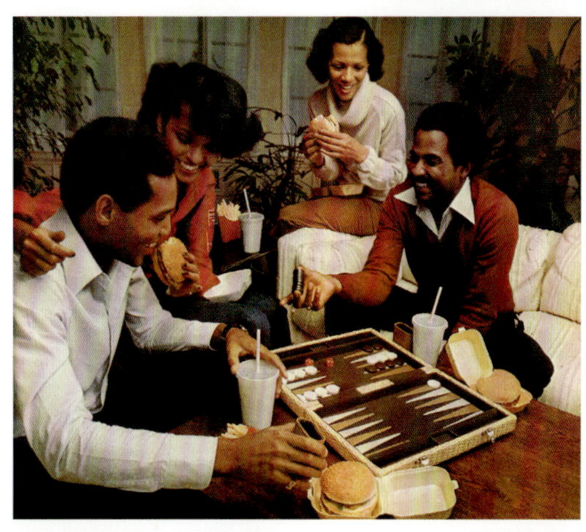
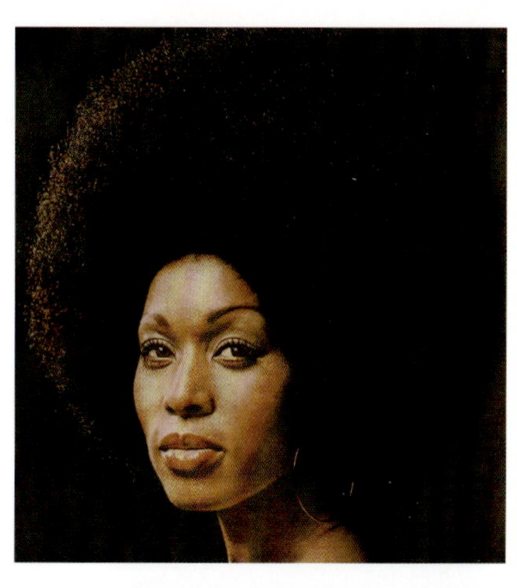
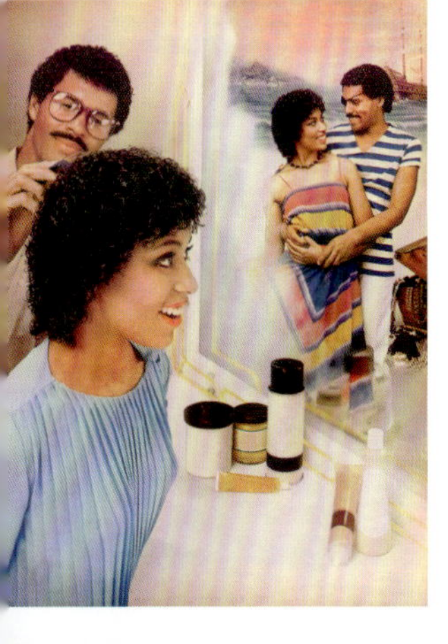
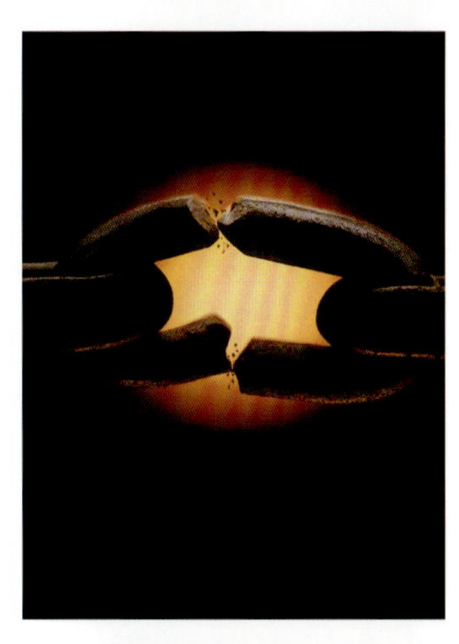
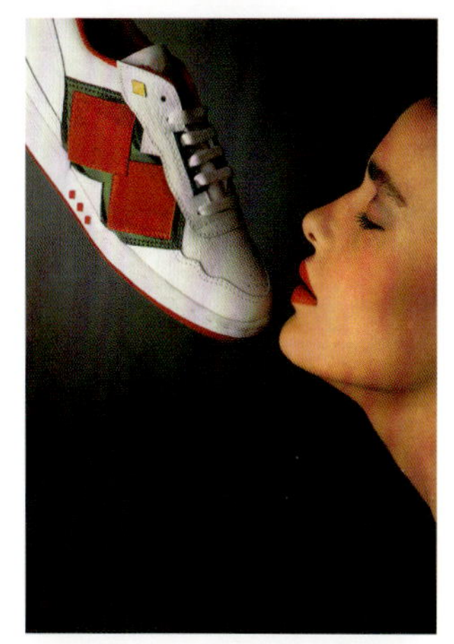
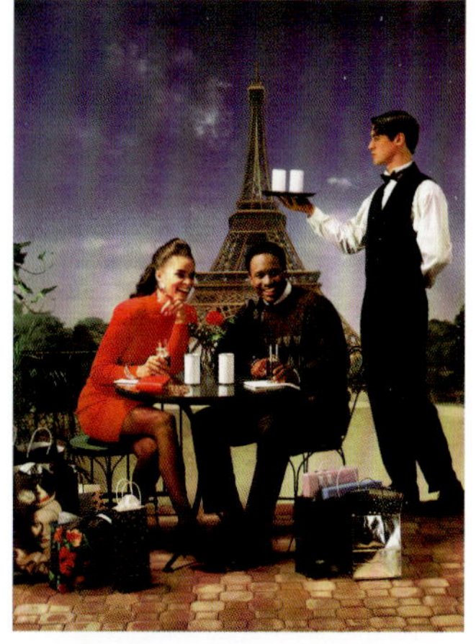
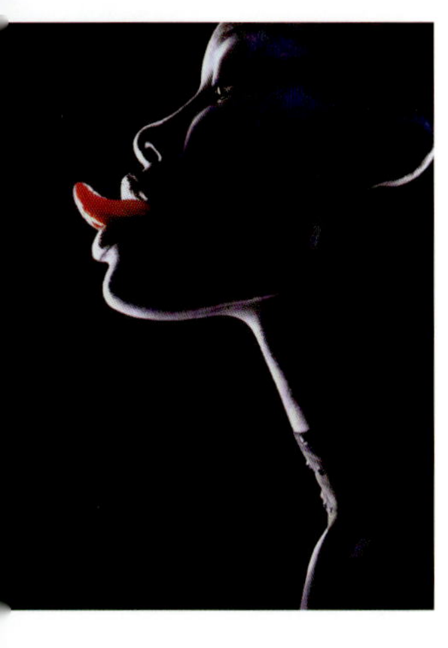
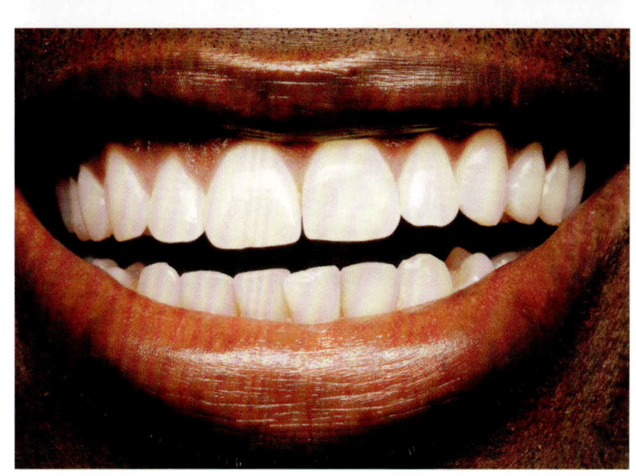
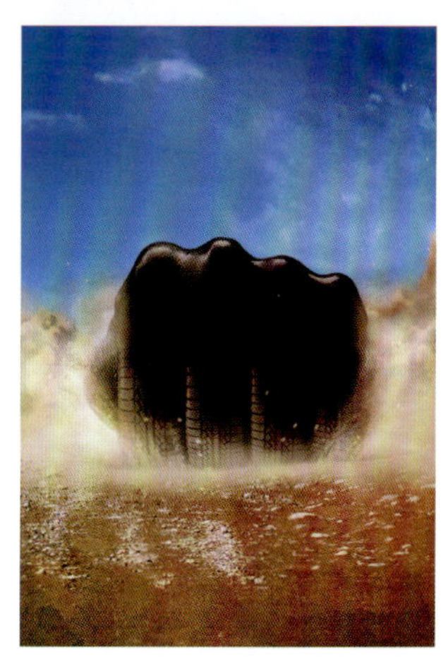

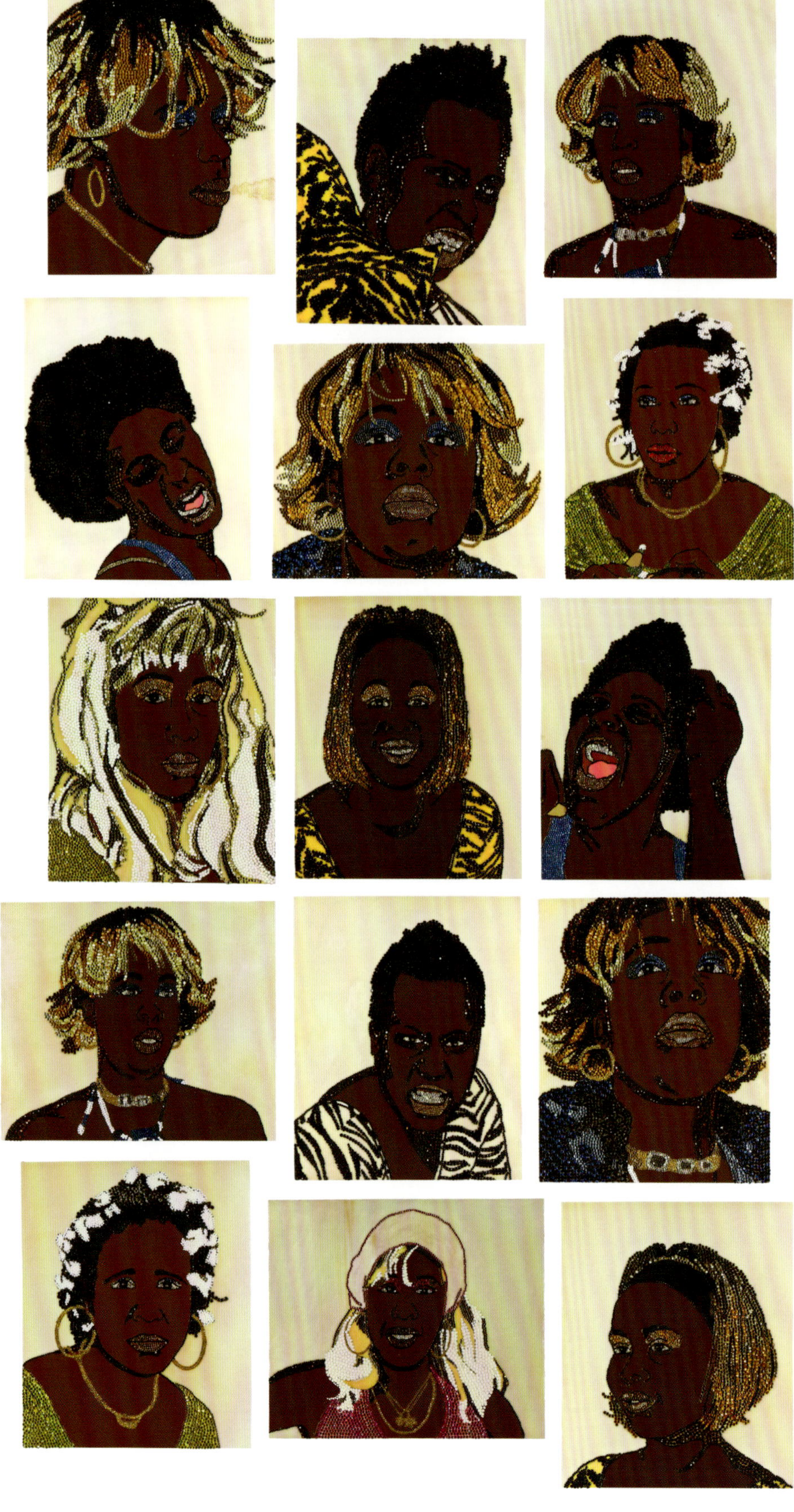

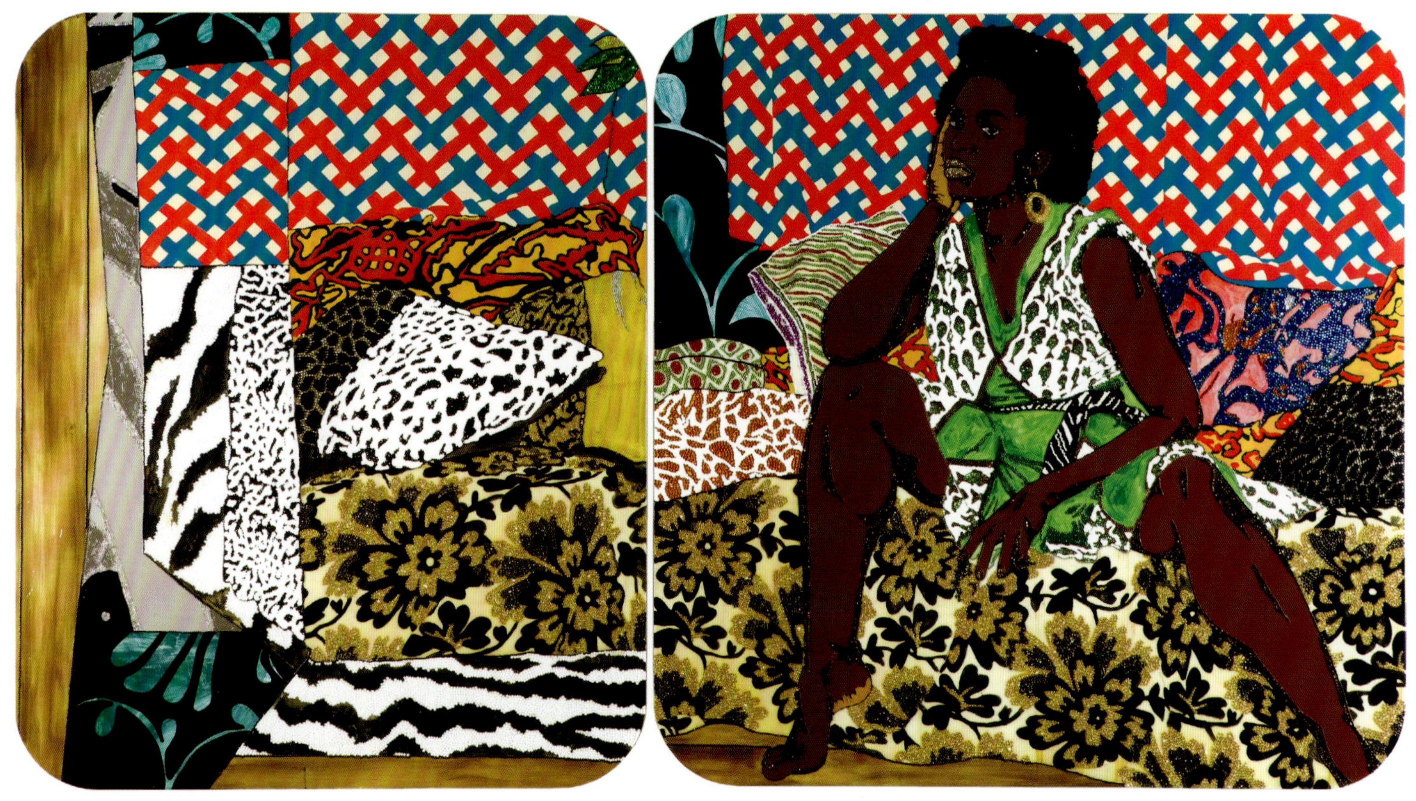

Portraits of Quanikah continues the deconstructive work of self-portraiture begun in the *Brawlin Spitfire* series. Each panel spotlights a different aspect of my own personality in the guise of my alter egos—Quanikah and the Amazonian wrestler. This piece heralds a formal shift in the paintings, breaking the pictorial space into different physical planes and using the grid as an overt reference to photo booth portraits, Pop Art and Andy Warhol in particular. These formal developments carry into my later paintings, further complicating and enriching the subject matter of self, muse, and painting. While *Portraits of Quanikah* is unmistakably a self-portrait, representative of an historical genre with specific parameters and traditions, it is a self-portrait that reflects a contemporary conception of the bifurcated self.

In *Baby I Am Ready Now*, the profusion of different, shifting patterns dominates. This painting is the first that I made working directly from a source collage. The method of collage naturally encourages the fracturing of spatial planes and breaks up the linear flow of composition. The basis of the work, however, rests firmly in the photograph taken in the installation I created as a specific interior space for the model. As a diptych, the piece sets up two opposing but complementary fields. On one side is a figure in an interior space, absorbed in her thoughts. On the other side, the space breaks down into abstract patterns without the centering presence of the figure, allowing her to be present and seen.

—Mickalene Thomas

Opposite page: *Portraits of Quanikah*, 2006, acrylic, rhinestones, and enamel on wood, 15 panels, each 24 x 20 in. (61 x 50.8 cm); overall 70 x 126 in. (178.8 x 320 cm), acquired in 2006
Baby I Am Ready Now, 2007, acrylic, rhinestones, and enamel on wood, diptych; left panel 72 x 60 in (182.9 x 154.2 cm); right panel 72 x 72 in (182.9 x 182.9 cm); overall 72 x 132 in. (182.9 x 335.3 cm), acquired in 2007

2020 Artist in Residence

Mother Saint Rebekah (2020) is the second piece that I created during my 2020 residency, and I'm so grateful for this piece. I would say this is a mother saint, and I've been referring to her as Mother Rebekah or Saint Rebekah. We're introduced to Saint Rebekah in the Book of Genesis. She is the wife of Isaac, and she is the mother of two very, very important sons—Jacob and Esau. Rebekah was a fine woman. She had an older man named Isaac, and she was about 40 years old when she gave birth to her kids. And to be honest with you, during this experience, I have been absolutely reminded about the strength that a woman offers the land. I truly believe that we are only, as a people, as strong as the women of our land are allowed to be. That was the inspiration going into the work, and that is the inspiration that drove a lot of the work that I was able to create while I was in my residency.

Throughout 2020, when I was making this work, there were so many children, women, and men who were lost, and our streets were turmoiled with Black, brown, and white marchers. I was given the unique and esteemed challenge of channeling all of the energy and all of the sadness that I felt when we lost Mother RBG, when we lost Brianna Taylor. You've got to put that energy somewhere really positive and into a space that gives back. I am so grateful when I am able to paint a mother saint. I feel challenged, I feel blessed, and I feel capable. I want to take a moment always to kiss and hug the mothers of our world—those who are seen and those who are unseen. I'm really more excited to offer you a piece that should lend toward empowerment.

When I was a little girl, I would go over to my grandmother's house every day after school. Nana, my grandmother, was a schoolteacher for over 30 years. As soon as she got home, Nana would start dinner, which meant that I was at the kitchen table drawing in between my homework pages and textbook pages, but, you know, getting my homework done. And my grandmother would sing and she would hum. And then the phone would ring, and then she'd pick up the phone, and she's still cooking. And then she would add a little of this, and then she'd open this cupboard and add some more of that. And you'd never see where she's pulling this magic from. You'd also never see a measuring cup. She would turn to me every now and again to make sure I was tending to my lesson, but she didn't miss a beat. It was absolutely magnificent. It was more than dinner. It was a process of caring, of loving the family, enriching the family. It was a process of art. I didn't know then that my grandmother was teaching me the process of layering. As a painter, it's almost a habit to create layer after layer. One layer feeds the next layer. One mistake feeds the next victory, which feeds the next blessing. I think one of the greatest things we can do as artists is make mistakes.

So often people have asked me how I know when to stop. Well,

how do you know when the food tastes good? You feel it in your gut. You taste it just a little bit. So, sometimes I lean into the piece, and I listen and I engage with each layer until it tells me I'm done, I've had enough. With *Mother Saint Rebekah* it stopped with a very rich, very light pink background in comparison to the strength of the mother saint. The piece, to me, feels very feminine and very complete. And it also feels incredibly necessary. Though it came as the second portrait I painted, it was the beginning of a new process while here. There are different materials in this piece than in the piece prior. So, again, those layers help me to get to the next point that God needs me to be at.

Hold on, I am Following (2020) is a portrait of Jacob. In the Bible, Jacob is said to have wrestled with God. When I was here in residency there were plenty of times when I wrestled with the Lord. I wrestled with the idea of success, with the idea of failure. I wrestled with the idea of family, of love, of loss. I needed this residency because it provided me a safe space to be all of me, and when is a woman offered a safe space to be vulnerable? Oh, my goodness—it's magic, truly. When you're given an opportunity to be blessed in that way, it allows you to be completely present for what it is you're being called to do. It definitely gave me a space to ask questions and to be really human because though these were saints that made great mistakes, they were still used by God. I just want to be used by God, so it's really encouraging for me to read the narrative of others who have come before me, whether it's real or not. It gives me strength, and it has helped me to build language in prayer, in paint, in song, in dance.

I think the risks we take as artists within the artist community are going to change the world. Jacob and Esau were born in the same womb. Why does it matter what the color of one's skin is if they were brothers? How dare we use something that God gave us as our greatest reason to separate. You can look at my skin and see us as different if you want to, but what this residency proved to me is that we are all in this boat together, and we had better be better by each other. This is the opportunity that God has given us to strengthen not just ourselves, but the person to your right, the person to your left, and especially the ones you don't know.

Covered by the Blood, Self-Reflection (2020) is the last painting I made during my residency. Juan had stretched two more 8-by-8-sized canvases for me. The studio was ready for me to come back to it, and I was very excited, except in my mind I was thinking that I'm really only supposed to paint one more—that's what I gained from prayer. And I did. I came in and I did what I was supposed to do, and a couple of nights before the end of the residency, I came in for closing prayer. And man, I really thought I was done, but when I came out of prayer, I had two brushes—one brush in each hand—and

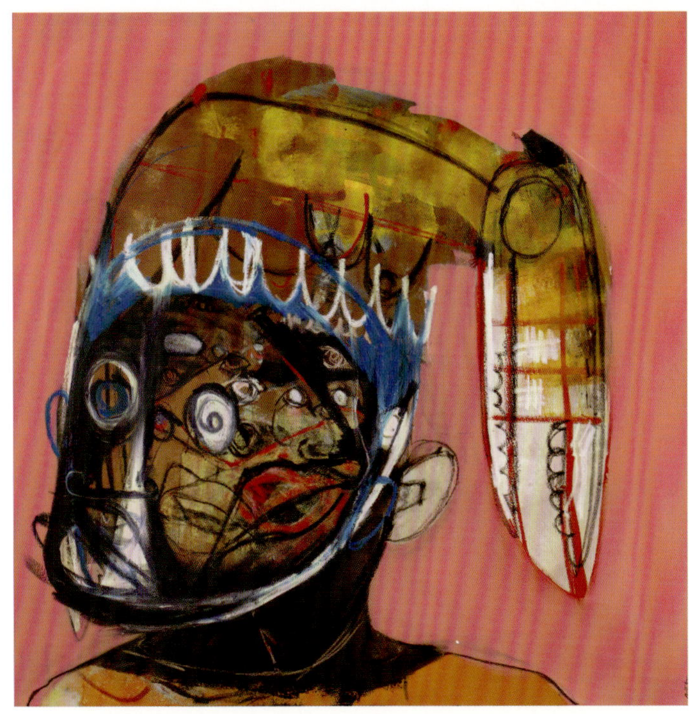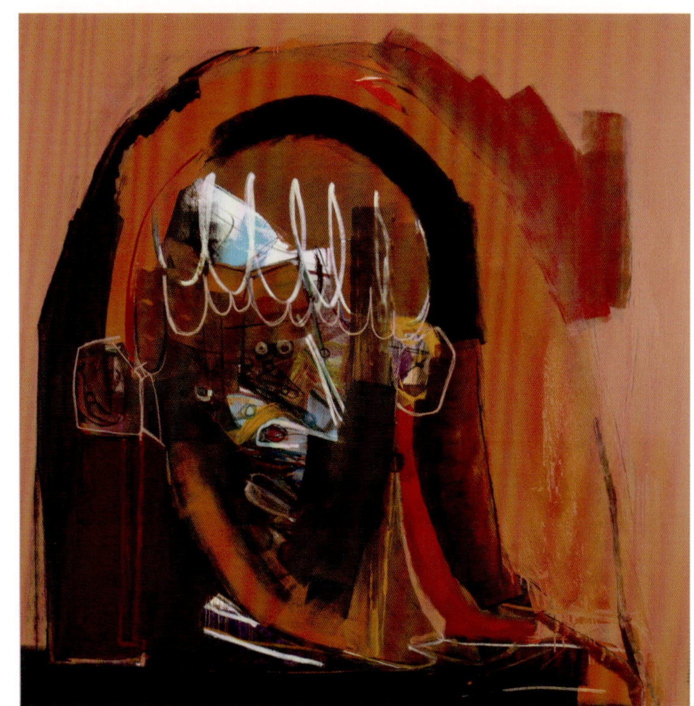

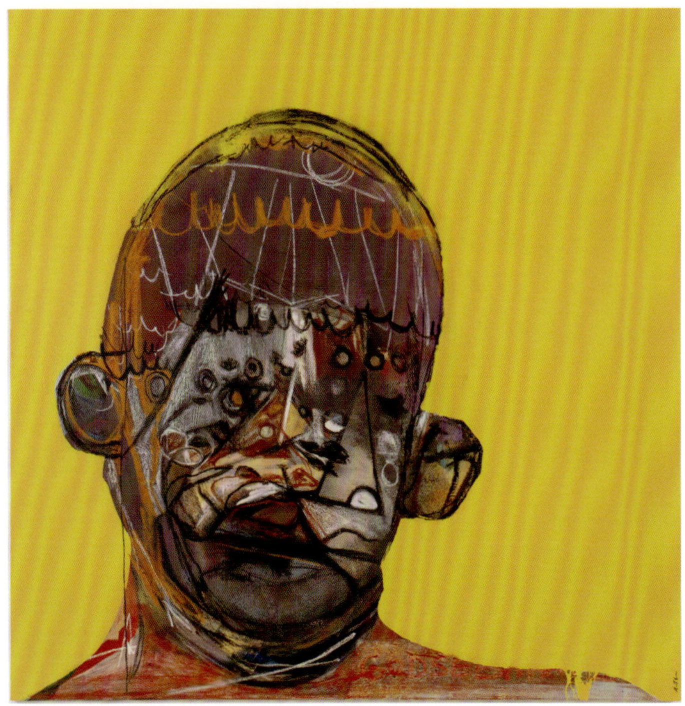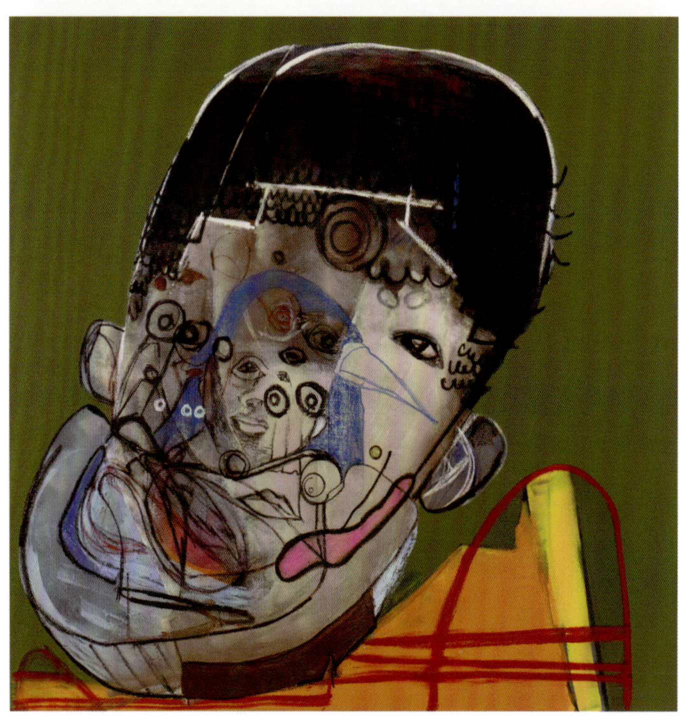

I was back at it. And I mean, I danced. Oh, my goodness. I remember lots of joyous tears. I gave such praise over the work. I gave such praise over the space I was closing, except I was closing in prayer, closing while working, while delivering. I remember a grave space of silence, and then I came out with a self-portrait, a self-reflection.

You cannot look at the story of Jacob and Esau without self-reflecting. Esau was the elder of a fraternal twin set; I am the elder of my siblings. The color red in this piece is most important because Esau was said to have been born with red hair. When I'm in the sun for too long, my hair and skin change, and since I've been in this beautiful Miami heat I've ntoiced this undertone of the color red. It is also said that when you go into a space, an unknown space, that it's okay to ask God to cover you with the blood, and so the name of the work is *Covered by the Blood, Self-Reflection*. —Genesis Tramaine

Clockwise from top left: *Mother. Saint. Rebekah*, 2020, acrylic, oil sticks, spray paint, oil pastels, and the Holy Spirit, 72 x 72 in. (182.9 x 182.9 cm), acquired in 2020; *Covered by the Blood, Self-Reflection*, 2020, acrylic, oil sticks, spray paint, oil pastels, Gravy Masters Browning Sauce, and the Holy Spirit, 96 x 96 in. (243.8 x 243.8 cm), acquired in 2020; *Hold on, I am Following*, 2020, acrylic, oil sticks, spray paint, oil pastels, and the Holy Spirit, 72 x 72 in. (182.9 x 182.9 cm), acquired in 2020; *Forgive Yourself*, 2020, acrylic, oil sticks, spray paint, oil pastels, Lawry's Sea Salt, and the Holy Spirit, 72 x 72 in. (182.9 x 182.9 cm), acquired in 2020

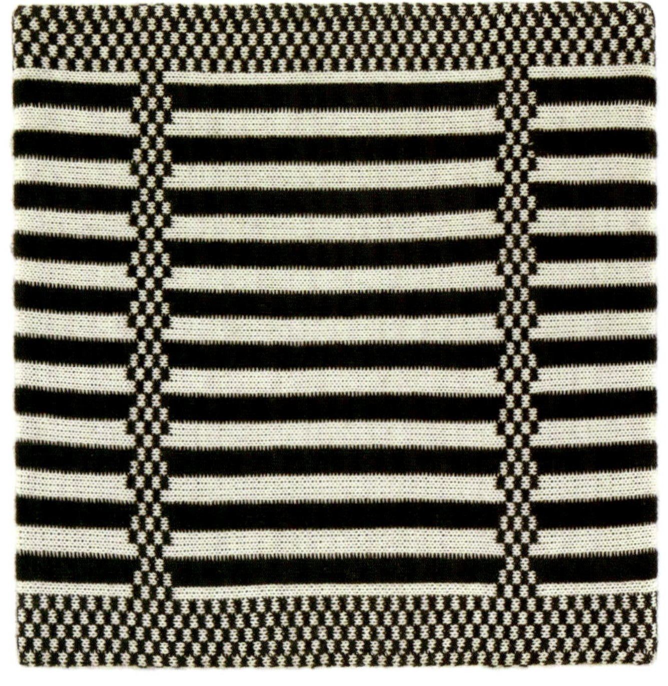

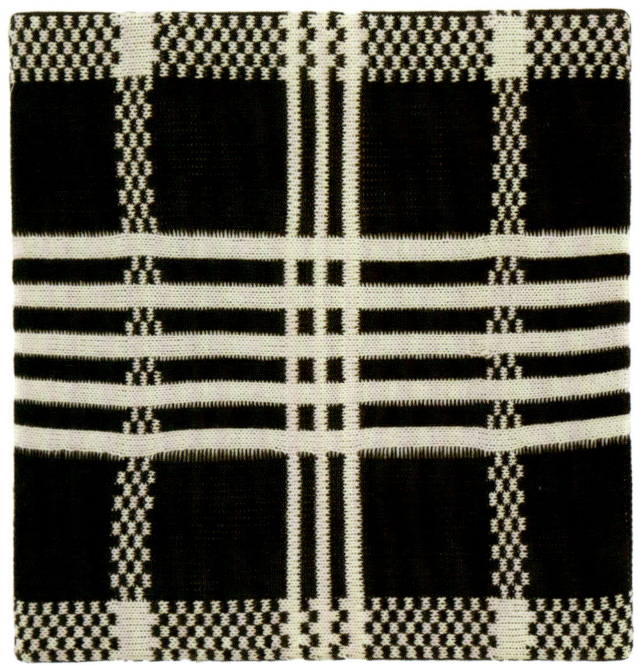
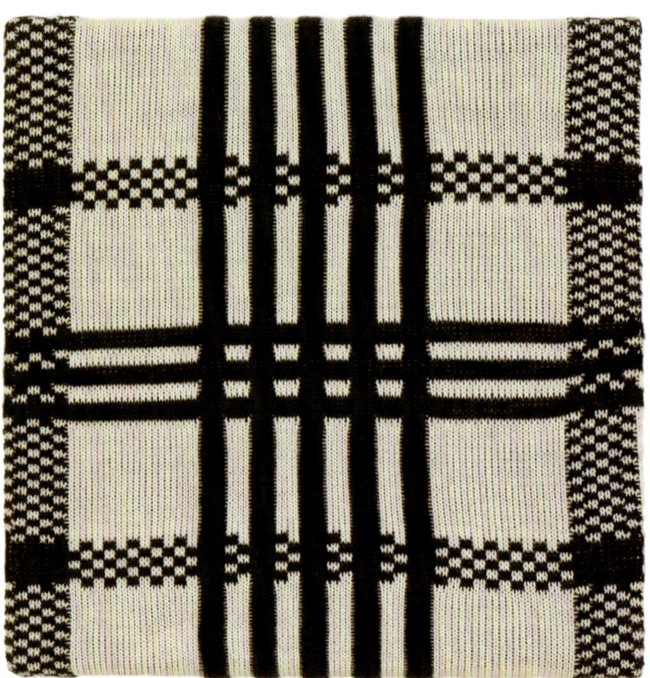

Untitled, 1986, wool, 14 1/2 x 14 1/2 in. (36.8 x 36.8 cm), acquired in 1986
Untitled, 1986, wool, 14 1/2 x 14 1/2 in. (36.8 x 36.8 cm), acquired in 1986
Untitled, 1986, wool, 14 1/2 x 14 1/2 in. (36.8 x 36.8 cm), acquired in 1986
Untitled, 1986, wool, 14 1/2 x 14 1/2 in. (36.8 x 36.8 cm), acquired in 1986
Opposite page: *Untitled*, 1990, wool, ed. of 5, 78 1/2 x 59 in. (200 x 150 cm), acquired in 2004

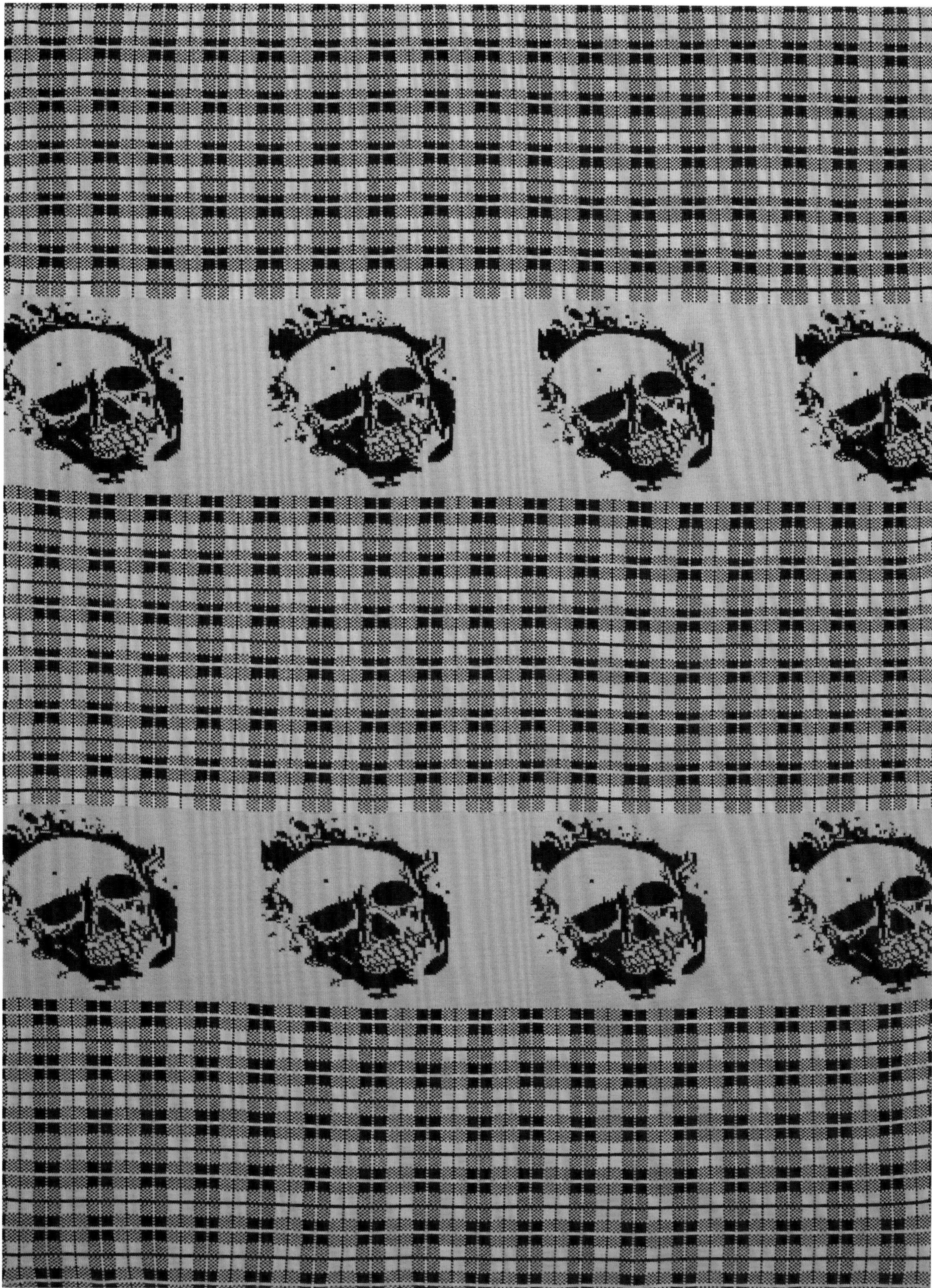

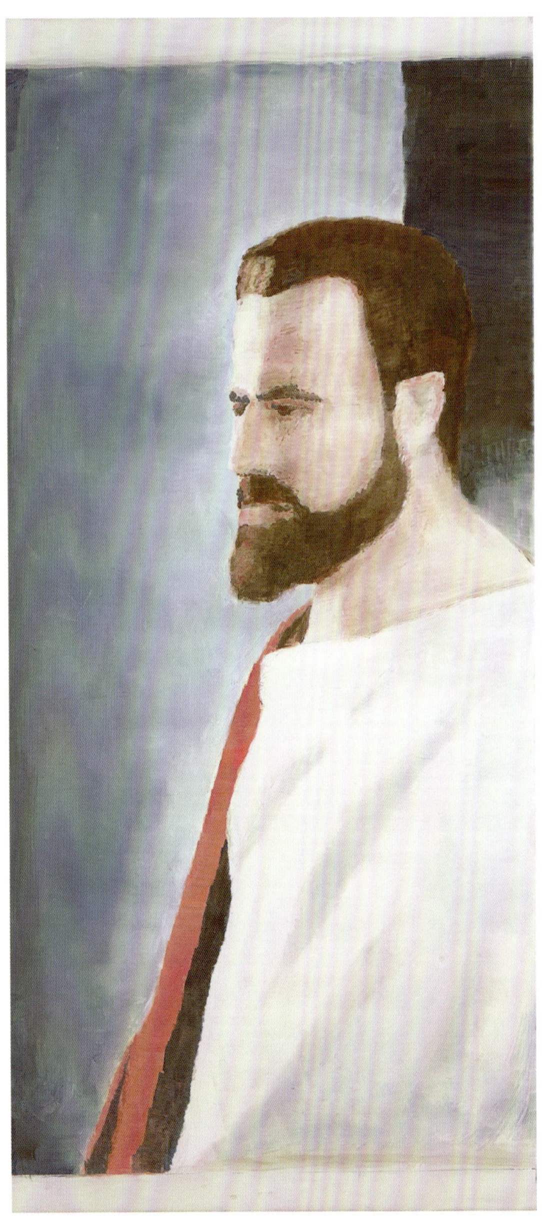

Christ is part of the *Passion* Series, which depicts scenes from the Passion Play in Oberammergau, Germany. The image of Christ comes from a brochure for the play, a source that implicates the role of advertisements and pamphlet publications in the distribution of religious subject matter. At the upper and lower edges of the canvas, white stripes reference the physical page from which the original photograph derived.

The painting is not specifically about Jesus Christ per se; but moreover, it is about the theatrical reenactment that is a longstanding tradition dating back to the 17th century. In this sense, the painting is an oblique representation of remembrance. The mimicry of the play is complemented by the handling of the paint, which imitates the style of the famous Dutch forger Hans van Meegeren. I have referred to my paintings as "authentic forgeries," but this series is the singular instance in which I have explicitly employed a style that is not my own.

The Oberammergau Passion Play was first performed in the 17th century as a plea to the Lord for protection from the bubonic plague. The townsmen survived and as a sign of their gratitude to God, they vowed to perform the play ritually every 10 years. Its legacy was badly tarnished during World War II when Adolph Hitler sat in attendance, and the play became associated with Nazi propaganda and anti-Semitism. The confluence of these disparate associations and backstory makes the series of paintings even more complex, dealing with issues of religious rituals, advertising and entertainment, propaganda and memory.

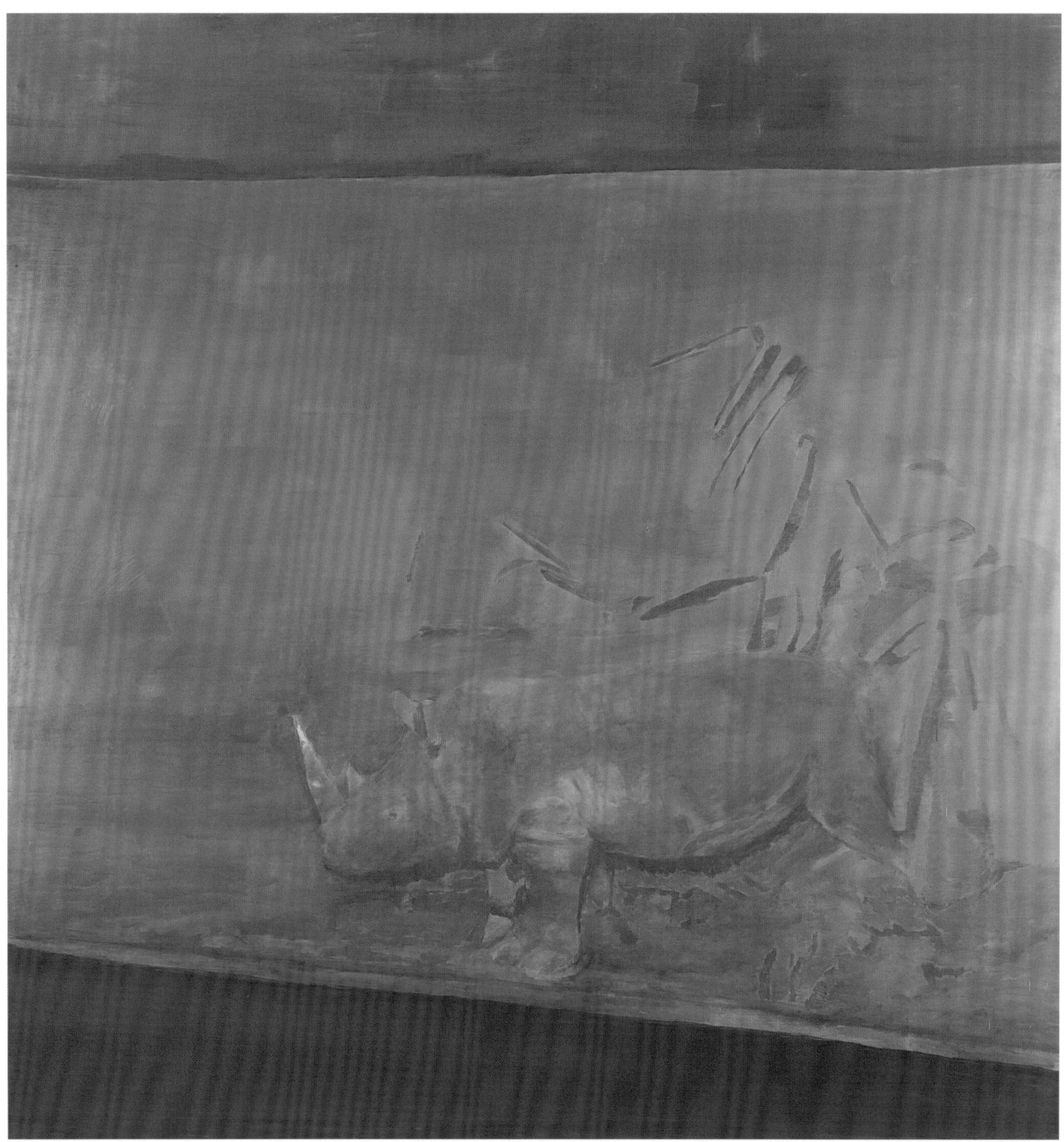

The work *Diorama* was the last work that concluded the series of works titled *Mwana Kitoko* and was specially made for my solo exhibition in the Belgian Pavilion of the Venice Biennale of 2001.

The work was by then the largest work I had ever made. *Diorama* deals with "historizing" the idea of colonization and is derived from my memory as a kid visiting the Africa Museum in Tervuren in the vicinity of Brussels.

Since it was impossible for me to take a satisfying photographic image of the taxidermied rhinoceros in the museum, I decided to use a toy rhinoceros and create a maquette that functioned as a diorama. I took several Polaroids of it, reworked them into watercolors, and finally into the painting itself.

—Luc Tuymans

Opposite page: *Christ*, 1998, oil on canvas, 48 x 22 3/4 in. (122.5 x 58 cm), acquired in 1999
Diorama, 2001, oil on canvas, 116 1/2 x 112 1/4 in. (296 x 285 cm), acquired in 2001

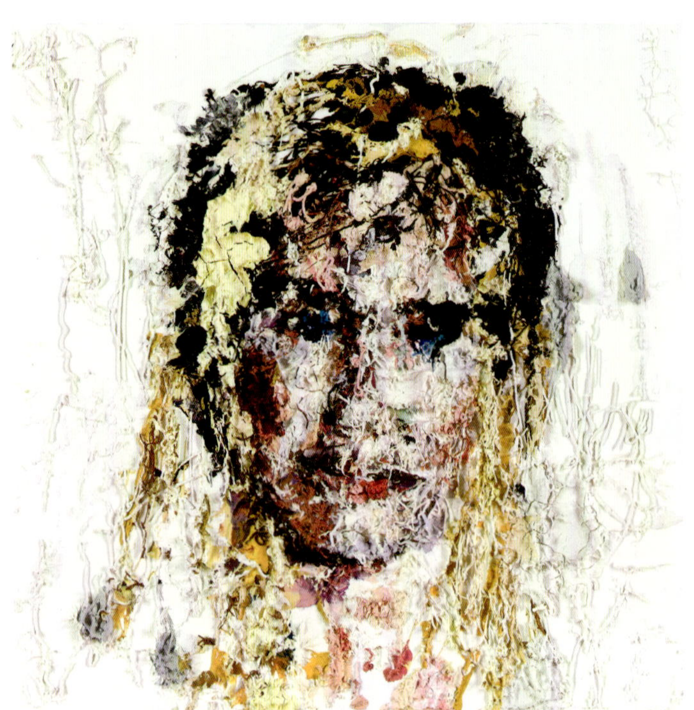 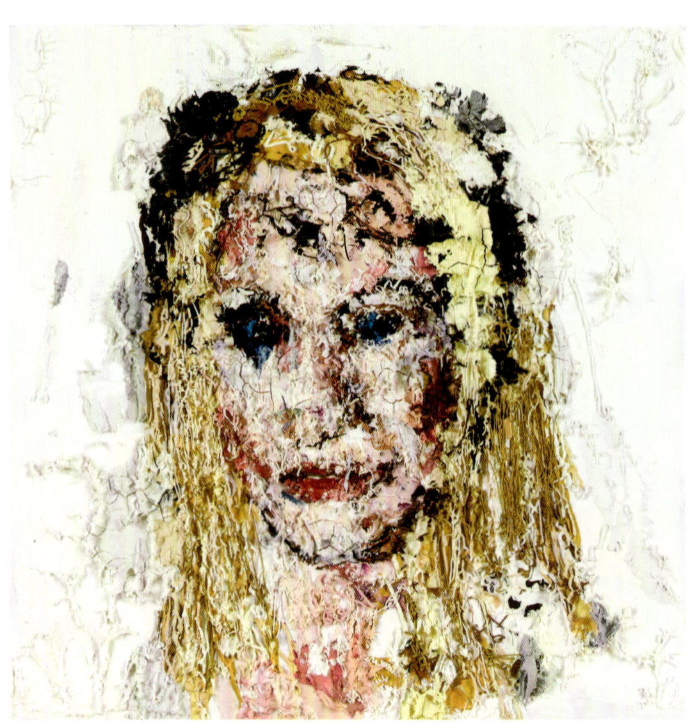

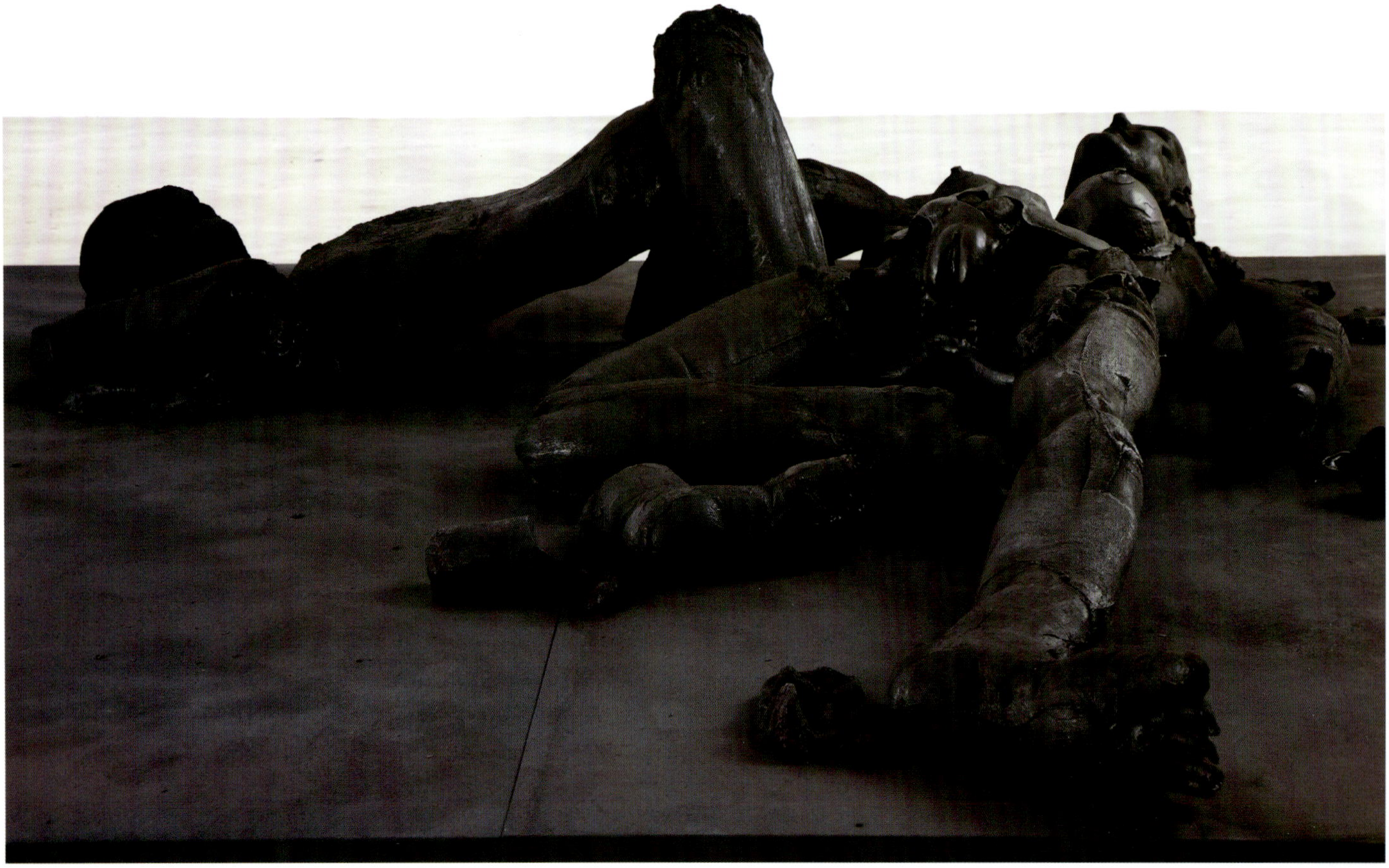

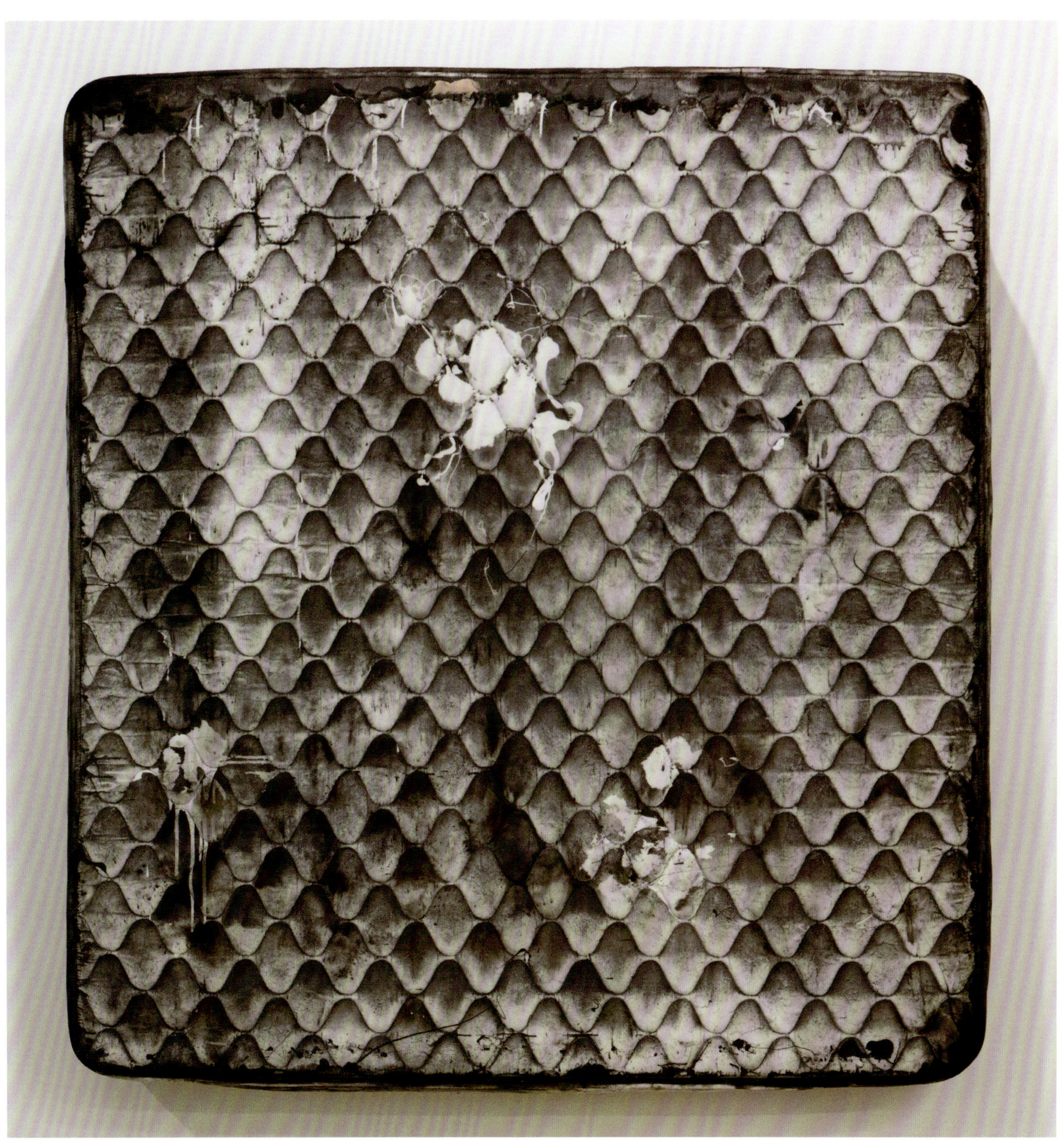

Opposite page, top to bottom: *Kiss 10*, 2008, oil on panel, diptych, each: 20 x 20 in. (50.8 x 50.8 cm), acquired in 2008
Untitled, 2009, charcoal and wax, 23 x 96 x 95 in. (58.4 x 243.8 x 241.3 cm), acquired in 2009
Above: *Rubells*, 2014, silicone, spandex, and fiberglass, 80 x 76 x 11 in. (203 x 193 x 27.9 cm), acquired in 2015

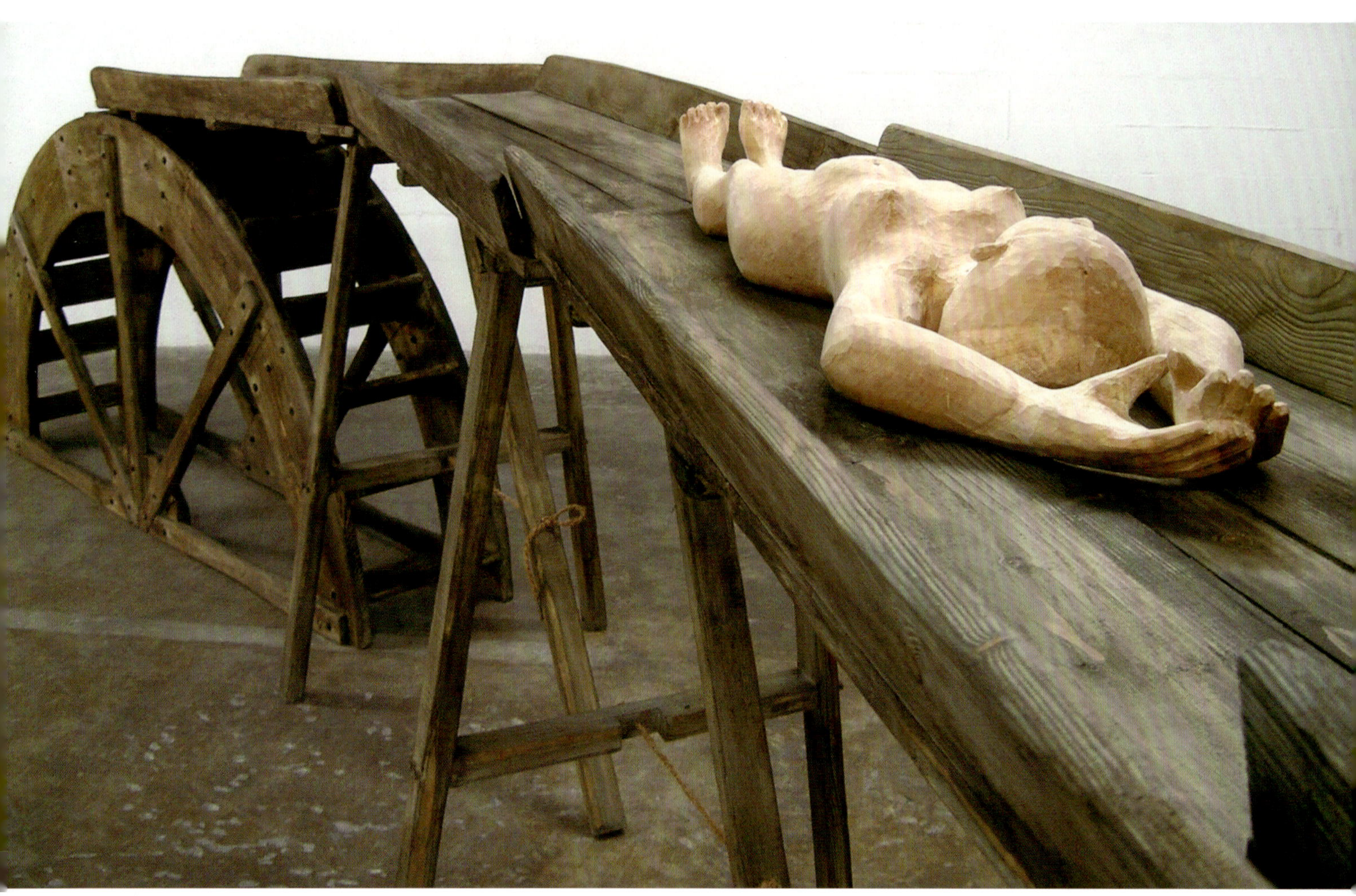

I made *Waldfrau* [opposite] while living in Bremerhaven, a very isolated city in the north of Germany. I was an artist in residence for one year and visited nearby Worpswede, a village that is very famous for its artists that had their careers around 1900—people like Otto Modersohn and Paula Modersohn-Becker. Along with others, they established a small artist colony there. My work was strongly influenced by these visits and the atmosphere surrounding the village. The moor landscape, the charm, and the works of the period strongly influenced and inspired me to create *Waldfrau*.

Again, for *Stubaifrau,* my work is deeply influenced by a geographic region. During my time working as an apprentice in wood carving and sculpture, I lived in the Alps. We would go to Austria, to the Stubai Valley, to buy our *schnitzeisen* ("carving tools") from the local knife grinders. The craftsmen that settled in this region were widely known for these tools that were made using waterpower—huge water wheels were installed behind the workshops along rushing streams. At the time I was very impressed by the seemingly untouched province. Sadly, upon visiting the region years later, not one of the huge water wheels was still intact and only one workshop was still producing the tools.

—Paloma Varga Weisz

Stubaifrau, 2002, limewood and stained pine, 63 1/2 x 360 x 36 in. (161.2 x 914.4 x 91.4 cm), acquired in 2003
Opposite page: *Waldfrau, getarnt*, 2002, limewood, larch tree, and camouflage fabric, figures 71 x 42 x 44 in. (180.3 x 106.6 x 111.7 cm) and 18 1/2 x 5 x 8 1/4 in. (46.9 x 12.7 x 20.9 cm); tree 27 1/2 x 165 1/4 x 24 1/2 in. (69.8 x 418.7 x 62.2 cm), acquired in 2003

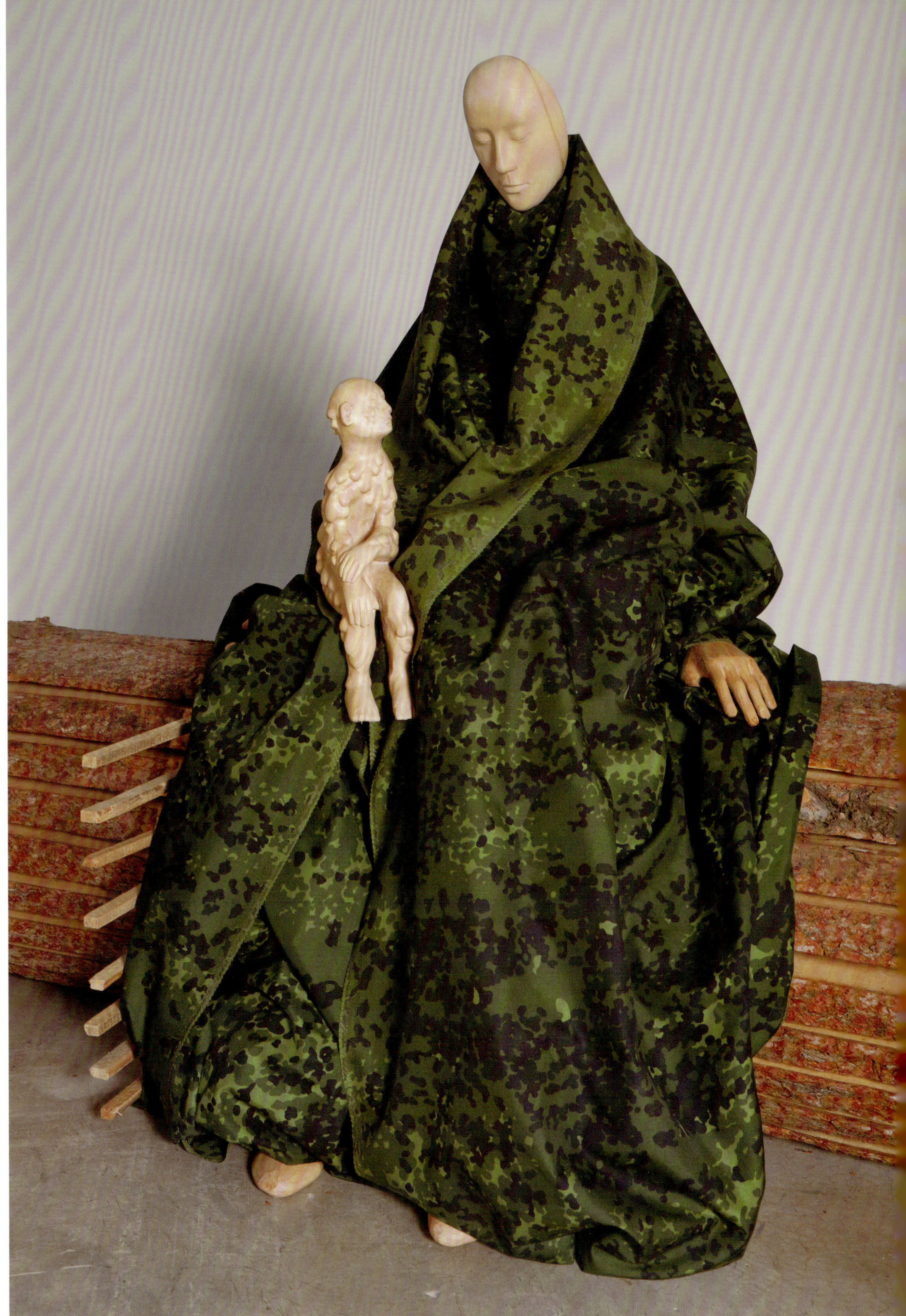

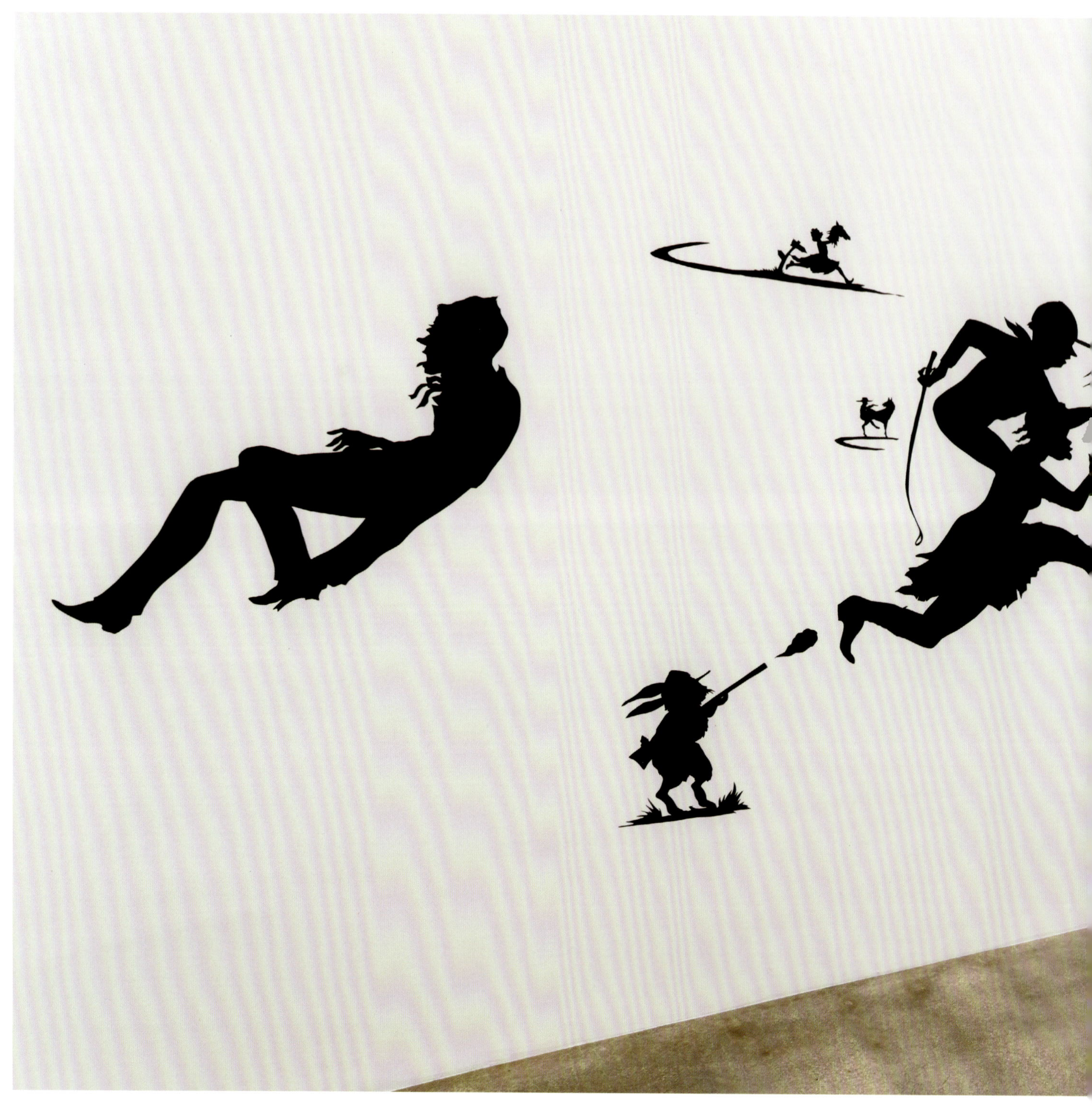

"Camptown ladies sing this song, dooh-dah! Dooh-dah! Camptown racetrack's five miles long, oh dooh-dah day!"

So goes the first line of Stephen Foster's popular minstrel nonsense song "Camptown Races," composed in 1850. A minstrel song, intended to be performed in blackface by white performers, in a raucous style intended to mimic African American folk traditions, "Camptown Races" is about nothing but *affect*. It's a jaunty, jumpy sing-along. The lyrics resist meaning and so I took this opacity as a starting point for an artwork: Who are the Camptown ladies? What is doo-dah? Why do they sing it? Is it a work song for runaway slaves? A sexual allusion? Magic language? And where is Camptown? Is it someplace or anyplace? Can I take the liberty of making a nonsense piece that recasts the caricatures of the minstrel stage? Change the tune away from the fantasy of racial harmonizing?

—Kara Walker

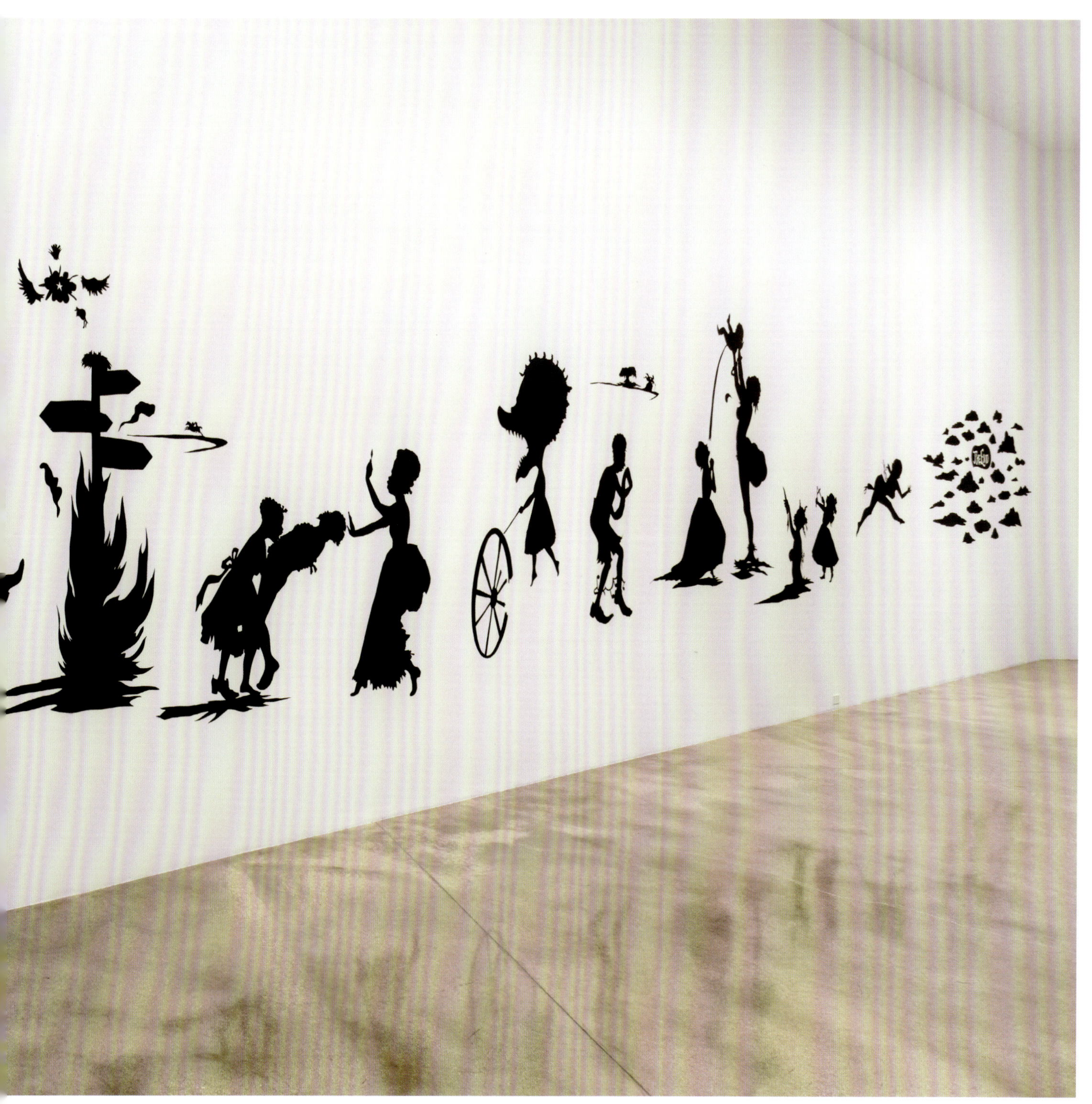

Camptown Ladies, 1998, paper and adhesive, 97 1/2 x 666 in. (247.7 x 1691.6 cm), acquired in 1998

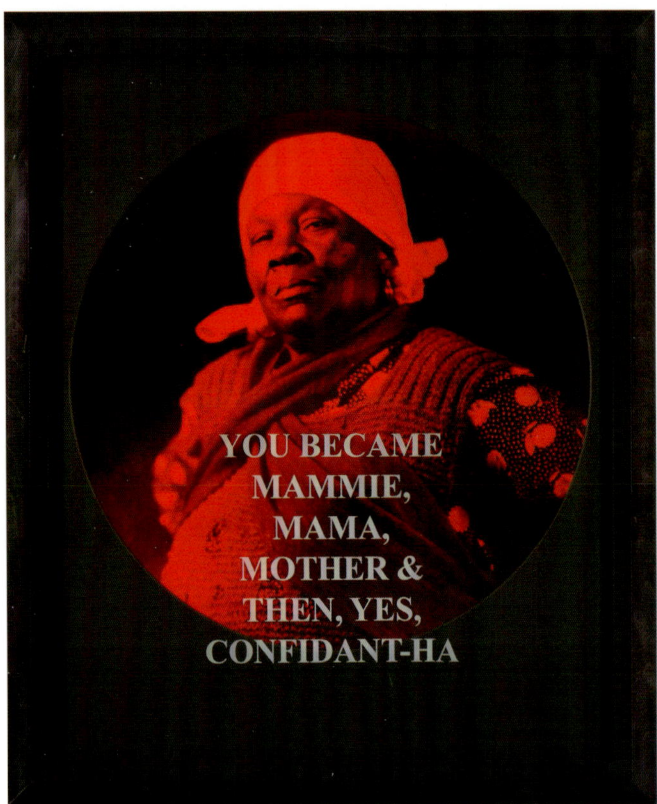

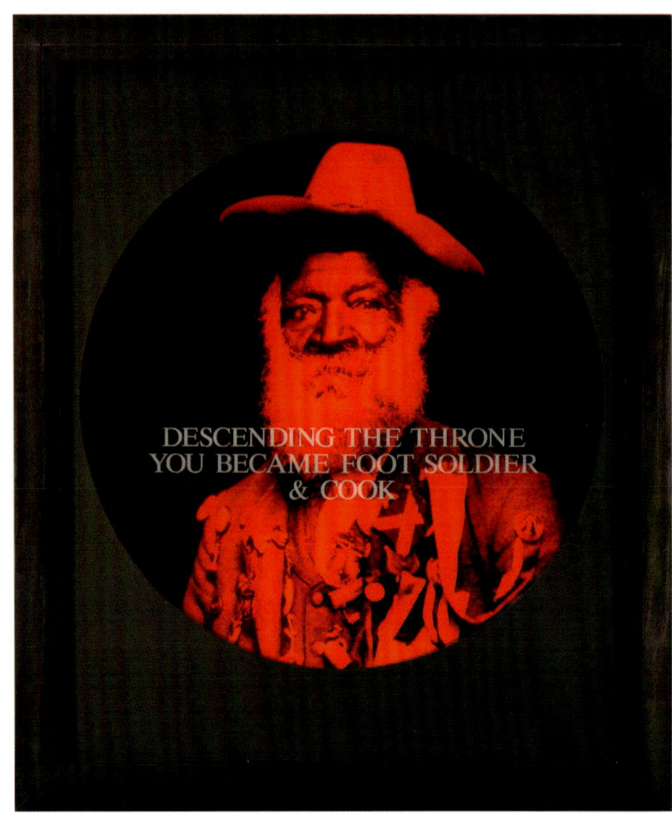

I was trying to look at the history of photography and the way in which African Americans had been particularly depicted and inscribed through, and in, American photography. I used images that were pre-existing, and my intervention was to reinscribe them by making them all consistent in terms of size and scale and format, and adding the use of color—for instance, I used the color red—to enunciate the image. I wanted to use oval or circular mats because I wanted to have that sense of looking through the photographic lens, which is a round surface.

When we're looking at these images, we're looking at the ways in which Anglo America, White America saw itself in relationship to the Black subject. I wanted to intervene in that by giving a voice to a subject that historically has had no voice. I use this idea of "I saw you" and "you became" as a way of both speaking out of the image and to the subject of the image. For instance, I say *You Became an Anthropological Debate & A Photographic Subject*. I'm trying to heighten a kind of critical awareness around the way in which these photographs were intended and then of course the way in which they are ultimately used by me, a strategy that I hope gives the subject another level of humanity and another level of dignity that was originally missing in the photograph.

From Here I Saw What Happened is perhaps one of the more painful pieces that I've made. When I look at it, when I study it, I cry. It is a very sad piece, and at the same time of course there's always hope that's located within sadness as well. The hope that in the end our mutual humanity will be understood and embraced.

—Carrie Mae Weems

You Became Mammie, Mama, Mother, & Then, Yes, Confident-Ha/ Descending the Throne (from From Here I Saw What Happened and I Cried), 1995-1996, two chromogenic prints with sandblasted text on glass, ed. 6/10, each 26 3/4 x 22 3/4 in. (67.9 x 57.8 cm), acquired in 2008.
Opposite page: *You Became a Scientific Profile/ An Anthropological Debate/ A Negroid Type/ & A Photographic Subject (from From Here I Saw What Happened and I Cried series)*, 1995-1996, four chromogenic prints with sandblasted text on glass, ed. 2/10, each 26 3/4 x 22 3/4 in. (67.9 x 57.8 cm), acquired in 2008

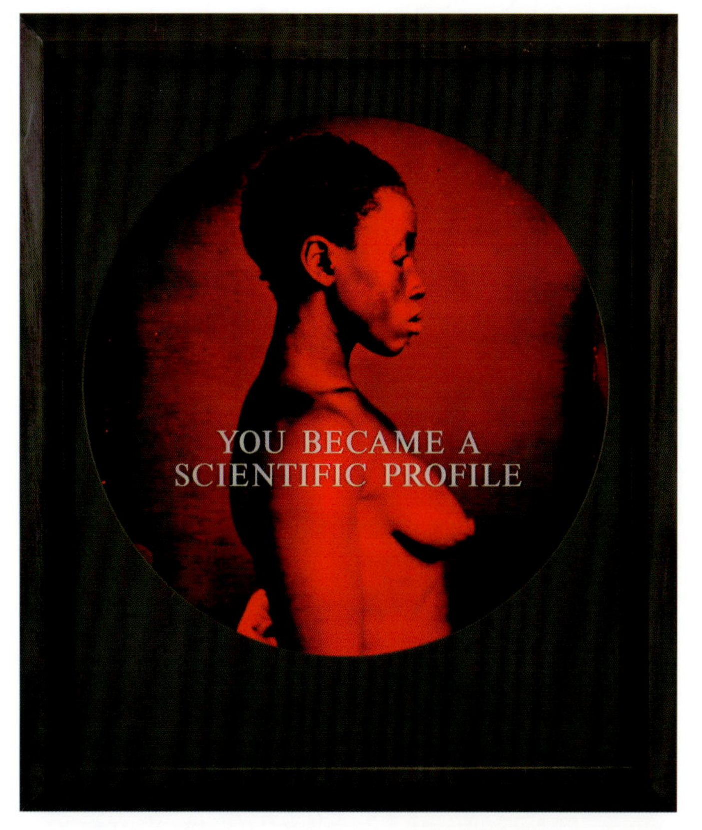
YOU BECAME A
SCIENTIFIC PROFILE
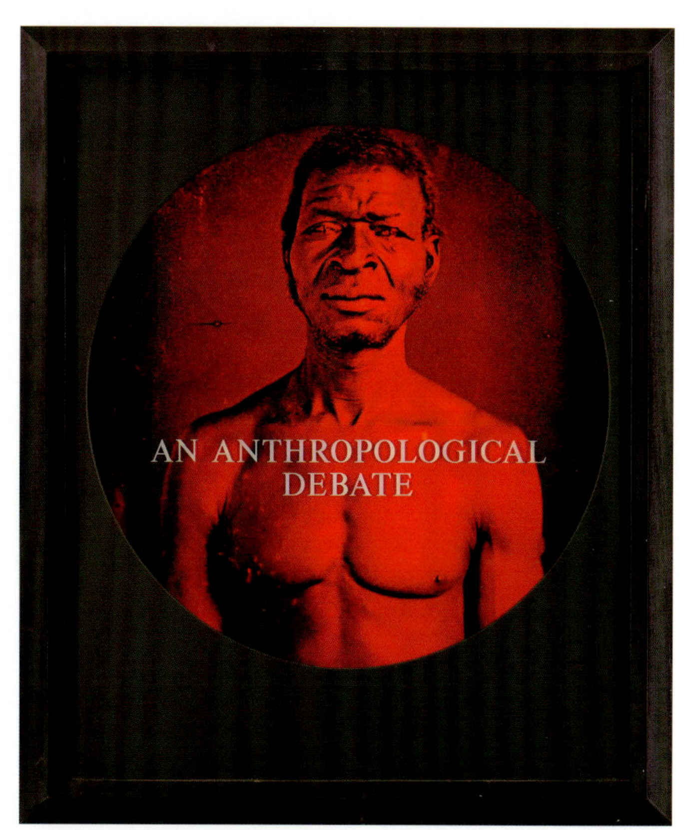
AN ANTHROPOLOGICAL
DEBATE
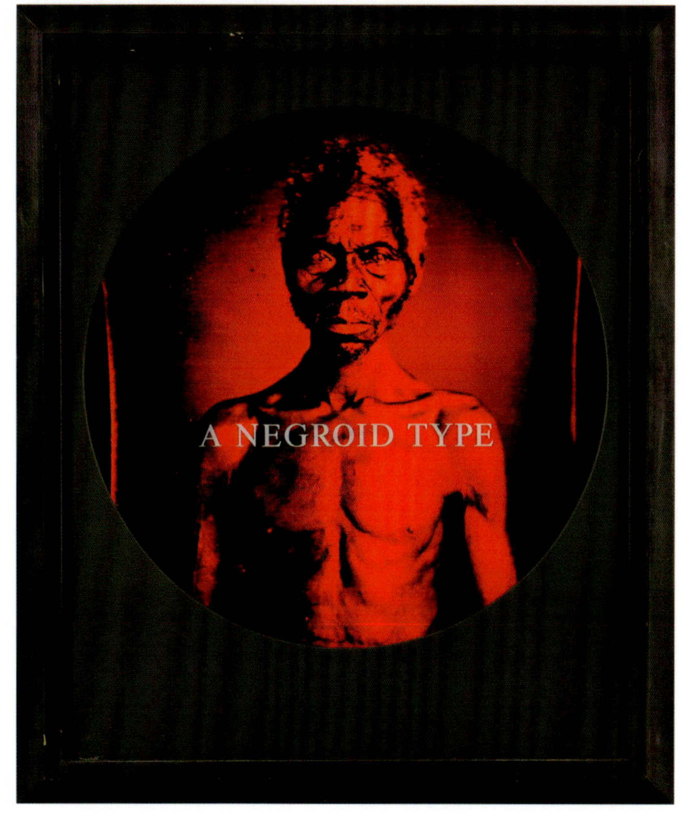
A NEGROID TYPE
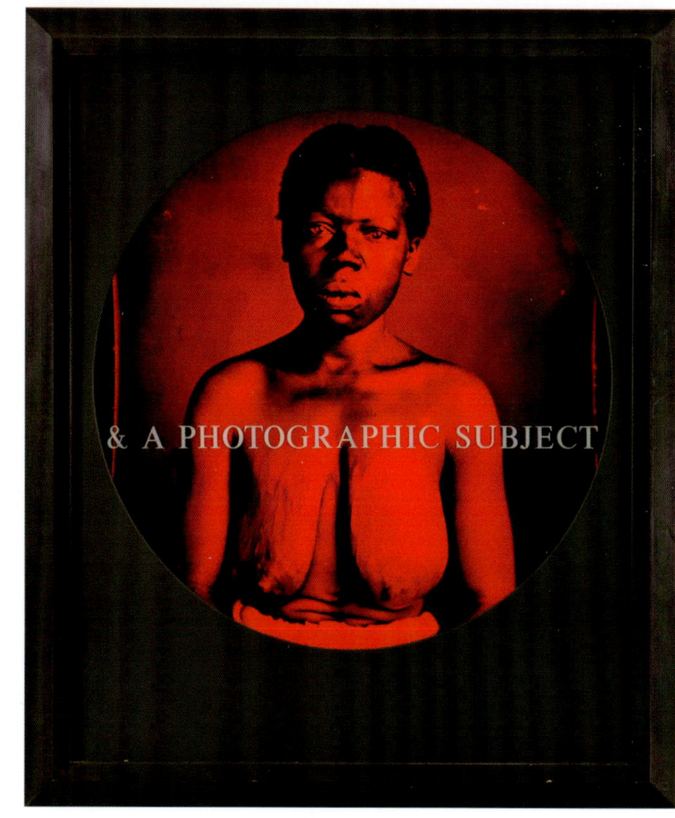
& A PHOTOGRAPHIC SUBJECT

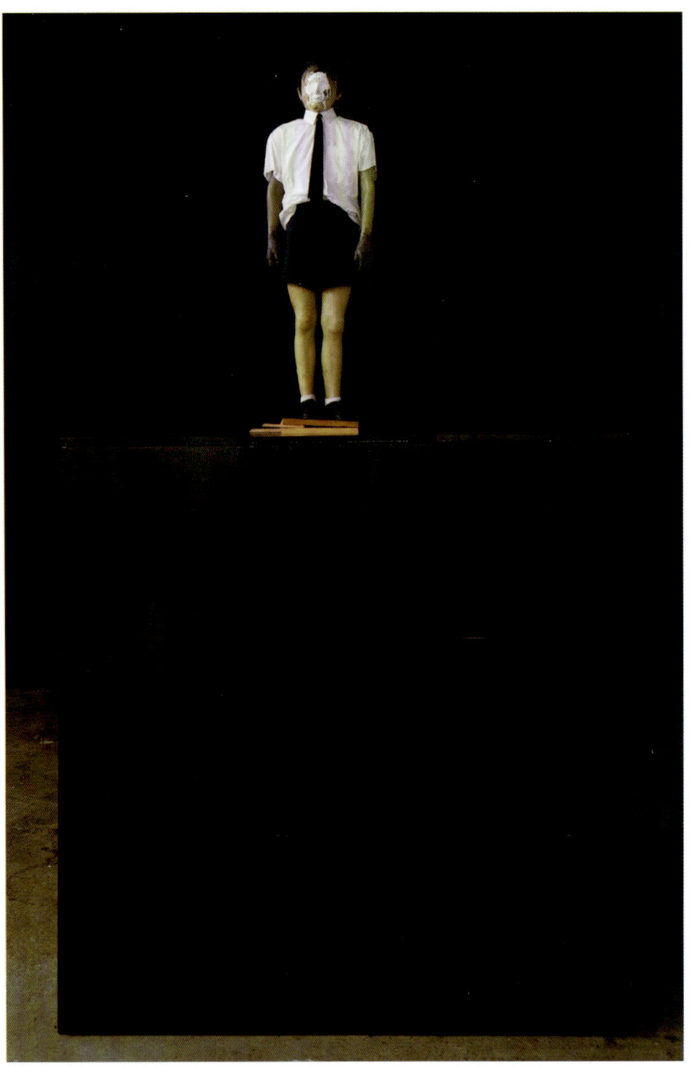

Wie heisst Du mein Kind? (What Are You Called, My Child?) was the second wax sculpture I made using the adolescent figure as a central subject; it is a particularly personal work based on a family photo of me as a child, and I assembled it myself. It is a very important, core work in my overall practice. The square, black structure that the sculpture stands on is very much like the black boxes on aircraft that contain all of the vessels' information; it's a physical object, it's a visible object, but all of the key information that it contains remains inaccessible. In contrast to the soft wax that the figure is made of, the surface of the box is hard and slightly reflective; it's less permeable because what's inside of it is vulnerable despite its immateriality. The large scale of the box means that the viewer is immediately confronted with it rather than with the figure; it is a protective gesture, and a way to ensure that the figure retains a slight distance from whoever happens to be in the room with it.

Untitled doesn't depict a specific person, but rather functions as a stand-in for the overall concept of adolescence, which to me indicates a state of waiting and anticipation. This in-between condition represents a person in the process of becoming, a liminal place between what will happen, and what has already occurred. I think of adolescence as a refugee state; it's a kind of transient placeholder that straddles who we were, and imagines who we will eventually become. This sculpture also incorporates technology, and the figure is animated from the outside, which implies that we are imprinted by the external experiences of our bodies. This suggestion of malleability repeats the material nature of the wax the work itself is constructed from. I think of this figure as a warrior who has been removed from a state of warfare; isolated from the context of battle, she is abstract, a kind of floating signifier between two worlds.

—Andro Wekua

Wie heisst Du mein Kind? (What Are You Called, My Child?), 2004, wax, fabric, leather, hair, lacquer, and ceramic, figure 53 1/2 x 16 x 10 1/4 in. (135.8 x 40.6 x 26 cm); pedestal 58 x 58 x 58 in. (147.3 x 147.3 x 147.3 cm), acquired in 2004
Opposite page: *Untitled*, 2014, synthetic hair, silicone, wax, polymer plaster, PU foam, steel, glass, synthetic rope, aluminum cast, fabric, motors, electronics, and mechanics, ed. 1/2 , 66 1/4 x 23 5/8 x 63 1/2 in. (168 x 60 x 161 cm), acquired in 2016

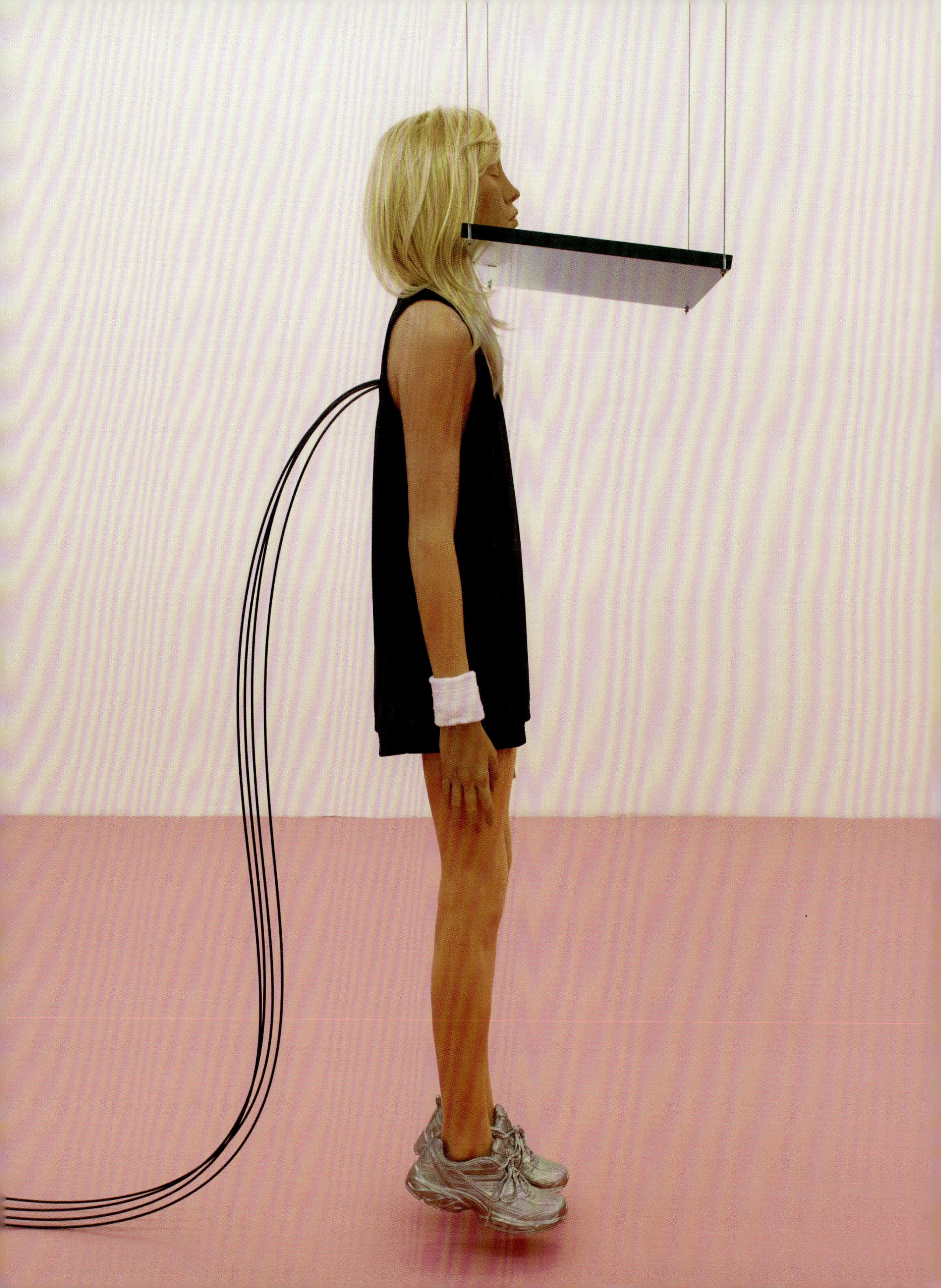

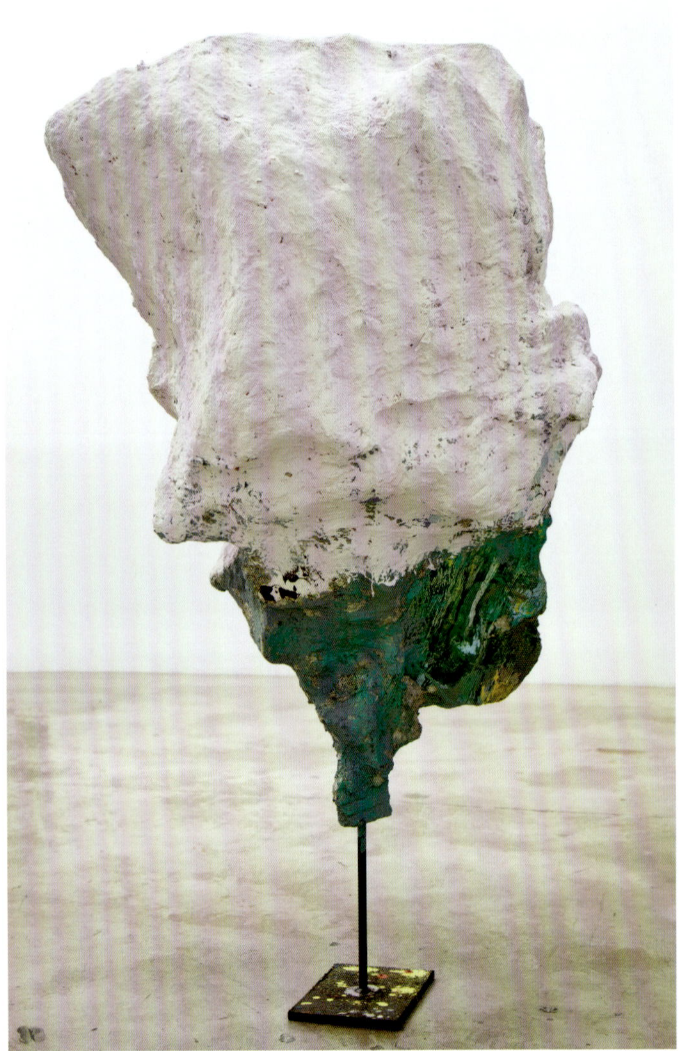

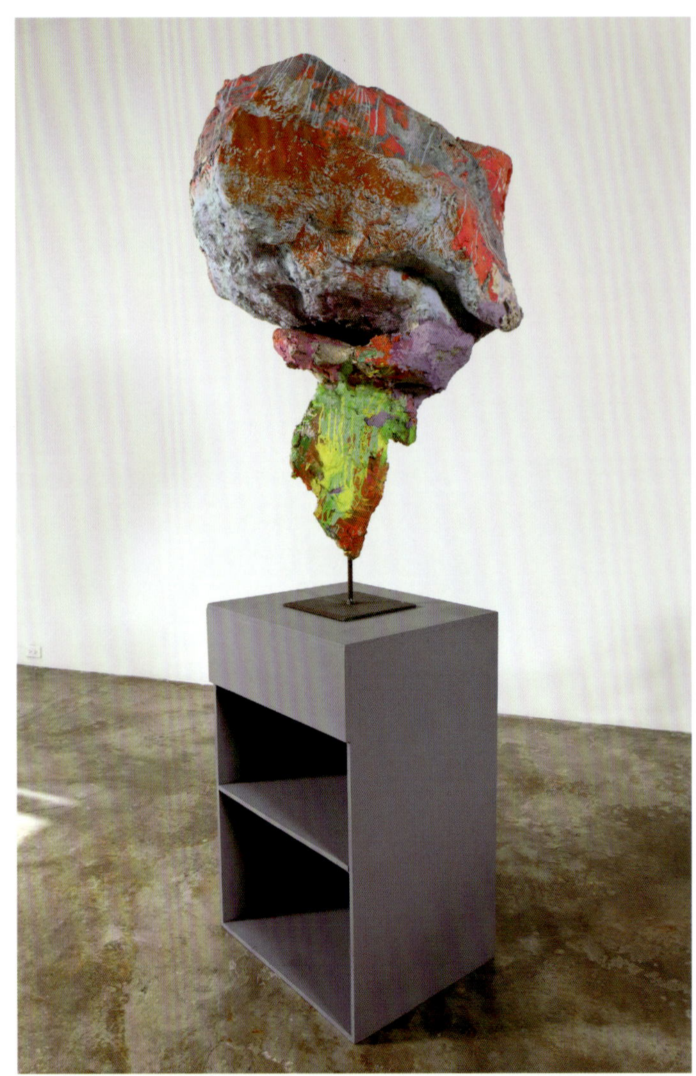

Art, to me, is an impetus, but one that cannot be articulated. You want to express something, but you have not yet learned how to do so. If you can express it, you do not have the impetus. Art is somehow suspended in between. Art is ultimately an impossible affair: if you don't learn it, you can't express it, and if you learn it, the substance vanishes before you.

—Franz West

Left to right:
Untitled (Rosa-Turquoise), 2007, papier-mâché and metal, 68 x 48 x 38 in. (173 x 122 x 96.5 cm), acquired in 2007
Goeschl, 2007, papier-mâché and metal with pedestal, 53 x 25 x 30 in. (135 x 65 x 78 cm), acquired in 2007
Untitled (Note with Table), 2005, papier-mâché and metal with table, 59 1/10 x 39 2/5 x 19 7/10 in. (150 x 100 x 50 cm), acquired in 2007

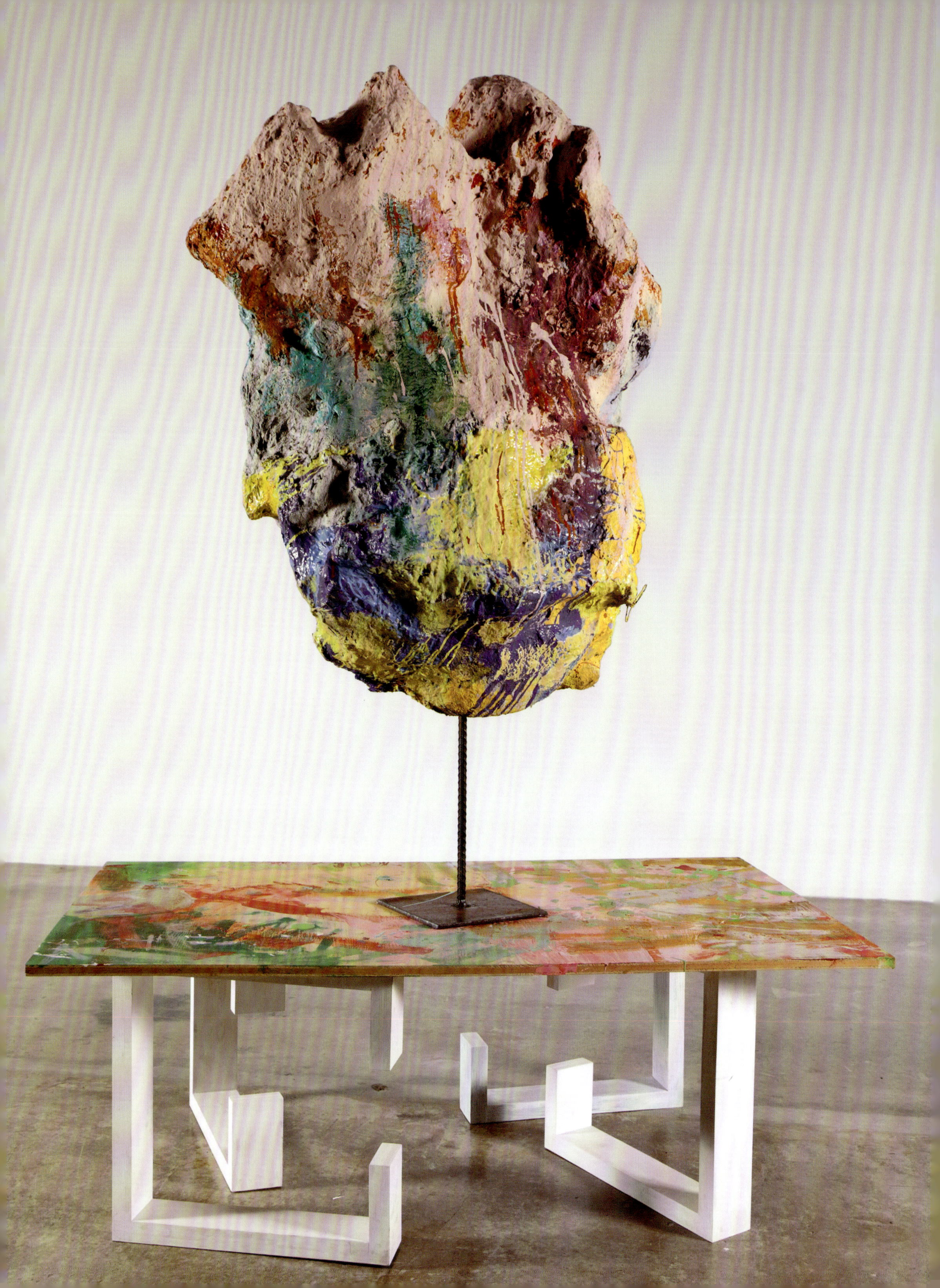

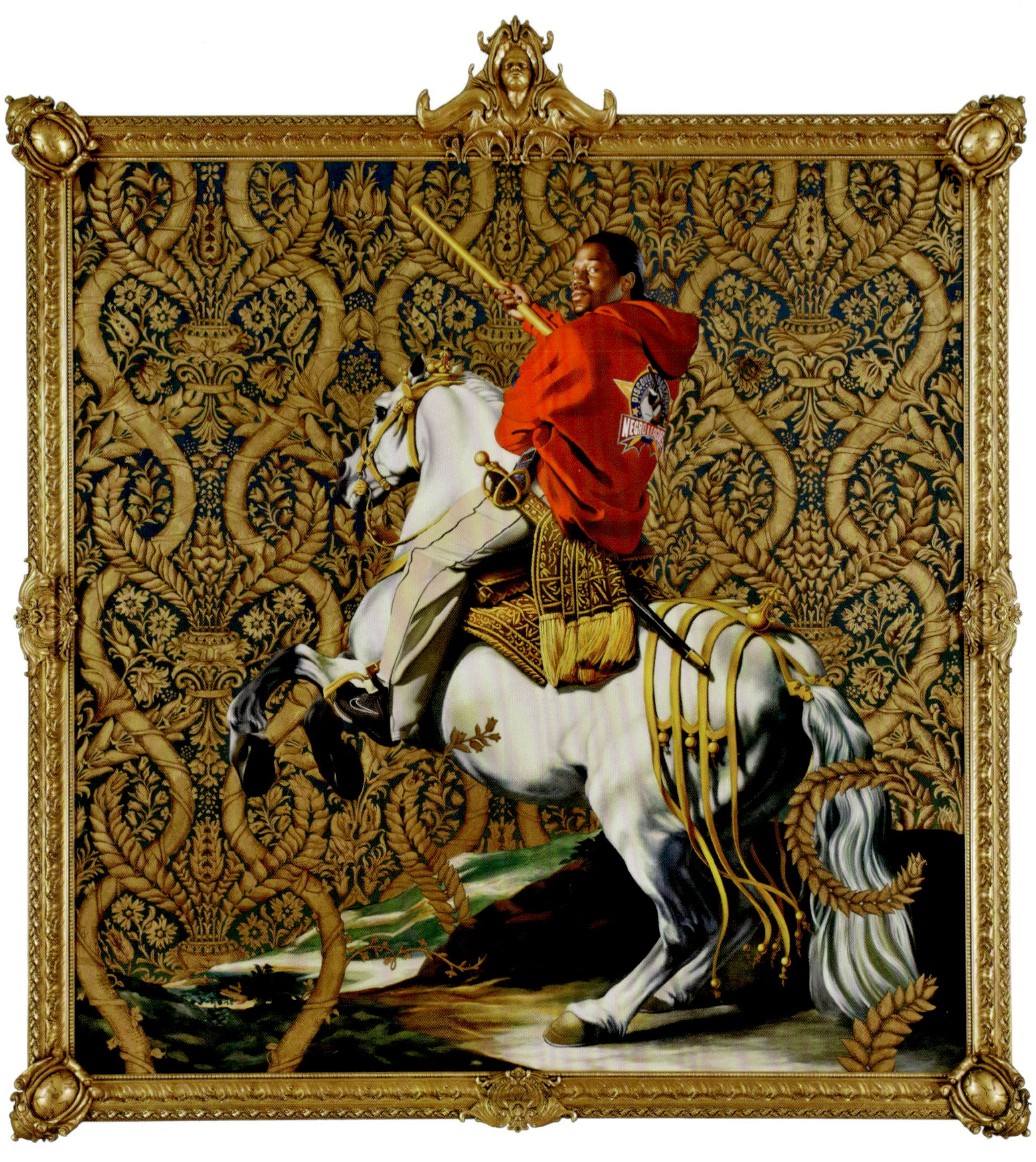

This painting is based on a Velázquez and comes out of a series of paintings titled *Rumors of War.* Rumors of War is a body of paintings concerned specifically with the depiction of large-scale military portraiture. Much of my work is devoted to the idea of distilling masculine power down to some of its most essential components within the history of Western easel painting, and in this case military portraiture stands in for the absolute proxy of that idea. The depiction and scale shifts are oftentimes misleading. In this painting I used a real horse stand-in only to find that, in the depiction of military equestrian portraiture, the male to animal ratio was erroneous, and so I followed suit. The background components are derived from decorative wallpaper elements spanning from the late French Rococo of the 18th century, to the Arts and Crafts movement of the late 19th and early 20th centuries. Independent of period style, I chose elements that connote a sense of pedigree and Europhilia.

Equestrian Portrait of the Count Duke Olivares, 2005, oil on canvas, 108 x 108 in. (274.3 x 274.3 cm), acquired in 2005

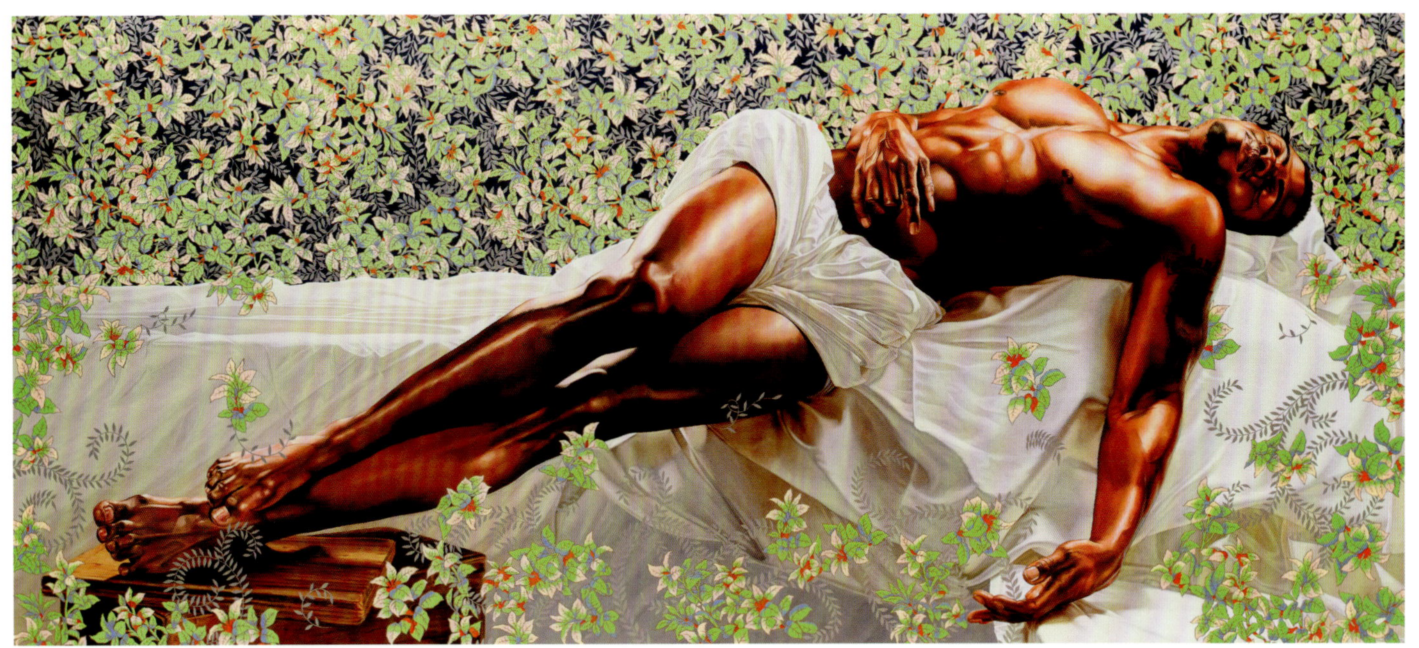

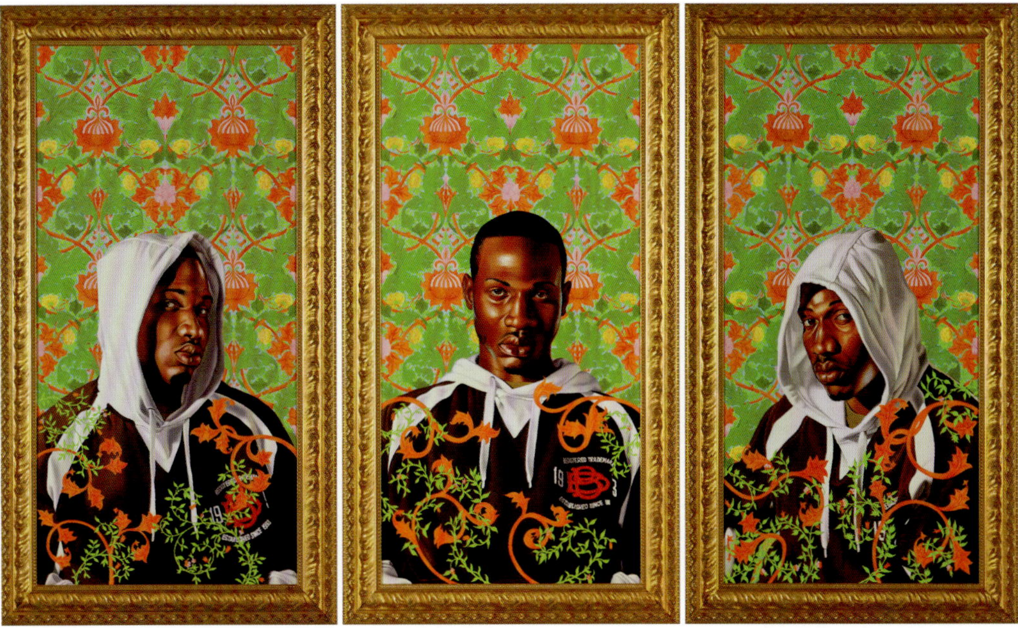

The *Triple Portrait of Charles I* was a preparatory painting designed to be a stand-in for use in the completion of formal portraits, be they sculptures or large paintings. In this case, three different angles were used to approximate the portrait so that other more complicated portraits could be made. In the painting I'm actually taking a nod to the mug shot profile photograph that inspired the *Passing/Posing* series of the early 2000s that gave rise to my career. Those were paintings that were inspired by the mug shot photo I found on the streets of a young Black man that made me question the mug shot as a type of portraiture, and whether or not portraiture connotes a certain amount of power about how you position yourself. The mug shot does not allow the model to position himself with all powers removed —side view, front view—and looking at the portraits of the land and gentry stands in stark contrast to that concept.   —Kehinde Wiley

Sleep, 2008, oil on canvas, 132 x 300 in. (335.3 x 762 cm), acquired in 2009
Triple Portrait of Charles I, 2007, oil and enamel on canvas, triptych, overall 82 x 135 in. (208.3 x 342.9 cm), acquired in 2007

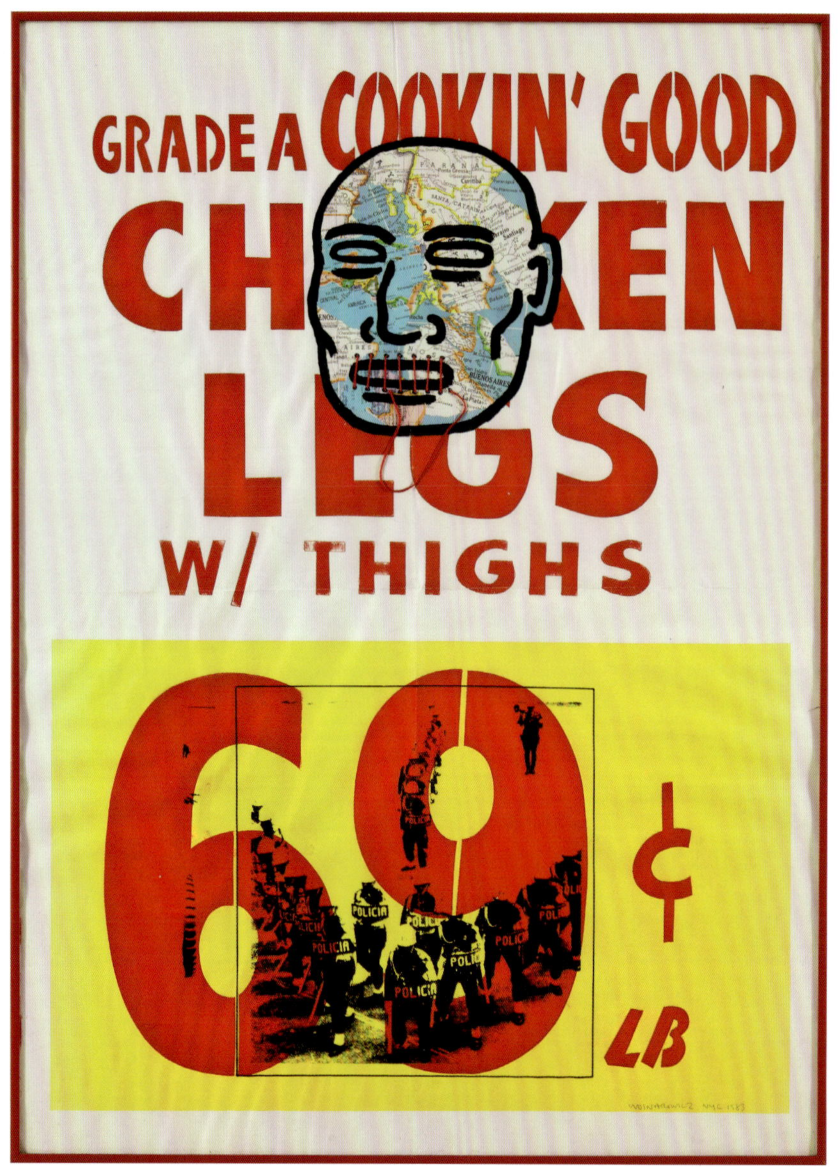

Barry Blinderman: Some people see things analytically; other people have a synthetic ability by which they are uniquely suited to putting things together. It seems that every art form you work with has to do with this putting together of elelments, for example, beginning with paper money or using maps, and then building images up…

David Wojnarowicz: I'll use pre-printed material in order to illustrate something of the structure behind those per-printed materials. These are things that we just blindly accept. Take the map: the concept of the map is contingent on people accepting that this is what landmasses look like from some point in outer space. Most people will never have that experience of being in outer space yet they accept as a given that this is what the world looks like. They don't stop to think that the borders are really psychic things rather than actual physical things. The North American continent is really just one big piece of land, but suddenly there's this arbitrary place where Mexicans have to stop and Americans can just saunter over.

You can think of the map as a metaphor for government— that this is what the world looks like, this is who you are, this is your job, this is how things have to run, etc. People take it as a given, and not always of their own accord, only because they're too exhausted from working meaningless jobs or they're too afraid. You question structures and you're suddenly in a minority and there's nothing as frightening as finding yourself a minority in a hostile environment.

So I use a map as a metaphor. By ripping the map into pieces I've suddenly erased all these borders and I've completely joined opposing governments. It's a metaphor for a sense of groundlessness and anarchy: No more governments no more borders. The most physically anarchic state would be literally upside down…

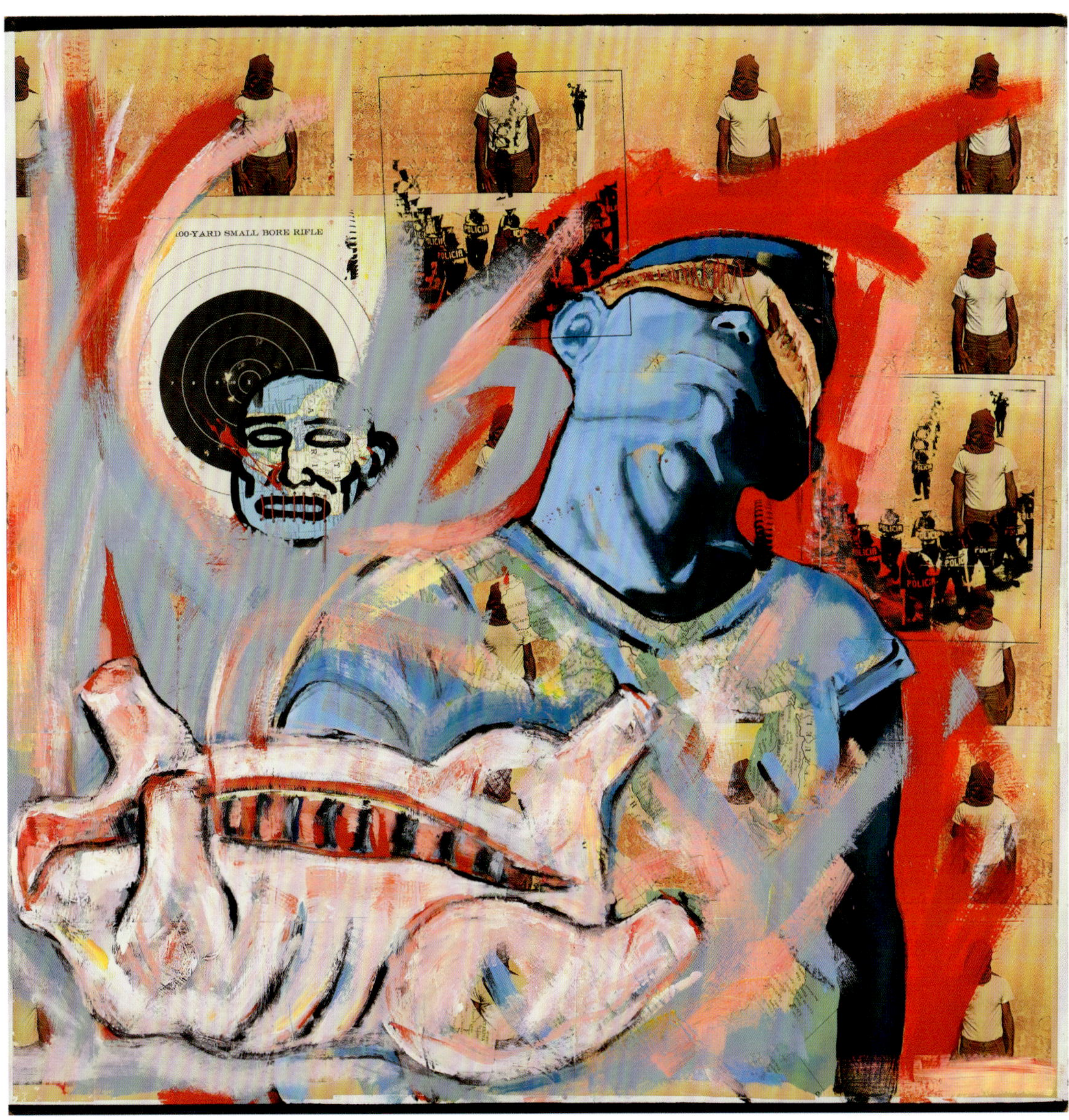

BB: What about the pre-printed food posters?

DW: They're symbols of consumption. I would think, Okay, what are images that we consume on a daily basis or that other people consume on a daily basis—people who live in places where there are wars or where there's murder on the streets by government forces, and I try to figure out a way of using that surface in a subversive way to look at the structure behind it. What supposes the society in which this food poster exists? What are the mechanics of that society?

The pressure of what we experience and what we contain in our minds and in our bodies from our environment is so intense that people do drugs, they fuck, they can do any of these things in order to achieve a weightlessness or something outside of the confines of their skin where all the pressure is. I mean, I felt like I should be 50 feet tall with everything that I contain inside my head; I wrote somewhere that I'm a 37-foot-tall person inside this six-foot frame. It's this pressure of information, of all this knowledge that I exist inside of a blind society where they try to deny or suppress what I'm experiencing. I think of whirling dervishes—they use that centrifugal motion of spinning and spinning and spinning to get into weightlessness, where weight and the polar gravity no longer exist.

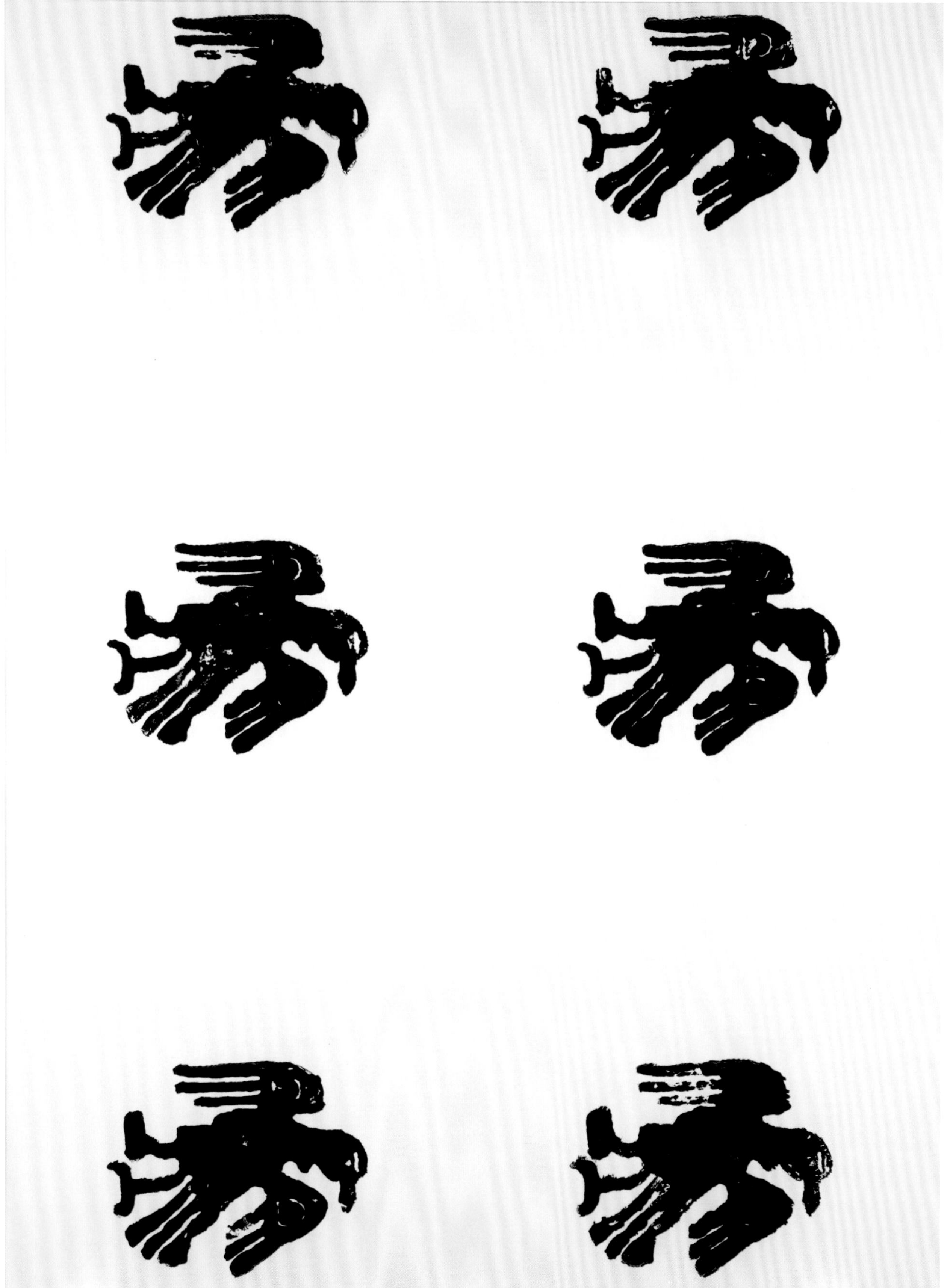

Untitled, 1990, alkyd and acrylic on aluminum, 96 x 72 in. (243.8 x 182.9 cm), acquired in 2000
Opposite page: *Untitled*, 2007, enamel on linen, 126 x 96 in. (320 x 243.8 cm), acquired in 2009

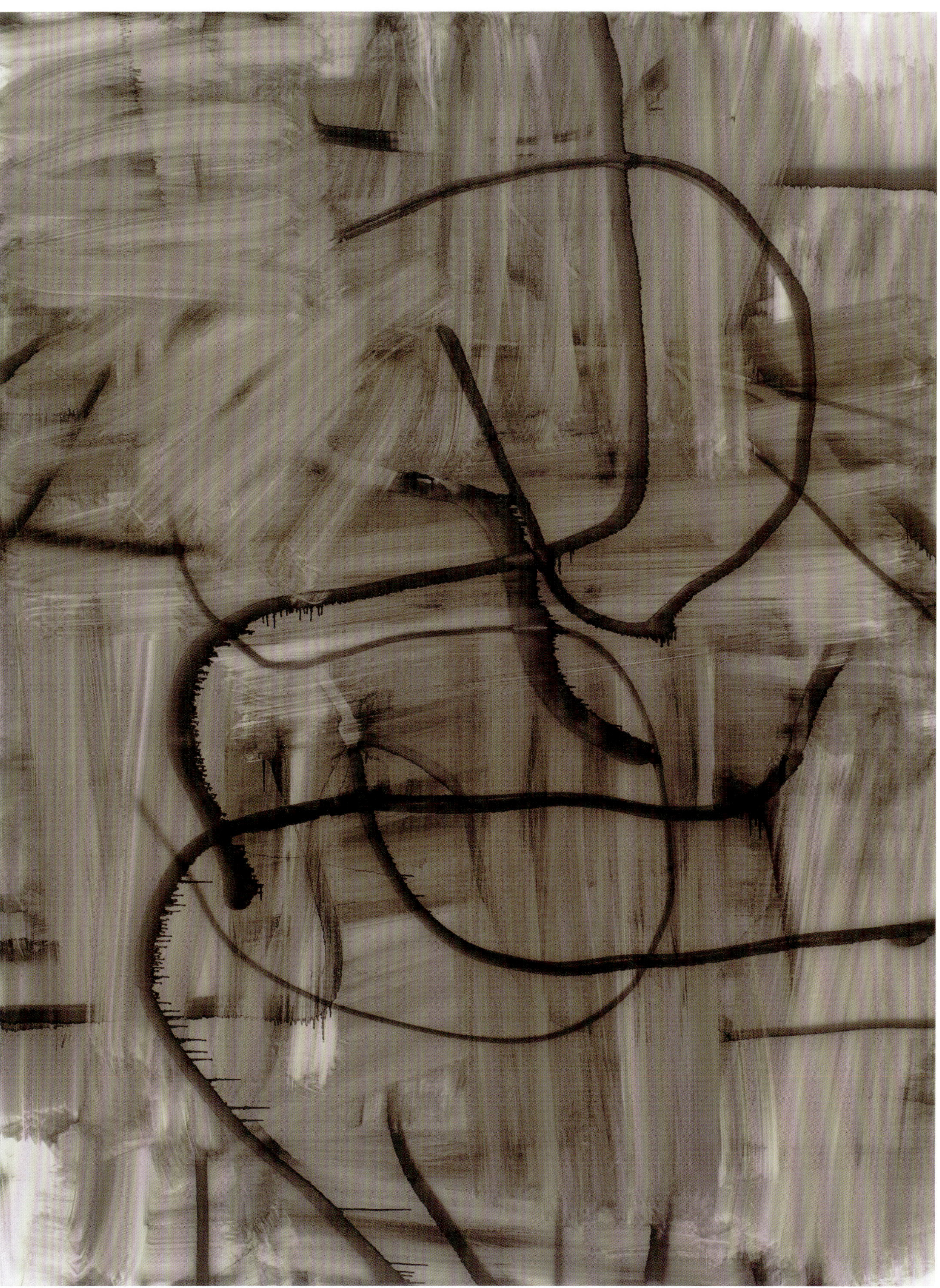

KENNEDY YANKO
b. 1988, St. Louis, MO / lives and works in Brooklyn, NY

2021 Artist in Residence

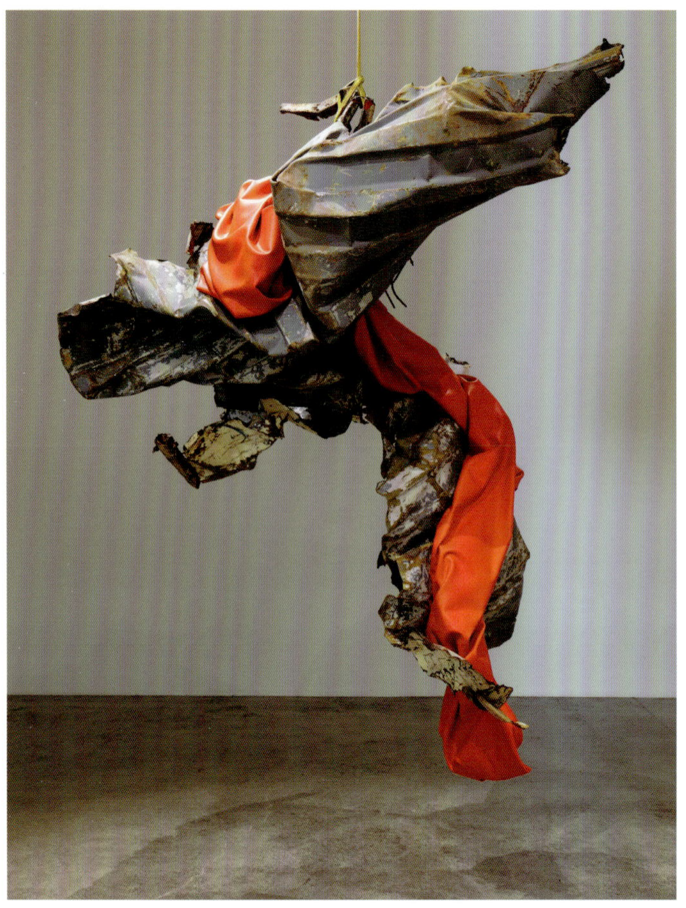

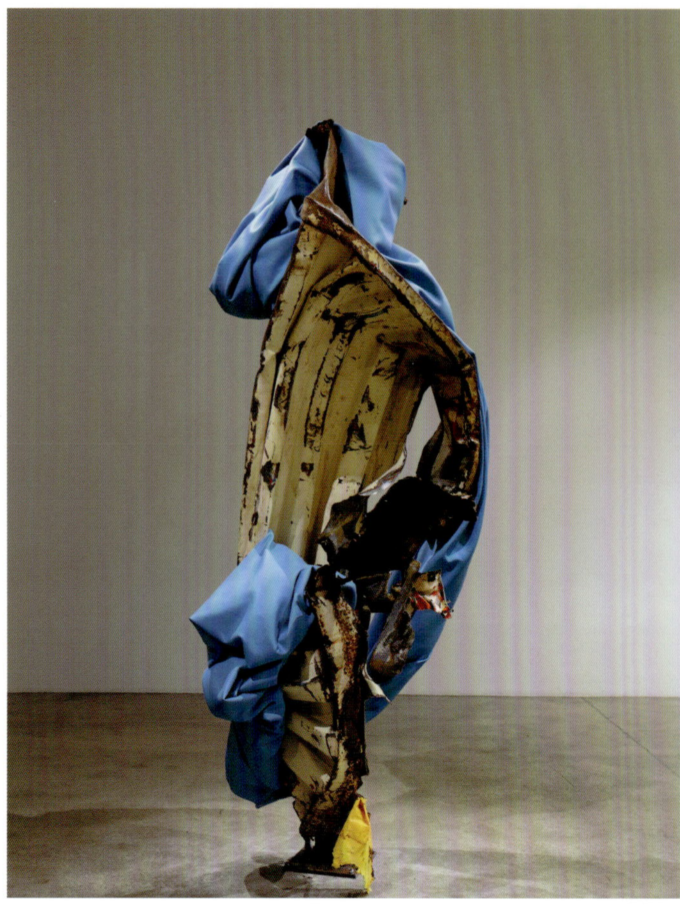

In Spring of 2021, I went to the Rubell residency with the intention to make the biggest works I'd ever made. Don and Mera had asked me what I wanted to achieve during my time there, and all I could imagine were big shapes soaring up and over me like tornadoes. When I got to Miami, I immediately started looking for my metal—the spines and frames of my sculptures that are the first impulse of what's to come. I found a white and gray, crumpled, and marked shipping container whose spots of blue and red and yellow caught my eye. The colors were primary and, in that, urgent. I began making the paint skins, pouring over 100 gallons of paint in response to the metal that so demanded its other: this smooth, supple, full and writhing body.

While making these pieces, I was simultaneously working on my graphic novel *Indelible Fluidity*. It is autobiographical, and it prompted me to look at myself, my story, my history, and my physicality in a way that my other artmaking has never so bluntly required. I had to look at my blond hair, green eyes, white-passing skin and not necessarily reconcile any part of that, but see it and feel it and sit with it. Working on this novel in tandem with the largest sculptures of my life was not only symbolic and intense, it was also revealing. I discovered a written language for my experience through developing this narrative while also realizing a visual language for the incommunicable parts of my existence in scale, form, and synchronicities within materials. The latter—the overlapping moments of the materials' experience, where metal and paint skin both bend and twist and sing—articulates dualities occurring within one moment, one person, one spirit.

There is light, dark, shadow, and reflection embedded in each of the three sculptures in *White, Passing*: *I am flower*, *I am water*, *I am that*. My Black American mother, my white American father, my biracial brother are among the swell of tension and togetherness passing through the space, transforming this matter alongside me. Heavy as the work is, there's a levity and even weightlessness to it—it's bright, kinetic, and will move with the wind. Its fluidity is its solidity. It is a rejection of definition and a welcoming of self.

—Kennedy Yanko

Left to right: *I am flower*, 2021, paint skin and Corten steel, 115 x 86 x 90 in. (292.1 x 86 x 228.6 cm), acquired in 2021
I am water, 2021, paint skin and Corten steel, 110 x 64 x 50 in. (279.4 x 162.6 x 127 cm), acquired in 2021
I am that, 2021, paint skin and Corten steel, 204 x 114 x 114 in. (518.2 x 289.6 x 289.6 cm), acquired in 2021

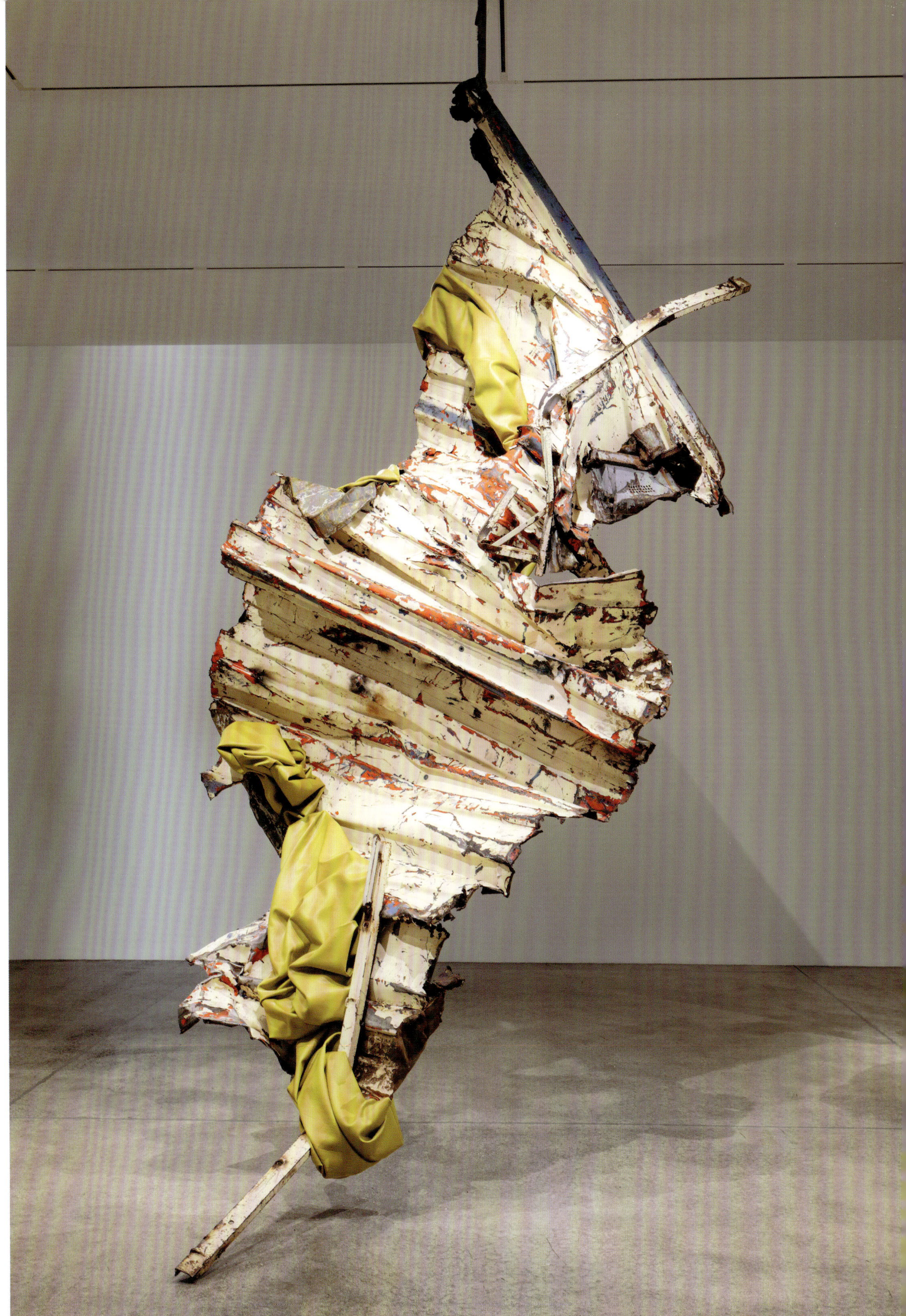

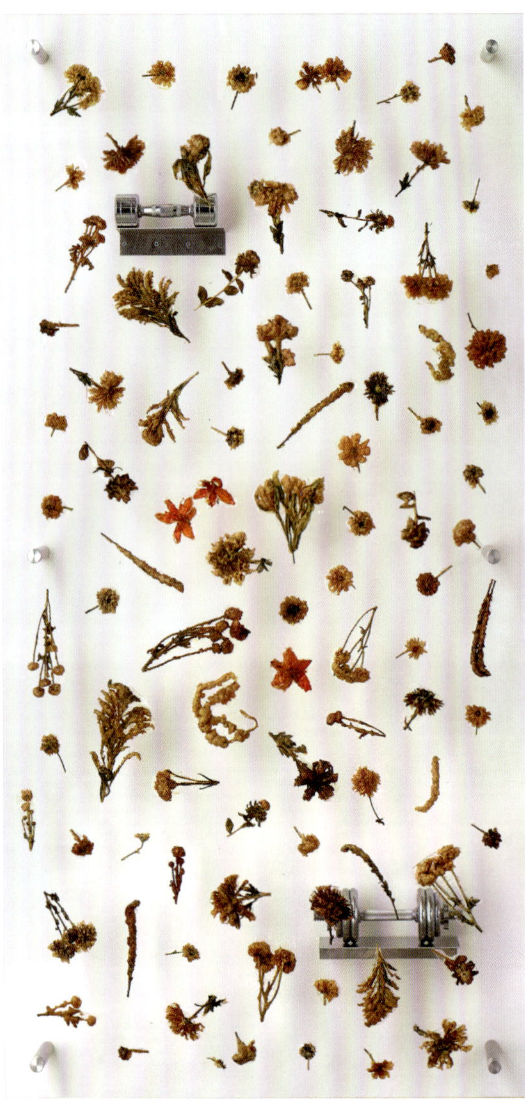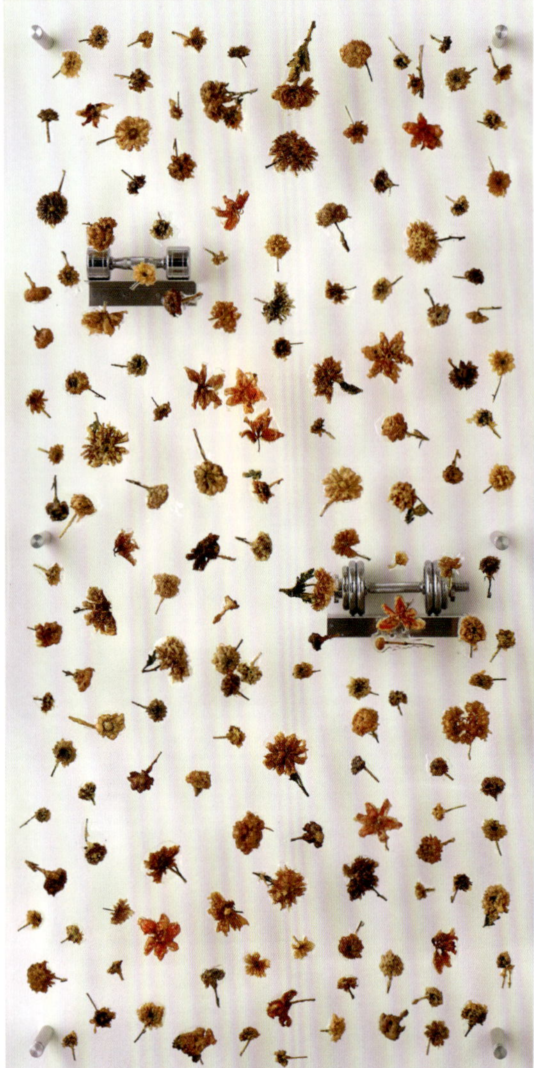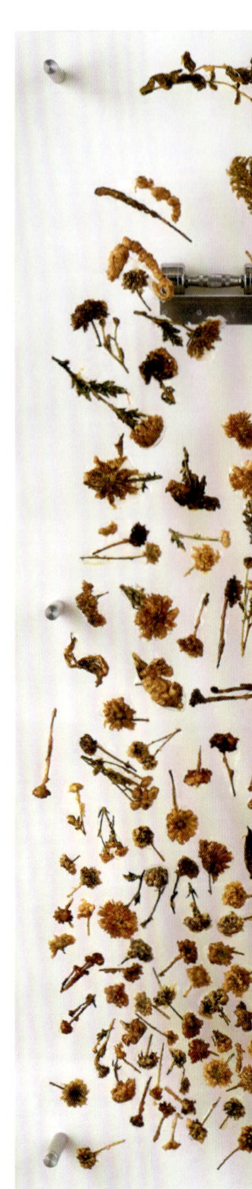

Humans have a fear of impermanence. We go against nature to try to preserve and stabilize and control something that resists all of that.

Around 2010, I started deep-frying flowers and plants. This very clunky batter is almost masking and destroying the flower itself, and then you subject it to 300-degree hot oil. The visual aspect of it was definitely something that I was aiming for but beyond that the odor of French fries, the odor of an *artwork* — that was very much compelling me, to fry up a batch of these.

There's always been an incredibly vulnerable aspect to my work. Many of my works use this element of deterioration and perishable materials. I'm interested in the kind of mutations that can take place in these changes.

I'm quite omnivorous in the areas and disciplines where I draw from. Before it's even a fully fleshed idea, I start small trials in the studio, much like you would do in a laboratory. As the trials start to bear fruit, we bring in the experts to help us, whether it's a software engineer or a forensic chemist or a perfumer. I look to the natural sciences, synthetic sciences, and artificial intelligence research. That seems like a very maximalist approach, but I think that we can't really discount how we are influenced by all of these different systems and ideas and information.

—Anicka Yi

Life Serves Up The Occasional Pink Unicorn, 2013, tempura fried flowers, resin, Plexiglas, stainless steel shelves, and chrome plated dumbbells, 96 x 248 x 6 in. (243.8 x 629.9 x 15 cm), acquired in 2014
ALZ/AZN, 2015, blower, Mylar, plastic, wood, resin, tempura fried flowers, LED lights, and Plexiglas, 60 x 120 in. (152.4 x 304.8 cm), acquired in 2015

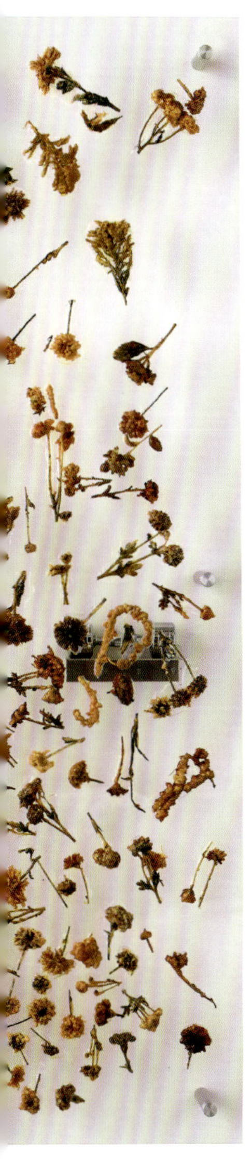
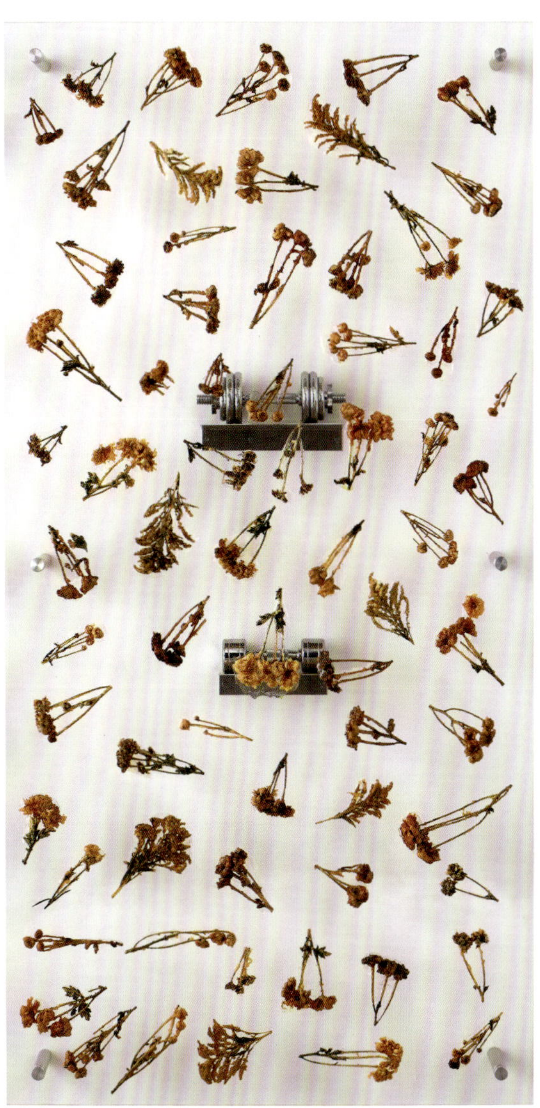
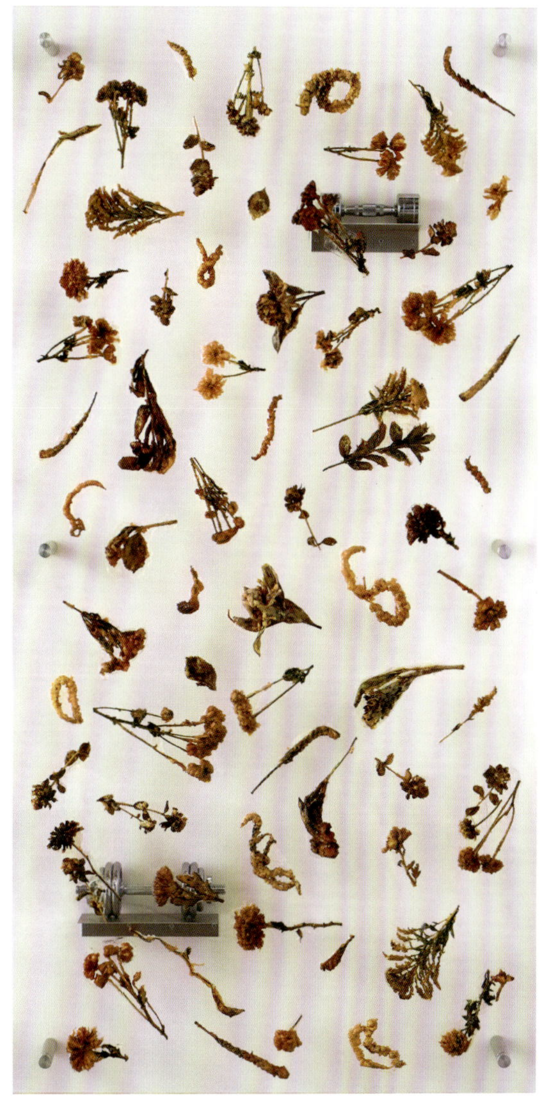
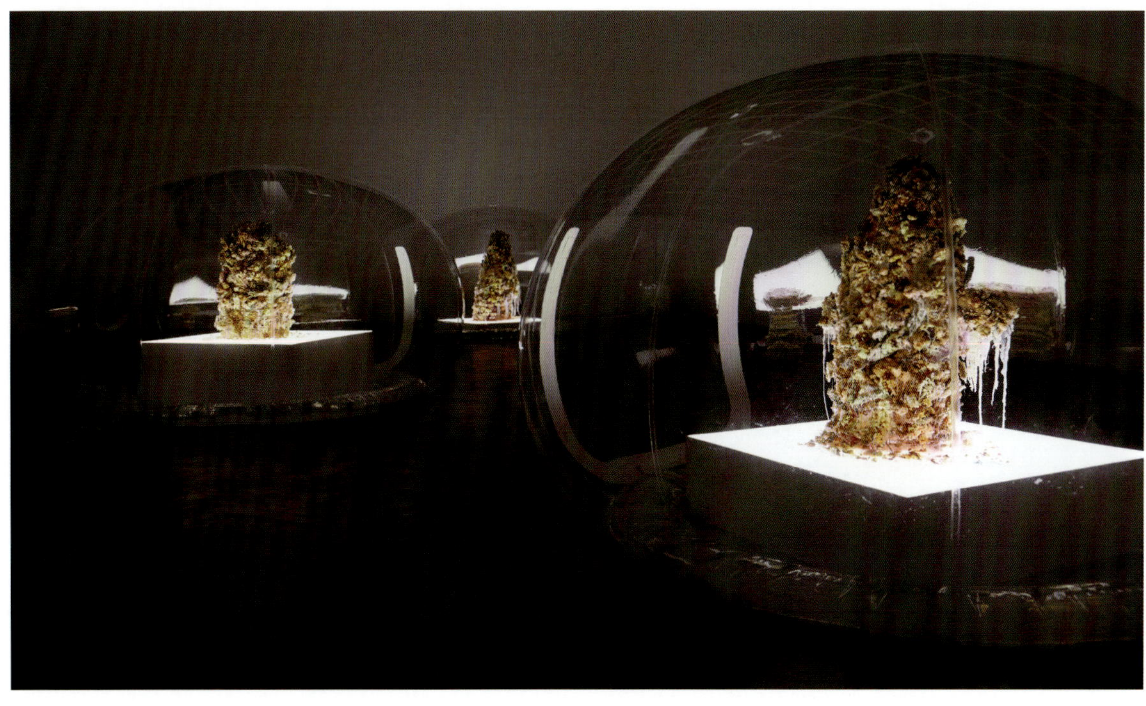

Hans Ulrich Obrist: I saw your great exhibition at the Rubell Collection. That's how I discovered your work for the first time. I was wondering if you could tell me a bit about this room, which was exhibited at the Rubells'.

Purvis Young: I must say, I paint the problems of the world— what I see in the world I paint it. Sometime I hope the world is a better place, but I just paint the problem. Sometimes I'll be around peoples and listen to them, you know, talk during the riots and like that. I didn't want to be nowhere near a painter, I just paint to paint. I started looking at the peoples and I start painting these things, what I see—it's problems, angels, sometimes I paint drugs with the angels trying to get rid of the drugs. As I get older, man, I kind of change when I see that. I listen to *The History Channel*—

HUO: Like on TV?

PY: Yeah, history always repeat itself. Sometime America is again like the Wild, Wild West, you know, and I just paint what I see, and it's some good things too. But my goal is one day to go to Europe, go somewhere and travel, man. I've been to New York about two or three times, and I don't get excited by New York. Go to Europe… and sometime I read about painters like Henri Toulouse-Lautrec...

HUO: I read that in an interview you said that when you started in the '60s to paint, that it had to do with politics and with Vietnam. Which got you started, the protests? So can one say that your painting grew out of protest?

PY: Yeah, it grew out of protest, but I looked at the *Wall of Respect* [1967 mural in Chicago]—how guys express their feelings painting murals on the wall. Then I paint sometimes my way, because some people probably think I'm happy, you know, that Purvis Young happy. But sometimes I paint to let them know that I have problems, because I'm human, and that's why I paint. But as I grow older, the round faces I do, when I wake up and go to sleep I can see faces in my dream. See, like me, I don't go to church or anything like that, the church in my heart. Like the American Indian, how he quote things and all like that. I don't know why I get older and the faces come to me.

HUO: Like the faces, which are also in many of the paintings?

PY: And in my drawing, it comes to me in a dream. As I get older, some say "Purvis, see the storms." Some tell me that they're going to destroy not only New Orleans…I've been to New Orleans two or three times and I cried when I see that.

But something tell me, a vision tell me, to get prepared.

HUO: And so how do you work? These faces, they visit you at night?

PY: They start visiting me. What I mean by that, it look like these faces come in real now as I sleep, and then when I wake up, I can see a face, you know. I tell peoples that, they probably say, "Ah man, you crazy as hell!" But I don't smoke dope or drugs. Actually, I wake up, I don't get nervous if I wake up and see something that I can't describe. I won't get afraid because this face will come and look at me like that.

HUO: Do you make sketches or do you directly paint on the material?

PY: Sometimes I make sketches. Sometimes it already be in my mind what I'm going to do. Sometimes I imagine making people work. I like to see people work, so sometimes I paint to develop the pictures, get big trucks carrying, doing work, dump trucks. I do that.

A lot peoples have been very good to me. Just like they setting up the show, different peoples, one took me to one state, to another one. And I never been to California, but as I look at America…I'm getting a look, man, it's a beautiful place! When you ride in Virginia—and I've been all through the South, New Orleans, and the landscape—I'm like a little kid, man, I'm like a little ol' child, been born again. I be looking at faraway places. Some say, "Damn Purvis! Look at you traveling!" Indiana and Ohio…oh man. I use to read about the Underground Railroad. I don't know why I am so interested in the Underground Railroad. Do you know what that is?

Slaves, slaves, and the people helped slaves. So when I was in Ohio, I look on the *The History Channel* about Ohio, how once you in Ohio you're free. I seen the Ohio River. I seen the peoples. I don't why, I don't know if I was here before or I was a slave, and I fantasize of being a Zulu warrior. I usually don't tell peoples my feelings.

HUO: A warrior?

PY: A Zulu warrior. I wasn't a chief, but I was a guy that obeyed. I put myself in battle, you know. As I get older, I see how the British came and colonized Zululand and I feel like I was a Zulu warrior.

Untitled, 1985-1999, paint on wooden tabletop, diameter 54 in. (137.2 cm) x 2 in. (5.1cm), acquired in 1999

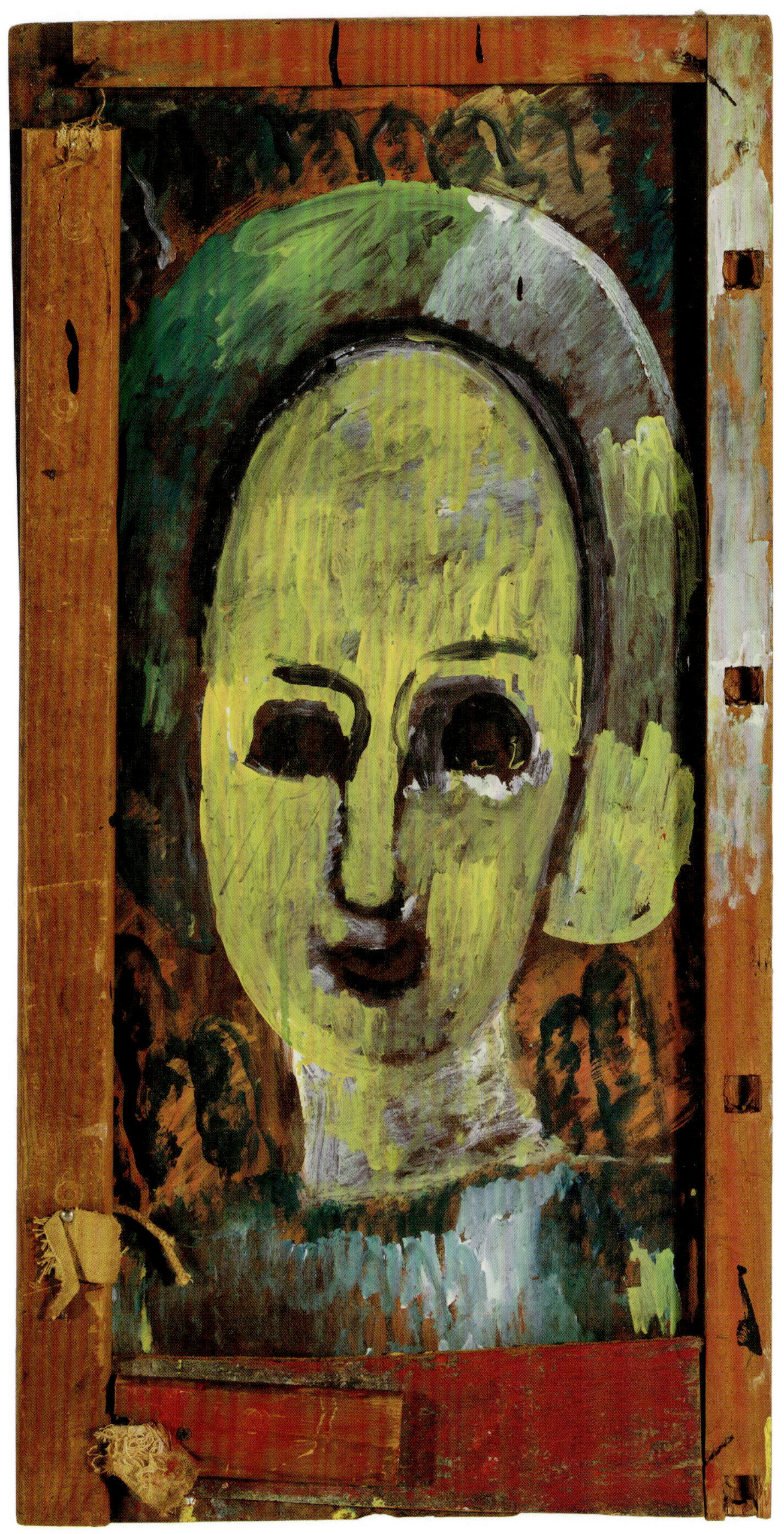

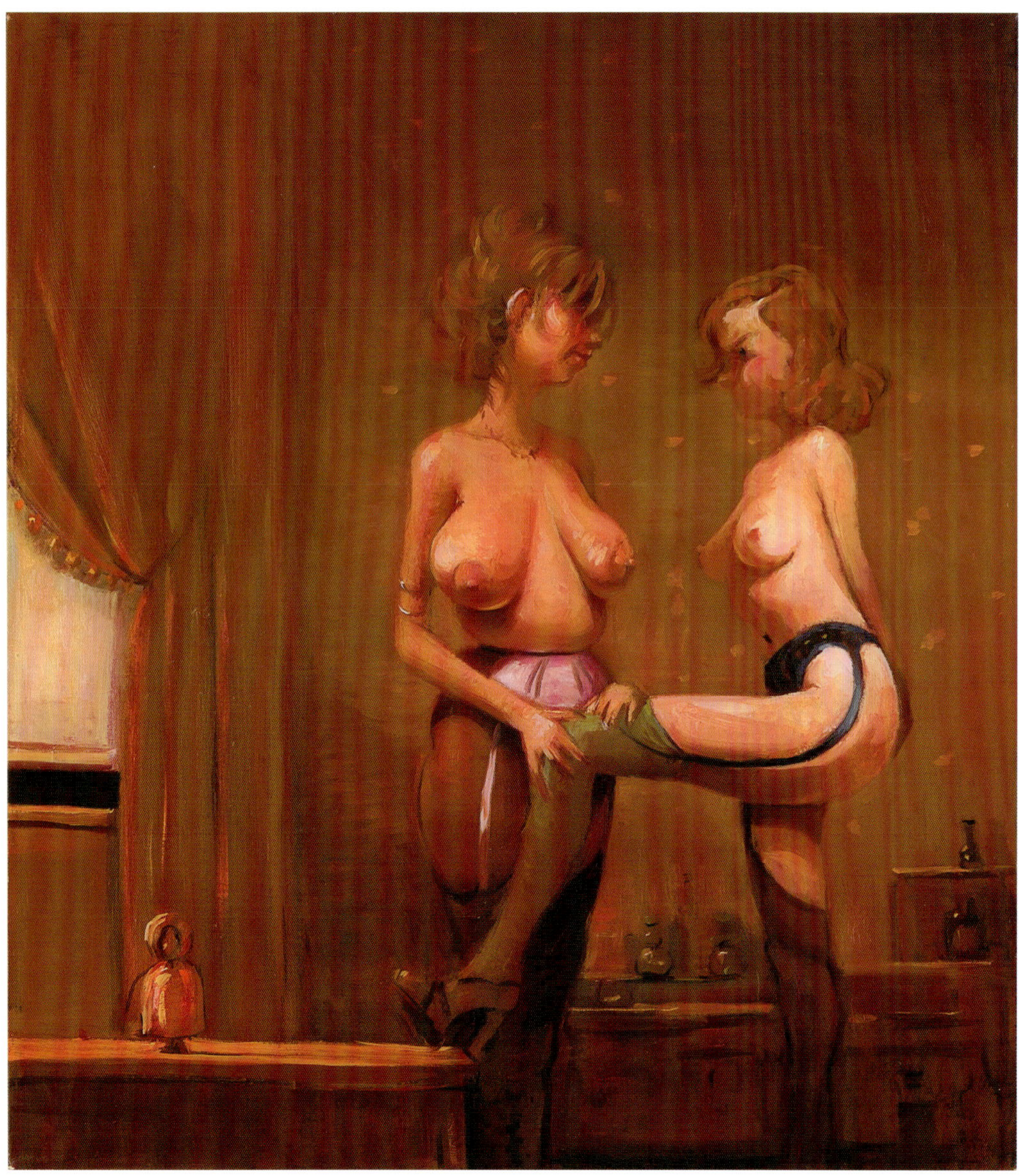

Northview [opposite] is one of five or six large canvases that I made from 1999 to 2001. I titled them all simply *Northview*. The title reflects the name of an estate in Westchester, New York. I had been researching how photographs in *Penthouse* from the 1970s were made, and I sent a fan letter to one of my favorite photographers among them (Bob Guccione having already passed away).

The photographer wrote back and I ended up in a long conversation with him about the way they worked and how their sets were borrowed mansions and beach houses. I had created a few paintings using borrowed images from *Penthouse* and felt uncomfortable continuing on that trajectory. Simultaneously, I was already beginning to work on

paintings (1997/1998) derived from simple sets in my studio with handmade costumes, props, and furniture. This idea of borrowing a location stayed in my mind, and shortly thereafter I was able to visit Northview with a friend whose mom lives there. I had also been reading about, and was interested in, the home of Laura Ashley. Her taste level and style were intriguing to me: über potent femininity. I brought models to Northview and made some pictures that I could take back to the studio to work from. This also marked a break in my work from the usual figure/ground relationship and got me more into the feeling of the ground being laced with the same intense feeling as the figure.

—Lisa Yuskavage

Lupe & Lola II, 2003, oil on linen, 20 x 18 in. (50.8 x 45.7 cm), acquired in 2003
Opposite page: *Northview*, 2000, oil on linen, 77 x 62 in. (195 x 157.5 cm), acquired in 2001

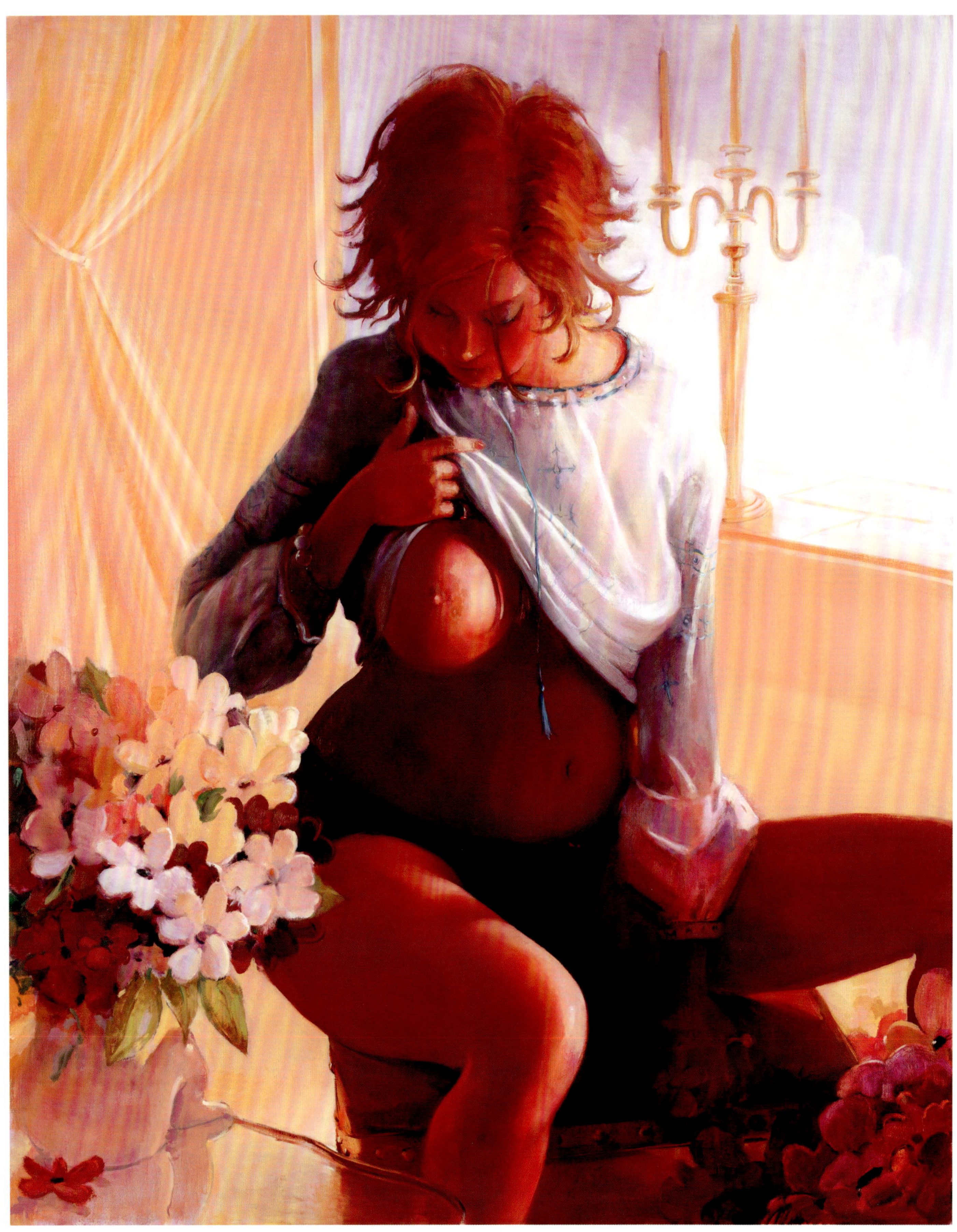

Post Me, Post You (2022) relates to an earlier piece of mine called *Messy Minors* (2010) that I made in Stockholm while I was pursuing my master's degree. Both pieces depict a group of girls in some sort of orgy, though *Messy Minors* was a group of plaster figures with references to classical sculpture. A few years back during COVID, I had changed materials and people were asking about older pieces. I always think it's so boring to show older pieces, so I did a remake of *Messy Minors*. It started with the piece *X Plus X Equals x* (2021) that I did for Kunsthalle Düsseldorf that was of a stripper. After making a new version of that and revisiting similar poses and the context of the work, I felt that this was actually really fun and thought to do the same for *Messy Minors*, one of my bigger pieces.

Post Me, Post You was made in the moment when I had just gotten pregnant, which I think is very funny. I was working with this very sexy scene and at the same time getting inseminated via IVF. It made so much sense because I really enjoyed having this synthetic pregnancy, and I feel that it relates back to the piece because the piece reflects a kind of synthetic sex. The figures are oddly not interested in each other, but they are interested in the images of themselves and in the kind of content that comes out of those camera lenses. They are not touching, but they are connected in this other world of social media. I wanted to capture the weirdness of being more interested in the portrayal of sex than in the actual thing. Now that I am using silicone and objects in my work, I knew that I wanted the technique and camera lenses to have reference to porn, but I wanted the figures to be in command. The lenses shoot out from their bodies instead of onto them. The figures' feet and fingers are growing into these pleasure objects, a kind of "*über* lesbian." I wanted to show how things are moving so fast that objects are growing into us. Just by thought, or by will, the figures are evolving that way.

I really have fun in the studio when I'm squeezing in materials that could easily fit into a whole show or layering ten different pieces onto one piece. I spent a lot of time during art school making big installations because I was always really keen on having the viewer walk into a situation and be a part of it. I think that's why when I make flat work, I end up ripping it into a thousand pieces. I have a really hard time relating to a frame. I love that with sculpture you're bodily there with something. You can walk around it; it has a butt. A painting doesn't have an ass and that bothers me. It's always confronting you with what it wants to say, and I think that's annoying. It can't take a break from communicating.

In Stockholm, classical sculptures in white marble are part of the city landscape. When I started working with sculpture, I wanted to refer to that but with more reference on my friends. We were sharing then the kind of "growing togetherness" that my sculptures are still sharing today where they're uncannily alike, almost clones of each other. When I work with a big piece that contains lots of characters, they have all tried each other's heads. They have all rotated their body parts until they end up like they do. Even though it's one piece with several people, I actually don't know how many people end up in the bed.

To create these figures, I cast friends, I always cast gay men, and I always work larger than life. I also sculpt the faces on my own. This comes from my earlier ways of working, which was very traditional, sculpting everything in clay or Styrofoam and then layering plaster on top. That's how I start off with a lot of the parts that are for the silicone pieces as well, casting from real bodies and parts of mannequins. I use it as a sort of puzzle. When you cast from silicone, it's like a thick skin and you can wrap it around a harder core made of foam or old mannequins just to build up the volume. Then I saw the figures into pieces to break up their poses to make them more flexible, or to make the legs more masculine or the torso more feminine. It's like a chopped-up body that is then reassembled. Then I dress it in silicone skin and sculpt all the parts that need to flow together. It takes a lot of sculpting to make it all come together into one full body again.

A shift happened to me when I started with silicone. I thought, I have the luxury of being an artist, so why am I not making the best out of it? Why am I not having as much fun as I want to have? And then I just closed that door and opened another one and rediscovered a lot of things, but with skills this time. People talk about my work as being so provocative. Back in the day I was happy to hear those words because it meant to me that I was being seen. But now I'm kind of surprised because that is not what I strive for at all. Obviously, I want people to be there and I love seeing when people meet my work, but it also says a lot about our time that we haven't developed that much. When you meet my work, I want that feeling of being slammed with information. I think that's a result of earlier in my practice trying to have control over what I release into the world and how that communicates with the viewer. I just let go of that leash. Let's just trust that people will have fun with not being able to solve this. Maybe it will spark something, whether it's good or bad.   —Cajsa von Zeipel

Post Me, Post You, 2022, aqua resin, silicone, fiberglass, faux eyelashes, glass eyes, synthetic hair, one Yeezy Boost, one Yeezy Foam Runner, acrylic nails, ball pins, camera lens, coffee cups, dirt bike helmet, horse goggles, dummy camera, earrings, elastic ribbon (LOVE), fill foam, flex foam, foam noodles, harness, GoPro accessories and harnesses, gray loungewear, gray sweatshirt fleece, halo ring light, hardware, hookah, horse sunshades, high density foam slabs, kayak oar holder, king-size memory foam mattress, knee brace, lenticular, MDF, medical inflatable walking boot, metal rods, mini projector, monitor desk mount, pigmented silicone, rubber tube, sex toys, shower sponge pouf, stone 3D air, spacer fabric, studs, T pins on bedframe, and video, 104 x 88 x 88 in. (264.2 x 223.5 x 223.5 cm), acquired in 2022

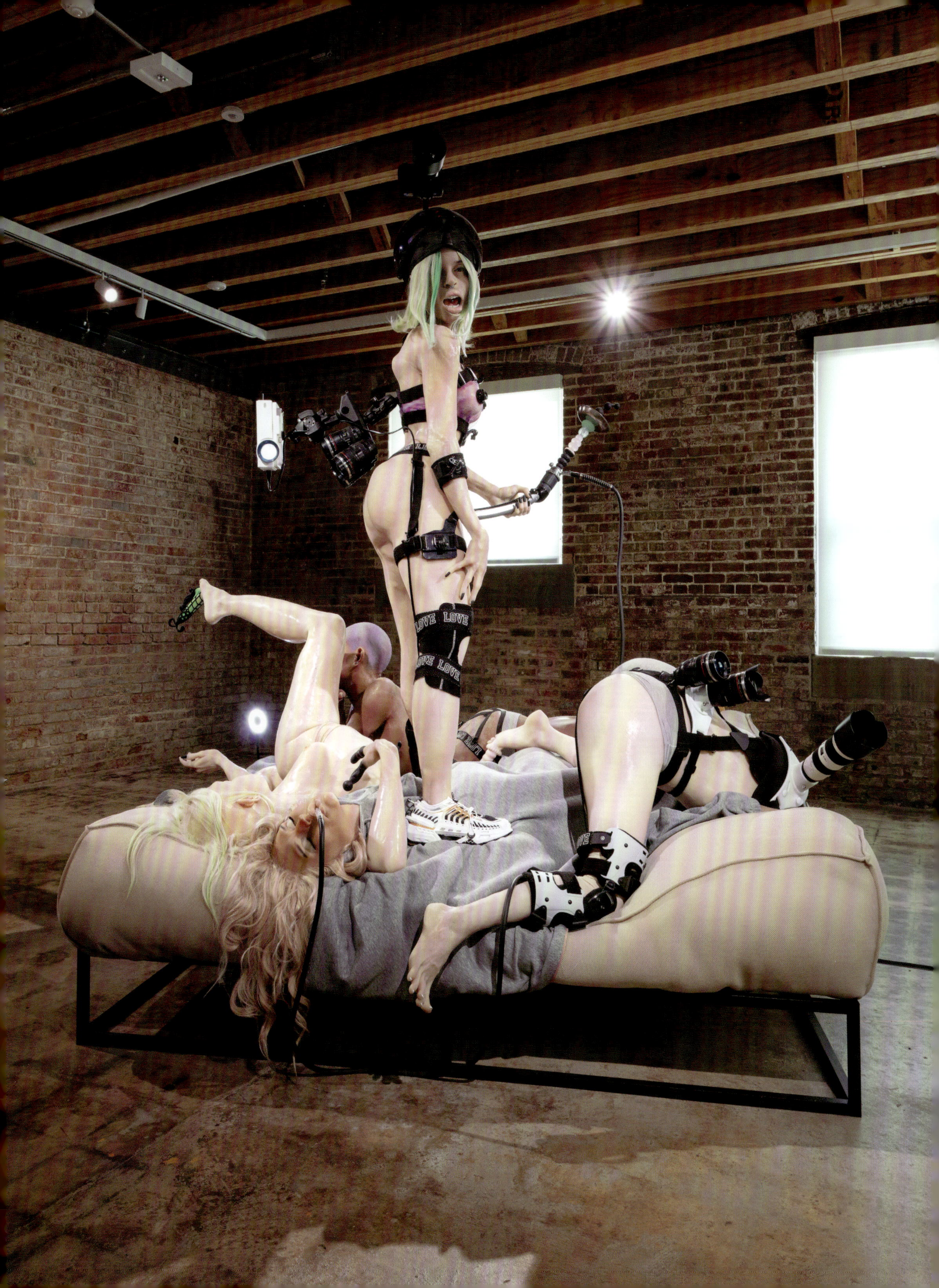

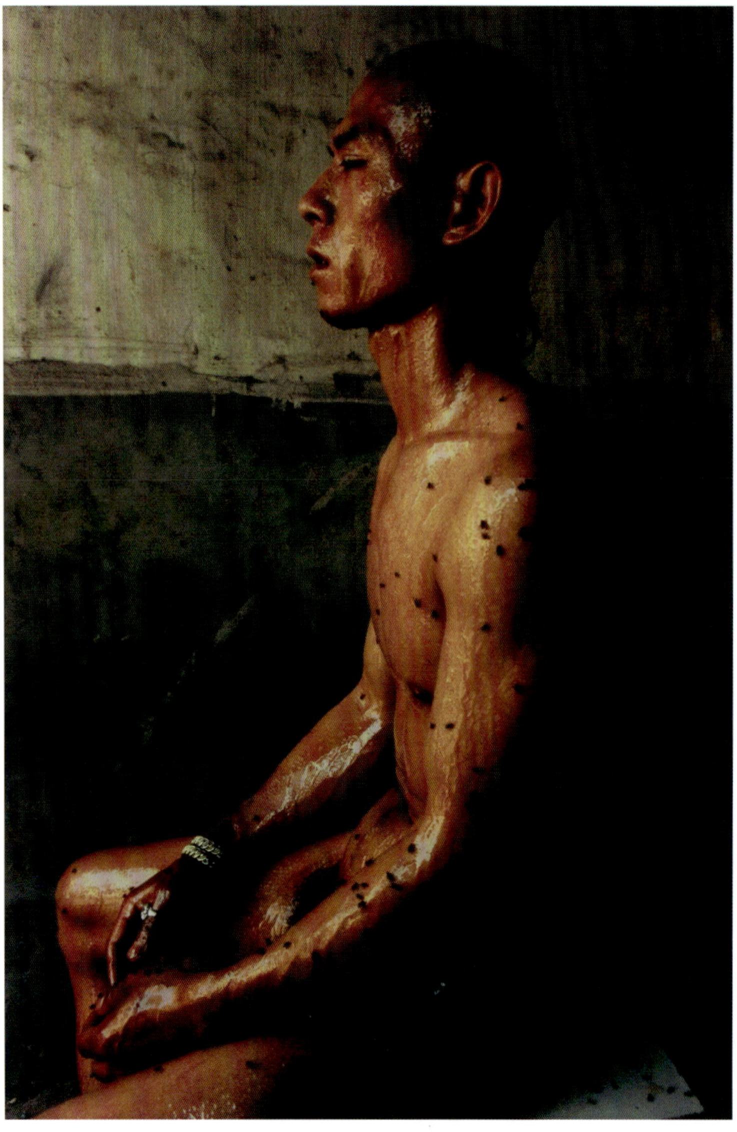

I created two works in 1994, *12 Square Meters* and *65 Kilograms*, to directly reflect our lives in the East Village. Twelve square meters is the area of the public toilets that are used every day in China. One day after lunch, I went to the toilet as usual. The sun had just come out following a rainstorm, but there was no place to stand in the toilet for it was flooded. I had to bike to another public toilet in the village. It was relatively cleaner. When I stepped in, thousands of flies swarmed toward me and I still had to squat down. This was my life, and no one could experience it but me. I was determined to make artworks about my life and suddenly came up with the idea of *12 Square Meters*. The next day, I experimented with pieces of paper: on one side of the paper I put honey and on the other side fishy-smelling liquid. When I left the coated papers in the courtyard, flies swarmed to them. Several days later, I realized the performance. I invited photographers with still and video cameras to document the piece. I remember a video camera almost fell into the toilet during taping, which was unnerving since we had rented the expensive machine from a TV station. I sat upright and unsupported in the middle of the toilet for an hour. My body was covered with honey and fish juice, and before long, flies were all over my body, even my lips and eyes. It was uncomfortable. Some people walked in accidentally during the course of the performance. When they saw me, they were embarrassed and surprised. They wanted to leave but couldn't because they had already begun to pee. They probably never would understand what they saw. In the course of the hour, I tried to forget myself and separate my mind from my flesh, but I was pulled back to reality again and again. Only after the performance did I understand what I experienced. An hour later, I walked out of the toilet and into a nearby pond that was polluted with garbage. I walked until water covered my head, and hordes of flies struggled on the water to save their lives.

12 Square Meters, 1994, c-print on Fuji archival paper, ed. 1/15, 60 1/2 x 40 3/4 in. (153.7 x 102.9 cm), acquired in 1999

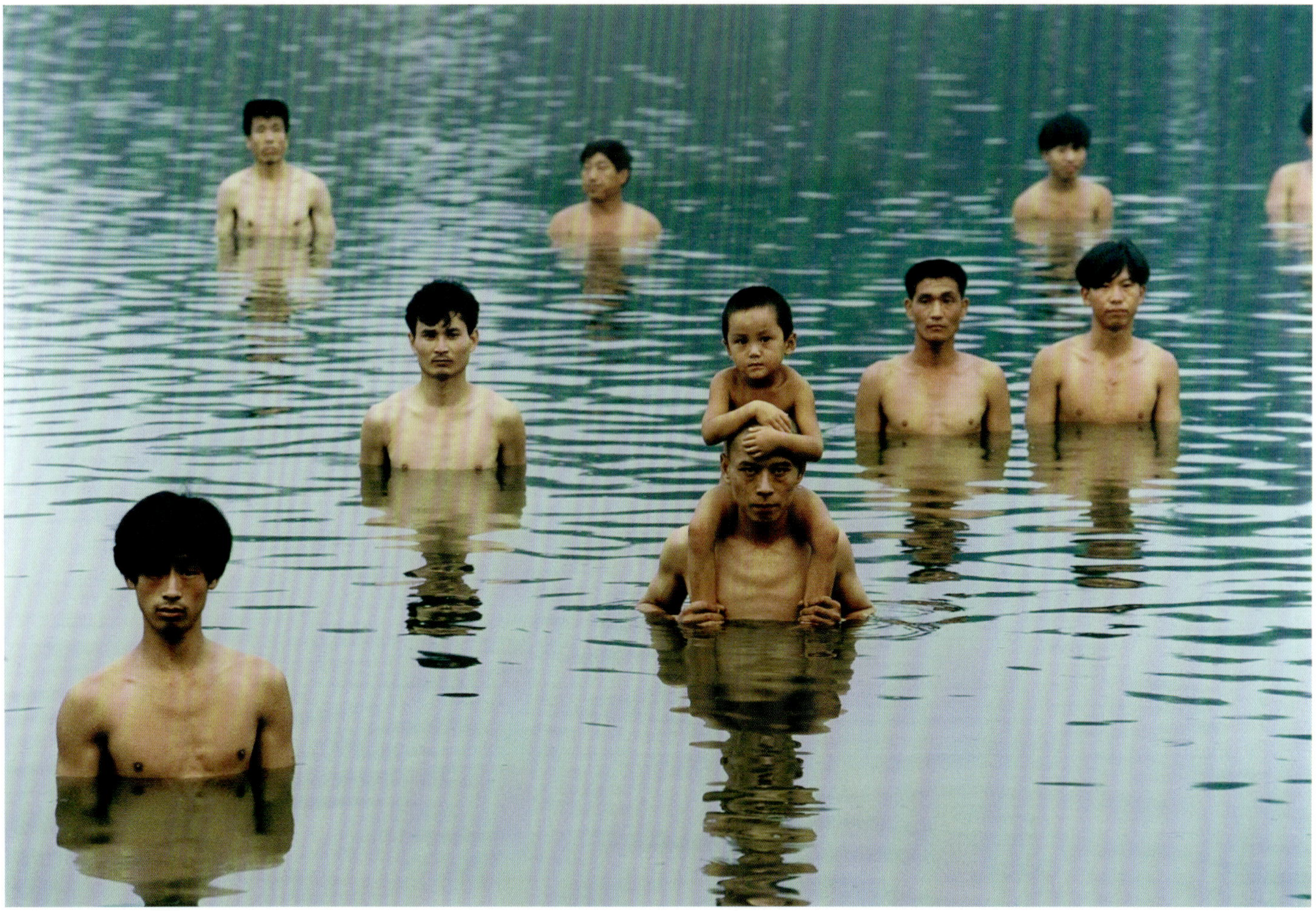

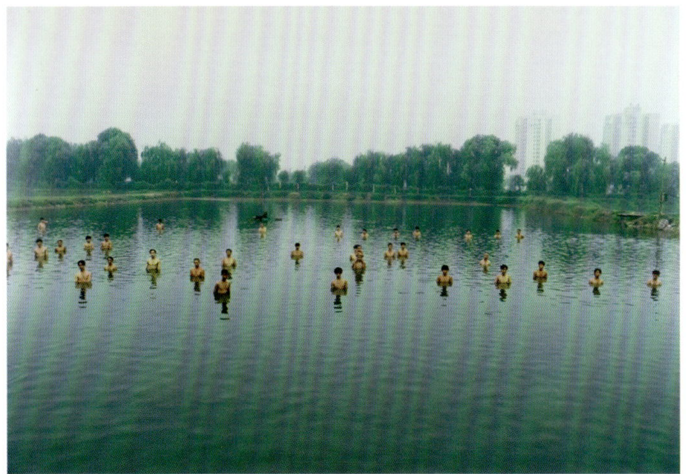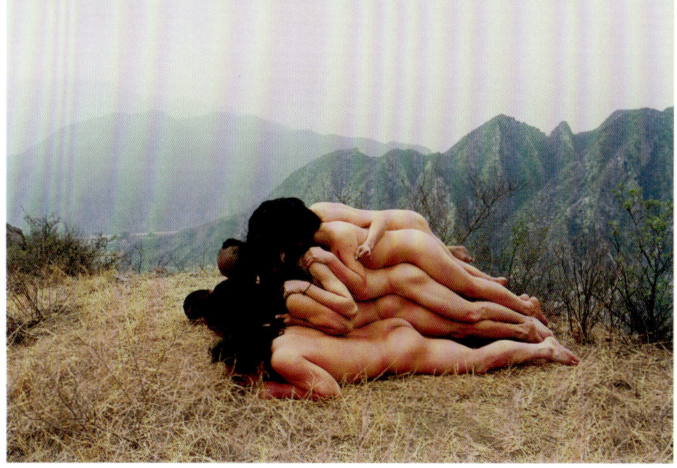

In the summer of 1997, I created *To Raise the Water Level in a Fishpond*. I invited more than 40 immigrant workers in Beijing to participate. They came from all over the countryside and ranged in age from 20 to 60. Some worked in moving companies and construction, while others sold fish. I went to many shabby tents (their homes) in order to find them. At the time, I lived within walking distance from a fishpond. The immigrant workers didn't understand what I was doing but simply followed my instructions. When I saw them, they reminded me of my uncles and brothers from my childhood.

The piece has three parts. First, we circled the pond with five to six meters between each person and faced the pond in silence. Next, we raised the water level of the pond. For the final part, we stood as a human wall to divide the fishpond in two. The boy on my back was the son of the fishpond owner and only five years old. Surprisingly, he did very well that day. I had created pieces related to mountains, so I wanted to make some related to water; this work fulfilled that desire. To my knowledge, it was the first time that an artist collaborated with immigrant workers. —Zhang Huan

Top to bottom right:
To Raise the Water Level of a Fishpond (Close-up), 1997, c-print on Fuji archival paper, ed. 4/5, 60 x 90 in. (152.4 x 228.6 cm), acquired in 1999
To Raise the Water Level of a Fishpond (Distant), 1997, c-print on Fuji archival paper, ed. 2/15, 40 3/4 x 60 1/2 in. (102.9 x 153.7 cm), acquired in 1999
To Add One Meter to an Anonymous Mountain, 1995, c-print on Fuji archival paper, Ed. 1/15, 46 x 65 in. (116.8 x 165.1 cm), acquired in 1999

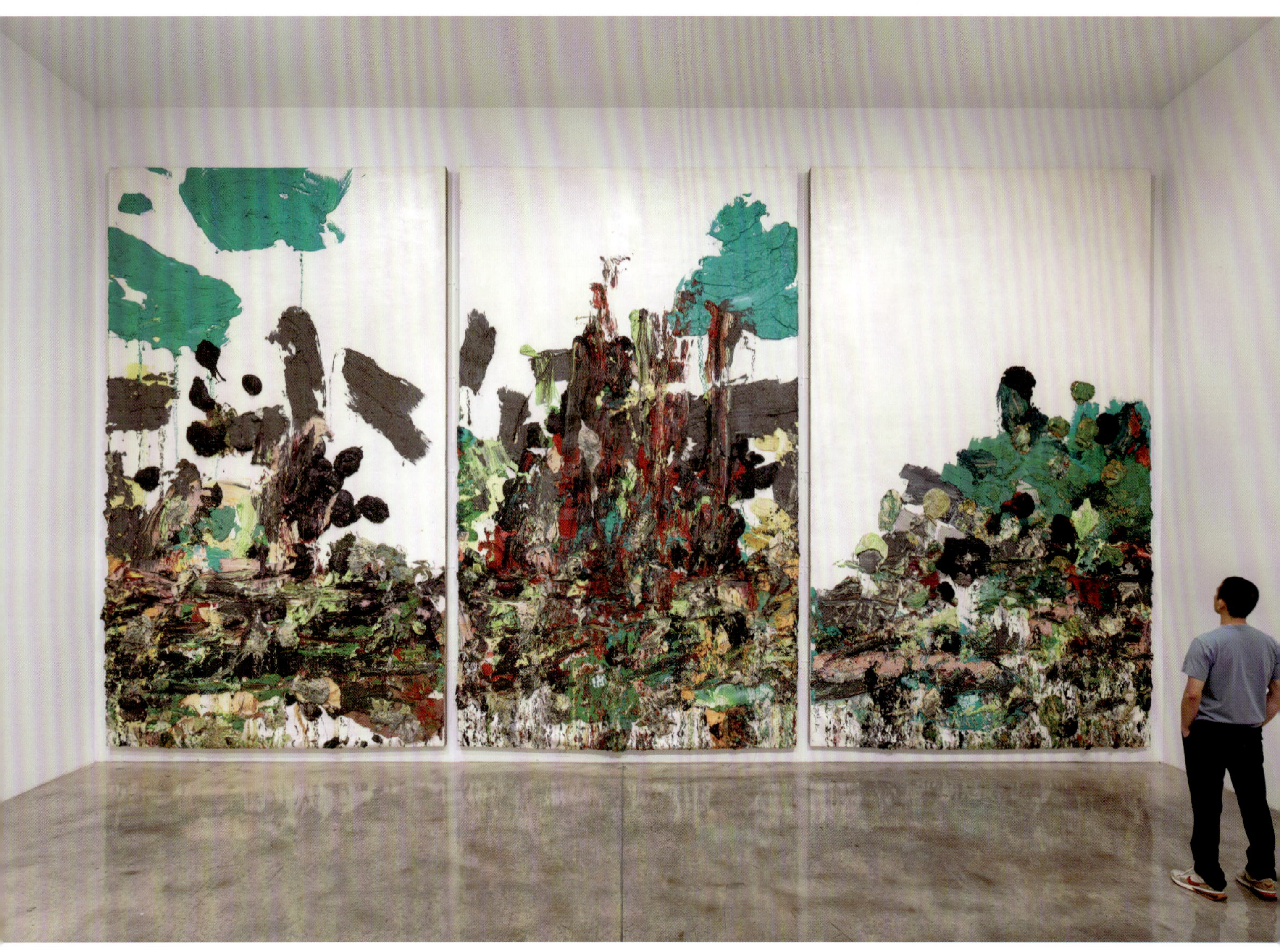

The triptych *Power and Country* was completed from 2007 to 2009, with an interlude in between. In 2008, when preparing installation works in Alario Gallery, one plan was that a Mercedes-Benz hit this work in the process of completion. After further consideration, it was replaced by ten tons of red oil paint, which could express the red political symbol of the country more.

The surviving unfinished work continued being developed after the exhibition of *Power and Country*. In the final stage, I used a giant shovel to work, cutting the paint on the painting horizontally, leaving its shovel marks everywhere.

This shovel has always been used to shovel the heating boiler coal in winter. Before the demolition of the studio, I fixed this shovel and the coal on the surface of a three-meter painting.

The entire work was completed without using a single paintbrush but only color palettes. This work used over 100 color palettes, which have been preserved in my studio until now.

—Zhu Jinshi

Power and Country, 2007, oil on canvas, triptych; each 191 x 117 x 6 1/2 in. (485 x 297 x 16.5 cm), acquired in 2011
Opposite page: *Boat*, 2012, Xuan paper, bamboo and, cotton thread, 590 x 137 x 165 in. (1500 x 350 x 420 cm), acquired in 2013

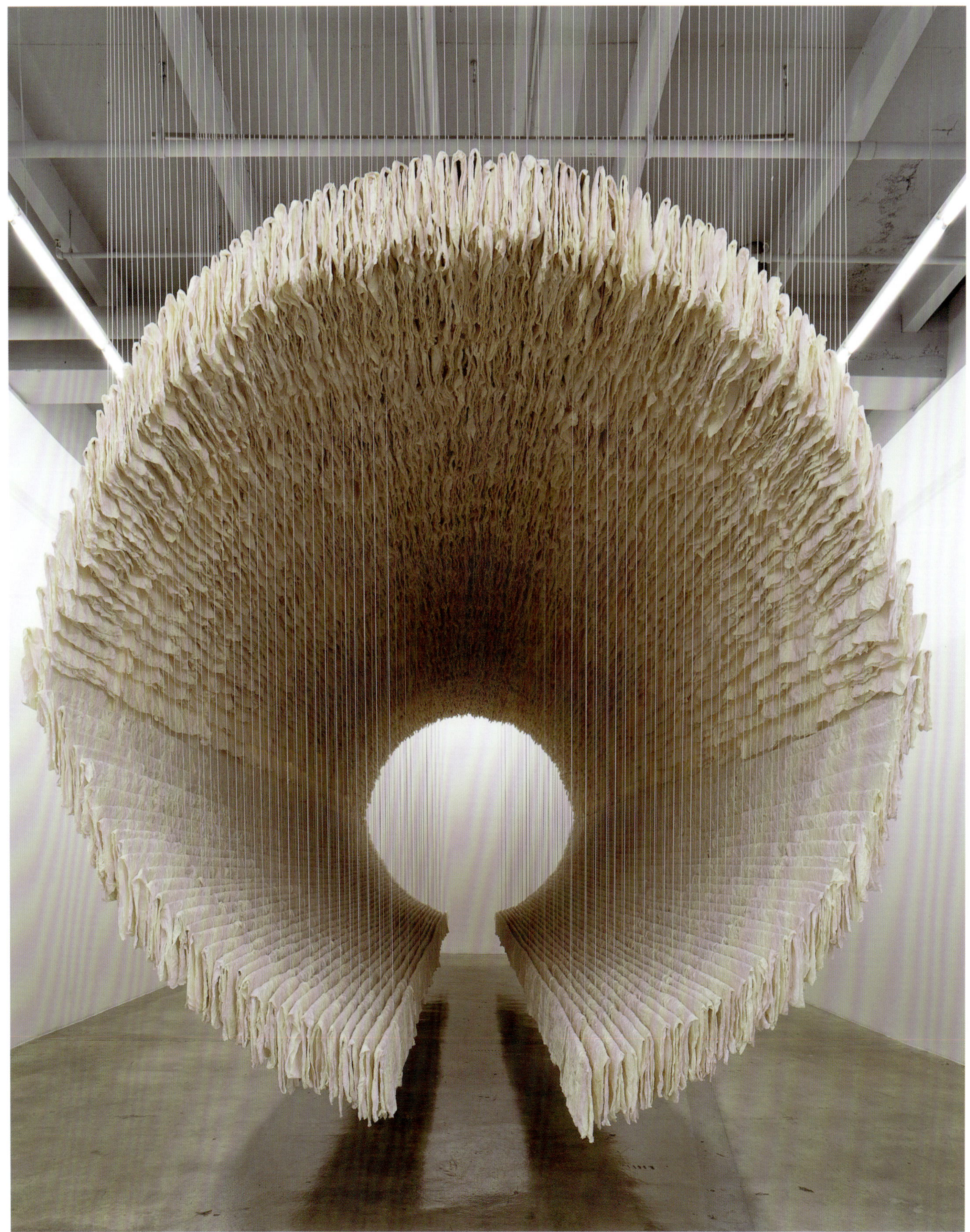

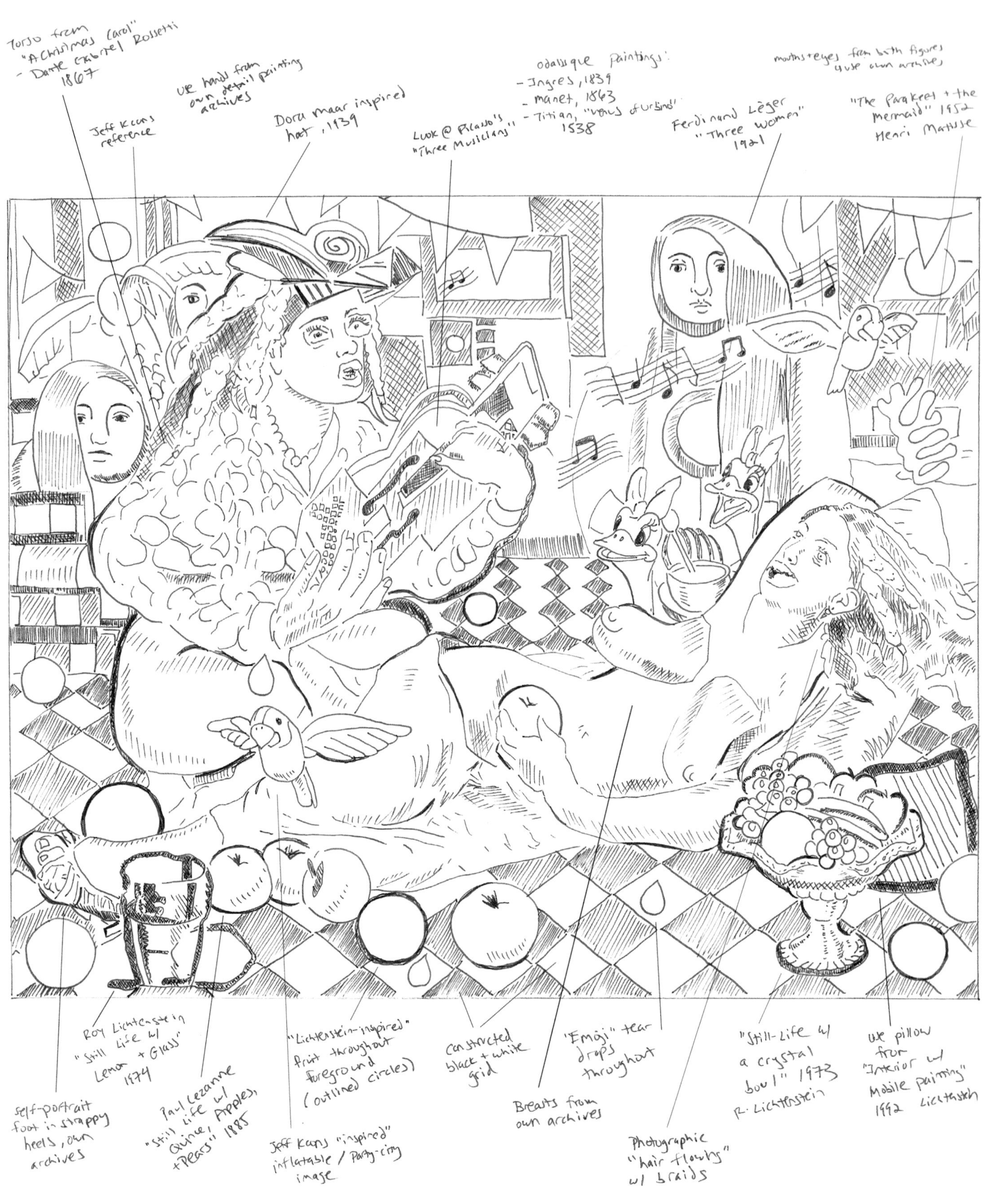
Torso from "A Christmas Carol" - Dante Gabriel Rossetti 1867
Jeff Koons reference
Use hand from own detail painting archives
Dora maar inspired hat, 1939
Look @ Picasso's "Three Musicians"
Odalisque Paintings:
-Ingres, 1839
-Manet, 1863
-Titian, "Venus of Urbino" 1538
Ferdinand Léger "Three Women" 1921
mouths+eyes from both figures use own archives
"The Parakeet + the Mermaid" 1952 Henri Matisse
Roy Lichtenstein "Still Life w/ Lemon + Glass" 1974
Self-portrait foot in strappy heels, own archives
Paul Cezanne "Still life w/ Quince, Apples +Pears" 1885
"Lichtenstein-inspired" fruit throughout foreground (outlined circles)
Jeff Koons "inspired" inflatable / Party-City image
constructed black + white grid
"Emoji" tear drops throughout
Breasts from own archives
Photographic "hair flowing" w/ braids
"Still-Life w/ a crystal bowl" 1973 R. Lichtenstein
Use pillow from "Interior w/ Mobile painting" 1992 Lichtenstein
"Serenade in the Courts"

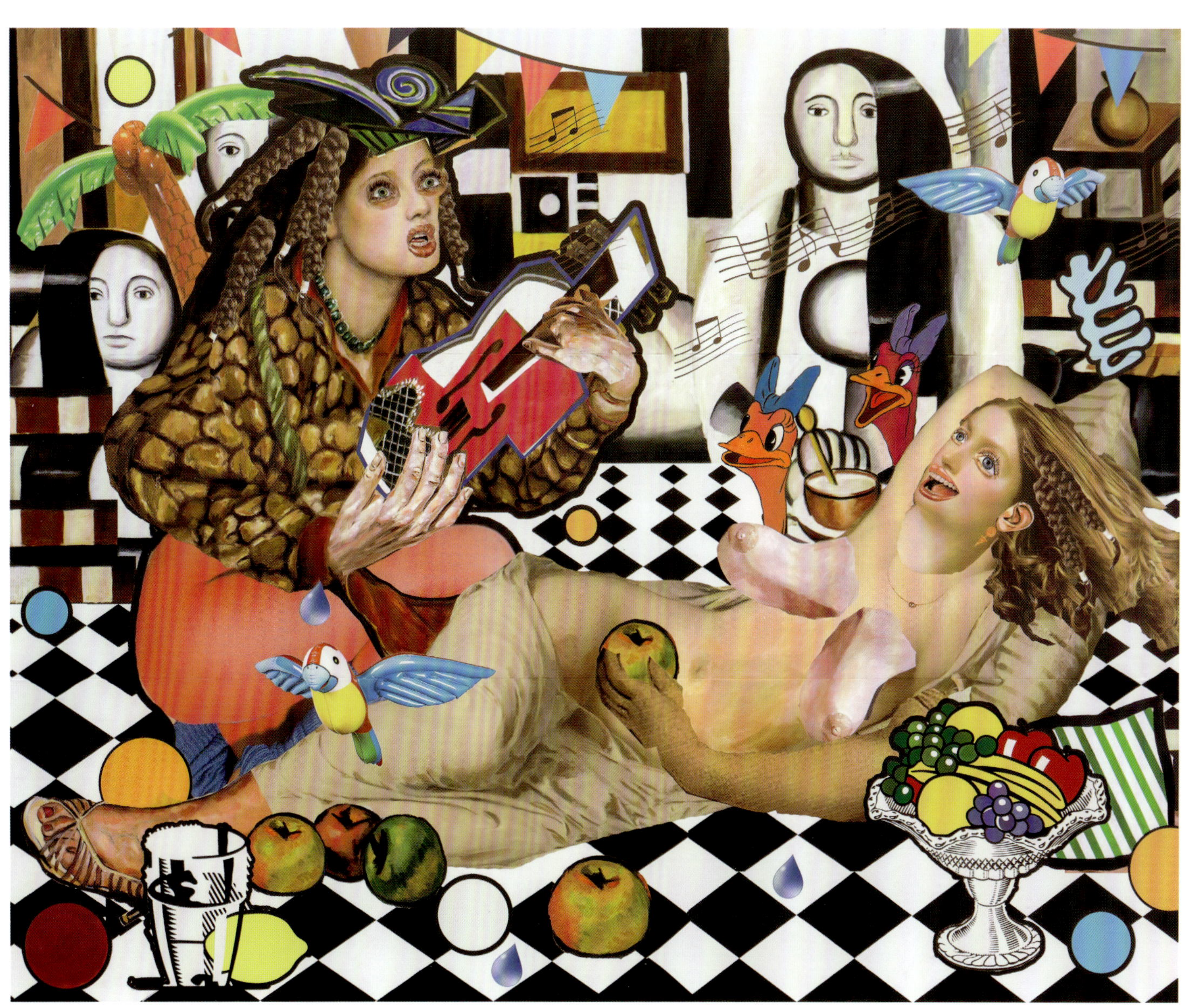

Serenade in the Courts, 2017, acrylic and inkjet on canvas, 193 1/2 x 155 1/2 in.(491 x 395 cm), acquired in 2017

THE ARTWORK IN THIS CATALOG WAS ACQUIRED FROM THE FOLLOWING

47 Canal, New York
56 Henry, New York
Galerie Paul Andriesse, Amsterdam
Luhring Augustine, New York
Atelier Cardenas Bellanger, Paris
Blum & Poe, Los Angeles/
    New York/Tokyo
Marianne Boesky Gallery, New York
Mary Boone Gallery, New York
Kathryn Brennan Gallery, New York
Gavin Brown's Enterprise, New York
Matthew Brown Gallery, Los Angeles
Galerie Buchholz, Cologne/
    Berlin/New York
David Castillo Gallery, Miami
Christie's, New York/London
Sadie Coles HQ, London
Company Gallery, New York
Contemporary Fine Arts, Berlin
Contrasts Gallery, Shanghai
Paula Cooper Gallery, New York
Pilar Corrias Gallery, London
Diego Cortez
Massimo De Carlo, Milan/
    London/Hong Kong/Paris
Elizabeth Dee Gallery, New York
Jeffrey Deitch, New York/Los Angeles
Anthony d'Offay Gallery, London
Dvir Gallery, Tel Aviv/Brussels/Belgium
Galerie Eigen + Art, Leipzig/Berlin
Zach Feuer Gallery, New York/
    Los Angeles
Konrad Fischer Galerie,
    Dusseldorf/Berlin
Frith Street Gallery, London
James Fuentes, New York/Los Angeles
The Fun Gallery, New York
Gagosian, New York/
    Los Angeles/London
Fort Gansevoort, New York/Los Angeles
Sandra Gering Inc., New York
Gladstone Gallery, New York/
    Brussels/Seoul
Thierry Goldberg Gallery, New York
Caren Golden Fine Art, New York
The Goodman Gallery, Cape Town
Marian Goodman Gallery, New York/
    Paris/Los Angeles

Jay Gorney Modern Art, New York
Half Gallery, New York
Pat Hearn Gallery, New York
Rhona Hoffman Gallery, Chicago
Galerie Hussenot, Paris
Sikkema Jenkins & Co., New York
Galerie Meyer Kainer, Vienna
Galerie Georg Kargl, Vienna
Galerie Peter Kilchmann, Zurich
Phyllis Kind Gallery, New York
Michael Kohn Gallery, Los Angeles
David Kordansky Gallery, Los Angeles
Tomio Koyama Gallery, Tokyo
Krakow Witkin Gallery, Boston
Kravets Wehby Gallery, New York
Andrew Kreps Gallery, New York
Galerie Krinzinger, Vienna
Yvon Lambert, Paris
David Lewis Gallery, New York
Maccarone, New York
Sprüth Magers, Berlin/
    London/Los Angeles
Lehmann Maupin, New York/
    Hong Kong/Seoul/London
Mazzoli Gallery, Modena/Berlin
Galerie Urs Meile, Beijing/Lucerne
Mendes Wood DM, São Paulo/
    Brussels/New York
Metro Pictures, New York
Victoria Miro, London/Venice
The Modern Institute, Glasgow
Greene Naftali Gallery, New York
Annina Nosei Gallery, New York
Overduin and Kite, Los Angeles
Roslyn Oxley9 Gallery, Sydney
Pace Gallery, New York/
    London/Hong Kong
Patrick Painter Gallery, Los Angeles
Franklin Parrasch Gallery, New York
Galeria Marga Paz, Madrid
Petzel Gallery, New York
Phillips, New York/London
Galerie Eva Presenhuber,
    Zurich/Vienna
The Project Gallery, New York
Max Protetch Gallery, New York
Almine Rech, Paris/New York/
    London/Brussels/Shanghai

Regen Projects, Los Angeles
Daniel Reich Gallery, New York
Meyer Riegger, Berlin/Karlsruhe/Basel
Roberts Projects, Los Angeles
Perry Rubenstein Gallery, New York
Semaphore Gallery, New York
Tony Shafrazi Gallery, New York
Jack Shainman Gallery, New York
Amir Shariat, Vienna
Sperone Westwater, New York
Stuart Shave Modern Art, London
Sister Gallery, New York
Fredric Snitzer Gallery, Miami
Sonnabend Gallery, New York
Sotheby's, London/New York
Spinello Projects, Miami
Sprüth Magers, Berlin/
    London/Los Angeles
Taxter & Spengemann Gallery,
    New York
Thread Waxing Space, New York
Jack Tilton Gallery, New York
Untitled, New York
Galerie Ferdinand van Dieten,
    Amsterdam
Vielmetter, Los Angeles
Civilian Warfare Gallery, New York
Shoshana Wayne Gallery, Los Angeles
Daniel Weinberg Gallery, Los Angeles/
    San Francisco
Galerie Barbara Weiss, Berlin
White Cube, London
Wilding Cran Gallery, Los Angeles
Workplace, London
Zeno-X Gallery, Antwerp
David Zwirner, New York/Los Angeles/
    Paris/Hong Kong

pp. 24-25: Jack Shainman Gallery, New York. pp. 26 photo: Martha Cooper. pp. 28-29: Galerie Urs Meile, Beijing/Lucerne. pp. 30-31: Victoria Miro, London/Venice. pp. 32-33: Jack Shainman Gallery, New York. pp. 35: Luhring Augustine, New York. pp. 36-37: Matthew Brown Gallery, Los Angeles. pp. 38-39: Marian Goodman Gallery, New York/Paris/Los Angeles. pp. 42-43: Fredric Snitzer Gallery, Miami; Victoria Miro, London/Venice; (pp. 42-43 photo: Markus Haugg). pp. 44-45: © The Estate of Jean-Michel Basquiat. pp. 46-47: Andrew Kreps Gallery, New York; Overduin & Co., Los Angeles; Sadie Coles HQ, London. pp. 48-49: © 2023 Amoako Boafo / Licensed by Artists Rights Society (ARS), New York. pp. 50-51: © 2023 Artists Rights Society (ARS), New York / ADAGP, Paris; Marian Goodman Gallery, New York. pp. 52-53: Zeno X Gallery, Antwerp. pp. 54-55: Hauser & Wirth, London/Zürich/New York. pp. 56-57: Gagosian, New York/Los Angeles/London. pp. 58-59: Meyer Riegger, Berlin/Karlsruhe/Basel. pp. 60-61: Marian Goodman Gallery, New York/Paris/Los Angeles; Perrotin, Paris/New York. pp. 62-63: Jack Shainman Gallery, New York (p. 62 photo: James Prinz Photography). pp. 64-65: Company Gallery, New York. pp. 66-67: Gagosian, New York/Los Angeles/London. pp. 68-69: © 2023 The Robert H. Colescott Separate Property Trust / Artists Rights Society (ARS), New York. pp. 70-71: © 2023 George Condo / Artists Rights Society (ARS), New York. pp. 72-73: Wilding Cran Gallery, Los Angeles. pp. 74-75: © Estate of Noah Davis, David Zwirner, New York/Los Angeles. pp. 76-77: Marian Goodman Gallery, New York/Paris/Los Angeles. pp. 80-81: © 2023 Artists Rights Society (ARS), New York; Tanya Bonakdar Gallery, New York/Los Angeles. pp. 82-83: David Lewis Gallery, New York; Sprüth Magers, Berlin/London/Los Angeles. pp. 84-85: Galerie Lelong & Co., New York/Paris. pp. 86-87: Galerie Paul Andriesse, Amsterdam; Frith Street Gallery, London; David Zwiner, New York/Los Angeles/Paris/Hong Kong. pp. 88-89: Galerie Eva Presenhuber, Zürich/Vienna. pp. 90-91: © 2023 Artists Rights Society (ARS), New York / VG Bild-Kunst, Bonn; Galerie Bucholz, Cologne/Berlin/New York; David Zwirner, New York/Los Angeles. pp. 92-93: Lehmann Maupin, New York/Hong Kong/Seoul/London. pp. 94-95: Matthew Marks Gallery, New York. pp. 96-97: Mendes Wood DM, São Paulo/Brussels/New York. pp. 98-99: © Estate Felix Gonzalez-Torres, courtesy Felix Gonzalez-Torres Foundation. pp. 100-101: Matthew Marks Gallery, New York. pp. 102-103: Almine Rech, Paris/New York. pp. 105: David Kordansky Gallery, Los Angeles. pp. 107: © 2023 David Hammons / Artists Rights Society (ARS), New York. pp. 108-109: Luhring Augustine, New York; Galerie Eva Presenhuber, Zürich/Vienna. pp. 110-113: © the Keith Haring Foundation, courtesy of the Haring Foundation and Gladstone Gallery, New York/Brussels. pp. 114-115: © Estate of Barkley L. Hendricks; Jack Shainman Gallery, New York. pp. 116-117: © Damien Hirst and Science Ltd. All rights reserved / DACS, London / ARS, NY 2023; White Cube, London. pp. 118-119: © 2023 Jenny Holzer, member Artists Rights Society (ARS), New York. pp. 120-121: © 2023 Artists Rights Society (ARS), New York / ADAGP, Paris; Gagosian, New York/Los Angeles/London. pp. 122-123: Pace Gallery, New York/London/Hong Kong. pp. 124-125: Hauser & Wirth, London/Zürich/New York; David Kordansky Gallery, Los Angeles. pp. 127: Galerie Krinzinger, Vienna. pp. 128-129: © 2023 Mike Kelley Foundation for the Arts. All Rights Reserved / Licensed by VAGA at Artists Rights Society (ARS), NY; Gagosian, New York/Los Angeles/London. pp. 130-131: Goodman Gallery, Cape Town. pp. 133: Atelier Anselm Kiefer, Barjac; Gagosian, New York/Los Angeles/London. pp. 136-137: 47 Canal, New York. pp. 138-139: Jeff Koons Studio; Gagosian, New York/Los Angeles/London; Pace Gallery, New York/London/Hong Kong. pp. 140-141: Sprüth Magers, Berlin/Cologne/London. pp. 143-145: Victoria Miro, London/Venice; David Zwirner, New York/Los Angeles. pp. 146-147: Victoria Miro, London/Venice. pp. 148-149: Metro Pictures, New York; Sprüth Magers, Berlin/London/Los Angeles. pp. 150: Regen Projects, Los Angeles. pp. 154-155: © 2023 Robert Longo / Artists Rights Society (ARS), New York. pp. 156-157: Sadie Coles HQ, London. pp. 158-159: Jack Shainman Gallery, New York. pp. 160-161: Hauser & Wirth, London/Zürich/New York. pp. 162-163: James Fuentes, New York/Los Angeles. pp. 164-165: 56 Henry, New York. pp. 167: Meyer Riegger, Berlin/Karlsruhe/Basel; Praz-Delavallade, Paris. pp.169: © muchaArchiv / Artists Rights Society (ARS), New York, 2023; (photo: John Berens). pp. 170-171: © 2023 Juan Muñoz Estate, Artists Rights Society (ARS), NY / VEGAP, Madrid. pp. 172-173: Gagosian, New York/Los Angeles/London. pp. 174-175: David Zwirner, New York/Los Angeles; Isabella Bortolozzi Galerie, Berlin. pp. 176-177: Vielmetter, Los Angeles; Victoria Miro, London/Venice. pp. 178-179: James Cohan, New York. pp. 180-181: Blum & Poe, Los Angeles/New York/Tokyo. pp. 182-183: Mendes Wood DM, São Paulo/Brussels/New York. pp. 184-185: Gagosian, New York/Los Angeles/London. pp. 186-187: Spinello Projects, Miami. pp. 189: Regen Projects, Los Angeles. pp. 190-191: The Modern Institute, Glasgow. pp. 192-193: Victoria Miro, London/Venice. pp. 195: Galerie Barbara Weiss, Berlin. pp. 196-197: Mendes Wood DM, São Paulo/Brussels/New York. pp. 198-199: Gagosian, New York/Los Angeles/London. pp. 200-201: Gagosian, New York/Los Angeles/London. pp. 202-203: Contrasts Gallery, Shanghai. pp. 204-205: Roberts Projects, Los Angeles. pp. 207: Pilar Corrias Gallery, London. pp. 208-209: © Courtesy Galerie EIGEN + ART, Leipzig/Berlin / Artists Rights Society (ARS), New York, 2023. pp. 211: Matthew Marks Gallery, New York. pp. 212-213: Gagosian, New York/Los Angeles/London. pp. 214-215: © 2023 Artists Rights Society (ARS), New York / VG Bild-Kunst, Bonn. pp. 216-217: © 2023 David Salle / VAGA at Artists Rights Society (ARS), NY. Courtesy of Gladstone Gallery, NY. pp. 218-219: © 2023 Julian Schnabel / Artists Rights Society (ARS), New York. pp. 220-221: © 2023 Artists Rights Society (ARS), New York / VG Bild-Kunst, Bonn. pp. 222-223: David Zwirner, New York/Los Angeles. pp. 224-225: Pilar Corrias Gallery, London. pp. 226-227: Metro Pictures, New York; Sprüth Magers, Berlin/London/Cologne. pp. 228: Hauser & Wirth, London/Zürich/New York (photo: Chan. T. Chao, Courtesy of the Corcoran Gallery of Art). pp. 231: Franklin Parrasch Gallery, New York. pp. 232-233: Almine Rech, Paris/New York. pp. 234-235: Dvir Gallery, Tel Aviv. pp. 236-237: Hauser & Wirth, London/Zürich/New York. pp. 238-239: Jack Shainman Gallery, New York. pp. 240-241: © 2023 Mickalene Thomas / Artists Rights Society (ARS), New York. pp. 243: Almine Rech, Paris/New York. pp. 244-245: © 2023 Artists Rights Society (ARS), New York / VG Bild-Kunst, Bonn. pp. 246-247: Zeno X Gallery, Antwerp. pp. 248-249: © Estate of Kaari Upson, Sprüth Magers, Berlin/London/Cologne. pp. 250-251: Konrad Fischer Galerie, Düsseldorf/Berlin. pp. 252-253: Sikkema Jenkins & Co., New York. pp. 254-255: Jack Shainman Gallery, New York. pp. 256-257: Gladstone Gallery, New York/Brussels. pp. 258-259: Gagosian, New York/Los Angeles/London; Galerie Meyer Kainer, Vienna. pp. 260-261: Roberts Projects, Los Angeles; Jeffrey Deitch, New York/Los Angeles. pp. 262-263: © Estate of David Wojnarowicz (p. 74 © Barry Blinderman). pp. 264-265: Luhring Augustine, New York. pp. 268-269: 47 Canal, New York. pp. 271: © 2023 The Larry T. Clemons Collection / Artists Rights Society (ARS), New York. pp. 272-273: David Zwirner, New York/Los Angeles. pp. 275: Company Gallery, New York. pp. 276-277: Pace Gallery, New York/London/Hong Kong. pp. 278-279: Pearl Lam Galleries, Hong Kong/Shanghai. pp. 280-281: Kravets Wehby Gallery, New York

Notes

p. 30-31: Akunyili Crosby, Njideka, Cheryl Brutvan, and Norton Museum of Art. 2016. *Njideka Akunyili Crosby: I Refuse to Be Invisible*, 21-29. West Palm Beach Florida: Norton Museum of Art.

p. 58: Cahn, Miriam, Anette Hüsch, Schweizer Kulturstiftung Prohelvetia, and Kunsthalle zu Kiel. 2016. *Miriam Cahn: Auf Augenhöhe = at Eye Level*, 98. Kiel: Kunsthalle zu Kiel.

p. 95: Gober, Robert, Theodora Vischer, and Schaulager (Art Museum: Münchenstein Switzerland). 2007. *Robert Gober: Sculptures and Installations 1979-2007*. 1st ed. Basel Switzerland Göttingen: Schaulager; Steidl.

p. 98: Gonzalez-Torres, Felix and Tim Rollins. 1993. "Interview by Tim Rollins." In *Felix Gonzalez-Torres*, edited by Bill Bartman, 5-31. New York: Art Resource Transfer.

p. 116-117: D'Argenzio, Mirta and Damien Hirst. 2004. "Nothing is Sacred." In *Damien Hirst: Napoli Museo Archeologico Nazionale*, edited by Eduardo Cicelyn, Mario Codognato, and Mirta D'Argenzio, 182. Napoli: Electa Napoli.

p. 126: Jungwirth, Martha. 2014. "the ape in me." In *Martha Jungwirth: Retrospektive = Retrospective*, edited by Hans-Peter Wipplinger, 53-55. Bielefeld Krems: Kerber; Kunsthalle Krems.

p. 128: Kelley, Mike. "In the Image of Man," Carnegie International Volume 1 (New York: Rizzoli and Pittsburgh: The Carnegie Museum of Art, 1991): 94.

p. 130-13: Christov-Bakargiev, Carolyn and William Kentridge. "Carolyn Christov-Bakargiev in conversation with William Kentridge." In *William Kentridge*, 31-34. London: Phaidon.

p. 132: Adriani, Götz, Georg Baselitz, Gerhard Richter, Sigmar Polke, Anselm Kiefer, Staatsgalerie Stuttgart, and Deichtorhallen Hamburg. 2019. *Baselitz Richter Polke Kiefer: The Early Years of the Old Masters*, 279-282. Dresden: Sandstein Verlag.

p. 142: Kusama, Yayoi and Ralph F McCarthy. 2013. *Infinity Net: The Autobiography of Yayoi Kusama*, 54-57. London: Tate Publishing.

p. 149: Lawler, Louise, and Douglas Crimp. "Prominence Given, Authority Taken." *Grey Room*, no. 4 (2001): 74–75.

p. 158: Marshall, Kerry James. 2016. "Shall I Compare Thee…?" In *Kerry James Marshall: Mastry*, edited by Helen Molesworth, 79. Chicago New York: Museum of Contemporary Art Chicago; Skira Rizzoli Publications.

p. 170: Muñoz, Juan, Iwona Blazwich, Andrea Schlieker, and James Lingwood. 1996. *Juan Muñoz: Monologues & Dialogues*, 66;126. Madrid: Palacio de Velazquez Museo Nacional Centro de Arte Reina Sofia.

p. 188: Ferguson, Russell and Catherine Opie. 1996. "'How to Think': An Interview with Catherine Opie." In *Catherine Opie: The Photographers' Gallery London*, edited by Kate Bush, 44. London: Photographers' Gallery.

p. 196-197: Munsell, Liz and Solange Pessoa. 2020. "Solange Pessoa in Conversation with Liz Munsell." In *Solange Pessoa*, edited by Alex Bacon, 95-96. Rio de Janeiro: Circle Books.

p. 214: Ruff, Thomas and Thomas Wulffen. "Reality so Real it's Unrecognizable." In *Thomas Ruff: 13 April-9 Juni 1996, 97*. Malmö: Rooseum.

p. 218-219: Schnabel, Julian. "Writings by Julian Schnabel." 1986. In *Julian Schnabel: Paintings 1975-1986 Whitechapel 19 September-26 October 1986*, edited by Nicholas Serota and Joanna Skipwith, 94-95. London: Trustees of the Whitechapel Art Gallery.

p. 220: Lingwood, James and Thomas Schütte. 2000. "Conversation with Thomas Schütte in Düsseldorf and London. July/December 2000." In *Thomas Schutte [Published on the Occasion of the Exhibition Held at the Sammlung Goetz Munich 19 March - 11 August 2001]*, edited by Rainald Schumachler, 84-85. Munich: Sammlung Goetz.

p. 234-235: Schwenger, Peter and Haim Steinbach. 2012. "Haim Steinbach by Peter Schwenger." *BOMB Magazine*, October 1, 2012. https://bombmagazine.org/articles/haim-steinbach/

p. 254: Weems, Carrie Mae. "Carrie Mae Weems. From Here I Saw What Happened and I Cried. 1995." The Museum of Modern Art, New York. https://www.moma.org/multimedia/embed/audio/207/2012.

p. 258: West, Franz. 2013. *Franz West: Where Is My Eight?*, 138. Publishers ed. Cologne Vienna: Verlag der Buchhandlung Walther König; Mumok.

p. 262-263: Wojnarowicz, David, Barry Blinderman, and Illinois State University University Galleries. 1990. *David Wojnarowicz: Tongues of Flame*, 61-63. Normal Ill: University Galleries Illinois State University.

p. 269: Yi, Anicka. "Bodies of Knowledge." Art in the Twenty-First Century, Season 11. June 23, 2023. https://art21.org/watch/art-in-the-twenty-first-century/s11/anicka-yi-in-bodies-of-knowledge/. (Transcript of an interview from Art 21, which has been slightly modified for clarity in print).

p. 270: Ulrich Obrist, Hans and Purvis Young. "Interview with Purvis Young." 2018. In *Purvis Young*, edited by Juan Roselione-Valadez, 23-31. Miami FL: Rubell Museum.

ACKNOWLEDGEMENTS

This book exists because our Director, Juan Valadez, believed it was possible.

We wanted to mark our 60th wedding anniversary and the 30th anniversary of the opening of our public space in Miami and Washington, DC, with a book that celebrated the artwork in the Collection, but Juan was convinced that the true story of these 60 years could only be complete if it included the words of the artists in it.

When Juan explained that he wanted to reach out to many of the artists in this catalog and ask them to write about a specific work, oftentimes the first work of theirs that we collected, we thought he was crazy. These artists are way too busy and famous to spend time reminiscing about events that, in some cases, occurred 30 to 40 years ago. He insisted and insisted, and so we told him to go ahead and try. We only said that because we knew he would never succeed.

We were so wrong.

Juan's belief and persistence brought this book into being. As we started to read the texts the artists sent in—often describing the first piece they ever sold, the first time they saw a piece of theirs hung in a collector's home —we understood that the artwork only tells part of the story of our collection. Our belief in the artists in our collection is fundamental to everything we do. We are so grateful for the artists' generosity in contributing. We are awed and moved.

For over two decades, Juan has committed himself to the museum with his broad knowledge, devotion, understanding, and care. He truly loves art and has the deepest appreciation for the artists who make it. He is relentlessly aware of the precious nature of these objects and is totally committed to preserving them physically and culturally.

We must also acknowledge the enormous accomplishment of Chi Lam, our designer and photographer. This is Chi's 22nd catalog for the museum, and nearly all the photographs in this catalog were executed by him.

Alexandra Perez provided amazing research and support for realizing this project. She is an extraordinarily knowledgeable professional who provides a depth of art-historical understanding that inspires our entire staff.

Acknowledgment and thanks to William Vargas and his colleague Leyden Ayure for installing and staging the complicated photo shoots of the artworks. We appreciate our team's focus, drive, and endless attention to detail.

We are also very grateful to Elizabeth Martinez for her meticulous research and work on all of our catalogs.

Every member of our team was crucial in creating the most extensive catalog of our Collection to date. It was a tremendous undertaking.

We are thankful and grateful.

RUBELL FAMILY

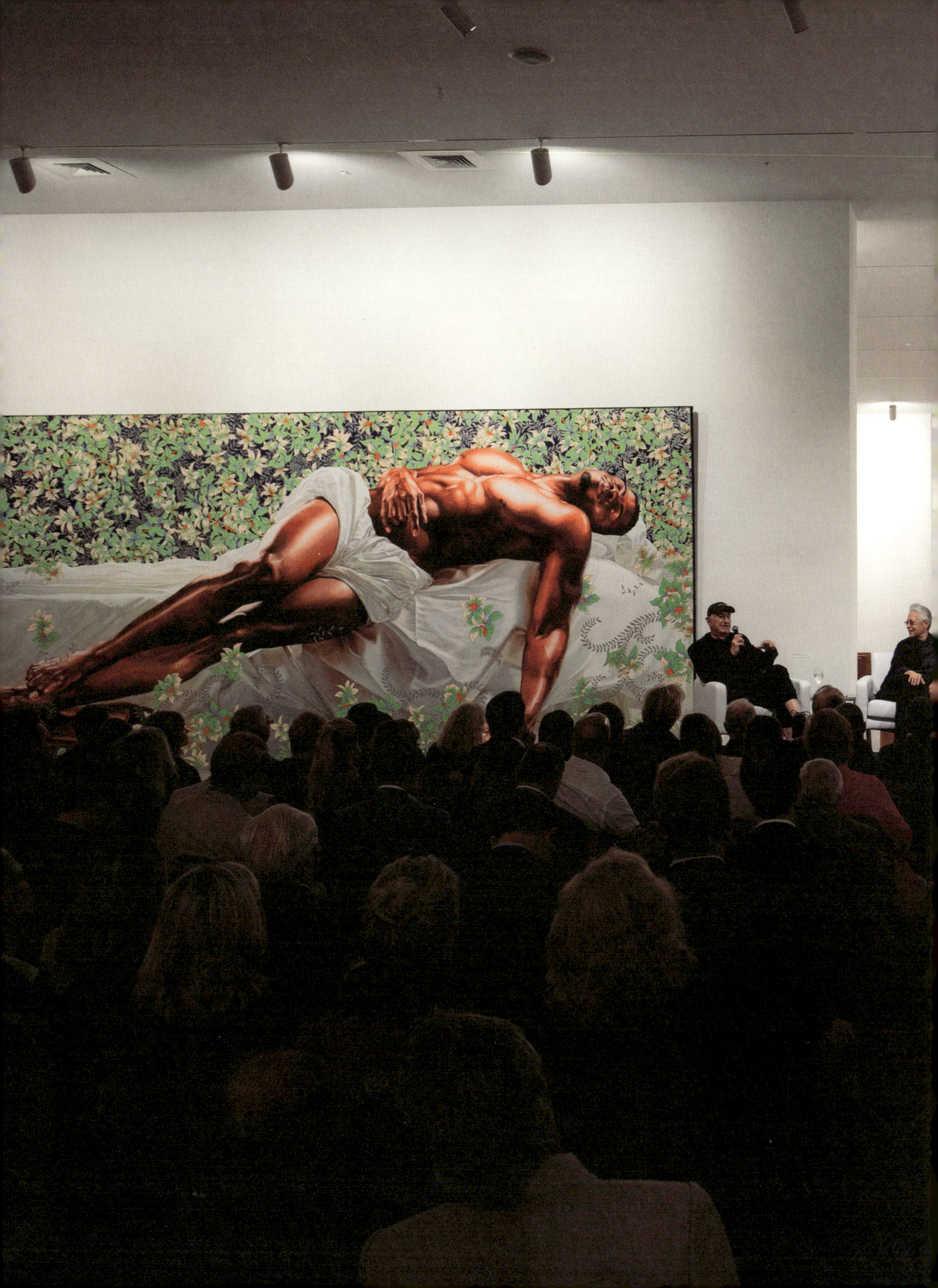